THE NATIONAL INSTITUTE OF
ECONOMIC AND SOCIAL RESEARCH

NIESR Students' Edition

4

BRITISH ECONOMIC POLICY
1960-74:
DEMAND MANAGEMENT

BRITISH ECONOMIC POLICY

1960-74:
DEMAND MANAGEMENT

BY

F. T. BLACKABY (*Editor*), M. J. ARTIS,
R. W. R. PRICE, J. H. B. TEW

CAMBRIDGE UNIVERSITY PRESS

CAMBRIDGE

LONDON · NEW YORK · MELBOURNE

Published by the Syndics of the Cambridge University Press
The Pitt Building, Trumpington Street, Cambridge CB2 1RP
Bentley House, 200 Euston Road, London NW1 2DB
32 East 57th Street, New York, NY 10022, USA
296 Beaconsfield Parade, Middle Park, Melbourne 3206, Australia

© The National Institute of Economic and Social Research 1978, 1979

Full-length edition first published 1978
This students' edition first published 1979

Printed in Great Britain
at the University Press, Cambridge

ISBN 0 521 29597 1 paperback
(Full-length edition ISBN 0 521 22042 4 hard covers)

CONTENTS

5 MONETARY POLICY – PART I 218

by J. H. B. Tew

TABLES

6 MONETARY POLICY – PART II 258

by M. J. Artis

TABLES

CHARTS

TABLES

CHARTS

SYMBOLS USED IN TABLES

..   not available

n.a.   not applicable

—   nil or negligible

roman numerals for quarters of the calendar year

PREFACE

This students' edition comprises the 'demand management' part of *British Economic Policy 1960–74*, together with the general policy appraisal which formed the conclusion of that book. The book was the joint product of a group which met regularly at the National Institute over a number of years. Its aim was to cover the whole field of economic policy over the period 1960–74 – except for regional policy, on which the National Institute has already published *The Framework of Regional Economics in the United Kingdom* by A. J. Brown. All the chapters went through a number of drafts, which were discussed by the group and amended in the light of the discussion; however, the final responsibility rests with the author of each chapter.

The chapters omitted from this edition are those on Planning, by P. Meadows; on Industrial Policy, by P. Mottershead; on Policy towards Nationalised Industries, by K. Jones; on Commercial Policy, by A. D. Morgan; and on Industrial Relations and Manpower Policy, by R. Elliott. All these authors contributed to the discussions on the chapters which are reproduced here. In addition, Pamela Meadows prepared a great deal of material for the chapters on monetary policy and incomes policy.

We are grateful to the large number of commentators from outside the National Institute – too numerous to mention individually – who have given us comments. We are also grateful to the Director, who painstakingly read through the whole book; to Miss Gillian Little, who undertook the immense labour of preparing the work for the printer, and by careful editing brought the book down to manageable length; to Mrs Evelyn McInulty, who was mainly responsible for typing the long succession of drafts and redrafts; and to Mrs Susan Price, who prepared the index.

The study was financed by a grant from the Treasury; this in no way impinged on the independence of those engaged on the work.

F.T.B.

NIESR
October 1977

'A government in modifying its laws . . . should collect with care documents necessary to prove, at a future date, whether the results obtained have answered their expectation. Laws are made and repealed with such precipitation that it is most frequently impossible to study their influence.'
(*A. Quételet,* Lettres à S.A.R. le Duc Règnant de Saxe-Cobourg et Gotha sur la Théorie des Probabilités Appliquée aux Sciences Morales et Politiques, *Hayez, Brussels, 1846. Translated by Olinthus Gregory Downes, London, 1849.*)

CHAPTER I

INTRODUCTION

by *F. T. Blackaby*

This book is a study of British economic policy from 1960 to 1974. Its starting-point is a description of what happened and its raw materials are government decisions and actions. The book is not addressed solely to an academic audience; we hope it will also be useful to those concerned with policy-making and we have tried to write it in a way that is relevant to their experience.

The study is not just descriptive, but includes explanation and assessment. The basic questions to which answers are sought in the descriptive material are: What was the government trying to do – what were its objectives – and why did it select the methods it did? Also, how far were its policies successful, and what were the reasons for the success or failure? Throughout the book, we have concentrated particularly on studying major changes in the direction of policy, such as the spasmodic adoption of incomes policies, the floating of the exchange rate in mid-1972, or the new approach to monetary policy which was inaugurated in May 1971.

In attempting to answer the question why the government chose certain policies, we have tried to trace any influence on these choices of the various views and theories current at the time. In answering questions about success or failure we have gone as far as we can, but we would not claim to have found many definitive answers; it is not so much a problem of evaluating effects as of deciding what they were. In many cases – indeed perhaps in most cases – the evidence on the effects of particular policies is thin, so that any conclusion about success or failure has to be highly tentative. In chapter 9 we survey and comment on the general appraisals of British economic policy which have been made during this period – a period in which the performance of the economy fell far short of the policy-makers' hopes.

COVERAGE

In the 1950s the study of economic policy was concerned mainly with demand management – with 'the practical application of...the broad rule – to stimulate demand when it is deficient and to restrain it when excessive. . .'.[1] This abridged edition is also primarily concerned with such policies, but during the period demand management lost its pre-eminent position – its semi-identity with economic policy.[2] For one thing economic growth became a dominant objective, and this was considered to need a quite different set of policies; to take another example – by 1962 the Prime Minister was reaching the conclusion that demand management was no longer effective in moderating inflation,[3] so he began the process of attempting to devise new institutions. At times policy-makers were almost wholly preoccupied with their incomes policy experiments; consequently the incomes policy chapter is included here.

There are a number of demarcation problems with the term 'economic policy'. There is no clear line between economic and other political decisions; virtually every government decision has some economic content, however small; thus if it is decided to turn the consulate in Peking into an embassy, government expenditure is fractionally increased. The most helpful criterion is probably that of the *main* objective of policy; if the government acts in any field *mainly* with an economic objective in mind, then that action can be counted as part of economic policy. Ideally all such actions should be considered in the study, since one of its purposes is to compare, and study the effectiveness of, the whole range of policies which were addressed to any particular objective. Economic policy is concerned with the selection of instruments to achieve certain objectives; it is not possible to evolve a sensible selection without a full inventory of the instruments available. A bird's eye view of the whole terrain of economic policy is needed for any attempt to answer questions such as: Which (if any) of the many measures adopted to encourage economic growth appears in retrospect to have had any success? Or, how far did policy in one area conflict with policy in another (for example, restraining prices of nationalised industries increase the public sector borrowing requirement)?

The term 'government' also raises a problem of border definition. There is local as well as central government, and there are many 'para-governmental' bodies – the Monopolies Commission, the Industrial Reorganisation Corporation (IRC), the National Board for Prices and Incomes (NBPI), the National Economic Development Office (NEDO), the Pay Board and the Price Commission – as well as the nationalised industries themselves. Some demarcation problems are fairly straightforward: business decisions by nationalised industries are excluded, but

---

[1] R. L. Hall in the Foreword to J. C. R. Dow, *The Management of the British Economy, 1945–60*, Cambridge University Press, 1964.

[2] This change of emphasis is illustrated by the coverage of W. Beckerman (ed.), *The Labour Government's Economic Record, 1964–1970*, London, Duckworth, 1972; of the nine chapters only one is specifically concerned with demand management.

[3] See page 20.

government policies towards them and directives to them are included; local authorities' expenditure is, of course, included in public sector expenditure, local authorities being considered essentially agents of the central government's economic policy. The harder problems are with bodies which the government sets up to execute particular strands of policy, such as the IRC, NBPI, or NEDO. It is particularly awkward when certain strands of policy are sometimes hived-off to separate bodies of this kind and sometimes kept within the administration itself. For example, the preparation of some kind of general economic plan was at one time the responsibility of the National Economic Development Council (NEDC); at another time it was the direct ministerial responsibility of the Secretary of State for Economic Affairs. In the same way, some of the functions of the IRC were later taken over by the Department of Trade and Industry. Consequently the work of bodies such as the NEDC or the IRC is taken as part of economic policy.

Government decisions and actions have been stressed in the discussion so far because we are particularly interested in the reasons for changes in the government's economic strategy, and changes are normally marked by some decision or action. However, in some areas of economic policy the process of government intervention is, as it were, continuous – in fiscal policy there is a continuous flow of taxation and expenditure – and inaction – the decision, for instance, not to make any changes in income tax in a time of rapid inflation – can be just as much a policy decision as action. It is sensible in these circumstances to talk about the stance of policy and changes in that stance; these changes may be discretionary – resulting, for instance, from government decisions to alter taxes – or they may be automatic – resulting from the application of the same tax rules to an economy which has changed in other ways. There may be particular statistical series which can be used as a measure of the stance of policy; the point is discussed on page 183 for fiscal policy, pages 280–5 for monetary policy.

FRAMEWORK OF THOUGHT

In the last decade, a good deal of academic work on economic policy has used the approach first developed by Professor Tinbergen:[1] that a government has a set of economic policy objectives and a range of instruments which it can use to try to reach those objectives.

Economic policy is intended to further a number of general *aims*; these give rise to a set of more precisely defined economic *objectives*. Governments, in attempting to achieve these objectives, employ a variety of *instruments*, and

[1] J. Tinbergen, *Economic Policy: principles and design*, Amsterdam, North-Holland, 1956.

take certain *measures*. . . The government's main policy problem is to select, from a wide range of instruments, the ones which will, in its opinion, most nearly achieve its objectives. The use of an instrument does not normally bring about changes in objectives directly; it operates on other economic quantities. For instance, a government may have expansion of production as its objective. It may choose to increase private consumption, investment or exports, and to effect these increases it can select from a large number of possible instruments – such as a guaranteed minimum wage or export subsidies.[1]

This approach, with multiple objectives instead of the single aim of maximising general welfare over time, certainly brought the analysis of economic policy closer to the real world. The objectives most often cited – full employment, economic growth, stable prices and an adequate balance of payments – were ones which policy-makers could recognise as corresponding to their experience. Further, Tinbergen's approach lent itself admirably to the kinds of quantification which econometricians and economic forecasters thought (rightly or wrongly) they could provide. So this framework not only made sense to policy-makers, it was one within which a large amount of the work done on economic relationships could be used.

Tinbergen's approach has been elaborated in a number of ways. First, with multiple objectives there is the problem of accommodating their complementarity or conflict. If two objectives are in conflict, how much of one must be sacrificed to get a given improvement in another? The practical development of this idea has been limited for a number of reasons. First, given the changing nature of the economic system and our imperfect knowledge of it, there is not much agreement among economists about the technical trade-offs; indeed, it is quite difficult to think of any trade-off between the four objectives listed above which could be said to be reasonably well established. Secondly, the trade-offs between any two objectives are not characteristics of the objectives themselves, they vary with the instruments used. To take one example: a possible instrument for achieving price stability is the lowering of tariffs, which would lead to a worsening of the balance of payments; on the other hand, the same objective might be pursued by a freeze on home prices, which would probably improve the balance of payments as manufacturers looked for higher prices abroad.

For a full model of Tinbergen's type, one would need to know not only all the possibilities of particular combinations of objectives (given a certain set of instruments), but also the preferences of the policy-makers – that is what the relative values are they give the various

[1] E. S. Kirschen *et al.*, *Economic Policy in Our Time*. Vol. 1: *General Theory*, Amsterdam, North-Holland, 1964. This book develops some of Tinbergen's ideas.

objectives. Attempts have been made to construct preference functions for policy-makers; questionnaires have been devised in which they indicate, for example, whether they would accept a rise in unemployment from 2 to $2\frac{1}{2}$ per cent if in consequence the rise in prices would be moderated from 4 per cent to 3 per cent.[1] There is, however, a certain artificiality about these exercises, since they try to make policy-makers think in a way which may be foreign to them. Further, it is difficult to conduct surveys about past changes in preferences; a questionnaire completed now cannot establish whether or not the emphasis given to economic growth increased during the 1960s. Changes in the relative importance of objectives have to be inferred from other evidence – for example, the varying levels of unemployment which at different times served as triggers for reflationary action. However, this is not straightforward, since belief in the efficacy of certain instruments may change over time; that is, policy-makers may become less (or more) confident about their ability to achieve the various objectives, even though these are still given the same relative values.

In this book we have used the general concepts of objectives and instruments, but we have not tried to put the whole of our description and analysis of what happened into this framework. The object of the book is not to build an ideal model of economic policy, but to describe, explain and assess what happened. The classification of actions according to the objectives served is of some help in explaining reasons for changes in policy – but of rather limited help (see page 406). Of a great many changes in the general direction of economic policy during this period comparatively few can be explained by changes in policy-makers' objectives; many have to be explained in other ways. The following section sets out some of the limitations of the 'objective' or 'instrument' classification for the purpose of this book.

OBJECTIVES AND INSTRUMENTS

It is not possible in practice to compile a satisfactorily comprehensive list of quantifiable objectives which describe past policy. Clearly in a book discussing actual policy, the objectives have to be what the policy-makers were trying to do, rather than some ideal set. The difficulty is that the policy-makers did not have a full set of quantified, published economic objectives by which their actions were determined.

In the field of demand management there were quantified objectives of a kind. At least it was generally accepted which series should be used as indicators of relative success or failure in respect of unemployment,

---

[1] E. S. Kirschen (ed.), *Economic Policies Compared: West and East*. Vol. 1: *General Theory*, Amsterdam, North-Holland, 1974, pp. 280 *et seq.*

the price level and economic growth. For the balance of payments –
which must also certainly be included in any assessment of the success or
failure of demand management in Britain in the 1960s[1] – there was
doubt about the appropriate measure; at times the emphasis was on the
level of the gold and foreign exchange reserves, at times on the current
account balance, at times on the current and long-term capital account
balance, and at times on the exchange rate itself.[2]

Sometimes explicit targets were set for the various objectives – as, for
example, in the National Plan.[3] However, policy-makers tended on the
whole to avoid publishing target figures for unemployment or for retail
prices. In practice there was, at any particular time, an upper limit for
unemployment, so that if it was exceeded it could be assumed that the
government would take some action. For both retail prices and unemployment it can reasonably be inferred that the targets shifted over
time; at the end of the period, policy-makers appeared to tolerate a
higher level of unemployment and a higher rate of price increase than
they would have done at the beginning.

For the four objectives relevant to demand management there was at
least a reasonably agreed measure of achievement, but this was not true
for other important objectives of economic policy. If these are taken to
be something which the government of the day considers desirable for
its own sake, and to which it devotes a significant amount of policy
action, then we should include regional development, an improvement
in the distribution of income, the promotion of competition, the
promotion of rationalisation, the protection of particular industries and
the extension of the international division of labour, but for none of
them was there a quantified target or measure of achievement. Any
precise comparison of objectives and achievements is possible, therefore,
only over a fairly narrow field of economic policy and, even in unquanti-
fied terms, it is not easy to establish a definitive list of economic policy
objectives apart from those relevant to demand management.

There is, moreover, a danger that making lists of 'ultimate' objectives,
and trying to allocate policy actions to them, may give a wrong impression of the way in which economic policy was in fact conducted. In
particular, in addition to the 'ultimate' objectives of the kind we have
just been considering, there were 'intermediate' objectives through

[1] In some 'normative' lists of objectives the balance of payments is not included on the
grounds that it should be considered an intermediate rather than a final objective: an
adequate balance of payments is needed only because without it economic growth and full
employment become impossible. In a description of economic policy, however, an objective
must be accepted as such if in fact a significant amount of policy action was directed towards
it. This was certainly true of the balance of payments in the United Kingdom.

[2] See pages 305–9.

[3] Department of Economic Affairs, *The National Plan*, Cmnd 2764, London, HMSO, 1965.

which the ultimate objectives were pursued. On occasions these intermediate objectives became ends in themselves – the all-important
guides to policy-making – without any reconsideration of ways of
reaching the ultimate objectives they had been supposed to serve. Thus,
on occasions economic policy seemed to be centred on the preservation
of a particular exchange rate, or on a particular figure for the public
sector borrowing requirement, or on the need to introduce legislation
to deal with unofficial strikes. Further, the historical section of the book
suggests that for fairly long periods economic policy followed the pattern
of 'one thing at a time, and one idea at a time', rather than the pattern
of a careful balancing of ultimate objectives.

Nor would any account of the objectives of economic policy be complete without some reference to elections. Certainly it is reasonable to
assume that a government which has general success in its economic
objectives will thereby improve its electoral chances – to that extent
there is no conflict between electoral and economic objectives. However, there are obviously times when the economic situation appears to the
electorate better than in fact it is – when, for example, an upswing has
increased real earnings and reduced unemployment, but has only just
begun to worsen the balance of payments. Obviously electoral considerations of this kind have influenced the timing of economic policy
measures; hence a certain general coincidence between the economic
cycle and the electoral cycle. Indeed it is rather surprising when, as in
1970, they do not coincide.

The clear distinction between 'instruments' and 'objectives' which
appears in most models of economic policy is also at variance with what
happens in practice. In most models, whereas the valuations put on
different objectives are for the politicians to decide, the choice of
instruments is assumed to be purely a technical matter. In real life
instruments are not neutral in this way, but are value-loaded, and both
Chancellors and Parties have shown strong preferences from time to
time for particular types of instrument. Sir Alec Cairncross has referred
to this complication:

The fact of political conflict means that what at first sight seemed purely
technical issues become the subject of party debate. Governments may be
inhibited from using particular instruments of policy such as bank rate by
ideological considerations or by the force of popular feeling which they have
stirred up earlier when in opposition. They may commit themselves publicly
to doctrines about how the economy should be run that rest on little more
than assertion and then find it impossible to retract when the doctrines are put
to the test.[1]

[1] Sir Alec Cairncross (ed.), *The Managed Economy*, Oxford, Blackwell, 1970, p. 21.

Any explanation of changes in policy would be incomplete unless it took account of these strong preferences for one type of instrument over another. Indeed, most of the more strongly expressed disagreements about economic policy have not been about objectives but about instruments: for example, about monetary policy or incomes policy, or investment allowances as against investment grants, or selective employment tax as against value-added tax (VAT). There is a more general difference which underlies many of these differences about the choice of instruments – with one Party showing, from time to time, a strong preference for reducing the amount of government intervention as much as possible and the other Party giving this consideration little weight.

For some acts of policy the metaphor contained in the term 'instrument' is inappropriate. It is suitable enough for a single change in some parameter, like the 10 per cent surcharge on indirect taxes, but for other actions, in particular all those which establish new institutions, or require some kind of negotiated consensus with interest groups, the metaphor is inappropriate. Over the period considered in this book, a growing proportion of economic actions consisted in bringing about institutional change of some kind, and it is especially difficult to establish the need for, or the effects of, this kind of change. The efficacy of the policy may depend upon the workability or acceptability of the new institution, and in such cases there is no satisfactory way at present of judging in advance what outcome is to be expected. So there is here a problem of assessment which is much more difficult than the problem of assessing the consequences of (say) a tax change.

UNCERTAINTY

Economic policy models tend to assume that the working of the economic system is known. If this had been so, actual economic policy in Britain would have been very different. If there were an agreed body of economic knowledge about the full effects of all major economic instruments, so that the technical trade-offs between particular objectives could be precisely calculated, there might be little reason for substantial disagreement about policy. Such a state of knowledge did not, and does not, exist. Admittedly there are some generally accepted calculations of the effects of particular tax changes on aggregate demand, but such cases are exceptional. Most of the wider effects are highly uncertain; that is, there is no general agreement among economists and there are rival views. For example, there is no agreement about the determinants of economic growth nor the kind of government actions which might accelerate it; we do not know which policies (if any) were responsible for such acceleration as there has been in the underlying trend of productivity – indeed there are differing views about whether this acceleration took place, and when; there is uncertainty about the effects of devaluation and about the possibility of preserving any competitive advantage so obtained; there is no agreement about the existence of long-term dynamic effects from joining the Common Market, nor about the sensitivity of rates of increase in wage rates or earnings to demand pressure as measured by unemployment.

A symptom of these uncertainties was that a number of conflicting views (or doctrines or theories) about the working of parts of the economic system were elaborated and presented by economists during this period. Policy-makers were subjected to a constant commentary on their actions – so long as their policies were successful the pressure to change was weak, but when their policies began to appear unsuccessful (as they usually did, since Britain's general economic performance was relatively poor) an alternative set of ideas, based on an alternative view of the working of the economy, was normally at hand. For example, when demand management by fiscal and monetary means appeared to be failing to control price rises, it was natural for policy-makers to turn to incomes policy; the idea had been extensively written about and widely discussed, and there was a theory of inflation to support it. Chancellors, it is true, were not much concerned with the theoretical backing – and in any case normally felt some obligation to explain that the new policy was essentially a continuation of the old policy in another form.[1] Nonetheless, policies were not normally developed far, or for long, without some theoretical backing, however rudimentary, to support them.

Part of the story of economic policy lies in links between changes in the direction of policy and the range of views and theories being discussed at the time. These links can only be explored in a general way; it is rarely, if ever, possible to identify the exact route by which an idea developed outside the government was eventually incorporated into policy. However, the absence of firm knowledge about the working of the economic system, and the presence of rival views and theories provided the background to such marked oscillations of policy as the rise and fall of planning, and the acceptance, rejection, and reacceptance of incomes policy.

---

[1] Conversely, when governments change, differences rather than similarities are emphasised, so that a policy which may be virtually identical with one pursued by a previous government is presented as being in some way basically different.

CONCLUSION

The description and analysis of actual economic policy therefore requires concepts rather more complex than simply a list of objectives and instruments. Policy-makers were uncertain about their objectives; they often pursued intermediate objectives, tended to concentrate on one thing at a time, and found that differences in political philosophy often revealed themselves in choices of instruments rather than objectives. Partly because knowledge of the working of the economic system was imperfect, policies were liable to considerable instability; as one set of policies appeared unsuccessful, another set, which implied a different view of the working of the economy, was ready and waiting in the wings.

CHAPTER 2

NARRATIVE, 1960–74

by *F. T. Blackaby*

INTRODUCTION

Most of this book is concerned with analysing particular strands of policy – either the use of a particular family of instruments (fiscal or monetary policy), or the examination of policies addressed to a particular area (the balance of payments, for example). Nonetheless a narrative chapter is needed to provide a general political framework for economic policy decisions – there were two changes of government during this period and six changes in Chancellors of the Exchequer – and, more generally, because there are important questions about economic policy – priorities and the dominance of particular themes at particular times – which the disaggregated analysis does not cover.

Economic policy is, after all, considered as a whole to some extent; the major decisions are either brought to the Cabinet or discussed among a small circle of Ministers. It would be going too far to say that at any point during this period there was a fully articulated and comprehensive economic strategy; certainly a good many policy decisions consisted of reactions to circumstances. However, by no means all economic policy can be explained in this way; Parties came to power with programmes and priorities which had some influence on their behaviour.[1] In addition, at various times particular issues appeared to become dominant and occupied the centre of the stage; this is clear from political biographies. An example is the attention paid by the Conservative government from the middle of 1972 until the election in 1974 to the problems of devising an effective incomes policy. It is the job of a narrative chapter to describe these shifting preoccupations and priorities.

Frequently in this account of the last twelve years a distinction has to be made between the picture as it appeared to policy-makers at the time, on the basis of figures then available, and the picture as it appears on the basis of revised figures now available. This certainly compli-

---

[1] Also, senior Civil Servants are diligent in attempting to establish in their own minds what the general line of policy is; indeed they sometimes appear to impose a more coherent philosophy on the policies than the politicians do themselves.

cates the narrative, but there is no way of avoiding it. The differences are sometimes substantial: for example, in the first half of 1961, 1960 was looked back on as a very disappointing year, during which national output between the fourth quarters of 1959 and 1960 had risen by only $1\frac{1}{2}$ per cent, whereas the best estimate available in 1977 was that the rise was $3\frac{1}{2}$ per cent. Revisions of this order are not uncommon.

It would not be fair, therefore, simply to use today's series in assessing policy; it must also be judged against the background of the figures available at the time. Further, there is no finality here; substantial revisions to the data are still likely, particularly for the later years covered in this book. It is an important point that the statistical foundations on which demand management is based are shaky; it makes a good deal of difference to the general conclusions drawn about economic policy in chapter 9.

THE YEAR 1960

Throughout 1960 – and indeed well into 1961 – although there were some long-term policy initiatives of importance, the decisions on short-term demand management were reactions to successive alarms (interspersed by short periods of reassurance) accompanying the publication of the figures for trade or reserves. Ministers were preoccupied with the reserves and the size of the trade gap; to a lesser extent, they were concerned with any weakening in the exchange rate. (Publication of the balance of payments accounts themselves seems to have had less influence, since they came out after quite a long delay.) It is clear from Harold Macmillan's account of economic policy in this period that, although other factors (such as the progress of wage demands) were minor background influences, what caught his eye (and were recorded in his diary) were exclusively trade or reserves statistics.[1] There was a change after mid-1961, when the 'battle of the pay pause' began.

The arguments within the government about the nature of the 1960 budget are worth elaborating in some detail, because it is one of the few cases where we have reasonably good documentation of a difference of opinion among Ministers and of the arguments deployed on either side. From early in 1960 the Chancellor of the Exchequer and the Governor of the Bank of England were both in favour of deflationary measures;[2] the Prime Minister was opposed.

[1] The references in this section to Macmillan's views are from chapter 8, 'A touch on the brake' in H. Macmillan, *Pointing the Way 1959–1961*, London, Macmillan, 1972.

[2] The Governor joined the Chancellor, it seems as an equal partner, in initial discussions with the Prime Minister on the economic situation in mid-February.

The Chancellor and the Governor were concerned at the risk of an inflationary boom. There was then nothing in the figures to indicate any slackening in the rise in demand: unemployment was continuing to fall, the trade gap had widened in the second half of 1959 and the reserves had fallen in the fourth quarter by substantially more than the annual payments of capital and interest on North American loans. It is true that the latest balance of payments figures available – for the third quarter of 1959 – still showed a current surplus, but they were by then four months out of date. The figures for the past which would have been under consideration are set out in table 2.1; the Chancellor probably had, in addition, a gloomy balance of payments forecast for 1960. These were the arguments for a tough budget.

The Prime Minister was disturbed at what he considered to be a 'loss of nerve'.[1] Only three months earlier he had led his Party to its third successive electoral victory, with an increased majority for the third time, and one of the themes had been the 'preservation of prosperity'. In a letter to the Chancellor, he presented these arguments:

(a) a deflationary budget would be 'either very foolish or very dishonest';

(b) an additional £50–£100 million of taxation would have practically no effect – 'after all, the national income is of the order of £20,000 million';[2]

(c) there would be a danger of companies changing their investment plans – for example, the motor companies might cancel their planned expansion on Merseyside;

(d) the balance of payments forecast on which the Chancellor based his desire to deflate was not to be trusted;[3]

(e) the economy was not yet at full stretch;

(f) if deflationary measures were needed, the best weapon was Special Deposits – 'if you like, add hire purchase, to taste'.

For all these reasons, Macmillan recommended a stand-still budget.

It is clear that the Prime Minister was most nervous of a budget – with all the publicity surrounding it – which appeared to reverse the previous one. To an economist it might seem sensible to use the budget to increase demand in one year and to reduce it the next. A politician, however, knows that he will be accused of cheating – as Butler was after

---

[1] He also surmised that Treasury officials were 'calmer' about the economic situation than the Chancellor.

[2] There is a certain inconsistency in his arguments. Here he is saying that the increase in taxation would not have much effect; elsewhere in the same letter he says: 'It cannot be sensible to cheer the economy on vigorously one moment and then push it violently back the next.'

[3] 'My confidence in the accuracy of figures of this sort is just about as much as I have in Old Moore.'

Table 2.1. *Some indicators available at various times during 1960*

	Monthly trade gap[a]	Gold and foreign exchange reserves[b]	Current balance of payments[c]	Unemployment[d]
	(£ million)	($ billion)	(£ million)	(%)
Available 25 January 1960				
1958	−36	3·15	+348	2·10
1959 I	−49	3·14	+19	2·51
II	−32	3·17	+96	2·22
III	−43	3·28	+48	2·06
IV	−53	2·74	..	1·92
October	−38	3·02	..	1·98
November	−72	2·97	..	1·92
December	−57	2·74	..	1·87
Available 25 March 1960				
1959 IV	−53	2·74	−18	2·03
1960 January	−48	2·68	..	1·73
February	−70	2·72	..	1·59
Available 25 July 1960				
1960 I	−56	2·78	+46	1·70
April	−65	2·83	..	1·65
May	−80	2·86	..	1·54
June	−71	2·89	..	1·55
July	..	..	..	1·56
Available 23 September 1960				
1960 II	−70	2·89	−9	1·58
July	−104	3·00	..	1·56
August	−74	3·07	..	1·62
September	..	..	..	1·53
Available 23 December 1960				
1960 III	−83	3·11	..	1·57
October	−133	3·14	..	1·59
November	−70	3·17	..	1·61
December	..	..	..	1·65

SOURCE: *National Institute Economic Review* (various issues).

[a] Seasonally adjusted and adjusted for dock strikes.
[b] At end of period.
[c] Not seasonally adjusted.
[d] Seasonally adjusted; for Great Britain only; includes temporarily stopped.

his autumn budget in 1955 – which is one of the political constraints on counter-cyclical action.

The figures which became available between the first discussions about the budget and the final decisions would have appeared, on balance, to support the Chancellor's thesis (table 2.1). Unemployment dropped sharply; in January and February the trade gap was running higher than in the fourth quarter of 1959, for which period a current deficit of £18 million was estimated for the balance of payments –

although negligible by today's standards, this was treated seriously at that time. Nonetheless the Prime Minister got his way about the budget (he was in a relatively strong position because the Chancellor had some time before indicated that he was anxious to return to private life) and the net tax change was negligible (see page 194). The Prime Minister even checked through the budget speech to make sure that there was 'no note of despondency or alarm; reversal of engines, end of expansionist policies, or any of the horrors which the Chancellor and the Treasury were threatening up to a few weeks ago'.[1] He reports 'I have won this battle quite definitely. I feel ... that we shall not *talk* ourselves into a crisis – as we did ... in 1957.' A public reversal of policies had been avoided.

During the rest of 1960 the statistical background to the decisions on demand management – dominated as always by trade and the balance of payments – was confused. The trade gap continued to widen and further measures were taken in response. On the other hand, the gold and foreign exchange reserves stopped falling and began to increase again; 1960 was a year in which the dollar rather than sterling was suspect and there was a substantial inflow of short-term capital (page 309). Curiously, when the first balance of payments figures for the year were published in July, they showed a return to a current surplus (table 2.1); revisions which turned this surplus into a deficit were not made until 1961. Unemployment continued to fall up to September.

By the end of April, reacting to the trade figures, the Prime Minister agreed to a 'touch on the brake' – Special Deposits at 1 per cent and the reimposition of hire purchase restrictions. He commented that he '... did not wish to be pressed to any panic measures; so many things can be done if they are done quietly and without confusion or alarm.' With a further widening of the trade gap, Bank Rate was raised from 5 to 6 per cent and Special Deposits from 1 to 2 per cent towards the end of June,[2] but there were no further restrictive measures that year.

At the end of July, Heathcoat Amory retired as Chancellor and was replaced by Selwyn Lloyd. The reserves survived an official shipping strike during August, and in October the situation was judged to have improved sufficiently for Bank Rate to be reduced from 6 to 5½ per cent. A Cabinet debate on the economic situation at the end of November led apparently to general bafflement, certainly to no new measures; various enquiries were instituted on different aspects of the balance of payments and the Prime Minister decided to preside over a committee

[1] The Prime Minister was even rather bothered at the thought that the speech would be delivered by the Chancellor in a very lugubrious voice.
[2] It is clear from frequent references that Macmillan considered that changes in Bank Rate had significant internal deflationary or reflationary effects.

on increasing exports. At the end of the year the trade gap seemed at least to have stopped increasing, and the Governor of the Bank of England declared that he was not particularly worried about the immediate future.

In the division of opinion between the Chancellor and Prime Minister, in one sense both sides were right and both wrong. The current balance of payments did worsen, as the Chancellor expected. After the first quarter, exports stopped rising. The American expansion came to an early end, the rise in world trade slowed down and, more important, the British share of world trade fell faster than before. The share of imports in national expenditure rose rapidly. On the other hand, the sharp rise in demand and output petered out after the first quarter without substantial deflationary measures. Consumers' expenditure rose little; the hire purchase and credit restrictions produced a slump in the demand for consumer durables, whose sales (in real terms) were 15 per cent lower at the end of 1960 than they had been at the end of 1959. These factors together brought about a virtual levelling off in total output after the first quarter. However, fixed investment was rising through the year, and investment in stocks stayed high up to mid-year.

During 1959 there had been an extraordinary gap in wage bargaining – the wage-rate indices hardly moved. 1960 was much more active, with unions pressing hard for reduced hours as well as for wage increases. The effect was to push up the hourly wage-rate index by $6\frac{1}{2}$ per cent during 1960, as against a rise of only 1 per cent during 1959. This, together with the slow rise in output in the second half of the year, pushed up wage costs, but the effect on final prices was small during 1960: retail prices went up through the year by less than 2 per cent, with import prices contributing nothing to this.

1961 TO MID-1962

In 1961, as in 1960, it was balance of payments considerations which were dominant. In 1960 the trade gap had widened, but an inflow of hot money had prevented any fall in the reserves. In 1961 this process was reversed: the trade gap narrowed but the hot money flowed out again, so that in July there was a balance of payments crisis, leading to a package of deflationary measures. The pattern was familiar; the only difference was that the inflow of hot money had postponed the crisis for a year.

Partly because it was a familiar pattern, it caused a good deal of discontent – among Ministers as well as the electorate. The simple principle which had governed demand management since the war – of reducing demand when it was excessive and increasing it when it was inadequate – began to appear more and more threadbare, so that moves were made to evolve longer-term policies – medium-term planning and new institutions for an incomes policy.

The first balance of payments crisis came in March, when the Deutschemark (and the Dutch guilder) were revalued by 5 per cent. Macmillan defines precisely the consequences of this:

(a) The *fact* of revaluation reminded all speculators and owners of hot money that fixed exchanges can, after all, be changed. If once, why not again?

(b) The fact that the up valuation is far too small to correspond to realities has led everyone to think the first move in this direction may be followed by a second. Since this could only be upwards, it's an absolutely safe bet to sell dollars and sterling in order to buy Deutschemarks. This has been done on an absolutely unprecedented scale. We lost £67 million [in] *one day* (£26 million was the worst post-Suez day). Altogether we have lost about £187 million of *hot* money from the reserves.[1]

The pound was supported under the Basle Arrangements (page 350).

This run on sterling was part of the background to the budget; in addition, revised balance of payments figures published on 1 April roughly doubled the estimate for the balance of payments current deficit in 1960 (table 2.2): in January this had been estimated at £150–£175 million; in April it was revised to £344 million. At home the signals were uncertain: by March the industrial production index had been flat for a year, but unemployment, which (on a seasonally adjusted basis) had risen a little in the fourth quarter of 1960, fell back again slightly in January and February. The budget was virtually neutral in its effect on demand: £5000 rather than £2000 of earned income was now exempt from surtax and two so-called 'regulators' were introduced. Powers were taken to increase the national insurance stamp by up to four shillings a week for each employee, also to vary most indirect taxes by 10 per cent up or down.[2] However, the idea of varying national insurance contributions was subsequently dropped.

Pressure on sterling continued. At the end of April and the beginning of May there was an unofficial London dock strike, so that when the May trade figures came out they showed a substantial widening in the trade gap. Further, in early June there were widespread rumours of a revaluation of the Swiss franc. It became clear that the Bank of England would have difficulty in arranging more help from the other central banks. Ministers were also getting more and more exasperated with difficulties on the labour front: Macmillan comments on ' . . . the

---

[1] Macmillan, *Pointing the Way*, pp. 371–2.

[2] Macmillan comments: 'We thus introduced into the management of the economy the now popular concept of the stimulant and the tranquillizer' (ibid. p. 373).

Table 2.2. *Some indicators available at various times during 1961*

	Monthly trade gap[a]	Gold and foreign exchange reserves[a]	Current balance of payments[a]	Unemployment[a]
	(£ million)	($ billion)	(£ million)	(%)
Available 22 March 1961				
1960 I	−54	2·78	+44	1·70
II	−69	2·89	−9	1·56
III	−82	3·11	−101	1·55
IV	−83	3·23	..	1·59
1961 January	−68	3·25	..	1·59
February	−65	3·19	..	1·47
Available 25 May 1961				
1960 I	−54	2·78	−37	1·70
II	−69	2·89	−42	1·56
III	−82	3·11	−148	1·55
IV	−83	3·23	−117	1·59
1961 I	−64	3·02	..	1·49
April	−41	2·95	..	1·41
Available 24 November 1961				
1961 I	−69	3·02	−68	1·49
II	−45	2·77[b]	−15	1·36
III	−33	3·55[c]	..	1·48
October	−55	3·53	..	1·74
November	..	..	..	1·74

SOURCE: as table 2.1.

[a] See notes to table 2.1.
[b] This fell to 2·45 at end-July.
[c] Includes drawing on the IMF stand-by, on which repayment began in November.

utter irresponsibility of labour in some of the *new* industries (motor cars, aviation and the like) and the *hopeless conservatism* of labour in some of the *old* industries (shipbuilding, etc.)'.[1]

There was a good deal of argument about the size of the deflationary package. The International Monetary Fund (IMF) was clearly pressing for cuts in government expenditure and on this Macmillan has an illuminating note: 'If we are to get our "drawings" from the International Monetary Fund, we shall have to make – or *pretend to make* – large savings on government expenditure.'[2] There was a division of opinion at home as well. The Governor of the Bank of England was pressing for a tightening of hire purchase terms and the use of the so-called 'payroll' tax. The Chancellor objected that hire purchase would hit the same industries as had been hit by the first regulator and that the payroll tax was so unpopular with both employers and trade unionists that it would militate against the success of his pay pause.

[1] Ibid. p. 375.   [2] Ibid. p. 376 (italics not in the original).

The issue was put to the Cabinet, which endorsed the Chancellor's position.

The July package had four components: fiscal measures, monetary measures, measures designed to affect the balance of payments directly, and the pay pause. The fiscal measures comprised the use of the new 'regulator' – a 10 per cent increase in indirect taxes – and public expenditure cuts. The monetary measures included a rise in Bank Rate, a call for Special Deposits and a discouragement of personal loans. On the balance of payments, new controls were introduced on private investment outside the sterling area, and British firms were to be encouraged to repatriate more of their overseas profits. Finally, a pay pause was imposed on wage increases in the public sector, in the hope that the private sector would follow suit.

These measures were successful in stopping the run on sterling. They also stopped the tentative recovery in output; after the middle of the year industrial production stopped rising and unemployment began to increase quite quickly. From July onwards there was a shift in ministerial preoccupations: the balance of payments was no longer immediately dominant, as the trade gap narrowed and the reserves rose, so that repayment of the IMF drawings began before the end of the year. The new battlefield was at home, with the objective of making the pay pause effective. As Macmillan saw it, 'The short-term measures ... will all be nullified if we put up personal incomes by £1,000 million in the next 12 months, as we have in the last 12 months.'[1]

The pay pause and incomes policy

The metaphor of a battlefield is not inappropriate. After the normal summer break in wage negotiations the government had a succession of skirmishes with various unions in the public sector. It also had a succession of encounters with the standard problems thrown up by a pay pause or freeze: for example, what should be done about any automatic cost-of-living clauses? Should arbitration procedures be suspended, or should there simply be a postponement of their judgements? What specific powers did the government have to control wage awards made by boards of nationalised industries?

The government's first major defeat was in November 1961 by the Electricity Board, which had informally agreed with Ministers the maximum offer it could make and that it should not be paid before 1 April, at the end of the pause. The negotiators then rang up the

---

[1] Ibid. p. 379. It is clear that in Macmillan's picture of the economy rises in wages had a 'real' reflationary effect. It was not until the early 1970s that the alternative view was widely accepted – that, after taking account of the effect on prices and taxes, the real reflationary effect of wage increases was, after a short interval, negligible and might become negative.

Minister of Power late one night to say that they had no alternative to offering more and to making payment as from 28 January, at which the Minister protested but took no further action. The Prime Minister publicly deplored this and the chairman of the Board was rebuked, but privately Macmillan admitted that it could be regarded as a tactical retreat from a salient which could not be defended.[1] However, in subsequent skirmishes the government was more successful. The Post Office workers' work-to-rule was called off, as was the threat of a go-slow by some of the Civil Service unions, on the promise that unfettered arbitration would be resumed when the pay pause ended.

As the pay pause continued, the Prime Minister became increasingly concerned with the policy which should follow it, for he had come round to the view that a permanent incomes policy of some kind was needed. He considered that the orthodox theory had in the past proved a good working rule: when the system became 'overheated' (the signs were over-employment, an unfavourable balance of payments, pressures on sterling, rises in wages unjustified by productivity increases) it had to be cooled down by deflationary touches of various kinds. But in 1962 for the first time a resistance had begun to appear. The 'conventional and lowering regimen' had been applied, but it seemed to be having no effect on wage demands. The Prime Minister complained that he got little support in developing new ideas from 'the practitioners of most repute', so he himself took on responsibility for evolving a more permanent incomes policy.[2] His plan was essentially for a 'guiding light' (page 363), together with a commission on pay, to be a permanent body; he considered at some length how to make the commission effective, and came down against compulsion (for example, a fiscal penalty, or depriving a recalcitrant trade union of the protection of the 1906 Trade Disputes Act) and in favour of the pressure which would arise from the 'full public disclosure of the facts'.

Meanwhile certain tentative moves had been made by the Chancellor and the Treasury. The Chancellor wrote to the General Council of the Trades Union Congress (TUC) early in January 1962, asking for their cooperation in keeping the increase in earnings during 1962 within the limits set by the probable increase in productivity, put by the Treasury at $2\frac{1}{2}$ per cent; in February the Treasury issued what was, in effect, a discussion paper,[3] mainly concerned with the criteria by which wage demands should be judged – should an increase in the cost of living be a justification, for example (see page 363)? However, the Prime Minister was becoming increasingly exasperated by the dilatori-

[1] H. Macmillan, *At the End of the Day, 1961–1963*, London, Macmillan, 1973, p 47.
[2] Ibid. pp. 84–5.
[3] Treasury, *Incomes Policy: the next step*, Cmnd 1626, London, HMSO, 1962.

ness of the Chancellor and the Treasury in working out concrete institutional proposals. He was concerned at the Party's loss of popularity in the country; also by June he was anxious about the need for some reflation, which he felt was impossible without an effective incomes policy. 'At present we dare not re-inflate, because our system is open at both ends – wages and imports. Increased wages mean (without increased productivity) more imports and less exports.'[1]

The Prime Minister's economic preoccupations of this period were, therefore, largely with trying to devise new incomes policy institutions, and it seems to have been this which led to his decision to replace Selwyn Lloyd as Chancellor; what is not clear, though, is how far 'dilatoriness' in this matter was due to a disbelief in incomes policies.

Establishing the NEDC

The initial proposal to do something about 'planning' had been made in a rather vague way by Selwyn Lloyd as part of the package of measures announced on 25 July 1961. The proposal clearly divided the Cabinet quite sharply and formal approval for an invitation to both sides of industry was not obtained until 21 September. The trade union side was nervous; they suspected that the invitation was part of an incomes policy trap and only eventually consented to join on condition that the Council was not used as an agent for wage restraint.

At this time policies for encouraging faster growth were being widely discussed. The *National Institute Economic Review* for February 1962 argued that 'a necessary, and almost sufficient condition for rapid growth is for businessmen in general to expect that the demand for their products will continue to grow rapidly'.[2] For this to hold true, businessmen must be confident that total demand in the economy as a whole would expand unhampered by balance of payments difficulties or excessive price rises. It was suggested that there were two distinct policy problems – how to achieve competitiveness in the first place and how to maintain it once it was achieved. For the first, devaluation was recommended while there was spare capacity. For the second, three suggestions were put forward:

(a) an incomes policy to ensure that relative costs did not get out of line;

(b) a policy to ensure that the higher investment needed was forthcoming;

(c) a planning mechanism to ensure, among other things, that the improved demand prospects were appreciated at key points in industry and that industry made its plans in the light of higher growth prospects.

[1] Macmillan, *At the End of the Day*, p. 89.
[2] *National Institute Economic Review*, no. 19, February 1962, pp. 55–6.

The NEDC's first meeting was in March 1962. The main contribution of the Council in its early days was (for good or ill) to establish a 4 per cent annual growth rate as the target for the British economy for the period 1961–6; this figure certainly influenced policy over the next two years.

The 1962 budget

The figures available at the time of the 1962 budget are shown in table 2.3. The trade and balance of payments figures were no longer particularly disturbing, but the recovery was fairly muted. The current balance of payments was still just in deficit in the third quarter of 1961, but the reserves had begun to rise again, apart from the IMF drawing; probably the best description of the balance of payments was 'convalescent'. On the other hand, the latest production figures available showed a distinct falling-off at the end of 1961 and seasonally adjusted unemployment had been rising since July to about 1¾ per cent at the end of the year.

Table 2.3. *Some indicators available at end-March 1962*

	Monthly trade gap	Gold and foreign exchange reserves	Current balance of payments	Unemployment	Index of industrial production	Quarterly change in:	
						Retail price index	Weekly wage rates
	(£m.)	($b.)	(£m.)	(%)	(1958=100)	(%)	(%)
1961 I	−69	3·02	−49	1·51	113	+0·5	+1·8
II	−45	2·77	−11	1·39	115	+1·3	+0·7
III	−33	3·55	−1	1·50	115	+1·3	+0·6
IV	−45	3·32	..	1·67	112	+1·1	+0·8
1962 Jan.	−68	3·61	..	1·82	111	+1·4	..
Feb.	−44	3·42	..	1·78	..	..	..

SOURCE: *National Institute Economic Review*, no. 20, May 1962.

Note: see notes to table 2.1.

Nonetheless the budget was essentially neutral. In his speech the Chancellor stressed the risk of excess pressure of home demand by the end of the year, for the official forecast was that output would be rising at some 3–4 per cent through the year, but this rested heavily on a very optimistic export forecast and on only a slight dip in private investment. Further, the Treasury at this time was probably more afraid of underestimating than overestimating demand; they certainly did not want unemployment to fall again and would not have been unduly disturbed if it had risen somewhat further.

MID-1962 TO OCTOBER 1964

The Prime Minister clearly considered that the change of Chancellor on 13 July 1962 and the Cabinet's adoption of an incomes policy provided the necessary conditions for a move towards expansion. Reporting on the economic debate held at the end of July 1962, he comments: 'We were now definitely set upon an expansionist course, and the whole purpose of the changes at the Treasury was to ensure that this should take place without further delay ... We regarded the Incomes Policy as essential in order to sustain expansion without incurring the evils which inflated costs following inflated wages had brought ...'[1]

However, there were in fact no immediate expansionary moves; no action was taken until the late autumn and then it was tentative and cautious. The main reason for this was that Treasury officials were reasonably confident, until the autumn, that output was rising satisfactorily. 'Throughout 1962 the big economic argument about expansion was not whether it was desirable, but whether it was happening.'[2] At the time of the budget the official forecast had been that by the end of the year there would be a greater risk of excess than of deficient demand, and the figures which became available up to August or September provided some support for this view – the seasonally adjusted industrial production index recovered from its dip at the end of 1961 and went on rising into the third quarter. But as the year wore on it became increasingly difficult to reconcile this with the general mood of business pessimism. If production was rising rapidly why were businessmen so gloomy? Further, there was some difficulty in reconciling the unemployment figures with relatively rapid expansion; there were precedents for unemployment continuing to rise after production had begun to recover, but it did seem surprising when October and November too showed quite sharp increases in seasonally adjusted unemployment. One suggestion was that a change in the underlying rate of increase in productivity explained the phenomenon; this change could have resulted from new policies on hoarding labour, an increased rate of introducing automation, and so on.

There were other reasons for official caution. A number of economists, both inside and outside the government, favoured trying to establish a rather wider margin of spare capacity than in the past; although by June unemployment had been rising for a year, it was still just under 2 per cent (according to the definitions then used), so that there were certainly those who were quite ready to see it rise a little further. Secondly, on the figures then available the balance of pay-

[1] Macmillan, *At the End of the Day*, p. 108.
[2] *National Institute Economic Review*, no. 23, February 1963, p. 4.

ments on current account had only just moved into a small surplus in the first quarter of 1962; also, the Chancellor's attempt at the IMF annual meeting to get an agreed increase in international liquidity had been unsuccessful.

Nonetheless some measures were taken. Special Deposits required from the banks were reduced from 2 to 1 per cent in early October and qualitative restraints on bank lending were abolished. In addition, on 3 October £42 million of postwar credits were released and an increase of £70 million in public investment was announced. Then in early November an attempt was made to stimulate investment, with increased investment allowances for industry, a quicker 'write-off' for heavy capital goods and an inducement to invest in research; to this was added a cut in purchase tax on cars from 45 to 25 per cent. The attempt to stimulate investment appears to have been the Prime Minister's idea; he noted in mid October: '... my fear is that in view of the uncertainty as to (a) Europe, (b) General Election, we have little chance of getting any natural increase in private investment during the next year unless we can stimulate it by some such means as I have proposed.'[1] It is quite possible that among officials in the Treasury there was a good deal of scepticism about the effectiveness of this kind of stimulus.

Developments during the winter of 1962/3 forced the government to more vigorous expansionist policies. First, official confidence that expansion was proceeding satisfactorily was punctured when the initial estimate of the industrial production index for October 1962 showed a fall of 3 per cent. This was a sharp shock and, although revisions later modified the collapse, they still showed a fall in October and November from the third quarter. Secondly, 1962/3 was a very bad winter; unemployment – seasonally adjusted in the normal way – rose to 3·3 per cent in January 1963 and to 3·6 per cent in February; it was very difficult to put the blame for these figures entirely on the cold weather. At the beginning of 1963 there were longer-term pressures too. Nearly a third of the period 1961–6, for which the NEDC had adopted a target annual growth rate of 4 per cent a year, had gone; to reach that objective the growth rate from 1963 to 1966 would have to be nearly 5 per cent. The case for a substantial stimulus was put in the *National Institute Economic Review* for February 1963, which recommended an additional budget stimulus of roughly £400 million.[2]

There were some further mild reflationary measures in early 1963, but the important question was the amount of reflation in the budget. Throughout the early months of the year the Prime Minister was clearly pressing for a high figure. He had his political difficulties: the

[1] Macmillan, *At the End of the Day*, p. 386.
[2] *National Institute Economic Review*, no. 23, February 1963, p. 43–6.

Labour Party was far ahead in the polls, and there was a substantial movement within the Conservative Party to replace him as Prime Minister. At the end of January he noted that the economy was still not responding; he also recorded his 'instinctive and violent' reaction against economists who accepted the higher level of unemployment. His strategy was firmly that of expansion with an incomes policy – that is, 'expansion without inflation', which was the budget theme.

In the event the budget tax reliefs were worth £261 million in the year 1963/4, mainly benefiting lower income groups, with the object of trying to obtain trade union support for an incomes policy. The full-year effect was, however, substantially greater (£406 million allowing for the effects of the additional investment reliefs introduced); further, the Chancellor's speech indicated that he was ready to meet by international borrowing, or by running down the reserves, any deficit caused by the temporary bout of stockbuilding which tends to accompany a recovery.[1] Of course this was much weaker than the statement made by another Conservative Chancellor nine years later, when Anthony Barber indicated that he was prepared to see the exchange rate go rather than forfeit expansion (page 64). Nonetheless Maudling's statement was an important milestone in the long progression by which 'the strength of sterling' was demoted from its position as a dominant objective of economic policy at the beginning of the 1960s.

In retrospect the recovery in output during 1963 seems clear enough; so also is the succession of stimuli which set it going. They began at the end of 1962 with the relaxations on bank credit, the repayment of postwar credits and the reduction in purchase tax on cars. At the beginning of 1963 purchase tax was also reduced on other durables and from the second quarter of 1963 there was some net stimulus from changes in national insurance benefits and contributions. By the third quarter of 1963 some effects were beginning to be felt from the rise in public investment intended for the fiscal year 1963/4. The tax concessions in the budget probably added some $1\frac{1}{2}$ per cent to consumers' expenditure in both the third and the fourth quarters.[2]

[1] 'Moreover, in so far as there is a stocking-up movement related to expansion, in effect the building up of working capital, then I think that it is perfectly reasonable and sensible to finance such a movement out of our reserves or out of borrowing facilities in the International Monetary Fund and elsewhere. This is surely what these various facilities exist for. It is wrong to use reserves or borrowing facilities to boost up an internal position which is unsound because costs, prices and incomes have got out of hand. But it is equally unsound to refuse to use reserves and borrowing facilities for the purposes for which they exist, namely, to deal with temporary situations and prevent temporary difficulties obstructing the proper long-term development of the economy' (*Hansard*, 3 April 1963, col. 471).

[2] However, one of the first of the expansionary measures – the improved terms for investment and depreciation allowances announced in November 1962 – seems not to have had much effect, certainly not immediately; private investment was only just beginning to recover at the end of 1963.

However, during 1963 there was much less certainty about the solidarity of the recovery, for two reasons. First, the high figures for the second quarter might simply have been a rebound from the effects of the very bad winter, so it was only as figures came in for the third quarter that confidence improved. Secondly, in 1962 there had been a recovery in the first half of the year which petered out in the second half – might not this pattern be repeated? However, by the late autumn it was clear that the recovery was well established – and by the beginning of 1964 – only a year after the turning-point – a cut-back in the rate of increase in output was already being suggested.

A useful summary of the background to policy decisions in 1964 is provided by the *National Institute Economic Review* for February of that year. Total demand was forecast to rise in real terms by some 5–6 per cent a year from the end of 1963 to the middle of 1965, the main driving forces being the upturn in private investment which had only just begun, the rise in public investment (intended to fill the gap caused by the drop in private investment) coming in late, substantial stock-building and a continuing rapid rise in exports. It was argued that this rate of increase in demand should be brought down because it would produce too low a figure of unemployment – perhaps about 1·3–1·4 per cent in mid-1965 and probably still falling – when incomes would be 'likely to rise considerably faster than productivity, even on fairly optimistic assumptions about the effect of a high pressure of demand on productivity trends'.[1] (The lagged relationship between output and employment, and therefore between output and unemployment, was by then well known.) The *Review* did not argue that the expansion up till then had been too fast, but that now it was 'sensible to look ahead to the point of full employment; and since there is no sign that the rise in demand is slowing down of its own accord, the government must be prepared to make the adjustment needed'.[2]

The argument for restraint at the beginning of 1964 was not based on any actual acceleration in price increases; indeed through 1963 the movements in both wages and prices had been moderate, even by the standards of the time. Between the fourth quarters of 1962 and of 1963 hourly wage rates had risen only 3½ per cent – virtually in line with the 'guiding light' – and over the same period the retail price index had risen only 2·2 per cent.

The balance of payments forecast took second place to unemployment in the argument for restraint. There were those who contended

---

[1] *National Institute Economic Review*, no. 27, February 1964, p. 10.

[2] Ibid. p. 11. When this was written, the estimate of the rise in national output between the fourth quarters of 1962 and 1963 was 5 per cent; on the latest figures now available, it is 6½ per cent. Had the latest figure been available at that time, the tenor of the passage quoted would probably have been rather different.

that, if at an acceptable level of unemployment Britain ran a balance of payments deficit, the remedy was not restraint but devaluation. The basis for discussion of the balance of payments in 1964 was the 'balance on current and long-term capital account, including a normal balancing item', which had already worsened during 1963: current estimates showed a change from a surplus of £43 million in the first half of 1963 to a deficit of £8 million in the second half, and this deficit was forecast to be £200 million in the first half of 1965. As to how far this emerging deficit might be considered temporary, it was conceded that some of it could be explained by stockbuilding, but probably not all of it.[1] (Throughout 1964, of course, successive balance of payments forecasts got steadily worse.)

The case presented, therefore, was for what Macmillan would have called 'a touch on the brake'. The standard argument was that it was better to take mild deflationary action early rather than severe deflationary action late. 'A policy of moderating the rise in demand, when it appears too high to be sustained, is not a "stop/go" policy: rather the opposite. The avoidance of "stop/go" does not mean that the Government should abandon the short-run regulation of the economy entirely, but rather that it should intervene in good time so that drastic action, leading to long periods of stagnation, is not needed.'[2]

The restraint urged was certainly moderate. Although it was argued that the forecast level of home output should be reduced by 2 per cent by mid-1965, a cut of only about 1 per cent was suggested for the rate of increase in real expenditure (public and private), on the grounds that if this was done soon further adjustments could be made later if needed. By mid-1965 perhaps a reduction in demand of the order of £400 million would be required, but a first instalment of £200 million was recommended. In the event the Chancellor halved this figure: he put up taxes on drink and tobacco to bring in an additional £100 million in 1964/5. He agreed that the growth rate of the economy should be reduced to 4 per cent, but judged that a relatively small amount of deflation was needed to do this.

During the rest of 1964, up to the election on 15 October, policy-makers and commentators were mainly preoccupied with the worsening balance of payments. Imports rose sharply and exports did not; by May 1964, the National Institute's forecast for the current and long-term capital deficit for the year was £300 million; by August this had risen to £500 million. In mid-October the estimate put before the new government was that the deficit was most unlikely to be below £700 million and might well reach £800 million; however, this last

[1] At that time it was assumed that stockbuilding had a particularly high import content.
[2] Ibid.

figure does not apparently take into account the 'balancing item', which was then assumed normally to provide a credit of some £60 million. Again, this was on a definition which is now not used; the figure we have in 1977 for the current deficit in 1964 is the much less formidable figure of £355 million.

The Chancellor's other concern in this period was with incomes policy. As unemployment came down wage rates began to move up rather faster and left the 'guiding light' behind; through 1964 the increase in weekly wage rates was about $4\frac{1}{2}$ per cent, and the rise in prices accelerated to about the same figure. It was too near an election for the TUC to come to any agreement with a Conservative government.

Partly because of the worsening overseas balance, the rise in output through 1964 was below the forecast; the figure now is that it rose about $4\frac{1}{2}$ per cent. Given that output rose less than expected, unemployment came down rather more sharply than forecast – to $1\frac{1}{2}$ per cent by the fourth quarter of 1964. The transition to a Labour government, therefore, came – conveniently for the narration – at the end of a period of re-expansion.

The years 1962–4 tend to be discussed as if they were in some important way different from other periods of re-expansion. However, the difference was more in words than in actions: first, there was an explicit statement that some balance of payments risks would be taken; secondly, there was a medium-term growth target of 4 per cent a year in the background, so that the relapse to a growth rate of under 3 per cent seemed more of a failure; thirdly, it was intended that an incomes policy should prevent the expansion worsening the price trend and thus the balance of payments, but this objective was never attained.

OCTOBER 1964 TO DEVALUATION

Introduction

In the period up to devaluation – and indeed until the middle of 1969 – economic policy was dominated to an even greater extent than usual by balance of payments considerations – more specifically, by the need to stop or to prevent runs on sterling. It is hard to think of any important demand management measures which were not taken with the balance of payments mainly in mind. This preoccupation comes out clearly in the first sentence of the Foreword to Harold Wilson's record of the Labour government, whose life he describes as dominated by an inherited balance of payments problem.[1]

Over this period there was a series of crises, followed by packages

---

[1] H. Wilson, *The Labour Government 1964–1970: a personal record*, London, Weidenfeld and Michael Joseph, 1971, p. xvii.

of crisis measures, often followed by false dawns, which then gave way to crises again. Nor was this pattern immediately broken by devaluation, which was, after all, to another fixed exchange rate that also had to be defended. For well over a year afterwards devaluation appeared to have been unsuccessful.

Policy decisions during this period give the impression that the government must have been struggling throughout 1965 and 1966 with a very large current balance of payments deficit. In fact, on the figures we now have, this was not so. There had certainly been a large current deficit in 1964. But from the beginning of 1965 to the end of the third quarter of 1967 the current account was virtually in balance on average. Over the whole of these eleven quarters, on the figures we have in 1977 there was in aggregate a balance of payments current surplus of £5 million. The problem was clearly not on current account at all, but on capital account.

There is a sharp divide between the policies which the Labour government found itself forced to pursue and the economic strategy which it had planned while in opposition, when four years of economic policy almost wholly constrained by the balance of payments had certainly not been envisaged.

Labour came to power firmly believing that it could improve on the Conservatives' growth record. Ministers had a clear picture of the 'stop-go' cycle, which they intended to replace by steady expansion: '... every four or five years a deliberately engineered consumption boom is generated which, after a few months, calls forth spectacular increases in national production ... A rapidly expanding home market exerts a dangerous pull on exports; a disproportionate rise in imports is needed to feed our factories and shops. So the green light changes to amber, interest rates rise, social programmes are cut back, and within a year the red light of economic crisis – with 7 per cent bank rates, additional taxation, and cuts in social expenditure – bring the economy grinding to a halt.'[1] In the discussion of ways of breaking out of the 'stop-go' cycle, Wilson put the emphasis on incomes policy and on selective intervention to improve the industrial structure. On industrial intervention he suggested, inter alia, a speedier write-off for plant (or special investment allowances) for exporting industries, 'decisive' investment allowances for particular types of automative equipment installed in manufacturing industry, help with research and finance when import-saving industries were being established, new, publicly owned industries based on science and the expansion of certain industries – such as chemical engineering and chemical plant

[1] H. Wilson, 'Labour's economic policy' in The New Britain: Labour's plan, Harmondsworth, Penguin, 1964, pp. 23-41.

manufacture; the expansion, also, of industrial training. Two new Ministries were proposed in the same speech: a Ministry of Technology and a Ministry of Economic Planning – which, in the event, became the Department of Economic Affairs. Clearly the intention was to reduce the Treasury's role in economic policy.

Thus the Labour Party came to power intending to give medium-term and long-term structural changes priority in its economic policy; instead, it found itself reacting to the day-to-day movements in the foreign exchange market.

The initial crisis

The new government made its major institutional change in the economic field straight away by establishing the Department of Economic Affairs under George Brown. The concordat which laid down the relative responsibilities of the new department and of the Treasury seems not to have been very clear, although, even if it had been, there would almost certainly still have been some struggle for power.[1] The original conception had been that the Department of Economic Affairs should lay down economic policy and the Treasury should be the administrative arm in financial matters, but since the new Chancellor of the Exchequer ranked third in the Party hierarchy it could hardly have worked out that way whatever the words of the agreement. The Civil Service put up a paper suggesting that the short term should be the Treasury's responsibility and long-term planning that of the Department of Economic Affairs, but the Prime Minister did not accept this; he wished the distinction to be between monetary matters and real resources. Either division would have been very difficult to define in terms of detailed responsibility for particular branches of policy. Most policies have both long-term and short-term effects and, in much the same way, virtually all policies have both real and monetary consequences. In fact, the new department had not been set up because Labour Party politicians saw a distinct division of responsibilities which they felt would be carried out more effectively if separated; rather it was that they distrusted the Treasury as being too pre-occupied with demand management and too little concerned with structural economic change, so that they wished for a countervailing power to champion the long-term cause in economic policy decisions. Inevitably, therefore, there was a large overlap in the responsibilities of the two departments, both of which had to be concerned in major

---

[1] 'We did manage to draft something that I called a "Concordat", but it never got itself formally accepted between Jim Callaghan, the Prime Minister and myself' (G. Brown, *In My Way*, London, Gollancz, 1971, p. 92). The use of the term 'concordat' is illuminating; it suggests an agreement between parties with potentially conflicting interests.

economic decisions. Eventually the Treasury dominated and the Department of Economic Affairs expired because the problems determining policy through most of this period concerned the balance of payments and foreign currency reserves, where the Treasury and the Bank of England could speak with authority and the Department of Economic Affairs could not.

Certainly the new division of responsibilities had little relevance to the government's immediate problems. The Treasury had presented to the Cabinet an appraisal and forecast of the economic situation which suggested that, in addition to the balance of payments deficit on current and long-term capital account of £800 million in 1964, there would be a continuing substantial deficit in 1965 a good deal higher than the published unofficial forecasts which had been available before the election. The Treasury indicated that, in addition to demand management measures, something was needed with a more immediate effect on the foreign balance. Three possibilities were put forward: devaluation of sterling, quantitative restrictions on imports, or a surcharge on a wide range of imports. The three economic Ministers chose the surcharge. The background to the decision not to devalue is set out on pages 311-12; it seems stranger now, in a world that has got used to exchange-rate changes, than it did then. Quotas were also rejected, probably mainly on the basis of Wilson's own experience of administering them in the 1940s, when he was President of the Board of Trade. This left the surcharge as the least damaging to the home economy of the three proposals, but the main objection to it was that it contravened international obligations, particularly those of the General Agreement on Tariffs and Trade (GATT) and of the European Free Trade Area (EFTA).

The government announced a 15 per cent surcharge on imports of manufactured goods on 26 October. This was accompanied by a published statement which included the estimate of a current and long-term capital deficit for 1964 of £800 million, but also indicated that the government did not consider the general pressure on resources excessive, so that there was no need to move to a higher level of unemployment.[1] Government expenditure was to be reviewed – Concorde was singled out – an export rebate system was announced and there were one or two other minor measures. The initial reaction abroad was rather sharp, particularly by members of EFTA, who had been given no advance warning. However, there was at this stage no run on sterling.

On 11 November the Chancellor introduced an autumn budget. He announced a big increase in pensions to take effect from March

[1] Prime Minister's Office, *The Economic Situation*, London, HMSO, 1964.

1965, together with an increase in national assistance benefits; prescription charges were abolished.[1] National insurance contributions were to be increased at the same time; in addition, petrol tax was put up and advance notice given that income tax would be raised in the 1965 budget. The Chancellor also gave notice that he would be introducing a capital gains tax and altering the system of company taxation. In crude terms, the increase in budget revenue was well in excess of the Exchequer contribution to the new benefits. However, the National Institute's analysis suggested that, since the rise in income tax would be at the expense of personal and company savings, and since employers' contributions work only partially and belatedly through to consumer prices, the combined net effect of the changes in benefits, the budget and the import surcharge would be to raise the demand for home output at the end of 1965 by around 1 per cent.

The budget started speculation against sterling, which continued into the next week. Bank Rate was, however, not raised on Thursday 19 November, as generally expected; according to Wilson, George Brown objected.[2] This was also the day on which other EFTA countries demanded and got a promise that the import surcharge would be reduced 'in a matter of months'. Bank Rate was eventually put up by 2 per cent on 23 November, but this still failed to check the speculative outflow.[3] Wilson describes a succession of interviews which took place during this period with the Governor of the Bank of England (Lord Cromer), who stressed the need for cuts in government expenditure as a necessary condition for stopping the outflow. The Prime Minister indicated that, rather than cut social expenditure in deference to foreign financial opinion, he would go to the country again and float the exchange rate; he asked Lord Cromer to see what he could raise from other central banks in support for sterling. Within a day the Governor announced that he had successfully raised £3 billion, thus ending the first of the Labour government's speculative crises.

It has been argued that the management of policy in these first two months was maladroit: that it was foolish to announce publicly the size of the expected deficit, to delay the increase in Bank Rate for four days, to announce in advance the introduction of capital gains tax and corporation tax without saying more precisely what their provisions would be, and so on. However, these errors of timing – if they were errors – cannot have mattered very much; in the light of the specula-

---

[1] The estimated cost of the changes in national insurance benefits and war pensions was £300 million. The other two measures were to cost much less: £23 million for the increase in national assistance benefits and £22 million for the abolition of prescription charges.

[2] Wilson, *The Labour Government 1964–1970*, p. 36.

[3] It is interesting that at that time it was considered necessary to inform the United States government in advance of the Bank Rate change; rather elaborate steps were taken to do this.

tion which took place against sterling during the next three years, it seems most unlikely that it would have been prevented just by the omission of a figure from a White Paper, or by raising Bank Rate four days earlier – there would have been some other trigger on some other occasion. The more serious criticism is that the initial deflation was inadequate, and that it would have been better if the government had begun in 1964 with the policies it eventually followed from 1966 onwards. If it was in any case going to take steps which increased unemployment to 2½ per cent, then it should have started on that policy right from the beginning. This is a much wider question. In 1964, of course, 1½ per cent unemployment was not considered abnormally low; it was only after 1966 that 1½ per cent was gradually replaced by 2½ per cent as a kind of norm.

The criticism of the Labour government's initial autumn budget is only part of a general criticism of the policy up to devaluation. That policy had, as its objectives, a substantial improvement in the balance of payments without the need to devalue the pound, and an acceleration of the growth rate. It failed on both counts, but it does not necessarily follow that more severe initial deflation would have been any better without other policy changes.

The second speculative crisis

International credit reinforcements stemmed the run on sterling, but did not stop it altogether; sales of sterling were still substantial in December. The pressure was eased further, however, when very good trade figures were announced for December. Throughout this period, and indeed right up to the present day, Ministers have repeated again and again that no weight should be attached to one month's trade figures, but this has made no difference to the tendency for confidence to swing according to the latest figure.

In the period between the two budgets, the Department of Economic Affairs made the first moves on an incomes policy; it also began to construct a National Plan. On incomes policy, employers' representatives and trade unionists were persuaded to sign a joint statement of intent on productivity, prices and incomes in the middle of December; by mid-February there was an agreed White Paper on the machinery of policy;[1] in mid-March Aubrey Jones was appointed chairman of the NBPI, and the TUC General Council agreed to a 3–3½ per cent norm for wage increases, which was endorsed in April by a conference of executive committees of affiliated unions. On planning, the target figure for the growth rate, announced well in advance of the National

[1] Prime Minister's Office, *Machinery of Prices and Incomes Policy*, Cmnd 2577, London, HMSO, 1965.

Plan itself, was a 25 per cent increase in output between 1964 and 1970. Linked to this ambitious target, the Chancellor announced in February that public expenditure was to increase in real terms by an average of 4½ per cent a year between 1964/5 and 1969/70.

However, in preparing for the budget the Chancellor was naturally concerned with the more immediate problems of the balance of payments. The credits from other central banks had been renewed for a further three months in early February and, in response to intense EFTA pressure, it had been announced that the surcharge on imports of manufactures would be reduced to 10 per cent in April. The National Institute continued to insist on the need for more deflation of home demand to allow a transfer of resources into the balance of payments. It argued that: 'The main aim for policy therefore must be to find ways of improving the balance of payments in 1966 by a figure of the order of £300 million, without adding to the total pressure of demand.'[1] A direct attack limiting investment and government expenditure overseas might conceivably produce a net improvement of £100 million, so that an increase in taxation sufficient to reduce final demand by £200 million from the level it would otherwise have reached was recommended.

In fact the budget followed this prescription fairly closely. United Kingdom residents who sold investments held outside the sterling area had to exchange 25 per cent of the proceeds for sterling at the official rate rather than the investment premium rate (see page 328), and there was a declaration of intent to save £50–£100 million in overseas military expenditure. In addition to the increase in income tax which had already been announced, higher taxes were imposed on drink and tobacco and motor vehicle licence fees were raised. The estimated effect on demand in 1966 was not far short of the figure which the National Institute had suggested.[2] Already an incongruity was beginning to appear between the declared growth target and the requirements of the balance of payments. The effect of the budget, according to the National Institute forecast in May 1965, would be to slow down the rise in output by the first quarter of 1966 to a rate of 2½ per cent a year.

After the budget the government felt, not unreasonably, that it had done enough to ward off further speculative attacks. Monetary policy was tightened in April, when there was an additional call for Special Deposits, and in May controls on bank advances were reimposed. Also in May there was a further drawing from the IMF, most of which was used to repay borrowings from the other central banks. Then in June,

---

[1] *National Institute Economic Review*, no. 31, February 1965, p. 12.

[2] About £150 million at factor cost in 1966 from the increases in taxation on drink, tobacco, and motor licences (*National Institute Economic Review*, no. 32, May 1965, p. 20).

when it seemed that there were neither external nor internal reasons for maintaining Bank Rate at 7 per cent, the Bank was persuaded to lower the Rate by a whole point, contrary to the old doctrine of 'up by ones, down by halves'. This also gave the government the option of increasing Bank Rate again if pressure developed on sterling in the autumn. But, presumably because of nervousness about foreign reaction, the Bank Rate reduction was coupled with tightening of hire purchase controls, to which the Department of Economic Affairs objected; the proposed measures were, however, endorsed by the Cabinet.

We know now that the current balance of payments improved very substantially between the second half of 1964 and the first half of 1965; on figures now available the current deficit fell from £251 million to £10 million. However, while the trade figures available at the time had improved very sharply to a deficit of only £13 million a month in the first quarter of 1965, in April this widened to £30 million and in May to £49 million – which was as bad as in the second half of 1964. A speculative run on sterling began again on publication of these figures and the June figure, at £33 million, was not sufficiently improved to stop the outflow.

The package of deflationary measures therefore announced on 27 July 1965 is generally accepted as 'tough', but, as with all packages which contain large cuts in public investment, it is hard to say just how tough in fact it was. Starts of public investment projects – except for industrial building, housing, school-building and hospitals – were postponed for six months; nationalised industries' investment and local authorities' building programmes were cut; local authority mortgages to private house-buyers were limited; building licences were introduced for commercial projects; hire purchase terms were tightened again and importers were required to make pre-payments on goods brought into the country. The whole package was supposed to reduce demand by £200 million in a full year, but it is very hard to say whether or not this figure was exaggerated. There was at the time a heavy load on the building industry, so that the postponement of starts may simply have accelerated completions. No public investment programme for 1965/6 had been published, so that, as the *National Institute Economic Review* remarked: '...cuts of an unknown size are being made in an unknown sum, to take effect at an unknown time'.[1] It is true that in August of that year the National Institute's forecast of output was significantly more pessimistic than in May, when it had

---

[1] Ibid. no. 33, August 1965, p. 8. The 1965/6 investment programme appeared in *The National Plan*, published in September; the impact of the investment cuts is appraised in this context on pages 113–14 below.

envisaged that output would be rising at about $2\frac{1}{2}$ per cent a year from mid-1965 onwards; by August that figure had been brought down to $1\frac{1}{2}$ per cent. However, the July measures were not the only reason for the change.

The third speculative crisis

As usual, it was uncertain for a time whether or not the measures would be successful in stopping the speculation. In the meantime the Prime Minister, the Chancellor and the Governor of the Bank of England discussed whether they could all go on holiday at the same time as planned, but sterling survived their simultaneous absence, helped by very good trade figures for July, with a deficit of only £3 million.

However, a great deal of the foreign lines of credit had been used up in the defence of sterling and there was no substantial reflux of short-term capital. It was clear that there would soon have to be further support for sterling and the American Secretary of the Treasury was a key figure in this operation. In particular, he pressed the British government to tighten up on its incomes policy because he doubted whether the voluntary policy would be able to withstand the pressure for wage increases.[1] The government therefore decided early in September to introduce legislation making the NBPI a statutory body, giving the Secretary of State power to defer any wage or price settlement while enquiries were continuing, and providing for an 'early warning' of price increases and wage settlements. The TUC General Council reluctantly accepted this Bill, but extracted the compromise that a special Order in Council would be required to activate the legislation; in the meantime the TUC had agreed to strengthen the voluntary system by requiring all wage claims to be submitted to their General Council for vetting by new machinery. The Bill was in fact introduced, but it had not passed through all its stages before the general election in March 1966, so that it lapsed and had to be reintroduced in the next Parliament. Enough had been done, however, to meet the American point and, on 10 September, further international support for sterling was announced.

On 13 September *The National Plan* was published;[2] two other longer-term measures of note at this time were the introduction of investment grants in place of investment allowances and the establishment of the IRC.

Throughout the second half of 1965 the trade figures were improving, with exports rising well. Unemployment stayed low, which seemed very surprising at the time, for the current estimates were that national

---

[1] Wilson, *The Labour Government 1964–1970*, pp. 131–2.
[2] Department of Economic Affairs, *The National Plan*.

output had only risen 1½ per cent in the year up to the fourth quarter of 1965. (The figures now available suggest a rise of 2½ per cent, and the failure of unemployment to rise becomes more explicable.) Thus the economic background for an election was not unfavourable: the government could claim significant progress in improving the balance of payments, unemployment was still very low and, in a pre-election statement of his assessment of the economic situation, the Chancellor suggested that there would be no need to increase taxation in the budget.

By the beginning of 1966 it was becoming clear that it would be very difficult to reconcile the two objectives of faster growth and improving the balance of payments. The National Institute throughout this period was putting forward the view insistently, and indeed repetitively, that on current policies there would be slow growth only, and for this to change it was necessary for export competitiveness to improve and the propensity to import to moderate. At the beginning of 1966 it was suggested that it might be better to revise the target figures for the National Plan, since it seemed probable that the annual growth rate in the first two years of the Plan would be at best 2½ per cent, which would leave an impossible requirement for the remaining four years.

From the beginning of 1966 the trade gap began to widen again. The government took monetary measures in February: the ceiling on bank advances was continued and restrictions on hire purchase tightened further. After the election the Chancellor found that the Treasury assessment of the economic situation had changed; unemployment had still not begun to rise – indeed it was lower in the first quarter of 1966 than in the fourth quarter of 1965 – so that a fairly substantial further reduction in demand was recommended. The form this took was the selective employment tax (discussed more fully on pages 150–3). The main disadvantage of its introduction in the 1966 budget was the time-lag before it could be implemented; collection did not start until September. The Chancellor also announced that the import surcharge would be removed in November 1966.

From the budget onwards events moved towards the third speculative crisis, of July 1966. The proximate cause was the seamen's strike, which started on 12 May and did not finish until 1 July. Again the background was not one of major underlying weakness in the balance of payments: when the 1965 crisis took place the balance of payments – as we now know – was running a very small deficit; at the time of the 1966 crisis there was a small current surplus of £84 million for the year as a whole.[1]

---

[1] The quarterly figures are distorted by the strike, so that the whole of the surplus is recorded in the fourth quarter of the year, but there was probably a small 'underlying' surplus by the second quarter.

The strike naturally caused a run on sterling. However, during the strike the pressure was contained at the cost of some loss to the reserves; the announcement of new swap facilities, agreed at the annual meeting of the Bank for International Settlements on 13 June, no doubt helped. When the strike ended on 1 July, it appeared to the policy-makers that they had weathered the storm. However, when the reserve figures were announced on 4 July there was a further rush to sell sterling; speculation had caused the fall in reserves, which in turn caused further speculation. Another possible factor was a French statement at the time of M. Pompidou's visit to Britain, which appeared to suggest that devaluation of sterling would be necessary before the idea of Britain joining the Common Market could be entertained.

The moves made in the attempt to handle the crisis have again been criticised. It is true that initially they failed, but in such a situation it is very difficult to know what moves might be successful. On 11 July stories of forthcoming deflationary measures were emphatically denied; on 12 July the Chancellor announced a continuation of a tight monetary policy – retaining the existing ceiling on bank advances, with no relaxation to help firms finance the interval between payments and refunds of selective employment tax; on 14 July Bank Rate was raised by 1 per cent, increased calls were made for Special Deposits and it was announced that deflationary measures would be introduced in about a fortnight's time. These moves were all unsuccessful; on 20 July a very substantial deflationary package was announced.

This time there was a devaluation party in the Cabinet. George Brown had come round to the view that further deflationary measures without a devaluation would finally dispose of any hope of significant economic expansion. For a while, in early July, it seems that the Chancellor too was willing to entertain the idea, but the Prime Minister persuaded him that there was no alternative to fighting on to the end in defence of the exchange rate. On 19 July the matter was discussed in the Cabinet, where there was some support for devaluing the pound and apparently some Ministers put the case for floating the pound, but the vote went heavily in favour of holding the exchange rate.

The package included a further tightening of hire purchase terms, the use of the regulator to raise indirect tax rates by 10 per cent, increases in Post Office charges, a surcharge on surtax for one year, an extension of the coverage of building licences, cuts in public investment and overseas expenditure, the introduction of a travel allowance and a six-month standstill on incomes and prices, to be followed by a further six months of severe restraint. The National Institute's assessment of the consequences of these measures was that they would put the economy on a 1 per cent growth path; however, at this cost – of virtually stopping any rise in output – the balance of payments should move into surplus in 1967 on current and long-term capital account.

The prelude to devaluation

After July 1966 there was a gradual return of confidence. Sterling received further support from abroad in September and the trade figures improved considerably. The impending abolition of the surcharge at the end of November explained a large part of the improvement: importers postponed purchases until the surcharge was removed. Nonetheless, in the winter of 1966/7 there was an appreciable reflux of short-term capital.

When George Brown, having piloted the Prices and Incomes Bill through the House of Commons, left the Department of Economic Affairs to be Foreign Secretary, it was probably the end of any substantial influence by this department on the main issues of economic policy. The TUC reluctantly acquiesced in the government's incomes policy, which was endorsed by a majority at the annual Congress in September. It remained a voluntary policy until October, when it was successfully challenged in the Courts by the Association of Supervisory Staffs, Executives and Technicians and the government activated the compulsory provisions of the Prices and Incomes Act (see page 372). There were in fact no strikes against the wage freeze.

It was at this time that the decision was taken to explore again the possibility of joining the Common Market; at the beginning of 1967 the Prime Minister and the Foreign Secretary began a tour of the six existing member countries of the European Economic Community (the EEC).

Early in 1967 official assessments of the economic situation and prospects became more confident. The reflux of short-term funds meant that by the end of March nearly all central bank assistance had been repaid. The trade gap in the first quarter of the year stayed small. The National Institute continued to forecast a surplus on current and long-term capital account in 1967; it also published a medium-term assessment which attempted to forecast export possibilities, deduce from them the volume of imports which could be purchased and so see what rate of expansion the balance of payments might allow. The conclusion was that: 'Allowing for a minor change in the competitiveness of British manufactures in home as well as export markets, the import availability...would be adequate, with a little to spare, for a 3 per cent growth-rate from 1967 to 1970.'[1]

The preoccupation with the balance of payments began to diminish a little and there were the first signs of concern about rising unemploy-

[1] *National Institute Economic Review*, no. 39, February 1967, p. 23.

ment. The budget was basically neutral; the Chancellor's message, introducing it on 11 April, was: 'We are back on course. The ship is picking up speed. The economy is moving. Every seaman knows the command at such a moment, "steady as she goes".'

There was a series of minor reflationary measures. As far back as November 1966 the Bank of England had indicated that credit was available to priority borrowers. In December the government had announced that there would be an additional 5 per cent on investment grants for investment undertaken in 1967 and 1968 only; then Bank Rate was reduced and restraints were tacitly eased on public investment programmes. In June the government announced increases in national insurance benefits to take effect from the end of October.

However, in the second quarter things began to go wrong: exports failed to rise and the trade gap worsened. The National Institute's forecast for the 'basic' balance in 1967, which had been £175 million in February, fell to £105 million in May and £35 million in August; from mid-May onwards confidence in sterling began to weaken again. Partly this was, of course, due to the Middle East war and the closure of the Suez Canal, but possibly also the British application to join the Common Market had led many people to conclude that the sterling parity would have to be changed before the application could be successful.[1]

In the third quarter of the year policy became uncertain: the balance of payments outlook was deteriorating but, on the other hand, unemployment was still rising. In July the Chancellor announced that the rise in public expenditure for three years from 1967/8 would be held to 3 per cent in real terms, but as late as the end of August there was further reflation – the restrictions on hire purchase terms were relaxed. The confidence which had been expressed earlier in the year was waning; the National Institute forecasts in August were for only a negligible basic balance in 1967, with no improvement in 1968; the appraisal noted:

If, looking further ahead, it turns out that with a 3 per cent growth-rate the balance of payments outcome is still inadequate, the Government could hardly meet this situation by deflating demand in the private sector once again. Last July, deflation by itself was a practicable alternative to devaluation or import controls, first because unemployment was still low; and secondly because there was the prospect of a very rapid rise in public sector expenditure which would partly counterbalance the check to private sector

[1] In the nature of things, suggested influences on the foreign exchange market have to be surmises. Reactions are not easily predictable; it was suggested, for example, that an increase in electricity charges had a bad effect (see S. Brittan, *Steering the Economy* (rev. edn), London, Penguin, 1971, p. 348).

spending. Now unemployment is high, and the increase in public sector spending is being cut back... If in such circumstances a further change of course is needed, and if the Government moved again to deflate private demand, the check might quickly slide into the first major postwar recession.[1]

However, at the beginning of October the position was still far from critical. Wilson states in his memoirs that the strength of the economy was not then in question. He clearly takes the view that we were forced to devalue, not by an underlying weak position, but by the particular circumstances of 1967.[2] It is doubtful, however, whether the Chancellor and the Treasury were so sanguine about the underlying position. Certainly between August and November the 'pre-devaluation' balance of payments forecasts by the National Institute deteriorated substantially: in November they were for basic deficits of £275 million in 1967 and £250 million in 1968. The official forecasts at the time are reported to have shown even larger deficits. Within the Treasury a number of people had long been in favour of running the economy with unemployment at about 2 per cent. Consequently they had been quite ready to accept the deflationary measures of July 1966, since they considered them desirable in any case and they regarded it as possible that if unemployment rose the balance of payments would improve sufficiently for devaluation to be avoided. In 1967 the position was different with unemployment above 2 per cent throughout the year, so that they were no longer prepared to advocate simple deflationary measures. Thus, the underlying situation cannot really be described as 'strong', but there is no doubt that it was made worse both by the dock strikes and by fairly wide-spread discussion in Europe of a possible British devaluation.

The dock strikes began in Liverpool, Manchester, London and Hull on 18 September, when the process of the de-casualisation began, and continued spasmodically for two months; the Merseyside dockers went back at the end of October, but in London the dockers at the Royal Group did not return until 27 November. In consequence, the trade figures announced in both October and November showed very large deficits. In October also a Common Market Commission reporting on the British application expressed substantial doubts about the sterling area and, by implication, about the sterling exchange rate. This theme was picked up by M. Couve de Murville in a speech where he compared the current British position with France's position in 1958, when the franc was devalued just before the Common Market began.

The actual sequence of meetings which led up to devaluation is best described in Harold Wilson's memoirs.[3] The Chancellor came to see

[1] *National Institute Economic Review*, no. 41, August 1967, p. 10.
[2] Wilson, *The Labour Government 1964-1970*, p. 439.   [3] Ibid. p. 447 *et seq.*

him on 4 November; pressure on sterling had increased because of rumours on the continent; the Ministerial Finance Committee of the Six, due to meet on 14 November, apparently had on its agenda an item on what the Six would do if Britain devalued. Wilson records that for the first time both he and the Chancellor expressed doubts about whether they could hold the position; he was concerned to avoid a major lurch into deflation, but also that too many other countries should not follow the pound if devalued. He stated that he favoured floating rather than a lower parity.

A number of moves were then made to consult other countries – asking them essentially whether they were ready to see sterling devalued, and if so whether they would want to follow us down, or whether they would promise help for sterling to avoid a disruption of world finance. The Chancellor had a meeting with the Secretary of the Finance Committee of the Six, and the Governor of the Bank of England consulted the European central bank Governors at their monthly meeting in Basle.

In Britain, further Ministers were informed of the possibility of devaluation on 8 November at a meeting of the Steering Committee on Economic Policy, where the agenda included a paper on import quotas, but the Prime Minister let it be known that alternative action could be discussed. Consequently devaluation *was* discussed and the Treasury began work on the deflationary package which would be needed to accompany it. The Treasury and the Bank also began to consider which countries might follow: they apparently suggested that the Scandinavians were likely to do so, but the Six were uncertain and so was Australia; if Australia devalued, Japan, Malaysia, Singapore and Hong Kong would do the same. If all these countries also devalued, gains from the change of parity would be problematical.

Of the foreign institutions consulted, it appears that the United States Treasury was the most horrified; they proceeded to try to organise an international package. However, it appears that the general opinion at Basle among the central bankers was that there should not simply be another set of stand-by facilities arranged between central banks; it should be routed through the IMF, the Secretary-General of which indicated that this would require intensive IMF supervision of the British economy – for example, strict credit control, a tighter prices and incomes policy, a limitation on growth, and an agreement not to float during the currency of the loan. A loan on these conditions was rejected and, although they were apparently qualified to some extent, under American as well as British pressure, the qualifications were insufficient. The decision to devalue was therefore taken on 13 November; the next day a group of Ministers met to decide on the accompanying deflationary measures; the Cabinet was informed on 16 November. By this time there were stories in the press about a massive $1 billion loan from foreign banks; a question was asked about this in the House of Commons and the Chancellor, while stone-walling in reply, appears to have given the impression that the stories were erroneous. Operators in the foreign exchange markets therefore leapt to the conclusion that the other possibility – devaluation – must be right and throughout the next day there was an enormous run on sterling. To allow time for the IMF Board to meet, the Treasury statement announcing devaluation was not issued until 9.30 on Saturday evening. In the event very few countries followed sterling down.

The demand restrictions which accompanied devaluation are widely reported to have been smaller than the Treasury or the Bank of England wished; the Prime Minister refused to accept a rise in the standard rate of income tax. They consisted of a moderate increase in hire purchase restrictions, a ceiling on bank advances and an increase of $1\frac{1}{2}$ per cent in Bank Rate; there were to be cuts in defence spending and also other public spending totalling £200 million a year; export rebates were to be withdrawn, also selective employment tax refunds to manufacturers except in development areas; corporation tax was increased. At the same time it was announced that an application would be made for stand-by credits of $1·4 billion from the IMF and $1·6 billion from other central banks.

THE AFTERMATH OF DEVALUATION

Introduction

Devaluation did not immediately transform economic policy. For a year and a half there was the same overriding preoccupation with the balance of payments; the same need was felt to defend the exchange rate which had, after all, moved to a new fixed parity. There were, as before, speculative runs on sterling, and again these forced the government to take deflationary measures. Until the middle of 1969 the government was waiting for the effects of devaluation to appear. Successive forecasts postponed the move into balance of payments surplus further and further into the future, until by the beginning of 1969 a number of people were doubting whether devaluation would ever improve the balance of payments.

The Treasury had warned the politicians from the beginning that the effect would not be immediate, that the balance of payments would get worse before it got better and that the improvement would not be apparent until the second half of 1968. In a Letter of Intent to the IMF on 23 November 1967, the Treasury stated the government's balance of payments target as: 'an improvement of at least £500 million a year... which on present prospects for world trade...should mean a surplus in the second half of 1968 at an annual rate of at least £200 million'. It was the failure of the balance of payments to improve in this way which dominated economic policy in this period. It is clear why the forecasts went wrong – they underestimated the buoyancy of imports.

'Making room'

The Letter of Intent of 23 November stated: 'The next review of the position and prospects of the United Kingdom economy...will, in the normal course of business, be carried out in February 1968. At this time, it should be possible to assess more accurately than can be done at present the effects of the decisions announced on 18 November 1967.' However, the government was forced to act earlier than this; undoubtedly one reason was that the reflux of short-term funds lasted for only a few days after devaluation, and at the end of November and the beginning of December there was renewed pressure on sterling. At this time there was a move into gold because the dollar was also suspect, and no doubt the speculators assumed that if the dollar were devalued sterling would go down with it. So in December the Prime Minister announced a very wide-ranging review of public expenditure.

In an *ex post* justification of the timing of the measures taken, published in mid-March 1968, the government claimed in effect that it was all part of a carefully planned strategy:

The Government recognised that further measures to release resources would be needed. But given the high level of unemployment,[1] and the necessary uncertainty about the timing and magnitude of the response of exports and imports to devaluation, it did not wish to engineer this release before the additional demand for exports (and import substitutes) induced by devaluation had started to come through. It proposed therefore to act during the course of the coming months, first on public consumption (since cut backs in that field necessarily take time to become effective) and later on private consumption.[2]

Or, as Roy Jenkins had put it more graphically in the House of Commons on 5 December 1967: 'We do not want to dig a hole and leave it empty. We want it to be there only when the export demand is ready to fill it.' This exposition is, however, not wholly convincing; certainly it is open to question whether the review of expenditure would have been so severe had there been a bigger reflux of short-term capital.

[1] Unemployment at 2·4 per cent (United Kingdom, excluding school-leavers) was then considered high.

[2] Treasury, *Economic Report on 1967*, London, HMSO, 1968, p. 7.

The public expenditure cuts occupied a long series of Cabinet meetings in early January 1968; the results were finally announced on 16 January. Cuts of this kind are always difficult to quantify sensibly, since they are reductions not from previous levels but from future programmes. The total decrease in expenditure plans estimated for 1968/9, including the £200 million cuts announced on 18 November, amounted to £500 million; larger reductions on existing commitments were estimated for subsequent years.

Chart 2.1. *Public expenditure on goods and services,[a] 1964–72*

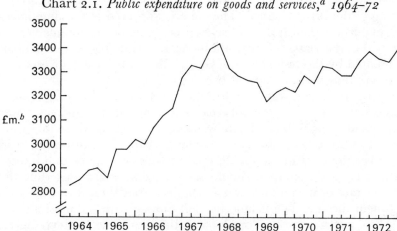

SOURCE: CSO, *Economic Trends, Annual Supplement 1976*, pp. 14, 46 and 47.

[a] Current and capital expenditure; iron and steel investment excluded throughout to avoid a discontinuity from nationalisation in 1967.

[b] At 1970 prices, seasonally adjusted.

The 1968 cuts are significant in two ways: first, they marked the end of British aspirations to be a world power, with accelerated withdrawal from east of Suez; secondly, superimposed as they were on previous reductions, they helped to bring about a sharp check in the rising trend of public authorities' expenditure on goods and services (current and capital) (chart 2.1). The first quarter of 1968 was a peak in the trend of this expenditure; from the beginning of 1964 to the beginning of 1968 it had risen at $4\frac{1}{2}$ per cent a year in real terms. From the beginning of 1968 the trend changed sharply; public expenditure on this definition was falling through the rest of 1968 and again in 1969. Many public expenditure cuts in the postwar period may be open to question, but there is no mistaking the genuine change in trend after the beginning of 1968.

In early March sterling came under pressure again in consequence of the rush into gold. At that time private buyers could purchase gold from the 'gold pool' at \$35 an ounce – the price collectively maintained by the gold pool countries.[1] Speculation increased when it became known that the chairman of the Federal Reserve Board was attending the meeting of the central bankers in Basle on 10 March, and statements both from Basle and the Bank of England that the gold price would continue to be held down failed to stop the movement. The drain from official reserves became formidable; it was decided to close the gold pool and create a two-tier market. The foreign exchange markets were closed on 15 March, a step which in Britain required a meeting of the Privy Council. The episode appeared at the time much more important than it does in retrospect; some of the comment even suggested that it was a major world monetary crisis. The whole incident was inflated by the resignation of George Brown from the government on the grounds that he had not been consulted.

The 1968 budget was perhaps the most formidable deflationary budget since the war; the full-year effect of the tax increases was estimated at £923 million. There was an immediate increase in a wide range of indirect taxes; selective employment tax was to be raised in September, by which time the delayed response in exports and import substitution to devaluation should have become more powerful; the standard rate of income tax was unchanged, but there was a levy on investment income. The Chancellor left himself with the possibility of using hire purchase restrictions later in the year. The tax increases, it was estimated, would reduce consumers' expenditure by about 2 per cent; the combined effect of the expenditure reductions and the tax increases was intended to keep the 'borrowing requirement' well below the upper limit of £1000 million mentioned in the Letter of Intent. For the first time the budget was accompanied by a quantified economic forecast.

Two further moves were made about this time. A new phase of incomes policy was announced: it provided for a nil norm;[2] a maximum increase of $3\frac{1}{2}$ per cent was allowed in exceptional circumstances, with additional exceptions for productivity bargaining, and the government's power to postpone settlements was extended to twelve months. By this time incomes policy was meeting with much stronger trade union opposition; in the autumn both the TUC annual Congress and the Labour Party conference rejected incomes policy legislation by overwhelming majorities.

Also in the spring of 1968 consultations were begun to protect

[1] At that time: Belgium, Italy, the Netherlands, Switzerland, the United Kingdom, the United States and West Germany. France had left the pool at the end of 1967.
[2] That is, the normal increase in wage rates should be nil.

sterling if sterling area countries, after devaluation, wished to diversify their reserves and reduce their sterling balances. These consultations resulted in September in the Basle Group Arrangement, under which a dozen other central banks offered credits to offset any reductions in sterling holdings by sterling area countries and the British government gave dollar-value guarantees on the bulk of the holdings. This effectively removed one threat to sterling.

Movements in the balance of payments

Improvement in the balance of payments was slow. It soon became clear that the target set in the Letter of Intent – a surplus in the second half of the year – would not be met; in successive forecasts, the estimated point at which the balance of payments would cross into surplus was shifted further and further into the future (table 2.4). The precise quantifications of the official forecast which accompanied the budget make it possible to compare the government's expectations with what actually happened (table 2.5). The volume of exports responded to devaluation as vigorously as expected; imports did not – partly, but only partly, because consumers' expenditure was maintained despite an expected fall.

Throughout 1968 the National Institute was arguing the case for import controls. The government tried tightening monetary policy in May: a ceiling was fixed on bank advances implying they should be held at roughly their existing level and the banks were asked 'especially to intensify restrictions on the granting of credit associated with imports of manufactured goods for home consumption or imports for stock accumulation'. The next moves were not made till November, when the balance of payments prospect looked much worse again and hire purchase restrictions were tightened. Then speculation in favour of the Deutschemark brought about the last of the series of speculative attacks on sterling which dominated economic policy under the Labour government.

A conference was called in Bonn, but the German government was not prepared to revalue. It introduced an export tax and an import subsidy equivalent to a 3 per cent 'back door' revaluation, and took steps to discourage the inflow of hot money. The Chancellor came back to announce a further deflationary package: the full use of the regulator, a further tightening of control on bank lending, with a 2 per cent reduction in non-exempt advances to be brought about by March, and an import deposit scheme which required importers to deposit 50 per cent of the value of goods for six months. There was, however, no immediate effect on confidence; at the beginning of December there were wide-spread rumours that the government was breaking up, with

Table 2.4. *Successive forecasts and estimates of the current balance of payments, 1967–70*

£ million

	1967		1968		1969		1970	
	1st half	2nd half	1st half	2nd half	1st half	2nd half	1st half	2nd half
By National Institute in:								
November 1967	−85	−265	−250	−125	..	..	..	..
February 1968	−108	−392	−75	+75	+200	..	..	..
May 1968	−99	−415	−335	−40	+175	..	..	..
August 1968	−514		−310	−140	+90	+260	..	..
November 1968	−404		−337	−169	−79	+121	..	..
February 1969[a]	n.a.		−430		+39	+89	+85	..
May 1969[a]	n.a.		−429		−96	+49	+125	+205
August 1969[a]	n.a.		−429		−14	+117	+91	+264
November 1969[b]	n.a.		−265		+93	+282	+327	+523
Latest official estimate (October 1976)	−298		−272		+150	+310	+416	+317

SOURCES: *National Institute Economic Review* (various issues); CSO, *Economic Trends, Annual Supplement 1976*, p. 98.

[a] Published forecasts excluded the cost of United States military aircraft and missiles; estimates for these are added to the above figures.

[b] The first figures which were corrected for the under-recording of exports disclosed in June 1969.

Table 2.5. *Some indicators for 1968: Treasury forecasts and actual out-turns*

Indices, 1967 (2nd half) = 100[a]

	1st half, 1968		2nd half, 1968	
	Forecast[b]	Actual[c]	Forecast[b]	Actual[c]
Consumers' expenditure	99·6	101·4	98·1	101·0
Public authorities' current spending	101·7	100·9	103·0	99·5
Gross fixed investment	102·7	103·5	105·7	104·6
Exports[d]	112·7	112·8	113·1	118·2
Imports[d]	102·3	105·6	100·6	106·4
GDP[e]	102·0	103·0	103·6	104·9

SOURCES: Forecasts from Treasury, *Financial Statement, 1968–69*, London, HMSO, 1968, table 13; actuals from CSO, *Economic Trends, Annual Supplement 1976*, p. 12.

[a] Seasonally adjusted.
[b] Based on 1958 prices.
[c] Based on 1970 prices.
[d] Of goods and services.
[e] Average of income, expenditure and output estimates.

resignations from the Prime Minister or the Chancellor. However, the November trade figures, announced on 12 December, chanced to be very good, and before the end of the year the speculative attack had spent itself.

The turning-point

On the figures we have now there is a clear turning-point in the balance of payments at the end of 1968:[1] in the first quarter of 1969 the current balance moved into surplus and in the second quarter this surplus – at an annual rate of nearly £400 million – was substantial. However, at the time things seemed to be getting worse rather than better. The trade figures, which had improved considerably in the three months from November 1968 to January 1969, got worse again after that; the trade figures for the three months February–April 1969, available in May, showed a deficit running a good deal higher than in the second half of 1968. Of all the balance of payments forecasts the National Institute made in the period after devaluation that of May 1969 was the most pessimistic.[2] However, there were no further speculative attacks on sterling in the first quarter; it was supported by some inflow of short-term money earning relatively high interest rates (Bank Rate was raised at the end of February) and a number of sterling area countries added to their reserves.

The budget introduced on 15 April was certainly not a confident statement of success. The Chancellor stated his objective in rather negative terms: 'what I must ensure is that there is certainly room for movement in the right direction, and that even a deviation in the wrong direction would not leave us in an intolerable balance of payments situation'; he acknowledged the possibility that he might have been on the wrong tack: 'It is, of course, the case that after a year of progress, real but disappointingly slow, no one in my position could dismiss without thought the views of those who urge some entirely different strategy.' The additional deflation in the budget was not substantial; rates of corporation tax and selective employment tax and a range of indirect taxes were increased, but this was estimated to have a fairly slow effect, perhaps reducing the growth rate of output by about $\frac{1}{4}$ per cent both in 1969 and again in 1970.[3] Taking public revenue and expenditure together, 1969/70 was a year in which the public sector moved into significant surplus on current and capital account combined (see page 203). Nonetheless, the economic forecast which accom-

---

[1] CSO, *Economic Trends, Annual Supplement 1976*, London, HMSO, 1976.

[2] This was before the announcement (in June 1969) of the discovery of under-recorded exports (see page 51).

[3] The effect was on a forecast which had, of course, already taken the public expenditure cuts into account.

panied the budget indicated the official view that output would be rising by just on 3 per cent between the first halves of 1969 and 1970. The National Institute had a lower forecast, of 2 per cent – which was, in fact, the actual outcome on the latest available figures (May 1977).

During the spring the government was concerned with refinancing the $1 billion remaining of the $1·4 billion IMF drawing made in December 1965, which was due for repayment in 1968–70. The conditions for this refinancing were set out in the Letter of Intent published on 23 June. This specified a target for 1969/70 of a £300 million current and long-term capital surplus on the balance of payments, a 1 per cent maximum increase in public expenditure in real terms over the 1968/9 planned level and a £400 million limit to domestic credit expansion (DCE).

However, the main preoccupation of policy-makers at this time was with the Industrial Relations Bill. The government's prices and incomes policies were clearly beginning to break down and the idea was spreading that, if some way could be found of dealing with unofficial strikes, this would be a major advance towards reducing the pressure behind wage demands. Following the publication of the Donovan Report,[1] Barbara Castle, Secretary of State at the re-christened Department of Employment and Productivity, produced a set of proposals published on 17 January.[2] The main contentious proposals were to give the Secretary of State discretionary powers:

(a) to require a ballot before an official strike which 'would involve a serious threat to the economy or public interest';

(b) in unconstitutional strikes or strikes where adequate joint discussions had not taken place, to order 'a conciliation pause' with a return to work for a period of 28 days.

There would be financial penalties for failure to comply.

There was strong opposition in the trade union movement and also in the Labour movement generally; when the proposals were debated in the House of Commons on 3 March some 57 Labour members voted against the government and an estimated 30 more abstained. Nonetheless the government decided to legislate immediately and announced at the same time that the statutory prices and incomes policy would be phased out. In the Industrial Relations Bill which followed the proposed ballot before an official strike was dropped.

Bargaining between the government and TUC over this Bill continued until early June. The TUC eventually produced alternative

[1] Royal Commission on Trade Unions and Employers' Associations, 1965–1968, *Report* [Donovan Report], Cmnd 3623, London, HMSO, 1968.

[2] Department of Employment and Productivity, *In Place of Strife: a policy for industrial relations*, Cmnd 3888, London, HMSO, 1969.

suggestions: on 12 May the General Council approved a 'programme for action', which gave them increased scope for intervention in unconstitutional strikes and inter-union disputes; this was endorsed by an overwhelming majority at a special Congress held on 5 June. Eventually the government, realising that there was a serious risk that it would be unable to get the Industrial Relations Bill through the House of Commons, negotiated a compromise, by which the TUC agreed to a 'solemn and binding undertaking' about the manner in which the programme for action was to be implemented. This was signed on 18 June.

The fact that a substantial balance of payments recovery was under way at last became apparent in June 1969. The trade deficit in May narrowed very considerably; then it was discovered that exports had been under-recorded for some time – the under-recording having built up to an annual rate of £140–£150 million by 1969; thirdly, there was a revised estimate of the rate at which net invisible earnings were running. The figure which perhaps finally persuaded the doubters that the position had been transformed was a visible trade surplus for August of £40 million; the declared balance of payments target figure, of a £300 million current and long-term surplus for 1969/70, was reached in the first half of that year.

The Labour government's final period

The government had thus at last achieved what it had set out to do and produced a substantial balance of payments surplus; it was in no hurry to change policies. The import deposit scheme was renewed in October, at the slightly reduced rate of 40 instead of 50 per cent; the first significant relaxation came with the abolition of the restricted travel allowance from the beginning of January 1970.

Given the slow rise in output, the slight upward movement in unemployment and the impending general election, the government might have been expected to reflate the economy significantly. One reason for caution, however, was that, with the effective ending of incomes policy, both wage rates and earnings were beginning to rise much faster. Possibly the official forecasts assumed that this would have some real reflationary effect; certainly they predicted a considerable rise in consumers' expenditure. Secondly, there were those who still held the view that if unemployment were allowed to fall significantly the increase in wage rates would accelerate even more. The budget made some income tax and surtax concessions, mainly on allowances, estimated at around £200 million for a full year, with an estimated net effect of increasing output by about $\frac{1}{2}$ per cent. The official post-budget forecast was again over-optimistic – a rise in output of $3\frac{1}{2}$ per cent between the first halves of 1970 and 1971 – in the event the rise was only a little over 1 per cent.

At the change of government, therefore, the economy was running with a considerable balance of payments surplus; however, output was increasing only very slowly and unemployment was gradually rising.

THE CONSERVATIVE PERIOD FROM MID-1970 TO SPRING 1972

Introduction

In 1964 the Labour government had come to power determined to change the course of the British economy and alter the pattern of economic policy by getting away from 'stop–go' towards planning for the medium term; the attempt failed. In 1970 the Conservative government came to power with equally high ambitions; as Edward Heath said in October 1970: 'We were returned to office to change the course of history of this nation – nothing less.'[1] Their policy had a rather different motif – to transform the economy by reducing the extent of government intervention, stimulating self-reliance and improving the efficiency of the government machine. This attempt must also be judged a failure.

During its period in opposition the Conservative Party had set up a number of policy study groups. (Such groups, of course, inevitably look for distinctive policies, sharply different from those of the Party in power.) A number of industrialists took part in these groups; many of these were present at one of the culminating conferences at Sundridge Park in September 1969; the final, better known, conference was at Selsdon Park in January 1970. At these conferences prospective Ministers were told how important it was to have reasonably detailed programmes, so that it would be easier to overcome bureaucratic opposition. This, again, is a common assumption of any opposition Party – that, in bringing about the changes it wants, it will have great difficulty in moving the bureaucratic establishment.

The philosophy put forward at these conferences, and as expounded to the Party conference in 1970, was not mainly concerned with techniques of economic management in the traditional sense. The emphasis was first on government withdrawal and, secondly, on improving the government's cost-effectiveness: 'less government, but of a better quality'.

Government was to withdraw 'from all those activities no longer necessary either because of the passage of time or because they are better done outside government, or because they should rightly be

[1] National Union of Conservative and Unionist Associations, *Verbatim Report: 88th Conservative Conference, Blackpool, 1970*, London, 1970, p. 129.

carried on, if wanted at all, by individual or by voluntary effort'. Individual citizens were to be made more self-reliant and encouraged 'to stand on their own feet, to accept responsibility for themselves and their families'.[1] In industrial relations, if firms gave way to irresponsible wage demands the government would not step in to rescue them from the consequences of their own actions. The functions of government and industry were different; the role of government was to create a framework, within which the free enterprise system should operate. There was not to be a partnership in the sense of mutual absorption or penetration. To make the government more efficient, new techniques would be used to bring about a systematic and continuous process of questioning and analysis of the objectives of the government's activity; new recruits from the business world would bring about a change of direction and attitude throughout Whitehall. The exposition of this new philosophy certainly persuaded commentators at the time that there was going to be a radical new approach to the running of the economy; there were frequent references to the end of consensus politics. The emphasis in this new approach was not so much in praise of the market economy, but in dispraise of government intervention. Further, it was the character-building virtues of government withdrawal which were emphasised, rather than the economic consequences.

The other main commitments of the Conservative Party were to bring the trade unions within the framework of the law and to renew the attempt to join the EEC. The process of negotiation with the EEC is not described in this chapter. The negotiations themselves are for the political rather than the economic history of the time and the actual accession on 1 January 1973 did not have significant economic consequences in the period covered by this book.

The first year

The economy which the new government inherited was in substantial current balance of payments surplus. However, the trade gap had widened between the first and second quarters of the year, so that the National Institute's forecast of the balance on current account in 1970 fell from £675 million in May to £475 million in August,[2] and, given the required debt repayments, current surpluses of this order were no more than adequate. Further, the new government had, on the one hand, an official forecast made at the time of the budget that national output would be rising in line with productive potential and, on the other hand, a slow but steady rise in unemployment from the middle of

[1] Ibid. pp. 131–2.
[2] Before these estimates are compared with actual figures they should be adjusted for the further under-recording of exports announced in November 1970.

1969. They were also in the middle of a wages explosion: basic hourly wage rates, which had risen only 5½ per cent between the fourth quarters of 1968 and 1969, were rising at 12–13 per cent during 1970; the price rise was also accelerating, though not so sharply.

Before the election future Conservative Ministers had clearly considered the possibility of breaking into the wage–price spiral by reducing indirect taxes, and possibly also by damping down nationalised industries' price increases, so reflating the economy and reducing prices at one and the same time. Once in office they decided against this; the reasons can be surmised. First, it was not as clear then as it is now that rapid increases in money wages have very little, if any, real reflationary effect. Secondly, and more generally, it seemed perverse to reflate at a time of rapid inflation. Although by 1974 the Treasury had come round to the view that the rise in wage rates was insensitive to the movement of unemployment within a fairly wide band, this was probably not their view in 1970. Further, there were still some anxieties about the balance of payments because the trade balance had worsened so much between the first and second quarters.

There was, in consequence, no significant reflationary action in the second half of 1970; indeed, at the end of July the Bank of England asked the clearing banks to slow down the growth of advances. The budget introduced on 27 October was in no sense primarily concerned with demand management; the Chancellor indicated that it was intended to be 'broadly neutral' in its effect upon demand in 1971/2, and to demonstrate this he quoted the estimated £329 million cut from public spending as against the £315 million cost to the revenue of the cut in income tax. The National Institute suggested that in fact there would be a small reflationary effect, with an increase in 1971/2 of the order of £120 million in gross domestic product (GDP) at market prices.

The main concern of this budget was putting into practical effect some of the principles of 'less government, but of a better quality' and of selective rather than general assistance. A long list of changes can be classified under these headings: the abolition of investment grants and their replacement by tax allowances; the announcement that the regional employment premium would be phased out; the repeal of the Industrial Expansion Act; the move from deficiency payments to British farmers to levies on imported food; the shift of emphasis in financial support for local authority housing from subsidising rents to subsidising individuals; the reduction of taxpayers' support for the Consumer Council and the British Productivity Council; the elimination of subsidies for London commuter trains; the introduction of admission charges for museums; increases in charges for school meals and dental treatment; the ending of cheap welfare milk and free school milk for the over-sevens. At the same time the income limit for free school meals and welfare milk for younger children was raised and a new scheme, the family income supplement, was introduced to benefit the poorest families. The intended net effect on the long-term trend in public expenditure between 1971/2 and 1974/5 was to reduce the annual rate of increase from 3·5 to 2·8 per cent. (This was the first of a long series of changes in public expenditure forward plans which are discussed on pages 117 *et seq.*) In the debate on 4 November 1970 the Secretary of State for Trade and Industry, John Davies, set out the principles according to which the government would be reducing the scale of its intervention in industry: '...the vast majority lives and thrives in a bracing climate and not in a soft, sodden morass of subsidized incompetence...We believe that the essential need of the country is to gear its policies to the great majority of people, who are not lame ducks, or do not need a helping hand...'.

The Chancellor had indicated when introducing the budget that in his view output over the next six months would be growing broadly in line with productive potential. However, the tone of his assessment suggested that he preferred to err on the side of caution: 'If one takes into account the continuation of the rapid rise in costs and prices which we have experienced over the past year or so, it follows that it would be wrong to take any steps likely to increase further the pressure of demand.' The National Institute's assessment at the time was that the trend of growth in real output would be nearer 2 per cent than 3 per cent, so that unemployment would continue its gradual upward movement. The upward movement did indeed continue, but soon ceased to be gradual (page 59).

Conservative policies towards inflation

During the winter of 1970/1 the pattern began to appear of the Conservative government's policies in the fields of inflation, industrial intervention and the trade unions.

In combating inflation the government was concerned to disengage itself from intervention in wage settlements. In November 1970 it announced that the NBPI would be wound up; it was left to employers ro resist excessive wage demands, given the risk that they might bankrupt themselves if they failed to do so. Indeed, as part of the process of disengagement, the conciliation work of the Department of Employment was reduced.

The problem for this policy lay in the public sector. The principle that responsibility for negotiating pay settlements must rest on employers applied in theory to the nationalised industries and the public services just as much as to private industry. In fact the government could hardly remain indifferent to settlements in the public sector and it gradually became more and more involved in them. It acted indirectly on the nationalised industries' finances by refusing to grant in full the price increases they requested (this happened with the Coal Board in the autumn of 1970 and with the Central Electricity Generating Board in the spring of 1971; it would have happened with the Post Office's increase in postal charges if the new stamps had not already been printed). The government also became increasingly identified with a view about the right kind of figure to be granted in specific cases, so that wage claims in the public sector came to be treated more and more as confrontations with the government.

In public sector negotiations in the winter of 1970/1, the government could at least claim it had not given way. The first episode – the 'dustmen's strike' – was a claim on behalf of 770,000 manual workers employed by local authorities. Here, the Department of Employment said that its conciliation services would only be available on the understanding that the settlement did not exceed 14 per cent and strike action began in September. After about four weeks both sides agreed to submit the case to a Committee of Inquiry under Sir Jack Scamp, which conceded most of the claim. At the end of November the miners voted in favour of accepting a 12 per cent increase offered to them by the National Coal Board. An increase of about the same size was offered to the electricity supply workers at the beginning of December, but they rejected it and began a work-to-rule and overtime ban. This caused considerable public irritation and in mid-December the union said they would call off their industrial action if the government would agree to a Court of Inquiry. The government was only prepared to accept this if the terms of reference included consideration of 'the public and national interest'; the unions were reluctant to agree, but eventually did so. However, the Court of Inquiry, under Lord Wilberforce, recommended an increase well above the Electricity Council's final offer; precise quantification is difficult, because the award included a lead-in payment starting at £1 a week to workers who accepted in principle an incentive bonus scheme.[1] Finally, the Post Office workers went on strike at the end of January, rejecting an 8 per cent offer. This strike was not successful; in the end the union agreed to the setting up of a Committee of Inquiry, which, on this occasion, added only

[1] Department of Employment, *Report of a Court of Inquiry into the Electricity Supply Industry*, Cmnd 4594, London, HMSO, 1971. The Department of Employment's *New Earnings Survey* (annual) shows that the average weekly earnings of manual workers in the electricity supply industry rose 14 per cent between April 1970 and April 1971, and 18 per cent between April 1971 and April 1972.

about 1 per cent to the 8 per cent offer. Thus, in this first round of settlements in the public sector, the government could generally be said to be holding its own.

Industrial intervention

The Conservative government's new policy on industrial intervention was also tested in the winter of 1970/1. In November the government refused to grant a bridging loan to the Mersey Docks and Harbours Board, intending it as a first lesson that they would not continue to rescue companies from the consequences of their own mistakes. Debenture holders of the Board's undertakings had always assumed that they had in effect a government guarantee for the security of their capital; when they discovered they had not this first move to industrial disengagement was not popular in the City. The second incident was on a much larger scale. In February 1971 Rolls-Royce was allowed to go bankrupt, but in spite of this rather extreme measure the government agreed to continue with the production of the RB 211 engine for Lockheed on terms which almost certainly implied a continuing Exchequer subsidy. The third problem for the government in this field came in June 1971, when further cash was refused to Upper Clyde Shipbuilders; this led to a sit-in and to an eventual solution in which all four yards – Govan, Linthouse, Scotstoun and Clydebank – continued in business, with Clydebank converted to building offshore drilling rigs.

The Conservative election manifesto had also indicated there would be significant 'hiving-off' of some of the peripheral activities of the nationalised industries. The moves made in the government's first year were not very far-reaching: in August 1970, as part of the process of establishing the second-force private enterprise airline which came to be known as British Caledonian, this airline was given British Overseas Airways' West African routes; then in January 1971 it was announced that Thomas Cook would be sold off, as also would be the state-owned public houses and bars in Carlisle, Gretna and Cromarty.

Industrial relations

The government in its first year was also getting through its Industrial Relations Bill, which was designed to bring the trade unions 'within the framework of the law'. The clauses which led to a struggle with the trade union movement over the whole period of this government were mainly those providing for the registration of unions, establishing the new concept of unfair industrial practices, with compensation for those injured by them, creating the National Industrial Relations Court (NIRC) and extending the existing Industrial Tribunals, and giving power to the government to apply to the NIRC for a 'cooling-off' period lasting up to 60 days, or to call for a ballot where industrial action would cause or continue a national emergency.

The TUC denounced the Bill and the General Council decided to embark on a course of outright opposition to it. In March 1971 a special Congress met at Croydon to decide the line the trade union movement should take. The General Council recommended that affiliated unions should be urged not to register – or if they did to inform the TUC of their reasons for doing so – and unions should not sign any legally binding contracts; trade unionists should not serve on the NIRC or the Commission on Industrial Relations (CIR) and should withdraw from the Industrial Tribunals. There were one-day protest strikes on 1 and 18 March, mainly in the engineering industry; it was estimated that $1\frac{1}{2}$ million workers were involved in the first stoppage and 2 million in the second.

The 1971 budget

The section in the Financial Statement for 1971/2 giving the economic background to the budget begins: 'During 1970 there was a rapid rate of cost and price inflation against the background of slowly rising output and a high and increasing level of unemployment.'[1] This summarises the Chancellor's dilemma. The government's anti-inflationary policy, of leaning on the public sector, had had some success, but there were as yet few signs that this success was being imitated in the private sector. Obviously the policy would only succeed if this occurred, for if the rise in earnings in the public sector was kept below that of the private sector for any length of time trouble would clearly build up. There was no certainty, therefore, that the rate of cost and price inflation was being brought down.

Unemployment had risen, but up to the spring of 1971 the rise had been fairly slow – in March 1971 the number wholly unemployed was 90,000 higher than a year earlier. In the National Institute's assessment of the situation before the budget, there seemed no prospect of any substantial reflationary force; it was assumed that the effect of devaluation on the volume of exports had come through and neither public nor private investment seemed likely to rise much. The Institute argued for a stimulus of the order of £500 million as a first step; in a judgement repeated a number of times during this period, it concluded that the effect of a reflation of this order on the trend of costs and prices would be roughly neutral on balance.

The Chancellor did in fact further reduce taxes so as to reduce expected revenue in 1971/2 by rather over £500 million. However, only about £160 million of this – arising from the increase in child

---

[1] Treasury, *Financial Statement and Budget Report, 1971–72*, London, HMSO, 1971, p. 5.

allowances – was quick-acting; three-fifths came from halving selective employment tax and from a further reduction in corporation tax, neither of which was likely to do much to stimulate effective demand immediately. The Chancellor considered that his measures would bring the economy back to a 3 per cent growth path by early 1972, but this proved, once again, over-optimistic; in any case something more would have been needed to check the rise in unemployment. During 1971 unemployment was reacting to the previous two years of slow growth – from the end of 1968 to the end of 1970 national output had been rising at around 2 per cent a year, which was below the country's productive potential.

The 1971 budget was again not simply an exercise in demand management. The main feature was the announcement of a two-year programme of fundamental reforms in the fiscal system, which included the replacement of purchase tax and what was left of selective employment tax by VAT. In addition, the Chancellor proposed to recast personal taxation, amalgamating income and surtax and replacing the earned income allowance by an investment income surcharge; corporation tax was to be reformed to eliminate disincentives to distribute. There were Green Papers on the proposals[1] and, in the case of corporation tax, a Select Committee of the House of Commons to consider alternative methods.

During the rest of 1971 it was the rise in unemployment which increasingly dominated economic policy. During 1970 unemployment had been increasing at 4000–5000 a month; from the beginning of 1971 this accelerated to around 20,000 a month. An objective of the budget had been to stabilise the level of unemployment; in his speech on 30 March the Chancellor said, 'I cannot make any promise that unemployment will fall until we get a substantial reduction in the level of pay settlements...I could have brought about a reduction in the level of unemployment by giving a still larger boost to consumer demand than I have. But everything I have said supports the view that it would have been irresponsible to do so.' In June he still held the view that the budget measures would slow down and eventually stop the increase in unemployment, but he also referred to the possibility that after the Treasury's regular summer review of the economy there might be a change. The main change in July appears to have been that the Treasury revised past figures rather than the forecast for the future; though they were firmly persuaded that an expansion was under way, they concluded that it was starting from a lower base than they had thought.

[1] Treasury, *Reform of Corporation Tax*, Cmnd 4630, and *Reform of Personal Direct Taxation*, Cmnd 4653, London, HMSO, 1971.

The package of measures introduced in the summer contained a £100 million public works programme for the development areas. In June there had already been a large increase (£46 million for two years) in the allocation for house improvement grants. Otherwise the measures were designed to have a relatively quick effect, and this was clearly right; also, perhaps more important, they formed part of an informal 'social contract' with the Confederation of British Industries (CBI), by which an attempt was made to break into the wage–price spiral from the prices side.

Hire purchase controls were abolished entirely, in line with the recommendations of the Crowther Report;[1] this was certainly a quick-acting measure. The improved capital allowances for industry also had a time-limit – the first-year tax allowance was increased from 60 to 80 per cent for expenditure incurred up to end-July 1973. Purchase tax was cut, clearly in line with the CBI price initiative; for, on the assumption – and indeed the condition – that the government would take action to reflate the economy, the CBI had asked its members to sign an undertaking if possible to avoid raising prices of products or services supplied in the United Kingdom, and to limit any unavoidable increases to a 5 per cent maximum within the twelve-month period ending 31 July 1972. By early September, 176 out of 201 leading companies in the United Kingdom had signed this undertaking. This had radical consequences for government policy towards the nationalised industries, because the CBI said that, if price restraint was to be implemented by the private sector, nationalised industries must be expected to do the same, and the government indicated to the nationalised industries that they should follow suit. This inevitably meant the abandonment of the financial targets which had been introduced in 1961, and from the beginning of 1972 subsidies to the nationalised industries, which had been held back between 1968 and 1971, began to rise sharply again, from £176 million in 1971 to £1308 million in 1974.

In 1971 also the structure of monetary policy was reformed: the Bank of England published 'Competition and credit control';[2] Bank Rate was lowered twice during the year, by 1 per cent in April and a further 1 per cent in September; then on 10 September the new regime for the control of banks and finance houses was announced. From 16 September all 'ceiling' limits on lending were removed and all institutions were required to observe a fixed minimum reserve ratio (page 244); the main consequence was a very sharp rise in bank advances to the private sector in general and to the personal sector in particular.

---

[1] Department of Trade and Industry, *Consumer Credit. Report of the Committee* [Crowther Report], Cmnd 4596, London, HMSO, 1971.
[2] *Bank of England Quarterly Bulletin*, vol. 11, June 1971.

This was not by any means the end of the sequence of reflationary measures. In November the Chancellor announced an acceleration of government expenditure amounting to £185 million over the next two years; in December he announced the repayment of all outstanding postwar credits (forced wartime savings), amounting to some £130 million. By the end of the year, therefore, the primary objective of government policy had become the checking of the rise in unemployment.

This period of anti-inflationary policy – from mid-1970 to end-1971 – can hardly be counted a success. It is true that the wage awards given in the public sector in the second half of 1971 were substantially lower than those given to the same groups a year earlier. However, there seems to have been no parallel moderation in the private sector which-ever index is used – basic wage rates, average hourly earnings excluding overtime, or wages and salaries per unit of output.[1]

The rise in retail prices did slow down after the middle of 1971; this was helped by reductions in purchase tax and selective employment tax, and by the CBI's price initiative, particularly in its consequences for prices in nationalised industries.

Finally, the policy of 'leaning on the public sector' foundered in a confrontation with the National Union of Mineworkers in the winter of 1971/2.

In September 1971 the National Coal Board offered increases which amounted to an average pay rise of 7 per cent. The president of the National Union of Mineworkers said the offer 'does not even provide us with a negotiating position', and the union imposed an overtime ban from 1 November, which effectively reduced output during December by 15–20 per cent; a ballot was held, which showed that 59 per cent of those who voted were in favour of strike action. The Board raised its offer to an average increase of 8 per cent, but this was refused and the first national coal strike since 1926 began on 9 January. The miners extending picketing from the pits to provide 24-hour cover at coal depots, open coal sites, ports and power stations. On 9 February the Board offered increases of £3 per week for surface workers and £3.50 for underground workers; this too was rejected. The government declared a state of emergency and power cuts were instituted; a Court of Inquiry was set up under Lord Wilberforce. On 14 February fuel rationing was tightened, most of British industry went on a three-day working week and the number of workers laid off amounted to 1½ million. The Court of Inquiry's Report, issued on 18 February, recom-

---

[1] Basic weekly wage rates rose 13 per cent, and wages and salaries per unit of output 10 per cent, between the fourth quarters of 1969 and 1970. Between the fourth quarters of 1970 and 1971 the comparable figures were 12·3 per cent and 8·8 per cent respectively. Average hourly earnings excluding overtime were 16 per cent higher than a year earlier in October 1970 and 14 per cent higher in October 1971.

mended £5 per week for surface workers and £6 a week for underground workers.[1] Then the union, in negotiations with the Prime Minister, won additional concessions in the attendance bonus and an extra five days' holiday a year, all of which cost another £8 million. A ballot showed a 96·5 per cent majority in favour of acceptance and on 25 February the seven-week strike was called off. The settlement raised average earnings in the mining and quarrying sector by some 17–20 per cent.

SPRING 1972 TO SPRING 1974

Introduction

At the beginning of 1972 the government's anti-inflationary strategy was in disarray. First of all, it had been intended simply to hold the level of unemployment at around half a million until the rise in wage rates moderated; it was no part of the strategy that the figure should rise to nearly a million. The government could hardly avoid the conclusion that unemployment had done very little to moderate the rise in basic wage rates. A second strand of anti-inflationary policy – that each successive settlement in the public sector should be lower than the previous one – had been broken by the miners' strike. Finally, the CBI initiative on price restraint showed few signs of encouraging similar restraint from the unions and, by forcing the nationalised industries to make losses, it had the incidental result of making it additionally obvious that unions in the public sector were negotiating with the government rather than with the boards of the industries.

Looking back now, the sequence of events gives the impression that during the first half of 1972 there was a major decision to change direction. Of course that was not in fact how things happened: the new policies emerged from the old gradually, so that it is hard to say for any particular policy when the transition from the old to the new approach was made. However, there is no doubt that, by the end of its period of office, the Conservative government's stance on economic policy was considerably changed from what it had been in 1970.

The new approach can be summed up as follows. Anti-inflationary policy changed, first, to a process of negotiation with the TUC and the CBI and, after about six months when that attempt was unsuccessful, to statutory intervention. Indeed in the last two years of the Conservative government the dominant economic objective was to make the new anti-inflationary policy effective. Then the high level of unemployment forced the government to take further substantial reflationary measures; this became a decision to aim for a higher rate of economic growth and

---

[1] Department of Employment, *Report of a Court of Inquiry into a Dispute between the National Coal Board and the National Union of Mineworkers*, Cmnd 4903, London, HMSO, 1972.

was accompanied by a declaration that the government would let the exchange rate go if necessary. Thirdly, the government's industrial policy changed – partly because with unemployment so high it was not easy to let large firms go bankrupt in high-unemployment areas, and partly because the government was dissatisfied with industry's investment performance and was therefore less willing than in 1970 to leave the amount of private manufacturing investment to be decided by the firms concerned.

The reflationary budget

Prominent in the background to the budget of 1972 was unemployment, which was, on the latest figures available to the Chancellor (seasonally adjusted) still rising – though a good deal more slowly than during 1971. The last count had been taken on 14 February just before the restrictions on power supplies, so that the figure was probably not much inflated by the effects of the coal strike.[1] The Chancellor would have had some justification for doubting forecasts that, on unchanged policies, it would soon begin to fall, for it had already risen much further than most forecasters had expected. On the other hand, the estimates which he had available suggested that there had already been quite a sharp recovery in national output in the second half of 1971, and there were forecasts on unchanged policies of a continuing rise by about $3\frac{1}{2}$ per cent a year between the second half of 1971 and the first half of 1973.[2] However, the Chancellor had to reckon with the possibility that a rise in output of this order would do no more than keep the level of unemployment roughly where it was at the beginning of the year. The estimate of national productive potential was probably quite high at the time, for productivity had, in an unprecedented way, improved in both 1970 and 1971. In previous periods of recession productivity had stayed low, but in 1971 it had risen by over 3 per cent, so that it seemed quite plausible that the rise during 1972 could be if anything higher.

The government was clearly not prepared to risk leaving unemployment near the million mark, and the explicit aim of the 1972 budget introduced on 21 March was to add 2 per cent to output in the first half of 1973. Quite deliberately, the Chancellor framed this policy in terms of a 5 per cent growth rate: 'The measures I shall put to the House are intended to ensure a growth of output at an annual rate of 5 per cent between the second half of last year and the first half of next...If my

[1] It showed unemployment at 3·8 per cent (Great Britain, excluding school-leavers and adult students).

[2] This figure was about the same in the Treasury 'unchanged policies' forecast and in the *National Institute Economic Review* for February 1972.

present expectations are correct, output will have risen by 10 per cent over the two-year period from the first half of 1971 to the first half of 1973.'[1] The Chancellor emphasised 5 per cent because he was concerned to get what stimulus to investment he could from the 'announcement effect' of a rapid rate of growth. For much the same reason, the budget speech contains the famous sentence which indicated that the exchange rate would be sacrificed if necessary: 'Moreover I am sure that all hon. members in this House agree that the lesson of the international balance of payments upsets of the last few years is that it is neither necessary nor desirable to distort domestic economies to an unacceptable extent in order to maintain unrealistic exchange rates, whether they are too high or too low.'

The 1972 budget has become a controversial one; the arguments are essentially about the objectives which the government chose – whether or not it was right to aim at accelerating the growth rate of national output to 5 per cent and bringing unemployment back to around half a million by the end of 1973. Given those objectives, a large stimulus in the budget was inevitable and, for achieving those objectives, the size of the stimulus was roughly right. The target of 5 per cent for the annual rate of growth of output for the eighteen-month period up to the middle of 1973 was in fact roughly achieved and by the end of 1973 unemployment had fallen to around half a million.[2]

The government was already committed to holding back the rise in public expenditure, and it is in any case difficult to get any quick effects in stimulating this element of demand, so that inevitably most of the reflation came from tax reductions aimed at raising personal consumption. The main measure was an increase in the income tax allowances for married and single people; also purchase tax was reduced. In addition the budget contained what the Chancellor termed 'the most powerful combination of national and regional investment incentives... since the war', but these, of course, were not expected to have any quick reflationary effect and certainly did not do so. However, the 1972 budget was notable for reasons other than the aggregate size of the tax reductions. Further major measures of tax reform were promised, with one Green Paper on the possible amalgamation of personal tax allowances with certain social security benefits, introducing in effect a negative income tax, and another on the transformation of death duties into an inheritance tax.[3] In addition there were some minor tax changes designed to benefit particularly those with middle-range incomes: loan

[1] On present figures (CSO, *Economic Trends, Annual Supplement 1976*) this is exactly what happened.
[2] Great Britain, seasonally adjusted, excluding school-leavers and adult students.
[3] Treasury, *Proposals for a Tax-Credit System*, Cmnd 5116, and *Taxation of Capital on Death*, Cmnd 4930, London HMSO, 1972.

interest of over £35 a year was to be tax deductible and, as from April 1971, the first £2000 a year of investment income was to be treated as earned income for tax purposes.

Industrial policy

The budget also took further a change in the Conservative government's industrial policy which had already begun. An original principle had been that enterprises should not be rescued unless there was a firm prospect of a viable independent future. Already, under pressure of unemployment, the government had broken with this principle in February 1972 in its rescue of all four Upper Clyde shipyards (page 57). Then in the budget there was a further retreat from general principles: to stimulate investment, free depreciation, which previously had been available in development areas only, was extended to the whole country. Since this meant that there were no longer any special incentives to invest in the development areas, a new system of 'regional development grants' was introduced, which seemed at least a partial reversal of the previous decision to replace investment grants with tax allowances. In addition, an Industrial Development Executive was set up in the Department of Trade and Industry, with wide powers to assist firms throughout the country.

The substantial change in the direction of industrial policy indicated by these moves is also strongly suggested by various ministerial changes at the Department of Trade and Industry about this time. Two junior Ministers who had been clearly identified with the previous industrial policy were moved and not long afterwards the Secretary of State himself, John Davies, left the department, his place being taken by Peter Walker.

Floating the exchange rate

The undertaking given in the budget speech – that a fixed exchange rate would not be allowed to stand in the way of economic expansion – was a promise which soon had to be taken up. However, before the rate was floated in June, there was in fact a move in the opposite direction. Towards the end of April the six members of the EEC took the first step towards a European Monetary Union by agreeing to narrow the range of fluctuations in their exchange rates.[1] On 1 May Britain, as a candi-

---

[1] Under the Smithsonian agreement of December 1971 rates for most currencies were allowed to fluctuate between margins of 2¼ per cent on either side of their parities against the dollar, so that the rate between any two could vary by 4½ per cent from their cross-parity. Under the agreement of 24 April 1972 EEC countries were committed to ensuring that the rates between any two of their currencies would not diverge from their cross-parities by more than 2¼ per cent.

date for the EEC, joined what came to be known as the 'snake in the tunnel'.

The United Kingdom balance of payments still appeared reasonably strong; the estimates available in the second quarter of 1972 suggested that there was still a substantial current surplus, although much reduced from the very high figures of 1971.[1] It is perhaps therefore a little surprising that substantial speculation against sterling developed during June. The reasons suggested for this are that the government appeared to be without any effective anti-inflationary policy and that the trade figures in April and May were judged to be bad.[2] The Labour shadow Chancellor, Denis Healey, forecast an early devaluation in a speech in the House of Commons in mid-June. When speculation threatened to force down the rate, under the new arrangements in the European Monetary Union the pound was supported by the central banks of the EEC countries, but Britain was under an obligation to repay these banks on the next settlement day.

Bank Rate was raised by 1 per cent on 22 June, which led a number of commentators to conclude that no action was going to be taken on the exchange rate. However, the next day the exchange rate was floated 'as a temporary measure'. The official line in presenting this change was that it was made necessary by illogical speculation, that there was 'nothing in the objective facts' to suggest that sterling was over-valued and that the United Kingdom still believed that a world system of fixed parities was desirable; by implication, therefore, once sterling had settled the government would be prepared to fix the parity again. Probably at that time the government did not envisage a virtually permanent floating; it may have had in mind previous German examples, in which the exchange rate for the Deutschemark was allowed to float for a few months and was then fixed again.

The move to a floating rate also marked the effective end of the sterling area. Up to June 1972 the only limit on capital flows to the overseas sterling area was the programme of voluntary restraint begun in 1966, and indeed this had been removed in the 1972 budget. After 23 June 1972 portfolio investors in the overseas sterling area had to pay the same premium as in other areas;[3] further, Bank of England approval was needed for official foreign exchange for direct investment in the overseas sterling area. These new rules were also presented at the time as temporary, but have in fact proved permanent.

The immediate effect of floating was a devaluation of the pound by

---

[1] Estimates now available suggest that in the first half of 1972 the current surplus in the balance of payments was running at an annual rate of rather over £500 million.

[2] In fact the current balance of payments surplus, seasonally adjusted, is now shown to have been larger in the second quarter than in the first.

[3] However, they did not have to surrender 25 per cent on liquidation.

roughly 7 per cent (on a weighted basis against other major currencies). This figure held through the summer, but the pound depreciated further in the autumn.

Negotiations with the unions

In the second half of the Conservative government's period of office the most important change was in anti-inflationary policy. From early 1972 onwards this became the central preoccupation of economic policy-makers: they were concerned, first, with devising a voluntary incomes policy and, when that attempt failed, with instituting and administering a statutory one. Just as at other times the balance of payments was wholly preoccupying, so in 1972 and 1973 the attention of the government was heavily concentrated on holding back the rise in money incomes. This section discusses the events leading up to the introduction of a statutory freeze on wages and prices on 6 November 1972.

The collapse of the government's previous anti-inflationary policy has already been described; from the spring of 1972 there was growing pressure by employers for some action to be taken on wages, because the CBI's price restraint code was due to expire in mid-July and the CBI was reluctant to extend it unless there was some move on the wages side. The first meetings after the miners' strike between the government, the CBI and the TUC took place on 9 and 10 March, but further moves were hampered by the operation of the Industrial Relations Act, which had been brought into full force at the end of February. The government twice invoked the Act during negotiations on railwaymen's pay. In April it applied to the NIRC for a cooling-off period, but in the fourteen days granted the negotiations made no progress. Then in May the government applied for and got an NIRC order for a ballot of railwaymen to see whether they supported the industrial action; the result was a six to one majority in favour, and the final settlement essentially conceded the claim. Thus, in this dispute the use of the Industrial Relations Act was a failure, and throughout the summer there were difficulties when private firms used the Act to bring unions to account for the behaviour of their shop stewards. The problem of 'union responsibility' was not a simple one. These situations did not improve the atmosphere for discussions between the TUC and the government; indeed, during this period the TUC was probably rather closer to the CBI. On 21 June the TUC and CBI reached an agreement on a new conciliation and arbitration service which was to be independent of the government.

Nevertheless, preliminary soundings were taken during the early summer and in early July more formal approaches began. The TUC General Council met the Prime Minister on 4 July – their main concern being to press him to repeal or suspend the Industrial Relations Act. The Prime Minister indicated he wished to discuss a wider range of subjects; he suggested the TUC and the government should meet to consider, as a matter of urgency, the problems of conciliation, low pay, and a link between collective agreements and the cost of living. Some members of the TUC Economic Committee, which considered the proposals, thought that there should be no talks with the government until the Industrial Relations Act had been suspended. As a compromise, however, they replied that the NEDC was a suitable forum, and pointed out, incidentally, that the idea of threshold agreements had been suggested by them back in 1971, but at that time the government had not been keen.

Three meetings of the NEDC held before the summer recess to discuss the Prime Minister's agenda appear to have been in the nature of preliminary skirmishes, discussing low pay and prices rather than wages. During August and early September evidence accumulated that the price rise was likely, if anything, to accelerate again. In the *National Institute Economic Review* for August a rise in retail prices of 7–8 per cent through 1972 (and perhaps another 9 per cent through 1973) was forecast. A number of formidable wage demands were being tabled at this time.

Negotiations began again in mid-September. At the first meeting the subjects were again price increases and low pay, but the idea of flat-rate pay increases was introduced and it was agreed that this should be on the agenda for the next meeting. On 26 September the government tabled its proposals:

(a) an extension of its commitment to a 5 per cent growth rate to cover the next two years;

(b) a limit of 5 per cent for the growth of retail prices resulting from increases in costs over the next twelve months (this would require a limit of 4 per cent for price increases of manufactured products, and matching performance from the nationalised industries);

(c) a £2 a week pay rise for everyone, together with 20p a week for each 1 per cent increase in retail prices above a threshold of 6 per cent. The government also undertook to do something about pensions, and tabled some arithmetic to show that the suggested £2 per week, which was assumed to lead in fact to a rise in average earnings of £2.60 per week, was compatible with a 5 per cent price rise and a 5 per cent growth in real gross national product (GNP), with a 61 per cent share of this product going to wages and salaries.

On 10 October the TUC presented counter-proposals. Their arithmetic suggested an increase of £3.40 per week in average earnings; about two thirds of the difference from the government figure of £2.60

was accounted for by different assumptions about the share of national income going to wages and salaries, and about one third by different assumptions about national productivity. Otherwise, as an initial bargaining move, they included virtually every demand they could think of: apart from an assurance on the non-operation of the Industrial Relations Act, they asked for price control, for VAT at $7\frac{1}{2}$ per cent rather than 10 per cent, for the increases in rents due to take place in 1973 under the Housing Finance Act to be abandoned, for a wealth tax, a surcharge on capital gains, and a restriction on dividend payments, and for the Consumer Council to be re-established as soon as possible. They pointed to some of the difficulties in any agreement on flat-rate payments – long-term agreements, the complexity of wage structures, existing incremental scales and the move towards equal pay. On land values, they suggested that betterment profits should accrue to the state and that there should be capital gains tax on speculative transactions; also that some action should be taken on estate duty, that family allowances should be increased, and that weekly pensions should rise by £2 for single people and £3.20 for a married couple, without being recouped to any substantial extent by increased national insurance contributions.

A brisk succession of meetings followed during the rest of October and early November. One working party made considerable progress on the problems of lump sum pay increases; they postponed consideration of what the figure should be by referring to it as £x. The main difficulty was on prices, where the TUC felt that a voluntary system was not strong enough. The Prime Minister put the view that any arrangement would have to be either statutory on both prices and wages, or voluntary on both of them. In a further negotiating move, the TUC tacitly withdrew its demand that there should be statutory price control, and asked instead for a guarantee from the government that the retail price index would not rise by more than 5 per cent in the next twelve months. They were concerned that the government's proposals referred only to price rises resulting from increased costs, which did not include rents, the introduction of food import levies, or any effects of changes in the exchange rate. They stressed the need for action on rents and food prices in particular; indeed they asked for an undertaking that the rise in food prices alone should be kept to 5 per cent.

The negotiations broke down on 2 November. The Prime Minister made a statement at that meeting in which he began by distinguishing between issues affecting prices and incomes, and other matters which were essentially matters of government responsibility. The Housing Finance Act and the Industrial Relations Act, for example, fell into the second category, and therefore could not explicitly be included in the negotiations. The proposals he outlined were basically the same as those which he had set out on 26 September, but he added some possibilities: an increase of 50p in the needs allowance to limit the effect of rent increases in 1973; an extension of the period for which family income supplement, free school meals and free welfare milk were awarded; a lump sum payment to be included in revised pensions; consultation with local authorities to moderate the increase in local rates. The TUC felt that the government had hardly moved from its original position – it had not, for example, taken any notice of the discussion on what the flat-rate pay rise should be – indeed they considered that the Prime Minister had retreated from his early position of offering the TUC a partnership in managing the economy.

The problems of reaching an effective voluntary agreement were indeed very formidable at that time; some concessions would have raised points of constitutional principle – for example, the Industrial Relations Act had passed through Parliament and it is an open question whether it would have been proper for the government to come to an agreement with the TUC that its operation should be suspended. There is no way of knowing how many concessions would have been needed to win TUC acceptance; if the government had given the prices guarantee for which the TUC asked, would this have been enough? Finally, it is not clear, if the negotiations had been successful, how the restrictions on wage and salary increases would have worked on a voluntary basis; what sanctions could the TUC have used against unions which successfully negotiated increases higher than had been agreed?

Statutory incomes policy: Stages I and II

On 6 November the government introduced a wages and prices freeze – the first step in the statutory incomes policy which was to preoccupy them for the rest of their period in office. (The details of the freeze are described on pages 378–9.) There was a gap after both the ending of the CBI period of price restraint (on 31 October) and the breakdown of negotiations with the TUC (on 2 November) in which a number of firms managed to put up their prices; also a number of important wage settlements were made, including the power workers, who settled for around 16 per cent, and about a million local government employees, who settled for around 13 per cent. Caught by the rule that awards had to be completed and operational on or before 6 November were settlements for agricultural workers and bank employees, which were both post-poned.

There were protests about the freeze, but no significant industrial action against it. The figures show quite clearly the check to the rise in wage rates, but the check to the rise in retail prices is not so clear, mainly because import prices had by this time begun to increase rapidly. Sharply rising import prices were in fact to bedevil this whole period of incomes policy. Some of this rise is accounted for by sterling's downward float, but the import price index still shows a very big upswing after correction for this.

At the turn of the year the government took action to slow down the rise in the money supply. Between 13 October and 22 December the minimum lending rate (which had replaced Bank Rate on 9 October – see page 252) was raised from $7\frac{1}{2}$ to 9 per cent, and in both November and December the Bank of England made calls for Special Deposits, which reached 3 per cent by January 1973. The government did not intend these measures to slow down the rise in real output. The argument was, first, that under the new incomes policy there would be no need for the money supply to rise as fast as before; secondly, that the very rapid monetary expansion earlier in the year, helped by the restoration of tax relief on interest in the budget, had led to a speculative rise in the price of property. The Bank of England consequently requested the banks to restrict lending for property and share speculation.

In beginning with a 90-day freeze the government had followed the pattern of policy in the United States, and it continued to follow the main outline of the American pattern in the general structure of the second stage of its prices and incomes policy announced on 16 January 1973.[1] The policy was to last from March through to the autumn; the main characteristics (described more fully on page 381) were that for each employee pay increases in a year were to be limited to £1 a week plus 4 per cent of the total wage bill for the employer, with a limit for any employee of £250 a year. A Pay Board and a Price Commission were to be set up; the basic principle of the price code was that only allowable cost increases could be passed on in the form of higher prices.

At the end of February a Green Paper was issued,[2] and some modifications were made, particularly to the proposals for price control, before legislation was enacted. The rules sought to control major settlements and the price policy of large firms in the belief that they set the pattern for the rest of the economy. The proposals also looked ahead to the need to sort out anomalies at some point; the deputy chairman of the Pay Board was required to produce reports on the treatment of anomalies by mid-September and on pay relativities by the end of 1973.

[1] In August 1971 wages, prices and rents in the United States had been frozen for three months. At the end of that period a Pay Board and a Price Commission were set up. One of the characteristics of the system of control – copied in the United Kingdom in 1972 – was that the price movements of large firms and large wage settlements were subjected to particularly close scrutiny; the requirements for small firms and small wage settlements were much less stringent.

[2] Treasury, *Price and Pay Code. Consultative Document*, Cmnd 5247, London, HMSO, 1973.

The trade union movement was, of course, officially opposed to Stage II. A number of unions tried industrial action – including the gas workers, hospital ancillary workers and teachers – but with little success. The provisions were stretched in a few instances – for example, the gas workers were allowed a reduction in pension contributions of 45p a week – but the bulk of settlements were within the rules. Perhaps the most important acceptance was by the miners who, when the National Coal Board's offer was put to a ballot in mid-March, voted against a strike. There were a certain number of protest strikes on 1 May, but these fell far short of a total national one-day stoppage.

Demand management during 1973

By the time of the 1973 budget, presented on 6 March, it was clear that activity was expanding rapidly. However, although unemployment had fallen and was still falling, the level in March (635,000, seasonally adjusted) was still high by historical standards and the Chancellor committed himself to continuing the 5 per cent annual growth rate for at least a further year. Indeed, it seemed that the government was still hoping that the underlying growth rate in the economy might have been shifted above its previous long-term path of 3 per cent a year. Because of the momentum of growth so far achieved as well as the further increases in public investment which were expected, the Chancellor judged that, with private manufacturing investment beginning to accelerate, no further stimulus to demand was required to achieve continued growth at 5 per cent during 1973.

The budget was, therefore, broadly neutral: VAT was brought in at 10 per cent, purchase tax and selective employment tax were abolished and, as promised in 1971, a unified income tax was introduced. However, this gave rise to criticism from some outside observers, who tended to point to the very large borrowing requirement of £4.4 billion which was officially forecast for 1973/4, despite the explanation by the Chancellor that £800 million of this could be accounted for by the once-and-for-all effect on the timing of indirect tax payments of the changeover to VAT. Then, as the output figures for the first half of 1973 were published, it became clear that the economy was growing very fast indeed. A good deal of this could be explained by large rises in consumers' expenditure in anticipation of the introduction of VAT and, rather fortuitously, by the simultaneous switch to positive stockbuilding after nearly two years of run-down. Not surprisingly, the rapid rise in output coming after a very long period of slow growth led to shortages of materials and components.

Policy therefore began gradually to move towards mild restriction of demand. On 21 May the Chancellor announced cuts in public expenditure of £100 million in 1973/4 and £500 million in 1974/5 (at 1972 survey prices[1]); this was partly because the counter-cyclical public spending which should have been maintaining demand some six to twelve months earlier was coming through long after the economy had picked up, when the demands of house-building and other private investment were also becoming very strong, and it was therefore sensible to cut back some of this expenditure. The government also took restrictive monetary measures in the middle of the year; when, in mid-July, the pound began to float down again, the Bank of England called for a further 1 per cent of Special Deposits and, by the end of July, raised the minimum lending rate to 11½ per cent – a record postwar level.

There was a good deal of argument about the extent to which the deterioration of the balance of payments in 1973 should be attributed to excess pressure of home demand, or to the quite exceptional rise in import prices. Non-oil commodity prices, as measured by the *Economist*'s dollar index, rose by 62 per cent in 1973, the largest year-on-year rise ever recorded (the updated index is published from 1860). Quantifying the effects of the commodity boom is complicated by the downward float of sterling during the year. Effectively, the devaluation between the fourth quarters of 1972 and 1973 was about 9 per cent. This must be set against a total rise (in sterling terms) of over 39 per cent in the import unit value index for goods, and of 32 per cent in the more comprehensive deflator for imports of goods and services.[2] Between the second halves of 1972 and 1973 the volume of exports and of imports of goods and services grew by almost equal amounts. The change in the terms of trade, therefore, accounted for virtually all the adverse change in the balance of payments, which hardly suggests an excessive strain on domestic resources.

Statutory incomes policy: Stage III

The TUC agreed to discuss the rules for Stage III with the government once they had been assured that no subject would be barred from discussion at the meetings. Fairly early in the discussions the Prime Minister announced that the government would propose linking wage rises with rises in the cost of living, both the CBI and the TUC having stressed the need for some such linking in principle. The government published its proposals as a consultative document on 8 October;[3] the TUC, while stating their disapproval of the proposals, did not suggest any particular alterations; some small concessions were made in

[1] See page 83, footnote 1 for an explanation of this term.

[2] These figures, which measure the prices of landed imports, are not significantly affected by the rise in the price of oil.

[3] Treasury, *Pay and Price Code for Stage 3. A Consultative Document*, Cmnd 5444, London, HMSO, 1973.

response to the CBI's comments. The new code became operative for prices, profits and dividends on 1 November and for pay on 7 November.

The basic provision for pay (discussed more fully on page 383) was a 'norm' of pay increases of up to 7 per cent for a group, or if preferred increases of up to £2.25 per head per week, with an individual maximum of £350 a year. There were various 'flexibility margins': a further 1 per cent was available in settlements which reduced anomalies and obstacles to the better use of manpower; extra payments were available under new efficiency schemes when genuine savings or a contribution to stable prices had been shown; there were also increased premium payments for those working 'unsocial' hours. The threshold provision was for flat-rate increases of 40p per week payable if, during Stage III, the retail price index rose 7 per cent, and similar increases for every 1 per cent above that level. The provisions on pay were to some extent specifically designed to enable the Coal Board to make a reasonably substantial offer to the National Union of Mineworkers; for prices they were essentially a continuation of Stage II (see page 384).

The last five months

In its last five months in office the Conservative government had to struggle with the problems created by the restriction on oil supplies, the trebling of the price of oil and, finally, industrial action against Stage III, first by the electricity workers and then by the miners.

The oil crisis was first to develop. War broke out in the Middle East on 6 October; on 16 October there was a 66 per cent rise in the posted price of oil and on 17 October the Arab oil Ministers announced a 5 per cent per month cumulative cut-back in oil production. This was further intensified in early November, when the Arab oil-producing nations indicated a minimum 25 per cent cut in supplies to the West; then, just before Christmas, the posted price of oil was doubled from 1 January, but this was coupled with an announcement that the cut-backs in production would be eased from 25 to 15 per cent of September output.

On the industrial front, the series of events which led up to the miners' strike began on 11 October, when the National Union of Mineworkers confirmed their negotiators' rejection of 7 per cent basic pay rises. On 1 November the 18,000 power engineers of the Electrical Power Engineers' Association began industrial action in support of a claim for increases in stand-by payments outside Stage III. The miners decided to start an overtime ban from 12 November and, on 28 November, a meeting between the National Union of Mineworkers and the Prime Minister failed to find a solution.

In reaction to these events the government declared a state of emergency on 13 November; electric advertising signs and floodlighting were prohibited, space heating was controlled in industrial and commercial premises. A week later oil company deliveries of all petroleum products were cut by 10 per cent. A 50 m.p.h. speed limit was imposed on 5 December, with further restrictions on street and office lighting; on 13 December the Prime Minister announced a three-day week from 1 January.

The government also took further steps to cut demand, though they were not, in fact, as formidable as they appeared. The minimum lending rate was raised from $11\frac{1}{4}$ to 13 per cent on 13 November and there was a further call for 2 per cent of Special Deposits. However, in a budget on 17 December the call for Special Deposits was reduced to 1 per cent; instead, new restrictions were placed on the growth of the banks' interest-bearing liabilities (see page 251). In this budget hire purchase controls were reintroduced; also a surcharge on surtax and taxation on property development were announced. However, the main measure was a cut in public expenditure amounting to some £1200 million for 1974/5 – by far the largest cut ever announced for a succeeding year. It was, of course, a cut in a programme announced previously; in the event it did not prevent a substantial rise during 1974/5 in public sector expenditure in real terms.

During January 1974 various attempts were made to solve the miners' dispute. The TUC suggested that other unions should agree that exceptional and distinctive circumstances existed in the mining industry, so that if the government made a settlement possible 'other unions would not use this as a lever in their negotiations'. On 16 January a special conference of trade union presidents and general secretaries overwhelmingly endorsed this initiative, but the government clearly held the undertaking in some doubt.

Meantime, on 10 January the National Union of Mineworkers had decided not to strike, but to keep their overtime ban. By the middle of January the prospect for fuel supplies was easing a little; the Secretary of State for Energy announced the immediate resumption of full electricity supplies for steel production and the likelihood of a four-day week for industry in the near future.

On 24 January the Pay Board's report on relativities was published;[1] the Prime Minister then invited the CBI and the TUC to immediate talks on setting up an independent pay relativities body to consider major claims including the miners'. However, on the same day the National Union of Mineworkers decided to call a strike ballot, and the result, declared on 4 February, showed an 81 per cent vote in favour of a strike to start from 10 February. On 7 February the Prime Minister

[1] Pay Board, *Advisory Report no. 2: Problems of Pay Relativities*, Cmnd 5535, London, HMSO, 1974.

announced a general election on 28 February. The National Union of Mineworkers rejected the Prime Minister's appeal to postpone their strike until after the general election; on 12 February they also rejected a pay offer made by certain industrialists whose identity was not revealed. During the strike, and during the election campaign, the Pay Board sat from 18 to 25 February as a special relativities board considering evidence on the relative pay of miners. Their Report was published on 6 March, after the result of the general election had been announced.[1]

This particular period of policy, therefore, came to a somewhat chaotic end. The attempt had been to combine a move to more rapid economic growth with a statutory incomes policy to prevent inflation at home and a floating exchange rate to protect the balance of payments. Unfortunately the second stage of this particular incomes policy coincided with a very sharp rise in world commodity prices and, in particular, with a trebling of oil prices. The oil price rise (and the accompanying cut-backs in production) did a great deal to strengthen the position of the National Union of Mineworkers in its confrontation with the government and the provision for indexation in the third stage of incomes policy ensured that the rise in commodity prices set off a price–wage spiral in the United Kingdom. (While the Labour government dismantled the Conservative government's incomes policy in general, they allowed the threshold agreements to run on until October 1974. This was one of the driving forces behind the wage and price explosion which followed the fall of the Conservative government, with average earnings rising 28 per cent and retail prices 25 per cent between the second quarters of 1974 and 1975.) The argument remains between those who conclude that the incomes policy experiment of 1972–4 should not have been tried and those who contend that it should not have been abandoned.

[1] Pay Board, *Special Report: Relativity Pay of Mineworkers*, Cmnd 5567, London, HMSO, 1974.

CHAPTER 3

PUBLIC EXPENDITURE

by *R. W. R. Price*

INTRODUCTION

This chapter is concerned with what the Musgraves call the 'stabilisation function' of managing public expenditure – its role in the management of demand.[1] The 'allocation' and 'distribution' functions, which relate to its role in the provision of social goods and the transfer of spending power between individuals, are not considered specifically,[2] although they are generally relevant because the coordination of all three is important in assessing the achievements of each. Combining social objectives with stabilisation policy can be successful, but conflict between the two has, perhaps, been more usual than harmony.

Public expenditure enjoyed an unchallenged pre-eminence in the original blue-prints for postwar stabilisation policy, but in practice it surrendered this position to taxation and the manipulation of consumer demand. If the postwar scene had been dominated by chronic under-investment or prolonged cyclical depression this might not have happened, but stabilisation turned out to require 'fine-tuning', to which variations in public expenditure seemed ill-adapted. By the end of the 1950s the avowed strategy had become to ensure that public spending was neutral *vis-à-vis* internal stability, with the public sector expanding at a rate consistent with the long-run growth of the economy, so that at least one sector would be free from cyclical disturbance. However, adjustments to programmes of a scale and frequency considerably beyond the limits of short-term flexibility originally allowed

---

[1] R. A. and P. B. Musgrave, *Public Finance: in theory and practice*, London, McGraw Hill, 1975, chap. 1.

[2] Concepts of welfare optimisation do not figure in the determination of expenditure and will not be pursued here. With respect to neither priorities for individual programmes nor the overall size of the public sector have governments 'tried to achieve the aims that welfare theories postulate for them, and . . . they are unlikely to do so in future. Consequently these prescriptive theories are simply not operational' (A. T. Peacock and J. Wiseman, *The Growth of Public Expenditure in the United Kingdom*, Princeton University Press, 1961, p. 14). Despite the creation (in the 1970s) of programme evaluation methods explicitly concerned with priorities and cost–benefit analysis (Programme Analysis and Review and the Central Policy Review Staff), fiscal politics and departmental log-rolling still decide most issues in determining expenditure.

for have still been a hallmark of the period covered here. Public expenditure has never wholly shed its short-term role.

It is not, of course, the principal object of public spending that it should act as a counterweight in balancing demand; rather, decisions about its volume and composition should reflect the economic and social considerations specifically attached to it. Concern that using it in a fully active short-term role may entail the sacrifice of these objectives has accompanied doubts about the physical costs of using it as an instrument. Adjustments to programmes (particularly increases) can be made to serve the needs of deficit finance and allocative policies, but only transiently, tending to be followed at short remove by conflict, as economic exigencies force *ad hoc* cuts across-the-board.

How can a framework for decisions on the volume and mix of public expenditure in the medium term be constructed to allow for a contribution to demand management without physical disruption and the sacrifice of other objectives? The principle of planning medium-term expenditure 'in relation to prospective resources', which was endorsed in the *Plowden Report*,[1] and established by the Public Expenditure Survey Committee (PESC), which began operation in 1961, was a first approach to a solution of the problem. This has, however, remained unsolved, so that continuing attempts to construct a more water-tight system are a dominant theme of the period.

The difficulties of applying any system effectively would be great in the best of circumstances; they are exacerbated by the multiplicity of agencies – central government departments, local authorities, nationalised industries and other public corporations – on which the Treasury has to rely both to supply the material on which decisions are based and to implement those decisions. The relationships between the Treasury and the departments, and between central government and the actual spending authorities, have been extensively debated during the period. It is hardly surprising that, despite the continued search for improvement and a number of significant innovations in techniques, the problem of dovetailing the allocative and stabilisation functions of government remains.

The first section of this chapter deals directly with the evolution over the period of public expenditure 'management' – to use a rather inadequate but handy term to describe the process and principles which govern the determination and control of public expenditure. Subsequent sections attempt to provide a quantitative and qualitative assessment of the impact of public expenditure as an instrument in the management of the economy.

[1] Treasury, *The Control of Public Expenditure*, Cmnd 1432, London, HMSO, 1961, p. 6.

THE MANAGEMENT OF PUBLIC EXPENDITURE

The search for improved methods of public expenditure control gives a certain continuity to its historical development, but this can conveniently be considered in three stages. The division between the first two is the *Plowden Report*, which set out the principles of medium-term planning and restricted short-term intervention.[1] Devaluation in 1967 provided a second watershed, because it led to a reappraisal of both medium-term and short-term ground rules; it was the most fundamental influence on policy until the oil crisis.

Public expenditure 1944–61

In 1944 a White Paper had recognised two means of achieving economic stability through regulating public investment. First, it was thought possible to 'maintain the stability of public investment when private investment is beginning to fall off', thus preventing sympathetic movements which tended to accentuate the trade cycle.[2] Secondly, public investment might be deliberately varied in a counter-cyclical way to compensate directly for disturbances in the private sector.[3]

The experience of the 1950s was a mixture of both strategies; so much so that there are two views about which was dominant. The *Radcliffe Report*, certain spokesmen for local authorities and nationalised industries, and the *Plowden Report* saw consistent medium-term planning being compromised by disruptive and destabilising short-term interventions.[4] The other view, expressed by Dow, Dennison and various official publications,[5] clearly allocates a subordinate role in counter-cyclical policy to public expenditure. Actually, during the

---

[1] Ibid.

[2] Ministry of Reconstruction, *Employment Policy*, Cmd 6527, London, HMSO, 1944, p. 21.

[3] The concept of deliberately destabilising public investment was criticised by Beveridge as introducing 'meaningless unprogressive fluctuation'; he advocated instead an expansion of the public sector 'so as to enlarge the area within which investment can be stabilised directly' (W. H. Beveridge, *Full Employment in a Free Society*, London, Allen & Unwin, 1944, pp. 183 and 269). This strategy was designed to maximise the longer-term contribution of expenditure policy to stability, and was reminiscent of Keynes, who foresaw 'the State, which is in a position to calculate the marginal efficiency of capital-goods on long views and on the basis of the general social advantage, taking an ever greater responsibility for directly organising investment' (J. M. Keynes, *The General Theory of Employment, Interest and Money*, London, Macmillan, 1936, p. 164).

[4] Treasury, *Committee on the Working of the Monetary System. Report* [Radcliffe Report], Cmnd 827, London, HMSO, 1959, pp. 167–8, and *Principal Memoranda of Evidence*, vol. 2, London, HMSO, 1960, pp. 183 and 186–7; Treasury, *The Control of Public Expenditure*, p. 10; Institute of Municipal Treasurers and Accountants, *Local Government Finance*, July 1961, p. 157.

[5] Dow, *The Management of the British Economy, 1945–60*; S. R. Dennison, 'Investment in the nationalised industries' (paper given to the Manchester Statistical Society, 11 February 1959) p. 4; Council on Prices, Productivity and Incomes, *1st Report*, London, HMSO, 1958; Treasury, *Public Investment in Great Britain*, Cmnd 1203, London, HMSO, 1960, pp. 6–7.

1950s spasmodic short-term interventions in public expenditure pro-grammes never seriously impeded the development of medium-term planning, which had explicitly become the axis of stabilisation policy by the early 1960s. Although short-term adjustments were made to pro-grammes of the nationalised industries, these were generally small, and became smaller still with experience. Some deflationary interventions – notably in 1956/7 – may have entailed a cost in terms of disruption, but in general they only affected programmes where ancillary schemes allowed some leeway, or where shortfalls from targets (often themselves due to changed levels of business activity) provided scope for notional cuts. Both the deflationary intervention of 1958/9 and the reflationary one of 1959/60 changed investment in nationalised industries by only 3 per cent; the most obvious characteristic of the period as a whole was the secular expansion of public industry, particularly fuel and power, as a proportion of the economy. Similarly, although there were five deflationary interventions by central government in local authority investment between July 1955 and October 1957, which evoked some local criticism, these had an extremely small overall impact on planned spending, partly due to reluctance to interfere with health and educa-tion programmes. To ease demand pressures, the government could accelerate the existing run-down in the public housing programme, while relying on local environmental projects to provide the remaining short-term restraint; thus, the natural conflict between central and local priorities probably accounts for most of the local authority complaints.

Throughout the 1950s public expenditure was tending, in practice, towards a stabilisation role that was neutral rather than actively compensatory. Since it was regarded as being unadjustable at short notice by more than 2–3 per cent either way without counter-productive consequences,[1] the characteristic two-year period from high to low was too short for variations in public investment to be effective. Hence Plowden's call for the 'greatest practical stability of decisions in public expenditure',[2] which was hailed by some as revolutionising the conduct of compensatory finance,[3] but, more properly, regularised what had already evolved as the *de facto* basis of policy.

[1] This was the official estimate of short-term flexibility in public investment programmes by the end of the 1950s (ibid; also D. H. Amory quoted in *Local Government Finance*, July 1960, pp. 161–2).

[2] Treasury, *The Control of Public Expenditure*, p. 7.

[3] See House of Commons, *Hansard*, 24 January 1962, col. 221; U. K. Hicks, 'Plowden planning and management in the public services', *Public Administration*, vol. 39, Winter 1961, p. 304.

Plowden and the planning era

Implementing Plowden's prescription for the medium-term planning of public expenditure with only the most marginal short-term variations depended on a number of factors which made the strategy difficult to put into effective practice. First, once the proper expenditure–resource relationship had been specified, the 'prospective development of income and economic resources' had to be defined and accurately estimated. The *Plowden Report* recognised that economic resources could be predicted five years ahead 'only within broad limits', and that regular surveys would not provide automatic criteria which could be substituted for judgement. Secondly, because targets were set in terms of fifth-year expenditure levels and growth paths in terms of an average rate of growth over the five years, early expenditure plans did not specify by what annual growth rates the average should be achieved. The problem of varying the rate of expansion around the average in order to suit the needs of economic policy was foreseen, but the difficulty was to prevent the timing profile from getting out of touch with short-term needs and the limits of flexibility.

Although the PESC began operation in a climate of restriction, its first tasks being to reduce expenditure to meet the 1961 external crisis, this was meant to be a prelude to a new secular course along a 3 per cent growth path,[1] which had become 4 per cent by mid-1962/3, whilst the 1963 PESC survey eventually projected a real annual average increase of 4·1 per cent between 1963/4 and 1967/8.[2] *The National Plan*, published in September 1965, went further, combining a $4\frac{1}{4}$ per cent annual average increase in public expenditure (except for investment in nationalised industry) with a 4 per cent annual average growth of GDP from 1964/5 to 1969/70.

In each case the rise in expenditure was to be kept roughly in line with resources, so that the public share of GDP was only scheduled to increase by about $\frac{1}{2}$ per cent in volume terms. In the event, as table 3.1 shows, the demand on resources increased much more than this: between 1963 and 1967 the public sector share of GDP grew by nearly 4 per cent in volume and nearly 5 per cent in value. Of this 0·33 per cent was a planned volume increase and 0·8 per cent a relative price increase;[3] of the balance of 3·65 per cent, over half can be attributed to defective control or policy changes, since by 1967 public expenditure had grown far ahead of schedule, and the rest to over-optimism about the growth of GDP. In the formative years of the PESC, then, the

[1] Selwyn Lloyd in the House of Commons, 17 April 1961.
[2] Treasury, *Public Expenditure in 1963–64 and 1967–68*, Cmnd 2235, London, HMSO, 1963.
[3] See page 85 below.

Table 3.1. *The share in GDP^a of public expenditure:^{b}*
planned and unplanned changes, 1963–7

Percentages

	Change 1963–7	Share
1963 share at current market prices		33·26
Planned increase in volume	+0·33	
Unplanned increase in volume:		
Due to GDP shortfall	+1·31	
Due to public expenditure excess	+2·34	
Total increase in volume	+3·98	
Relative price effect	+0·80	
Total increase in value	+4·78	
1967 share at current market prices		38·04

SOURCES: Treasury, *Public Expenditure in 1963–64 and 1967–68*; Department of Economic Affairs, *The National Plan*; CSO, *National Income and Expenditure 1963–73*, London, HMSO, 1974; NIESR estimates.

^{a} At market prices.

^{b} Excluding imputed rents, net purchases of existing assets (real and financial) and debt interest.

attempt to relate expenditure to resources was not successful and the lessons learnt were negative ones. The subsequent development of expenditure control since devaluation may, indeed, be seen as a reaction to two factors which had become apparent immediately after the *Plowden Report* – the tendencies both to overestimate the resources available and to underestimate public sector demands on them. The PESC procedures relating to these two issues merit further comment.

Since the purpose of the PESC is to provide a framework for taking decisions regarding public expenditure over the medium term, the critical elements have been seen as establishing what prospective resources are available and the 'cost' of pre-empting them for public sector use. Crucial to the former is the concept of the growth of productive potential, or the path of 'constant employment' output from which variations in capacity utilisation have been abstracted.[1] It is this concept rather than the growth of GDP itself which in practice constrains expenditure strategy and determines the growth of expenditure in the medium term.[2] However, since at any base date expenditure may be 'off-trend' in either direction (implying a short-term share of resources greater or smaller than that considered normal or desirable in the

[1] Productive potential increases with both productivity and the labour supply, and 'constant employment' implies absorbing the growth of the latter.

[2] For a discussion of this point see House of Commons, *Seventh Report from the Expenditure Committee, Session 1971–72. Public Expenditure and Economic Management*, London, HMSO, 1972, especially pp. vi–viii and 113–16.

Table 3.2. *Official projections for growth rates of GDP and public expenditure*

Percentages[a]

Forecasts[b]		GDP growth assumed	Public expenditure[c] growth		
Published	Period		Volume[d]	Total cost[e]	Net resource cost[ef]
Dec. 1963	1963/4–1967/8	4·0	4·10	4·85	4·85
Sept. 1965	1964/5–1969/70	4·0	4·25[g]	5·00[g]	5·00[g]
Dec. 1969	1968/9–1971/2	3·0–4·0	2·80	3·00	3·20
Jan. 1971	1970/1–1974/5	..	2·20	2·60	3·10
Nov. 1971	1971/2–1975/6	..	2·20	2·70	3·20
Dec. 1972	1972/3–1976/7	3·5–5·0	2·20	2·50	3·00
Dec. 1973	1973/4–1977/8	3·5–4·5	1·50	2·00	2·50

SOURCES: Treasury, *Public Expenditure in 1963–64 and 1967–68*; Department of Economic Affairs, *The National Plan*; Treasury, *Public Expenditure 1968–69 to 1973–74*, *Public Expenditure 1969–70 to 1974–75*, *Public Expenditure 1969–70 to 1975–76*, *Public Expenditure to 1976–77* and *Public Expenditure to 1977–78*.

[a] Annual average growth rates.
[b] From sources in order given.
[c] Including contingency reserve and shortfall allowance from December 1969 forecast, and excluding investment grants from January 1971 forecast.
[d] At constant survey prices.
[e] At constant out-turn prices, including the relative price effect.
[f] Demand on output in cost terms, as defined, for example, in Treasury, *Public Expenditure to 1977–78*, table 3.1.
[g] Excluding investment in nationalised industries.

longer run), it is legitimate to specify medium-term growth rates for the public sector which diverge somewhat from growth rates in productive potential proper.

Table 3.2 lists these projected official growth rates, as published since 1963, together with the various medium-term output assumptions which accompanied them. From the third and fourth columns it can be seen that there is a fairly consistent decline in the projected volume growth rates of expenditure, both absolutely and relative to the growth of GDP.[1] At first sight this would seem to imply a comparable decline

[1] These volume growth rates are expressed in terms of constant 'survey prices'. The PESC system is integrated with the annual estimates cycle, which forms the basis for financial control: departmental estimates for spending in the next financial year are submitted to the Treasury on 1 December, and the Parliamentary 'Vote on Account' to meet these estimates takes place in mid-February. Including local authority grants, this covers about 55 per cent of government spending, and the components provide the basis for the first year of the PESC survey which follows from March to November. For this expenditure, therefore, 1973 survey prices, for example, mean the pay and prices used to cost the 1973/4 budget estimates, and would refer very roughly to October–November 1972. For other categories of expenditure the precise base point varies, but would normally relate to February–March 1973 (See Treasury, *Public Expenditure White Papers: handbook on methodology*, London, HMSO, 1972,

in the share of the public sector in GDP, but in fact short-term programme increases and GDP shortfalls meant that public expenditure
was being forced into an 'above-trend' position in the short run
and an important reason for the lower projected growth rates for
later periods is the attempt of medium-term policy to correct for
this.

However, the contrast between projections made before and after
devaluation is unambiguous; indeed, the growth of productive potential
had a rather different meaning as a constraint in the two periods. Both
the NEDC experiment and the National Plan were based on the
premise that public expenditure demands would help create their own
supply, thus making the resource 'constraint' endogenous to the growth
path for public expenditure. Following devaluation there was a reaction
from this optimism; projections made in February and December 1969
envisaged an increase in total output of between just under 3 per cent
and about 4 per cent a year over the medium term, with the expenditure plans based on the lower figure.[1] This 'wedge' approach is still
used in expenditure plans, even though the growth objective has
periodically reasserted itself. In 1972/3 and 1973/4 the prospect of
above-average growth was not allowed to influence the longer-run
public expenditure allocation; instead, provision for other demand
items, particularly private investment, was increased.[2]

Generally speaking, the strategy of expenditure management between
1968 and 1973 revolved around a medium-term growth path of
approximately 3 per cent, which the Treasury has described as 'proceeding in a majestic and unvarying way',[3] and which was deduced from
the historical growth record from 1958 to 1970. This has been criticised
by the more optimistic as leading to a self-perpetuating restraint on
growth, but the Treasury has viewed it as 'imprudent to assume a faster
growth rate of available resources without a very clear idea of where the
growth was to come from.'[4]

We have seen in table 3.2 that the National Plan implied a small
increase in the volume of public expenditure relative to GDP, but the
growth of expenditure volume and of GDP were not far from propor-

---

pp. 23 et seq., and W. A. H. Godley, 'The measurement and control of public expenditure',
Economic Policy Review, no. 2, March 1976, pp. 58–63).

[1] Department of Economic Affairs, The Task Ahead (Economic Assessment to 1972), London,
HMSO, 1969; Treasury, Public Expenditure 1968–69 to 1973–74, Cmnd 4234, London,
HMSO, 1969.

[2] See Treasury, Public Expenditure to 1976–77, Cmnd 5178, p. 10, and Public Expenditure
to 1977–78, Cmnd 5519, p. 10, London, HMSO, 1972 and 1973.

[3] House of Commons, Seventh Report from the Expenditure Committee, Session 1971–72, p. 52.
In exact terms, the growth of productive potential was derived as 3·2 per cent per annum,
comprising a 3 per cent increase in productivity and a 0·2 per cent increase in the labour
force (ibid. pp. 113–19).   [4] Ibid. pp. ix and 75.

tional as originally conceived by both administrations. There appears, however, to have been something of a doctrinal divergence between the two Parties on this matter, with Labour coming to regard proportional growth as too low and the Conservatives as too high. Although this latter view was not apparent during Maudling's 'growth experiment', it asserted itself in 1970,[1] when the new approach was 'to consider the need of public expenditure and for what it will be required...first, rather than trying to predict the rate of growth of total output and then seeking to justify the rate of growth of public expenditure in reference to it.'[2] At the root of the difference lies a value judgement about private and public spending and about taxation.

To maintain a given share of national output, the government sector demand for finance (and therefore taxation) has to advance more than proportionately. This is because the productivity increase in the government sector is deemed to be zero,[3] so that the cost of output increases faster than in the 'enterprise' sector, where it is not – the so-called 'relative price effect'. This ensured that public expenditure plans laid down in the early 1960s entailed a continuous rise in their share of GDP at current prices between 1963 and 1967 (0·8 per cent, see table 3.1). This disproportionate demand for finance was recognised from the start;[4] it was at the heart of Chancellors' warnings in the House of Commons about increased longer-term taxation in 1964/5.[5] It was also the basis of the post-devaluation reversal of strategy; the cost of services rather than the level provided having become central to public expenditure planning since 1968. In December 1969 the 3 per cent growth rate for public expenditure was fixed in terms of its cost not its volume (fifth column in table 3.2).[6]

Public expenditure has therefore come to be explicitly identified with the resource transfer (and hence taxation) necessary to finance public spending. But what is the correct measure of this transfer? Public expenditure as it stands is net of charges (for medical prescriptions, for example), but gross of income and expenditure taxes. Direct taxes are generated by some types of current grant and by interest paid on public debt; there is also a significant indirect tax element in government

---

[1] Treasury, *New Policies for Public Spending*, Cmnd 4515, London, HMSO, 1970.
[2] House of Commons, *Hansard*, 22 February 1971, col. 127.
[3] The failure to measure productivity increases in public services means that (identifiable) output increases come from increased public employment; also, the long-run cost of public services goes up relative to the GDP deflator at a rate equal to average productivity growth in the economy (provided public and private sector earnings increase at the same long-run rate). A constant level of public service output then gives a lower volume share in GDP, but a fixed value share, as the relative price of public services increases at the same rate as GDP.
[4] Treasury, *Public Expenditure in 1963–64 and 1967–68*, p. 10.
[5] Reginald Maudling, 14 April 1964, and James Callaghan, 22 February 1965.
[6] Treasury, *Public Expenditure 1968–69 to 1973–74*.

purchases.[1] Further, where the same function can be fulfilled by either expenditure or tax allowances, changes in spending may involve off-setting changes in revenue (as when switching from investment grants to allowances), so that estimates of the rate of increase in resource demands should take both sides into account. Again, certain items are transactions in existing assets and, while these are significant in them-selves, they do not constitute claims on current production. Finally, since part of transfer expenditure is saved by the recipients, this also can be discounted as a claim on output. By adjusting for all these factors,[2] we can obtain estimates of public expenditure which may be described as 'demand on output at factor cost', changes in which measure the net resource transfer necessary to finance both the growth in public services provided and the redistribution of private spending power (including that to public authority employees through the relative price effect).

This 'weighted' measure of public expenditure – its net resource cost rather than its gross cost – first attained planning significance in 1971/2; as may be seen from the last column of table 3.2, the growth path of public spending was constrained by linking the growth of its net cost to the (past) growth rate of productive potential. In the process, the gross cost projections fell below this by about 0·5 per cent per annum (although the exact difference between the two depends on the com-position of expenditure). Granted that planned public expenditure should be evaluated in this way, the magnitude of public spending is, of course, still a matter for political and economic decision. A proportional (3 per cent) constraint on growth in resource cost can be regarded as a proxy for longer-run (non-inflationary) revenue poten-tial, but as a rule of thumb it cannot have the same force as an explicit long-run income–expenditure budget. It has been advocated that expenditure should be matched directly to tax revenue projections so as to provide a better and more comprehensive method of coordinat-ing public spending with available resources, but here too there have been differences over what rules or datum lines should be specified, and the proposals have not been systematically implemented.[3]

---

[1] In the national accounts charges are netted out of public spending and treated as personal consumption, and the PESC follows this practice. Most of the indirect taxes are included in purchases of goods and services, but selective employment tax introduced a large tax element into the public wage and salary bill, which meant, at the time, an artificial increase in the gross cost of services.

[2] For a fuller description of the adjustments see pages 95–6 below.

[3] The integration of the public expenditure descision-making process with longer-term policy towards taxation was advocated by Sir Richard Clarke, one of the chief architects of the *Plowden Report* (see *The Management of the Public Sector of the National Economy*, London, Athlone Press, 1964, p. 24). It was endorsed in a Green Paper – Treasury, *Public Expenditure: a new presentation*, Cmnd 4017, London, HMSO, 1969 – but the revenue projections in this document were discontinued after the White Paper of the same year (until restored in the

Policy since 1968: medium-term demands and short-term needs

The failure to delineate the growth path of public expenditure between base and target years was recognised with hindsight as a defect of planning in the period 1963–7.[1] It contributed to a tendency to excess spending and made the fifth-year target unachievable without drastic intervention;[2] public expenditure was uniformly ahead of the specified average growth path in 1967/8 (see charts 3.3 and 3.4 on pages 108–10 below) and, though an initial 'hump' in expenditure had been foreseen,[3] its magnitude was an expression of the general fault – that plans were precise five years ahead, but vague as one came nearer to actuality. Since devaluation, therefore, the annual growth path by which the fifth-year target is supposed to be reached has been delineated. This was intended to ease the difficulties of phasing public expenditure to suit the needs of demand management. Inability to manipulate public expenditure in the short term to any marked degree was blamed for the stabilisation problems of the National Plan;[4] a consistent medium-term growth path would therefore help to prevent destabilising variations in the public sector itself and to keep expenditure policy within the bounds of short-term flexibility.

Two further innovations were also supposed to increase the contribution of public expenditure planning to stability. The first was the concentration on the third year, rather than the more nebulous fifth, as the focal point for decision-making. This was portrayed as the most convenient stage at which to confirm or modify provisional expenditure decisions, because it was the year when there was real scope for substantial changes up or down without too great a cost through disruption.[5]

White Paper of January 1978). The innovation was dropped chiefly on the grounds that public expenditure decisions should not be taken on the basis of arbitrarily defined revenue projections (see House of Commons, *Third Report from the Expenditure Committee, Session 1970–71. Command Papers on Public Expenditure*, London, HMSO, 1971, pp. 6–10). Partly this reflected the belief of the incoming Conservative administration that taxation was already too high and ought to be reduced. But there are obvious problems regarding inflationary and real fiscal drag – should tax rates be specified in indexed form or not, and if not what rate of inflation should be assumed? – which may tend to make revenue projections arbitrary unless based on a consistent long-term taxation strategy and/or rules regarding the full-employment budget balance (Cf. R. R. Neild and T. Ward, *The Budgetary Situation: an appraisal*, Department of Applied Economics, University of Cambridge, 1976, and Godley, 'The measurement and control of public expenditure', p. 62).

[1] House of Commons, *Hansard*, 22 January 1970, col. 743.

[2] See H. Heclo and A. Wildavsky, *The Private Government of Public Money*, London, Macmillan, 1974, p. 211.

[3] Treasury, *Public Expenditure: planning and control*, Cmnd 2915, London, HMSO, 1966, pp. 13–14; House of Commons, *Hansard*, 22 January 1970, col. 743.   [4] Ibid.

[5] Treasury, *Public Expenditure: a new presentation*, p. 8; House of Commons, *First Report from the Select Committee on Procedure, Session 1968–69. Scrutiny of Public Expenditure and Administration*, London, HMSO, 1969, pp. 150 *et seq.*

The Treasury have not wished by this approach to create the impression that options are closed before the focal point and open after it, but have emphasised that the inflexibility of programmes diminishes the further one looks ahead to the end of the planning period.[1] However, the PESC system of annual reviews tends to emphasise that the third year is the point at which medium-term and short-term needs converge.[2]

It was hoped that the second innovation would also help with short-term stabilisation; plans were to be made on the basis that it was 'less disruptive later to bring forward plans if there proves to be room for them than it is to stop what has been started if this proves to have been too much'.[3] But the relative merits of reflation over deflation are not so clear-cut; they rest, particularly, on the lower relative *cost* of increasing programmes at short notice than of cutting them – cost being here interpreted as the financial, political and psychological diseconomies of altering existing commitments. In terms of the actual physical and contractual difficulties of changing programmes at short notice, it is doubtful so far as capital expenditure is concerned whether either reflation or deflation has a distinct advantage. Cuts have to be restricted to programmes not yet 'committed' (the last formal stage before the scheme moves to tender); they do not extend to projects already contracted, and only exceptionally to those out to tender.[4] Short-term deflationary potential thus excludes any effect on work-in-progress, which is accepted as zero; it is confined to cuts in orders, which means that a given change in capital expenditure necessitates a much larger alteration in project starts.[5] Against this, reflation has to rely on the extent to which longer-term projects are ready to be put into effect,[6] or on the existence of frustrated demand in, for example, local environmental schemes.

[1] House of Commons, *Third Report from the Expenditure Committee, Session 1970–71*, p.67; Treasury, *Public Expenditure 1969–70 to 1974–75*, Cmnd 4578, London, HMSO, 1971, p. 6.

[2] It is beyond the short-term horizon of $1\frac{1}{2}$–2 years, but allows for positive cyclical phasing within the context of the medium-term economic assessment, as well as minimising the possibility of public expenditure plans becoming cyclically perverse and thus straining the capacity for short-term stabilisation proper.

[3] Roy Jenkins in the House of Commons, 21 January 1970.

[4] Even so, land may be held unproductively and designs shelved or scrapped. The effects on morale and efficiency have frequently been cited by local authorities as one of the costs of programme reductions (see *Local Government Finance*, September 1970).

[5] Occasionally the government may intervene in the 4–6 month period between commitment and commencement, but in the case of local authority projects it has, in fact, no legal right to do so. It took a 50–60 per cent cut in starts to achieve the 20 per cent across-the-board planned investment cut in December 1973 (see NEDO, Building and Civil Engineering Economic Development Committees, *The Public Client and the Construction Industry*, London, HMSO, 1975, p. 22; House of Commons, *Fourth Report from the Expenditure Committee, Session 1974. Expenditure Cuts in Health and Personal Social Services*, London, HMSO, 1975, p. ix).

[6] The possibility of a 'shelf' of partially prepared projects has been mooted at various times, in particular in OECD, *Fiscal Policy for a Balanced Economy* by W. Heller *et al.*, Paris, 1968, p. 110. The Treasury objections to such a scheme are set out in House of Commons, *Seventh Report from the Expenditure Committee, Session 1971–72*, pp. 8–9.

With suitable incentives for spending within a particular time (as in 1971–3), reflationary policies can be effective, but persuasion is not equivalent to the direct controls available for implementing cuts – the system acts better as a bridle than a spur. This being so, it has remained the opinion of the Treasury that it is physically 'easier to postpone than to bring forward'. [1]

The real advantage of reflation lies, in fact, in current expenditure. Transfer payments tend to be rigid downwards and elastic upwards, and for technical reasons instruments such as increasing national insurance benefits or government consumption have a more immediate impact on demand than either taxation or investment, which makes them almost irresistible. [2] The trouble is that these instruments tend to be self-defeating in the sense that much of their short-term effect compromises the medium-term strategy from which their usefulness devolves. Except for the peculiar case of postwar credits, repayments of which can be confined within a given period, transfer payments cannot be phased, but necessitate an upward shift in the medium-term expenditure schedule; [3] the same thing applies to current expenditure on goods and services. Short-term cuts may also imply medium-term shifts, but these can be contained more easily than upward changes.

This difficulty of phasing reflations so that they do not spill over inopportunely into the medium term is one reason why there tend to be successive reversals of stance in stabilisation policy. The tendency for reflation to result in increased medium-term commitments, which then have to be cut back, may be partly the result of laxer control during reflations, so that there is an unintentional spill-over, but the documentary evidence on 1972/3 shows that, in fact, discretionary policy decisions are more important in this respect than a looser Treasury hold on the reins.

Reflation began in 1971/2, with the Treasury looking for things which could be started quickly but completed within two years; it was not the intention to 'prejudice the whole of public expenditure for five years ahead'. [4] During the course of 1972, however, conjunctural policy took on a new dimension and as a result there were large programme increases for 1973/4 and beyond. [5] It seems that the authorities had decided

---

[1] Ibid. p. 9.

[2] The impact multipliers for the first year of intervention are relatively large because the lags are shorter and the savings and import offsets smaller. In the case of an uprating the impact effect is also much greater than the eventual leverage because the negative effect of increased contributions (especially those by employers) takes longer to work through than the positive effect of increased transfers.

[3] It is true, however, that, to the extent that they are fixed in nominal terms, the higher the rate of inflation the faster the rate at which increments in transfer payments will be eroded in real terms.   [4] Ibid. pp. xi, 3, 4 and 11.

[5] Treasury, *Public Expenditure to 1976–77*.

that 'there were two ways to go about relieving [unemployment] by means of public expenditure policy. One was the straight counter-cyclical deviation from the plan which would otherwise have been in being. The other was an addition to the programme which would be acceptable in the medium-term.'[1]

The situation is illustrated in chart 3.1. The specifically counter-cyclical action initially scheduled to taper off during 1973/4 constituted an increase of about 1·7 per cent on total 1972/3 expenditure; the

Chart 3.1. *Counter-cyclical and other policy increases in public expenditure[a] between the 1971 and 1972 surveys*

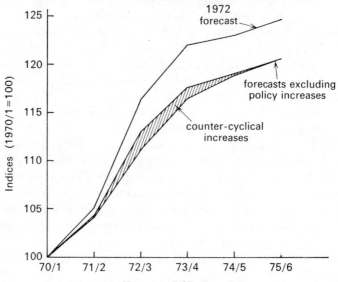

SOURCE: Treasury, *Public Expenditure to 1976–77.*

[a] Expenditure volume of total programmes excluding investment grants.

medium-term or secular increases more than doubled this, adding 2·8 per cent to that year;[2] they also shifted the expenditure schedule upwards by about 3½ per cent in the following years. In such a process there is a danger that medium-term strategy may be undermined even though the planning constraint fixed in terms of the average annual rate of growth from the base year is not exceeded. In this case the projected rate of growth (the slope of the schedule) was actually reduced from 2·7

---

[1] House of Commons, *Fifth Report from the Expenditure Committee, Session 1972–73. The White Paper 'Public Expenditure to 1976–77'* (*Cmnd 5178*), London, HMSO, 1973, pp. 4–5 and 8–9.

[2] In 1972/3 conjunctural policy increases formed about 40 per cent of the total and in 1973/4 25 per cent.

to 2·5 per cent in cost terms, the latter, of course, being from a larger base. The facility with which shifts in the expenditure schedule can be compensated for by more shadowy adjustments to the longer-term profile of expansion must be counted a defect of the control system.[1] Even if the intention is to restore the balance later by downward shifts, this might be at a cost, and there is the danger of imbalances in the programmes because the elements which are flexible upwards, and useful in reflations, are not necessarily those available for deflation. Counter-cyclical action proper has concentrated on investment, while (in 1972/3 at least) medium-term action has been through increases in current expenditure (transfers, goods and services). Since the latter are least operable in a deflation, capital reductions are often called upon to compensate.

Whilst the refinement of the PESC system has undoubtedly brought some notable gains in the costing of public expenditure – the focus on the third year and the provision of appropriately cautious datum lines – these cannot be said to have solved the basic problem of making room for contra-cyclical variation of plans within a viable medium-term programme. Since, moreover, the system has been called upon to provide a degree of flexibility substantially and increasingly beyond that envisaged at the beginning of the period, it must remain a cause for serious concern that failure to solve this problem may result in programme imbalances and successive reversals of policy.

Control of the spending authorities

The multifarious agencies actually responsible for the programmes which make up public expenditure exacerbate the problems. Since it is principally upon investment that contra-cyclical adjustments fall, it is the nationalised industries and the local authorities rather than central government which carry the onus of adjustment. Some observers have accordingly criticised the government machine for lack of coordination, with local authority spending a 'rogue elephant'[2] responsible for periodic over-loading of the economy;[3] the belief is also prevalent that short-term adjustments can never be adequately enforced on either the local authorities or the nationalised industries.

Certainly as regards current spending, it is officially admitted that the mechanism of rate support grants constitutes 'strong influence' rather than control.[4] Local authorities have the right to levy their own rates, so

---

[1] For a discussion of the 'fine art' of bartering long-term cuts for short-term increases, see Heclo and Wildavsky, *The Private Government of Public Money*, pp. 236–7.

[2] A. R. Prest, 'Sense and nonsense in budgetary policy', *Economic Journal*, vol. 78, March 1968, p. 5.

[3] Sir John Hicks, *After the Boom*, London, Institute of Economic Affairs, 1966, p. 16.

[4] Treasury, *Public Expenditure White Papers: handbook on methodology*, p. 19.

that their expenditure must be autonomous at the margin, the main constraint being the inflexibility and unpopularity of the rates themselves. But local authority expenditure is in many ways similar to that of the central government, except insofar as priorities determined centrally may call for relative expansion of programmes in the local authority domain (particularly housing and education); some of these (housing, again, in particular) may pose special planning and control difficulties.[1] In respect of capital expenditure local authorities are, in fact, almost satellites of the central government, chiefly as a result of their inability to raise loans without government sanction.[2] Up to 1970/1 loans had to be approved for financing each project, despite the fact that 80 per cent or so of local capital spending was also subject to direct departmental control of some form or another and despite local authority complaints that meticulous control over the other 20 per cent was unwarranted in spheres of essentially local interest. The reforms of November 1970 rationalised the system, so that for 'key sector' programmes – housing, the bulk of education and roads – direct departmental sanction carried automatic borrowing approval; in the 'locally determined' sector local authorities may now set priorities within the framework of a block capital allocation which is fixed annually. It is here – in the environmental sector and the smaller road and education projects[3] – that counter-cyclical policy has traditionally been concentrated, since such projects have low priority and are thought, in the main, to have shorter planning horizons.

[1] See NIESR evidence, 'Local authority finance and the management of the economy', Appendix 6 to Department of the Environment, *Local Government Finance. Report of the Committee of Enquiry* [Layfield Report], Cmnd 6453, London, HMSO, 1976, pp. 48–80. The housing programme, for which local authorities are mainly responsible, largely accounts for the unpredictability which sometimes characterises local authority investment. Otherwise, neither this nor current expenditure has differed in regard to shortfalls, overruns or relative price effects from central government spending. Moreover, the *National Institute Economic Review*, no. 75, February 1976, pp. 86–9, shows that, for the period between 1970/1 and 1974/5, central and local spending did not display separate features *vis-à-vis* the expansion which occurred. The local authority contribution to the excess of 1974/5 spending levels over those planned in November 1971 appears to have been about 17 per cent – cf. Q. Outram, 'The significance of public expenditure plans' (unpublished working paper, Centre for Studies in Social Policy), London, 1975, pp. 16 and 34. There is strong evidence that difficulties in controlling programmes are linked more to the level of capital expenditure and to open-ended subsidies and transfers than to institutional factors, though time and cost overruns also vary significantly (see NEDO, Building and Civil Engineering Economic Development Committees, *The Public Client and the Construction Industry*, pp. 79 *et seq.*)

From the point of view of demand management, of course, it should be noted that rate-financed expenditure has only a second-order effect on fiscal leverage, since the financial balance of the authorities is not affected.

[2] This system was established in 1933 to prevent local authorities from burdening themselves with debt; it provided a readymade instrument for carrying out postwar employment policies (see Ministry of Reconstruction, *Employment Policy*, p. 21).

[3] 'Other environmental services' make up 50–60 per cent of the locally determined sector, education, libraries and the arts about 20 per cent, and roads 25 per cent.

Investment in nationalised industries presents special problems of control; its usefulness as a short-term instrument is limited by its strong market-orientation. The 1944 White Paper mentioned only that ways were being considered by which 'the programming of capital expenditure by public utility companies' could be used for counter-cyclical purposes;[1] local authority investment was supposed to be the principal instrument. In the event governments have been unable to ignore possible contributions to demand management from the nationalised industries, because of the impact of their capital spending on heavy engineering and transport. Public service investment, on the other hand, is predominantly in new building and works, so that the two sectors have complementary roles in stabilisation. The effectiveness of interventions in nationalised industries is, however, particularly questionable, not so much because the system of control is inadequate, nor because the industries do not try to respond to the wishes of the central government, but because their capital programmes are subject to forces – from the market and from suppliers – which tend to make marginal short-term adjustments futile. This is reflected in shortfalls of spending from planned levels, which disguise the effects of cuts and may nullify increases.

It is no doubt true that the control of public expenditure suffers from the divorce of responsible agencies from the centre, but the cause cannot be traced to inadequate institutional procedures. In the control of the purse strings and the legislative determination of priorities, the central government is more-or-less dominant in relation to both nationalised industries and local authorities, with the proviso regarding rates (see page 91 above). The problems lie rather in the efficient use of funds which are spent locally but raised mainly nationally. Agencies outside the central government are responsible for the detailed evaluation of projects and their execution is subject to market pressures. This gives scope for forecasting errors and for putting local and technocratic considerations before national economic ones. When things are favourable this may lead to over-compliance, while in adverse circumstances there may be a tendency to protect plans from short-term restrictions. It is doubtful, however, whether this resistance is any greater than the Treasury experiences within the central government from the spending Ministers and their departments.

[1] Ministry of Reconstruction, *Employment Policy*, p. 21.

PUBLIC EXPENDITURE AND RESOURCES
1959/60 TO 1973/4[1]

Introduction

There is nothing absolute about the share of resources to be pre-empted by the public sector, nor about its measurement. Measuring the public sector by reference to its own output or employment may be valid for some purposes, though there is no direct link between these magnitudes and the expenditure and revenue requirements of the budget. As an employer, the public sector has, during the period under review, used between 24 and 26 per cent of resources at a cost of 29–31 per cent of all employment income, but in spending terms 35 to 41 per cent of resources have passed through government hands.

Table 3.3. *The public sector's employment and wage bill, 1959–73*

Percentages

	Employment/working population				Wages and salaries/total employment income			
	1959	1964	1970	1973	1959	1964	1970	1973
Central government	7·71[a]	7·01	7·55	7·71	9·64	9·09	9·58	9·70
Local authorities	7·04	8·24	10·11	11·28	7·85	8·52	9·73	11·15
Public authorities	*14·75*	*15·25*	*17·66*	*18·99*	*17·49*	*17·61*	*19·31*	*20·85*
Public corporations	9·46[a]	8·22	7·95	7·27	11·56	10·26	10·14	10·00
PUBLIC SECTOR	24·21	23·47	25·61	26·26	29·05	27·87	29·45	30·85

SOURCE: CSO, *National Income and Expenditure 1964–74.*

[a] The Post Office is classified throughout as a public corporation, although it was part of central government until 1961.

Table 3.3 shows public sector employment as a proportion of the total working population (employed and unemployed) and the public sector's wage and salary bill as a proportion of total income from employment. The observations refer to years which were political dividing lines, since there have been quite explicit differences between the Parties on public expenditure and nationalisation. Nevertheless,

[1] For an analysis of trends in public spending in a historical context see Peacock and Wiseman, *The Growth of Public Expenditure in the United Kingdom* (for the period 1890–1955); J. Veverka, 'The growth of government expenditure in the United Kingdom since 1790' in A. T. Peacock and D. J. Robertson (eds.), *Public Expenditure: appraisal and control*, Edinburgh, Oliver & Boyd, 1963, pp. 111–27. Inter-country comparisons of expenditure growth between the years 1957 and 1965 are given in OECD, *Public Expenditure Trends in OECD Countries* by M. Garin-Painter, Paris, 1970. A discussion of the definition and measurement problems is to be found in T. E. Chester, 'The public sector – its dimensions and dynamics', *National Westminster Bank Review*, February 1976, pp. 31–44.

such trends as there are appear to hold for all three periods. The public corporations' share of the total workforce declined steadily from 9·46 per cent in 1959 to 7·27 per cent in 1973, despite the nationalisation of steel and as a result of the run-down in the coal industry and rail transport. Central government employment stayed fairly steady throughout, chiefly because the armed forces were reduced; without this it would have expanded fairly continuously, as did local authority employment, which went up over the period from about 7 per cent to over 11 per cent, with its wage bill matching this quite closely. However, the central government workforce is more expensive, so that for public authorities as a whole in 1973 the proportion of income was 21 per cent compared with a proportion of manpower of 19 per cent.

The public sector's demands on resources

Public employment is not an adequate measure of the public sector's impact as a supplier of social goods, as a distributor of resources among sections of the community, or as a vehicle of stabilisation policy. Current expenditure by public authorities includes purchases of goods and services from the private and overseas sectors which amount to about half as much again as is paid in direct wages and salaries. Only a very small fraction of their wage bill (about $1\frac{1}{4}$ per cent) is charged to capital accounts, since private contractors are used for most public investment projects. Conversely, some public sector employment goes towards satisfying private wants; certain elements of public service are charged for, and may be treated as private goods. Also, the operating accounts of the public corporations do not involve the use of public resources – only their surpluses (as revenue) and deficits (as subsidies to be met by public expenditure) appear in the published accounts, together with their capital spending and debt interest paid to non-government sources. Consolidated with public authorities' spending, these items provide a definition of public sector expenditure which is the basis of the analysis below.[1]

Translated into demands on resources at factor cost (which includes the relative price effect), direct public spending accounted for about 28 per cent of national resources in 1973/4 (slightly less than the 31 per cent public share of employment income), but to this must be added

[1] To comply with international practice, since 1977 a sharper distinction has been drawn – for both PESC and national accounts purposes – between 'general government' spending and that of the public enterprises. The former corresponds to central and local government expenditure; it includes government grants and loans to the public corporations, but not that part of their capital spending which is met by loans from other sources, nor their corresponding payments of debt interest. The use of the 'public sector' definition, which includes both of these, is justified here by the practice of both demand management and public expenditure control over the period under review, as well as by the fact that *all* public investment contributes to the borrowing requirement and to fiscal leverage.

Chart 3.2. *Public sector demands on resources relative to full-employment GDP,*
1959–1973/4

SOURCE: NIESR estimates.

Notes: (i) Public expenditure excludes investment grants and steel industry investment.

(ii) Full-employment GDP defined as maintaining a level of 325,000 unemployed, with underlying productivity growth of 3·2 per cent per annum. Imputed rents of private and public sectors are excluded.

(iii) Resource demand = total public expenditure net of net lending, imputed rents, indirect taxes on public expenditure, direct taxes on current grants, net purchases of land and existing buildings, estimated private sector savings out of current grants and stock appreciation.

(iv) Marginal resource share is the year-to-year change in resource demand (at constant 1970 factor cost) as a ratio of the year-to-year change in real full-employment GDP.

(v) Elasticities in the lower section are the ratios of year-to-year percentage changes in public expenditure (at 1970 factor cost) to the annual growth rate of full-employment GDP (3·2 per cent).

transfers and subsidies – publicly financed private expenditure – which raised the public share of resources to about 41 per cent. The necessity of raising revenue constrains both direct and indirect public expenditure, so that, in the context of the budget and fiscal policy, it makes sense to combine them into a single measure of aggregate public sector demand on resources. For estimates of this aggregate demand (shown in chart 3.2), the raw expenditure figures have been refined in various ways. First, variations in expenditure associated automatically with changes in the level of activity have been neutralised by recalculating the relevant expenditure at a full-employment level of activity; the items concerned are unemployment benefits and debt interest.[1] Secondly, some items of public expenditure are automatically associated with tax receipts and in such cases (for example, taxable current grants or government purchases subject to indirect taxes) expenditure is taken net of tax. Thirdly, the expenditure figures have been converted into terms of actual demand by allowing for savings offset against current transfers and netting out expenditure on the purchase of existing assets (for example, land). Finally, the short-run consequences for domestic output clearly depend on the import content of the demand for resources and a further adjustment is made for this.

Chart 3.2 therefore shows public expenditure redefined in 'weighted' terms, which enables it to be evaluated directly in relation to full-employment GDP at factor cost. Two measures are important: the estimates of *total* claims, including expenditure abroad, and of the direct demands on domestic production. While 'resource demand' is a measure of total resources pre-empted by public expenditure as a ratio of full-employment GDP, the 'marginal resource share' shows the resources allocated to the public sector out of GDP *growth* – that is, the year-to-year increment in public spending as a ratio of the corresponding increment in full-employment GDP (both at constant prices). The domestic output content is derived, also as a ratio of GDP, by deducting the net import content of expenditure.[2] Again we are talking in terms of

[1] Full-employment GDP is defined on the basis of 325,000 unemployed with an underlying growth rate of 3·2 per cent per annum. Expressing public expenditure in terms of constant employment abstracts from it items which involve no opportunity cost (since unemployment-related expenditure does not, by definition, pre-empt resources from alternative employment), while also netting out spending which is 'non-discretionary' through being related to the level of economic activity. The concept of the full-employment budget and its measurement are discussed further in chapter 4. Expenditure is not as sensitive to the level of unemployment as revenue, though unemployment benefits are significant. The adjustment for debt interest is small, being an estimate of the extra interest paid on the difference (in a particular year) between the full-employment deficit and the actual one (see *National Institute Economic Review*, no. 77, August 1976, pp. 21–4).

[2] This includes direct expenditure abroad, indirect imports in the form of inputs into domestic purchases and an allowance for the import content of purchases made by the recipients of current grants. So defined, the import content of public expenditure has crept

public demands on output, but overseas expenditure is excluded, because this does not (in the short run) contribute to domestic activity – that is, we have an estimate of the content of public spending which exercises demand 'leverage' on the domestic economy.[1] Changes in leverage occur both directly (by changes in public sector demand) and indirectly (through the multiplier) when the output content of expenditure changes. The *direct* changes involved in this process are shown in the lower part of chart 3.2 in the form of elasticities, which express the percentage change in the domestic output content of public expenditure as a ratio of the percentage change in productive potential. For comparison, changes in the resource measure of expenditure – gross of import content – are also shown in similar proportionate terms, and the two series can be seen to track each other quite closely.

The chart shows very clearly the profile of expansion up to 1967 (with the elasticity measure almost always in excess of unity), the turn-round after devaluation and the subsequent resurgence. Between 1959 and 1973/4, the total resource cost of public expenditure rose from some 35 to 41¼ per cent of potential GDP – a rate of increase about 1 per cent per annum above the underlying economic growth rate of 3·2 per cent. Indirect claims were the fastest growing element, their share of potential GDP expanding from 10·3 to 14·1 per cent, but direct claims also raised their share from 24·7 to 27·2 per cent. At the peaks of public sector expansion, in 1961/2, 1963/4, 1967 and 1973/4, demands on resources emanating from the public sector increased by between 72 and 130 per cent of the real absolute change in full-employment GDP, or 2–3 times the percentage change. All of these expansions involved a discretionary contra-cyclical element, although in the middle years the expansion was also a function of a conscious longer-run shift in policy.

---

up from 15 to 20 per cent as shown in the chart. In the resource definition of expenditure (as used for planning purposes), the import content is counted as an element of demand, on the basis that in the long run the balance of payments must be zero; consequently, any increase in net public sector demands for imports must be met by a corresponding decrease in the private sector's net imports. In terms of the leverage exerted by public expenditure on domestic output, the import content is given a zero weight, there being no presumption that the net imports of the private sector adjust so as to keep the external balance the same.

[1] Leverage refers to the *net* effect of the budget in raising or lowering aggregate demand. Like expenditure, some elements of taxation have a larger effect on production than others, so these have to be weighted too, the balance of expenditure and revenue then being the 'weighted' budget balance (see chapter 4, pages 183–9). It would be possible to define leverage as the difference between *actual* weighted expenditure and *actual* weighted receipts, but the measure implied here is one which nets out the non-discretionary element associated with the cycle (see R. A. Musgrave, 'On measuring fiscal performance', *Review of Economics and Statistics*, vol. 46, May 1964, and R. A. and P. B. Musgrave, 'Fiscal policy' in R. E. Caves and Associates, *Britain's Economic Prospects*, London, Allen & Unwin, 1968, pp. 40–2). The choice of an 'elasticity' measure to depict direct changes in leverage in the following analysis is presentational, since it perhaps best expresses the degree of expansion and contraction in public spending relative to the underlying expansion of the economy.

Public sector output and the volume of expenditure

The demands of public expenditure on resources include the cost of maintaining the relative incomes of public employees in the face of lower (recorded) productivity growth for the public authorities, which leads to the deflators for public expenditure increasing faster than those for GDP as a whole – the relative price effect. Part of the expansion in public demand relative to GDP has thus been due to (adverse) price trends, not to increases in public output, as may be seen from table 3.4, which shows the annual average growth rates of expenditure for a number of categories over the period 1959–73. Increases in the total volume of expenditure (first column),[1] which represent the growth in the supply of public services, were achieved at an average annual rate of 3·55 per cent per annum (an elasticity of 1·17 with respect to the underlying GDP growth rate), while the total cost of programmes increased at an average rate of 4·3 per cent.[2] The difference of 0·75 per cent can be ascribed to the relative price effect, which is shown in the second column. The *net* resource cost of expenditure, as we have seen above, grows at a slightly different rate from the gross cost, and this is also shown as being 4·15 per cent over this period.

The chief source of adverse relative price effects can be traced to public authority wages and salaries (table 3.3). Current expenditure on goods and services, to which most of this applies, increased by an average of 2·45 per cent in volume from 1959 to 1973, compared with 3·85 per cent in terms of cost (table 3.4); military defence was the main programme held back, whereas the provision of education and other services increased relative to GDP (note *e*). But the slower growth of the health services shows that the relative price effect is an important constraint on expansion. Overall, public authority current expenditure on goods and services has pre-empted an increasing proportion of resources, while forming a diminishing part of output; *ex-post*, it

[1] The derivation of expenditure *volumes* depends on the existence of price indices relating to the various services provided. As far as the national accounts are concerned, deflators are available for current expenditure on goods and services in four sectors – defence, health, education and 'other'. Capital expenditure deflators may be derived for the various assets on which money is spent (new buildings and works, plant and machinery, etc.). Transfers are evaluated notionally, according to the purchasing power of income in the hands of the general public (that is, by reference to the consumer price index, or to the GDP factor cost deflator in the case of items like debt interest). From these deflators it is then possible to derive deflators applicable to the various programmes and spending authorities by referring to the economic analysis of public sector programmes (CSO, *National Income and Expenditure 1964–74*, London, HMSO, 1975, table 58) and to the asset composition of capital spending programmes. For a discussion of the difficulties involved in creating estimates of public sector output, see Godley, 'The measurement and control of public expenditure'.

[2] The price index relevant to the *real* cost of public expenditure is the GDP factor cost deflator.

Table 3.4. *Public expenditure by category in volume and cost terms: changes, 1959–73*

	Volume[a]	Relative price effect	Total cost[b]	Net resource cost[bc]	Volume growth/ GDP growth[d]
	(annual average percentage changes)				(ratios)
Current expenditure					
On goods and services					
Central government	1·10	1·40	2·50	2·65	*0·34*
Local authorities	4·70	1·40	6·10	5·90	*1·46*
Public authorities[e]	2·45	1·40	3·85	3·80	*0·77*
Transfers					
Current grants to persons	5·80[f]	−0·25	5·55	5·70	*1·80*
Subsidies	5·15	—	5·15	4·80	*1·72*
Total transfers[g]	4·75	−0·15	4·60	4·90	*1·48*
TOTAL CURRENT EXPENDITURE	3·40	0·80	4·20	4·20	*1·07*
Capital expenditure[h]					
Central government[i]	6·00	1·05	7·05	6·55	*1·88*
Local authorities[j]	5·90	0·90	6·80	6·55	*1·84*
Public corporations[k]	1·20	−0·15	1·05	1·30	*0·38*
Public sector GDFCF	3·95	0·45	4·40	4·25	*1·23*
TOTAL INVESTMENT	4·30	0·40	4·70	4·55	*1·34*
TOTAL PUBLIC EXPENDITURE[hl]	3·55	0.75	4·30	4.15	*1·17*

SOURCES: CSO, *National Income and Expenditure 1964–74* and *National Income and Expenditure 1970* London, HMSO, 1970.

[a] Expenditure deflated by own-price indices (base 1970), but see notes *f* and *g*.

[b] Expenditure deflated by the GDP factor cost deflator.

[c] As total cost, but 'weighted' to allow for the true demand effect.

[d] GDP growth taken as 3·2 per cent.

[e] Public authorities' current expenditure on goods and services can be disaggregated as follows:

	Volume	Relative price effect	Total cost	Net resource cost	Volume growth/ GDP growth
	(annual average percentages changes)				(ratios)
Military defence	−0·80	1·55	0·75	0·75	*−0·25*
Health	2·80	1·50	4·30	4·30	*0·88*
Education	4·80	1·40	6·20	6·20	*1·50*
Other	4·10	1·15	5·25	5·20	*1·28*

[f] Expenditure deflated by the consumer price index.

[g] Including debt interest and grants abroad which (with subsidies) are deflated by the GDP factor cost deflator.

[h] Excluding net lending and investment grants.

[i] Including grants to universities.

[j] Including housing improvement grants.

[k] Excluding British Steel Corporation.

Table 3.4 cont.

[l] Total public expenditure can be disaggregated as follows:

	Volume	Relative price effect	Total cost	Volume growth/ GDP growth
	(annual average percentage changes)			(ratios)
Military defence	−0·95	1·70	0·75	−0·30
Health	3·25	1·65	4·90	1·56
Education	5·50	1·15	6·65	1·72
Roads	4·70	1·80	6·50	1·47
Housing*	6·25	0·75	7·00	1·95
Environmental	6·40	1·20	7·60	2·00

* For 1959/60–1973/4, see 'Treasury analysis of public expenditure' in CSO, *National Income and Expenditure 1964–74*, p. 132.

seems that about half of the relative price effect has been met by allowing the cost of such spending to grow at 0.7 per cent per annum above underlying GDP, while the volume growth has been kept below GDP to an equal extent.

Current transfers have been relatively expansionary, the more so in volume terms because of a favourable relative price effect. The increase in current grants and subsidies can be traced to reasons of social and economic policy. Social security benefits have been a method of redistributing income and of reflation, while subsidies combine both these uses with the further one of combating inflation. Neither grants nor subsidies grew very smoothly, both being subject to recurrent bouts of expansion and inflationary erosion.

Despite the popularity of capital expenditure as a short-term defla- tionary instrument, it has been relatively fast-growing in volume terms (an average annual increase of 3·95 per cent). Fixed investment by central government and by local authorities provided the chief momen- tum, both expanding at a rate of about 6 per cent per annum. Invest- ment in nationalised industries, on the other hand, was a declining pro- portion of GDP for the period as a whole (despite a favourable relative price effect of −0·15 per cent); up to devaluation its expansion was very rapid, being based on the unrealised economic growth target of 4 per cent, but this was followed, from 1968 onwards, by a substantial decline. Public authority investment is relatively concentrated on land and construction, where prices rose very fast in the period 1971–3, so that the relative price effect was positive. In general, this effect is less important in capital spending than on the current side, though it is subject to more cyclical fluctuation, making it less predictable. How- ever, there also tend to be 'unforeseen' relative price effects on current spending when public sector incomes are successively held back and given free rein – as happened in the period 1971–4.[1]

The programme which expanded most consistently was education, both this and the National Health Service being subject to medium-term plans, but it has been in housing and the environment that the greatest increases have taken place, both sectors being subject to cyclical fluctuation (note *l*). The housing programme particularly was successively restricted (up to 1962/3 and between 1969 and 1971) and allowed to expand (from 1963 to 1967 and from 1972 through to 1976). Investment in water and sewerage has been the most consistent impetus to the environmental programme, while sub-sectors with lower priority have been restrained or exhorted to expand according to the short-term economic climate; for such elements, average rates of growth would be quite different if a different period was taken.

Growth of public expenditure: its determinants

Ideas vary about the causes of the relative expansion observed in the public sector, with a tendency to seek explanations that are universally valid in the long run for what is considered a general process, rather than to view it against the background of the time. The particular circumstances of the period seem to provide at least an adequate explanation of experience in the United Kingdom, especially the mis-specification of planning constraints, the inadequate appreciation of relative price effects and the displacement effects of counter-cyclical policy.[2] But perhaps these are also expressions of a more general tendency for the sector to expand and there are other more fundamental factors at work as well. Other commentators have stressed in turn:

(a) structural factors linked to the process of growth, industrialisation and demographic trends;

(b) institutional and financial control factors;

(c) behavioural imperfections by consumers of public goods;

(d) 'social disturbance' and factors which force the government to assume temporarily greater responsibilities, but which have displacement effects leaving some of the increase as permanent.

This last hypothesis has been put forward by Peacock and Wiseman as a possible explanation of longer-run historical developments.

In the much shorter historical perspective of the postwar years the applicability of the last theory would seem to be limited, though there are undoubtedly displacement effects resulting from economic contingencies, particularly reflationary reactions to unemployment. Displacement effects linked to changes in administration (the electoral

[1] See *National Institute Economic Review*, no. 75, February 1976, pp. 87–9.

[2] Peacock and Wiseman, *The Growth of Public Expenditure in the United Kingdom*, pp. 24 *et seq.*

cycle) also offer a possible explanation, though it is doubtful whether this goes deep enough. Of the structural biases tending to increase public expenditure, the most obvious is the tendency towards a lower real level of public service for a given outlay. This may be partly due to the adverse relative price effect on public output, but may also derive from demographic trends;[1] if these produce (as in the United Kingdom) an increasing proportion of the population above retiring age, an increase in the public sector proportional to GDP would mean a lower growth of services per recipient, so that maintaining a given quality entails a relative expansion in health and social services. On the other hand, a fall in the school population (as experienced in the 1970s) has the opposite effect. Similar arguments stress the effects of economic growth – industrialisation and urbanisation – on the expansion of government activity; others have suggested that the growth of income has a similar effect on public services to that on all services, which tend to have a relatively high income elasticity of demand.[2] But while it is easy to see how all these factors may influence individual programmes, their effect on aggregate public spending is impossible to quantify.

So far as institutional and financial factors are concerned, the analysis above has emphasised the deficiencies of strategic control, which seems to be effective so long as it is negative and restrictive, but less so when it is a matter of positive planning for systematic expansion.[3] The role of the local authorities as *causal* factors in the growth process has been discounted, though the system of local authority finance cannot be said to make for an efficient allocation of resources. The authorities' expenditure functions bear no relation to their income, which comes substantially from the central government, so that the system facilitates over-expansion even when the cause is central legislation. This suggests the wider question of whether (as is frequently argued) the separation between the expenditure and revenue-raising functions of government generally leads to over-expansion of the public sector due to the lack of any short-term budget constraint. As we have seen above, public spending shifts are associated with budget deficits, but this is connected with the stabilisation role of the budget and governments cannot escape from a longer-term budget constraint. The fact that they can do so in the short-term, however, may mean that the inevitable correction in the longer term will be made partly by higher tax rates, leaving a net expansion. If this argument is correct it leads us to discard an alternative

[1] For a list of demographic factors affecting the size of the public sector see OECD, *Public Expenditure Trends in OECD Countries*, p. 54.

[2] Peacock and Wiseman, *The Growth of Public Expenditure in the United Kingdom*, p. 22; C. T. Sandford, *Economics of Public Finance*, Oxford, Pergamon, 1969, pp. 228–31.

[3] Cf. C. T. Sandford and P. N. Dean, 'Public expenditure: the paradox of control', *The Banker*, vol. 120, April 1970, pp. 377 *et seq*.

theory about the expansion of public spending – that it is linked to a process of 'natural budget reaction', by which expenditure responds to the buoyancy of tax receipts.[1] This does not seem to fit the case of the United Kingdom, though fiscal drag is useful *ex post* in financing the net growth of expenditure once deficit-financing has become cyclically inopportune.

The detachment of costs from the benefits of public expenditure may affect individuals as well as governments. If public services benefit particular sub-groups, while tax costs are more widely shared, then over-supply can result because part of the cost can be shifted to non-beneficiaries.[2] Alternatively, there is a more politically influential hypothesis of under-expansion put forward by Professor Galbraith.[3] Whether or not one accepts his idea that individual choices may be distorted from a true preference system by advertising, the possibility that legislators have been influenced to correct for this is very real.[4] Behavioural arguments about a built-in bias in either direction cannot readily be verified, but it is interesting that either may lead to the growth of the public sector – the first automatically, the second by discretionary correction. Like the structural arguments, their net impact is impossible to translate into figures, so that how far the more observable and quantifiable effects of shortcomings in planning and control are proxies for more deep-rooted expansionary impulses remains undetermined.

IMPLEMENTING POLICY: INTENTIONS AND OUT-TURNS

Earlier we set out changes in total public expenditure after adjustment for the automatically stabilising elements within it. As so defined these figures include shortfalls and overruns in comparison with plan; further, changes in the level of spending may be due as much to autonomous factors (such as demographic trends) as to discretionary policy decisions about the 'quality' of service provided. All these elements are important in determining the reliability and flexibility of public expenditure as an instrument of demand management; by the same token, they complicate the task of diagnosing policy success by obscuring both the true nature of 'policy' changes themselves and the extent to which they are implemented. (It was understandable, for example, that the House of

---

[1] OECD, *Fiscal Policy in Seven Countries, 1955–1965* by B. Hansen, Paris, 1969; however the United Kingdom is not cited as one of the countries subject to this phenomenon. The case that public spending is induced by inflationary tax buoyancy has been used in the argument for indexation (see D. R. Morgan, *Over-taxation by Inflation*, London, Institute for Economic Affairs, 1977, p. 16).

[2] See Musgrave and Musgrave, *Public Finance*, pp. 98–100, for a fuller discussion.

[3] J. K. Galbraith, *The Affluent Society*, London, Hamish Hamilton, 1958.

[4] See M. J. Artis, 'Fiscal policy for stabilization' in Beckerman (ed.), *The Labour Government's Economic Record 1964–1970*, p. 265, and Sandford and Dean, 'Public expenditure', p. 376.

Table 3.5. *Demand management and short-term interventions in public expenditure, 1960–73*

Date of announcement	Effect in financial year	Current expenditure, announced effect Current prices	1970 prices	Public investment Announced effect Current prices	1970 prices	Discretionary factor[a]	Realisation factor[b]
		($£$ million)				(%)	(%)
23 June 1960	1961/2	—	—	..	—75	—	10
25 July 1961	1962/3	—175	—265	..	—25	—	—
9 Oct. 1962	1962/3	—	—	+15	+21 }	35	100
	1963/4	—	—	+83	+115 }		
27 July 1965	1965/6	—7	—9	{—65^c / —50^d	—80^c / —70^d}	50	100
	1966/7	—6	—8	—70^d	—100^d }	100	85
20 July 1966	1967/8	—100	—130	—150	—175	70	60
18 Nov. 1967 } 16 Jan. 1968	1968/9	—129	—138	—163^e	—184^e	67	94
	1969/70	—275	—294	—213	—239	74	100
July 1971 to May 1972	1971/2	+3	+2	+33	+30 }	100	100
	1972/3	+147	+124	+270	+241 }		70
	1973/4	+62	+53	+197	+180 }		—
21 May 1973	1973/4	—14	—11	—92	—68	10	100
	1974/5	—198	—152	—341	—254	—	100
8 Oct. 1973	1973/4	—19	—15	—97	—72	10	100
17 Dec. 1973	1974/5	—329	—250	—851	—655	60	55

SOURCES: House of Commons, *Hansard* and Expenditure Committee Reports; Annual Reports of Department of Education, Ministry of Housing and Local Government, British Transport Commission, Electricity Council, Gas Council and National Coal Board; Department of Economic Affairs, *The National Plan* (Cmnd 2764); Treasury, *Public Investment in Great Britain* (Cmnd 1203), *Public Investment in Great Britain, October 1961* (Cmnd 1522, London HMSO, 1961), *Public Investment in Great Britain, October 1962* (Cmnd 1849), *Public Investment in Great Britain, October 1963* (Cmnd 2177), *Public Expenditure: planning and control* (Cmnd 2915), *Public Expenditure in 1968–69 and 1969–70* (Cmnd 3515), *Public Expenditure 1968–69 to 1973–74* (Cmnd 4234), *Public Expenditure 1969–70 to 1974–75* (Cmnd 4578), *Public Expenditure 1969–70 to 1975–76*, (Cmnd 4829), *Public Expenditure to 1976–77* (Cmnd 5178), *Public Expenditure to 1977–78* (Cmnd 5519) and *Public Expenditure to 1978–79*, Cmnd 5879, London, HMSO, 1975).

[a] The proportion of the announced effect which cannot be attributed to estimating changes – identified from discrepancies between programme forecasts and out-turns and from Annual Reports of departments and nationalised industries.

[b] The proportion of the announced effect actually achieved – aggregated from an analysis of individual programmes. Offsetting changes in exempted programmes (e.g. housing in 1967/8 and 1974/5) not included.

[c] For public corporations.

[d] For public authorities.

[e] Excluding a cut of £80 million in investment grants.

Commons Expenditure Committee should mistrust the 1973 cuts,[1] which were announced at a time when public expenditure was falling short of planned totals.) In what follows an attempt has been made to estimate the authenticity and effectiveness of announced variations in public expenditure after taking account of such elements. The results, summarised in table 3.5, are inevitably subjective to some extent.

Ministerial speeches and White Papers provide a series of announcements of cuts or increases, for each of which, as it affected capital expenditure, two factors have been calculated. The 'discretionary factor' estimates the proportion of the announced intervention which can properly be termed 'discretionary'; it discounts the announced figure for changes due simply to revised estimates for a given programme, or to changes in a programme which would have occurred anyway (for example, a change in school building due to revised demographic forecasts). The 'realisation factor' estimates the proportion of an announced intervention (whether properly discretionary or not) which was carried through. The basis for evaluating each of these components for the various interventions is discussed below in a historical context.

However, it would be a mistake to view the contribution of public expenditure to short-term demand management solely in the light of *announced* interventions. Short-term changes are frequently accompanied by shifts in longer-term programmes, which are relevant to the stabilisation function of the budget because they involve changes in the budget balance. Taking account of these, public expenditure makes a contribution to demand management which is sometimes larger than the announced change, or sometimes in the opposite direction. Table 3.6 therefore shows the announced public expenditure changes in the context of realised changes in both the budget deficit and overall public spending, all expressed as proportions of full-employment GDP.[2]

The effectiveness of policy – both long-term and short-term – depends substantially on the reliability of long-term plans and how far they are implemented. Charts 3.3 and 3.4 therefore show both planned expenditure and short-term deviations from plan against the realised growth paths of the major categories of expenditure, in order to appraise the effectiveness of expenditure management.[3] The hatched areas indicate

[1] House of Commons, *Eleventh Report from the Expenditure Committee, Session 1972–73. The May 21st Expenditure Cuts*, London, HMSO, 1973, pp. viii and 14.

[2] A further discussion of this weighted budget impact is to be found in chapter 4; the expenditure figures correspond to those given in chart 4.7.

[3] Public Expenditure White Papers have been published annually since 1969, so that there is a series of plans from that date. Previously, there was a plan from the NEDC, *Growth of the United Kingdom Economy to 1966*, London, HMSO, 1963, and from the Department of Economic Affairs, *The National Plan*; early in the 1960s there were also regular Public Investment White Papers looking two to three years ahead. Budget forecasts have contained one-year forecasts of the major economic spending categories since 1966/7. The plans are

Table 3.6. *Short-term interventions in public expenditure and changes in the budget deficit,[a] 1959/60–1974/5*

Percentages of full-employment GDP

	Public expenditure[b]		Change in budget deficit
	Change in total	Announced intervention(s)	
1960/1	+0·03	—	+0·28
1961/2	−0·75	+0·18	+0·55
1962/3	+0·49	+0·53	+0·64
1963/4	−1·17	−0·24	−1·76
1964/5	−0·76	—	−0·13
1965/6	−0·18	+0·30	+1·47
1966/7	−0·72	+0·34	−0·14
1967/8	−0·89	+0·32	−0·35
1968/9	+1·13	+0·53	+2·75
1969/70	+1·10	+0·84	+2·69
1970/1	−0·38	—	−0·95
1971/2	+0·26	−0·05	−1·09
1972/3	−0·50	−0·55	−1·86
1973/4	−0·85	−0·20	−0·88
1974/5	−2·05	+1·85	−1·93

SOURCES: as table 3·5; NIESR estimates.

[a] Public expenditure and the budget deficit both output-weighted.

[b] The contribution of changes in public expenditure to budgetary leverage, as shown here, is of the opposite sign to the actual spending changes.

announced short-term deviations from plan, while the difference between the plans and the out-turn are shortfalls or overruns. In the light of these it is also possible to make an impressionistic judgement of the true nature of the adjustments as a background to table 3.5.

The first Conservative administration, 1959/60–October 1964

The first two interventions of the period covered by this study seem to have had little effect. The first, in June 1960, was an announcement that public investment programmes for 1961/2 would be kept to the same real level as in 1960/1. Allowing for a possible 3 per cent growth rate, this probably represented a potential saving of £75 million (at 1970 prices),[1] but no short-term adjustment was needed – the savings were to come from an autonomous decline in nationalised industries' programmes, with public authority investment still scheduled to increase

all expressed in terms of constant survey prices, while the out-turns are in terms of 1970 prices. The charts therefore refer to the volume of expenditure and do not contain the relative price effect.

[1] All the intervention figures given below are in volume terms at 1970 prices, though table 3.5 also gives them in current prices.

Chart 3.3. *Public authorities' current expenditure, planned and out-turn,*
1959–1974/5

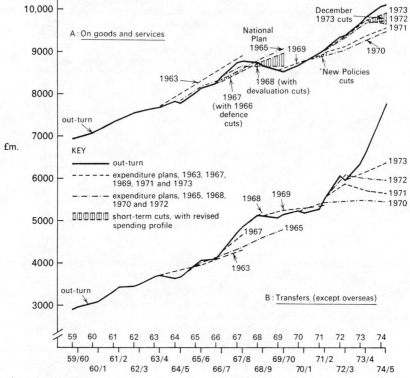

SOURCES: CSO, *National Income and Expenditure 1964–74* and *Economic Trends, Annual Supplement 1975*, London, HMSO, 1975; Department of Economic Affairs, *The National Plan*; Treasury White Papers as table 3.5.

Notes: (i) Expenditure is in volume terms at 1970 prices.
(ii) Expenditure planned in 1971 shown after short-term increases.
(iii) Expenditure on goods and services planned in 1972 shown after cuts in May and October 1973.

substantially. In addition, the pressure of demand in 1960, to which the intervention was a response, began causing shortfalls, so that the real discretionary element in the intervention must have been very small. The extent of the shortfall could not have been accurately known at the time, but, in conjunction with the ceiling, it implied an eventual increase of 5 per cent in public investment for 1961/2. In fact, investment increased by about 8 per cent – some £75 million over the imposed limit – so that even the nominal saving was negligible.

In the summer of 1961 further intervention was needed to salvage the

Chart 3.4. *Public sector capital expenditure, planned and out-turn, 1959–1974/5*

A: *Central government*

KEY
— out-turn
- - - - expenditure plans, 1960, 1962, 1965, 1968, 1970 and 1972
-·-·- expenditure plans, 1961, 1963, 1966 (or 1967), 1969, 1971 and 1973
short-term cuts
short-term increases

B: *Local authorities*

KEY: See chart 3.4 A

Chart 3.4 *cont.*

C: *Nationalised industries*

SOURCES: CSO, *Economic Trends, Annual Supplement 1975, Financial Statistics*, October 1975, and *Annual Abstract of Statistics, 1974*, London, HMSO, 1974; Department of Economic Affairs, *The National Plan*; Treasury White Papers as table 3.5.

Notes: (i) Capital expenditure is gross domestic fixed capital formation in volume terms at 1970 prices.

(ii) Expenditure planned in 1971 shown after short-term increases.

(iii) Planned expenditures by the central government and local authorities do not include the provision for shortfalls made since December 1969 because no separate figures available.

(iv) Local authority investment includes capital grants to the private sector, also health and water investment throughout (although the functions were removed in 1973/4).

(v) December 1973 cuts by local authorities take no account of increases in housing investment.

(vi) Planned investment by nationalised industries excludes steel up to 1966/7 and includes investment by the British Steel Corporation thereafter.

'critical external situation', but the effect realised was, like that of the previous adjustment, indistinguishable from zero. It was announced that total capital expenditure by local authorities in 1962/3 'should not significantly exceed the (real) level of the current year'. The nationalised industries were excluded because they were now seen as obliged to make a commercial return on capital, so that it was proposed to allow them the investment needed to reach their financial targets.[1] At the same time, however, current expenditure was to be controlled in the medium term in the way that Plowden had suggested by being restricted to a $2\frac{1}{2}$ per cent real increase, which, in fact, reduced it by £265 million. This

[1] House of Commons, *Hansard*, 26 July 1961, col. 435.

saving was part of a general move to bring expenditure into a 'proper relationship with resources likely to be available in the long term'.[1]

Whether the adjustments to investment were intended to be cosmetic or not, they were certainly ineffective; before the year was out strategy was reversed towards reflation, but even before that local authority programmes were expanding faster than was compatible with the restriction. However, the intention to restrict current expenditure was undoubtedly real; although Selwyn Lloyd was to express concern as to whether the objective was being met in the House of Commons on 27 February,[2] the historical record confirms that its volume growth was constrained to $2\frac{1}{2}$ per cent.

The intervention of 1961 was made otiose by the falling off in economic activity which became apparent after the 1962 budget. During the summer and autumn of that year additional investment was authorised for local authorities and nationalised industries, to be phased over the remainder of 1962/3 and 1963/4, with most of the impact in the latter year, when the increases were to be 6 per cent for local authorities and 2 per cent for the nationalised industries. The additions scheduled for 1962/3 were forestalled by the severe winter, but would otherwise have been achieved. As can be seen from charts 3.4B and C, the conjunction of reflationary and growth objectives provided an impetus to the programmes of both local authorities and nationalised industries which carried public expenditure forward (with the help of the National Plan) to 1967. The intervention in nationalised industries looks small in comparison with the subsequent secular additions, while part of the short-term increase in public authority programmes was really a secular adjustment; in housing, for example, there was a prior commitment to an increase to solve the housing and slum-clearance problem of the big cities.[3] A significant characteristic of this reflation was the large secular upswing in expenditure which went with it and dwarfed the actual counter-cyclical (phased) element. The projected public investment increase for 1963/4 was raised from 8 to 22 per cent between October 1962 and October 1963,[4] which must be attributed to the conjunction of short-term needs with the revised medium-term goals implied by the higher growth objectives.

Of these three interventions, therefore, the first two were subject to shortfalls and the third to a large additional upswing, which made the

[1] Ibid. 25 July 1961, col. 224.
[2] The estimates for 1962/3 exceeded the target set by £111 million (current) or about 60 per cent of the real intended saving.
[3] Ministry of Housing and Local Government, *Housing in England and Wales*, Cmnd 1290, London, HMSO, 1961.
[4] Treasury, *Public Investment in Great Britain. October 1962*, Cmnd 1849, and *Public Investment in Great Britain. October 1963*, Cmnd 2177, London, HMSO, 1962 and 1963.

realised profile of public investment different from what was intended. Chart 3.5 shows the actual and intended annual growth rates of public investment as ratios of the long-run growth rate of GDP, to give an elasticity measure of the pressure being exerted on the economy by this sector.[1] Defining neutrality as an elasticity of 1, the intention in 1960/1 can be seen to have been neutral, although the actual out-turn was deflationary because supply constraints led to programme shortfalls. The out-turn in 1961/2 was expansionary (an elasticity of nearly 3), although supposed to be moderately restrictive. In 1962/3 the bad winter aborted contradictory attempts at stabilisation; on the other hand, the reflationary strategy of 1963/4 was compounded by secular programme increases, which gave an elasticity of nearly 6 when the real counter-cyclical impact was supposed to have been a third of this.

The medium-term forecasts of public expenditure as a whole which were published in December 1963 envisaged a 4·1 per cent average growth rate after 1963/4 up to 1967/8, with a 5½ per cent average growth rate for public investment;[2] together with the large increase which had already occurred in 1963/4, this represented an expansion of 8·6 per cent per annum over the period from 1962/3. Thus, by 1963 public investment had well and truly taken off.

Labour administrations, October 1964–June 1970

On assuming office in October 1964, the Labour government found in its predecessor's plans 'a lack of balance and absence of proper social and economic priorities'.[3] But the purpose of most expenditure was 'sound enough', so that outside the spheres of defence and social security little was to be altered. In public investment, the strong momentum in nationalised industries' and housing programmes was to be maintained under the National Plan. Both were considered crucial to faster growth,[4] and both were to play a critical part in the expansion of the public sector up to devaluation and subsequently.

The reappraisal of defence expenditure aimed at a saving of £550 million up to 1969/70, with a reduction of £50 million in 1965/6 from cancellation of the TSR-2.[5] Expenditure on defence was to be kept at the same real level as 1964/5 and up to 1967/8 this was almost achieved – the real annual average growth being 0·7 per cent (although this was

---

[1] See below page 117 and cf. the lower part of chart 3.2.

[2] Treasury, *Public Expenditure in 1963–64 and 1967–68.*

[3] Prime Minister's Office, *The Economic Situation*, p. 2.

[4] The evidence suggested 'that the most successful housebuilding countries lead the United Kingdom at least partly because they have chosen to devote a greater proportion of their national resources to housing' (Ministry of Housing and Local Government, *The Housing Programme 1965–1970*, Cmnd 2838, London, HMSO, 1965, p. 3).

[5] House of Commons, *Hansard*, 6 April 1965, col. 280. At 1965 prices the figures were £400 million and £35 million respectively.

only what it had been over the preceding three years). Nevertheless, partly because of this, the National Plan was able to show a reduction in the annual average growth rate of current expenditure on goods and services to 3 per cent (from 3¾ per cent in the Conservative plan). However, despite this downward shift (chart 3.3), the out-turn up to 1967/8 was 4 per cent not 3 per cent. Moreover, the shift in the schedule probably had as much to do with the shortfall in expenditure in 1964/5 (for which defence expenditure was largely responsible) as with discretionary action.

Compensating for this reduction, the new administration calculated on increasing current transfers to the personal sector (particularly social security benefits) at a rate of 6 per cent per annum between 1964/5 and 1968/9 (chart 3.3B). A feature of the period up to devaluation was the constant upward revision of this target; in the event this component of current expenditure grew at a real average rate of 9¾ per cent per annum up to 1967/8.

There was no substantial attempt at short-term intervention in the current sector until January 1968. Meanwhile, however, there were two deflationary packages aimed at public investment. The first, on 27 July 1965, followed large increases in taxation in the 1965 budget and, while there were no further revenue increases, included tighter hire purchase terms and a six-month moratorium on project starts by public authorities – housing, schools and hospitals being excepted, so that road and local authority environmental expenditure bore the brunt of the adjustment. The cuts were to save £70 million in 1965/6 and £100 million in the following year.[1] This seems to have fallen short of the Treasury's original target,[2] but appears to have been almost fully implemented (see table 3.5). By 8 February 1966 the Chancellor was able to announce that the cuts 'had achieved their purpose'; in particular, the rate of expenditure on capital projects had been appreciably reduced. Though the moratorium did not apply to the nationalised industries, these were urged 'to follow a similar course of action', in deferring the purchase of goods to the 'maximum possible extent' without compromising projects essential for economic growth and the National Plan.[3] Expenditure of £80 million was ostensibly deferred in 1965/6, but a substantial element of this might have come from shortfalls in the electricity programme.

Observers at the time and subsequently have tried to identify this intervention as the moment when the government abandoned its

[1] Small savings of £9 and £8 million were announced in current expenditure.
[2] '... by the time we had made exemptions for the things which were either contracted for, or had been committed... its effect was not nearly as big as it was designed to achieve' (House of Commons, *Seventh Report from the Expenditure Committee, Session 1971–72*, p. 9).
[3] Treasury, *Public Expenditure: planning and control*, p. 14.

growth objective.[1] In terms of its public expenditure plans, however, this is not true. First, the deferments did not affect the major programmes at the heart of the National Plan and excess housing investment was to compensate for 40 per cent of the cuts. Secondly, there was the shortfall in central government investment and the nationalised industries' programmes, where the responsiveness of the electricity programme to market factors and to the secular increase in investment in natural gas was to provide a reservoir of readymade 'cuts'. Thirdly, deferment was really what it said – a rephasing – which meant that road and education schemes would be reallocated over the remaining period of the Plan. This was done at the beginning of 1966 and restraint continued only in local authority environmental programmes.

Public investment in 1966/7 still came to a 'formidable total', and the objective of demand management in 1966 remained the moderation of consumption to finance the expansion of the public sector. Though the Chancellor believed that 'government expenditure would not make excessive new claims on the economy', some observers did not agree.[2] The intervention of July 1966, however, was as much a response to the sterling crisis of June – a result of the seamen's strike and the world liquidity shortage – as to inflated demand *per se*. The cuts were in 1967/8 programmes. Reductions of £130 million in defence and overseas spending were to help the balance of payments directly. Public authority investment was to be cut by £65 million, with the same exceptions and priorities as in 1965. Though there is little doubt that environmental investment was restrained, the cuts in the road programme were intended to 'reduce the extent to which we shall be making up ground lost as a result of the 1965 deferment measures'.[3] Part of these cuts might therefore be considered notional, since the same items were being deferred as in the previous year. More important, housing and social services, the main engines of expansion, were not affected, and the intervention looked small in comparison with the eventual excess of £125 million on the housing programme. The nationalised industries were to contribute £110 million, but though these cuts were supposed to exclude slippage, the electricity industry could clearly meet the government's demands, and more, out of autonomous revisions to its programmes;[4] as with public authorities, adjustment to parts was only as effective as the control over the whole body of investment, which in

---

[1] See Brittan, *Steering the Economy* (rev. edn), p. 309.

[2] Public investment was to increase by 7½ per cent and public corporation investment by 14 per cent (House of Commons, *Hansard*, 1 March 1966, cols. 1115–16, and Bank of England, *Report for the year ended 28 February 1967*, p. 6).

[3] Harold Wilson in the House of Commons, 3 August 1966.

[4] Ministry of Technology, *Electricity Council. Annual Report and Accounts 1967–68*, London, HMSO, 1968, p. 11.

1966 and 1967/8 was influenced especially by the development of natural gas.

Nationalised industries' investment, though reduced, remained at a level above that projected in the National Plan. Public authority total investment was to be only $2\frac{1}{2}$ per cent below the National Plan level in 1967/8, so that, overall, the public sector was still expected to show substantial leverage. As it turned out, public authority investment exceeded the Plan's target by 1 per cent; this was due to the excess housing investment and despite a continuing rigid control over environmental investment, where restrictions on loans effectively curbed expansion. The total impact of the 1966 'cuts' was, therefore, not all that great, though certain component cuts were achieved.[1] Moreover, it was not long before a projected decline in private investment seemed to call for reflation,[2] so that the incentive to implement the cuts disappeared. It is thus difficult to attribute a positive overall impact to the intervention of 1966.

At the same time large increases were being planned in public sector transfers, while current expenditure on goods and services was to turn out almost 3 per cent higher than planned (chart 3.3). The reductions that were achieved have thus to be taken in the context of aggregate increases which were to prove particularly large in 1967. The impetus to public expenditure was still very much intact, despite the attempt at cuts. This problem was highlighted in the negotiations for the first biennial rate support grant in December 1966. The forecasts for local authority current expenditure in 1967/8 and 1968/9 showed increases over the previous year of about 9 and $6\frac{1}{4}$ per cent respectively (at constant prices). These were considered too high, and the grant was fixed to allow local current expenditure on goods and services to increase by $1\frac{1}{2}$ per cent in 1967/8 (compared with a forecast increase twice as big in the same category of central spending). The eventual excess in this area was wholly attributable to the local authorities, whose spending actually grew by $5\frac{3}{4}$ per cent, but it is noteworthy that the over-spending was financed wholly by the central government, not from local revenue.

Much of the heat generated in the Cabinet by the 1966 intervention was due to a dispute over the relative merits of devaluation and of public expenditure cuts. With hindsight, it is evident that the structural imbalance created by framing public expenditure programmes against over-optimistic growth rates, which reached its culmination in 1967/8 (see chart 3.2), could be corrected only by a drastic shift in the public

[1] It is only these component cuts which are evaluated in the column for realisation factors in table 3.5, the offsetting changes in exempt programmes being omitted from the calculation.

[2] House of Commons, *Hansard*, 20 March 1967, col. 1313.

expenditure schedule. This was accomplished at the beginning of 1968 in conjunction with devaluation. Immediate cuts of £84 million were made in the nationalised industries' programmes for 1968/9, and this was followed by reductions in other programmes of £238 million, 60 per cent being current expenditure on goods and services.[1] Total public expenditure was planned to increase by 4·8 per cent in 1968/9, compared with the rate of 6·9 per cent scheduled previously, while over the two years to 1969/70 the average rate of growth was to be 2·85 per cent compared with 4·25 per cent. In practice the fall was more severe – demands on real resources (chart 3.2) increased negligibly in 1968/9 and declined by 1 per cent over the two years.

The secular switch of resources away from public expenditure is seen most clearly in the case of current expenditure on goods and services (chart 3.3); in the event the scheduled cuts were exceeded, though current transfers were slower to make a contribution. Once it was acknowledged that the National Plan growth targets were unattainable, there was bound to be a reaction in public investment plans which had been based on those targets. Nationalised industries' investment fell by twice as much again as the announced cuts; housing investment too reacted to devaluation and the high level of activity in previous years, leading to a large shortfall in 1968/9 and four years of continuous decline.[2]

Because most of the overt interventions in the period 1964 to 1967 entailed expenditure cuts and tax increases, the whole tenor of demand management has been interpreted as deflationary. A closer study of the leverage exerted by public spending contradicts this quite emphatically.[3] Chart 3.5 shows that the intended rate of growth of public investment in the years 1965/6 to 1967/8, even taking account of short-term interventions, was still about 2 to $3\frac{1}{2}$ times that of productive potential. The 1965 intervention emerges clearly as a pause (emphasised *ex post* by an underestimate of the expansion in 1964/5), while, for the 1966 intervention to be interpreted as effective, it must be seen as reducing the intended growth of public investment from 5 times to $3\frac{1}{2}$ times that of productive potential. After devaluation, policy was supposed to be neutral in 1968/9 and deflationary the following year. A substantial proportion of the deflationary leverage which emerged in both years is thus attributable to the involuntary reaction of investment in nationalised industries and housing.

[1] Treasury, *Public Expenditure in 1968–69 and 1969–70*, Cmnd 3515, London, HMSO, 1968. These figures exclude a scheduled cut of £80 million (1967 prices) in investment grants in 1968/9.

[2] For a discussion of this and the education programme, where the cuts were not achieved in 1968/9, see NIESR evidence to the Layfield Committee.

[3] Cf. Artis, 'Fiscal policy for stabilization', p. 267.

The second Conservative administration, June 1970–February 1974

The new Conservative administration was at pains to emphasise the differences between its attitude to public spending and that of its predecessors. An immediate review had as its object 'to reduce substantially previous plans for public spending and to permit taxation to be reduced',[1] and resulted in a White Paper in October 1970.[2]

Chart 3.5. *The growth of public sector capital expenditure relative to the growth of full-employment GDP, planned and out-turn, 1960/1–1974/5*

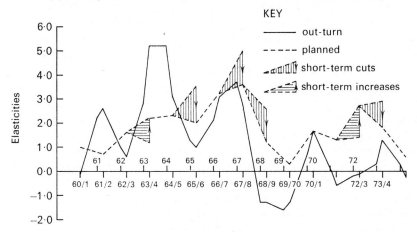

SOURCES: as chart 3.4.

Notes: (i) Capital expenditure is gross domestic fixed capital formation in volume terms (at 1970 prices) excluding steel investment and housing grants.
  (ii) Full-employment GDP taken as growing at 3·2 per cent per annum.
  (iii) 'Planned' growth observations based on estimates made immediately (0–6 months) before the financial year. 1974/5 level taken before December 1973 cuts.

The objective, as announced by the Chancellor in the House of Commons on 27 October, was the long-term restructuring of public expenditure, with an imputed saving of £394 million in 1971/2 supposed to be 'broadly neutral' in its effect upon the economy when taken with the £315 million reduction in income tax liability.[3] Though by the end of 1969/70 the 'great shift of resources' away from public spending had been completed, and the previous Chancellor had announced on 21 January 1970 the beginning of a period 'when public expenditure can grow as fast as national resources – but not, in the near future, faster',

[1] Treasury, *Public Expenditure 1969–70 to 1974–75*, p. 5.
[2] Treasury, *New Policies for Public Spending*.
[3] After setting off estimation revisions, the net announced impact was £330 million (Treasury, *Public Expenditure 1969–70 to 1974–75*, pp. 4–5).

this was regarded with suspicion. The estimates having been revised upwards, it was stated by Maurice Macmillan in the House of Commons on 22 February 1971 that the calculations of the previous government had been undermined by the 'falling off of industrial investment and the wages explosion'; also, Conservative philosophy on the control of expenditure was different – proportionality with the growth of GDP was considered too high.[1] Although the cuts were not explicitly linked to conjunctural circumstances but rather to secular objectives, it is difficult not to conclude that some deflation to help in combating rising money incomes and prices would have been welcome as a side-effect.

However, the downfall of 'New Policies' was certainly a reversal of conjunctural stance. By 30 March 1971 the Chancellor could announce that increased unemployment had removed the danger that 'demand inflation would be added to the inflation stemming from rapidly rising costs', and the budget aimed to stabilise the situation – that is, to prevent the pressure of demand from falling further. By the summer the government was prepared 'to use the level of public spending and the programmes to which it is applied to meet urgent and immediate needs as an instrument of policy',[2] which involved a series of interventions to increase public investment. Despite attempts to reconcile this expansion with 'New Policies', in practice the principles of that document were being abandoned.

Although some of the reflationary measures which spanned the period from June 1971 to May 1972 were supposed to have a general effect (the repayment of postwar credits, for instance), most of the interventions were aimed at particular sectors (naval shipbuilding, purchases of machine tools and the replacement of rolling stock). The intermediate and development areas featured prominently, as did the construction industry, including housing investment. The impact was to be concentrated over the period up to mid-1973/4, with just over half (£365 million) in 1972/3 and 35 per cent (£233 million) in 1973/4. The effect of this phased leverage seems to have exceeded the Treasury's expectations; there was found to be 'much greater flexibility in public expenditure than people had supposed in the past, or we have ever been able to achieve in the past'.[3] Local authorities' and nationalised industries' capital programmes were increased by 5 per cent, thus substantially exceeding the limit of 2–3 per cent previously entertained in the conventional wisdom on the subject (see page 80 above). The increase in central government investment was slightly less, at 4 per cent.

[1] See above, page 85.

[2] Maurice Macmillan in the House of Commons, 8 December 1971.

[3] House of Commons, *Third Report from the Expenditure Committee* (*Public Expenditure* (*General*) *Sub-Committee*), *Session 1971–72. Changes in Public Expenditure*, London, HMSO, 1972, p. 9.

Including housing, the counter-cyclical increase in local authority investment alone was intended to be 7 per cent in 1972/3. Improvement grants were thought to be 'quicker-acting than new building, and more labour intensive',[1] so that, in June 1971, such grants (for local authority and private improvements in assisted regions) were increased for work which could be completed within two years.[2] This policy was misconceived; improvements are intensive of *skilled* labour, which is not an important element in the pool of unemployed. The counter-cyclical increases, with the simultaneous switch from new dwellings to improvements, resulted in an overload and a sharp increase in tender prices, so that by the spring of 1972 the two-year limit was extended to three.[3] An important element in the upturn of 1972–4 was the way in which a modest counter-cyclical impulse to the housing market grew; in 1972/3 alone the impact, initially estimated at approximately £40 million, was raised to nearer £140 million, with the impetus carried forward into the medium term. Because of this, the housing intervention is not incorporated in the figures in table 3.5.[4] The reflationary impact could not be contained and the concentration on improvements ensured that housing investment reached capacity at a level of output and employment below that which had obtained in 1964 or 1967.[5]

Were the other reflationary measures more effective, or did they too founder on supply constraints that they themselves created, thus leading to the cut-backs of 1973? Prima facie evidence against the reflation constituting a net *ex post* addition to demand is given by the fact that in all three investment programmes there were shortfalls in 1972/3 and 1973/4 greater than the extent of the intended intervention.

In the nationalised industries the shortfall was fairly large, but the Treasury was alert to the problem of ensuring that the measures had their forecast effect at the forecast time. The accelerations were monitored and, by the beginning of 1972, 95 per cent of the work had been authorised, let and started within the time envisaged.[6] Pressure on supplies does not seem to have been as important a factor in the subsequent overall decline in investment as the more endemic problem of

[1] House of Commons, *Seventh Report of the Expenditure Committee, Session 1971–72*, p. 6.

[2] House of Commons, *Hansard*, 22 June 1971, cols. 271–2.

[3] Ibid. 21 April 1972, col. 164; House of Commons, *Tenth Report from the Expenditure Committee, Session 1972–73. House Improvement Grants*, vol. 1: *Report*, London, HMSO, 1973, p. xxix. The switch of emphasis to improvements dated from the Housing Act of 1969.

[4] The White Paper of December 1972 (Treasury, *Public Expenditure to 1976–77*) also dropped the housing intervention from its 'counter-cyclical' definition, in contrast to Treasury, *Public Expenditure 1969–70 to 1975–76*, Cmnd 4829, London, HMSO, 1971.

[5] In 1972 the building labour force was still only 80 per cent of its 1967 level.

[6] House of Commons, *Seventh Report from the Expenditure Committee, Session 1971–72*, pp. 10–11.

the 'planning and execution of major projects'.[1] Attributing a net effect of zero to these measures on the grounds that they pre-empted other projects is probably less realistic than applying to them the usual element of structural shortfall, giving a realisation factor in 1972/3 of about 80 per cent. Supply constraints were more evident in the construction and civil engineering industry, where a large part of the environmental and 'infrastructure' increases was concentrated.[2] Certainly, some of the shortfall in the road and environmental programmes must have been due to excess demand, which makes it doubtful if all the counter-cyclical increases were a *net* addition to demand. About 60 per cent of the authorised short-term increases in public authority investment would seem to have been attained in 1972/3, making a 70 per cent realisation factor for the public sector as a whole.

A substantial proportion of the 1972/3 and 1973/4 shortfalls was due not to supply constraints but to price increases. The price of land, particularly, caused delays in land-intensive programmes (environment and roads),[3] while in other sectors there is evidence of a reaction to increased tender prices.[4] But, to the extent that price increases were a symptom of excess demand, it may be wrong to label shortfalls as the result of one *or* the other. (Equally it would be wrong to equate the two, since increases in the relative cost of investment cannot be categorically attributed to public expenditure policy.)

The first intervention of 1973, in May, seems mainly to have been a reaction to criticism of the December 1972 White Paper.[5] The medium-term increases were attacked for being potentially destabilising – particularly in late 1973/4 and 1974/5[6] – so that £79 million was taken from the 1973/4 programme and £406 million from the following year, in order to make way for the 'strong expansion of industrial investment and exports which we can now expect'.[7] This again evoked criticism on two counts: the first, that the successive shifts of policy for 1974/5 was

[1] House of Commons, *Expenditure Committee (General Sub-Committee), Session 1973–74. Minutes of Evidence, Monday, Jan. 28, Public Expenditure to 1977–78 (Cmnd 5519). Public Expenditure and the Balance of Resources*, London, HMSO, 1974, p. 25; House of Commons, *Fifth Report from the Expenditure Committee, Session 1972–73*, pp. 29–32.

[2] House of Commons, *Eleventh Report from the Expenditure Committee, Session 1972–73*, p. vii, and Anthony Barber in the House of Commons, 21 May 1973.

[3] House of Commons, *Expenditure Committee (General Sub-Committee), Session 1973–74. Minutes of Evidence, Nov. 12, 1973. Control of Road Programme Expenditure*, p. 15, and *Minutes of Evidence, Dec. 3, 1973. Public Expenditure in 1972–73 and 1973–74: forecasts, revisions and out-turn*, pp. 14–16, London, HMSO, 1973.

[4] Ibid. *Minutes of Evidence, Dec. 3, 1973*, pp. 15 and 18; NEDO, Building and Civil Engineering Economic Development Committees, *The Public Client and the Construction Industry*, p. 19. In the environmental sector, the reorganisation of local government and the transfer of functions to the regional water authorities (from 1974/5) may also have contributed to the shortfall.   [5] Treasury, *Public Expenditure to 1976–77*.

[6] House of Commons, *Fifth Report from the Expenditure Committee, Session 1972–73*, p. vii.

[7] Anthony Barber in the House of Commons, 21 May 1973.

contrary to the principle of medium-term stability; the second, that the cuts had come after the belated identification of the large 1972/3 short-fall, so that there was no assurance that they would not merely reduce the shortfall rather than actual expenditure.[1]

The rephasing of building contracts which followed in October 1973 was explicitly a reaction to excess demand – an overload in the con-struction industry had led to increased tender prices – and was intended to avoid the 'partial frustration' of some programmes.[2] The saving of £87 million imputed for 1973/4 was quite outside the possible time-scale for an adjustment to real demand. The proposition that the 1973 measures relied on a 'built-in shortfall that comes to the rescue when-ever there is pressure to reduce public expenditure'[3] is thus difficult to refute, though equally it is not clearly demonstrable in the terms expressed by the Expenditure Committee. Because expenditure is unrealised in one year does not mean it will be unrealised the next, and the Treasury's view of how far programmes would be realised in 1973/4 proved more accurate than that of its critics, who expected an even larger shortfall.[4] But, if the cuts were illusory, could they also be disrup-tive? Paradoxically, the case that the 1973/4 cuts depended on short-falls is strongest when based on the maintenance rather than the disrup-tion of a given medium-term stance. As can be seen from table 3.7, before the emergence of the 1972/3 shortfall public investment was due to increase by 7·3 per cent in 1973/4 and 2·5 per cent in 1974/5; with the emergence of shortfall these percentages were increased to 10·6 and 5·1 per cent respectively, and the effect of the May and October cuts was only to revert to the *status quo*, with implied increases of 7·0 per cent for 1973/4 and 2·6 per cent for 1974/5. (The discretionary factor for the 1973 policy adjustments has therefore been shown as minimal in table 3.5.)

Current expenditure cuts, which made up 37 per cent of the total in 1974/5, seem to have been more disruptive of medium-term policy, because it was in this area that secular changes were most evident in the reflation of 1972 (chart 3.3). Although there was a shortfall on transfers in 1972/3, current expenditure in 1973/4 exceeded the forecast level even after the cuts, so that it would be difficult to argue that they had been constructed out of a shortfall.

[1] House of Commons, *Eleventh Report from the Expenditure Committee, Session 1972–73*, pp. viii, x and 14.
[2] Treasury, *The Counter Inflation Policy: Stage 3*, Cmnd 5446, London, HMSO, 1973, pp. 9–10.
[3] House of Commons, *Eleventh Report from the Expenditure Committee, Session 1972–73*, p. 14.
[4] See House of Commons, *Expenditure Committee (General Sub-Committee), Session 1973–74. Minutes of Evidence, Dec 3, 1973*, and *Minutes of Evidence, Monday, Jan. 28;* also Treasury, *Public Expenditure to 1977–78*, pp. 147–8.

Table 3.7. *Volume of public sector capital expenditure: projections of gross domestic fixed capital formation and the 1973 programme cuts*

Percentages

	Forecast Dec. 1972[a]	Forecast December 1973[b]			Out-turn[c]
		Excluding cuts	After May and Oct. cuts	After Dec. cuts	
Change from previous year:					
1973/4	+7·3	+10·6	+7·0[d]	+7·0	+3·0
1974/5	+2·5	+5·1	+2·6[d]	−12·2	−1·0
Change from 1972/3:					
1974/5	+10·0	+16·2	+9·8	−5·9	+2·0

SOURCES: Treasury, *Public Expenditure to 1976–77* and *Public Expenditure to 1977–78;* CSO *Economic Trends, Annual Supplement 1975.*

[a] At 1972 survey prices.   [b] At 1973 survey prices.   [c] At 1970 prices.
[d] Allowing for £100 million shortfall by nationalised industries.

By the beginning of December 1973 public expenditure was planned to increase by 1·4 per cent overall in the year 1974/5, with an intended elasticity of 0·44 in relation to the secular growth of GDP, a strategy designed to make way for a projected increase in industrial investment and exports.[1] This was, however, to prove unattainable. On 17 December 1973, as a reaction to the oil embargo, 20 per cent cuts across-the-board were made in capital programmes (except housing, fuel and power) and there were large accompanying decreases in current expenditure. These cuts reduced the 1974/5 programme by £905 million in total. The reductions were based on a new output forecast, which had been significantly revised downwards, and on the inevitability of increased unemployment.[2] They were, therefore, a real reaction to changed external circumstances and a radical shift in policy beyond anything that had gone before. For capital expenditure, for example, the ostensible result of the intervention was to translate a 2·6 per cent increase into a 12·2 per cent decrease (table 3.7), but two factors make this an overestimate of discretionary change. First, the original forecast was based on quite large increases in investment by central government and nationalised industries, which looked suspiciously optimistic in view of the shortfalls of the previous years (and that of 1974/5 as it turned out). Secondly, reductions in local authorities' investment were accompanied by a switch to housing investment, so

---

[1] Ibid. p. 10.   [2] House of Commons, *Hansard*, 17 December 1973, cols. 954 and 963.

Table 3.8. *Public expenditure on goods and services: annual growth rates relative to full-employment GDP, 1971/2–1974/5*

Ratios[a]

	Volume			Net resource cost		
	Current	Capital[b]	Total	Current	Capital[b]	Total
1971/2	1·05	−0·70	0·50	1·50	−0·50	0·85
1972/3	1·20	−0·50	0·65	1·25	0·05	0·90
1973/4	1·35	1·30	1·30	1·80	4·20	2·50
1974/5	0·70	−0·45	0·35	3·35	0·70	2·50

SOURCES: CSO, *Economic Trends, Annual Supplement 1975*.

[a] Percentage annual change in expenditure at 1970 prices divided by 3·2 per cent.

[b] Gross domestic fixed capital formation, plus capital grants for housing and universities.

that the volume of public investment was, in the event, hardly to decline in 1974/5, even though it was a deflationary influence on the economy.

Characteristic of the period 1970/1 to 1974/5 was the substantial negative leverage exerted by the volume of public investment, which in no year (as charts 3.4 and 3.5 show) matched the planned profile of reflation and deflation. However, in terms of demands on resources, as described in table 3.8, the picture was substantially different, with adverse relative price effects causing the net resource cost of public invest-ment to increase at 4·2 times the growth of full-employment GDP in 1973/4. The explanation of the persistent gap in this period between planned volumes and out-turns must be found substantially in this relative price shift.

Although current spending on goods and services was expansionary in both cost and volume terms up to 1973/4 (with the severely adverse relative price effect coming through in this sector in 1974/5), taking capital and current spending together, table 3.8 shows a profile of expenditure growth quite different from that intended at the start.[1] Though most of the growth was supposed to come through in late 1971/2 and 1972/3, growth of public expenditure was still lower than that of potential GDP in those years; the impetus was greatest in 1973/4, by which year it was actually meant to level off. The incon-gruity is particularly marked in terms of total direct leverage derived from net demands on resources; in 1973/4 and 1974/5 these were a substantial expansionary influence – they grew by 2·5 times the growth of potential GDP in both years.

[1] For a discussion of the unforeseen relative price effects operating at this time see page 130; public sector earnings moved ahead of private in an unprecedented fashion in 1974 and 1975 (A. J. H. Dean, 'Earnings in the public and private sectors 1950–1975', *National Institute Economic Review*, no. 74, November 1975, pp. 60–70).

THE PHASING OF PUBLIC EXPENDITURE AND
THE OBJECTIVE OF STABILISATION

There are two reasons why the above analysis cannot be interpreted directly in terms of the effect of public expenditure on economic stability. First, it is arguable that to test a government's stabilisation policy it is necessary to take into account not only the expenditure but also the revenue side of the budget – also, indeed, monetary policy. In other words, one should look at the net impact of all the instruments of economic policy and not confine the analysis to the operation of a single one. Secondly, to appraise the effectiveness of varying public sector demand as an instrument of stabilisation, it has to be considered in the context of private sector demand.

For the first reason economic analysis is properly reticent about attempting to quantify the stabilising properties of public expenditure in aggregate.[1] Nevertheless, it can be argued that stabilisation need not extend to the entire economy, but could also apply to parts of it; in particular, the stabilisation of investment is a subsidiary objective which should not be overlooked. It then becomes legitimate to analyse the impact of counter-cyclical investment policy in its own right, since it has, from time to time, been the express intention to balance demand and supply in investment goods. The direct correlation of movements in public investment with private sector fluctuations can then be defended as valid insofar as the latter may be taken as autonomously determined – or at least unaffected by public investment plans.

Chart 3.6A therefore measures the deviations of public and private investment from their respective linear trends (at constant 1970 prices).[2] Strictly speaking, for stability the requirement would be that the value of the deviations should be equal and opposite in sign. Since, however, the two sectors have been approximately equal in size,[3] the deviations are expressed as percentages of trend, which makes it easier to identify the amplitude of the fluctuations. We shall therefore assume that an optimal result would be for the percentage deviations of the public sector to offset those of the private sector, so that the two summed to zero; a necessary (but not sufficient) condition for a completely stabilis-

[1] Such an exercise was, however, undertaken by A. R. Prest for the period 1955–66, cf. 'Sense and nonsense in budgetary policy', p. 5. For a criticism of the procedure used see G. D. N. Worswick, 'Fiscal policy and stabilization in Britain' in Sir Alec Cairncross (ed.), *Britain's Economic Prospects Reconsidered*, London, Allen & Unwin, 1970, pp. 36–60.

[2] Here the private and public sectors display different characteristics: the former approximates most closely to a fixed percentage rate of change (4·7 per cent per annum), while the latter is best described in terms of a constant elasticity because of the 'hump' in the mid-1960s.

[3] In 1970 investment the private sector (as here defined – see notes (iii) and (iv) to chart 3.6) formed approximately 55 per cent of the total and the public sector 45 per cent.

Chart 3.6. *Stabilisation in the capital goods sector, 1959–1973/4*

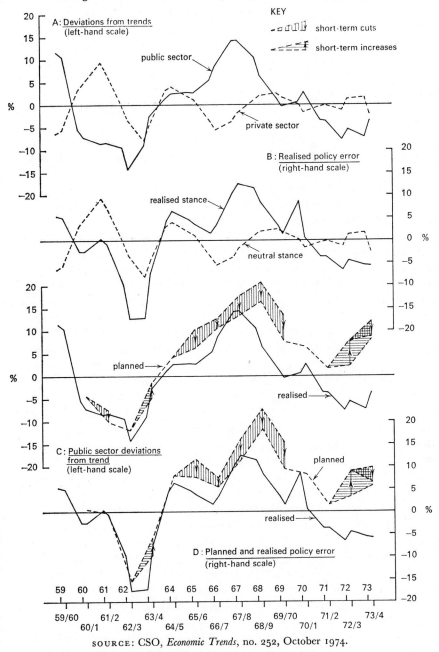

SOURCE: CSO, *Economic Trends*, no. 252, October 1974.

Notes: (i) For definitions of trends, see text.
(ii) Policy errors in parts B and D equal to sum of public sector and private sector deviations from trend as a proportion of public sector trend.
(iii) Steel is treated as part of the private sector throughout.
(iv) Capital grants to universities and grants for housing improvement included in the public sector.

ing investment stance would then be that the elasticity of public sector deviations with respect to private should equal -1.

For the data shown in chart 3.6A the coefficient works out at -0.677, which is statistically significant, although the negative correlation with private sector movements is only about 10 per cent.[1] While policy thus seems to have responded correctly to the private sector's cycle, only a small amount of the fluctuations in public investment are explained (or offset) by private sector fluctuations. Thus, the greater source of cyclical deviations in the investment market has been public sector demand, as may be deduced directly from the fact that the trend accounts for 96 per cent of all movements in private investment but only for 87 per cent of public sector movements.

The implications of this generalisation may be best appreciated from chart 3.6B, which expresses the total investment cycle as the sum of private and public sector deviations, which may be interpreted as an index of the realised policy stance. For a perfectly stabilising policy the deviations would always be zero, but where stabilisation is incomplete the index shows how far the actual public sector deviation from trend departed from the optimum and, as may be seen immediately, it has almost always done so. On the other hand, has it increased instability? Had public sector investment followed the 'neutral' policy of trend growth without fluctuations, the cycle in total investment would reduce to the deviations in private investment alone. The 'neutral stance' line in chart 3.6B thus repeats the private sector line of chart 3.6A; it can be seen to run, for the most part, closer to the zero line of optimal stabilisation than the actual total of private and public sector deviations from trend, the exceptions being chiefly at the beginning of the period, but including 1966/7. The early years exhibit a clear counter-cyclical effect, as do the periods 1966–8/9 and 1970–3. Marked pro-cyclical behaviour is limited to 1962–5, but destabilisation is characteristic of all three later periods – in the first the existing cycle was amplified (1962/3) and reinforced (1964/5); in the second and third (especially the former) the public sector created its own amplified counter-cycle.

It appears, therefore, that the degree of public investment has been destabilising, though not uniformly or unequivocally so; a tendency towards over-correction is revealed. This is not necessarily a consequence of short-term demand management; the public investment profile is a mixture of short-term interventions and medium-term influences, which may even contain elements of 'planned' instability

---

[1] $y = x^{-0.677}$ ($t = 1.96$; DW $= 1.02$; $R^2 = 0.12$) where y = public sector deviations and x = private sector deviations. There are 30 observations for the 15 years (calendar and financial) between 1959 and 1973/4.

(as for instance during the growth experiments).[1] Nor is it necessarily discretionary; the deviations are those that were *realised* and need not represent intended phasing. In particular, failures in the specification of policy may distort the original stance; for example, supply constraints may impose a counter-cyclical pattern in practice.[2]

Charts 3.6C and D attempt to separate short-term from medium-term policy, and discretionary from realised stance. In these charts any immediate (non-cumulative) forecasting errors have been added back to the realised deviations to give an *ex ante* estimate of the effectiveness of stabilisation,[3] including the impact of any short-term changes made. Chart 3.6C is related to 3.6A in that it too shows the amplitude of public sector deviations from trend, not only as they occurred, but as they would have occurred had spending plans been fully realised.[4] Chart 3.6D repeats the test in chart 3.6B for the intended stance of policy before and after short-term changes; that is, it shows the deviations of private (realised) investment added to those of public sector investment, as realised and as intended.

Three general conclusions emerge. First, due to the opportune effects of shortfalls and overruns, policy out-turns proved less destabilising than the original expenditure plans in nine of the fourteen years covered by the chart. Secondly, short-term interventions have been a mixed benefit: where the arrows point towards the zero line they may be taken as stabilising, while a movement away is destabilising. Perverse counter-cyclical reactions can then be identified in 1961/2 and the period 1972/3–1974/5. In later years the intended expenditure plans erred towards reflation, though the realised stance does not show this. The cuts in May and October 1973, however, partly cancelled out the original short-term increases for that year (the cross-hatched area) and can be seen to have been opportune. This also applies to the whole series of interventions from 1963/4 until devaluation; policy was correctly reversed towards reflation in the first of these years, while the deflationary interventions which followed from 1965 can be justified as tending to restore to a proper balance an economy which had embarked upon an extended period of above-trend investment. This brings us to

[1] M. C. Kennedy, 'Employment policy: what went wrong?' in Joan Robinson (ed.) *After Keynes*, Oxford, Blackwell, 1973, pp. 83–4.

[2] Such constraints may also affect private investment, though there seems to be a tendency in some supplying industries to give priority to private sector demand, so that the strain is taken by the public sector.

[3] Adding back the forecasting error naturally affects the trend itself, so that the graph slightly misconstructs the forecast deviations. *Ex ante* policy is thus not the intended deviation, but short-term public investment intentions, expressed as functions of the trend realised between 1959 and 1973/4.

[4] Thus the 'realised' line in chart 3.6C corresponds to the public sector line in chart 3.6A, whilst the 'realised' stances in charts 3.6D and B are also identical.

the third conclusion: that medium-term changes accounted for the major part of policy error, particularly the tendency to over-reflation juxtaposed with the National Plan targets which occurred in the mid-1960s. It is interesting to note that the large devaluation cuts, though opportune, were not initially sufficient to restore balance in investment, given the degree to which the public sector was above-trend and the fact that the private sector had also entered an expansionary phase.

CONCLUSIONS

Expenditure growth and control

The period under review is one in which the public sector has expanded a good deal more rapidly than the economy as a whole. Its share of total full-employment resources rose from 35 per cent in 1959 to $41\frac{1}{4}$ per cent in 1973, implying that exactly half of the extra resources created during the period were allocated to public spending of one kind or another.

It is, on the face of it, paradoxical that a period which began with concern over the need to contain public expenditure, which has seen important reforms in the management of public spending and which has stressed the need to relate public demands to the availability of total resources should have encountered such expansion. It is, of course, essential to note that the *amount* of services provided by the public sector (at least as measured in the national accounts) has increased much more slowly than its cost – an annual average growth rate of 3·55 per cent compared to 4·15 per cent (table 3.4). The relative price effect has been one of the most important influences on the longer-run expansion of the public sector, particularly in the mid-1960s. However, following devaluation not only were resources more realistically defined, but also the relationship of public expenditure to them; the assumptions about the rate of economic growth were more pessimistic, while the cost, not the volume, of public spending was constrained to grow at the same rate as prospective resources. This switch of emphasis involved recognising the fact that an adverse relative price effect must entail a volume growth of public services slower than that of GDP if the current-price resource share of public expenditure is not to rise indefinitely.

Even so, still to be explained are the continuing rise in public spending in the 1970s (after the pause at the end of the 1960s), the failure of the 'New Policies' approach and, although it is really a postscript to the period, the remarkable further expansion of the public sector in the mid-1970s, which raised the ratio of public spending to full-employment

GDP to about 46 per cent in 1974/5.[1] Some commentators have emphasised general underlying factors as the cause of public expansion – for example, the income elasticities of various public services – and political factors are obviously important, but because public spending is subject to fits and starts, one looks for an explanation in the system of control. A whole series of circumstances has made the PESC and the concept of forward planning vulnerable to events. In the first place, the balance of medium-term growth in expenditure tends to be upset when the instrument is used to reflate or maintain demand. Short-term changes tend to imply medium-term shifts in expenditure schedules and to have displacement effects. Once expenditure is raised it is not easy to reverse the process because of the tendency for current expenditure to be flexible upwards but rigid downwards; imbalances then result from the different instruments used to cut back, capital spending being particularly vulnerable. Phasing errors can also help to raise public expenditure in the long term if, as in the period 1972/3–1973/4, reflation is followed by a period of falling activity which, far from allowing a relaxation of public demand, actually calls for a further stimulus.

In any case, the PESC is only as effective as the determination (political and economic) to use it as a control rather than as a signpost to the medium-term horizon – to decide what the direction *should be*, as well as what it *is*. The vulnerability to vertical shifts of the spending schedule is paralleled (and compounded) by doubts over what the longer-run path of public spending should be – in particular, what its relationship should be to the secular growth rate of GDP. This has been respecified several times – in 1963–8 it was more than proportional, in 1969–70 proportional and from 1970 less than proportional – with the Treasury view tending towards the middle strategy. The difficulty is that any such rule can only be defended on pragmatic grounds, since there is no reason why the rate of growth of public expenditure, or its size, should be immutably related to GDP. Yet without some rule there is no clear idea of how far public expenditure should expand and, in the absence of other criteria (such as those provided by output and objective budgeting and the welfare analysis of public expenditure, for which medium-term rules are a somewhat inadequate proxy), it may expand by default. However, the system is not without its built-in constraints; medium-term economic assessment provides a perspective for assessing the claims on GDP of the various categories of expenditure, and it is useful for appraising how far public demands are compatible with the longer-term availability of resources. This check could perhaps

[1] See *National Institute Economic Review*, no. 75, February 1976, p. 88, and no. 77, August 1976, pp. 21–4. In January 1977 the aim was to bring this down to about 43 per cent by the end of the decade (Treasury, *The Government's Expenditure Plans*, Cmnd 6721, London, HMSO, 1977).

be made more effective if revenue forecasts were calculated and published, so that the medium-term budget constraint became more apparent – a development invited by the 1969 Green Paper,[1] but not consistently pursued thereafter.

Further, the planning of public expenditure is framed in terms of constant prices with an allowance for the relative price effect. This is, in conception, a relative productivity effect, and otherwise there is no presumption that the cost of public sector expenditure will increase faster or slower than the general rate of inflation. Since public expenditure has been presumed to play no causal role in inflation, it has been a precept of the PESC, as of the rate support grant, that any increase in the general price level will be financed automatically.[2] This system was upset in 1973/4 and 1974/5, when there was a substantial 'unforeseen' relative price effect, which raised the total cost of programmes by an unplanned £1700 million (current) by 1974/5. Not only had the general rate of inflation been underestimated by an amount not included in the £1700 million, but there had also been relatively greater inflation in the price of public goods. Much of this was due to increases in the cost of land and construction, but £500 million was the effect of relatively larger increases in public authority wages. In these circumstances it became necessary to alter the rules, so that changes in the relative price of public goods brought a compensating change in the volume of expenditure (as was evident in the public investment shortfalls of 1973/4) and so that public spending was not seen to be fuelling the fires of inflation. As a bolster to the control of expenditure volume by the PESC, cash limits were introduced in 1975, together with closer monitoring of cash flows on a month-to-month basis.[3] Provided the general rate of increase in earnings can be accurately foreseen and the rate of cash settlement is linked to it, this would cover the normal relative price effect, but not any further adverse changes in the relationship between earnings in the public and private sectors. At the same time, growth in the volume of public spending is constrained, since the application of cash limits implies that the *cost* of public spending increases propor-

---

[1] Treasury, *Public Expenditure: a new presentation*.

[2] Cf. Godley, 'The measurement and control of public expenditure', p. 58; the use of constant prices is an essential component of any system of medium-term expenditure management, since 'it insulates public expenditure from variations in the *general* rate of cost inflation'.

[3] See House of Commons, *Twelfth Report from the Expenditure Committee, Session 1974–75. Cash Limit Control of Public Expenditure*, London, HMSO, 1975; the intention to use cash limits on expenditure to back up the pay policy was announced on 11 July 1975 and incorporated in the rate support grants for 1976/7 announced on 21 November 1975. Up to 1975/6 the Treasury received quarterly information on cash flows from the spending departments; from 1976/7 this was changed to monthly. From April 1977 it has been supplemented by information on spending volumes and price changes supplied five times a year.

tionately to GDP. In these circumstances, the precise identification and control of the benefits (in terms of output) received from public spending becomes increasingly important if the standard of public services is not to fall; a regime of cash limits on a long-term basis means that 'positive planning' is necessary so that the results of programmes can be appraised other than by measuring public sector output with its conventional assumption of fixed productivity.

Again, the stresses caused by expanding public expenditure tend to be felt most acutely at the local level because of the inelasticity of local revenue and because of the historical tendency for local expenditure to grow faster than that of central government. The PESC has, of course, only incomplete control over local authority current expenditure through the rate support grant, but this accounts for only a small part of the overall deficiency in control, which tends to be general and strategic in origin rather than institutional.

Finally, it is still possible to point to particular deficiencies in control which lead to mis-estimations – either excesses or shortfalls – and serve to underline a basic weakness of the PESC – that the whole is only as strong as the sum of its parts. Certain areas of expenditure are not amenable to control by ceilings; they depend on forecasts. This applies to public transfers in particular, where once the rates of benefit and subsidy have been set, total spending is determined by the rate of take-up, so that expansion of this sector (as from 1972) does not help the cause of aggregate control. Some capital programmes – by nationalised industries and in housing especially – are also not subject to control in any basic sense, but to market and supply conditions. Errors in extrapolating such expenditure add an arbitrary element to attempts at effective demand management – public and national.

The PESC, as a system of control, has not been conspicuously effective as judged by results; on the other hand, it has developed defences against some of its weaknesses. Paradoxically, periodic breakdowns in control only serve to emphasise (as immediately after devaluation) the overwhelming necessity for the concept of the PESC and for a commitment to its effective working.

Short-term demand management

A feature of the period under review is the contrast between the scale of public expenditure interventions at the beginning and the end. Part of this was due to force of circumstances – devaluation and the oil crisis, for instance. But there has also been a calculated reaction against the limited scope for short-term action which was accepted as a fact in the early 1960s. While the Treasury still says that 'short-term management of the economy by fiscal means should primarily be carried out by changes in taxation', it has also discovered greater scope for using public expenditure to this end.[1] On the other hand, there has been continuing doubt about its effectiveness in such a role and concern over disruption and destabilisation.[2]

In the early 1960s the instrument almost atrophied entirely; the interventions of these years were a mixture of rather ineffective medicines and placebos. The need for something stronger arose primarily from the failure of the medium-term strategy advocated by Plowden. Up to devaluation the successive interventions (starting with reflation in 1963 and turning to deflation from 1965) were concerned as much with offsetting the instabilities inherent in public expenditure itself as with counter-cyclical action, but the experience of those years only seemed to confirm the rigidity of the system – particularly the limited scope for cuts. The reversal of strategy after devaluation was based on the belief that it would be easier to reflate, if necessary, than to deflate; the safe margin for the upward adjustment of public expenditure would be greater than for cuts. The extent to which this was confirmed in 1971/2 led to a new found optimism in the Treasury over the potential of public expenditure as an instrument of demand management (and a selective one). Although it would be difficult to argue that this optimism was wholly justified by events, especially given the problems of shortfalls in public spending, it seems safe to say that public expenditure had, by the early 1970s, acquired a somewhat greater potential as a short-run instrument than would have been admitted in the early 1960s.

Certainly experience may have delineated more clearly those areas where little can be expected from attempts at short-term adjustment. The problem of controlling nationalised industries' investment, with its perpetual shortfalls, would seem to prevent action here from having much effect. Housing investment has also proved difficult to predict, and this programme, together with that of the nationalised industries, comprises the major unpredictable element in public spending; forecasting errors in these areas (as may be seen, for example, from chart 3.4) often exceed the scale of short-term interventions. On the other hand, it does not seem that short-term policy is frustrated at the local government level. On environmental projects, where all loans must be sanctioned by the Treasury, control is very effective, while intervention to stabilise demand for new buildings and works appears to have been fairly effective.

Adjustments to current expenditure, insofar as they entail longer-run

[1] House of Commons, *Fifth Special Report from the Expenditure Committee, Session 1974–75. Public Expenditure, Inflation and the Balance of Payments*, London, HMSO, 1975, p. 5.

[2] House of Commons, *Ninth Report from the Expenditure Committee, Session 1974. Public Expenditure, Inflation and the Balance of Payments*, London, HMSO, 1975.

changes in expenditure plans, obviously have a meretricious quality, but in certain respects they may have dependable and desirable short-term effects; this applies particularly to current transfers and even subsidies. On the other hand, much of current spending on goods and services is in the hands of the local authorities, which have much more discretion here than over capital expenditure. Most local spending appears to be in response to central legislation, but in the short run the system of rate support grants gives only limited central control, the government having to rely on the unpopularity of the rates to force local authorities to spend less.

Historically, as table 3.5 shows, it is possible to identify a rather mixed performance in achieving announced changes in spending. Overall, there is not a great deal of evidence that such packages have been merely window-dressing for the sake of opinion abroad, though they do offer potential in this respect and one finds some references to 'pretended cuts'. But instances of under-implementation are probably less common than the opposite tendency, for interventions to lead – frequently with a lag – to an over-reaction. At all events, the picture given is one of effectiveness in some sectors, but this is more than offset by ineffectiveness in others.

As with implementation, the stabilisation record has been mixed. The devaluation cuts could not be said to be destabilising, for instance, and nor could those in 1965, but there is evidence that some attempts at fine-tuning have actually accentuated the cycle in the short-term, while others, though rightly timed in terms of immediate trends in private demand, have had adverse repercussions on stability in the medium term. The problem of timing reflations was brought into particularly sharp perspective in the period 1971–3, and forecasts of private investment – particularly in dwellings – have not proved accurate triggers for intervention. Had it been possible to ensure that public investment exactly followed a consistent medium-term trend, this would have been by some margin superior to the policy actually followed in contributing to economic stability. But it has to be remembered that medium-term planning is itself difficult; it is by no means easy to ensure that such plans do not eventually cause short-term trouble as a result of the difficulties of control listed above.

Since short-term expenditure changes invariably involve cost in terms of disruption, the doubts attached to their potential benefits seem to call for public spending to be relegated to the position of a 'tool of last resort'. It may be more profitable to devote resources to improving the consistency and reliability of medium-term planning than to making the instrument more effective in the fine-tuning of the economy. But this could be to learn the wrong lesson, for if the amplitude of the cycle is to be greater than it was to 1973/4, counter-recessionary contributions from public spending cannot be ruled out. Nor should selective intervention – in particular sectors, with particular skills and inputs of resources – be ignored.

Depending on the scale of the stabilisation problem with which the government is confronted, there would seem to be two possible courses open to it. In the kind of circumstances which faced demand management up to 1973/4 there is little doubt that public expenditure policy would have gained by ignoring the short-term and adjusting programmes only on a planned long-term basis. This would have entailed following a fairly rigid and consistent growth path, in order to minimise the chance of the stance of policy becoming perverse and necessitating short-term action. The second possible course is perhaps more apposite to the period since the oil crisis. If short-term expenditure changes are to make an important counter-cyclical contribution the problems are twofold: first, to establish medium-term rules which prevent unforeseen financing difficulties from emerging as plans get nearer to actuality; second, to adjust any short-term role for the instrument to longer-term needs and resources – the deficit-financing which initially accompanies the use of public expenditure as a short-term instrument must be brought down to more normal levels by phasing expenditure to fit in with medium-term revenue and borrowing potential. This would seem to call for a system of medium-term budgeting, where prospective public sector claims on resources are constrained in the longer run by the limits of non-inflationary taxation potential, and by the need for domestic savings to finance investment and an external surplus. This is already partially accomplished through the medium-term assessment, but would be improved by a more comprehensive regime of full-employment budgeting, which, in the medium term, implies planning against the prospect of economic resources being, at some stage, 'fully' employed.[1] In the past it has never been exactly clear how much of a deficit-financed increase in public spending was supposed to be temporary and how much permanent; grafting a full-employment budgeting system on to the existing short-term one would undoubtedly make this clearer, so helping to prevent an inflationary conflict between stored-up resistance to expenditure cuts and equal resistance to tax increases. In this respect, a full-employment budgeting system may be seen as an important *desideratum* if not the *sine qua non* of an effective counter-cyclical expenditure policy.

[1] For a discussion of the full-employment budget, and the distinction between its medium-term and short-term use, see pages 183–5 below.

CHAPTER 4

BUDGETARY POLICY

by *R. W. R. Price*

OBJECTIVES AND INSTRUMENTS

Economic policy and demand management: a historical perspective

Fiscal policy and public finance are not interchangeable terms. The former refers to government action as a 'balancing factor' in the economy at large;[1] the latter is wider-reaching, embracing, for example, the distribution of costs and benefits. These allocative issues are an important sub-theme to the basic concern of this chapter, which is with macroeconomic management; the precise method by which budgetary policy seeks to balance demand has often been based on the desired shape of the fiscal system in terms of its contribution to income redistribution, enterprise and efficiency. Indeed, the allocative content of budget-making has tended to grow in importance, though with some controversy over the degree of 'neutrality' or 'interventionism' involved – the one philosophy being based on classical beliefs in the efficiency of the market and the need to minimise distortions by the tax system, the other on the belief that the tax system can act in a positive way to improve economic performance.

On the other hand, the tax structure has also tended to develop in an *ad hoc* and even inconsistent way because of the requirements of demand management and because of the absence of longer-term policies concerning either the internal harmony of the tax system or the overall size of the tax take. The character of fiscal policy has been derived primarily and initially from the needs of short-term demand management, the clearest objective of which has always been the maintenance of full employment. But in practice this has borne little resemblance to the diagnosis of Keynes's *General Theory*.[2] Postwar variations in demand were less violent than expected, and by 1960 it had come to be believed that the 'pre-war problem of mass unemployment had gone'.[3] What remained was the problem of responding to cycles of much smaller amplitude and duration, to which the answer appeared to be greater flexibility and rapidity of action – that is, 'fine-tuning'.

---

[1] Keynes, *General Theory of Employment, Interest and Money*, p. 220.
[2] Ibid.   [3] Treasury, *Public Investment in Great Britain*, Cmnd 1203, pp. 6–7.

Accompanying this, there was the problem of reconciling 'expansion and price stability'.[1] The possibility of a link between demand pressure and inflation encouraged the use of demand management to maintain price stability by the creation of unemployment – a prescription which, though never an overriding basis of policy, occasionally emerged as a reinforcing rationale for deflating demand, most notably in 1961/2 and 1970/1. By the end of the period the belief that wages responded gradually to unemployment was explicitly rejected by the Treasury,[2] but even at the beginning disillusionment with 'stop–go' led to a search for alternative prices and incomes policies. Partly this was in response to a growing belief that inflation was cost-induced and thus outside the scope of demand management, but more explicitly the problem had become one of 'limiting the rise in incomes associated with a given level of unemployment to a rate lower than that which would occur on the basis of past experience'.[3]

Similar considerations applied to reconciling expansion with balance of payments equilibrium, which re-emerged, with price stability, as the central problem of economic management in 1960 and 1961. The solution of the two was linked; of the instruments available to affect the balance of payments in the short term, only reducing the rate of cost and price increases appeared not to have any serious international disadvantages. Otherwise, the external consequences of expansion could be tempered by *ad hoc* measures like export rebates, cuts in government expenditure overseas, quantitative restrictions and surcharges on imports, but basically the short-run balance of payments problem was regarded as insoluble because of the temporary flows of imports needed for stockbuilding and re-equipment.[4] However, if the imbalance was temporary only, demand management might achieve longer-run growth provided that the 'virtuous circle' of growth, productivity increases and export competitiveness could be entered from expansion rather than from a shift in the demand schedule for exports.[5] This was the strategy on which the expansion of 1963/4 was based. In this respect, though, policy was also turning towards a more directly structural approach to growth, linked with planning, which was to dominate demand management from the end of 1964 to 1967. On the other hand, the allocative

[1] Ibid. p. 7.
[2] Wages and prices, it came to be believed, do not react to the level of unemployment over a wide range until very high levels are reached (House of Commons, *Ninth Report from the Expenditure Committee, Session 1974*, p. 136).
[3] NEDC, *Conditions Favourable to Faster Growth*, London, HMSO, 1963, p. 45.
[4] Ibid. pp. 32–4 and 47.
[5] The direction of causation between export growth and GDP growth was ambivalent, but 'to some extent, the rapid increase in exports was due to the same factors that led to growth in the economy as a whole' (ibid. p. 34).

effects of public expenditure and the tax system came in for increasing scrutiny.[1]

The development of incomes policy and planning as economic instruments was a reaction to the waning belief that fiscal policy could achieve all economic objectives simultaneously – a belief that tended to flourish in the upswing and wither with the reserves. But up to 1967 no instrument proved sufficient to solve the conflict between full employment and the balance of payments. Devaluation was a landmark in this respect and from that time the proper balance between fiscal policy and exchange-rate policy which was needed for external and internal stability with (demand-led) growth has been an important consideration. In general terms, fiscal policy is usually assigned the role of maintaining internal stability and the exchange rate that of achieving external balance; the two are not taken as independent, but policy tends to be regarded in this way because exchange-rate effects are treated as partial equilibrium relative price effects, with income changes the province of fiscal policy.[2] But the impact of devaluation on the balance of payments depends on the income effects of the extra demand generated by the change – the absorption[3] and savings out of increased income earned abroad – as well as on export and import price elasticities. To gain the maximum effect from devaluation, additional savings should equal the increase in demand resulting directly from the change in relative prices. At levels of employment below the optimum the increase in demand will itself generate some additional private savings, but at full employment fiscal policy must create all the necessary savings to prevent devaluation from producing pure inflation.[4] Thus, at full employment, one cannot have a flexible exchange rate without an active fiscal policy to reconcile full-employment domestic savings with the target balance of payments;[5] in this sense, fiscal policy determines absorption and hence the balance of payments. But below full employment the respective importance given to one or other instrument is dependent on the multiplier; if this (and the marginal propensity to save) is unity, it is the exchange rate that fully secures the balance of payments objective.

[1] The first time the tax system was considered in relation to growth was in Inland Revenue, *Report of the Committee on Turnover Taxation* [Richardson Report], Cmnd 2300, London, HMSO, 1964.

[2] See C. P. Kindleberger, *International Economics* (3rd edn), Homewood (Ill.), Irwin, 1963, pp. 211–12.

[3] Where b is the balance of payments, y output and a expenditure, $\Delta b = \Delta y - \Delta a$ and Δa is termed absorption.

[4] Devaluation can increase real savings at full employment if there is money illusion, or if income is redistributed to relatively high-saving areas, among which export industries may be important.

[5] See N. Kaldor (ed.), *Conflicts in Policy Objectives*, Oxford, Blackwell, 1971, p. 12.

The greatest area of dispute over the combined role of fiscal and exchange-rate policy has concerned the amount of domestic savings forthcoming – the income effects of devaluation. The strategy of 1968/9 involved a large turn-round in budgetary savings, from financial deficit to surplus, and the main question is whether the initial correction was sufficient, or whether the delayed effects of devaluation were symptomatic of excessive domestic absorption. Since there was a rise in unemployment, the usual verdict is that the correction was sufficient and a lagged response by demand to prices can explain the delay, but other features point to the possibility of excessive absorption in 1968 (page 202 below). In any case, the 1972/3 reflation was built upon the lagged effects of devaluation for, domestic demand having been increased, sterling was floated in mid-1972 with the objective of a viable and sustained expansion. This combination of deficit budgeting and a flexible exchange rate gave rise to the so-called 'New Cambridge' controversy, which centred initially on the possibility that the potential gains from floating were being dissipated by domestic absorption – specifically, by budgetary dis-savings which private sector savings (interpreted here as the surplus of current savings over investment) could not be reliably expected to offset and which, as the economy reached capacity, would spill over into the balance of payments.[1]

Pessimism about the private surplus to be expected at the peak of the cycle in 1973/4 then led to a more universal proposition – that the private sector spends all (or almost all) its income in the longer run and cannot *at any time* be relied upon to supply more than a small amount of savings.[2] As a result, even below full employment fiscal policy becomes both necessary and sufficient to determine the balance of payments; the exchange rate (or a similar device) can affect output but not the external balance (that is, absorption offsets completely the price effects of exchange-rate changes). It is this extension of the complete absorption theory from a full-employment context that constitutes the 'new' in New Cambridge. It differs from orthodox Keynesian theory in its different view of the behaviour of private savings,[3] so that within the same framework it arrives at a series of 'elegant paradoxes'; the first is the direct link between the budget deficit and the balance of payments, the second that short-term interventions in demand management are unnecessary, because the private sector is not a source of instability and does not call for compensatory action. But the theory

---

[1] N. Kaldor, *The Times*, 30 March and 21 August 1973; see also page 190 below.

[2] R. R. Neild, *The Times*, 19/20 July 1973, 30 January 1974; W. A. H. Godley and F. Cripps, *The Times*, 22 January 1974; House of Commons, *Ninth Report from the Expenditure Committee, Session 1974.*

[3] Insofar as the original thesis postulated a negligible amount of private sector savings, it has also been seen as a reversion to Say's Law.

stands or falls on empirical proof and in this respect it has not been substantiated.[1] The recession after the oil crisis showed that instability in the economy can stem from changes in overseas or private sector surpluses, and that when such changes are incompatible with domestic full employment fiscal policy reverts to its traditional role of stabilising employment rather than determining the full-employment external balance. However, the danger of absorption from the conjunction of large-scale deficit budgeting and cyclical upturns in domestic and world demand – when the full-employment surpluses of the private and overseas sectors tend to be eroded – suggests that as the economy actually nears full employment the budget balance should be framed more explicitly than in the past to secure the balance of payments objective.

Taxation and compensatory finance

The principle of compensatory finance is that fiscal policy should match public and private savings (or dis-savings) to ensure that aggregate savings are compatible with full employment, but only rough guidance is provided as to the balance of policies; capital expenditure should be used to offset fluctuations in private investment, for instance, but when demand generally is unbalanced the particular mix of policies is indeterminate.

There was, however, a fairly distinct – and asymmetric – pattern of policy response in the period up to the early 1960s, according to which it was by a more restrictive monetary policy, increases in voluntary savings, and short-term and longer-term cuts in public expenditure, as well as through the automatic buoyancy of the revenue, that relief could be found from excess demand; deficient demand, on the other hand, could be countered by tax concessions, chiefly in the personal income tax – where discretionary changes were synonymous with reductions – and purchase tax.[2] Up to 1963/4 the dominant view was that taxation was too high and should be used to balance demand only where that was consistent with reductions. From 1963/4 the situation changed: the background to taxation policy became the rising revenue requirements of the expanding public sector. The Conservatives' return to office in 1970 then brought a restoration of something like their earlier strategy (which was, in turn, reversed by the Labour administration which followed), so that taxation policy shows a marked oscillation, which is described in fuller detail below.

---

[1] See Lord Kahn and Michael Posner, *The Times*, 17/18 April 1974; G. D. N. Worswick, *The Times*, 5 March 1973 and 28 January 1974; *National Institute Economic Review*, no. 64, May 1973, pp. 20–4; House of Commons, *Ninth Report from the Expenditure Committee, Session 1974*.

[2] The asymmetry of expanding by fiscal policy and retarding by monetary policy was criticised by Paish and others (see J. M. Buchanan, 'Easy budgets and tight money', *Lloyds Bank Review*, no. 64, April 1962, pp. 17–30).

Personal income tax

There have been two influences on the development of the personal income tax system[1] – the level of taxation and the graduation of the tax structure – and in both contradictory forces can be identified. First, the tendency for the public sector to demand resources for its expansion and increase the tax burden accordingly has conflicted with the intuitive but not empirically established view that a progressive tax system acts as a disincentive to work, initiative and growth. Secondly, the administrative convenience of a smaller number of rates and larger steps from one marginal rate to the next (particularly at the threshold) has conflicted with, and largely overridden, the arguments for a more highly differentiated structure; these have been seen as enhancing the progressiveness of the system and mitigating its harmful side-effects on the labour supply and possibly on wage bargaining.

There has, in fact, been an element of all-Party consensus over the possibly stultifying effects of direct tax increases.[2] Nevertheless, there have been noticeable differences between the Parties in the weight given to the argument. The problem is that, whilst the effects of an increase in the marginal rate may well be to substitute leisure for work, any change in average rates which accompanies it will have an 'income effect', so that people may work more to maintain a given post-tax income.[3] This may account partially for the marked difference between income tax policy in the period 1964–70 and the years before and after. The Conservatives' policy was characterised by reductions in income tax rates and rises in income tax and surtax thresholds. Under Labour the expansion of public spending and the switch into exports after devaluation called for an increased standard rate (from

[1] Until they were merged in 1973/4 this incorporated two taxes – income tax and surtax; 94 per cent of the yield in 1972/3 was from income tax and 6 per cent from surtax. National insurance contributions have becoming increasingly akin to an income tax with their transformation from a flat rate to a graduated income-related levy; their position in aggregate personal taxation is described on pages 161–3. Capital gains tax is another element of personal taxation which should be taken into account, but its development has coincided with reform of the company tax structure; it is discussed in the context of taxing retained and distributed profits in the next section.

[2] Cf. Roy Jenkins (in the House of Commons, 19 March 1968), who rejected the case for increasing income tax in the budget after devaluation on the grounds that, even if the disincentive effect of high tax rates was 'more allegation than reality', it was inadvisable to ignore the possibility.

[3] See Royal Commission on Taxation of Profits and Income, *Second Report*, Cmd 9105, London, HMSO, 1954, pp. 42–5. Subsequent studies have confirmed the possibility that this 'income effect' is likely to be stronger than the 'substitution effect' caused by lowering the opportunity cost of leisure (see C. V. Brown and E. Levin, 'The effects of income taxation on overtime: the results of a national survey', *Economic Journal*, vol. 84, December 1974, pp. 833–48, where it was found that the overall effect of tax was very small but led to a slight increase in the hours of overtime worked).

Table 4.1. *Statutory rates of tax, 1955/6–1973/4*

	Personal income taxes[a]				Company taxes[b]		Indirect taxes	
	Thresh-old	Lowest rate	Basic rate	Highest rate	On reten-tions	On distri-butions	Purchase tax	SET per head
	(£)	(%)	(%)	(%)	(%)	(%)	(%)	(£)
1955/6	566	8·75	33·06	92·50	45·00	70·00[cd]	5–90[c]	—
1956/7	566	8·75	33·06	92·50	45·50	72·50[d]	5–90	—
1957/8	630	8·75	33·06	92·50	45·50	72·50[d]	5–90	—
1958/9	630	8·75	33·06	92·50	48·75		5–60	—
1959/60	630	6·80	30·14	88·75	48·75		5–50	—
1960/1	630	6·80	30·14	88·75	51·25		5–50	—
1961/2	630	6·80	30·14	88·75[e]	53·75		5½–55[c]	—
1962/3	630	6·80	30·14	88·75	53·75		{10–45 / 10–25[c]}	—
1963/4	771	15·60[f]	30·14	88·75	53·75		10–25	—
1964/5	771	15·60	30·14	88·75	56·25[c]		10–25	—
1965/6	797	15·60	32·08	91·25	40·00	64·75	10–25	—
1966/7	797	15·60	32·08	96·25[cg]	40·00	64·75	11–27½[c]	1·25
1967/8	797	15·60	32·08	91·25	42·50	66·22	11–27½	1·25
1968/9	797	15·60	32·08	91·25[c]	45·00	67·69	{12½–50 / 13¾–55[c]}	1·88
1969/70	842	23·33[h]	32·08	91·25	42·50[c]	66·22	13¾–55	2·40
1970/1	958	32·08[i]	32·08	91·25	40·00	64·75	13¾–55	2·40
1971/2	1061	30·14	30·14	75·44	40·00	63·25	11¼–45[c]	1·20
1972/3	1234	30·14	30·14	75·44	40·00	63·25	11¼–25	1·20
1973/4	1245	30·00	30·00	75·00[e]	52·00		(VAT, 10%)	

SOURCES: Treasury, *Financial Statement and Budget Report* (annual); Inland Revenue, *Report of the Commissioners* (annual); Customs and Excise, *Report of the Commissioners* (annual).

[a] On earned income. The threshold is that applicable to a married man with two children aged 11–16.

[b] Maximum rates applicable to company accounting periods (or portions thereof) ending in the financial year. [c] Changes announced other than in the annual budget.

[d] Only applicable if companies paid their taxes out of reserves. Since the maximum distribution ratio was only about 65 per cent if taxes were paid out of current income, the maximum rates of tax in practice were 61·7 per cent (1955/6) and 62·9 per cent (1956/7 and 1957/8) (see A. R. Prest, *Public Finance* (1st edn), London, Weidenfeld & Nicolson, 1960, p. 165).

[e] Changes in surtax, including its threshold (see also note g).

[f] Number of reduced rates cut from three to two. [g] 10 per cent surcharge on surtax.

[h] Number of reduced rates cut to one. [i] Reduced rates abolished.

1965/6), surtax and investment income surcharges and a resistance to maintaining the real value of allowances, but also, a general reluctance to increase tax rates, even if not to reduce them like the Conservatives.

As a result, as table 4.1 shows, the basic rate on earned income (defined up to 1972/3 as the 'standard rate' reduced by the full earned income relief of two ninths) was the same (30 per cent) in 1973/4 as in 1959/60, but on higher and lower incomes there were fundamental changes. Until 1970/1 the highest rate of tax on earned income was the standard rate plus surtax because of the cut-off point for earned income relief, but this maximum was reduced in the 1971 budget to 75·44 per cent by extending a 15 per cent earned income relief to all higher incomes. The rate structure was rationalised further in April 1973, when income tax and surtax were unified, the 30 per cent standard rate on earned income being redefined as the 'basic' rate, with 75 per cent as a maximum. At the same time, investment income (above a specified minimum) was surcharged at 15 per cent, the concept of earned income relief being abolished.

Formerly, earned income relief, together with the system of reduced rates, had made income tax appear more graduated, but the elimination of reduced rates in the budgets of 1963, 1969 and 1970 (there is, again, some bipartisanship here) and the absorption of earned income relief into the basic rate imply that administrative simplicity – a relatively low tax threshold, a high initial rate and simple proportionality over a large range of income – has taken precedence over a more graduated income tax.[1] Because increases in personal allowances roughly kept pace with inflation in the end, the real value of the tax threshold was maintained, but the real value of the threshold at which the basic rate became payable was reduced by about half by the elimination of the reduced rate bands.[2]

[1] The width of the basic band had been justified by the need to avoid adjustments at the end of the year and the abolition of the reduced rate bands, which removed small income earners from the tax net, by the uneconomical cost of collecting small amounts of tax. By 1963 it had come to be believed that the starting point for liability was 'too low for modern conditions' (Reginald Maudling in the House of Commons, 3 April 1963). However, by 1970/1 the proportion of the working population liable for income tax had regained its 1962/3 level despite the intervening abolition of reduced rates; despite also the increased allowances in the 1971 and 1972 budgets, the proportion grew over the period as a whole.

The negative income tax scheme suggested in the 1972 Treasury Green Paper, *Proposals for a Tax-Credit System*, would have extended simple proportionality below the tax threshold.

[2] The 1973/4 tax thresholds as proportions of their 1959/60 equivalents were (with 1959/60 allowances, including earned income relief, multiplied by an index of consumer prices to convert them to 1973/4 terms):

	Value in 1973/4	Proportion of 1959/60 threshold for:	
		Initial rate	Standard rate
	(£p.a.)	(%)	(%)
Single person	595	*163*	*45·6*
Married couple	775	*124*	*49·5*
Married couple with 2 children	1245	*97*	*56·2*

In terms of the threshold and the initial rate of tax (raised to 35 per cent in 1975/6) the United Kingdom tax structure compares disadvantageously with that of other industrial countries, where the average starting rate is about 14 per cent and the threshold level two thirds higher (House of Commons, *Hansard*, 25 March 1976, col. *247*).

The increased tax rates that these changes implied at lower income levels and the reduction in the higher rates can be clearly seen from chart 4.1, which compares the tax structure in 1959/60 and 1973/4. The marginal and average (also called 'effective') rates of tax are shown for a 'representative' taxpayer – one with income all earned and claiming the marriage allowance. Progressiveness, as measured by an average rate of tax which increases continuously with income, has remained a characteristic of the system, though the reforms of the period

Chart 4.1. *Marginal and average rates of tax on earned income for the 'representative' taxpayer,[a] 1959/60 and 1973/4*

SOURCES: Inland Revenue, *Report of the Commissioners* (annual); NIESR estimates.

Notes: (i) 'Representative' taxpayer defined as a couple with all income earned, claiming only the married person's allowance.
(ii) 1959/60 translated into 1973/4 income terms by multiplying allowances and rate bands by an index of consumer prices.

have mitigated this. However, a significant aspect of progressiveness, especially in an inflationary economy, is the consistency of the rate of change of the average rate. If everyone's tax liabilities increased in the same proportion as incomes increased, the average rate schedule would be a straight line (since it is drawn to a log scale), but its slope is steeper at the lower end, in both 1959/60 and 1973/4, implying that effective rates of tax increase faster for lower income earners. In this respect the system tends to become less progressive as incomes increase (a factor explored more fully below), and this was enhanced by the reforms of the period, since the average rate schedule can be seen to rise more rapidly in its early stages in 1973/4 than in 1959/60.

The taxation of company income and capital gains

Changes in company taxation showed a great deal of purely conjunctural variation, while there were also major structural reforms on grounds of growth, efficiency and equity. Rates of company tax are a flexible instrument for short-term demand management, particularly popular at times of economic stringency, while investment incentives, operating through allowances or grants, have been prominent in reflations. The relative merits of grants and allowances has been a source of some dispute, as has the issue of differential tax rates on retained and distributed profits.

Up to 1957/8 retained profits were favoured by differential rates of profits tax. Income tax, to which companies were also liable at the standard rate, was levied on the same base as profits tax, but insofar as profits were distributed to the personal sector the income tax already paid was regarded as deducted at source and set off against the liability of the recipient.[1] There were, therefore, three salient features of the system before 1958: first, the company and personal income tax systems were not entirely separate; secondly, payments of income tax by companies counted as payments by the recipient of dividends; thirdly, there was (in 1957/8) a 27 per cent differential in favour of retentions through discriminatory profits tax rates (of 3 and 30 per cent), which, with income tax at 42·5 per cent, meant overall rates of 45·5 per cent on retentions and 72·5 per cent on distributions (table 4.1).[2]

The 1958 budget removed this discrimination through a single 10 per cent rate of profits tax, but left the income tax system unchanged. Capital gains also remained exempt from tax. This reform stemmed from the majority recommendation of a Royal Commission.[3] The minority agreed that in the long run a private enterprise economy was likely to function better without discrimination against dividends, but recommended that the existing differentiation should be abolished only if a capital gains tax was introduced;[4] on equity grounds, however, (which were not accepted by the majority) they were prepared to introduce double taxation of dividends by separating the company and personal tax systems and subjecting distributed profits to both. They

[1] The standard rate is not necessarily the actual rate payable by a recipient on his dividends, since the tax is refundable if his liabilities are less, or surtax may be added. The marginal rate of tax on dividends was about 52 per cent (a quarter more than the standard rate) in 1969/70 (see page 168 below, and cf. A. J. H. Orhnial and L. P. Foldes, 'Estimates of marginal tax rates for dividends and bond interest in the United Kingdom, 1919–1970', *Economica*, vol. 42, February 1975, pp. 79–91).

[2] If all profits were distributed this would have involved a penal rate of tax in the sense that it would have had to be paid out of reserves (see table 4.1 footnote *d*).

[3] Royal Commission on Taxation of Profits and Income, *Final Report*, Cmd 9474, London, HMSO, 1955.   [4] Ibid. pp. 354–70 and p. 388.

recommended that, after the introduction of a capital gains tax, a 'corporation profits tax' should be introduced at a uniform rate and, while income tax should not be levied on companies as such, they should act as agents and deduct income tax at the ruling standard rate from dividends.[1]

The reforms introduced by the new Labour administration in the 1965 budget followed exactly this prescription. The company tax system was separated from the personal by the creation of corporation tax, while a 'classical' system of double taxation on distributions was introduced, with companies being made responsible for deducting the standard rate of income tax at source.[2] While the 1962 budget had already made short-term capital gains subject to income tax and surtax, the 1965 budget made realised long-term gains (on assets held for more than a year) subject to a capital gains tax of 30 per cent.[3]

With corporation tax at 40 per cent the new system implied a differential of 24·75 per cent in favour of retentions because of the double taxation of distributions. But the issue remained in dispute and, when returned to office in 1970, the Conservative government announced they would abolish double taxation, and with it discrimination. After some discussion an imputation system was introduced with effect from 1973/4,[4] under which distributions carried a liability to advance corporation tax. This is a payment in advance equivalent to the standard rate of income tax; it counts against the company's eventual corporation tax liability and is 'imputed' to the shareholder by means of a 'tax credit' against his income tax liability.[5] By this reform the separation of the two tax bases was confirmed and it has now become an established principle of British taxation that company profits are

[1] Ibid. pp. 384 and 389.

[2] Treasury, *Corporation Tax*, Cmnd 2646, London, HMSO, 1965.

[3] Treasury, *Taxation of Capital Gains*, Cmnd 2645, London, HMSO, 1965. Company capital gains are chargeable to corporation tax; the distinction between short-term and long-term gains was removed by the 1971 budget.

[4] The absence of debate on the 1965 reforms was seen by many observers as an indictment of the governmental process (see A. R. Prest, *The Capital Gains Tax and the Corporation Tax*, London, Woolwich Polytechnic, 1967), so that the 1973 reforms were preceded by a Green Paper (Treasury, *Reform of Corporation Tax*), the proposals of which were considered by a Select Committee of the House of Commons, which reported in October 1971 (House of Commons, *Report from the Select Committee on Corporation Tax*, London, HMSO, 1971). The White Paper followed in April 1972 (Treasury, *Reform of Corporation Tax*, Cmnd 4955, London, HMSO, 1972).

[5] An alternative method – treating the tax on distributions as income tax and charging corporation tax on distributions at a correspondingly lower rate – was the one favoured initially, but it was considered disadvantageous in respect of distributions overseas and this tipped the balance in favour of an imputation system (see House of Commons, *Report from the Select Committee on Corporation Tax*, pp. ix–x; A. R. Prest, 'The Select Committee on corporation tax', *British Tax Review*, no. 1, 1972, pp. 19–20; J. F. Chown, *The Reform of the Corporation Tax*, London, Institute for Fiscal Studies, 1971, and 'The reform of the corporation tax: some international factors', *British Tax Review*, no. 4, 1971, pp. 215–29).

sui generis, calling for a separate tax regime which is 'something more than a mere attempt to collect personal income tax in advance';[1] hence there is the distinction between 'mainstream' corporation tax, which cannot be set off against income tax, and the imputed element, which can.[2] The reintroduction of a system which is 'neutral' as between the taxation of retained and distributed profits has remained, however, a divisive issue. Advocates of fiscal neutrality have held, on equity grounds, that the personal and company tax systems should be considered in their combined effect and the burden of taxation for a shareholder equalised between his benefits from received and from retained income.[3] There is, however, no determinate answer to the problem of fairness and neutrality. It depends, first, on the true incidence of company taxes, where the evidence is inconclusive but tends to indicate that such taxes are not passed on to the consumer;[4] secondly, on the extent of capital gains and the taxation of these – for a shareholder to be indifferent between distribution and retention of profits, he should be liable to pay company and personal income tax on the one equal to his potential liabilities by way of company and capital gains tax on the other.[5] For a taxpayer at the standard rate, realised capital gains would have borne tax at half the standard rate from 1965, while it appears that for shareholders as a whole both the marginal rate of income tax on dividends and the rate of capital gains tax would have been higher – 50 and 28·5 per cent on average in 1973/4.[6] For the standard rate taxpayer, therefore, distributions would have been taxed at an aggregate rate of 52 per cent (table 4.1), while realised capital gains would have borne a total effective rate of 59 per cent – a bias in favour of distributions. However, the 1973 system appears to have

[1] House of Commons, *Hansard*, 6 April 1965, col. 255; Royal Commission on Taxation of Profits and Income, *Final Report*, p. 164.

[2] With corporation tax at 52 per cent and all profits distributed, the 'mainstream' rate would be 31·4 per cent and the imputed rate 20·6 per cent (three sevenths of the distribution).

[3] The opposite case is that, if company income is *sui generis*, principles of equity require that profits tax should be set off against the individual's tax no more than other payments such as rates (ibid. p. 383). See also the viewpoints of Prest and Kaldor in House of Commons, *Report from the Select Committee on Corporation Tax*, p. vii.

[4] See M. T. Sumner, *The Effect of Taxation on Corporate Saving and Investment*, London, Institute for Fiscal Studies, 1976.

[5] Accounting for the fact that the imputation system allowed income tax at the standard rate to be offset against the grossed-up value of the dividend (that is, the dividend multiplied by $10/7$), this condition is $\mathrm{CT} + (1-\mathrm{CT})(10/7)(\mathrm{IT}-0\cdot3) = \mathrm{CT} + (1-\mathrm{CT})\,\mathrm{CGT}$, or $(10/7)(\mathrm{IT}-0\cdot3) = \mathrm{CGT}$, where CT is the rate of company tax and $0\cdot3$ is the standard rate of income tax, IT is the marginal tax rate on dividends and CGT the rate of capital gains tax. Of course, retained profits are not systematically related to capital gains, which accrue and are realised in an erratic manner. The analysis here is thus fairly simplistic.

[6] See table 4.6 below and *Inland Revenue Statistics 1974*, table 107. For a standard rate taxpayer capital gains tax liability (on the first £5000 of gains) is restricted to the amount that would be due if half of this gain was added to his income as assessed for income tax.

been more neutral than either of the two previous regimes insofar as it removed the discrimination between retained and distributed profits for the *average* shareholder, who would have been taxed at (approximately) 66 per cent on both retentions and distributions. Both of the previous regimes involved a bias against distributions, despite the one operative from 1958 to 1964 being neutral towards the standard rate taxpayer.[1]

The issues of economic management which have entered into the differential tax debate have concerned the effects on aggregate savings and on inflationary pressure. The problem is not so much whether retentions – and hence company savings – are increased, it is rather to quantify the extent of the increase.[2] The *net* savings effect is, however, a different matter. The majority of the Royal Commission was much more hopeful than the minority that increasing distributions would not add much to demand,[3] and the proponents of discrimination have continued to argue that the propensity to save out of distributions is considerably lower than out of (realised or unrealised) capital gains,[4] but the differential may be as low as 10–15 per cent according to one calculation.[5] This might be taken as implying that the economic gains from discrimination are tentative, but part of the argument has

---

[1] For the period as a whole, the company tax system displayed the following properties *vis-à-vis* retentions and distributions:

	Standard rate taxpayer	Average shareholder
1958–64	neutral	bias against distributions
1965–72	bias against distributions	greater bias against distributions
1973	bias against retentions	neutral

When there is no capital gains tax, as in 1958, neutrality would actually demand a higher rate of tax on retentions than on distributions, both to force profits into the surtax net and to act as a proxy for an accrued capital gains tax (see Royal Commission on Taxation of Profits and Income, *Final Report*, p. 163; A. R. Prest, *Public Finance: in theory and practice* (5th edn), London, Weidenfeld & Nicolson, 1975, pp. 362–3).

[2] For a résumé of the evidence see Sumner, *The Effect of Taxation on Corporate Saving and Investment*.

[3] Both majority and minority were of the opinion that restoring neutrality would increase distributions and hence, *in the short term*, share values. The pessimism of the minority over the inflationary pressures that this would cause seems to have been shared by the Treasury, since the discrimination against distributions remained for three years afterwards, and was even increased in 1956.

[4] Kaldor in House of Commons, *Report from the Select Committee on Corporation Tax*, p. 251. See also, T. Balogh, 'Differential profits tax', *Economic Journal*, vol. 68, September 1958, pp. 529–30.

[5] M. S. Feldstein and G. Fane, 'Taxes, corporate dividend policy and personal savings: the British postwar experience', *Review of Economics and Statistics*, vol. 55, November 1973, pp. 399–410.

rested on the 'undoubted psychological link between dividend payments and wage claims'.[1]

However, the weight of the arguments for and against discrimination have come to centre on its effects *vis-à-vis* the size and character of investment. The Royal Commission's finding that retentions did not necessarily encourage ploughing back, but did interfere with the raising of new capital on the market by firms which needed it, implied a net discouragement to investment. The neutralist case, however, has rested on allocative efficiency – the correction of a system which discriminates in favour of monopoly and inefficiency by benefiting existing (large) corporations and encourages investment in relatively unprofitable channels. The reasons put forward for the 1958 reform (which were to be echoed by Anthony Barber in 1971) were that it would 'improve the supply of capital to firms who needed it most, and help remove the distortions in company finance';[2] that the previous system short-circuited the market seems to have been generally agreed on at one time. Among the arguments for reintroducing discrimination in 1965, the most powerful was thought to be that it would shift the tax burden away from 'the faster growing companies, which are generally low distributors, and thus enable them to expand faster'.[3] Empirical evidence is short on this subject, though a good deal of the neutralist case has been based on the finding that companies which retain a relatively high proportion of profits select relatively unprofitable investments.[4]

Theoretically, too, the issue is not clear-cut.[5] In particular, if the marginal rate of tax relevant to investment decisions is the rate on retentions, then the 1965 reform gave an added incentive to invest, as was claimed by the Chancellor at the time, by reducing the operative marginal rate from over 50 to 40 per cent.[6] But this obviously has to be considered in the context of the change from investment allowances to grants, a move prompted by disillusionment in the new administration over the effectiveness of investment incentives given through the tax system.[7] In January 1966 grants replaced investment allowances,[8]

[1] Royal Commission on Taxation of Profits and Income, *Final Report*, p. 387; A. Rubner, 'The irrelevancy of the British differential profits tax', *Economic Journal*, vol. 74, June 1964, pp. 350–1.   [2] D. H. Amory in the House of Commons, 15 April 1958.
[3] James Callaghan in the House of Commons, 6 April 1965.
[4] I. M. D. Little, 'Higgledy piggledy growth', *Bulletin of the Oxford University Institute of Statistics*, vol. 24, November 1962, pp. 387–412.
[5] See Sumner, *The Effect of Taxation on Corporate Saving and Investment*, for a summary of the theoretical issues.
[6] House of Commons, *Report from the Select Committee on Corporation Tax*, p. 249; *Hansard*, 6 April 1965, col. 255.   [7] Ibid. cols. 256–7.
[8] Department of Economic Affairs, *Investment Incentives*, Cmnd 2874, London, HMSO, 1966.

and here there is a second source of dispute. The arguments against grants were of the same genre as those against discriminatory tax rates; they were believed to distort the relationship between investment and returns by benefiting firms irrespective of profitability. The reintroduction of allowances in October 1970 was thus based primarily on the danger of 'uneconomic investment leading to waste of resources', though the discrimination against the service industries built into the grants system and the larger element of central administration and direction (not to mention public expenditure) were also considerations.[1] The 1970 reform introduced accelerated depreciation through increased initial and annual allowances (making 60 per cent the 'first-year' allowance on plant and machinery); there was no return to the system of investment allowances which had periodically reinforced initial allowances in the 1950s and early 1960s. It was followed in 1972 by the system of 100 per cent initial allowances (or 'free depreciation').

Indirect taxation

The late 1950s and early 1960s saw a substantial fall in expenditure tax rates on income-elastic goods, prompted by a belief in the economic efficiency of a more uniform tax incidence and greater 'fiscal balance'. By 1959/60 the number of purchase tax rates had been reduced to four, with a range of 5–50 per cent (table 4.1), and this tendency continued up to 1963/4, when there were three rates with a range of 10–25 per cent. Though purchase tax increases were occasionally used in contractions, its absolute and relative impact on a restricted range of goods was a drawback recognised by all Chancellors;[2] in Conservative periods this acted as an incentive to reduce and standardise rates and in Labour periods as a disincentive against increases, though expediency sometimes prevailed (as in 1968).

Debates on the expansion of the tax base which accompanied expenditure tax increases usually brought suggestions of substituting a turnover tax for purchase tax. This, having been rejected in 1958, was raised again in March 1963, but received no encouragement from the Richardson Report, which saw no benefits sufficient to offset the added burden of administration.[3] If a further expansion of the tax base was desirable, this could best be achieved by extending and modifying purchase tax; the committee found that VAT did not, any more than purchase tax, promote exports or growth. However, because of the small amount of purchase tax on industrial inputs such as cars and

---

[1] Treasury, *Investment Incentives*, Cmnd 4516, London, HMSO, 1970.
[2] See particularly the budget speeches on 6 April 1965 and 3 May 1966.
[3] Inland Revenue, *Report of the Committee on Turnover Taxation*, chap. 5.

stationery which enter into export costs, and because of the discrimination in favour of services (which a sales tax cannot easily cover) such
a reform continued to be favoured in some circles;[1] it became official
Conservative policy in preference to selective employment tax and as
a step towards harmonisation with the EEC. The introduction of VAT
in 1973/4 at a standard rate of 10 per cent was represented as reducing
the 'distortion of consumer choice' which led to allocative inefficiencies,
and as benefiting the balance of payments because the hidden element
of purchase tax and selective employment tax on exported services
could now be refunded in full.[2] Because VAT provided a broader and
more uniform tax base, it was also supported as making stabilisation
policy more effective (the selectivity allowed by purchase tax having
come to be considered as of dubious value).[3] From the late 1950s the
need for more flexible and broader based demand interventions had
become apparent, which led to the introduction of an expenditure tax
regulator in the 1961 budget, so that adjustments to expenditure taxes
as a whole could be made between budgets to a limit of 10 per cent of
existing duties.[4] In 1964 this was altered to allow variations in any one
or more of five groups of duties – purchase tax, tobacco, alcoholic
drink, hydro-carbon oils, and betting and other minor duties – the
object being to exclude items which were thought to be near their
taxable capacity.

While the degree to which the excise tax base as a whole responds to
changes in real income is not as low as sometimes supposed, all the
excise duties decline in real value through inflation and this is probably
the biggest single reason for the prominence of excise duties in discretionary tax increases. There is, though, an important drawback in that they
achieve their effect only by raising consumer prices, with the danger
that they will accelerate the price–wage spiral. Partly for this reason
there was a growing reluctance to correct the declining real value of
excise duties between 1968/9 and 1973/4.

The introduction of selective employment tax in the budget of 1966
was the product of both expediency and refined economic logic, in
that it reflected the need for more revenue and faster long-term growth.
It was a poll tax, levied as a flat-rate surcharge on employers' national
insurance contributions, with broad distinctions as to age and sex.
It was to be refunded to all industries except services and construction;
manufacturers and institutions engaged in scientific research related to
manufacture received premiums.

[1] For example, NEDO, *Value Added Tax*, London, HMSO, 1969.
[2] Treasury, *Value Added Tax* [Green Paper], Cmnd 4621, London, HMSO, 1971.
[3] NEDO, *Value Added Tax*.
[4] Excluding protective duties, television licence fees and excise licence duties.

Apart from its structural aspects, selective employment tax was intended to raise revenue for the expansion of the public sector. While its potential as such was welcomed in some quarters,[1] it was not the descendent of the 1944 payroll regulator, which had been revived as a proposal in 1961, but had foundered because it had none of the necessary qualities for flexible action. As the delayed starting date for selective employment tax showed (it was to be effective from 5 September 1966) the instrument could only be slow-acting, while the economic efficiency of a tax on *employers'* contributions could not be great, since its effects on prices and consumer spending were ambivalent and delayed.[2] As a means of eliminating the bias of the tax system in favour of services the new tax could be supported by economic liberals; but it also had strong directional aspects in its discrimination in favour of visible exports, manufacturing and (with the subsequent introduction of regional employment premiums) the regions.

An implicit subsidy for exports was contained in the general rebate to manufacturing industry; the rationale being the relatively high export content of manufacturing in comparison with construction and (allegedly) services. It can be traced to a memorandum submitted to the Committee on Turnover Taxation by Kaldor in 1963;[3] here the suggestion was a value-added tax, the proceeds of which would be used to pay a general subsidy to enterprises on their wages bill. From the point of view of exports and the balance of payments this was claimed to be 'just as effective as a devaluation'. The effect of the premium ($37\frac{1}{2}$p per male worker) in stimulating exports was, however, small. The National Institute estimated the net effect on exports as virtually nil and other commentators did not differ substantially.[4]

The further positive ingredients in the system, which aimed to affect export growth and achieve lasting expansion, were the employment base and the restriction of the base to services and construction. The idea of a permanent payroll tax (of which the poll tax is a variant) had arrived in official circles by way of Sir Robert Hall's diagnosis of the structural weakness in the British economy during the boom of 1960/1.[5] At that time a great degree of spare capacity existed side-by-side with over-employment, preventing output and productivity gains.[6] There was also evidence of labour hoarding, one remedy for which was seen as a tax disincentive, and selective employment tax was a logical solution.

---

[1] See *National Institute Economic Review*, no. 36, May 1966, p. 10.

[2] See Brittan, *Steering the Economy*, pp. 249–50.

[3] N. Kaldor, *Essays on Economic Policy*, vol. 1, London, Duckworth, 1964, pp. 291–4.

[4] *National Institute Economic Review*, no. 36, May 1966, pp. 18–19; S. Brittan, 'The selective employment tax', *The Banker*, vol. 116, June 1966, p. 367.

[5] See Brittan, *Steering the Economy*, p. 248.

[6] Sir Robert Hall, 'Britain's economic problem', *Economist*, 23 September 1961, p. 1133.

Perhaps the more sophisticated argument, which related to the choice of services and construction to bear the burden of selective employment tax, had been set out by Kaldor in 1966.[1] Here a high growth rate for manufacturing output was laid down as the *sine qua non* of high productivity increases, fast-growing exports and high levels of economic growth. The crucial element in Britain's growth performance was distilled from the premise that 'over a run of years it was the rate of growth of production which determined the rate of growth of our exports and not the other way round'.[2] Neither high rates of export demand, nor large amounts of industrial investment were regarded as sufficient in themselves to procure expansion (though necessary) and the conclusion was that 'once it is recognised that manpower shortage is the main handicap from which we are suffering...we shall...tend to concentrate our efforts on a more rational use of manpower in all fields'.[3] Thus selective employment tax aimed to transfer manpower to manufacturing as a potentially more productive sector, emulating the effect that large reserves of agricultural labour had had upon growth in other countries.

This thesis did not gain universal acceptance. A Brookings report found the link between growth and the labour supply unconvincing;[4] moreover, it was disputed that a tax on an employment base was a better means of increasing productivity than one based on total cost or output. Selectivity was considered questionable in its effect on export competitiveness because of the adverse effects on invisible trade and service inputs into merchandise trade,[5] while devaluation reduced the need for such expedients in any case; it also discriminated against investment insofar as construction was not exempt. For these reasons the Conservative government abolished selective employment tax (in two steps, in 1971/2 and 1973/4) as part of a wider programme involving the introduction of VAT.[6]

Reports on the effects of the tax find some savings in manpower in the service industries (particularly distribution),[7] but these results are ambiguous in that the introduction of the tax coincided with the

---

[1] N. Kaldor, *Causes of the Slow Rate of Economic Growth of the United Kingdom*, Cambridge University Press, 1966.   [2] Ibid. p. 25.   [3] Ibid. p. 31.

[4] Musgrave and Musgrave, 'Fiscal policy' in Caves *et al.*, *Britain's Economic Prospects*, p. 64. See also J. N. Wolfe, 'Productivity and growth in manufacturing industry', *Economica*, vol. 35 (new series), May 1968, pp. 117–26; N. Kaldor, 'Productivity and growth in manufacturing industry: a reply', *Economica*, vol. 35 (new series), November 1968, pp. 385–91.

[5] '... this was bound to be true if the field of tax was defined in terms of establishments, rather than by reference to activities' (W. B. Reddaway, *Effects of the Selective Employment Tax: final report*, Cambridge University Press, 1973, p. 172).

[6] House of Commons, *Hansard*, 30 March 1971, cols. 1392–4.

[7] Reddaway, *Effects of the Selective Employment Tax*; Treasury, *Effects of the Selective Employment Tax. First Report: the distributive trades*, London, HMSO, 1970.

abolition of resale price maintenance and the withdrawal of investment allowances to service industries; also, productivity gains in service industries were accompanied by similar 'abnormal gains' in manufacturing, which may imply that some common factor, such as a shake-out of labour, was at work during the period.[1] The case for selective employment tax – apart from redressing the erstwhile tax imbalance between service and goods industries, now accomplished by VAT – thus remains unproven.

BUDGETARY STRATEGY:
DISCRETIONARY AND BUILT-IN CHANGES IN REVENUE

Introduction

Budgetary policy in the United Kingdom has been based on short-term discretionary action through changes in tax rates. This derives from the historical procedure of annual budget-making, and from the constitutional and political realities of Cabinet government, which have normally ensured the prompt enactment of Finance Bills by Parliament. This is in marked contrast to the American system, for Congress has a more influential role, so that statutory tax changes there are introduced only infrequently and have a Congressional delay of twelve to eighteen months.[2] To compensate, the United States places greater emphasis on automatic stabilisation and has committed resources to improving its effectiveness. In Britain, on the other hand, more attention has been concentrated on enhancing legislative and administrative flexibility in the interests of 'fine-tuning'.

Although British practice has never had explicit rules for operating automatic stabilisers, these have great analytical relevance to fiscal policy. They not only provide the 'built-in flexibility' which damps cyclical movements in the economy, they also define the automatic properties of the system *vis-à-vis* growth and inflation; that is, they specify budgetary rules to identify and even neutralise the biases arising from 'fiscal drag', through either indexation or the direct specification of the level of the full-employment budget balance. Some prescriptions for setting this balance attempt explicitly to eliminate the

---

[1] The attribution of productivity gains to selective employment tax has been questioned by J. D. Whitley and G. D. N. Worswick from a study of the corresponding trends in manufacturing (see 'The productivity effects of selective employment tax', *National Institute Economic Review*, no. 56, May 1971, pp. 36–40; W. B. Reddaway, 'The productivity effects of selective employment tax – a reply', *National Institute Economic Review*, no. 57, August 1971, pp. 62–8, and Whitley and Worswick, 'The productivity effects of selective employment tax – a rejoinder', *National Institute Economic Review*, no. 58, November 1971, pp. 72–5).

[2] On the implications of this lag for stabilisation see P. R. Portney, 'Congressional delays in U.S. fiscal policymaking: simulating the effects', *Journal of Public Economics*, vol. 5, April–May 1976, pp. 237–47.

need for discretionary fiscal intervention,[1] but the concepts of fiscal drag and the 'full-employment surplus' may be better interpreted as delineating discretionary action by providing benchmarks for a 'neutral' policy. In British budgetary practice, for instance, a neutral budget may be defined as one leaving statutory tax rates and allowances unaltered, but because of fiscal drag the effective tax burden may still rise automatically and it has been at the discretion of Chancellors to offset this or not.[2] Discretionary policy should therefore be defined to include both active changes in statutory rates and passive changes due to fiscal drag. In this respect, also, the use of the full-employment surplus can be shown to identify more closely the criteria by which the overall neutrality of the budget is judged, in that it measures the combined effect of fiscal drag and other discretionary policy influences, undisguised by the automatic damping effects on budget revenue which less than full employment has on the actual budget balance.

Accordingly, the following analysis attempts to measure discretionary and built-in policies as they conform to various definitions of neutrality. The definitions used in British budgetary practice are followed in measuring the demand effect of budgetary changes; these statutory changes are then traced through the resultant changes in effective rates and analysed in the context of the accompanying automatic changes in tax rates. Not all such automatic changes are built-in – some are haphazard or non-recurring – so finally we attempt to specify the structural element they contain through their relationship with income. The approach here is to derive first the marginal tax rates applicable to built-in flexibility, then, secondly, the non-proportional effects (elasticities) which are the basis of fiscal drag. Later in the chapter the total stance of budgetary policy is measured with reference to the neutrality rules applicable to the full-employment budget balance.

Discretionary interventions in British budgetary practice

Changes in tax rates and allowances are generally accompanied by an estimate of their revenue effects on both a current-year and a full-year basis.[3] In addition, the Financial Statement issued at budget time shows the total revenue from the various classes of taxes expected to be received during the financial year; it thus provides the basis for break-

[1] Cf. M. Friedman, 'A monetary and fiscal framework for economic stability', *American Economic Review*, vol. 38, June 1948, pp. 245–64.

[2] This was recognised in the 1977 Finance Act, which laid down that personal income tax reliefs be changed in following years 'by not less than the same percentage as the increase in the retail price index for the previous calendar year'; to prescribe lesser reliefs the Treasury needs Parliamentary approval.

[3] The difference between the two reflects the lag of accruals on payments and, where the intervention occurs part-way through the financial year (as with the regulator), the fact that the tax change is not operative for the whole of the current year.

ing down the change in total tax between discretionary and automatic effects. The procedure may be clarified by considering a proportional tax system, with tax base B, statutory rate of tax μ and a total yield T; thus:

$$T_t^t = \mu_t B_t \qquad (1)$$

$$T_{t-1}^{t-1} = \mu_{t-1} B_{t-1} \qquad (2)$$

and

$$T_t^{t-1} = \mu_{t-1} B_t \qquad (3)$$

T_t^t being the accrued yield of tax in year t (subscript) derived from the tax function actually operative in that year (denoted by superscript t). Similarly, T_{t-1}^{t-1} is the accrued yield in the previous year, derived from the tax rates which operated in that year, and T_t^{t-1} the yield which would have accrued had the previous year's tax rates operated in the current year. All three estimates appear in the Financial Statement.[1] The first is the actual forecast for the year, and the difference between this and the provisional out-turn for the past year (2) is the total expected change in yield $(T_t^t - T_{t-1}^{t-1})$. The third estimate is the pre-budget forecast, and the difference between this and the actual forecast is a measure of the discretionary change introduced in the budget: $T_t^t - T_t^{t-1}$. The automatic change in yield which would have occurred without budgetary intervention then emerges as the difference between the pre-budget forecast and the past year's out-turn: $T_t^{t-1} - T_{t-1}^{t-1}$. The total change can then be expressed as:

$$
\begin{aligned}
T_t^t - T_{t-1}^{t-1} &= (\mu_t B_t - \mu_{t-1} B_t) &&+ (\mu_{t-1} B_t - \mu_{t-1} B_{t-1}) \\
&= (\mu_t - \mu_{t-1}) B_t &&+ \mu_{t-1}(B_t - B_{t-1})
\end{aligned}
\qquad (4)
$$

or

$$\underbrace{}_{\substack{\text{total} \\ \text{change}}} \qquad \underbrace{}_{\substack{\text{discretionary} \\ \text{change}}} \qquad \underbrace{}_{\substack{\text{automatic} \\ \text{change}}}$$

However, the tax base B can change both independently and as a result of discretionary changes in tax rates. It is conventional to ignore induced effects on the tax base so far as income tax is concerned, although if the repercussions of a change on labour supply or any other relevant behaviour were known with some certainty and were not negligible it would be proper to incorporate them. The case of expenditure taxes is quite different, and Treasury estimates of revenue changes allow for the effects of budget-induced relative price changes on the composition of consumers' expenditure, since the post-budget forecast is evaluated at levels of the tax base which take account of substitution effects. Under the previous tax regime the base in year t would have

---

[1] These figures are in terms of tax payments rather than accruals, so that some adjustment is necessary to the published figures to obtain estimates of accruals (*National Institute Economic Review*, no. 65, August 1973, pp. 53-4).

Table 4.2. Discretionary tax changes,[a] 1959/60–1973/4

£ million

	1959/60	1960/1	1961/2		1962/3		1963/4	1964/5		1965/6	1966/7	
	Budget	Budget	Budget	Regulator	Budget	Other[b]	Budget	Budget	Other[c]	Budget	Budget	Regulator
Personal income taxes[d]												
Rates of tax	−61		−83		−4		−77[e]		+90	+2		+25[f]
Allowances, etc.	−105	−20	−15				−218			−10		
Total												
Current year	−135	−7	−12		−9		−221			−8		
Full year	−166	−20	−98		−4		−295		+90	−8		+25
Expenditure taxes												
On alcoholic drink	−34	−4		+31	−6			+49		+52		+38
On tobacco	+40	+40		+71	−4			+55		+75		
On hydro-carbon oils			+50	+43	+42			−2	+93		+3	+72
Purchase tax	−82			+45		−77						+40
SET[h]											+240	
Others	−12	−7	+33	+6	−18		−53	−6		+54	+17	
Total												
Current year	−103	+29	+79	+130	−1	−31	−36	+91	+32	+172	+323	+94
Full year	−128	+29	+83	+196	+14	−77	−53	+96	+93	+181	+257	+150
(Full-year out-turn)	−153	+20	+83	+191	+7	−77	−53	+78	+104	+206	+350[k]	+180
Company taxes[l]												
Income tax[d]	−63	+65	+70					+5				
Profits tax	−3		+3									
Corporation tax									+32		+75[m]	
Investment allowances	−9					−53[o]	−57[e]			+48	−35[f]	
Total												
Current year	−57	+1	+1				−3	+3			+3	
Full year	−75	+65	+73			−53	−57	+5	+32	+48	+40	
Capital taxes												
Capital gains tax										+125		
Estate duty		−2					−1				+1	
Total												
Current year		−1					−1					
Full year		−2					−1			+125	+1	
TOTAL TAXATION												
Current year	−295	+22	+68	+130	−10	−31	−261	+94	+32	+164	+326	+94
Full year	−369	+72	+58	+196	+10	−130	−406	+101	+215	+346	+298	+175
(Full year at 1970 prices)	−541	+103	+80	+268	+13	−172	−639	+130	+266	+422	+352	+206

£ million

	1967/8	1968/9		1969/70	1970/1		1971/2		1972/3	1973/4
	Budget	Budget	Regulator	Budget	Budget	Other^c	Budget	Other^b	Budget	Budget
Personal income taxes[a]										
Rates of tax	—	+100[f]	—	—	-5	-350	-38	—	-14}	-316[g]
Allowances, etc.	-4	+123	—	—	-186	—	-241	—	-1227}	—
Total										
Current year	-3	+164	—	-6	-150	-350	-184	—	-982	-316
Full year	-4	+223	—	—	-191	-350	-279	—	-1241	-316
Expenditure taxes										
On alcoholic drink		+15	+33	+10						
On tobacco		+30	+44	+45						
On hydro-carbon oils	+2	+76	+97	+52						
Purchase tax		+163	+76	+130			-245	-235	-175}	-64[i]
SET[h]	-10	+152		+12	-13[j]		-3		-175	
Others		+156								
Total										
Current year	-2	+548	+65	+212	-13		-292	-110	-141	:
Full year	-8	+592	+250	+249	-13		-248	-235	-175	-64
(Full-year out-turn)	-8	+581	+296	+236			-299	-236	-175	..
Company taxes[l]										
Income tax[d]										
Profits tax										
Corporation tax		+98		+105		-90	-105		-60	-77[n]
Investment allowances						-90		p	-205[p]	
Total										
Current year		+57		+75		-60	-55		-17	:
Full year		+98		+105		-90	-105		-265	-77
Capital taxes										
Capital gains tax				-10			-16		-15	-2
Estate duty		-1		+2	+2		-53		-123	-5
Total										
Current year		-1		-9	+6		-15		-71	-2
Full year		+11		-8	+2		-69		-138	-5
TOTAL TAXATION										
Current year	-5	+774	+65	+272	-144	-60	-546	-110	-1211	:
Full year	-12	+923	+250	+346	-202	-440	-701	-235	-1819	-462
(Full year at 1970 prices)	-14	+1027	+270	+368	-285	-430	-618	-202	-1464	-340

SOURCES: Treasury, *Financial Statement and Budget Report* (annual); NIESR estimates.

[a] Full-year budget forecasts on tax accruals unless otherwise defined. Current-year figures are for effects on tax payments in the year of intervention. For extra-budgetary interventions and changes (such as SET) operating part-way through the year, differences between current-year and full-year effects arise from both partial operation in the year and an adjustment for accruals.
[b] Changes made by Treasury Order (other than the regulator) in October 1962 and July 1971.
[c] Supplementary budgets in November 1964 and October 1970.
[d] Income tax on distributions is allocated to the personal sector.
[e] Includes abolition of schedule A tax on imputed rent of owner-occupation equivalent to −£48 million.
[f] Surcharges on surtax (1966/7) and investment income (1968/9).
[g] Effect of unifying income tax and surtax.
[h] Excludes SET allocated to public authorities' expenditure.
[i] Effect of replacing purchase tax and SET by VAT.
[j] Excludes the effects of the import surcharge (1964/5) and import deposits (1970/1).
[k] Difference from budget estimate due to discrepancies between payments and accruals of tax refunds.
[l] For income tax and corporation tax, rates are on income assessed in the financial year – usually earned in the previous-but-one calendar year. Profits tax rates were, however, set in advance on income to be earned in the financial year.
[m] Estimated effect of change to corporation tax, with double taxation of distributions.
[n] Nil included for effect of reverting to single taxation of distributions, because with the increase to 52 per cent corporation tax it did not affect overall liabilities (Treasury, *Financial Statement and Budget Report 1972–73*, p. 28).
[o] Effects expected in 1964/5.
[p] Effects of substituting investment grants for allowances (1966/7) and allowances for grants (1970/1–1972/3).

been B_t^{t-1}; post-budget it becomes B_{t}^t, where superscripts again refer to the tax function and subscripts to the year's income considered. Equation (4) then needs to be modified slightly and, as applied to an individual instrument whose base is sensitive to changes in budget parameters, it becomes:

$$\underbrace{T_t^t - T_{t-1}^{t-1}}_{\substack{\text{total} \\ \text{change}}} = \underbrace{(\mu_t B_t^t - \mu_{t-1} B_t^{t-1})}_{\substack{\text{net discretionary} \\ \text{change}}} + \underbrace{(\mu_{t-1} B_t^{t-1} - \mu_{t-1} B_{t-1}^{t-1})}_{\substack{\text{automatic} \\ \text{change}}} \qquad (5)$$

Treasury estimates of discretionary change prepared on this basis are presented for the principal expenditure taxes in table 4.2, also the income tax changes as derived from equation (4). They are defined as 'full-year budget estimates' of change and are accompanied, for the major categories of taxation, by estimates of the change occurring in the current year. For expenditure taxes the 'out-turn' effects of tax changes on a full-year basis are also given; these may be used to check the accuracy and consistency of the budget estimates themselves, as well as to provide a breakdown according to the sector affected.[1] A change in personal income tax can be attributed wholly to the personal sector, but the proportion of a change in an expenditure tax which affects consumers directly varies substantially. Duty on hydrocarbon oils and selective employment tax particularly impinge to a large extent on industrial inputs, which makes their effect on price levels and spending more diffuse than that of beer or tobacco excise duties, which fall almost wholly on consumers.

The substitution effects on the tax base which cause B_t^t to differ from B_t^{t-1} as a result of discretionary budget changes – equation (5) – may be quite complex and on them depends the efficiency of a particular tax instrument in raising extra revenue. The net discretionary change in equation (5) can actually be divided into a tax rate change and a tax base change, the second usually offsetting to some degree the *ex ante* effect on revenue of the first:

$$\underbrace{\mu_t B_t^t - \mu_{t-1} B_t^{t-1}}_{\substack{\text{net discretionary} \\ \text{change}}} = \underbrace{(\mu_t - \mu_{t-1}) \, B_t^{t-1}}_{\text{\textit{ex ante} effect}} + \underbrace{\mu_t (B_t^t - B_t^{t-1})}_{\substack{\text{substitution and} \\ \text{income effects}}} \qquad (6)$$

[1] The disaggregated tax model used for simulating the effects of tax changes over a period is based on a regression analysis of the various tax bases between 1955 and 1972. The allocation to consumption is given in table 4.8 on page 174 below. The out-turn figures also incorporate the income effects on consumption, which are usually smaller than the substitution effects. The complexities do not allow an *ex post* check of the Inland Revenue estimates of discretionary changes in allowances, but the effects of standard rate changes can be deduced from published figures of taxable income. For example, the effect of the 1970 change was put at −£350 million; the out-turn shown in table 4.8 for 1971/2 was −£380 million.

The *ex ante* effect is the rate change evaluated at unchanged forecast levels of the tax base. The substitution effect depends on how much tax changes are shifted into final prices, the 'tax content' of prices and the relevant substitution elasticities. A further effect derives from the reaction of consumers to the real income changes caused by the tax change and this may be quite substantial on occasions. The more tax changes are shifted and the higher the tax content of final prices, the greater will be the absolute and relative price change for a good arising from a given tax change, and this, together with the price elasticity, determines the substitution effect.

Table 4.3. *Effects on the tax yield from consumers' expenditure of a 'regulator' change in indirect taxes*

	Relative price elasticity[a]	Substitution effect	Income effect	Net discretionary tax change
		(percentage of *ex ante* tax change)		
Excise duties	−0·35	−20·5	−16·5	+63·0
Beer	−0·25[b]			
Spirits	−2·10[b]	−41·5	−17·0	+41·5
Wine	−0·70			
Tobacco	−0·30[c]	−14·0	−7·5	+78·5
Petrol	—	—	−38·5	+61·5
Purchase tax	−1·00	−1·0	−12·5	+86·5
Total regulator	−0·80	−15·5	−15·5	+69·0

SOURCE: NIESR estimates.

[a] Estimated from a regression analysis for the period 1956–72, using annual Customs and Excise data; see also note *c* to table 4·7.

[b] There is also a strong substitution effect between beer and spirits. The elasticity for drink as a whole is −0·95.

[c] The budget estimates in table 4.2 imply an elasticity of −0·5 in the mid-1960s and of −0·3 in later years. A value of −0·15 is quite plausible (see A. B. Atkinson and T. C. Skegg, 'Anti-smoking publicity and the demand for tobacco in the UK', *Manchester School of Economic and Social Studies*, vol. 41, September 1973).

The extent of the substitution effects will also depend on whether the instrument is used singly or in a package. Even an across-the-board tax change, such as accompanies the use of the regulator, will, however, have quite large substitution effects because of the differing tax content of the various goods affected.[1] As an illustration, table 4.3 presents the substitution effects accompanying the 1968 regulator surcharge of 10 per cent. These, the corresponding income effects on the tax base and the net discretionary effects are all expressed as percentages of the

[1] Cf. W. A. B. Hopkin and W. A. H. Godley, 'An analysis of tax changes', *National Institute Economic Review*, no. 32, May 1965, pp. 33–42.

initial *ex ante* change (as defined in equation (6)). This being 10 per cent, it can be seen that the net effect on tax receipts was 6·9 per cent,[1] with the substitution and income offsets accounting equally for the difference between this and 10 per cent. Overall, excise duties seem to have been less effective than purchase tax in raising revenue, and this is associated, in particular, with the extremely price-elastic duty base for spirits. The sensitivity of the tobacco base to the effect of duty changes seems to have led to some pessimism on the part of the authorities in the mid-1960s about the usefulness of this instrument in raising revenue and to its exclusion from the 1966 regulator. But since the relevant elasticity is −0·3, and might well be as small as −0·15, this pessimism seems to have been overdone.

Overall, as may be seen from the budget estimates and out-turns in table 4.2, indirect taxes are a fairly reliable instrument of policy, with an average range of prediction error of ± 10 per cent only in the interventions of the period. The unpredictability can, however, be as high as 20 per cent of the announced discretionary change, and this factor, together with the caveats attached to individual instruments, qualifies the verdict somewhat.

Effective rates of tax

Discretionary budget changes may be partly determined by the need to offset unwanted automatic changes in tax incidence. Or, if they are opportune, automatic changes may make discretionary interventions unnecessary. In this respect, effective rates of tax derive from a combination of automatic changes (the parameters of the tax system being taken as fixed) and statutory changes in tax rates or allowances. The relative contribution of each is summarised in chart 4·2.[2] Parts B and C

---

[1] This applies to the 80 per cent or so of the regulator surcharge falling directly on consumption; the element falling on industrial inputs and other final expenditures would not be subject to substitution and income effects.

[2] Direct and indirect taxes are here evaluated in relation to a base of aggregate personal income (Y), or consumers' expenditure, which are national income concepts and have no statutory existence. The effective rate of tax therefore changes as the ratio of the statutory to the national accounts base changes, even with an unchanged tax rate. In year t, the average rate $\overline{ar}_t^t$ will actually be $\mu_t(B_t/Y_t)$; if the statutory rates operating in year t had applied to the previous year's income, the effective rate would have been $\overline{ar}_{t-1}^t = \mu_t(B_{t-1}/Y_{t-1})$, so that the average rate would have changed automatically if the base had grown at a different rate from income. The actual average rate in the previous year being $\overline{ar}_{t-1}^{t-1} = \mu_{t-1}(B_{t-1}/Y_{t-1})$, the total change in the average rate emerges as:

$$\underbrace{\overline{ar}_t^t - \overline{ar}_{t-1}^{t-1}}_{\text{total change}} = \underbrace{(\overline{ar}_t^t - \overline{ar}_{t-1}^t)}_{\substack{\text{automatic} \\ \text{change}}} + \underbrace{(\overline{ar}_{t-1}^t - \overline{ar}_{t-1}^{t-1})}_{\substack{\text{discretionary} \\ \text{change}}}$$

In general terms, the automatic change derives from the fact that the average rate differs from the marginal rate, a measure of which is given by $\overline{MR}_t = \mu_t(\Delta B_t/\Delta Y_t)$, where

Chart 4.2. *Effective rates of personal sector taxes, 1955/6–1973/4,
with automatic and discretionary changes*

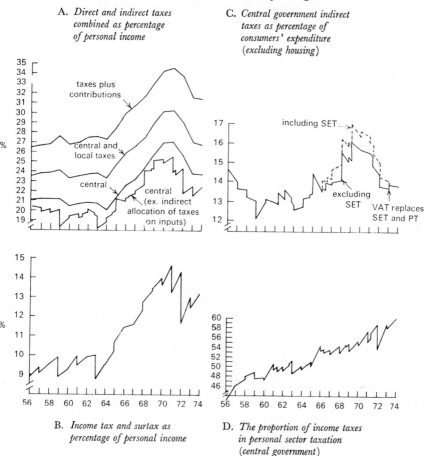

A. *Direct and indirect taxes
   combined as percentage
   of personal income*

C. *Central government indirect
   taxes as percentage of
   consumers' expenditure
   (excluding housing)*

B. *Income tax and surtax as
   percentage of personal income*

D. *The proportion of income taxes
   in personal sector taxation
   (central government)*

SOURCES: Inland Revenue, *Reports of the Commissioners* (annual); Customs and Excise, *Reports of the Commissioners* (annual); NIESR estimates.

Notes: (i) Automatic and discretionary changes are as defined on page 158; the former are shown by lateral shifts and the latter by vertical shifts. Discretionary changes are measured at the income level at the time of intervention. Automatic changes in indirect taxes include all influences on consumption not stemming directly from budgetary changes. Where changes did not take effect from the beginning of the financial year, the actual-year effect is given at the point of intervention and the residual is added to the subsequent year's change.

(ii) 'Personal income' includes national insurance contributions in measuring rates of tax plus contributions and excludes them in measuring tax rates alone.

(iii) Indirect taxes exclude the indirect allocation to consumption of taxes on industrial inputs and local authority rates.

(iv) Horizontal scales refer to financial years ending 31 March (e.g. '74' indicates the end of 1973/4).

show the aggregate average or effective rates of tax on personal income and consumers' expenditure respectively; they are summed and referred to personal income in Part A and table 4.4; the relative movements in each are reflected in the changing mix of direct and indirect taxes illustrated in part D.

Table 4.4. *Changes in the average rate of tax (direct and indirect) on total personal income,[a] 1955/6–1973/4*

Percentages

	Discretionary change	Automatic change	Total change
Budget 1955/6 to October 1964	−2·98	+2·51	−0·47
Budget Nov. 1964 to end-1970/1	+4·45	+1·50	+5·95
Budget 1971/2 to end-1973/4[b]	−5·34	+2·23	−3·11
Budget 1955/6 to end-1973/4	−3·87	+6·24	+2·37

SOURCES: Inland Revenue, *Report of the Commissioners* (annual); Customs and Excise, *Report of the Commissioners* (annual).

[a] Excludes rates and indirect allocation to consumption from taxes on industrial inputs.

[b] Includes changes announced in October 1970 effective from 1971/2.

The average rate of personal income tax has been influenced by the persistent upward bias imparted by rising incomes under a progressive rate structure (as shown in chart 4.1). This was counteracted up to 1963/4 by discretionary reductions, so that the effective rate remained fairly steady at around 9·5 per cent,[1] but thereafter there was a strong and consistent rise until the end of 1970/1, when the rate reached 14·7 per cent. Of this increase of 5·2 per cent, a small amount (0·6 per cent) was attributable to budget changes, while the bulk was due to automatic changes in yield. In the second Conservative period attempts were made to bring the rate down, but three quarters of the substantial discretionary reductions of 4·5 per cent merely offset the increasing automatic buoyancy of income tax revenue, so that the effective rate of 12·2 per cent in 1973/4 still represented a significant increase over the beginning of the period.

The ratio of central government indirect taxes to consumers' expenditure (chart 4.2C) has the opposite pattern: increases have been effected

---

$\Delta B_t = B_t - B_{t-1}$ and $\Delta Y_t = Y_t - Y_{t-1}$. The marginal rate can differ from the average because of a progressive rate structure, or because the tax base changes at a different rate from income. The automatic changes in the average rate discussed in the text can thus be understood as:

$$\overline{ar}_t^t - \overline{ar}_{t-1}^t = (\overline{MR}_t - \overline{ar}_{t-1}^t)\,(\Delta Y_t / Y_t)$$

[1] See chart 4.2B. The effective rate is here calculated with respect to personal income as defined in the national accounts (see note (ii) to chart 4.2).

by discretionary action and decreases (apart from purchase tax) have largely resulted from the fact that the quantum base of excise duties fails to keep pace with inflation. The period 1956/7–1964/5 saw the overall rate fall slightly from 14 to about 13 per cent of consumer spending.[1] Between 1964/5 and 1970/1, however, the effective rate increased emphatically, reaching 15·5 per cent, with oil duty, purchase tax and selective employment tax the principal instruments (see table 4.2).

The effects of automatic factors on the combined (direct and indirect) effective rate of tax (chart 4.2A) have been less consistent, chiefly because the buoyancy characteristics of the two types of taxation were partially offsetting, but the effects have almost always been fairly consistently positive and were significantly so overall (table 4.4). They explain the net increase in the tax rate between the late 1950s and 1973/4, when central government taxes accounted directly for about $22\frac{1}{2}$ per cent of personal income. With indirect taxes on inputs into consumption and local rates, the tax take was 27 per cent; with national insurance contributions it was almost 32 per cent. At the same time the proportion of personal taxation derived from income taxes rose from 45 to 60 per cent (chart 4.2D), the consistency of this movement being remarkable, in that automatic biases making for greater dependence on income taxes (the lateral upward movements) were accompanied, but only partially offset, by a discretionary bias towards expenditure taxes (the vertical downward shifts). This significant change in the tax-mix seems to have been at odds with prevailing ideas about the relative merits of direct and indirect taxes.

It was shown in the Richardson Report that the burden of company taxation – as expressed in the effective rate of tax on the income of that sector – had fallen between the mid-1950s and early 1960s despite statutory increases in rates of profits tax;[2] the improvement in capital allowances (especially the introduction of investment allowances in 1954), together with the increase in investment, was largely responsible. Chart 4.3 shows, however, that this trend ceased to operate in the 1960s, despite the increase in investment allowances at the end of 1962 and notwithstanding the switch to investment grants in 1966. The average rate of United Kingdom tax on gross company income (including that on distributions)[3] increased from 23·5 per cent to a peak of

---

[1] This excludes local authority rates and the indirect allocation to consumption from taxes on industrial inputs. Housing expenditure, which bears rates, is correspondingly excluded from consumer spending.

[2] Inland Revenue, *Report of the Committee on Turnover Taxation*, pp. 48–50.

[3] The effective rate is defined in terms of *accruals*, that is taxes levied on income earned during the year irrespective of when they are paid. This broadly corresponds to the national accounts definition, except that that includes additions to reserves made according to anti-

Chart 4.3. *Effective rates of tax on company income, 1959–73*

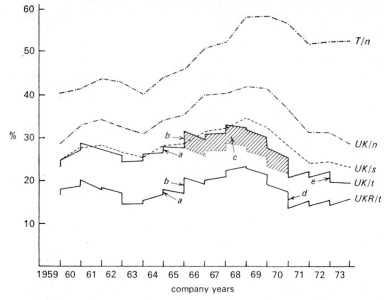

company years

SOURCES: CSO, *National Income and Expenditure 1965–75*; Inland Revenue, *Inland Revenue Statistics* (annual); NIESR calculations.

Notes: Automatic changes shown by lateral shifts and discretionary changes by vertical shifts; the latter are shown at the beginning of the company year in which they started, and any difference between actual and full-year effects at the beginning of the next year.

T = total taxation: United Kingdom accruals (payments plus addition to reserves), with adjustments for retrospective tax changes, and overseas taxes on a payments basis.

UK = United Kingdom taxes as in T, including those on distributions, at standard rate.

UKR = United Kingdom taxes as in T, excluding those on distributions, at standard rate.

t = tax base of total company income net of interest payments.

s = tax base as t less stock appreciation.

n = tax base as s less capital consumption.

a = effect of changing to corporation tax, with double taxation of distributions (see footnote 1, page 165).

b = effect of abolishing investment allowances.

c = estimated accrued value of investment grants, calculated on an 18-month lag in payment, less the effect on depreciation allowances.

d = effect of changing back to investment allowances.

e = change including the effect of reducing the standard rate of tax from 0·3875 to 0·3.

---

cipated tax rates (the rate of corporation tax being fixed retrospectively), whereas here the tax yield refers to actual not expected liabilities. Overseas taxes are given in payment terms. Company income is net of interest payments (debenture and loan interest, cooperative society dividends and interest, building society interest and other interest paid by banks etc. – all as defined in table 5.1 of CSO, *National Income and Expenditure 1965–75*, London, HMSO, 1976). Correspondingly, the income tax on such interest deducted at source is netted out from company tax liabilities.

28 per cent in 1968 (a figure which nets out the tax equivalent of investment grants from the actual effective rate of 32·5 per cent, as shown by the shaded area in the chart). Net of income tax on distributions, the rate on gross profits rose from 16·5 to 23 per cent, while, if taxes paid abroad are taken into account, the aggregate effective tax rate rose from 33 to 38·5 per cent. Discretionary budget changes – increases in the rate of profits tax (in April 1960 and 1961), a rise in the standard rate of income tax (affecting 1964 company income), the net effect of switching to corporation tax with double taxation of distributions (effective from 1966/7)[1] and the increases in the rate of corporation tax which followed devaluation – wholly accounted for this extra burden. The net effect of automatic changes on the company tax rate seems to have been negative, though fluctuating with the rate of investment and tending, with a falling distribution ratio, to become increasingly negative towards the end of the decade.[2]

This and the retrospective reductions in statutory rates introduced in October 1970 and April 1971 caused the effective rate to fall between 1968 and 1970; the downward momentum was kept up by a further series of discretionary measures – the dismantling of the investment grant system, leading to the introduction of free depreciation in 1972/3; the reduction in the standard rate of income tax in 1971/2 and the further reduction in 1973/4 (from 0·3875 to 0·30); finally, the return to equal treatment of distributed and retained profits, also in 1973/4.[3] These later changes seem, however, to have been partly offset by a tendency to greater buoyancy, mainly because investment was failing to keep pace with gross company income, while stock appreciation (part of the base for company taxation) was forming an increasing proportion of gross profits.[4] The result, as table 4.5 shows, was that United Kingdom taxation formed a lower proportion of gross company income in 1973 than in 1959 (19 per cent including tax on distribu-

[1] It was announced in the 1965 budget that the intention was not to increase the burden of tax but to redistribute it; for this purpose a 35 per cent corporation tax was thought to suffice (House of Commons, *Hansard*, 6 April 1965, col. 257). Ideas about the correct equivalent rate were subsequently revised upwards, but the actual rate of 40 per cent probably still represented a 1½ per cent increase in overall effective incidence (ibid. 3 May 1966, cols. 1449–50).

[2] A feature of the two-tier tax on distributions operating between 1965 and 1972 is that the buoyancy of the tax is a function of the distribution ratio: a fall in the ratio leads, *ceteris paribus*, to negative buoyancy.

[3] The effect of reducing the standard rate was to reduce tax liabilities on distributions (and with it total liabilities) by £160 million, though part of this was recouped by the 15 per cent surcharge on investment income over £2000. The effect of eliminating double taxation was neutral, since the revenue loss was recovered by the change from 40 to 52 per cent in the rate of corporation tax.

[4] A measure of tax relief on stock appreciation was introduced in the November 1975 supplementary budget.

Table 4.5. *Effective rates of company taxation,[a] 1959 and 1973*

Percentages

	United Kingdom tax		Total (including overseas)
	Excluding tax on distributions[b]	Including tax on distributions[b]	
On gross income[c]			
1959	16·5	23·5	33·0
1973	15·5	19·0	35·0
On gross income less stock appreciation			
1959	16·5	24·0	33·5
1973	18·5	23·0	42·0
On gross income less stock appreciation and capital consumption			
1959	20·0	28·5	40·5
1973	23·0	28·5	52·5
Change 1959–73			
Discretionary	+ *1·5*	− *1·5*	− *1·5*
Automatic	+ *1·5*	+ *1·5*	+ *13·5*
Total	+ *3·0*	—	+ *12·0*

SOURCES: CSO, *National Income and Expenditure 1965–75*; Inland Revenue, *Inland Revenue Statistics* (annual); NIESR estimates.

[a] United Kingdom accruals, overseas payments (see text).
[b] At the standard rate of income tax.   [c] Net of interest payments.

tions, $15\frac{1}{2}$ per cent without). But this reduction can be seen as partly illusory by substituting true economic profit – the maximum level of payments which a company could make while maintaining its ability to produce the same level of goods and services – for the conventional accounting definition;[1] that is, company income should be net of stock appreciation and capital consumption at replacement cost. As can be seen from table 4.5, United Kingdom effective rates in relation to profits net of stock appreciation were only slightly lower in 1973 than in 1959; netting out capital consumption as well, the effective rate of United Kingdom tax was the same in both years. However, the effective tax burden on companies, including tax paid abroad and offset against corporation tax (double taxation relief), increased quite emphatically from 40·5 to 52·5 per cent and this is perhaps the most accurate indicator available.[2] Moreover, since the net effect of discretionary

[1] See M. A. King, 'The United Kingdom profits crisis: myth or reality?', *Economic Journal*, vol. 85, March 1975, pp. 35–7.
[2] It is not strictly possible to derive the effective rate of taxation on United Kingdom *domestic* income because of lack of data on the amount of United Kingdom tax borne by

changes was slightly beneficial, this increase occurred automatically as a result of a slower investment trend and stock appreciation – adverse influences which would have caused the United Kingdom effective rate to rise were it not for the growing element of double taxation relief. The net automatic changes in the United Kingdom effective rates were small, so that fiscal drag as applied to the buoyancy of United Kingdom revenue was negligible; as applied to company tax liabilities the effect was much more marked.

Marginal rates of tax and built-in flexibility

A positive marginal rate of tax damps the multiplier and reduces the amplitude of the economy's response to exogenous demand disturbances. If tax revenue fluctuates positively with income, the system is said to contain 'built-in flexibility', which is usually measured by the marginal rate of tax – that is, the amount of any change in income which adds to or subtracts from government revenue rather than personal disposable income. The extent to which this built-in flexibility also constitutes built-in stability depends upon the damping effect which the marginal rate has through its inclusion in the multiplier.[1] Where an increase in wages and prices is related to increased activity, built-in stability may also imply greater price stability, but here it is necessary to consider how far built-in flexibility applies to movements in money incomes which are offset by price rises ('inflationary' income movements). Estimates of the marginal rates of both direct and indirect taxes on personal incomes are given separately for movements in real income and 'inflationary' income in table 4.6.

The concept already developed of the automatic change in revenue in any particular year provides the first means of estimating marginal rates of tax. The automatic change in tax yield divided by the change in income which accompanies it is the simplest definition of a marginal rate,[2] but it is subject to two deficiencies. First, such a rate has no

income earned abroad. However, on the assumption that no United Kingdom taxes were charged on such income, then the effective tax rate (including taxes on distributions) on domestic income net of stock appreciation and capital consumption would have risen in similar proportion to the third column of table 4.5 – from 38.5 per cent in 1959 to 54.5 per cent in 1973. The effective rates of tax on United Kingdom manufacturing companies may, however, have behaved somewhat differently, the rate at the end of the period probably lying in the range 25–30 per cent (ibid. p. 46).

[1] Built-in stability is measured by the fraction of the change in income which is prevented by the existence of built-in flexibility (see, inter alia, R. A. Musgrave and M. H. Miller, 'Built-in flexibility', American Economic Review, vol. 38, March 1948, and, in a British context, A. T. Peacock and G. K. Shaw, The Economic Theory of Fiscal Policy, London, Allen & Unwin, 1971, pp. 115 et seq.; E. T. Balopoulos, Fiscal Policy Models of the British Economy, Amsterdam, North-Holland, 1967).

[2] Following the methodology described above: $MR_t^i = (\mu_t \Delta B_t / \Delta B_t)(\Delta B_t / \Delta Y_t)$. In this formulation built-in flexibility is the product of two factors – the flexibility of the tax base and

Table 4.6. *Marginal rates of tax,*[a] *1959/60–1973/4*

Percentages

	Income tax rates on personal income[b]			Expenditure tax rates on disposable income[c]		Total personal tax rates[d] on personal income[b]		Tax plus NI rates on total personal income[e]	
	'Average' for year	Year-beginning	Year-end	Real income	'Inflationary' income	Real income	'Inflationary' income	Real income	'Inflationary' income
1959/60	17·0	16·5	17·3	12·7	5·2	27·9	21·6	28·1	21·8
1960/1	18·0	17·3	18·4	12·5	4·9	28·6	22·4	28·8	22·6
1961/2	18·0	17·6	18·5	12·5	4·9	28·6	22·3	29·2	23·0
1962/3	13·5	17·7	18·6	12·2	4·8	28·6	22·6	29·5	23·4
1963/4	18·0	17·5	18·0	12·5	4·8	28·2	22·5	29·7	23·4
1964/5	18·5	18·0	18·7	13·6	5·1	29·9	22·8	30·8	23·8
1965/6	20·0	19·4	20·9	14·3	5·1	32·2	24·9	33·1	25·9
1966/7	17·5	19·9	20·3	14·7	5·2	32·1	24·5	33·2	25·5
1967/8	21·5	20·2	21·2	15·6	5·3	33·6	25·4	34·6	26·6
1968/9	22·0	21·3	22·2	16·8	5·7	35·4	26·6	36·3	27·7
1969/70	23·0	22·0	22·9[f]	17·9	6·1	36·8	27·6	37·9	28·8
1970/1	25·0	23·0	25·1	17·7	6·2	38·4	29·5	39·7	31·0
1971/2	23·0	22·9	24·9	16·9	5·8	37·6	29·0	39·1	30·7
1972/3	23·5	21·7	23·4	16·2	5·4	35·8	27·5	37·4	29·6
1973/4	23·0	20·5	22·4	15·7	5·9	34·6	26·9	36·7	29·4

SOURCES: Inland Revenue, *Survey of Personal Incomes 1969–70*, London, HMSO, 1972; CSO, *Economic Trends*, no. 264, October 1975 and *National Income and Expenditure 1964–74*, tables 21–7; NIESR estimates.

[a] Tax accruals not including capital gains tax.

[b] Personal income as defined in the national accounts, including the income of non-profit-making bodies and life and superannuation funds, but excluding contributions to national insurance, etc.

[c] Personal income less accrued income taxes, but including the indirect allocations to consumption from expenditure taxes on industrial inputs.

[d] The combined marginal rate is $\overline{mr} + (1 - \overline{mr})\overline{mr}^*$, where $\overline{mr}$ is the marginal rate of income tax and $\overline{mr}^*$ the marginal rate of expenditure tax, the base for which has to be adjusted by $(1 - \overline{mr})$ to make it equivalent to personal income.

[e] As personal income, but including contributions to national insurance, etc.

[f] For 1969/70 for example, this rate is the weighted average of the following marginal rates on different categories of income: employment income, 24·6 per cent; self-employment income, 25·3 per cent; current grants, 5·1 per cent; other personal income (excluding imputed rents), 36·8 per cent. Within this last category, the marginal rate on dividends received by persons was 52·5 per cent, on rental income 41·75 per cent and on occupational pensions 8·05 per cent.

the statutory marginal rate of tax (see L. Cohen, 'An empirical measurement of the built-in flexibility of the individual income tax', *American Economic Association Papers and Proceedings*, vol. 49, May 1959, pp. 532–41; J. A. Pechman, 'Yield of the individual income tax during a recession' in National Bureau of Economic Research, *Policies to Combat Depression*, Princeton University Press, 1956, pp. 123–48).

operational significance: for instance, for an individual taxpayer who crosses the 30 per cent threshold half way through the year, his marginal rate at the beginning would have been zero and at the end 30 per cent, whereas expressing the annual change in his tax liabilities as a ratio of his change in income would give a marginal rate of 15 per cent. The latter could be described as his average marginal rate for the year and, in similar vein, this is how the first column of table 4.6 should be interpreted for the economy as a whole; the rates actually operative at the beginnings and ends of financial years would be rather different. The second deficiency relates particularly to indirect taxes, the yield of which can fluctuate for a number of reasons beside their relationship to income and still be reflected in the automatic change over the year. These fluctuations make the marginal rates erratic; they cannot, in any case, be interpreted strictly in terms of built-in flexibility, which is an income-related concept;[1] average marginal rates are therefore not given for indirect taxes in the table.

The problems of estimating the marginal rates of income and expenditure taxes operating at any particular time are principally those of aggregation (since statutory rates are known for individuals and commodities) and (particularly for indirect taxes) the specification of the relationship between the tax base and the national accounts definition of personal income. For income tax the required aggregate marginal rates can be derived from Inland Revenue statistics as weighted averages of the rates for individuals, which is how the estimates in table 4.6 were generated. The Inland Revenue's annual *Survey of Personal Incomes* collects tax and income data by income range; within each range the average tax paid per person (x_i) is T_i/N_i (where T_i is the total tax paid and N_i the number of tax units in income bracket i). The average effective rate is also immediately apparent as $(T_i/N_i)/(Y_i/N_i) = T_i/Y_i$, but the marginal rate has to be derived by a regression analysis of the average tax paid per person against the average income per person: $x_i = f(y_i)$.[2] Since such a function only operates when the parameters of the tax system are unchanged, a series of functions must be calculated,

[1] Automatic changes in yields of expenditure taxes can be due to factors such as hire purchase restrictions or the impact of anti-smoking campaigns. Such effects introduce an apparent randomness into the marginal relationship between expenditure taxes and personal income, and *seemingly* impair the built-in stability of the system (see OECD, *Fiscal Policy for a Balanced Economy*, p. 67).

[2] This relationship is a proxy for the progressive structure of the income tax system and on estimation yields a marginal rate rising with income: $x_i = \alpha + \beta_1 y_i + \beta_2 y_i^2 + \beta_3 y_i^3 + \beta_4 y_i^4$, where $x_i = T_i/N_i$ and $y_i = Y_i/N_i$. The marginal rate is then

$$\hat{mr}_i = \beta_1 + 2\beta_2 y_i + 3\beta_3 y_i^2 + 4\beta_4 y_i^3$$

and the aggregate marginal rate can be deduced as

$$\overline{mr} = \Sigma_{i=1}^n \hat{mr}_i w_i$$

where $w_i = Y_i/\Sigma_{i=1}^n Y_i$ (see R. W. R. Price, 'Some aspects of the progressive income tax structure in the UK', *National Economic Institute Review*, no. 65, August 1973, pp. 52–63).

yielding a tax schedule and a set of income-class marginal rates, $f'_t(y_{it})$, for each budgetary year. The rates given in the third column of table 4.6 are then calculated by weighting these according to the proportion of income accruing to each income class. Each tax function thus generates a marginal rate of tax applicable to the level of personal income during its year of operation; specifically, since income is to be thought of as a flow, a rate applicable to the level of income reached at the *end* of that year. Applying the same function to the level of income at the beginning of the year (the end of the previous year), as in the second column, the difference between the two estimates will be the automatic change in the marginal rate, and the two estimates should approximately bracket the average marginal rate for the year given in the first column (which they do in most cases[1]). The discretionary change in the marginal rate in any year is given by the difference between the figure in the second column and the previous year's figure in the third column. [2]

In the light of the large differences between the marginal rates of tax on different kinds of income (as noted in the table for 1969/70),[3] it might be expected that changes in the distribution of income as between sources would contribute to instability in the aggregate marginal rate. In fact there is a high degree of consistency in the pattern of its development over time; like the average rate of income tax, the marginal rate was kept fairly steady by discretionary tax reductions, at 17–18 per cent during the late 1950s and early 1960s; it was allowed to rise to 25 per cent in 1970/1, and from then until 1973/4 its tendency to increase automatically was more than offset by discretionary tax cuts. At the end of the period the rate was just over 22 per cent, which still represented a significant increase.

Marginal rates of income tax relate to both real and inflationary income because tax rates are set in money terms. This is not so for

---

[1] The major exceptions are 1962/3 and 1966/7. In terms of automatic changes in the tax yield, the differences involved are, respectively, £60 million (2·7 per cent of the tax yield) and £30 million (0·9 per cent of the tax yield).

[2] These relationships can be clarified by denoting end-year estimates as

$$\overline{mr}^t_i = \Sigma^n_{i-1}[f'_i(y_{it})\ w_{it}]$$

and beginning-year estimates as $\overline{mr}^t_{i-1} = \Sigma^n_{i-1}[f'_i(y_{i\overline{i-1}})\ w_{it}]$, where the subscript denotes the year's income taken and the superscript the tax function used. The year-to-year changes in the third column can then be broken up into:

$$\underbrace{\overline{mr}^t_i - \overline{mr}^{t-1}_{i-1}}_{\text{total}} = \underbrace{(\overline{mr}^t_i - \overline{mr}^t_{i-1})}_{\text{automatic}} + \underbrace{(\overline{mr}^t_{i-1} - \overline{mr}^{t-1}_{i-1})}_{\text{discretionary}}$$

Since the two estimates used to calculate the automatic change are based on the same income weights (and therefore imply a fixed distribution of income), it is perhaps interesting that there have not been more occasions on which they have not bracketed the average marginal rate.

[3] The differences are the result partly of different tax rates – on investment income for example – partly of the pattern of exemptions and partly of the size of incomes within each category.

expenditure taxes, where some rates are set in quantum terms and where, at an aggregate level, improved living standards have markedly different effects on spending patterns from income changes which merely offset increases in the cost of living. Aggregate marginal rates of total taxation on consumer spending are therefore presented in both real and 'inflationary' terms in table 4.6;[1] the figures are derived from regression analysis of the individual tax bases;[2] they show a stable and consistent increase in the built-in flexibility of the indirect tax structure. Some elements of tax on consumers' expenditure may be fairly income-inelastic, but the marginal rate with respect to real disposable income rose from 12·7 per cent in 1959/60 to 15·7 in 1973/4, as consumption patterns changed towards income-elastic and highly taxed goods. Combined with the marginal rate of personal income tax, the aggregate marginal rate of tax on real personal income increased steadily from under 28 per cent to about 38½ per cent in 1970/1, three quarters of the increase being due to income tax; budgetary changes subsequently brought the rate down to about 35 per cent in 1973/4. Taking national insurance contributions into account,[3] the marginal rate of all deductions from real personal income also increased substantially, from 28 to nearly 37 per cent. A change of this order, most of which can be traced to underlying automatic increases, represents a significant restructuring of the built-in properties of the system; like the effective rates of income tax and indirect tax, and the tax-mix, the structure of marginal rates has developed automatically rather than by design.

Much the same process occurred in the marginal tax rates applicable to 'inflationary' income changes, though here the increase was almost wholly due to income tax. Despite the introduction of VAT, the marginal rate for indirect taxes rose only from 5–5½ per cent at the beginning of the period to 6 per cent at the end. Including national insurance contributions, the total rate of tax on 'inflationary' income changes was just over 29 per cent in 1973/4 compared with 22 per cent in 1959/60.

Income elasticities and fiscal drag

While built-in flexibility is defined in terms of the marginal rate of tax, the concept of fiscal drag has come to be defined in Britain in terms of the change in the average rate which takes place as incomes rise. This

---

[1] These estimates refer to either central government or public authority taxation, since local authority rates have a zero marginal relationship with respect to both real and money income.

[2] Since the relationships of the individual tax bases have been specified mainly in constant elasticity form, the procedure was to weight these elasticities (see below page 173) in order to create an aggregate expenditure tax elasticity $(\bar{e}_t)$ and to derive the marginal rate as a product of the elasticity and the average rate: $\overline{mr}_t = \bar{e}_t \bar{ar}_t$. Measured at the levels of income obtaining *in* the year, the rates are calculated on the same income basis as the third column of the table. [3] See note 1, page 174.

can be thought of in terms of the difference between the marginal rate of tax and the average rate, since this determines the 'elasticity' of the tax yield – the proportionate change in taxes relative to a proportionate change in income. To the extent that this elasticity exceeds unity, an increase in (real or money) incomes will generate an increase in the average rate of tax and fiscal drag is produced.[1]

In the presence of fiscal drag, calculations of the full-employment budget balance would show that in a growing economy the deficit (surplus) was falling (rising) as a proportion of national income, even if the growth of public expenditure was keeping pace with the underlying growth rate of the economy.[2] If fiscal drag is associated with inflationary increases in money incomes (real incomes being constant) the full-employment budget deficit (surplus) will tend to fall (rise) as a proportion of income, causing real changes in the balance.[3] When fiscal policy is measured by changes in the full-employment budget deficit, therefore, fiscal drag is the agent of automatic fiscal tightening in the context of income growth, while negative drag (which emerges when the tax elasticity is below unity) causes automatic fiscal relaxation. The measurement of fiscal drag is therefore of obvious and direct significance to the analysis of fiscal policy.

Since the presence of fiscal drag is identified by tax yield elasticities in excess of unity, this propensity can be shown, as in table 4.7, by computing the relevant elasticities; these are derived in the same way as the marginal rates in table 4.6 and correspond to them. Estimates of fiscal drag in value terms are given in table 4.8.

It emerges that the income elasticity of the income tax yield has fluctuated between 1·6 and 1·9, with a tendency to decline as incomes rise partly accountable (together with the introduction of lower

---

[1] That is, where the elasticity of the tax yield ($\bar{e}$) at any point in time is $\overline{mr}/\overline{ar}$, the proportionate change in the average rate of tax from a proportionate change in incomes will be $(\overline{dar}/\overline{ar})/(dY/Y) = \overline{mr}/\overline{ar} - 1$.

[2] Where national income grows at a constant longer-run rate, aggregate demand must keep pace if unemployment is not to occur, and net public demand (revenue less expenditure) must keep pace for the stance of stabilisation policy to remain unchanged. For the same reason, a neutral growth path of public receipts may be taken as one which maintains proportionality with potential national income. Ultimately, however, fiscal drag has to be measured with reference to the neutrality rules governing the longer-run planning of public expenditure (which are described in chapter 3), so that, from a balanced budget position, net fiscal drag would occur if $\bar{e} > \bar{g}$, where $\bar{g}$ is the ratio of the longer-run growth of public expenditure to the longer-run growth of national income; only if this was unity would fiscal drag be the same in gross and net terms. For a further discussion of fiscal drag in the context of expenditure plans, see below, page 184, and A. S. Blinder and R. M. Solow, 'Analytical foundations of fiscal policy' in *The Economics of Public Finance*, Washington (DC), Brookings Institution, 1974, p. 19.

[3] Tax receipts may rise in proportion to the price level without causing real tax rates to change; the non-proportional element in taxation will, however, have consequences for real incomes (ibid. p. 20 and page 179 below).

Table 4.7. *Income elasticities of personal sector taxes,[a] 1959/60–1973/4*

Ratios

	Income taxes[b]	Expenditure taxes[c]		Total personal taxation[b]		
		Real income	'Inflationary' income	Real income	'Inflationary' income	Average[d]
1959/60	1·87	1·03	0·42	1·36[e]	1·05[e]	1·35
1960/1	1·85	1·04	0·41	1·38	1·08	1·28
1961/2	1·84	1·03	0·40	1·37	1·07	1·09
1962/3	1·86	1·02	0·40	1·37	1·09	1·20
1963/4	1·89	1·06	0·41	1·39	1·09	1·31
1964/5	1·84	1·09	0·40	1·40	1·07	1·19
1965/6	1·81	1·13	0·40	1·42	1·10	1·17
1966/7	1·75	1·12	0·39	1·38	1·05	0·86
1967/8	1·72	1·15	0·39	1·39	1·05	1·22
1968/9	1·66	1·17	0·40	1·37	1·03	1·07
1969/70	1·63	1·19	0·40	1·37	1·02	1·07
1970/1	1·71	1·22	0·42	1·42	1·09	1·18
1971/2	1·74	1·26	0·42	1·45	1·12	1·18
1972/3	1·80	1·29	0·43	1·50	1·15	1·31
1973/4	1·67	1·31	0·48	1·45[e]	1·13[e]	1·18

SOURCE: NIESR estimates.

[a] Accruals of central government taxes, not including capital gains tax.

[b] With respect to personal income as defined in note b to table 4.6.

[c] With respect to disposable income as defined in note c to table 4.6. Elasticities for individual expenditure taxes are calculated in R. W. R. Price, 'A model of the indirect tax system in the UK, 1956–72' (unpublished NIESR working paper), 1977.

[d] The responsiveness of the tax yield to total (real and 'inflationary') income changes during the year.

[e] Elasticities of total taxes including national insurance contributions with respect to total personal income (see note e to table 4.6) were as follows:

	Central government		Total public authority	
	Real income	'Inflationary' income	Real income	'Inflationary' income
1959/60	1·17	0·90	1·05	0·81
1973/4	1·28	1·02	1·16	0·92

statutory rates) for the 1973/4 elasticity being at the lower end of this range. Indirect taxes, on the other hand, have tended to become more buoyant as spending patterns have changed in favour of goods with a high tax incidence and high income elasticity of demand, like petrol, wines and spirits, and durables. The real income elasticity applicable to the excise yield rose from only 0·87 at the beginning to 1·53 at the end of the period and, while statutory reductions in tax rates on income-elastic goods brought down the elasticity of purchase tax quite

Table 4.8. *The effects of fiscal drag and discretionary tax changes on personal sector taxes,[a] 1959/60–1973/4*

£ million

	Income taxes		Expenditure taxes			Total personal taxation		
	Discretionary change	Fiscal drag	Discretionary change[b]	Fiscal drag	Other effects[c]	Discretionary change	Fiscal drag	Total automatic effects[d]
1959/60	−166	+90	−129	−10	+125	−295	+80	+205
1960/1	−20	+140	+20	−35	−85	—	+105	+20
1961/2	−98	+90	+149	−60	−40	+51	+30	−10
1962/3	−4	+110	+59	−60	−45	+55	+50	+5
1963/4	−295	+140	−39	−35	+65	−334	+105	+170
1964/5	—	+175	+121	−90	+60	+121	+85	+145
1965/6	−8	+225	+216	−115	−145	+208	+110	−35
1966/7	+25	+55	+329	−90	+110	+354	−35	+75
1967/8	−4	+210	+58	−80	+40	+54	+130	+170
1968/9	+223	+200	+517	−160	−150	+740	+40	−110
1969/70	—	+225	+335	−175	+5	+335	+50	+55
1970/1	−191	+435	−7	−210	+75	−198	+225	+300
1971/2	−659	+485	−345	−255	+90	−1004	+230	+320
1972/3	−1241	+690	−218	−160	—	−1459	+530	+530
1973/4	−316	+760	−64	−355	—	−380	+405	+405

SOURCES: Treasury, *Financial Statement and Budget Report* (annual); NIESR estimates.

[a] Full-year effects on tax accruals.

[b] Extra-budgetary changes apportioned between the year of intervention and the following year.

[c] Effects stemming from automatic changes in effective rates which are not attributable to income changes.

[d] Other effects on expenditure taxes plus total fiscal drag.

markedly (from 1·32 to 1·17), there was a continuous trend towards a higher overall elasticity of indirect taxes – from just above unity to 1·3. Together with the growing importance of income taxes in the tax-mix, this accounted for an increase in the real income buoyancy of overall personal taxation from an elasticity of 1·36 in 1959/60 to about 1·45 in the early 1970s. On the other hand, local rates and the flat-rate element in national insurance contributions have, in principle, an elasticity of zero with respect to income.[1] The downward bias that this seemingly imparts to overall fiscal drag is, however, somewhat illusory, for both forms of tax are regularly increased in line with prospective

[1] Apart from the responsiveness of flat-rate contributions to employment, the relationship to national income has depended on graduated contributions, introduced in April 1961. These have made up an increasing proportion of the whole, being 13 per cent in 1961/2 and 48 per cent in 1973/4; from April 1975 the whole system became earnings-related. As can be seen, the overall elasticity has risen with the proportion of graduated in total contributions.

expenditure, which can be regarded as having some relationship to income, though not a rigid one.

The 'inflationary' income buoyancy of the revenue system is quite different from its real income buoyancy. Excise yields, which react to inflation only through its effects on consumer spending patterns, maintained a fairly constant elasticity of 0·2,[1] and the overall buoyancy of expenditure taxes fluctuated narrowly around 0·4 until the introduction of VAT raised it nearer to 0·5. Any increase in buoyancy in personal taxes overall (1·13 at the end compared with 1·05 at the beginning of the period) is due to this and the increasing incidence of progressive income tax.

Together, personal income and expenditure taxes displayed an emphatically positive real income drag and an only slightly positive inflationary income drag. The extent of the bias in terms of receipts depends both on the rate of change in money incomes and on the real and inflationary composition of this change. The estimates in table 4.8 measure the aggregate annual effects on the tax yield of both real and inflationary income movements,[2] while the 'average' column in table 4.7 shows the implied overall elasticity of tax receipts with respect to total 'money' income changes – in effect, an average of the real and inflationary income elasticities weighted by the proportions of real and inflationary income changes in the total change for the year. As can be seen from comparing the fiscal drag estimates with the effects of discretionary tax changes, the former have made an important contribution to budgetary stance throughout the period, the revenue gain in the 1960s being between £30 and £130 million, with overall revenue elasticities between 1·07 and 1·35 (last column, table 4.7).[3] The indirect tax base has, however, behaved rather erratically from year to year due to influences not systematically related to income, and these 'other effects' in table 4.8 have to be set against fiscal drag proper. In the early 1970s – due to increasing inflation and the gradual rise in tax elasticities – the contribution of fiscal drag to the Exchequer rose to about £700 million from income taxes and between £400 and £500 million in total (net of the negative drag associated with indirect taxes). Budgetary policy had thus to offset a substantial – and growing – bias

[1] Prices of goods subject to specific duties rise more slowly than the general price level and so their relative price falls; their consumption therefore increases (cf. table 4.3) and excise yields expand by about a fifth of the rate of inflation.

[2] The calculations are made on the same basis as the automatic changes in average rates defined in footnote 2, page 160; i.e. fiscal drag (£ million) = $(\overline{ar}_t - \overline{ar}_{t-1}) Y_t$. Since fiscal drag is defined as a function of income, this leaves the effects of other factors on the average rate of tax, which are particularly important in the case of indirect taxes (table 4.8).

[3] Because the inflationary buoyancy of the revenue was not enough to offset the effects of the fall in real income in 1966/7, the amount of drag accruing in that year was (exceptionally) negative and the average elasticity of the revenue less than unity.

in the tax system before it could achieve a net reduction in effective tax rates.

Distributional effects of fiscal drag

Fiscal drag has important consequences for the distribution of the tax burden and of post-tax incomes. This section analyses these effects for income tax, which has been the centre of greatest controversy.

A progressive tax system implies that the tax burden is concentrated on higher income earners, so that post-tax incomes are more equally dispersed than pre-tax ones. Chart 4.4 tests the income tax system for these attributes. It shows, first, cumulative percentages of the income tax burden (plotted vertically) ranked against cumulative percentages of pre-tax income; a proportional tax system would give a curve linking the two along the diagonal, while the more progressive the system the more the curve is pushed to the right.[1] The chart shows, for example, that in 1973/4 the lower 50 per cent of incomes yielded 32·5 per cent of taxes, while the top 50 per cent of incomes accounted for 67·5 per cent of taxes. But in 1959/60 the tax burden had a more marked concentration as measured by the gap between the tax distribution curve and the diagonal; here, the lower 50 per cent of incomes bore only 19 per cent of taxes. By this measure the degree of progressiveness has thus declined quite markedly and, although this was partly due to discretionary changes in the tax system, automatic changes accounted for a substantial part also.

The effect of taxation in redistributing income may be deduced from Lorenz curves of pre-tax and post-tax incomes; chart 4.4, however, gives a shorthand account of this by also ranking cumulative percentages of pre-tax and post-tax incomes against each other. Again a proportional tax system would give a curve linking the two along the diagonal, which in this context is to be interpreted as a line of unchanged income distribution; taxation reduces income inequality if these curves are to the left of the diagonal.[2] In both 1959/60 and 1973/4, the first 50 per cent of gross incomes received about 53·5 per cent of post-tax incomes and neither the 1973/4 curve nor the 1959/60 one is unequivocally more progressive, since they intersect in the fifth decile of pre-tax incomes. Below this level the 1973/4 curve distributes incomes more equally, whilst the 1959/60 curve shows greater equality above this level. It

---

[1] In contrast to a conventional Lorenz diagram, which ranks cumulative gross incomes against cumulative income units and where deviations to the right of the diagonal reflect inequality and inequity, an unequal distribution of the tax burden by concentration on higher incomes is progressive and equitable.

[2] As with the tax distribution curves, movements *away* from the diagonal (this time to its left) are progressive so long as the income distribution is not reversed.

appears that the regressive structural reforms of the period have been partly offset by the compensating changes which have taken place automatically as incomes have risen.

Chart 4.4. *The distribution of the tax burden and of post-tax incomes with respect to cumulative gross incomes, 1959/60 and 1973/4*

SOURCES: CSO, *National Income and Expenditure 1965–75*, table 4.8, and *National Income and Expenditure 1969*, London, HMSO, 1969, table 23; NIESR estimates.
[a] Post-tax/pre-tax income distribution curves.   [b] Tax distribution curves.

Intuitively it might be expected that fiscal drag would be accompanied by a tendency to greater concentration of the tax burden and a fairer distribution of income as taxpayers were pushed into higher tax brackets; that is, that a progressive system would become more progressive over time as incomes rose. Yet, with the advent of high rates of inflation, this was qualified by concern that rising money incomes were shifting the tax burden relatively on to lower income earners, which became one of the chief arguments for index-linked allowances.[1] At first sight, however, this is difficult to square with the fact that post-tax incomes became more dispersed for the lower 45 per cent of incomes between 1959/60 and 1973/4.

To resolve this paradox it is necessary to review the criteria for a stable tax system – that is, one which maintains the distribution of the tax burden and of post-tax incomes in the face of proportional increases in gross incomes. It can be shown that for the distribution of the tax burden to remain stable and progressive it is necessary and sufficient that the elasticity of the average rate schedule (as defined for chart 4.1 – the proportionate change in average tax rates relative to income) should be positive and constant.[2] This follows intuitively from the fact that, for the proportion of aggregate tax each person pays to remain the same, his tax liability should increase at the same rate as everyone else's. With a given growth in money incomes, a declining elasticity causes the effective rate of tax to increase proportionally faster for lower income earners, so that their contribution to the overall tax burden rises, and this can be shown to apply in large measure to the income tax system. Chart 4.5 plots the elasticity of the average rate of tax for the 'representative' taxpayer (as defined for chart 4.1). Corresponding to the definition of aggregate fiscal drag given above (page 172), we have here a measure of the extent of fiscal drag on individuals' tax liabilities:

$$ar' = \frac{dar}{ar} \bigg/ \frac{dY}{Y} = \frac{mr}{ar} - 1 \qquad (7)$$

It can be seen that, whilst initially (up to the threshold) the elasticity is zero, it rises to infinity at the point of the threshold and then declines towards zero, because the average rate increases while the marginal rate is fixed. Then, as higher tax rates are reached, each new marginal rate causes a discrete jump in the curve, giving a 'saw-tooth' effect as the rate declines towards zero within each band. This imparts a certain amount of consistency to the elasticity of the average rate, which does not deviate markedly from 0·5, but this is lower than the responsiveness to income changes of tax on incomes under (about) £2000. For a given proportionate change in money incomes, the increase in the effective tax rate would be greater below this level than above it, the more so the nearer to the threshold the income is.

Furthermore, since the elasticity can be defined as the *non*-proportional change in tax yield that accompanies automatic income changes (the difference between the tax yield elasticity and unity), it can also

[1] See Morgan, *Over-taxation by Inflation*; R. I. G. Allen and D. Savage, 'Inflation and personal income tax', *National Institute Economic Review*, no. 70, November 1974, pp. 61–72.
[2] See U. Jakobsson, 'On the measurement of the degree of progression', *Journal of Public Economics*, vol. 5, Jan.–Feb. 1976, pp. 161–8.

be shown to measure the increase in real tax liabilities which arises from inflationary fiscal drag. Tax yields can, of course, increase at the same rate as inflation (covered by offsetting increases in money incomes)

Chart 4.5. *The responsiveness to changes in income of average tax rates and the ratio of pre-tax to post-tax income: 'representative' and 'average' taxpayers, 1973/4*

SOURCES: table 4.1; CSO, *National Income and Expenditure 1965–75*, table 4.8; NIESR estimates.

Notes: (i) 'Representative' taxpayer defined as for chart 4.1; 'average' taxpayer defined in terms of average tax liability for all persons with a given gross income (derived from Inland Revenue, *Survey of Personal Incomes*, see text).

(ii) elasticities: above zero, the proportionate change in the average tax rate from a proportionate change in income; below zero, the proportionate change in the ratio between pre-tax and post-tax incomes from a proportionate change in pre-tax income.

without affecting real tax liabilities; so the curve for the representative taxpayer can be interpreted in terms of the consequences of inflation for the tax distribution. The elasticity of the yield applicable to aggregate United Kingdom income tax in 1973/4 was 1·67; that is, for an 'inflationary' change in money incomes of 1 per cent, the real increase in the yield would have been 0·67 per cent, as also would have been the percentage increase in the effective rate of tax. But a 'representative' taxpayer receiving less than £2000 a year would have suffered a larger real increase than this; at an income of £1000, for instance, the increase in the effective rate would have been approximately 3·5 per cent.

It does not necessarily follow that the distribution of post-tax incomes has also become less progressive. A necessary condition for this distribution to remain stable is that the proportionate change in the ratio of post-tax to pre-tax incomes should be negative and constant.[1] By increasing the government's share of income more than proportionally, fiscal drag automatically reduces the proportion retained by recipients, so that this decrease should occur at the same rate for all income earners if their share of post-tax income is to remain unchanged. It is, however, possible for the burden of taxation to be thrown increasingly on lower income earners – through a declining tax elasticity – while the post-tax income distribution remains constant or improves. Whether or not this is the case in the United Kingdom is a matter for some debate. The lower part of chart 4.5 shows the proportionate reduction in the ratio of post-tax to pre-tax income from a proportionate growth in gross incomes for the 'representative' taxpayer; it also measures the proportionate reduction in real post-tax income that occurs with inflation, since

$$xr' = \frac{d(1-ar)}{(1-ar)} \bigg/ \frac{dY}{Y} = \frac{(1-mr)}{(1-ar)} - 1 \tag{8}$$

where $(1-mr)/(1-ar)$ is the 'residual income elasticity', defined as the proportionate change in post-tax income with respect to a proportionate change in pre-tax income.[2] This would be less than unity under a progressive tax system. But if real post-tax incomes are to maintain their value they *must* keep pace with inflationary income increases, when xr' would be zero; the further below zero this value falls, the more the rate of increase in post-tax incomes is falling behind the rate of inflation.

Up to the threshold, recipients retain all their income and pay no tax to be affected by inflation. At the threshold the ratio of post-tax to pre-tax income begins to fall, the proportionate increase in post-tax income being 70 per cent of the proportionate increase in pre-tax income and, if this was an inflationary increase, the proportionate decline in real income would be 30 per cent of the rate of inflation. But after this the responsiveness of the ratio to income growth begins

[1] Ibid.
[2] R. A. Musgrave and T. Thin, 'Income tax progression, 1929–48', *Journal of Political Economy*, vol. 56, December 1948, pp. 498–514.

to decline, reaching a low point at the end of the basic rate band, where the decline in real post-tax income would be only 5·5 per cent of the rate of inflation. After that responsiveness changes in a saw-tooth manner with increases in marginal rates and the curve reaches a high point at the beginning of the top rate of tax, where a 1 per cent inflationary increase would cause a 0·49 per cent decline in real post-tax income.

Using the aggregate marginal and average rates derived above for 1973/4, it would be expected that 1 per cent inflation would lead to a 0·12 per cent decline in real spending power (as measured by total personal post-tax incomes). Compared with this overall effect, it can be seen from chart 4.5 that those with annual incomes less than £2500 or more than £5775 suffer a greater decline, while those within this range suffer less. The fact that lower income earners appear to suffer more than average has been a fundamental part of the case for indexing tax allowances to prevent inflation from increasing tax liabilities more than proportionally.

However, while the validity of these conclusions is not in doubt for taxpayers with different incomes but identical circumstances, it is not strictly possible to generalise from this to what would happen to the relationship between post-tax and pre-tax incomes as shown in the distribution diagram, where the horizontal axis cumulates the incomes of people with the same gross incomes but different allowances. A part of such allowances is income-related (payments of mortgage interest, life assurance premiums, etc.), so that at any particular level of gross income there is an array of taxpayers facing different average rates and even different marginal ones. Thus, for any given movement up the scale of gross incomes there will be people on both the rising and falling parts of the curves for the representative taxpayer in chart 4.5 – they may be moving either across the threshold or into higher tax brackets. If sufficient people are being drawn into new tax brackets to offset the automatic decline in elasticity experienced by those who are not, the average effect will be to maintain the post-tax income elasticity and with it the existing post-tax income distribution. But to estimate whether or not this is the case, it is necessary to calculate the average elasticities at each level of gross income. For these it is again possible to rely on the Inland Revenue's *Survey of Personal Incomes* and the income-class marginal and average rates used to derive the aggregate tax rates described above. From the relationship between these it is possible to calculate the average of the tax and post-tax income elasticities which apply at various points on the income scale.[1] These

---

[1] From footnote 2 page 169 above we already have the marginal rate $\hat{mr}_i$; the corresponding average rate is $\hat{ar}_i = \alpha y^{-1} + \beta_1 + \beta_2 y + \beta_3 y^2 + \beta_4 y^3$. The elasticities of the system are then derived as $\hat{ar}' = \hat{mr}_i/\hat{ar}_i - 1$ and $\hat{x}r_i' = (\hat{ar}_i - \hat{mr}_i)/(1 - \hat{ar}_i)$.

calculations provide the 'average' taxpayer elasticities for 1973/4 shown in chart 4.5, and may be taken as determining the effects of proportional gross income changes on the tax and post-tax distribution lines in chart 4.4. It can be seen that the tendency for the tax burden of the average taxpayer to increase faster at lower levels of income is confirmed, but to a more limited extent than for the 'representative' taxpayer. Nevertheless it is marked and accounts for the flattening of the tax distribution curve towards the line of equal tax distribution in chart 4.4. But the effect on the post-tax income distribution expected from the curve for the average taxpayer is predominantly progressive; the responsiveness of the post-tax income ratio to changes in income increases for an annual income above (about) £1000, though it diminishes for the short range between the threshold and this point. People at or very near the threshold are still relatively badly affected, but for most of the range up to £2500 per annum inflation would have caused a lower proportionate decline in real incomes than for those above £2500. The effect of inflation and real income growth seems, therefore, unequivocally progressive for the upper 90 per cent of incomes, not the converse as would be expected from the 'representative' curve. The distribution curves corroborate this insofar as the 1973/4 post-tax income distribution is more progressive for the lower 45 per cent of incomes than the 1959/60 distribution; the fact that for the upper 55 per cent the curve became less progressive reflects reforms in higher rates which offset the automatic progressive tendencies of the tax system.

The effects of fiscal drag on income tax liabilities seem therefore to be, for the most part, progressive *vis-à-vis* disposable incomes (income tax being the principal adjustment in calculating personal disposable income as defined in the national accounts). But other factors, including indirect taxes and benefits from subsidies and transfers, obviously need to be considered. Taking account of expenditure taxes on consumption, in 1973/4 a 1 per cent growth in real incomes would have led to a 0·86 per cent growth in real personal disposable incomes, while a 1 per cent growth in inflationary incomes would have led to a 0·04 per cent decline (compared with the 0·12 per cent decline due to income taxes alone).[1] Although the distributional effects are indeterminate without knowing individual indirect tax elasticities, the conclusion that automatic income changes are biased towards a more progressive distribution of disposable income is still likely to hold.[2]

[1] The income tax effect is related to disposable income at market prices, the total effect to disposable income net of indirect taxes.

[2] The assumption behind the aggregate expenditure tax elasticities in table 4.7 is one of constant elasticities for the individual tax bases, leading to an increasing elasticity overall as the consumption of income-elastic goods increases. This is not necessarily the best description of the way elasticities change over a scale of gross incomes, but the implication is that the

THE PUBLIC SECTOR FINANCIAL BALANCE
AND FISCAL LEVERAGE

Introduction

In this section the taxation and public expenditure sides of fiscal policy are brought together to give measures of the full-employment budget.

In one form or another, the balance of total public sector receipts over expenditure as an indicator of public sector (dis)savings probably represents the most concise summary of the stance of fiscal policy. However, two important considerations suggest that the raw data which emerge as the public sector financial balance should be modified: first, tax receipts vary (to an extent already explored in the previous section) with the growth of incomes and fluctuations in economic activity; secondly, a given change in the balance may occur as a result of changes in receipts or expenditures which are offset by private sector savings in varying degrees.

Taking the first consideration, it is clear that changes in the actual budget balance will occur both as a result of fiscal interventions and because of the two types of automatic change described above – fiscal drag and built-in flexibility.[1] The weakness of the public sector financial balance as an indicator of fiscal stance is that it fails to distinguish the influence of the budget on the economy from the influence of the economy on the budget.[2] The concept of the full-employment budget balance seeks to resolve these problems by normalising the level of

distribution of tax and of post-tax incomes will become more progressive as incomes rise. So far as the 'inflationary' income elasticities of the indirect tax system are concerned, there is little reason to suppose that these change much in aggregate and, this being so, inflation would not be expected to have a noticeable effect on the distribution of the indirect tax burden.

[1] Using the distinction between discretionary and automatic budget changes developed on page 160 and distinguishing between long-run and short-run changes in income, the change in the balance (P) can be separated into four components:

$$P_t - P_{t-1} = \Delta \overline{ar}_{t-1}^{\Delta t} Y_{t-1} + \overline{MR}_t(Y_t^{fe} - Y_{t-1}^{fe}) + (\overline{MR}_t - \overline{G}_t)(U_t - U_{t-1}) - (G_t - G_{t-1})$$

| total change | discretionary tax change | long-run automatic tax change | automatic stabilisers | public expenditure change |

where $\Delta \overline{ar}_{t-1}^{\Delta t}$ = the discretionary change in the effective tax rate evaluated at the level of income in year $t-1$ (as defined in footnote 2 page 160), $\overline{MR}_t$ = the average marginal rate of tax in year t, Y^{fe} = full-employment income, $U_t = Y_t - Y_t^{fe}$ (the difference between actual and potential national income: the 'GDP gap'), $\overline{G}$ = the marginal rate of change in public expenditure relative to changes in U, and G = other government expenditure.

[2] It can be demonstrated that as a target of fiscal policy it may lead to perverse fiscal action, in that a shortfall in employment will lead to a shortfall in receipts, thus increasing the deficit and prompting *deflationary* action to correct for this (see *National Institute Economic Review*, no. 79, February 1977, pp. 43–4).

economic activity and real income at which the balance is measured; this nets out the effects of built-in flexibility and leaves an index of fiscal policy containing the effects of discretionary changes and long-run automatic changes in revenue.[1] The 'weighted' full-employment balance attempts to account for the differential incidence of private savings on different forms of revenue and expenditure by scoring the items in question according to their net impact on demand and output; the weights used are discussed below and in chapter 3.

The full-employment budget balance represents the initial (or *ex ante*) stance of the budget in regard to savings at the full-employment level of income; it is initial in the sense that, if there is an imbalance of aggregate savings intentions, the multiplier will generate a different level of national income and employment and a new level of public receipts, in which process neither full employment nor the full-employment balance need be realised. Changes in the full-employment balance thus reflect changes in fiscal stance which, with the multiplier consequences, cause aggregate demand to diverge from or gravitate towards its full-employment level. Since the economy grows at a certain underlying rate over time with productivity increases, a fixed policy stance would normally be one where the proportion of public savings in full-employment income remained the same; a change in policy would then be reflected in a change in this proportion, causing demand to diverge from its long-run growth path and so altering the rate of unemployment. Such a change would be composed of discretionary interventions and net fiscal drag. The weighted full-employment balance represents the initial demand leverage of the budget;[2] it is interpreted in the same way as the unweighted balance, the only difference being that the weighted variant translates the budget balance into a 'first round' demand impact by netting out budgetary transactions which do not represent claims on output. The full leverage of the budget is determined by this and the multiplier.

Because it nets out the secondary demand and revenue effects which

---

[1] Discretionary changes in tax rates are evaluated as the change in yield which would occur at full-employment income; expenditure plans (G) and long-run automatic tax changes are not affected. Thus (where P^{fe} is the full-employment balance):

$$\underbrace{P_t^{fe} - P_{t-1}^{fe}}_{\text{total change}} = \underbrace{\Delta \overline{ar}_{t-1}^{\Delta t} Y_{t-1} + \Delta \overline{MR}(Y_{t-1}^{fe} - Y_{t-1})}_{\substack{\text{discretionary change at} \\ \text{full-employment income}}} + \underbrace{\overline{MR}_t(Y_t^{fe} - Y_{t-1}^{fe})}_{\substack{\text{long-run automatic} \\ \text{tax change}}} - \underbrace{(G_t - G_{t-1})}_{\substack{\text{public expenditure} \\ \text{change}}}$$

The discretionary change is thus the *actual* discretionary change, plus the difference in yield which would accrue by evaluating the GDP gap at the new marginal rate, where $\Delta \overline{MR} = (\mu_t - \mu_{t-1})(\Delta B_t / \Delta Y_t)$.

[2] This balance can be interpreted as the multiplicand (M_{fa}) in Musgrave's measure of 'fiscal leverage' (see Musgrave, 'On measuring fiscal performance', pp. 216–17).

disguise the original stance of policy, the full-employment balance has obvious advantages over the actual balance as an indicator of fiscal policy, but it still suffers from two potential drawbacks. First, because errors occur in forecasting public expenditure and receipts, policy will be imperfectly implemented. A distinction should thus be drawn between the intended initial stance of policy and its out-turn. Insofar as it is possible to derive the intended stance – from forecasts of actual GDP and the actual balance made at budget time – these are presented, with the out-turn, in table 4.9 on page 187 below. The second drawback is due to the fact that the overall change in GDP leverage exerted by a change in the weighted full-employment balance is a function not just of that change but also of the multiplier attached to it, which in turn depends on the marginal rate of tax. It is possible for the total effect on GDP leverage to be in a different direction from the initial change in the full-employment balance if changes in the marginal rate of tax cause a change in the multiplier which more than offsets the change in the initial leverage. In this case changes in the full-employment balance would even mislead as to the direction of change in fiscal stance.[1] Although, over our period, the multiplier has been reduced by the steady increase in marginal tax rates, it does not appear that the direction of change implied by changes in the full-employment balance was, in fact, ever contrary to the change in total leverage; however, when allowance is made for this, at the end of the period the leverage implied by a given change in the full-employment balance was about 10–15 per cent below that at the beginning.

[1] For example, assuming zero full-employment balances in other sectors, and thus an equilibrium full-employment budget balance of zero, the change in GDP leverage exerted by the budget is $-(P_t^{fe} k^t - P_{t-1}^{fe} k^{t-1})$, where $k^t =$ the multiplier with post-intervention tax rates and $k^{t-1} =$ the previous multiplier. Alone, a discretionary tax change would give a leverage change of:

$$\Delta GDP^{\Delta t} = -\Delta \overline{ar}_{t-1}^{\Delta t} Y_{t-1} k^t = -[\Delta \overline{ar}_{t-1}^{\Delta t} Y_{t-1} + \overline{\Delta MR}(Y_{t-1}^{fe} - Y_{t-1})] k^t - P_{t-1}^{fe} \Delta k$$

discretionary change in GDP	tax yield effect calculated at full-employment income	multiplier change

Where, from a position of unemployment (full-employment surplus), a cut in the effective rate also involves an increase in the marginal rate, the change in the full-employment multiplicand may (depending on the GDP gap) show a change towards greater surplus. The reflationary stance of policy is not picked up by the change in P^{fe}, but is actually contained in the effect of a lower multiplier on the existing full-employment surplus ($P_{t-1}^{fe} \Delta k$). The further the economy is from full employment, the more this possibility must be taken into consideration (see Blinder and Solow, 'Analytical foundations of fiscal policy', p. 17; W. H. Oakland, 'Budgetary measures of fiscal performance', *Southern Economic Journal*, vol. 35, April 1969, pp. 347–57; OECD, *Fiscal Policy in Seven Countries, 1955–1965*, pp. 25–6).

The public sector financial balance, 1959/60–1973/4

The out-turn and forecast levels of the actual and the full-employment public sector financial balance are set out in table 4.9.[1] The actual balance was in surplus only during the two years after devaluation, while the full-employment balance was also in surplus in 1970/1. Initial public savings were at a peak during 1969/70 and 1970/1 (at about £1200 million), though it was the latter year which saw the most restrictive intended stance of policy, as reflected in a forecast full-employment surplus of £1580 million. Differences between the forecasts and out-turns of the actual balance reflect, among other things, the effects on income-related receipts and expenditure of mis-estimating economic activity; differences between the forecasts and out-turns of the full-employment balance, on the other hand, arise principally from short-falls and overruns in public expenditure, from mis-forecasts of inflation and from mis-estimating the pattern of demand in its effect on revenue. The differences illustrate the ambiguity involved in treating changes in the out-turn of the full-employment balance as policy changes; this is especially marked for 1972/3 – the year which (with 1973/4) shows the largest realised deterioration in the full-employment balance (−£1545 million) and an intended change in fiscal stance of −£2105 million. In 1973/4, on the other hand, the full-employment balance was almost exactly as intended, despite the difference of −£800 million between the intended *actual* balance and its out-turn, which was almost wholly attributable to the GDP shortfall in that year.

The estimates of the weighted full-employment balance follow the principles set out in calculating the domestic output content of public expenditure in chapter 3. The changes in private savings set off against tax changes are the obverse of those allowed against transfers and subsidies, though substantially more important. Government direct expenditures are not affected by such offsets, while the recipients of grants and transfers tend to have a lower propensity to save than tax-payers as a whole, and a good deal lower than surtax payers or recipients of unearned income. The 'economic efficiency' (to use Kaldor's term for the output-content of public sector transactions) of surtax seems to be about 64 per cent, of taxes on 'other personal income' about 74 per cent, of taxes on wages and salaries 90 per cent, and of taxes on

---

[1] For the definition of full-employment national income see above, page 84. Since the full-employment balance is derived by measuring what the budget would be at full-employment *income* under existing tax rates and expenditure plans – including existing expenditures by other sectors of the economy, where only consumption is taken as income-related – compositional errors in its calculation are confined to errors in the allocation of full-employment income between companies and persons (which are subject to different marginal rates of tax). The composition of full-employment expenditure is not an issue here.

Table 4.9. *The public sector financial balance with full-employment corrections,[a] 1959/60–1973/4*

	Actual balance		Full-employment balance		Weighted full-employment balance[b]	
	Forecast[c]	Out-turn	Forecast	Out-turn	Out-turn	Proportion of full-employment GDP
	(£ million)					(%)
1959/60	..	−620	..	−560	−1619	−7·61
1960/1	..	−720	..	−460	−1644	−7·33
1961/2	..	−619	..	−680	−1612	−6·75
1962/3	..	−602	..	−460	−1549	−6·11
1963/4	..	−1098	..	−1020	−2102	−7·87
1964/5	..	−857	..	−670	−2273	−8·00
1965/6	..	−697	..	−450	−1989	−6·53
1966/7	−473[d]	−1169	..	−810	−2174	−6·67
1967/8	−1317	−1828	..	−1120	−2425	−7·02
1968/9	−857[d]	−548	−530[d]	−270	−1570	−4·27
1969/70	+538	+662	+900	+1290	−625	−1·58
1970/1	+1138	+114	+1580[d]	+1165	−1117	−2·52
1971/2	−378[d]	−508	+1285[d]	+780	−1827	−3·61
1972/3	−2441	−1994	−1325	−765	−2992	−5·23
1973/4	−2853	−3646	−2415	−2375	−4056	−6·30

SOURCES: CSO, *Economic Trends, Annual Supplement 1975, National Income and Expenditure 1970* and *1975* and *Annual Abstract of Statistics 1975*; NIESR estimates.

[a] Full employment is defined as the 1960 level of 325,000 unemployed and the full-employment growth rate is taken as 3·2 per cent per annum (see text). The full-employment correction is calculated on the basis that inflation, the exchange rate, exports and investment are exogenous and fixed, the adjustment being to derive discretionary, or *ex ante*, public sector savings. The responsiveness of public sector receipts to a 1 per cent change in GDP has risen from 0·94 to 1·02 per cent over the period.

[b] Net of steel industry investment. The savings offsets are derived from regression analysis and the import weights from CSO, *Input–Output Tables for the United Kingdom* (various issues). The expenditure figures are as defined in chapter 3, pages 97–8 above. The results should be taken as representing orders of magnitude rather than absolute expressions of the economic impact of the budget, with year-to-year changes more relevant than actual levels. The accruals adjustments have been given a weight of zero.

[c] Forecasts of the actual balance have been given officially in the Financial Statement only since 1966/7 and official forecasts of GDP (needed to convert the actual figures to a full-employment basis) only since 1968/9.

[d] Excluding subsequent extra-budgetary interventions.

transfers 99 per cent, compared with an overall 85 per cent efficiency for across-the-board tax changes such as general adjustments to expenditure taxes.[1] Allowing for these and other offsets on the receipts side, the net impact of the budget on demand will always tend to be

[1] See M. J. C. Surrey, 'Personal incomes and consumers' expenditure' in K. Hilton and D. F. Heathfield (eds.), *The Econometric Study of the United Kingdom*, London, Macmillan, 1970, p. 108; J. C. Dorrington and G. A. Renton, 'A study of the effects of direct taxation on consumers' expenditure' in G. A. Renton (ed.), *Modelling the Economy*, London, Heinemann, 1975, pp. 557–609.

greater than is apparent, the weighted balance being on the negative side of the actual balance, with greater implied leverage.

More attention should be paid to changes in the weighted full-employment balance than to its actual level, but its impact in 1959/60–1960/1 is estimated at about $7\frac{1}{2}$ per cent of full-employment GDP, declining to about 6 per cent in 1962/3;[1] the upturn of 1963/4–1964/5 then brought it to a peak of 8 per cent, which declined to between $6\frac{1}{2}$ and 7 per cent in the next three years. The extreme reaction which followed devaluation and lasted until 1972/3 is quite apparent: the weighted full-employment balance fell to a low of about $1\frac{1}{2}$ per cent of full-employment GDP in 1969/70, rising gradually to 3·6 per cent over the next two years. The reflation of 1972/3 relaxed the budgetary stance by 1·6 per cent (the intended increase was nearer to 2·5 per cent) and the supposedly 'neutral' budget of 1973/4 further increased the weighted full-employment deficit to 6·3 per cent of full-employment GDP.

These year-to-year changes in the weighted full-employment balance are shown in chart 4.6 in terms of the separate contributions of changes in expenditure and in revenue. Since decreases in receipts have the same expansionary effects as increases in expenditure, all changes plotted to the right of the diagonal 'neutrality' line, where expenditure changes exactly offset revenue changes, add to budgetary leverage, while leverage is diminished to the left.[2] During the 1959/60 and 1963/4 reflations, and in the upturn of the 1970s, both sides of the accounts acted in the same direction (tax decreases being relatively more important in stimulating the economy in 1959/60 and 1972/3, and expenditure dominating in 1963/4). Similarly, the deflationary leverage exerted in 1968/9 and 1969/70 was the product of both sides. On the other hand, the combination of expansionary expenditure policies and restraining taxation changes was a dominant feature of the period 1964/5–1967/8, with only 1965/6 showing net deflationary leverage. In 1971/2 there was an example of the opposite – expansionary revenue policies (tax cuts) offset, in leverage terms, by restraint on the expenditure side (to which shortfalls on capital spending made an unintentional contribution).

[1] The budgetary impact in first-round terms is, of course, positive where the budget balance is negative.

[2] This exposition follows in some respects that of Artis, 'Fiscal policy for stabilization' pp. 292–4, as described in M. J. Artis and R. H. Wallace, 'Assessing the fiscal impact' in, N. Runcie (ed.), *Australian Monetary and Fiscal Policy: selected readings*, London University Press, 1971, pp. 378 *et seq*.

Chart 4.6. *Changes in budgetary stance (with full-employment corrections),[a]*
1959|60–1973|4

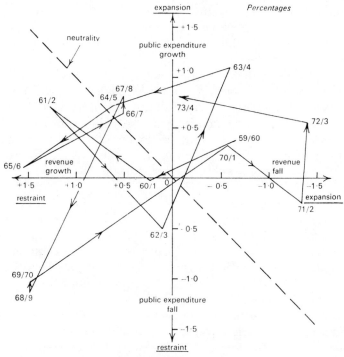

SOURCE: NIESR estimates.

[a] Changes in the ratios of weighted full-employment receipts and expenditure to full-employment GDP.

Sector balances and 'fiscal adequacy'

Estimates of the full-employment budget balance, as developed here, do not in themselves contain any built-in judgement about the adequacy or appropriateness of the fiscal stimulus which they measure. To develop such a judgement at least two further ingredients are required: comparable full-employment estimates of the private sector and overseas balances, and a view on the appropriate rate of adjustment from the current position to full employment.

The full-employment budget balance is a comparative static concept. It says nothing about lags in the response of the economy to changes in fiscal policy. The time-path of response to alternative fiscal stimuli can only be illustrated by appropriate simulations on an econometric model. However, when measuring the full-employment adequacy of the budget, short-run dynamic responses can reasonably be set aside;

then, comparably calculated full-employment balances for the private and overseas sectors can, in principle, be set against the full-employment budget balance to test the adequacy of a given fiscal policy for realising full employment, or the likelihood that it will generate excess demand (relative to the full-employment target). The test to be applied is whether the intended full-employment budget balance is equal and opposite in sign to the sum of the intended overseas and private sector balances, also evaluated at full-employment income levels. If the net result is a deficiency of aggregate intended savings, there is a presumption of excess demand; if it is a surplus, deficient demand is presumed. In either case, the implication is that fiscal policy is inadequate in the short term to achieve either full employment or the full-employment budget balance as measured, though in the medium term such a balance may become appropriate and sustainable as the private and overseas sectors vary cyclically.[1]

In this context the particular contribution of the 'New Cambridge' school was to suggest that the private sector surplus could be taken as being a small and stable fraction of GDP.[2] Granted an exchange rate or 'degree of competitiveness' sufficient to ensure an acceptable balance of payments (the inverse of the overseas sector's balance) at full employment, the approach determines an appropriate full-employment public sector balance for a balance of payments target of zero as the obverse of the long-run private sector surplus. The private savings behaviour implied in this approach has, however, remained contentious, no less than the assumption that the overseas sector could be relied upon to provide no marked destabilising influence.[3]

For purposes of evaluating short-run policy, however, if some assumptions can be made about the full-employment values of the potential overseas and private sector balances, the comparative static

[1] Where, for instance, a calculation of the full-employment balances reveals both a surplus in the public sector and a greater savings surplus in the economy at large, there will be a shortfall in demand and GDP which can be corrected by fiscal action only at the expense of the full-employment surplus itself; that is, the public sector balance must be altered so that its deficit offsets the surplus of potential savings in other sectors. In the context of medium-term budgeting and resource planning, however, the full-employment public sector balance has a somewhat different significance, since the assumption is that full employment can be sustained at the peak of the cycle, when 'full-employment budgeting' actually implies a planned public sector balance compatible with fully employed resources.

[2] See pages 138–9 above. Subsequently this was adjusted to a 'small and predictable' rather than a 'small and stable' fraction (see House of Commons, *Ninth Report from the Expenditure Committee, Session 1974*, p. 15).

[3] The claim that fluctuations in output have been '*entirely* the consequence of stabilisation measures' (ibid. p. 5) clearly rests as much upon assuming stability in the overseas sector balance as in the private sector surplus. It was the claim of the 'New Cambridge' school in this regard that 'during the past twenty years or so, purely by chance, the fluctuations of UK exports, to the extent that these were induced by changes in world trade, have been roughly offset by changes in import prices attributable to the same cause' (ibid. p. 5).

adequacy of fiscal policy can be appraised, but the extent to which it is useful to do this hinges on the difficulty of estimating such values, or proxies for them, and on the confining framework of the comparative static analysis itself. The approach does not produce hard and fast quantification, but it does suggest that it might be fruitful to view fiscal policy in the light of the state of world demand and the implied changes in the (full-employment) overseas sector balance. Such considerations feature in the next section, which is devoted to a narrative account and running assessment of fiscal policy; they are subsequently brought to bear in a test of the cyclical appropriateness of fiscal policy.

IMPLEMENTING BUDGETARY POLICY

An account of fiscal policy in terms of full-employment budget balances is inevitably abstracted from the sequence of short-term pressures under which fiscal policy decisions are actually made. The purpose of this section is to correct the perspective by giving a narrative account of the background to fiscal changes.

The formulation of fiscal policy in the short run hinges on the forecasting of real demand variables to the relevant horizon (usually eighteen months to two years), and an account of policy must clearly aim to distinguish failures due to forecasting errors from those which have their roots in other causes. Official forecasts were not published explicitly until the 1968/9 budget; before that we have to rely on the indications (frequently only qualitative) given in budget statements by Chancellors of the Exchequer. An alternative is the published National Institute forecasts, which have been used in place of official ones up to 1967/8; they were available to the Chancellor and, though they are not likely always to have been identical with those on which policy was based, it has been assumed that by and large the differences were not marked.

The rate of growth of GDP is the most critical element in any demand forecast, since this must be the same as the growth in productive potential for the unemployment rate to remain constant. Growth rates are generally expressed as percentage changes from the same period in the previous year,[1] though the average year-on-year change is also emphasised on occasions. Chart 4.7 presents both, together with the errors in forecasting GDP, which are the sum total of errors in forecasting its components. Consumers' expenditure is, of course, the principal component, so that forecasts and forecast errors are also given for this. Since errors in forecasting imports have also been important

---

[1] In the Financial Statement the Treasury publishes forecasts based on half-year to half-year percentage changes, while the *National Institute Economic Review* analyses quarterly changes, with particular emphasis on fourth quarter to fourth quarter (year-end to year-end).

Chart 4.7. *Total final demand: quarterly and annual percentage changes, forecast and out-turn, 1959–73*

A: *Total final expenditure*

B: *Gross domestic product at factor cost*

Chart 4.7 (*cont.*)

C: *Consumers' expenditure*

SOURCES: CSO, *Economic Trends, Annual Supplement 1975*; Treasury, *Financial Statement and Budget Report* (since 1968); *National Institute Economic Review* (May issues) to 1967; Neild and Shirley, '*Economic Review*: an assessment of forecasts, 1959–1960'; M. C. Kennedy, 'How well does the National Institute forecast?', *National Institute Economic Review*, no. 50, November 1969, pp. 40–52.

Notes: (i) Quarterly changes are changes from the same quarter of the previous year; annual changes are changes over four quarters up to the end of the calendar year in question.

(ii) Forecasts at budget-time (including the budgetary intervention) are corrected for subsequent interventions, including variations in hire purchase controls. Up to 1968, data from *National Institute Economic Review*, except where there is evidence (as in 1962) that this conflicted with the Treasury's unpublished forecasts; since 1968, forecasts are half-yearly ones published in the *Financial Statement*.

(iii) The compromise (average) estimate of GDP is used.

to managing the economy, forecasts of aggregate demand (total final expenditure) are given in part A of the chart, the difference between these and the GDP forecasts consisting of the import (and net indirect tax) content of expenditure.

The first Conservative period, 1959/60–October 1964

By the beginning of 1960 the economy had been expanding rapidly for some time and, following the reflationary boost given in April 1959, people were beginning to look for signals indicating the need for budgetary moderation.[1] Such signals began to appear when figures for

---

[1] *Economist*, 2 January 1960.

GDP showed that the pace of the expansion had been far greater than anticipated – in the final quarter of 1959 GDP was over 6 per cent higher than in the same quarter of 1958, as against an increase of about $2\frac{1}{2}$ per cent forecast previously.[1] The unwelcome result of this was a weakening in the balance of payments, which dominated budget-making up to July 1961.

The 1960 budget, resting on the prognosis of a diminishing rate of growth towards the end of the year, was, however, absolutely neutral. Profits tax was raised by $2\frac{1}{2}$ per cent, but this was not intended to cut back private investment, for which capital allowances remained unchanged. Because of the balance of payments weakness, this budget involved a 'balancing of risks', but as far as total demand was concerned the forecasts appear to have been correct. However, they were wrong in regard to the balance of payments: the propensity to import was underestimated, while the falling off in export demand (due to a decline in world activity) was not foreseen. These two circumstances led to demand management packages in the spring and early summer which relied on credit controls and public expenditure cuts. But the altera-tions in hire purchase terms, which had proved 'prompt and substantial' in their effects, bore too heavily on a certain range of goods, particularly consumer durables. In the 1961 budget the Chancellor deduced the need for the more extensive and uniform use of the existing expenditure tax base through an 'economic regulator' – a device enabling the Treasury at any time to institute across-the-board changes in duties up to a maximum of 10 per cent.[2]

The 'wait and see' possibilities offered by this innovation helped to make the budget fairly neutral once more. Apart from raising an extra £68 million of revenue in the current year (principally from the oil duty), the opportunity was taken to mitigate the effects of higher rates of tax on earned incomes, where the surtax threshold was raised from £2000 to £5000;[3] this was scheduled to cost £83 million in 1961/2 and was to be paid for by an increase in profits tax from $12\frac{1}{2}$ to 15 per cent.

With final demand expected – correctly – to increase by about $2\frac{3}{4}$ per cent in 1961, and with imports levelling off as predicted, the forecasts

[1] On the failure to foresee the upswing in demand see R. R. Neild and E. A. Shirley, 'Economic Review: an assessment of forecasts, 1959–1960', National Institute Economic Review, no. 15, May 1961, pp. 12–29.

[2] Treasury powers to surcharge or rebate revenue duties 'with a view to regulating the balance between demand and resources' (Finance Act 1961, s. 9) have to be renewed in each Finance Act. The 1961 Act also contained a provision for the Treasury to introduce sur-charges on employers' national insurance contributions, up to a maximum of 4s. per week per employee, but this power was not subsequently renewed (see page 17 above).

[3] Earned income relief was extended from income tax to surtax and a further earnings allowance of £2000 was introduced.

for both an improved external balance and output growth matching productive potential would have been fulfilled for the year as a whole. But this did not prevent the introduction on 25 July of a 10 per cent regulator surcharge which, together with measures affecting public expenditure and credit, increased taxation by £130 million in 1961/2. This coincided with the end of the boom, for from the last quarter of 1961 GDP fell below the rate necessary to maintain full employment.

How far this denouement was deliberate and how far an unintentional coincidence of deflation with a declining trend in activity is open to question.[1] In favour of the latter interpretation are the statements about increased demand forecasts which accompanied the intervention,[2] but, on the other hand, the Chancellor spoke of the need for a 'pause' in activity. However, the episode gives rise to a more fundamental question of the soundness of the decisions to reflate in 1959 and to stay neutral in 1960, since these implied coincidence of the budgetary cycle with the world demand cycle (chart 4.8) and a deterioration in the current account; this might have been avoided or diminished by more cautious policies, but in the event led to speculative losses from the reserves and the eventual deflationary 'stop'.

The crisis of 1961 encouraged a re-evaluation of the adequacy of demand management for achieving growth with stability. The future need for new instruments – incomes policy and planning – was officially accepted in the July intervention and the budget of 1962. In the meantime, though, it was the deflationary school arguing for a higher margin of unused resources whose ideas appeared to be in the ascendant.[3] The output pause became endowed with strategic significance, since a period of lower demand pressure was seen in some quarters as a means of keeping money wage increases below the world level, thus restoring competitiveness.[4] The deflationary strategy was not, in the event, long-lasting, but the episode illustrates how demand management interventions tend to be seen as turning-points when new strategic approaches to the achievement of *all* the major objectives of policy are adopted. This was to be even more true of the subsequent reflation, which was not merely an exercise in balancing aggregate demand and supply, but an attempt to break through into the 'virtuous circle' of growth and stability on all fronts.

---

[1] See Brittan, *Steering the Economy*, pp. 251 *et seq.*

[2] Selwyn Lloyd in the House of Commons, 25 July 1961. Though correct as to the year-on-year growth of output, the budget forecast itself had tended to overestimate output growth in the second half of 1961 (chart 4.7).

[3] This school might, in general, be termed 'Paishite', but Brittan (*Steering the Economy*, p. 254) refers to the spare capacity argument as a 'recurrent intellectual fashion' to which *some* Treasury officials were drawn.

[4] On this argument see *National Institute Economic Review*, no. 19, February 1962, p. 56.

Chart 4.8. *Changes in initial fiscal leverage, and the export and investment demand cycles, 1958/9–1973/4*

SOURCES: table 4.9; chart 3.6; United Nations, *Monthly Bulletin of Statistics* (various issues); NIESR estimates.

Note: Annual changes (financial and calendar years) in the ratios to full-employment GDP of:

  (*a*) the (intended) weighted full-employment budget balance – initial fiscal leverage;

  (*b*) export demand, deduced from fluctuations around their trend of world exports of manufactured goods;

  (*c*) private investment demand, represented by fluctuations around the trend described in chapter 3.

The Treasury forecast for 1962 anticipated a growth in output through the year of some 4 per cent and on the strength of this the budget itself was neutral in its overall impact, though, in consolidating the regulator surcharge of the previous July, it was decided to continue reshaping purchase tax by extending the tax base and rearranging the existing rates to keep the same yield. A new rate of 15 per cent was introduced on confectionery, soft drinks and ice-cream and the range of existing rates was changed from 5½–55 per cent to 10–45 per cent (table 4.1). At the same time, the anachronistic 'breakfast table duties' were abolished[1] and speculative capital gains were brought within the

---

[1] These were duties on tea, cocoa, coffee and sugar, yielding a revenue of about £15 million.

charge to income tax. By September it had become clear that the budget demand forecasts were optimistic. Public investment increases announced in early October were accompanied by increased investment allowances for the private sector, while the two highest rates of purchase tax were reduced to 25 per cent at a cost of £77 million in a full year.[1]

The process of reflation was continued in the 1963 budget in order to make up the ground lost on the (by then) official growth target of 4 per cent per annum. £218 million of taxation was remitted by way of increased personal and child allowances, though this rise in the tax threshold was accompanied by the elimination of the lowest reduced rate of tax, which increased the initial rate from 6·8 to 15·6 per cent (table 4.1). A further £77 million was remitted through the abolition of income tax on personal owner-occupation (schedule A), which had actually been announced in the previous budget. Overall, the budget concessions amounted to tax cuts of £349 million in a full year (£257 million in 1963/4), to which should be added the effects of improved investment allowances (table 4.2).

In terms of aggregate demand the developments of 1963 were almost identical with those of 1959, though this time the expansion was, for the most part, intentional, being based on the explicit acceptance of the balance of payments deficit likely to occur in the early stages of growth. [2] The circumstances of budget-making in 1964 were therefore remarkably similar to those in 1960, except for the crucial commitment to continue the expansion through 1964. There were certain differences, however, in that the forecasts were showing a faster year-end rate of growth for 1964 than had been predicted for 1960 (5½ per cent growth of GDP compared with 3 per cent), with investment (particularly public investment) mainly responsible for the difference. In these circumstances, the budget strategy for 1964 was based on the need to effect 'the transition to 4 per cent, and to avoid the danger of "overheating" '.[3] However, the extra £100 million raised by the budget seems to have been more influenced by the danger of 'checking expansion rather than moderating it'.[4]

---

[1] The duty on cars was reduced with effect from 6 October; other goods formerly taxed at 45 per cent were affected from 1 January 1963. It is interesting that the regulator was *not* used.

[2] Given the actual annual growth of GDP of nearly 4 per cent in 1963 as a whole and of 6¼ per cent as the year-end rate, against a post-budget forecast of 5½ per cent, the extent of the upswing was still underestimated. This was true of consumption, where the year-end rate was 4¼ per cent against an anticipated 3, of exports, where the out-turn was 4¾ per cent to the forecast 3, and of total investment, where the final quarter increase of 20 per cent over the final quarter of 1962 was extremely similar to the situation in 1959/60.

[3] Reginald Maudling in the House of Commons, 14 April 1964.

[4] Ibid. There seems to have been an emphasis here on the importance of not giving 'confidence' an untoward jolt; the National Institute in its February forecast and policy

The overall out-turn for 1964 – with the rather critical exception of the balance of payments, where the current deficit was about twice what had been expected – lay well within the limits of forecasting accuracy, so that, whilst the errors of the 1959 reflation could largely be attributed to forecasting mistakes, the errors of the period 1963–4 are essentially the result of the medium-term strategy which was adopted. That strategy consciously provided for maintaining expansion by running down the reserves and using additional policy instruments to modify the trade-off between external stability and internal expansion;[1] the rapid deterioration of the basic balance[2] and the change of administration ushered in a policy package in November which contained just such an instrument in the form of an import surcharge and export rebate. In contrast to the 1961 'stop', policy throughout 1964 sought, quite directly, to avoid a deliberate output pause, whilst intending to deal with the balance of payments problem by alternative means. The difficulty with this policy – as it was with the overall growth strategy which had been adopted – was that, though providing a short-term solution to the problem of 'stop-go', it still gave no permanent answer to the reconciliation of faster growth with a stable currency and the transfer of resources into the balance of payments.

The November 1964 budget effectively marks the end of the second of the two cycles which characterised the period 1959–64. Both of the upturns on which these were based derived from experiments in domestic demand-led growth, which sooner or later created a need to free resources for investment and the balance of payments, and this was likely to prejudice the momentum of growth itself. While the ensuing balance of payments difficulties may have been a matter of fundamental competitive inadequacies, it is possible that they were also, to some extent, expressions of excess demand resulting from the type of strategies actually followed. Both budgetary cycles shadowed those in world demand, so that policy (partly by commission, partly by omission, since export demand was frequently misread) failed to

appraisal for 1964 was quite explicit about this. Having calculated that the transition to 4 per cent growth required the extraction of some £400 million from demand, it went on to recommend a smaller adjustment (of £200 million as compared with the Chancellor's £100 million) on the grounds that considerations of confidence argued against so large a change (*National Institute Economic Review*, no. 27, February 1964, p. 11).

[1] In his budget speech on 14 April 1964 Maudling entertained the use of import controls 'if we should be facing severe balance of payments difficulties which could not be dealt with in better ways'. Work had been put in hand on alternative schemes of import quotas or a surcharge, which the ex-Chancellor claimed he would have used rather than deflation (see Brittan, *Steering the Economy*, pp. 284–5).

[2] The deficit on current account was similar, in real terms, to that in 1961 – at 1970 factor cost the current deficit in 1964 was £450 million as compared with about £400 million in 1961.

exploit the balance of payments and growth possibilities from this direction.

Demand management deficiencies also played a part in the pattern of pro-cyclical budgeting which seems to have emerged. Forecasting performance was mixed; although policy-makers seem to have been given the right signals for much of the time, the exceptions were rather critical – the 1959/60 upturn was not foreseen and the extent of the recession in 1962/3 was underestimated, both of which led to reflationary over-reaction. The upturn having once started, it is probable that strategic (growth) considerations did most to determine the budgetary inaction which tended to follow.

Labour administrations, October 1964–June 1970

The new administration in October 1964 sought a wide-ranging contribution from fiscal policy towards the realisation of its economic and social objectives,[1] while endorsing the trend towards 'new' instruments of policy. The character of fiscal policy itself became more interventionist, with a greater emphasis on income redistribution. Corporation tax and capital gains tax, which became effective in 1966/7, introduced, for reasons of equity and economic policy, extra tiers of taxation on income accruing to shareholders; investment grants, which replaced allowances against tax in January 1966, were designed to give more discretionary power over the direction of investment and, like selective employment tax, were strongly *dirigiste* in conception.

The prognosis accompanying the November 1964 budget was that 'there was no undue pressure on resources calling for action', though there were specific areas of imbalance.[2] The overall demand impact of the fiscal changes – with increases in social security benefits countering the effect of an increase in the standard rate of income tax (due to take effect in 1965/6) and a further rise in duties on hydro-carbon oils – was in fact broadly neutral;[3] it was consistent with the latest output forecasts, which foresaw GDP growth slowing down from 5 per cent in 1964 to about 3 per cent in 1965.[4]

By the time of the 1965 budget, however, the estimates of consumers' expenditure had risen and the tax increases of £164 million (on a

---

[1] 'In all these ways', the Chancellor stated in November 1964, 'budgetary policy must contribute to our objectives: a healthy foreign balance, stable prices and full employment, social justice for the needy, fair play for all taxpayers, sound planning of public expenditure, rewards for the energetic and sustained economic growth' (House of Commons, *Hansard*, 11 November 1964, col. 1025).

[2] Prime Minister's Office, *The Economic Situation*, para. 7.

[3] See *National Institute Economic Review*, no. 30, November 1964, p. 8.

[4] Ibid.

current year basis) which were introduced,[1] brought its forecast growth (of 2 per cent through 1965) back down to the levels forecast in November. GDP was expected to rise by $3\frac{1}{2}$ per cent up to the end of 1964 ($2\frac{1}{2}$ per cent through the financial year), so no effect was anticipated on unemployment,[2] and since the balance of payments was forecast to improve, there were favourable indications for the compatibility of external and internal stability, which the record shows were justified (charts 4.7 and 4.8). Nevertheless, speculation against sterling and supply pressures in the construction industry resulted, in July, in measures using credit restrictions (but not taxation) to hold consumption to a forecast 1 per cent growth rate through 1965. With the accompanying public investment cuts, these were intended to hold GDP to $2\frac{1}{2}$ per cent growth through 1965/6, with an $8\frac{1}{2}$ per cent growth in exports partially offsetting the less expansionary stance of the budget (table 4.9 and chart 4.6).

The strategy of transferring resources into the balance of payments without cost to employment seems to have been successful initially and the prospects for 1966 seemed reasonably favourable. The momentum behind public expenditure was maintaining the leverage exerted by the budget, though relying on the public sector to sustain demand while private expenditure bore the brunt of the adjustment necessary to safeguard the balance of payments was to create special difficulties. Excise duties on alcohol and tobacco were thought to be near their taxable ceiling, whilst income tax increases were ruled out as prejudicial to savings and investment. Hence the hasty introduction, in the 1966 budget, of selective employment tax (to become operative only in September), which supplied most of the extra £326 million revenue to be raised in 1966/7. In the meantime however, disappointing balance of payments figures and the seamen's strike provoked more precipitate action; the deflationary package of July aimed at raising an extra £94 million in 1966/7 through the regulator (tobacco duties were exempted on this occasion), with a surcharge on surtax liabilities expected to bring in a further £25 million in 1967/8. In the context of the continuing growth of public expenditure, however, direct fiscal leverage remained very much the same as in the previous year, of the order of $6\frac{3}{4}$ per cent of full-employment GDP (table 4.9). The balance of taxation and spending increases by which this was achieved implied the strict

---

[1] The reliance on excise duties derived from the worry that purchase tax increases would prove damaging to industrial investment (House of Commons, *Hansard*, 6 April 1965, cols. 288–90).

[2] With the trend in productive capacity at $3\frac{1}{4}$ per cent a year the National Institute diagnosed some shortfall, but did not expect to see this translated into unemployment because employment was at the time 'a good deal out of adjustment' (*National Institute Economic Review*, no. 32, May 1965, p. 4).

restraint of private consumption; originally forecast to rise by some 1½ per cent through 1966/7, after the July measures a fall of a similar magnitude was forecast (reduced, in the event, to an actual decline of about ¼ per cent).

With the private sector depressed, the Chancellor chose not to intervene in the budget of 1967, relying on the recession for further improvement in the balance of payments, while restricting the decline in activity by means of public expenditure and automatic stabilisers. The actual budget deficit was intended to increase by £450 million in the calendar year 1967, with an improvement in the current balance of £200 million.[1] In the event, the current balance deteriorated by some £400 million, an outcome accounted for partly by disappointing export results, partly by an underestimate of the buoyancy of internal demand, in which an overrun by public expenditure played a role. The 2·1 per cent GDP growth in the year as a whole was double the 1 per cent originally forecast, aided in part by a relaxation of credit in June and August. The expansionary leverage of the public sector is particularly notable in retrospect, rising to 7 per cent on a weighted full-employment basis (table 4.9).

Devaluation in November was followed by fiscal adjustments designed to release resources in appropriate amounts at the appropriate time, thus combining the transformation of the balance of payments into surplus with continued high utilisation of resources. Initially cuts were announced in public expenditure plans; then taxes were increased in the 1968 budget, which was brought forward to March for that purpose – revenue being increased by £923 million. Apart from the commitment to recover the full amount of the recent increase in family allowances from income tax, the Chancellor was keen to avoid using this instrument, concern over possible adverse effects on savings being by this time fairly pronounced. However, since profits and equity prices were expected to increase, corporation tax was raised by 2½ per cent, but an increase in the rate of capital gains tax was ruled out because it was thought that its use as a short-term instrument might cause an immediate reluctance to realise profits and thus possibly a fall in yield. Instead, a special surcharge on investment income was added to surtax for 1967/8, yielding a once-and-for-all £100 million. The economic impact of these measures seems to have been less important to the Chancellor than the effects on equity and the financing requirement. Spending power was constrained by raising indirect taxes (beer duty being excepted because it was considered regressive); in all £923 million was added to tax accruals in 1968/9, the effective rate of personal sector taxation (chart 4.2A) being raised by 1½ per cent.

[1] See *National Institute Economic Review*, no. 40, May 1967, p. 8.

The financial deficit in 1968/9 was expected to be about £1000 million less than in 1967/8. In terms of demand aggregates, the effects of this were to be reflected in consumption growing at 0·25 per cent in 1968, with private investment recovering by 4½ per cent; exports were forecast to increase by 7¾ per cent in volume and imports by 1¾ per cent, giving a GDP increase of 3 per cent over 1967. All these figures turned out to be underestimates, which necessitated reinforcing measures, in the shape of a regulator surcharge, in November. This was to have a full-year impact of £250 million, so that consumption growth through 1968 was eventually held to 1·2 per cent.

The balance of payments turned round slower than expected (the improvement in the year was only £26 million compared with earlier forecasts of improvements as large as £500 million[1]) which, together with the underestimates of consumption and the necessity for supplementary intervention in November, raised questions about the effectiveness of the original fiscal strategy. This had been planned with the tax measures delayed until 1968 on the calculation that the 'elasticity effects' of devaluation would not begin to make themselves felt until the second half of that year.[2] In fact it was not until late in 1968 that the public sector financial balance began to show substantially less expansionary leverage than it had in 1967[3] and, although this was consistent with the strategy, it seems less appropriate in the light of the underestimate of the upturn in domestic and world demand (charts 4.6 and 4.7), and the capacity constraints that emerged in early 1968.[4]

The 1969 budget aimed at raising an extra £272 million in 1969/70, again through indirect taxation because income tax was ruled out.[5] The Chancellor considered whether 'even in a year as difficult as this, it would be justifiable for incentive reasons and for the encouragement of savings,

---

[1] *National Institute Economic Review*, no. 43, February 1968. By May this forecast had been trimmed back to an expected improvement of £140 million.

[2] Ibid, no. 42, November 1967, pp. 10–11.

[3] At an annual rate (for the four quarters up to and including the quarter in question) the public sector balance was as follows:

£ million

1967 II	1967 III	1967 IV	1968 I	1968 II	1968 III	1968 IV	1969 I
−1227	−1447	−1648	−1828	−1795	−1608	−1136	−548

[4] The situation at the time was confused. Unemployment still seemed high, but the relationship between unemployment and vacancies had changed and the latter, like the statistics of capacity utilisation and overtime rates, suggested that demand pressures in 1968 were quite as high as they had been in the boom years of 1961 and 1964 (see *London and Cambridge Economic Bulletin*, November 1968 and January 1969).

[5] There were also a number of constraints on indirect taxation. Duties on tobacco and spirits could not be raised because it was feared that this would diminish revenue. It was also preferred to expand the base of purchase tax rather than to increase rates, which might have been seen as encouraging those who had tried to anticipate this by pre-budget spending.

to mitigate slightly the rates of tax on high earned incomes';[1] an increase in the earned income allowance was regarded as a high priority for a later budget.[2] Meantime, the tax threshold was raised by a combination of higher personal allowances and the abolition of the lowest reduced rate (which raised the initial rate to $23\frac{1}{3}$ per cent) without any net effect on demand. The public sector financial balance as a whole, which had improved by £1280 million in 1968/9, was meant to improve by about a further £1100 million, bringing a surplus of over £500 million despite an unexpectedly large increase in unemployment (table 4.9).

In the two years following devaluation, the discretionary budgetary leverage provided by the public sector was greatly reduced, from 7 per cent of full-employment GDP to about $1\frac{1}{2}$ per cent, the contribution of changes in taxation and in public expenditure being about equal (chart 4.6). Further, a current account surplus of £727 million was achieved and GDP grew at an annual average rate of about 3 per cent, so that in this respect fiscal policy and devaluation may be said to have worked. It is possible that the immediate budgetary action accompanying devaluation was inadequate viewed from the cyclical situation at the time, but, this apart, the most salient point about the devaluation strategy was that even the somewhat tardy turn-round in the full-employment public sector balance was uniquely stabilising, in that *for the first time* (as chart 4.8 shows) the domestic budgetary cycle was inversely phased with the world demand cycle – a characteristic which has otherwise been conspicuously absent in the United Kingdom.[3] This implied, however, that at some time after the 1969 budget fiscal policy should have been relaxed to compensate for the relative falling-off of world trade and investment which then ensued. Because the consolidation of an external surplus appeared paramount this was not done, and the fact that no reflationary action was taken (despite the advice of outside commentators such as the National Institute) until the other sectors of demand were picking up again (chart 4.8) is crucial to the understanding of stabilisation policy in the early 1970s.

The second Conservative period, June 1970–February 1974

The legacy of the planning era was thus potentially beneficial as well as detrimental to the economy. On the detrimental side there was the excessive growth of the public sector, so that from 1969/70, when both the public sector balance and the overseas balance moved into surplus, fiscal policy could turn to reducing the accumulated burden on the private sector. A good deal of this had been built up through hidden

---

[1] House of Commons, *Hansard*, 15 April 1969, col. 999.   [2] Ibid. cols. 1031–2.
[3] This is not to say that exploiting the world cycle is an answer, in itself, to competitive inadequacy, but it is potentially a factor to compensate for the inadequacy.

increases in the average rate of income tax, with company taxes and indirect taxes being increased by discretionary means. (The first relaxation had come in Roy Jenkins' 1970 budget, which reduced the personal income tax by £191 million; this reform followed the 1969 pattern by raising the tax threshold and abolishing the one remaining reduced rate, so raising the initial rate of tax to 32 per cent (table 4.1).)[1] The move towards reducing income tax – and taxation in general – was taken much further by the incoming Conservative administration, which undid several of the structural tax reforms introduced during Labour's period of office. A series of structural measures was announced in the 1971 budget: the unification of the personal income and surtax systems, with lower marginal rates on earned income; the substitution of VAT for purchase tax and selective employment tax; the abolition of the second-tier tax on company distributions; the proposed unification of the social security and income tax systems through the mechanism of tax credits; the immediate substitution of investment allowances for grants (in October 1970).

Demand management continued for a time in the same cautious vein, aimed at keeping demand roughly in line with productive potential. The stimulus to export demand had continued throughout 1969/70 (the volume increase being 11 per cent), but was expected to fall to 4 per cent through 1970/1. The budget, though introducing a measure of relaxation, implied the same weighted *ex ante* leverage as in the previous year: at $1\frac{1}{2}$ per cent of potential GDP (table 4.9), this was extremely deflationary in view of the lack of stimulus from other sources. The projected $3\frac{1}{4}$ per cent growth rate was, in the event, optimistic, and the realised budget surplus, not least because of the downturn in activity, was £1000 million less than forecast.

The emergence of the two evils which were to plague economic policy in the 1970s – cost inflation and unemployment – was rather ambivalently contributing to the cautious stance of budgetary policy at this time. On the one hand there was a belief that the two were causally connected,[2] so that reduced public spending plans tended to be rationalised partly on grounds of the slower growth of the economy and the increased cost of programmes.[3] On the other hand, it was the

---

[1] Such had been the alteration in the balance of direct and indirect taxation (chart 4.2) that the Chancellor even considered substantially raising indirect taxes in order to finance even larger reductions in income tax, but he was dissuaded by the belief that price rises occurring as a result would be a stimulus to inflation (House of Commons, *Hansard*, 14 April 1970, cols. 1242–3).

[2] The rise in unemployment in 1970/1 was due to the relatively slow growth of output, but it also reflected 'rapidly rising wage costs', which had forced employers to cut down on labour (House of Commons, *Hansard*, 30 March 1971, col. 1362).

[3] Treasury, *New Policies for Public Spending*.

Chancellor's belief that the fight against inflation would not be aided by a further reduction in the pressure of demand, even though fiscal policy should avoid creating the additional danger of demand inflation.[1] Budgetary policy, as expressed in the interventions of October 1970 and March 1971, was cautious, preferring to err towards a lower pressure of demand, though trying to maintain a rate of growth equal to productive potential.

The first package was avowedly neutral in its effects on demand, the projected cut in the standard rate of income tax in 1971/2 nominally offsetting the expenditure cuts. The decrease in the rate of corporation tax was, however, intended to have a longer-term effect on investment;[2] on a weighted basis the whole package was slightly reflationary. The out-turn leverage of the budget was still, however, only 2·5 per cent of full-employment GDP – much less than even in 1962/3.

Maintaining such a stance through 1971/2 would have meant a shortfall from potential, so the 1971 budget introduced some correcting measures to increase the growth rate from a projected 2 to 3 per cent. Through a combination of income tax changes (amounting with the cut in the standard rate in October 1970 to £500 million in 1971/2), a further reduction in the rate of company tax and the partial abolition of selective employment tax, the total discretionary revenue decrease in 1971/2 was over £850 million. Even so, the change in the weighted *ex ante* leverage was slight, partly because of the effects of fiscal drag. It required a further reduction in purchase tax rates on 19 July 1971 and a series of public expenditure measures to increase budgetary leverage from 2·5 to 3·6 per cent of potential GDP in 1971/2 (table 4.9). This was sufficient, with a recovery in export demand in the second half of the year, to keep GDP growth up to the original target of 3 per cent in 1971, with an increased current account surplus. (The real extent of the employment gap implied by four years of growth below potential, had, however, caused a revision of the growth target in mid-1971, to 4–4½ per cent through 1971/2, so that the out-turn represented a shortfall from this.)

In the 1972 budget the Chancellor chose to continue the momentum he saw in the economy by raising the growth target to 5 per cent between the second half of 1971 and the first half of 1973. To achieve this, £1200 million was to be remitted in taxation and the budget deficit was expected to increase substantially to £2441 million. To safeguard the balance of payments the exchange rate was to be allowed to float if necessary – a significant factor in view of the sharply rising tide of

[1] House of Commons, *Hansard*, 30 March 1971, col. 1369.
[2] The cut in the rate applied to taxes on 1969 profits and involved refunds where payments had already been made.

imports, which had begun to swell towards the end of 1971/2 and was accounting for much of the shortfall in domestic output through that year.

The Chancellor relied mainly on income tax for reflationary effect, £982 million being remitted through an increase in personal allowances (against which should be set fiscal drag of about £700 million). A boost to consumption greater than its nominal value (£7 million in a full year) was given by allowing loan interest over £35 against tax – a concession that did not apply to hire purchase debt. The rest of the package was made up of cuts in purchase and company tax (table 4.2). Overall, the budget introduced the largest discretionary change in leverage of the whole period by a considerable margin. The intended stance, in weighted full-employment terms, was approximately 6·15 per cent of full-employment GDP and, though this represented a return only to the 1965–7 level of intervention, the implied change in direct budgetary leverage from the previous year was – at about 3 per cent of GDP – without precedent. Neither this nor the growth objective were, in the event, achieved; GDP increased only at a 3¼ per cent annual rate over the eighteen months to mid-1973, and the full-employment budget balance turned out at 5·23 per cent in 1972/3 because of substantial shortfalls in public expenditure. The current account balance deteriorated by £1215 million to −£237 million.

At the time of the 1973 budget the erosion of the external position was already apparent, although the output target still seemed achievable.[1] The budget therefore followed a strategy of 'no change', maintaining the objective of 5 per cent growth through 1973/4, while being 'broadly neutral' on the tax front.[2] April 1973 was, however, the date for the inception of several tax reforms announced previously, and these were to cost about £460 million in a full year. The unified income tax system entailed a tax reduction of £300 million, though the savings content of this must have been fairly high because much of the benefit was to unearned incomes and higher levels of earned income; on the other hand, both the changeover to an imputation system of company taxation and the introduction of VAT at a standard rate of 10 per cent were fairly neutral in effect. The extra leverage exerted by the full-employment balance in 1973/4 was in fact to come from the expenditure side, with the nominal deficit increasing to an intended £2853 million and the weighted full-employment balance to 6·3 per cent of full-employment GDP (an increase of about 1 per cent over the 1972/3 out-turn). Expecting an upturn in manufacturing investment, the

[1] The 1973/4 Financial Statement gave a GDP growth rate of 6·8 per cent between the second half of 1971 and the first half of 1973.
[2] House of Commons, *Hansard*, 6 March 1973, col. 249.

Chancellor avoided demand cuts which would prejudice this; in addition, export demand was expected to recover strongly. In 1973, which turned out to be the peak of the world demand cycle (chart 4.8), there was thus a reversion to the pre-devaluation pattern, by which burgeoning export and investment demand coincided with expansion in other sectors of the economy led by a fiscal deficit. This time the output targets were achieved for 1973, though the oil crisis and the three-day week gave a different result for the financial year, but it was at the expense of, or in conjunction with, a further deterioration of £1263 million in the current balance, which reached −£1500 million.

Whether this conjunction of expansionary budgeting and a deteriorating payments position was causal or coincidental is a matter of some dispute among economists, the 'New Cambridge' school being only the most prominent of the critics of the official position. The basic judgement of policy-makers and those who supported their position throughout this episode was that the economy began by carrying very substantial excess capacity (estimated by the National Institute at 6 per cent of GDP in 1971[1]) and the continued 5 per cent growth target (granted that underlying productive potential was growing at over 3 per cent per annum) was no more than consistent with the steady removal of this unused capacity. The floating of the exchange rate was seen primarily as a protection against the contingency that the recovery would be prematurely halted by speculation against the pound. The initial diagnosis of excess capacity is, however, disputable, because the behaviour of unemployment was inconsistent with that of other indicators; by other measures (vacancies, capacity utilisation, etc.), the margin of excess capacity was not great in 1973 – it was indeed comparable to that existing in the boom year of 1964. Moreover, there is no doubt that, whatever the 'aggregate' margin of spare resources, there were numerous specific bottlenecks encountered at this time.

A second problem is that, even if there were a clear agreement on the margin of spare resources, this does not readily translate into an agreement over policy, which involves a calculation not only of the added amount of demand required, but also of the rate at which demand should be augmented. It is not implausible to argue that the rate of change of demand is as significant as the level for its inflationary potential;[2]

[1] Assuming 'full employment' at a registered unemployment rate of 1½ per cent (cf. *National Institute Economic Review*, no. 63, February 1973, pp. 44-5).

[2] There is not much empirical evidence on this issue. However, the argument is eminently plausible that if demand is added to an economy at a high rate this will exceed the rate at which production schedules can easily be raised and the gap will be filled by imports, rationing and price rises. On the importance of the *speed* of the upswing in creating pressures and bottlenecks, see F. P. R. Brechling and J. N. Wolfe, 'The end of stop-go', *Lloyd's Bank Review*, no 75, January 1965, pp. 23-30; for a sceptical viewpoint, see P. M. Oppenheimer,

here, it is important to note not only that the turn-round in fiscal policy attempted in those two years was very large,[1] but also that it was accompanied by an expansive convulsion in monetary policy of an unparalleled kind.

These considerations suggest that fiscal policy in this period may very well have attempted too much too quickly. The 'New Cambridge' school were more definite in their criticism, which was based upon the proposition that the projected public sector deficit (£2853 million in 1973/4) could not be matched by private sector savings at the foreseen output levels and therefore could only be realised if there was a direct spill-over into the balance of payments (excess demand was here put in the region of £500–£600 million).[2] The uniqueness of this view – and the source of greatest dispute – rests on the precision with which private sector savings are held to be predictable and hence the precision with which the spill-over can be identified.

Another element of 'New Cambridge' criticism was of earlier origin and more general validity. It was that domestic demand-led growth is a chimera, for in the long run the growth of the economy must be determined by the growth of exports.[3] Relying on domestic demand for reflation disposes towards budgetary immobility at the top of the cycle, since 'governments have been plagued with the dilemma whether to restrain consumption so as to provide more resources for investment or exports, or to allow relatively free rein to consumer demand to ensure the growth of capacity'.[4] By relying on export growth, the confidence effects on investment (such as they are) caused by reining back domestic demand may be avoided and the greater scope for productivity gains thought to attach to the export sector exploited. The 1972/3 episode was the last and perhaps the most dramatic of the attempts to use domestic demand to break through to the 'virtuous circle' of demand-induced growth and investment. As history stands it failed.

BUDGETARY POLICY AND STABILISATION, 1959/60–1973/4

It would be a mistake to see the conduct of demand management as related immutably to one particular objective of policy. At times, it has been used (with and without the added help of other instruments)

'Is Britain's worsening trade gap due to bad management of the business cycle?', *Bulletin of the Oxford University Institute of Economics & Statistics*, vol. 27, August 1965, pp. 177–83.

[1] Out-turns were less expansive than intended (especially in 1972/3) largely because of shortfalls in expenditure, some of which may have been due to market difficulties.

[2] R. R. Neild, *London and Cambridge Economic Bulletin*, July 1973; W. A. H. Godley and F. Cripps, *The Times*, 6 September 1973. See also pages 137–8 above.

[3] W. A. H. Godley and F. Cripps, *The Times*, 9 January 1973; Kaldor (ed.), *Conflicts in Policy Objectives*.   [4] Ibid. p. 15.

as a means of achieving all the major economic objectives; at other times there has been a conscious trade-off between them – particularly unemployment and the balance of payments. Nevertheless, there remains a dimension to demand management which is summed up in its effectiveness as a stabiliser, in which it is dependent on the reliability of short-term forecasts. It is true that such forecasts can be overridden by political expediency, but the process of budget-making in the United Kingdom is based on the belief that aggregate demand can be forecast, and then balanced by appropriate intervention.

Fiscal neutrality

In assessing fiscal policy the first requirement is to establish some concept of neutrality.[1] One such rule specifies neutrality as unchanged tax rates; that is, statutory tax rate changes provide indices of deviations from neutrality. This is attractive because the budget is the ultimate balancing exercise. Tax changes are, however, frequently made in order to pay for public expenditure changes, so that they cannot be thought of simply as means of offsetting changes in other components of demand; more to the point, we have seen how powerful automatic tax movements can be, so that effective rather than statutory tax rate changes might be more logical indicators of changes in fiscal stance. Fiscal drag would then be implicitly defined as discretionary, which conforms with policy-makers' frequent use of the buoyancy of the revenue as a substitute for (or supplement to) discretionary action proper.

Even so, changes in revenue can only be partial indicators of policy action, so that the public sector financial balance can be regarded as the best measure of fiscal policy stance, provided that it is translated into full-employment terms and, according to the form of analysis to which it is subjected, weighted or not for the differential impact on demand of different types of revenue and expenditure.

The record of stabilisation

Discussion of the success of budgetary policy in stabilising the economy usually starts from Dow's pessimistic conclusion for the 1950s that 'budgetary and monetary policy must be regarded as having been positively destabilising'.[2] Tests of stabilising adequacy, however, conventionally require an estimate of the domestic output cycle in the absence of intervention. Policy is then presumed to have damped fluctuations in the economy if this cycle (net-of-policy) shows greater variation than the actual cycle. Representing fiscal policy by discretion-

[1] Worswick, 'Fiscal policy and stabilization in Britain', p. 50, and page 154 above.
[2] Dow, *The Management of the British Economy, 1945–60*, p. 384.

ary tax changes,[1] the results of such tests have been ambiguous. Whereas, for the period 1955–65 Bristow's verdict was that policy had been marginally stabilising, Artis's results for the periods 1958–70 and 1965–70 showed it to have been slightly destabilising.[2] However, perhaps most noticeable was the smallness of the effects either way (as well, indeed, as the smallness of the fluctuations to be offset). The effects of total budgetary leverage were also found to be slightly destabilising by the OECD country study of the period 1955–65, which concluded that the United Kingdom was unique in this respect.[3] The 'pure cycle' (net-of-policy) appeared to have been amplified by 11 per cent for the public sector or 13 per cent for the central government. Following a different approach, the Brookings Institution also criticised budgetary policy for being destabilising: from a reaction function analysis of policy changes over the period 1951–65, it appeared that interventions had been triggered by changes in unemployment – an indicator which lags GDP changes by about a year and which, if used as a basis of policy formulation, must of necessity lead to instability.[4] Despite the methodological and other misgivings attached to all tests of demand management, there remains a consensus against a positive contribution to stability from budgetary policy.

Simulation procedures used for testing the impact of interventions

[1] Testing for the stabilising effectiveness of policy by comparing fluctuations in the economy with and without discretionary tax interventions is not strictly a test of counter-cyclical policy, since the changes in tax may, in fact, be compensating for variations in the public sector itself (cf. chapter 3, page 124). It is, however, a test of short-term budgetary adequacy as practised in the United Kingdom, where tax changes are ultimately called on to balance *all* sources of excess or deficient demand.

[2] J. A. Bristow, 'Taxation and income stabilisation', *Economic Journal*, vol. 78, June 1968, pp. 299–311; Artis, 'Fiscal policy for stabilization'. Bristow's analysis was based on Hopkin and Godley, 'An analysis of tax changes', while Artis analysed the model described in J. R. Shepherd and M. J. C. Surrey, 'The short-term effects of tax changes', *National Institute Economic Review*, no. 46, November 1968, pp. 36–41, which included an allowance for accelerator effects on investment, whereas the previous model did not. Bristow found that for the cycle net-of-policy the ratio of GDP to its logarithmic trend was 0·90, compared with a ratio of 0·91 for the actual cycle; that is, that 0·01 of instability had been offset by policy. Artis's results showed that for both periods policy had increased instability by 0·01 (1958–70 : 0·99 net-of-policy, 0·98 with-policy, and 1956–70 : 0·97 net-of-policy, 0·96 with-policy).

[3] OECD, *Fiscal Policy in Seven Countries*, pp. 69–71. Of the countries studied, the United States appeared to be the only one which offset over half of the exogenous fluctuations in the economy, the others having been mainly 30–40 per cent successful.

[4] Caves *et al.*, *Britain's Economic Prospects*, p. 489. Changes in total public sector leverage and in tax rates appear to have been expansionary when unemployment was increasing and deflationary when unemployment was falling (the statistical significance of the relationship between total leverage and unemployment being quite small). The general methodology of the Musgraves has been criticised by Worswick, 'Fiscal policy and stabilization in Britain', pp. 42–7, but it is true that up to the 1960s the lagged relationship between employment and output was not well known. There was a formal reappraisal of reactions between these two indicators in the early 1960s, so that after this it cannot be said that policy was premised on ignorance of the lags involved (cf. W. A. H. Godley and J. R. Shepherd, 'Long-term growth and short-term policy', *National Institute Economic Review*, no. 29, August 1964).

call for a full-scale model of the economy and a knowledge of the lags involved. On pages 190–1 above an alternative method of testing budgetary adequacy was set out which overcomes the problem of lags.[1] If the (intended) full-employment public sector balance is accepted as the indicator of fiscal policy, fiscal adequacy can be assessed by comparing changes in the value of that indicator with changes in the overseas and private sector balances, also evaluated at full employment. A regression using the intended change in the weighted full-employment balance (P'^{fe}) and, as proxies for the *ex ante* changes in overseas and private sector financial balances, world exports of manufactures (X) and investment in the private sector (I) (all expressed as ratios of full-employment GDP) gave the following result:[2]

$$\Delta P'^{fe} = 0.52\Delta(I+X) \quad (\text{SE} = 0.20, \quad t = 2.49, \quad R^2 = 0.21). \quad (9)$$

The negative sign expected if fiscal policy was stabilising does not appear;[3] indeed, discounting the two years after devaluation, the budgetary cycle appears to have been positively phased with the private investment and export cycles, as is borne out by chart 4.8. As far as the relationship of the budgetary cycle with the investment cycle is concerned, reflationary budgeting has tended to lead (in 1959/60, 1963/4 and late 1971), but with a tendency for an overlap as the upturn in activity takes hold. At this point budgetary leverage usually ceases to exert any *extra* demand leverage, though the budgetary stance (for reasons considered below) tends to be maintained at peak level by so-called 'neutral' budgeting (1960/1, 1964/5 and 1973/4). This conjunction of peak budgetary leverage and investment demand has then tended to be followed by reinforcing downturns (1961/2–1962/3 and 1965/6). The pattern seems to have been broken in 1966/7 and 1967/8, when the budgetary turn-round was checked, and by devaluation in 1968/9, though this favourable conjunction gave way in 1970/1 to an unfavourable one, when reflationary action was delayed – a reversion

---

[1] Musgrave 'On measuring fiscal performance', p. 261. However, the caveats attached to the use of a 'reaction function' analysis of this comparative static type should be kept in mind (page 189 above).

[2] Changes in the intended *ex ante* balances should be used to avoid problems caused by forecasting errors, but in practice the precise data required are not available. The proxies used here are the *ex post* figures of the (change in) deviation from trend of gross domestic capital formation in the private sector (as described in chart 3.6) and world demand for exports (given by the United Nations volume index for manufactures). Both cycles being translated into GDP terms (chart 4.8), perfect stabilisation would give a coefficient of -1.

[3] Regressions were also run against each of the two proxies separately:

$$\Delta P'^{fe} = 0.69\Delta I \quad (\text{SE} = 0.39, \quad t = 1.79, \quad R^2 = 0.12)$$
$$\Delta P'^{fe} = 0.72\Delta X \quad (\text{SE} = 0.34, \quad t = 2.16, \quad R^2 = 0.17)$$

All the equations discount the extremely stabilising budget changes of the two post-devaluation years and are based on the calendar and financial year data in chart 4.8.

to the usual pattern of reinforcing recessionary pressures. There has been a similar tendency for the budgetary cycle to reinforce the world demand cycle, except immediately after devaluation, and in this case the conjunction in trends has tended to appear almost immediately (1959/60, 1963/4 and 1972/3), with a degree of symmetry also appearing at the top of the two cycles as domestic and external leverage is maintained (1960/1, 1964/5 and 1973/4).

Pro-cyclical budgeting

However, the less than beneficial effect of fiscal policy on domestic stability needs two qualifications: first, it is not implied that stability has been markedly worsened, only not improved, since public demand can fluctuate at least as much as non-government demand before the impact becomes worse than if the cycle applied to the economy as a whole. Secondly, variations around the trend of output in the United Kingdom have not, including demand management effects, been as great as in other (faster-growing) countries.[1] Nevertheless,.it still has to be explained why demand management has been pro-cyclical, and one can advance three hypotheses: first, the techniques and instruments of demand management may have been insufficient, and forecasting inaccuracies may have misled policy; secondly, demand and output instability might be explained by the electoral cycle; thirdly, since the tactics of demand management have not been applied in an unchanging strategic framework, output stability may have been sacrificed from time to time to the balance of payments, or risked by 'growth experiments'. The performance of stabilisation policy seems explicable in terms of each of these factors, though it is a matter for subjective judgement which was most important.

As instances of forecasts misleading policy, there were the wrong diagnosis in 1962 and the underestimate of the downturn in 1970, while the 1959/60 and 1972/3 reflations seem to have been guided by pessimistic views of the actual demand forces in the economy. However, once the economy gets off course it becomes increasingly difficult to withstand political pressures for action, so that there has also been a tendency for output forecasts to be overruled for short-term gains. Excessive reflation, for instance, has been explained by reference to the electoral cycle[2] – the expansions of 1953/4, 1958/9 and 1963/4 closely preceded elections, though that of 1972/3 did not. Moreover, 'neutral' budgeting at the height of the boom might be partly attributable to

[1] See A. Whiting, 'An international comparison of the instability of economic growth', *Three Banks Review*, no. 109, March 1976, pp. 26–46.

[2] See memoranda by G. D. N. Worswick in House of Commons, *Ninth Report from the Expenditure Committee, Session 1974*, pp. 28–33.

reluctance to be seen altering course once an election has taken place, particularly if it might appear in breach of a pre-election declaration; the 1960 dispute between Macmillan and his deflationist Chancellor comes into this category, as does the budget of 1966. But interventions for immediate economic and political ends can come to be represented as strategic changes. Deflations may be seen as transferring priorities towards the balance of payments, or as lowering the pressure of demand to mitigate inflation and even improve export performance.[1] Correspondingly, reflations tend to become opportunities not just for filling a particular demand gap, but for solving all the problems of economic policy by expansion, which may be part of the explanation of reflationary over-reaction. Although it may also depend on the under-forecasting of upturns, consumption-led growth (possibly mixed with public expenditure-led growth, as in 1963/4) has been the dominant philosophy behind expansionism in the United Kingdom and it is a characteristic of such a strategy that it becomes difficult to rein consumption back once the upturn is under way, because it is believed that to do so would adversely affect investment.

The idea that the British economy has been subject to recurrent bouts of 'planned instability' arising from deliberate deflationary policies[2] may be extended to the successive switches between expansion and contraction, during which stabilisation policy proper has been compromised. In this sense, it may have been that too much has been expected of demand management and that, if the successive policies have failed, it is because productive potential has not been pushed up as hoped, secondary export expansion (through increased competitiveness) has not been achieved and the balance of payments constraint has never been overcome. Because faster growth has been impossible to achieve, stability has also been impossible.

To summarise, it seems that the pro-cyclical tendency of budgetary policy may be ascribed to a combination of all three factors. Forecasting errors have certainly played their part, but are by no means more important than the other elements, for the political pressures accompanying adverse employment and balance of payments indicators have always been powerful enough to override, in the last analysis, any mechanistic forecast-linked demand management policy; at the same time, it has been a notable feature of fiscal policy that it has been used not simply for 'fine-tuning' of demand but to try to break through supply constraints. Domestic stability appears to have been compromised by failure to raise the growth of productive potential in this way.

---

[1] On the 'toothpaste tube' approach to exports – that when demand is squeezed exports are extruded – see Worswick, 'Fiscal policy and stabilization in Britain', p. 53.

[2] Kennedy, 'Employment policy: what went wrong?'.

CONCLUSIONS

The operation of budgetary policy

Budgetary policy in the United Kingdom has been characterised both by an active short-term policy towards tax rates and by the pursuit of longer-run structural reform. Discretionary interventions have been largely identified with income tax decreases and expenditure tax increases, but this asymmetry has to be seen in the context of the automatic biases in the system associated with inflationary fiscal drag. These have resulted in increases in the effective rate of personal income tax and decreases in indirect tax rates, with the net result that the overall reliance of the system on personal income tax has increased, though not as a conscious act of policy.

With respect to both real and inflationary income movements, the aggregate yield of taxes on personal income (direct and indirect) has exhibited an elasticity greater than unity, which tends to increase without discretionary correction. The net fiscal drag which has resulted has been behind the increase over the period in the aggregate effective rate of tax; the rapid inflation of the early 1970s accelerated this, so that budget-making became increasingly involved with offsetting, rather than exploiting, the bias. This factor, together with the unwanted changes in the tax-mix, the augmented 'patronage powers' of Chancellors who can remit large increases in taxes, and the fact that automatic movements disguise the true discretionary stance of the budget, formed the basis of the case for 'indexing' the tax system – that is, fixing tax rates in real terms to eliminate inflationary fiscal drag. The case for this has also been argued from other points of view, most notably because of the regressive effects which fiscal drag may have on the distribution of the tax burden and of post-tax incomes. But, though inflation tends to have especially adverse effects on lower income earners at and near the tax threshold, fiscal drag has actually been associated, by and large, with a movement towards a more progressive distribution of post-tax incomes.

Whilst discretionary budgetary policy has become increasingly preoccupied with the offsetting of automatic biases, the built-in properties of the system have themselves grown in relative strength. British budgetary practice has never explicitly employed automatic stabilisers, preferring to adjust tax yields in order to balance demand, but the built-in damping potential of the tax structure tends to be augmented unless corrected by discretionary action, as marginal rates and elasticities automatically increase with the growth of incomes. This has been particularly marked in the case of marginal rates (built-in flexibility), which determine the strength of automatic stabilisers; it has also, to a lesser extent, been a feature of the aggregate elasticities of the tax system, which determine fiscal drag.

The period has seen a substantial overhaul of the tax structure. The personal income tax system has been simplified administratively by the abolition of reduced rates of tax and the unification of income tax and surtax. The relatively high maximum rates of tax on earned income have been abated and the graduation of the system at its lower end has been reduced; among advanced industrial countries the British tax threshold has become one of the lowest and the 30 per cent initial rate of tax (raised to 35 per cent in 1975/6) one of the highest. The indirect tax system has also been simplified (the revised rate structure being associated with increased costs of collection). Doubts on economic grounds about discriminating against income-elastic goods led to a reduction and standardisation of purchase tax and eventually to the introduction of VAT at a single standard rate. But this trend was not consistent: selective employment tax, while removing one element of discrimination by taxing services, was still based on a preference for manufacturing industry. The clash between 'interventionist' and 'neutralist' attitudes towards the role of the tax structure in resource allocation, which was evident here, had a parallel in the shaping and reshaping of company taxes to be neutral towards or discriminate against distributions. Here, and in the tax system at large, the net outcome over the period was in favour of a more 'neutral' and uniform structure, a process in which efficiency (either administrative or economic) has been advanced over the redistributive functions of the system, which might be better served by a more highly differentiated and progressive structure.

The reforms and counter-reforms of the period have been criticised as introducing a degree of uncertainty and instability. A number of fundamental changes sprang 'fully armed from the Chancellor's head',[1] with no prior public discussion and little chance of consensus. In this respect, the practice of issuing consultative documents in the form of Green Papers in the latter part of the period extended the boundaries of debate and increased the possibilities of reform with stability. Parallel improvements can be identified in the operation of budgetary policy, where the reform of the Exchequer accounts was followed, in 1968/9, by publication of forecasts for the financial balance and borrowing requirement of the public sector, enabling the overall leverage of budgetary policy to be interpreted more easily. There still exists, however, no coordinated longer-term strategy with respect to either the internal balance and structure of the tax system, or the balance of public spending and taxation, such as would emerge from a medium-term (or full-employment) budgeting system (see page 130 above).

[1] Prest, *The Capital Gains Tax and the Corporation Tax*, p. 19.

The effectiveness of budgetary policy

The effectiveness of short-term fiscal action has been questioned to a considerable degree. Besides criticisms which depend on alternative models of economic behaviour, there are judgements on the performance of fiscal policy within its own terms of reference *vis-à-vis* the objectives of demand management. Full employment (in some degree) has been achieved, but only associated with balance of payments deficits and inflation which have made it unsustainable for more than a short period. However, it has long been recognised that price stability needs a separate instrument, while it is difficult to reconcile full employment with balance of payments equilibrium when the economy is competitively inadequate. Fiscal policy should not, therefore, be judged by objectives which it could not be expected to achieve.

Nevertheless, budgetary policy has exerted a pro-cyclical influence; indeed, fluctuations in the economy would have been reduced if budgetary leverage had not fluctuated. However, whilst forecasting errors (including those relating to public expenditure trends) have at times been misleading and encouraged policy-makers to leave correction too late, fiscal (and other) policy has not always aimed at stabilising demand in a mechanistic way. Political pressures and external crises have sometimes evoked responses which sacrificed domestic stability, while deliberate attempts to induce faster growth (as opposed to cyclical recovery) have fundamentally compromised stability; because domestic demand was the instrument chosen to influence growth, there was a tendency for excess demand to emerge at the peak of the cycle, with some spill-over into the balance of payments. In this respect policy is particularly open to the criticism that it did not (part knowingly at least) exploit the periodic upswings in world demand as opportunities to improve the balance of payments and growth simultaneously. Only at the time of devaluation was there a conjunction of deflationary budgeting and output growth based on the world and domestic output cycles, but this advantage was lost by delaying the subsequent reflation.

The short-term element in demand management, as practised in the United Kingdom and epitomised in the term 'fine-tuning', was the product of the circumstances in which it has operated. The cycles in activity up to 1973/4 were not in fact very deep, so that conclusions about the period 1959/60–1973/4 may be peculiar to the circumstances of the time; even if the verdict were unfavourable, it would not rule out using budgetary policy when the troughs of activity were deeper (as after the oil crisis), or where there was a secular unemployment problem. It may be, however, that the short-term horizon of eighteen months to two years is too short, which is an argument for extending medium-term budgeting techniques.

In budgetary circumstances similar to those which obtained up to 1973/4 it might be that there should be a greater emphasis on medium-term policy, with correspondingly less on balancing demand in the short term. This at any rate is a possible verdict of experience, but such a conclusion cannot be drawn unambiguously from the record of stabilisation. Short-term policy *has* actually been subordinated, from time to time, to strategies for economic growth which may to some extent be called medium-term, and stabilisation has been compromised. Requiring that budgetary policy be framed around medium-term consistency therefore somewhat begs the questions of what the rule should be, how it should be maintained against immediate political and other pressures, and how it can be prevented from eventually becoming destabilising in the short run.

If a solution is to be found to the relative roles of short-term and medium-term policy, it is probably neither in continuing what has gone before nor in adopting some unbending rule of medium-term neutrality. Past expansions have been pro-cyclical because the strength of exogenous demand forces – world demand and investment – have been underestimated and because relying on domestic demand-led growth involved a conscious policy choice. In other words, policy has never been intentionally counter-cyclical in any very meaningful sense, so that there remains the option of clearly adhering to this aim in future. This, in turn, would mean greater reliance on the medium-term (cyclical and trend) prognosis, so as to ensure (as was not the case in the past when expansions started from balance of payments surplus) that any upturn can be sustained in the longer run and does not entail competition for resources between deficit-financed expenditure, investment and exports.

CHAPTER 5

MONETARY POLICY

PART I

by *J. H. B. Tew*

INSTRUMENTS AND OBJECTIVES

The 'new approach' to monetary policy, inaugurated by the Bank of England's consultative document 'Competition and credit control' of May 1971,[1] did not represent a break in the continuing objectives of that policy. But there were changes in the instruments by which the authorities sought to achieve their objectives and in the views of officials about the mechanism by which their actions are transmitted through the economy so as to achieve the desired objectives.

In the postwar period the objectives of British monetary policy have indeed changed very little. The two main external objectives, both treated in chapter 7, were (until June 1972) to peg the spot exchange rate for the dollar by official transactions in the foreign exchange market and to discourage excessive capital outflows. The predominant internal objective has always been demand management. In the 1950s there was also the potentially conflicting objective of keeping down the interest burden of the national debt, but by the mid-1960s this had been sub-ordinated to demand management,[2] which has meant in practice avoiding a level of demand either so low as to lead to a politically unacceptable amount of unemployment or so high as to drain away our international reserves.

The instruments of British monetary policy are official regulations and official transactions. In both cases there were changes under the 'new approach', so initially we shall consider the evolution of such instruments prior to 1971.

There were then (apart from exchange controls, to be considered in chapter 7) three main groups of *regulations*, of which the first were the balance sheet ratios observed by the clearing banks. From 1946 the London clearing banks had observed an 8 per cent minimum cash ratio,[3]

[1] Reprinted in *Bank of England Quarterly Bulletin*, vol. 11, June 1971.
[2] 'Official transactions in the gilt-edged market', *Bank of England Quarterly Bulletin*, vol. 6, June 1966; see especially p. 146.
[3] 'Cash' included notes, coin and demand deposits at the Bank of England. 'Liquid assets' included cash, call money and Treasury and commercial bills. 'Call money' here means

and from 1951 they also undertook to observe a liquid asset ratio somewhat vaguely defined as 28–32 per cent of their deposit liabilities.[1] In 1957 this was made more precise, as a minimum of 30 per cent, reduced in 1963 to 28 per cent. From 1960 the authorities attempted to improve the efficiency of the minimum liquid asset ratio by activating a scheme for Special Deposits, under which part of the liquid assets of the London clearing banks could be rendered non-liquid by being blocked in Special Deposit accounts at the Bank of England. A variant of the scheme applied to the Scottish clearing banks, which also undertook to maintain whatever liquid asset ratio each had observed hitherto. The second group of regulations took the form of lending requests. From the early 1950s onwards the banks had been accustomed to receive from time to time official advice on the composition, and subsequently also on the total amount, of their sterling lending to the private sector. In the 1950s requests were addressed only to the London and Scottish clearing banks, but as from 1961 they were extended to other banks and to the larger finance houses. The third group of regulations – controls on hire purchase terms for consumers' durable goods – were exercised with only short intermissions from 1952 to 1971. In addition to these official regulations, the London clearing banks, with the support of the authorities, operated an interest-rate cartel, which related their deposit and lending interest rates to Bank Rate.

Official *transactions* are conducted in three markets – the foreign exchange market, the money market and the gilt-edged market. There are also transactions in national savings media, but these appear not to have been used to any significant degree as an instrument of monetary policy.

From the reopening of the London foreign exchange market in the early 1950s up to the floating of the pound in 1972, the spot pound–dollar rate was pegged by official transactions in the market and, though the peg was changed from $2.80 to $2.40 in 1967, the technique of intervention remained much the same throughout the period. In the forward market, however, there was an important change in official tactics as from November 1964 (see chapter 7).

In the money market, official policy from 1951 onwards has been for the Bank to control money market rates, especially the Treasury bill rate, by acting as the residual supplier of finance to the discount houses, whether by purchases (and occasionally by sales) of bills

---

short-term lending to discount houses, bill brokers, Stock Exchange jobbers and money brokers, and the banks' own holdings of tax reserve certificates.

[1] European Communities Monetary Committee, *Monetary Policy in the Countries of the EEC. Supplement 1974 (The United Kingdom)*, Brussels, EEC, 1974, p. 22.

through its bill broker, or by transactions through the discount office. In this way the Treasury bill rate has been held on a target by broadly the same means as the pre-1972 exchange rate, though in this case the target has been readily varied since 1951, if needs be from day to day, instead of being changed only rarely and reluctantly as with the exchange rate.

In the gilt-edged market, however, official transactions, conducted by the Government Broker, have not aimed at holding the bond rate on a target – at all events not since Hugh Dalton's 'cheap money' target of $2\frac{1}{2}$ per cent was abandoned. What the Government Broker has sought to do instead was affected by policy shifts at about the beginning of the 1960s and again towards the end of the decade (culminating in the 'new approach' of 1971). In the period between these two shifts, official policy in the gilt-edged market was to 'lean against the wind': that is, to buy as well as to sell in the market, and to do so in such a way as to moderate and slow down the fluctuations in interest rates which market forces tended to bring about, while still always permitting any persistent pressure of market forces to move rates upwards or downwards.

The way in which the various instruments of British monetary policy are matched with the objectives is in many cases straightforward, as is also the transmission mechanism[1] by which the former serve to achieve the latter. Thus, prior to the floating of the pound in 1972, the objective of exchange transactions in the spot market was to peg the exchange rate; the objective both of exchange control and of exchange transactions in the forward market was to mitigate excessive external capital movements; the objective of hire purchase restrictions and of lending requests was demand management. Credit extended by the clearing banks was also controlled for purposes of demand management by the imposition of the minimum liquid asset ratio and by calling for Special Deposits.

However, the 8 per cent cash ratio imposed on the London clearing banks was not a demand management device like the liquid asset ratio. As we have already seen, the main aim of the Bank of England's transactions in the money market was to achieve control of interest rates, especially the Treasury bill rate.

Treasury bills can therefore always be turned into cash without much disturbance of the market rates of discount on them. It follows that the Bank cannot restrain the lending operations of the clearing banks by limiting the creation of cash without losing its assurance of stability of the rate on Treasury bills. It is because of this circumstance that the effective base of bank

---

[1] The term is not here used in the technical banking sense of the cheque clearing system.

credit has become the liquid assets (based on the availability of Treasury bills) instead of the supply of cash.[1]

What, then, was the purpose of the cash ratio? It seems to have served no purpose other than to stabilise the London clearing banks' demand for cash and thus to enable the Bank of England to forecast more accurately the amount of finance which the discount houses could expect from these banks, and hence how much would have to be provided by the Bank of England to achieve its desired level of interest rates in the money market. Thus, the cash ratio, together with the fixing of Bank Rate and the transactions undertaken by the discount office and the Bank's bill broker, were all instruments for controlling the level of rates prevailing in the money market.

A further instrument for controlling short-term rates – more specifically the London clearing banks' rate on 'regular' call money lent to the discount houses,[2] their overdraft rates and the rates they paid on deposit accounts – was the cartel interest-rate agreement, by which the London clearing banks, at the instigation of the authorities, used Bank Rate as the basis for determining the rates at which they themselves borrowed and lent. By making use of these various devices, the Bank had a very effective control over what may be called 'traditional' short-term rates, in particular the rates in the traditional money market – broadly those on the discount houses' assets (other than certificates of deposit) and on their liabilities.[3] On the other hand, this control did not extend to the rates prevailing in 'London's new markets for money',[4] which expanded rapidly in the 1960s, nor to deposit rates paid by the non-clearing banks, whose business was expanding no less rapidly (table 5.1).[5]

In their control of short-term rates the authorities had a mixture of objectives: to keep down the cost of the short-term national debt; to regulate demand insofar as capital expenditure was sensitive to variations in short-term rates;[6] to avoid undermining confidence in the

---

[1] Treasury, *Radcliffe Report*, para. 376.

[2] 'The rate of interest on "regular" money lent to the market by the clearing banks does not normally vary with the week-to-week fluctuations in the Treasury bill rate: it is only changed when Bank Rate is changed' (Treasury, *Radcliffe Report*, para. 360).

[3] See the evidence of the Chief Cashier as quoted in para. 360 of the *Radcliffe Report*.

[4] *Midland Bank Review*, August 1966, p. 3. See table 5.6 on page 243 below.

[5] 'Banks' in this chapter means banks in respect of which the Bank of England publishes statistics (listed in *Bank of England Quarterly Bulletin*, vol. 12, December 1972, pp. 573–5). They subdivide into 'deposit banks', 95 per cent of whose sterling deposits were at the London and Scottish clearing banks, and the following categories of other banks which will be collectively labelled the 'non-clearing banks': accepting houses; British overseas and Commonwealth banks; American banks; foreign banks and affiliates; other overseas banks; other banks in the United Kingdom.

[6] The Radcliffe Committee clearly thought that capital expenditure was fairly insensitive to variations in short-term rates.

Table 5.1. *An analysis of bank deposits,*[a] *1963–9*

£ million

	Held by UK residents		Held by overseas residents	
	At deposit[b] banks	At non-clearing[b] banks	At deposit[b] banks	At non-clearing[b] banks
1963	8,734	738	408	2,374
65	9,669	1,137	429	3,397
67	10,702	1,610	426	5,395
69	11,330	2,500[c]	459	12,883[d]

SOURCE: Bank of England, *Statistical Abstract*, no. 1, London, 1970, p. 28.

[a] At end-years; includes both sterling and other currencies, but excludes inter-bank deposits and certificates of deposit.
[b] See footnote 5 page 221.   [c] Of which approximately £2000 million in sterling.
[d] Of which a little over £1000 million in sterling.

bond market by undue irregularities in bill rates; to influence short-term external capital movements by variations in London short-term rates relative to those in foreign centres.[1] Nevertheless, although motives were mixed, it is apparent from the timing of the actions taken by the authorities that by 1960 the last objective had come to predominate.

There remains to note the purpose of official transactions in the gilt-edged market and in sales of savings certificates and other national savings media. Both are potentially relevant to demand management; the former was actively used to this end, though with disappointing results, in preference to pursuing other possible objectives; the latter was, however, very little used – the terms and yields on the various national savings media being adjusted, often belatedly and inadequately, to those prevailing in the private sector.

OFFICIAL REGULATIONS IN THE 1960s

Balance sheet ratios

Prior to the new approach of 1971 the only innovation in officially imposed balance sheet ratios was the introduction of the Special Deposits scheme to improve the effectiveness of the liquid asset ratio. Throughout the history of this scheme the Bank of England was

---

[1] There was a fifth objective in the second half of the 1950s, namely to create a demand for Treasury bills among the non-bank public by increasing the Treasury bill rate relative to the clearing banks' deposit rate, thereby depriving the clearers of liquid assets. However, with the availability of higher yielding local authority temporary debt and later of other 'new' money market assets, industrial companies and other large non-bank investors mostly lost interest in Treasury bills.

constantly expressing the hope that Special Deposits could be used as a substitute for control of advances; the hope was constantly frustrated. When the scheme was first activated in 1960, the Chancellor hoped that the banks would moderate advances rather than sell gilt-edged stock, but there was nothing in the scheme to prevent them doing this and the Government Broker's strategy of leaning against the wind[1] enabled them to unload their gilt-edged stocks without serious capital losses. So the initial intention to use the new instrument on its own was abandoned. In July 1961 the call for Special Deposits, effective as from 16 August, was part of a package which included restrictions on advances; thus Special Deposits were used as a reinforcing rather than a substitute measure. The banks were specifically told that the impact should fall primarily on advances.

During the remainder of the decade this pattern continued; nevertheless, the authorities still from time to time expressed the hope that they would be able to use Special Deposits without recourse to lending ceilings and in April 1967 actually applied such a regime to the clearing banks, the Chancellor explaining that Special Deposits would be used in future in a new and more flexible manner so as to maintain a continuous control over bank lending. He did not, however, remove the ceilings from non-clearing banks, because there was no alternative system of control for them in existence at that time.[2] The experiment lasted only until November, when a lending ceiling was again applied to all banks.

The use of Special Deposits as a means of reinforcing the Bank of England's directives on lending was given a new twist in May 1969. For some time lending by the clearing banks had been above the ceiling imposed in November 1968; they had been given until the middle of March to attain it, but in April and May were still exceeding it. The Bank therefore halved the rate of interest paid on Special Deposits. This provoked a strong reaction from the clearing banks, who protested that they were already carrying out official instructions to the best of their ability. The full rate of interest was restored in April 1970, when the ceiling was raised somewhat; the banks were then within the new ceiling.

One of the problems of the Special Deposits scheme was that part of the banking sector was exempt from imposed balance sheet ratios; the growth of this part (the non-clearing banks) had exceeded all expectations during the 1960s (table 5.1). The Bank of England was therefore concerned to find a means of controlling over 150 diverse non-clearing banks, with differing liquidity needs and practices. The Cash Deposits scheme announced in February 1968 was designed to

[1] See page 231 below.   [2] *Midland Bank Review*, May 1967, p. 26.

fill this role,[1] although it never actually came into operation. As with Special Deposits, Cash Deposits had to be made in frozen accounts at the Bank of England at the request of the Bank; they were to be levied as a percentage of all sterling deposits and all foreign currency deposits switched into sterling. Interest would normally be paid at the Treasury bill rate, but the Bank reserved the right to pay a lower rate if the response to official guidance on the development of bank credit was deemed insufficient.[2] This penal aspect of the scheme was important, since, unlike Special Deposits, Cash Deposits could not act in any way other than as a penalty on profits; the non-clearing banks did not observe a conventional liquid asset ratio and so in their case there was no fulcrum against which the authorities could press.

Lending requests

Formally at least the institutions receiving requests have cooperated on a voluntary basis; indeed in one instance they voluntarily acquiesced in penalties for infringement (page 223, above). Implicit statutory backing is, however, provided by the Bank of England Act, 1946, which gives the Bank qualified powers to 'direct' the commercial banks.

The *Radcliffe Report* regarded lending restrictions as an instrument only suitable for use in emergencies, although in such circumstances it foresaw the possible need to widen the coverage of requests to include institutions such as hire purchase finance companies. However, it was confident that in normal circumstances official market transactions could be made to exercise sufficient influence over the lending of financial institutions; moreover, though necessary in a serious crisis, in the longer term credit rationing would be subject to substantial slippage and would lead to a loss of efficiency in the capital market. The Bank's testimony to the Radcliffe Committee also made clear its distaste for restrictions on advances as a permanent or semi-permanent instrument of control.

In the event, far from withering away, lending restrictions were operative in the 1960s whenever official policy was to restrict demand. The first request was in July 1961; in its published form it was not quantified, and only a behind-the-scenes suggestion by the Bank of England led the clearing banks to interpret it as a ceiling on advances at the mid-June level.[3] Commercial bills were to be restricted as well as advances, though not by an explicit ceiling. From May 1965 onwards quantified ceilings were made explicit for both advances and commercial bills; the latter had become very necessary, since firms denied

---

[1] 'Control of bank lending – the Cash Deposits scheme', *Bank of England Quarterly Bulletin*, vol. 8, June 1968.   [2] Ibid, p. 170.
[3] *Midland Bank Review*, May 1962, p. 17.

access to overdraft finance were turning increasingly to bill finance, as is apparent from table 5.2.

The lending requests in the 1950s were addressed only to the London and Scottish clearing banks, but that of July 1961 also went to the non-clearing banks; moreover, the Finance Houses Association was advised that their members should not seek to attract deposits to finance business other than that to which they were already committed and that restrictions of credit should fall primarily on consumers' expenditure.[1] Subsequent requests went to the clearing banks, 'the other lending banking associations' and the larger finance houses.

Throughout the period non-sterling lending and lending to the public sector were excluded from the ceilings. In the six months preceding May 1968 medium-term shipbuilding credits and all lending which could be identified as going to finance exports were also excluded. This wide concession was then discontinued; from May to November 1968 the ceiling covered all sterling lending to the private sector. This was relaxed in November 1968 to exclude advances made under special schemes for exports and shipbuilding.

With each request priorities were laid down. Exports were given high

Table 5.2. *Holdings of commercial and other bills (excluding Treasury bills),[a] 1958–69*

£ million

	London clearing banks		Discount market
	UK commercial bills[b]	Other[c]	Sterling bills
1958	135	..	70
59	141	23	118
1960	133	22	117
61	195	57	183
62	197	71	189
63	231	74	249
64	343	83	302
65	356	100	339
66	354	120	404
67	347	142	437
68	302	223	560
69	258	350	629

SOURCE: Bank of England, *Statistical Abstract*, no. 1, pp. 22, 37 and 39.

[a] At December each year.

[b] Includes medium-term export credits refinanceable at the Bank of England and likewise refinanceable shipbuilding credits. See below, chapter 7, pages 357–9.

[c] Includes Treasury bills of Commonwealth and foreign governments.

[1] *Midland Bank Review*, November 1965, p. 7.

priority on every occasion; in November 1967 this was extended to cover import-saving. Regional policy also had priority, but after May 1968 it was dropped because of the overriding importance of the balance of payments. The same thing happened to productivity-increasing investment in industry and agriculture, and to bridging finance for house purchase. Low priority categories included, in all but one of the requests, lending to personal borrowers; building and property development was similarly classified up to 1967. The financing of imports was added to the low priority list as from July 1965, as was the financing of import deposits in 1968 (chapter 7 below).

Hire purchase restrictions

Although hire purchase regulations are usually regarded as a monetary instrument, they are not administered by the Bank of England and the Treasury, but by the Ministries which have at various times been responsible for trade and consumer affairs. The controls have never been applied to industrial plant and machinery, and their provisions have always regulated the minimum down-payment and the maximum period over which the purchaser has to repay the balance. The problem with the use of this instrument has always been that it has strong directional effects on particular industries. In evidence submitted to the Radcliffe Committee, the Board of Trade argued that as a general principle when restrictions have to be applied, 'measures of wide and general application are preferable to selective measures of narrow application'.[1] They added that the two main reasons for restrictions were to cut down consumer demand and release more capacity for exports, but restricting credit might well redirect consumers' expenditure into other channels and 'the result may well be that the pattern of the economy, e.g. in investment, is distorted in favour of industries which, while being of no greater importance to the national economy, are fortunate enough to escape from the hire-purchase restrictions'.[2] In oral evidence the representatives of the Board of Trade took it that a change in controls would have a once-and-for-all effect on consumer spending on durables, but they thought that a new equilibrium level would be reached after a delay of approximately twelve months.[3]

Controls on hire purchase terms were removed in 1958 and reimposed in April 1960. The demand for cars was increasing and there were regional labour bottlenecks along with a worsening in the balance of payments. The controls were aimed at cutting back demand specifically

---

[1] Treasury *Committee on the Working of the Monetary System. Principal Memoranda of Evidence*, vol. 1, London, HMSO, 1960, p. 232, para. 8.   [2] Ibid. p. 236, para. 71.

[3] Treasury, *Committee on the Working of the Monetary System. Minutes of Evidence, July 11, 1957 to April 30, 1959*, London, HMSO, 1960, question 3159.

in the industries affected, which was a return to the sort of use prevalent in the early 1950s, when they were intended to reduce the excess demand for durable goods. By January 1961 it was clear that the demand for consumer durables had been depressed more than could be justified by the need to restrict domestic expenditure as a whole; the terms were therefore relaxed.[1] In his budget speech the Chancellor admitted that the discriminatory consequences of hire purchase controls were undesirable, but did not propose any alternative. In the summer of 1965, when the controls, having been slightly relaxed in January 1961 and June 1962, were again tightened, the intention was not to depress differentially the demand for consumer durables; rather the measure was part of a general deflationary package and this was true of all hire purchase restrictions in subsequent years.

In 1968 the Crowther Committee was set up to investigate all aspects of consumer credit and its Report was published in 1971. It accepted that there were several reasons why governments liked hire purchase controls: for one thing, unlike taxes, they did not affect the retail price index; they also had an immediate psychological effect and became effective without appreciable delay. Nevertheless, the Committee condemned the use of the instrument:

It remains true that changes in terms controls have to be very sharp to produce any effect that is significant in relationship to total economic policy, and the industries affected... have the right to enquire whether the net benefit to the community is commensurate with the undoubted damage done to them, particularly since they have not been selected (latterly, at least) for their suitability to play this role, but solely by the accident of being affected by a particular control which is easy to apply.[2]

In addition they pointed out that people of means could avoid the restrictions by paying cash, by taking out personal loans or by second mortgages. They concluded that hire purchase controls should find no place among the weapons of economic policy.

In July 1971 all hire purchase controls were lifted, but there was no commitment to abolish them permanently; in fact restrictions were reimposed in December 1973 (page 251 below).

[1] *Bank of England Quarterly Bulletin*, vol. 1, March 1961, p. 9.
[2] Department of Trade and Industry, *Crowther Report*, p. 352, para. 8.2.4.

OFFICIAL TRANSACTIONS IN THE 1960s[1]

Transactions in the money market

Treasury bills, issued to cover the government's residual need for sterling finance, are offered for tender every Friday. The members of the London Discount Houses Association tender a syndicated bid to cover the whole of each week's issue; in practice they never secure the whole issue. The other tenderers are mostly non-clearing banks and the Bank of England (mainly acting on behalf of other central banks). The London clearing banks do not tender on their own account, but buy their Treasury bills from the discount houses. By agreeing to cover the whole tender the discount houses ensure that each week's issue is taken up, but the size of the tender is usually large enough to cause the discount houses to be short of finance on at least some days every week unless the Bank either buys bills or lends to the market. The Bank can be relied upon to relieve a shortage in one way or the other, though on terms of its own choosing, and by choosing the appropriate terms it determines interest rates in the traditional money market.

In the early 1960s the Bank's practice was to relieve a shortage either on penal terms (traditionally at Bank Rate) at the discount office, or on more favourable ('market') terms by purchasing Treasury bills through its bill broker. But in the course of the 1960s the Bank began to lend at the discount office also at non-penal interest rates. The first step was taken in 1966, when the Bank lent overnight at the market rates charged by the clearing banks.[2] In August 1967 for the first time loans at market rates were given for seven days and in September for five days.[3]

Though the arrangements just described normally kept the discount houses dependent on help from the Bank, it could happen on particular days that the market had an excess of funds, and on such occasions the Bank might well mop them up. In the early 1960s this was done by the Bank's bill broker coming into the market as a seller, but as from 1964 the Bank adopted the additional technique of regulating the maturities of its lending to the discount houses so as to mitigate foreseen fluctuations in the daily balance of their books. In December 1964 the Bank advanced the discount houses £24½ million, half for six and half for eight days,[4] instead of the traditional seven days, and a further development was when in June 1966 the Bank advanced money at Bank Rate overnight, to 'balance out a shortage of money on one day

---

[1] Official transactions in the foreign exchange market are treated in chapter 7.
[2] *Bank of England Quarterly Bulletin*, vol. 6, September 1966, p. 216.
[3] *Bank of England Quarterly Bulletin*, vol. 7, December 1967, p. 342.
[4] *Bank of England Quarterly Bulletin*, vol. 5, March 1965, p. 7.

with an expected surplus on the next'. Such operations 'serve to keep money short, the discount houses' repayments transferring the initial shortage from day to day'.[1]

Transactions in the gilt-edged market

In the 1950s and up to the late 1960s, save on a few brief occasions of seriously inadequate effective demand, the overwhelming preoccupation of the authorities responsible for official transactions in stocks was with what may be termed the 'flooding problem'. To Peter Thorneycroft the monetary system appeared 'like an antiquated pumping machine, creaking and groaning, leaking wildly at all the main valves, but still desperately attempting to keep down the level of the water in the mine',[2] and this preoccupation with flooding is no less apparent in the speeches of the Governor of the Bank, in the official evidence to the Radcliffe Committee and in subsequent articles in the *Bank of England Quarterly Bulletin*.

Table 5.3. *Domestic borrowing, and stock repayments and conversions, by the central government, 1955–73*

£ million

	Domestic borrowing	Stock repayments and conversions
1955–9[a]	252	909
1960–4[a]	152	854
1965–9[a]	69	1274
1970	663	1771
71	3438	1949
72	34	1414
73	2562	1735

SOURCES: Bank of England, *Statistical Abstract*, no. 1, table 1; Bank of England, *Report* (various years); *Bank of England Quarterly Bulletin*, vol. 15, March 1975, table 2, and vol. 17, September 1977, p. 321.

[a] Annual averages.

The water which is seen as flooding into the mine corresponds to the sum of two financial flows (table 5.3). The first is the government's domestic borrowing requirement, which, to the extent that it is not offset by government debt taken up by the public, has to be met by borrowing from the banks. The second flow comprises gilt-edged maturities which have to be refinanced; in the United Kingdom these are unusually large due to our unusually large national debt (table 5.4).

[1] *Bank of England Quarterly Bulletin*, vol. 6, September 1966, pp. 215–16.
[2] P. Thorneycroft, 'Policy in practice' in *Not Unanimous*, London, Institute of Economic Affairs, 1960, p. 1.

If the refinancing cannot be wholly covered by placing new stock with the public, the banks are again called upon to finance the balance.

Table 5.4. *Comparative sizes of national debts,[a] 1968/9*

	Percentages of GNP
Canada	29
France	13
Germany	13
Italy	15
Japan	6
Netherlands	20
United Kingdom	59
United States	29

SOURCE: *Bank of England Quarterly Bulletin*, vol. 14, December 1974, p. 433.

[a] Excluding official holdings and IMF notes.

The Radcliffe Committee, in line with most academic opinion, took the view that the flooding problem could always be resolved by making gilt-edged stock cheap enough to attract the investing public. But witnesses from the Bank of England and the Treasury had taken the contrary view, insisting that 'the market in long-term securities is dominated by expectations of future prices and is therefore seriously liable to react perversely to a movement of prices'.[1] In their oral evidence to the Radcliffe Committee, the Chief Cashier and the Government Broker made it quite clear that they would never hope to sell more stock by reducing its price; not only would it be ineffective, it would also be a breach of faith with people who had bought stock when it was originally issued.[2] Thus, official witnesses to the Radcliffe Committee clearly believed that the Government Broker's role as a salesman, though not wholly passive, gives him little scope for initiative. If the market is rising his skill as a dealer enables him to exploit his opportunity, but if it is not rising he has no opportunity to exploit.

On this issue, despite the criticisms expressed by the Radcliffe Committee, there seems to have been, at any rate up to 1975, no subsequent change in official opinion, which was re-stated with emphasis in an article, 'Official transactions in the gilt-edged market',[3] and was in no way disowned in 'Competition and credit control'.[4]

The shifts in the Government Broker's strategy, which occurred both

[1] Treasury, *Radcliffe Report*, para. 563.
[2] Radcliffe Committee, *Minutes of Evidence*, questions 11967 and 12009.
[3] *Bank of England Quarterly Bulletin*, vol. 6, June 1966.
[4] *Bank of England Quarterly Bulletin*, vol. 11, June 1971.

at the beginning of the 1960s and at the time of the new approach, were not in his selling but in his buying. In the early 1960s the strategy was to lean against the wind in *both* directions: the Government Broker would not only seize the opportunity to sell when demand increased, but would also come in as a buyer when the market was weak. The main reason advanced for supporting a weak market was that otherwise investors 'would be seriously discouraged from investing their funds...the capacity of the market would be permanently reduced and with it the ability of the Government to borrow at long term.'[1]

It is clear that intervention of this kind, in support of a weak market, was not practised to any extent in the decade before 1958; the evidence of the Bank to the Radcliffe Committee in November 1958 suggested that there had been only one occasion since the late 1940s when support of this kind had been given.[2] Yet by 1960 a new strategy of supporting the market was being practised, much to the Prime Minister's displeasure. Referring to the first call for Special Deposits on 28 April 1960, Harold Macmillan noted in a letter to Selwyn Lloyd that the banks, which had promised to adhere to the Special Deposits scheme, had been selling gilt-edged securities to do so and the Government Broker had been frightened into buying.[3] The implication of market support which alarmed Macmillan (the weakening of official control over the behaviour of the banks) does not seem to have troubled the authorities very much before the 'brakes-on' phase of demand management in the second half of the 1960s; indeed in the preceding period of slack demand they reduced the minimum liquid asset ratio from 30 to 28 per cent lest it should unduly constrain bank lending. Macmillan's point was, however, publicly taken by the Bank in 1969, when it admitted that the policy of leaning against the wind had enabled the banks to change their holdings from one form of government debt to another in the short term without much loss.[4] Hence, it was variations in the banks' total holdings of government debt relative to their deposit liabilities, rather than the details of the division between cash, Treasury bills and gilts, which largely determined whether their balance sheets were becoming more or less liquid.[5] The significance of this admission will be apparent from table 5.5, which shows that the London clearing banks' ratio for liquid assets and investments combined, though on a declining trend until 1969, was always in excess of 40 per cent and hence well in excess of the minimum liquid asset ratio, which was consequently ineffective as an instrument of control.

---

[1] *Bank of England Quarterly Bulletin*, vol. 6, June 1966, p. 147.
[2] Radcliffe Committee, *Minutes of Evidence*, questions 12029–33.
[3] Macmillan, *Pointing the Way, 1959–1961*, p. 361.
[4] *Bank of England Quarterly Bulletin*, vol. 9, June 1969, p. 177.   [5] Ibid. p. 178.

The twin precepts, that the Government Broker should never attempt to sell more gilts by dropping their price and that he should lean against the wind when the market was weak, clearly had far-reaching implications for monetary policy. First, though this strategy was regarded as the best one for maximising official sales of bonds in the longer run, it accepted that in the short run the Government Broker's transactions were largely in response to market conditions and not to the immediate requirements of monetary policy. Hence, unless the market was sufficiently buoyant to enable the Government Broker to sell enough stock to the public to match maturities plus the government's domestic borrowing requirement, the balance sheets of the banks would inflate, with deposits rising on the liabilities side (hence a corresponding increase in the quantity of money) and with public sector debt (in the form of cash, Treasury bills, call money advanced against Treasury bills, and government stock) rising in balance on the assets side. Secondly, the natural reaction of the banks to the increases in their liquidity implicit in this change in their balance sheets would certainly not be to cut their lending to the private sector; rather they would want to lend more to the private sector, which would thereby bring about a secondary increase both in their deposit liabilities and in their assets (this time in the form of advances). Thirdly, since the Govern-

Table 5.5. *London clearing banks' liquid assets and investments as a proportion of gross deposits,[a] 1958–71*

Percentages

	Liquid assets	Investments[b]	Total
1958	33·9	32·9	66·8
59	31·0	29·1	60·1
1960	31·5	21·3	52·8
61	30·4	16·5	46·9
62	32·6	14·8	47·4
63	30·5	16·0	46·5
64	29·7	14·6	44·3
65	29·5	12·0	41·5
66	30·1	12·0	42·1
67	29·5	13·7	43·2
68	28·7	13·2	41·9
69	29·4	11·7	41·1
1970	29·7	11·8	41·5
71	32·4	10·2	42·6

SOURCES: Bank of England, *Statistical Abstract*, no. 1, pp. 36–9; *Bank of England Quarterly Bulletin*, vol. 11, March 1971, p. 98, and June 1971, p. 246.

[a] At mid-March, which is near the seasonal minimum for liquid asset holdings.

[b] Mainly gilt-edged stock. In March 1969 £1064 million out of a total of £1232 million were British government stocks.

ment Broker has so much difficulty in selling enough gilts, his problems should not be exacerbated by an expansionist budgetary policy. Finally, leaning against the wind in order to maximise official sales in the long run must preclude, save in fortuitously favourable circumstances, a demand management policy based on using official national debt transactions to manipulate the pattern of interest rates, as favoured in the *Radcliffe Report*. The Bank of England's article 'Official transactions in the gilt-edged market' is quite explicit on this: one of a number of possible subsidiary aims of national debt management was 'to assist economic policy by promoting or sustaining the most appropriate pattern of interest rates', but these subsidiary aims must not be pursued at the risk of causing damage in the long run to the health and capacity of the market – a limitation that may sometimes preclude all but a fairly narrow choice of policies in the short term.[1]

There was a transitional period of a number of months up to 24 February 1960 when the Government Broker set a floor to bond prices – this being done to stimulate the then depressed economy by making it easy for the banks to unload their bonds in order to increase their advances. But, as from February 1960, leaning against the wind did not imply, save in rare circumstances, that the Government Broker would hold rates to a target.[2] When the market was buoyant his sales would mitigate the rise in prices but not stop it altogether; in this way he reassured investors in gilts that it was possible to make capital gains. When the market was weak his purchases usually served to slow down the fall in prices, rather than to support them with a firm floor.[3] Exceptionally, and then only for short periods (December 1964, May and June 1967, and November 1968[4]) he set a floor to steady a demoralised market; otherwise leaning against the wind meant mitigating short-term fluctuations but not resisting market pressure. The operations of the Government Broker were indeed compatible with a long-term upward trend in yields and appreciable fluctuations from month to month and year to year.

[1] *Bank of England Quarterly Bulletin*, vol. 6, June 1966, p. 146. The Governor had made the same point in 1958; he said, 'It would still not be true to say that the Bank were aiming at any particular range of rates' (Radcliffe Committee, *Minutes of Evidence*, question 11919).

[2] Bank of England, *Report for the year ended 29 February 1960*, p. 12.

[3] See *Bank of England Quarterly Bulletin*, vol. 1, September 1961, p. 12: 'On the 2nd August rumours began to circulate to the effect that the authorities intended to withdraw their support. The Bank therefore reminded the market that it was not the practice of the authorities to support the gilt-edged market in the sense of pegging it at any particular price level: that the authorities would continue to be concerned to ensure orderly market conditions so that dealings at a price could continue; and that prices would continue to depend upon general market conditions.'

[4] *Bank of England Quarterly Bulletin*, vol. 5, March 1965, p. 9; vol. 7, September 1967 pp. 227–8; vol. 9, March 1969, p. 15.

TRANSMISSION MECHANISMS

Changes in the choice of instruments of monetary policy, and in the way they are used to pursue various objectives, may derive from revisions to official views about transmission mechanisms; in the period treated in this book there were such revisions. As from 1972 there was official rethinking about how external balance might better be achieved by greater reliance on variations in the exchange rate.[1] Previous to this, however, rethinking about transmission had been confined to the means for achieving just one of the official policy objectives – demand management. Nor is it surprising that official views on this particular aspect of the transmission mechanism should be specially subject to revision. For the channels by which official action in the monetary sphere may influence the level of demand for goods and services are complex and tortuous; they are, moreover, very imperfectly understood by economists and have, throughout the postwar period, been the subject of inconclusive controversy, in the United Kingdom and elsewhere, in both academic and official circles. Official rethinking about this issue was especially active in two periods – at the time of the *Radcliffe Report* and again towards the end of the 1960s. In both periods the stimulus came from academic economists: in the earlier period from the two academic members of the Radcliffe Committee, Richard Sayers and Alec Cairncross; in the later period (partly via the IMF officials who were engaged in negotiations with the British authorities) from the American monetarist school, which, under the leadership of Milton Friedman, had in the course of the 1960s become increasingly influential in the United States. However, the outcome in the two periods was dissimilar: the new views advanced by the Radcliffe Committee had only a small impact on official action – the Bank's new strategy in the gilt-edged market in the early 1960s did not follow from the *Radcliffe Report's* recommendations. On the other hand, the rethinking which began in the late 1960s was an important element leading up to the new approach of 1971.

In the period up to the late 1960s, when the British authorities were so obsessed with the flooding problem, they seem not to have committed themselves to any particular version of the transmission mechanism by which official transactions in the gilt-edged market might be supposed to influence the demand for goods and services. Though the Radcliffe Committee tried to give a decisive lead on several facets of this issue, it was in response not to their lead but to the influence of the American monetary school that the authorities eventually began rather gingerly to commit themselves.

[1] Chapter 7, below.

Let us look briefly at some of the crucial features of the transmission mechanism on which the *Radcliffe Report* took a definite stand but on which the authorities seem to have maintained an eclectic position. It is common ground that, for the monetary authorities of any country, 'it is not possible to choose the direction of movement of interest rates and of the quantity of money independently',[1] but some economists believe that the authorities should conduct their transactions with their eyes on interest rates as their main target variable, while others (including the quantity theorists and more recently Friedman) believe that their target variable should be the quantity of money. The *Radcliffe Report* strongly backed the former point of view. It argued that a change in interest rates had considerable effect on the readiness of lenders to lend and a slower, more partial, influence on the readiness of borrowers to borrow.[2] The Bank's written evidence to the Radcliffe Committee clearly gave rather greater weight to the latter effect, but also attached some importance to the effect of interest-rate changes on the readiness of lenders to lend.[3] Subsequently the authorities seem to have paid little attention to the issue, if for no other reason than because they did not believe that (given the need to sell as many bonds as possible in the long run) they were free to exercise much influence over gilt-edged rates, apart from ironing out short-term fluctuations.

On the other hand the Radcliffe Committee strongly questioned the value of the quantity of money as a target variable:

...spending is not limited by the amount of money in existence; but it is related to the amount of money people think they can get hold of, whether by receipts of income (for instance from sales), by disposal of capital assets or by borrowing.[4]

and later:

In a highly developed financial system the theoretical difficulties of identifying 'the supply of money' cannot lightly be swept aside. Even when they are disregarded, all the haziness of the connection between the supply of money and the level of total demand remains.[5]

The official evidence to the Radcliffe Committee had attached much more importance than this to the quantity of money. The Bank maintained that 'the basic need remains the ability to regulate the total quantity of currency and bank deposits',[6] and quoted from a communiqué issued after a meeting of the Governor and Chancellor on

---

[1] Radcliffe Committee, *Principal Memoranda of Evidence*, vol. 1, Bank of England's submission, p. 36, para. 14. [2] Treasury, *Radcliffe Report*, para. 983.
[3] See Radcliffe Committee, *Principal Memoranda of Evidence*, vol. 1, p. 37, paras, 22, 24, 25 and 29. [4] Treasury, *Radcliffe Report*, para. 390.
[5] Ibid. para. 523.
[6] Radcliffe Committee, *Principal Memoranda of Evidence*, vol. 1, p. 36, para. 11.

24 July 1956, which indicated that the government would press on with measures influencing the supply of money.[1] All the same, the Bank was certainly not committed to any view as specific as the quantity theory: 'a change in the supply of money is not rigidly associated with a similar change in the amount of spending'.[2] Or again: '...but addition to the money supply is by no means the only factor which increases demand and so puts up costs and prices. There is bound at any time...to be a large volume of spendable money, in the form of bank deposits, cash or easily-realisable assets'.[3] Here the inclusion of the last item, 'easily-realisable assets', indicates that the Bank was concerned with the quantity of money only as one component of the public's total holding of liquid assets, along with, for instance, national savings and building societies' shares and deposits.[4] Significantly, the growing short-term debt of local authorities was a cause of official anxiety.[5] Thus the pre-Radcliffe official view attached importance to the quantity of money because one of the many factors determining the level of demand was the public's holding of liquid assets, of which the stock of money is one component; there is, however, no suggestion that the authorities at this time thought that 'the behaviour of the money supply is an important indicator of the thrust of monetary policy', as the Chief Cashier put it in November 1971 in his explanation of the 'new approach'.[6]

The Radcliffe Committee's view that the quantity of money was unimportant led them to conclude that 'regulation of the banks is required not because they are "creators of money" but because they are the biggest lenders at the shortest (most liquid) end of the range of credit markets'.[7] The official evidence to Radcliffe included a memorandum, 'The control of bank credit in the United Kingdom', which also stressed the role of bank advances;[8] moreover, this official view continued into the 1960s, as witnessed by the fact that, when bank lending to the private sector could not be adequately controlled by official sales of gilt-edged, the authorities did not hesitate to impose lending ceilings.

To summarise: apart from interest rates in the traditional money market, the only target variable which we know for certain the authorities adopted up to the late 1960s was one for bank and finance house lending to the private sector. We know this for certain because, in the credit squeezes which occurred from May 1965, such a target was

---

[1] Ibid. p. 31, para. 114.   [2] Ibid. p. 36, para. 9.
[3] The Governor's Mansion House Speech, 8 October 1957, quoted ibid. p. 50, para. 65.
[4] Ibid. p. 17, paras. 6 and 7.
[5] See the Bank's oral evidence to the Radcliffe Committee on 27 November 1958 (*Minutes of Evidence*, questions 12061–2).
[6] Sykes Memorial Lecture, 10 November 1971.   [7] Treasury, *Radcliffe Report*, para. 504.
[8] Radcliffe Committee, *Principal Memoranda of Evidence*, vol. 1, pp. 9–10.

explicitly incorporated in official requests to the institutions concerned. This does not mean that officials thought the quantity of money or the level of bond rates to be of no consequence, but whatever they thought had little impact on their actions.

THE CHOICE OF INSTRUMENTS OF POLICY IN THE 1960s

Though in the 1960s the authorities came to rely more and more on lending ceilings, this instrument was always very much a second-best one, which the authorities resorted to only because their preferred instrument, the limitation of liquid assets available to the banks, could not be relied upon to ensure an adequate degree of restraint. Early in the decade the Bank optimistically hoped that lending ceilings could be reserved for emergency use, or even dispensed with altogether. The proportion of public sector debt in the clearing banks' assets was following a downward trend, and the availability of liquid assets to the banks (see table 5.5) contracted so greatly that, in 1963, a year in which the stance of official policy was to stimulate demand, the authorities reduced the minimum liquid asset ratio from 30 to 28 per cent.[1] Yet, whatever optimism the authorities may have felt gave way to disillusionment, and lending ceilings, withdrawn in the recession of 1962, had to be reapplied from December 1964 onwards, with only one brief respite (for the clearing banks only) in 1967. The clearing banks' liquid assets, supplemented by their cushion of gilts, which (thanks to the Government Broker's readiness to support the market) could be 'liquefied' without serious loss, never fell low enough to press against the 28 per cent minimum. Special Deposits were invented precisely to deal with this situation, by converting liquid assets into illiquid ones, but such Deposits were never called on a scale sufficient to make the minimum liquid asset ratio really bite.

Why were the authorities thus forced back on their second-best technique for limiting bank lending? One explanation is the rapid rise in the popularity with British industry of bill finance, which (since such commercial bills usually qualified as liquid assets) added to the liquid assets available to the banking system (table 5.2).[2] However, this problem could presumably have been overcome if the authorities had redefined the liquid assets which counted towards the 28 per cent

---

[1] In March 1963 the banks were permitted to go for the time being 'somewhat below' 30 per cent (*Bank of England Quarterly Bulletin*, vol. 3, June 1963, p. 88). Later in the year this became 28 per cent (*Bank of England Quarterly Bulletin*, vol. 3, December 1963, p. 295).

[2] Commercial bills held by the discount market contributed to the increase in the clearing banks' liquid assets because they increased the market's need for call money, which counted as a liquid asset.

minimum to exclude commercial bills altogether, or at any rate to exclude any in excess of a prescribed amount – as indeed they eventually did in 1971 as part of the new approach (see footnote to page 244 below). A more intractable problem was that the 28 per cent minimum applied only to the London clearing banks, and the authorities saw great difficulty in extending it to cover other banks, which in the course of the 1960s were expanding much faster than the clearing banks, even in their domestic business (table 5.1). Eventually, however, under the new approach, the nettle was grasped and a common 'reserve asset' ratio applied to all banks. Last, but most important, was the fact that the Government Broker's strategy in the 1960s (page 232 above) meant that the amounts of his sales or purchases were, at any rate in the short run, determined by prevailing market conditions and not by the need to regulate the liquid assets available to the banks in the interests of demand management. It was in recognition of this problem that, under the new approach of 1971, official support to the gilt-edged market was to be limited, as in the 1950s, to exceptional circumstances.

THE NEW APPROACH

The new approach to monetary policy, inaugurated in May 1971 with the publication of the Bank of England's consultative document 'Competition and credit control', and put into operation later in the year, can best be described as a change of instruments, and a change in the use of existing instruments, for the purpose of demand management. Lending ceilings on banks and finance houses, which had been in almost continuous operation since 1964, were discontinued, although the possibility of qualitative guidance was retained, and in July hire purchase restrictions were also discontinued for the time being. From September the balance sheet ratios previously imposed on the clearing banks were changed, and their application was extended to the non-clearing banks and to the finance houses. The London clearing banks' interest-rate cartel was discontinued from October 1971; henceforth their borrowing and lending rates were no longer automatically related to Bank Rate. The London Discount Houses Association continued to make a joint bid each week to cover the Treasury bill tender, but no longer at one agreed rate of discount for all members of the Association. The Government Broker's technique for dealing in the bond market was changed; he was no longer in normal circumstances to support the gilt-edged market, although he would continue to buy maturities of under one year.

All these changes, introduced more or less simultaneously, reflected a rethinking by the authorities over a number of years, as we can judge from earlier official actions (sometimes rather trivial in themselves) and also from official pronouncements over the period from 1967 to May 1971. The actual timing of the new approach was influenced by several factors. The change of government in June 1970 returned to power a Conservative administration which wanted to encourage competition and free enterprise. There had been a change in the attitudes of officials towards monetary policy instruments. There had been a rapid falling off of effective demand, so that the time was right to institute a change which would be expansionary in its initial impact.[1] Finally, the external deficit had at last turned into a surplus, so that monetary policy was no longer constrained by the external situation and could for the time being be directed exclusively towards the expansion of the economy.

There are three interrelated strands in the evolution of official thought in the late 1960s. There was a determination to infuse a new spirit of competition into the British banking system. There was a growing optimism that the flooding problem might be less intractable than it had earlier seemed and a willingness to tackle it with a new strategy for conducting official transactions in the gilt-edged market. There was, finally, a 'reinstatement of the money supply as more than just one in a whole range of liquid assets'.[2]

Competition

'Competition and credit control' quoted with approval the Chancellor of the Exchequer's statement in his March 1971 budget that 'it should be possible to achieve more flexible but still effective arrangements basically by operating on the banks' resources rather than by directly guiding their lending'. The idea that the imposition of lending ceilings could be harmful to competition and to the structure of the monetary system had long been recognised by the authorities, in particular in the Bank of England's evidence to the Radcliffe Committee,[3] but also on many subsequent occasions.[4] The authorities had indeed been seeking an alternative solution for some years before 1971. However, the experiment in 1967 with the use of Special Deposits without a lending ceiling for the clearing banks[5] came to an untimely end with the devaluation crisis in November, when severe lending ceilings were reimposed

---

[1] The removal of lending ceilings could be expected to lead to an increase in bank advances to the private sector. Also, the minimum reserve asset ratio imposed on clearing and non-clearing banks alike had to be fixed at a level which was tolerable to the latter and hence might be unrestrictive to the former.

[2] Chief Cashier, Sykes Memorial Lecture, 10 November 1971.

[3] Radcliffe Committee, *Principal Memoranda of Evidence*, vol. 1, p. 39, para. 7. See also the Governor's reply to question 1818 in the *Minutes of Evidence*.

[4] For example, *Bank of England Quarterly Bulletin*, vol. 9, June 1969, p. 179.

[5] Page 223, above.

and not discontinued until the new approach of 1971. There was even then a proviso in 'Competition and credit control' about qualitative, as distinct from quantitative, guidance on bank lending:

Notwithstanding the abandonment of quantitative ceilings...the authorities would continue to provide the banks with such qualitative guidance as may be appropriate. For example, so long as hire purchase terms control remains in force, banks will be asked that personal loans related to the purchase of goods subject to terms control should be made on terms no easier than those permitted...for hire purchase contracts.[1]

In the event this particular need for qualitative guidelines soon disappeared for the time being with the discontinuance in July 1971 of all restrictions on hire purchase, credit sale and rental agreements.

The authorities took longer to come round to the view that the London clearing banks' interest-rate cartel was also seriously harmful to competition in banking services. As early as April 1963 the Governor of the Bank of England had made a speech in praise of increased competition, which was at the time widely interpreted as inviting the clearing banks to abandon their cartel on interest rates. However, he did not explicitly make this point; his words could be taken to mean simply that the cartel rates should be more competitive with those of the non-clearing banks and other financial intermediaries.

In October 1963 the clearing banks, possibly in response to the Governor's speech, put forward a proposal for an increase of $\frac{1}{2}$ per cent in their overdraft rates, combined with the simultaneous introduction of special savings deposit accounts (maximum holding £500) paying a higher interest rate than the then deposit rate ($3\frac{1}{2}$ as against 2 per cent). This proposal was, however, not welcomed by the authorities, presumably because its aim was competition for deposits mainly with national savings media and building societies; moreover, a rise in overdraft rates was politically unattractive. The banks were therefore told not to proceed with the scheme.

The clearing banks themselves drew a distinction between competition for deposits with other private sector institutions and with public sector institutions. Competition with the latter, for example the Post Office and Trustee Savings Banks, brought them obvious advantages. As the NBPI subsequently put it: 'These public sector institutions lend largely to the Government...cheques [of depositors] will be drawn on the clearing banks with a resultant fall in the latter's reserves with the central bank...',[2] and with a consequent reduction in the clearing banks' liquid assets. Thus competition to retain depositors who might

---

[1] 'Competition and credit control', para. 14.
[2] NBPI, *Report no. 34: Bank Charges*, Cmnd 3292, London, HMSO, 1967, para. 59.

be tempted to redeposit at public sector institutions was to the clearing banks' collective advantage; the obstacle here was that the government did not welcome such competition.

Competition with private sector institutions mainly involved kinds of business (especially 'wholesale' banking in large transactions) which are not transacted through a clearing bank's provincial branch network. In such cases the clearing banks preferred to acquire or establish subsidiary or associated banks,[1] which could compete with independent non-clearing banks on equal terms without having to observe imposed balance sheet ratios. In addition, there was at this time a wide-spread view, which the NBPI did not accept, but which it nonetheless thought it necessary to elucidate, that competition for deposits with other private sector institutions brought no advantage to the clearing banks as a whole, in that they could not as a group 'lose' deposits to other financial institutions in the private sector. For when someone transfers a deposit to such an institution from a clearing bank, then a deposit in that person's name at a clearing bank will be transferred to the other institution's account at a clearing bank and, when the other institution lends on the deposit, the borrower will also bank at a clearer, so 'what is involved is merely a transfer in the ownership of the bank deposits [at the clearing banks]...The logical corollary of this line of argument would be that the payment of any deposit rate is a needless cost for the banks.'[2] The clearing banks seem at one time to have attached importance to this argument, though progressively less so in the course of the 1960s.

There matters rested until the publication in July 1968 by the Monopolies Commission of a Report on the proposed merger between Barclays Bank, Lloyds Bank and Martins Bank, which came out strongly against the practice of regulating the banks by lending ceilings.[3] This, taken together with the NBPI Report, made out a strong indictment against the cartel and also a case, again with the aim of encouraging competition, for banks to reveal their inner reserves and true profits in their published accounts. The indictments of the cartel in

[1] The subsidiary or associated banks of the clearing banks did their English banking business from London, not from provincial offices.

[2] NBPI, *Report no. 34*, para. 58. The Board's own (critical) appraisal of this argument is in para. 59, which, after dealing with competition with public sector institutions, reads as follows: 'Secondly, there are the private sector financial institutions – e.g. hire purchase companies. Deposits transferred to them from a clearing bank will enable them to increase their lending, thus driving down interest rates and tending to raise the level of spending and income, with possible adverse effects on the balance of payments. In such a case the monetary authorities would need to take offsetting action, e.g. the sale of bonds, so as to reduce the lending power of the clearing banks themselves ... the reserves and deposits of the clearing banks suffer in the last analysis a decline.'

[3] Monopolies Commission, *Barclays Bank Ltd, Lloyds Bank Ltd and Martins Bank Ltd. Report on the Proposed Merger*, London, HMSO, 1968.

the two Reports may be briefly amalgamated into the following line of argument. The cartel had a soporific effect; it also led to excessive non-price competition, especially in the opening of too many branches. Moreover, its abolition would enable the clearing banks to regain ground lost to the non-clearing banks; this would, of course, require them to take over a higher share of total bank lending, as well as a higher share of total deposits. Finally, the NBPI maintained that some of the business then conducted by the clearing banks through subsidiaries was conducted in this way, and not directly in their own names, solely because of the cartel agreement and because of official restrictions imposed on the clearers alone; some such business could, however, be more efficiently conducted by the clearers in their own right. Hence there was a case not merely for abolishing the cartel, but also for assimilating the regulatory balance sheet ratios imposed on different kinds of banks and finance houses.

The case for reform did not go unheeded. Pressed by the authorities, the London and Scottish clearing banks agreed in 1968 to observe the full disclosure provisions of the Companies Act, even though banks are, under the Act, specifically exempted; the first annual accounts on the new basis were in respect of 1969. Action on the other impediments to competition was delayed until 1971, but it is clear from a speech by the Governor of the Bank on 17 October 1968 that the issue was under official review.[1]

There were difficulties in the way of reform, both as regards the abolition of the interest-rate cartel and as regards the imposition of more or less uniform balance sheet ratios on all banks and finance houses. In the case of the cartel, the original official fear that freer competition for deposits would reduce the flow of savings into national savings media and the building societies remained to the end. Even in 'Competition and credit control' the Bank envisaged the possibility of imposing official controls (having an equivalent effect to that of the cartel) on the terms offered for savings deposits.

Another problem was that the Treasury continued to fear that the abolition of the cartel would mean unacceptably high interest rates on advances to industrial firms.[2] A further problem was that the abolition of the cartel would break the automatic link between Bank Rate and the London clearing banks' deposit and lending rates, and thus cut off one route (traditionally regarded as of considerable importance) by which the authorities could influence the economy. However the importance of this bit of transmission mechanism was being eroded by the development in the course of the 1960s of London's new markets for

[1] *Bank of England Quarterly Bulletin*, vol. 8, December 1968, p. 411.
[2] Monopolies Commission, *Report*, para. 206.

money (table 5.6), in which interest rates were settled by unfettered competition.[1] The rapid growth in the 1960s of the non-clearing banks, who took in 'wholesale' deposits at interest rates uncontrolled by the London clearing banks' cartel and lent on to the private sector within the limits of their lending ceilings, or otherwise to local authorities, was further developed by their issuing, as from October 1968, sterling certificates of deposit (table 5.6).[2] One result of these developments was that the new 'free' rates became the important ones for a significant part of the British economy. Hence, when in 1971 the authorities decided to press for the abolition of the London clearing banks' cartel, this was to weaken a policy instrument which had already become much weaker than it had been in the 1950s.

Table 5.6. *New money markets: sterling funds outstanding, 1961–73*[a]

£ million

	Local authorities' temporary money[b]	Inter-bank deposits	Certificates of deposit	Finance houses' deposits
1961	1079	..	—	337
62	1142	260	—	337
63	1349	350	—	390
64	1712	462	—	494
65	1740	588	—	654
66	1728	712	—	648
67	1854	924	—	591
68	1870	1333	165	612
69	1896	1728	442	636
1970	1879	1978	1089	688
71	1974	2200	2372	823
72	2408	4760	4930	437[c]
73	3368	7694	5983	477[c]

SOURCES: European Communities Monetary Committee, *Monetary Policy in the Countries of the European Economic Community. Supplement 1974 (The United Kingdom)*, table 11; CSO, *Financial Statistics*, February 1975, tables 31, 41 and 66.

[a] At end-year.

[b] Deposits and revenue bills of up to one year. In the years 1965–71 inclusive, deposits taken net of bank deposits by local authorities.

[c] Excluding figures from institutions recognised or confirmed as banks in January 1972 and previously classified as finance houses.

[1] Of the markets distinguished in table 5.6, the local authority short-term market dates from the 1950s. The inter-bank market developed somewhat later; its main dealers were the merchant banks, foreign banks in London and British banks operating abroad, together with some subsidiaries of clearing banks. The clearing banks themselves did not take part, though it was deposits at the clearing banks which the non-clearing banks, operating as principals, transferred from one to another in their inter-bank market operations (*Midland Bank Review*, August 1966, p. 6). Subsequently, under the regime of 'Competition and credit control', the clearing banks also began to operate in this market as principals, and on a large scale.

[2] The advantage of a certificate of deposit as against a time deposit of the same maturity is that the former is a negotiable instrument which can be traded in a secondary market conducted by the discount houses.

A final problem posed by the abolition of the cartel was that the London clearing banks could represent its existence as a reasonable *quid pro quo* for the favourable terms they extended for medium-term export credits and for their observance of two onerous balance sheet ratios (the 8 per cent cash ratio and the 28 per cent liquid asset ratio) from which non-clearing banks were exempt. Of these objections, the first was eventually met by an upward adjustment of the relevant interest rate,[1] while the second was met in 1971 by imposing uniform reserve and Special Deposit ratios on all banks.

The need for uniform ratios had not been readily admitted. The Bank of England had initially shied away from it; in the 1968 proposal for a Cash Deposits scheme (which remained a dead letter)[2] it was represented as impractical to have the same balance sheet ratios imposed on such a diverse collection of institutions as banks. There was also the problem that controlling banks through imposed balance sheet ratios requires that the prescribed reserve assets should be in inelastic supply. This condition could not be fulfilled if reserve assets were to include 'new money market' assets (such as local authority deposits), and in the 1960s the non-clearing banks normally relied for their liquidity on such assets and on the inter-bank market, rather than on traditional money market assets such as Treasury bills. Yet in the end the Bank overcame its scruples; the new approach replaced the 28 per cent liquid asset ratio hitherto imposed on the London clearing banks by a $12\frac{1}{2}$ per cent ratio for all banks of 'reserve assets' (not including 'new money market' assets) to liabilities.[3] A common Special Deposit ratio, fixed from time to time at the discretion of the Bank, was also to be imposed on all banks. Finance houses with liabilities over £5 million also had to observe a minimum reserve asset ratio of 10 per cent and became liable to calls for Special Deposits, which in practice have been at the same percentage rate as in the case of banks.

The uniformity of these regulations was mildly infringed by the fact that the London clearing banks, but not other banks, were required

---

[1] The rate was raised from $5\frac{1}{2}$ per cent to 7 per cent in October 1970.

[2] See above, pages 223–4.

[3] Reserve assets comprise balances with the Bank of England (other than Special Deposits); Treasury bills; money at call with the discount houses, bill brokers, Stock Exchange jobbers and money brokers; British government stocks with one year or less to final maturity; local authority bills and (up to a maximum of 2 per cent of eligible liabilities) commercial bills eligible for rediscount at the Bank of England.

Liabilities are taken to comprise the sterling deposit liabilities of the banking system as a whole, excluding deposits having an original maturity of over two years, plus any sterling resources obtained by switching foreign currencies into sterling. Inter-bank transactions and sterling certificates of deposit (both held and issued) are taken into the calculation of individual banks' liabilities on a net basis, irrespective of term.

to hold $1\frac{1}{2}$ per cent of their $12\frac{1}{2}$ per cent reserve asset ratio in the form of (zero-interest) demand deposits at the Bank of England. In addition, the fact that notes and coin were not to be counted towards the reserve asset ratio, as they had been towards the old 28 per cent liquid asset ratio, involved what might be regarded as discrimination against the clearing banks, the nature of whose business requires them to hold a higher proportion of their assets in these forms than the non-clearing banks.

The flooding problem

Towards the end of the 1960s the authorities came to have doubts as to whether supporting the gilt-edged market in the face of selling pressure was a necessary, or even a desirable, element in the Government Broker's dealing technique. The Bank's paper of October 1969 on 'The operation of monetary policy since the Radcliffe Report'[1] noted that a more flexible policy on interest rates had given more scope for flexible tactics in debt management. In particular, as from May 1969 the official buying price for stocks within three months of maturity was no longer tied to the Treasury bill rate, and from July the authorities no longer announced the price at which they were prepared to sell tap stocks but instead considered bids made by the market.[2]

The change of dealing technique proposed in 'Competition and credit control' was explained as follows:

(i) the Bank will no longer be prepared to respond to requests to buy stock outright, except in the case of stocks with one year or less to run to maturity;
(ii) they reserve the right to make outright purchases of stock with more than a year to run solely at their discretion and initiative;
(iii) they will be prepared to undertake, at prices of their own choosing, exchanges of stock with the market except those which unduly shorten the life of the debt;
(iv) and will be prepared to respond to bids for the sale by them of 'tap' stocks and of such other stocks held by them as they may wish to sell.[3]

This modification by the Bank of their mode of operation in the gilt-edged market represented a return towards the position which they had occupied in the 1950s. Looking back in 1971 on the market support which the Bank had provided in the 1960s, the Chief Cashier suggested that it

...probably contributed to the attrition of the market's resources. So long as the Bank were prepared in effect to put substantial resources into ensuring the marketability of gilt-edged there was no particular reason why others should do so...Also, it is the essence of a market that there should be a

[1] *Bank of England Quarterly Bulletin*, vol. 9, December 1969.   [2] Ibid. p. 456.
[3] 'Competition and credit control', para. 13.

variety of views among operators of similar size. The Bank's close presence in the market often meant that in practice there were only two views – those of the Bank and those of everybody else.[1]

All the same, the Bank's close presence in the market was not something that could be spirited away by the new tactics of official intervention. Year in and year out the Government Broker still had to sell stock on an enormous scale, and he continued to do this, as in the 1960s, by waiting for a rising market, not by dropping his price ahead of the market in an attempt (futile, as the authorities continued to believe[2]) to tempt more buyers for his wares. The only time when his presence was less in evidence than in the 1960s was in a weak market, for under the new approach he became less ready to afford support and then only at the Bank's discretion. Thus, his transactions still continued to be determined very largely by the state of the market, even if not quite so closely as in the 1960s.

The quantity of money

The first sign accepted by outside commentators that the British authorities might have come to regard the money supply as more than just one in a whole range of liquid assets was the official Letter of Intent sent to the IMF in connection with the stand-by drawing right negotiated just after the devaluation of sterling in November 1967. This stated that the growth in the money supply in 1968 should be limited to its estimated growth in 1967, both absolutely and as a proportion of GNP. Then in 1968 and 1969 the British authorities became unusually receptive to the idea of relying more heavily on monetary policy, since in both Britain and the United States deflationary fiscal policies seemed disappointing in their results. In Britain the post-devaluation deflationary measures were unaccountably slow in taking effect, while in the United States the 10 per cent surcharge on income taxes, imposed in 1968, was no less disappointing. The views of Milton Friedman and his American followers had begun to be reflected in United Kingdom publications as from 1968. Thus in December 1968 *The Banker* invited leading proponents of differing points of view, among them Milton Friedman, to put their cases,[3] and Samuel Brittan wrote a number of articles in the *Financial Times* in 1968 and 1969 on the control of the money supply.[4] A. A. Walters, in a pamphlet published in January 1969, argued that monetarist theory explained

---

[1] Sykes Memorial Lecture, 10 November 1971.   [2] At any rate up to 1975.
[3] M. Friedman, H. Wincott and F. W. Tooby, 'The money supply debate', *The Banker*, vol. 118, December 1968.
[4] For example, 'Money supply: the great debate' in the *Financial Times*, 25 October 1968; 'Four propositions about the money supply' in the *Financial Times*, 23 January 1969, and other articles in the *Financial Times* of 8 and 10 July, and 13 November 1969.

the behaviour of the British economy very well up to 1945, although less well in the postwar period.[1] The Governor of the Bank of England in his Mansion House speech in October 1968 showed that he was aware of the monetarist school of thought, though he was not prepared to accept its teaching without due reservations,[2] and the same may be inferred of the Chancellor of the Exchequer, in the light of his budget speech in April 1969.

One of the chief catalysts of official thought was a seminar held in London in October 1968 for Bank of England and Treasury officials and representatives from the IMF.[3] Its main subject was DCE, a concept which had been invented by a senior IMF official,[4] who was himself one of the IMF representatives at the seminar. The new concept became important with the second Letter of Intent to the IMF of May 1969, which set a quantitative target for DCE in the year ending 31 March 1970 of not more than £400 million.[5]

How did those responsible for British monetary policy make use of the new concept? It would seem that they regarded it as just one of a number of diagnostic devices at their disposal, but in no sense a prescription for treatment. If a DCE target were exceeded, this was prima facie evidence that something might be amiss with the United Kingdom economy; in such circumstances all other available evidence should be analysed in the hope of achieving a correct diagnosis and then (but only then) a suitable course of treatment should be prescribed.[6]

In his April 1970 budget statement Roy Jenkins was able to report that DCE had been negative in 1969/70, so that his expectation that the expansion would be less than £400 million had thus been more than fulfilled. Looking forward to 1970/1, his expectation was for an expansion of domestic credit of under £900 million, and he expected the money supply to rise by less than DCE.[7] In his 1971

---

[1] A. A. Walters, *Money in Boom and Slump*, London, Institute of Economic Affairs, 1969. Other contributions to the public debate in 1969 were Anna Jacobson Schwartz ('Why money matters', *Lloyds Bank Review*, no. 94, October 1969), Judith A. Waters ('Money supply and credit – theory and practice', *National Westminster Bank Review*, November 1969), and Laurence Harris, 'The Chicago school of thought', and P. R. Herrington, 'Walters on money – a review article', (both in *The Bankers' Magazine*, vol. 208, July 1969).

[2] *Bank of England Quarterly Bulletin*, vol. 8, December 1968, p. 410.

[3] *The Banker*, vol. 118, December 1968, p. 1094.

[4] J. J. Polak, 'Monetary analysis of income formation and payments problems', *IMF Staff Papers*, vol. 6, November 1957; see also page 50 above.

[5] DCE corresponds to the change in the money stock on its M_3 definition (see footnote to table 5.7 below) plus the balance of payments deficit (defined for this purpose, broadly speaking, as the deficit on current account less net private sector borrowing overseas).

[6] See Treasury, 'Money supply and domestic credit', *Economic Trends*, no. 187, May 1969, p. xxi; also the Governor of the Bank of England's Jane Hodge Memorial Lecture in December 1970 (*Bank of England Quarterly Bulletin*, vol. 11, March 1971, pp. 43–4).

[7] In the event, DCE in 1970/1 was £1400 million and the increase in the money supply (M_3) £2031 million.

budget the new Chancellor did not lay down a specific money supply target, but he thought it would be inconsistent with his budget judgement to restrict the growth of money supply much below 3 per cent per quarter.

The DCE concept is so defined as to include not only the current deficit in the balance of payments (which is appropriate in an indicator to be used as a guide to demand management), but also a wide variety of external capital movements (for example, much of the short-term capital inflow which occurred in 1971). If therefore such capital movements are erratic and unpredictable, DCE becomes to that extent an unreliable indicator for demand management purposes, and the case for having a DCE target would have to rest on the control of the external balance being no less important as a policy objective than the control of effective demand – a presumption which was unquestionably invalid in 1971, when our external position was unusually strong. Hence it is not surprising that in his 1971 budget speech the Chancellor adduced the strength of sterling as a reason for not setting a DCE target. However, when in 1972 and 1973 our external balance deteriorated, official interest in DCE as an alternative monetary indicator to the stock of money was not resumed (though it came into use again in 1976).

Though officials lost interest in DCE, they did not in the money stock. A greater emphasis on the money supply was an ingredient in at least some of the official rethinking which characterised the new approach of 1971. Thus the Chief Cashier, in his Sykes Memorial Lecture of November 1971, spoke of a theoretical reappraisal,[1] which had led to the conclusion that the Bank's operations in the gilt-edged market should have more regard to quantitative effects on monetary aggregates; hence there was a need for a better official dealing technique in the gilt-edged market to give the authorities a better control over the monetisation of the national debt. The greater emphasis which some officials now gave to the money supply also supported a presumption against forms of control which affected only certain kinds of credit, for example bank advances and hire purchase contracts. It equally supported a presumption in favour of imposing a uniform control over all private sector institutions whose liabilities are conventionally regarded as 'money'; hence the imposition of uniform reserve asset and Special Deposit ratios on all banks.

[1] Some at least of the results of the Bank's 'theoretical reappraisal' have appeared in its Quarterly Bulletin. See in particular 'The importance of money', *Bank of England Quarterly Bulletin*, vol. 10, June 1970, 'Timing relationships between movements of monetary and national income variables', vol. 10, December 1970 and 'The demand for money in the United Kingdom: a further investigation', vol. 12, March 1972.

THE NEW APPROACH IN OPERATION

The period from the adoption of the new approach in 1971 until the general election in February 1974 saw an intensification of competition in banking, as had of course been intended by the authorities. Among the developments within the banking system was the entry of the London clearing banks in their own right into the market for certificates of deposit, both as issuers and as holders. Moreover, besides offering their traditional seven-day deposit account facilities through their branches to their regular customers, they now negotiated competitive terms for large 'wholesale' deposits and participated in the inter-bank market, both as deposit takers and as lenders.

The period also saw many changes in the use of the various instruments of monetary policy. Finally, it saw a complete change in the stance of official policy, since the pressure of effective demand moved from inadequate to adequate, or even excessive, and the balance of payments deteriorated from favourable to unfavourable, or even alarming. The main preoccupation of the authorities throughout the period was with demand management – initially to stimulate demand and later to restrain it. During most of the stimulation phase the balance of payments was not a constraint; though it deteriorated rapidly after 1971, the floating of the pound in June 1972 gave a further year's respite, so it was not until July 1973 that there arose any conflict between internal and external objectives.

The first touch on the monetary brakes, a slightly belated touch in retrospect according to views of the Governor of the Bank in October 1972,[1], occurred in mid-1972 with an abrupt upward movement in interest rates in the two months between the end of May and the end of July. Then about a year later, with the first indication that concern for the balance of payments was beginning to operate as a constraint on official action, the Bank of England took steps in July 1973 to bring about 'a sharp upward shift in short term rates in London', which, in the words of the Governor, 'achieved our primary objective of stabilising the sterling exchange rate...Apart from the external need I should have preferred a less sudden change.'[2]

[1] Address prepared by the Governor and delivered by the Deputy Governor at the Lord Mayor's dinner on 19 October 1972; *Bank of England Quarterly Bulletin*, vol. 12, December 1972, p. 516.

[2] Speech at Lord Mayor's dinner on 18 October 1973; *Bank of England Quarterly Bulletin*, vol. 13, December 1973, p. 476.

Official regulations

The period we are now considering was one of rapid increase in bank deposits and bank advances, likewise (see table 5.7) in the money stock, whether defined narrowly (M_1) or broadly (M_3). Up to the middle of 1972 all the evidence points to monetary policy being unrestrictive. Even after mid-1972 the figures of actual reserve ratios suggest that banks were being allowed to continue on a fairly loose rein. However, the behaviour of short-term interest rates after mid-1972 seems to suggest that the banks were beginning to compete more actively for reserve assets. Under the new approach every bank, including the London clearing banks, was now free to bid for wholesale deposits or to issue certificates of deposit at competitive interest rates as a means of preserving, or improving, its share of the total available reserve assets. Hence a rise in certificate of deposit and inter-bank interest rates in relation to rates on reserve assets, such as occurred very markedly from mid-1972 until February 1973, can probably be interpreted as implying that the discipline of the $12\frac{1}{2}$ per cent minimum reserve asset ratio was making itself felt, even though the figures of actual reserve asset ratios remained appreciably above $12\frac{1}{2}$ per cent.

Table 5.7. *Growth rate of the money supply, 1968–73*

Percentages

	$M_1{}^a$	$M_3{}^b$
1968	5·0	7·3
69	—	3·2
1970	9·3	9·4
71	15·4	13·5
72	14·4	28·1
73:^{c}		
March	10·1	26·8
June	12·3	23·8
September	8·0	28·2
December	5·8	27·9

SOURCE: *Midland Bank Review*, May 1974, p. 4.

^{a} Defined to include notes and coin in circulation with the public plus sterling current accounts owned by the private sector.

^{b} Includes notes and coin in circulation with the public plus all United Kingdom private and public sector deposits, both sterling and other currencies, with banks and discount houses.

^{c} Percentage change on 12 months earlier.

In the second half of 1973 official restrictions were progressively tightened. In August the Special Deposit ratio was increased by 1 per cent to 4 per cent, which immediately touched off a rise in certificate of deposit and inter-bank interest rates,[1] both absolutely and in relation to the rates on reserve assets. Further increases in Special Deposits followed in November.

In August 1972 the Bank had reverted to lending priorities, with a request that property and Stock Exchange speculation were to be accorded low priority. This request was later made more forcibly and supplemented by other measures: in December 1973 hire purchase controls were reintroduced and at the same time a new device, Supplementary Deposits – which could even less be reconciled with the competitive philosophy of the new approach – was introduced. This new device provided for non-interest bearing deposits to be made with the Bank whenever the interest-bearing sterling deposit liabilities of each bank (or finance house) grew at more than a certain rate, which was fixed at 8 per cent for the next six months.[2] Thus, the Supplementary Deposit scheme (like the old ceilings on advances) imposed a limitation on each individual bank, not just on banks as a whole, so that competition between banks (for depositing customers in this case, for borrowing customers under the old lending ceilings) was inhibited or at any rate discouraged.

Finally, though the banks' freedom to indulge in competition for deposits was encouraged by the abolition of the interest-rate cartel in 1971, an official ceiling of $9\frac{1}{2}$ per cent was imposed in September 1973 on interest payable on bank deposits of under £10,000. The official justification was:

In the consultative document of May 1971, the Bank recognised (paragraph 15) that the greater freedom of the banks to compete for personal savings could have implications for the savings banks and the building societies. The increases in short-term interest rates which took place in the first half of the year under review curtailed the flow of funds into the building societies, which were constrained in raising their own rates because of the effect on the cost of mortgages.[3]

The imposition of so many restrictive controls in the second half of 1973 provoked a comment in the following year from Lord O'Brien, who had then just retired as Governor of the Bank of England, to the effect that the recent changes in the credit control mechanism had brought the money supply under control, but they carried some of the same dangers to competition in the banking system as did the old techniques.[4]

[1] *Midland Bank Review*, May 1974, p 8.
[2] For details, see 'Credit control: a supplementary scheme', *Bank of England Quarterly Bulletin*, vol. 14, March 1974, p. 37.
[3] Bank of England, *Report and Accounts for the year ended 28 February 1974*, p. 7.
[4] *Financial Times*, 13 September 1974.

Official transactions in gilt-edged

Though under the new approach there was not the systematic support for the gilt-edged market that occurred in the 1960s,[1] support was afforded in June and July 1972, following the floating of sterling on 23 June, and again from time to time in 1973. In 1972 the Bank made facilities available to the banking system for the temporary sale and repurchase of short-dated gilt-edged stocks, under which it bought £358 million of stocks on 30 June which were resold to the banks on 14 July.[2] In 1973 there were some sharp fluctuations in the market, which, on occasion, involved moderate net purchases by the Bank, particularly during the period early June to mid-September.[3] However, despite the Bank's occasional support for gilt-edged, prices in the market in 1972 and 1973 fluctuated much more than in the 1960s. This seems to have been at least partly responsible for three firms of jobbers withdrawing from the gilt-edged market in July 1972; however the Bank was not unduly concerned.[4]

Official money market transactions

Since 1971 there have been three changes in official tactics in the money market. First, in October 1972 the Bank's traditional rediscount rate, Bank Rate, was superseded by an automatically determined 'minimum lending rate', which had the advantage of avoiding the dramatic announcement effect of changes in Bank Rate. The new arrangement was practicable because the significance of Bank Rate as a conventional reference point for other money market rates had been reduced, notably because the clearing banks had ceased to tie their deposit and lending rates to it and instead had each announced its own 'base' rate from time to time. The Bank's new minimum lending rate was to be determined every Friday at $\frac{1}{2}$ per cent above the average rate of discount for Treasury bills at the tender, rounded to the nearest $\frac{1}{4}$ per cent above, but a change in the rate independent of these arrangements was not excluded if this was required to signify a shift in monetary policy.[5] In fact such a change was made in 1973, when in November the Bank raised the rate (from $11\frac{1}{4}$ to 13 per cent) by specific announcement rather than in accordance with the new formula.

Secondly, the balance sheet constraint, initially imposed on the discount houses in 1971 with the aim of limiting the undue expansion of call money (a reserve asset) for the finance of non-public sector debt,

---

[1] Except in the case of bonds maturing within one year.
[2] Bank of England, *Report and Accounts for the year ended 28 February 1973*, p. 15.
[3] Bank of England, *Report and Accounts for the year ended 28 February 1974*, p. 14.
[4] *Bank of England Quarterly Bulletin*, vol. 12, September 1972, pp. 318–19.
[5] Bank of England, *Report and Accounts for the year ended 28 February 1973*, p. 6.

was amended in July 1973. Under the original arrangements the discount houses had undertaken to hold at least half their assets in specified forms of public sector debt, thereby artificially stimulating the demand for such assets (page 254 below). Under the revised arrangements, holdings of non-public sector debt were limited to a maximum of twenty times each house's capital and reserves.

Thirdly, the tradition under which the Bank did not undertake transactions in the new money markets was broken in late 1973 and early 1974.[1] It is perhaps too soon to judge whether these will be seen to have created an important precedent; so far they seem not to have done so.

There can be no doubt that under the new regime the Bank's transactions in the traditional money market, whether at the discount office or through its bill broker, continued to afford the Bank as effective a control over rates on reserve assets as it had enjoyed in the 1960s.[2] The transition from Bank Rate to the new minimum lending rate in October 1972 was not intended to abdicate the Bank's control over rates on reserve assets. As regards interest rates in the new money markets, it has become very apparent that, with the new reserve asset ratio, the differential between the rates prevailing in the traditional and new money markets (as measured, for example, by the excess of the certificate of deposit rate over the Treasury bill rate) is very sensitive to whether or not the banks are experiencing, or expect to experience, a shortage of reserve assets. When there is no shortage, as for instance in the first half of 1972, the differential can be very small, but when the banks fear that they are going to be squeezed the differential increases, since the way that the banks compete for scarce reserve assets is to offer higher rates on the 'wholesale' deposits which they borrow and on certificates of deposit which they issue.[3] This is what happened in the second half of 1972 and early 1973, and then again in the course of roughly the same months one year later.[4]

[1] Bank of England, *Report and Accounts for the year ended 28 February 1974*, pp. 12 and 13.
[2] Bank of England, *Report and Accounts for the year ended 28 February 1973*, p. 12.
[3] The clearing banks' rates on 'retail', i.e. seven-day branch deposits, are conventionally related to their base rates, as pre-1971 they were to Bank Rate.
[4] The following table permits a comparison of the differential:

Percentages

	Treasury bill rate	3-months CD rate
25 February 1972	4·36	5·19
23 February 1973	8·06	10·81
22 February 1974	11·82	14·31

SOURCE: *Bank of England Quarterly Bulletin*, vol. 14, September 1974, table 30.

The Bank's amendment in July 1973 of its restriction on the discount houses' portfolios was probably intended to mitigate the tendency for the differential between the certificate of deposit and Treasury bill rates to widen at times of a squeeze on reserve assets. In the preceding squeeze it had been found that the differential had been increased not only because the banks competed for reserve assets by bidding up the certificate of deposit rate, but because the discount houses, in attempting to supply the banks with more reserve assets (in the form of call money they borrowed from the banks), bid more fiercely for Treasury bills, since they could take £2 more call money for every additional £1 of Treasury bills in their portfolios.[1] Thus, up to the reform of July 1973 both the banks and the discount houses had an incentive to widen the differential between the certificate of deposit and Treasury bill rates. However the reform did not improve matters much; during the next period of squeeze, which began in mid-1973 and reached a climax at about the turn of the year, the differential between the certificate of deposit and Treasury bill rates was as wide as ever.

The quantity of money

The practice of announcing monetary targets lapsed in 1971 (page 248 above), and was not resumed until 1976. By the time of the first budget after 'Competition and credit control', in March 1972, the authorities had adopted a policy of reflating demand and the Chancellor was prepared to accept a growth of money supply high by standards of past years to ensure that adequate finance was available for the extra output; he rejected the constraint of a numerical target. In fact, an accelerating rise in the money stock was tolerated, even though (according to Patrick Jenkin, Chief Secretary at the Treasury) it was accepted that an excessive expansion of money supply could store up trouble in the future, since the full effects of monetary policy are likely to be felt only after a lag of perhaps a year or even more.[2] A rapid increase in the money supply was at the same time tolerated on econometric grounds, in that the Bank of England's research on demand functions for money (on various definitions of the money stock) strongly suggested that when real income is increasing a much more rapid rise is needed in the money stock than in money national income if unacceptably high rates of interest are to be avoided.[3] This conclusion

---

[1] Since one half of their portfolios had to be in public sector debt, for example Treasury bills, their acquisition of £1 of such debt enabled them to acquire a further £1 of private sector debt, for example certificates of deposit, so that they could then make use of £2 additional call money. [2] Reported in the *Financial Times*, 17 July 1972.

[3] L. D. D. Price, 'The demand for money in the United Kingdom: a further investigation', *Bank of England Quarterly Bulletin*, vol. 12, March 1972. An earlier version of this paper had been presented at a conference in September 1971.

reconciled the Bank for the time being to a remarkable fall in the velocity of circulation (GNP divided by M_3), which brought its value down from a plateau of about 3·0 in 1970 and 1971 to about 2·7 in the third quarter of 1972.

The first sign of a change from acquiescence by the authorities in an increase in the money supply came in mid-1972 with a sharp rise in short-term rates (page 249); then in mid-September 1972 came a warning that the highest priority must now be given to the reduction of the rate of inflation, since the real growth of the economy had speeded up to the government's target rate of 5 per cent and concern had shifted to the rapid rise in prices. Moreover, in the course of 1973 confidence in the Bank's demand functions for money was undermined; the econometric case for tolerating a rapid rise in the money stock was weakened by the recognition that recent structural changes in the financial system had decreased the reliability of the M_3 statistical series as a useful measure of the money stock.[1] In particular:

(1) Six years of lending ceilings had driven some business out of banking channels, for example into inter-company loans. This had now come back into the banks and helped to swell the figure for bank deposits and hence for the money stock.

(2) The new competitive environment allowed the banks, especially the clearing banks, to extend their range of deposit facilities, including sterling certificates of deposit, and thus provide new homes for funds awaiting investment. Bank deposits, unlike some of the alternative homes for such funds – such as deposits with local authorities – are included in the figures of the money stock.

(3) Towards the end of 1973 some bank customers came to believe that the Bank and the government – faced with this rapid expansion in money and credit – would be forced to reintroduce credit ceilings. This led to some precautionary borrowing, with customers making use of their facilities for advances while the going was good, and thereby causing an equivalent increase in bank deposits.

(4) At times a perverse relationship developed between clearing bank borrowing and lending rates, so that borrowing became relatively cheap, and bank customers were able to draw upon their facilities for advances and use them to build up their deposits – sometimes drawing money solely in order to reinvest it in sterling certificates of deposit or in large wholesale deposits which earned relatively high market rates.

[1] The alternative series for measuring the money stock, M_1, was no less unsatisfactory. As the Deputy Governor explained in an address on 11 April 1973, the Bank's estimates of M_1 were inherently of poorer quality than those for M_3 and had been available on a consistent definition for little more than a year. Hence the Bank had during 1973 become increasingly sceptical of the value of either M_1 or M_3 as intermediate variables in the formulation of monetary policy (*Bank of England Quarterly Bulletin*, vol. 13, June 1973, p. 198).

This was the process which came to be known as the 'merry-go-round' or 'round-tripping'.[1] The reasons why this occurred included: first, the existence of the overdraft system, which gave customers sizable unused facilities which they could draw upon at will; secondly, the fact that the cost of those facilities was related to base rates which the banks were reluctant to raise – partly because they were already embarrassed by the high profits they were known to be making as a result of the generally high level of interest rates. In this situation the banks preferred to respond to pressure on the reserve ratio by bidding aggressively for large amounts of wholesale deposits rather than by raising rates on advances. And the more deposit rates rose in relation to lending rates, the greater the demand for credit and the greater the pressure on reserve ratios. Hence there was a vicious circle of rising market rates, associated with an expansion of bank advances and deposits, and also of the quantity of money.

The rise in the money stock had eventually to be slowed down – even though some of the rise may have been only a statistical distortion – and clearly Special Deposits were an inappropriate instrument for this purpose since they would merely aggravate the pressure on reserve ratios. So, in December 1973, the Supplementary Deposit scheme was introduced, which imposed a direct limit on the rate of growth of the banks' interest-bearing liabilities, which are a substantial component of the money stock. This scheme allowed a reasonable rate of growth in the banks' balance sheets, while discouraging them from bidding for funds and creating the distorted interest-rate pattern described above. It was also intended to encourage the banks to be more cautious in extending facilities for advances, for there is no doubt that in the first flush of freedom following the introduction of 'Competition and credit control' in 1971 many banks took on lending commitments far beyond what they could have reasonably expected to have the resources to finance.

As compared with the lending ceilings of the 1960s, which applied to a particular area of bank lending (namely the private sector), the new arrangements had the advantages of allowing banks more freedom to arrange their assets as they wished and to run their own business within the given overall rate of growth, and of providing more control over the money stock. It was also hoped that the scheme would be more easily applied for a temporary period than the lending ceilings had proved to be. (It was, in the event, suspended for the time being in February 1975.)

---

[1] The merry-go-round effect was the subject of an initiative by the Bank later in 1973, which led to decisions by the clearing banks to adjust their base rates to respond more rapidly to movements in market rates and to link their lending rates to certain customers (in particular local authorities, finance houses and other banks) to money market rates rather than to base rates.

The Supplementary Deposit scheme did its job well, in the sense that the growth in the money supply was quickly checked. After a few months the scheme was made less necessary by the falling demand for credit from the private sector; in the event very few banks came up against the prescribed limits. Yet in the first half-year of its operation it was thought by the Bank to be contributing to the banks' greater restraint in extending credit.

CHAPTER 6

MONETARY POLICY

PART II

by *M. J. Artis*

INTRODUCTION

This chapter is addressed principally to the problem of evaluating the effects of monetary policy. As such, it would ideally incorporate, if not summary statistics measuring these effects, then at least orders of magnitude illustrating the importance of monetary measures. In fact, it is only for a few types of measure and a limited range of monetary variables that this ideal can even be approached, and then not often with great confidence. However, the consequent rather uncertain and patchy verdict on monetary policy is consistent with the findings of other investigators;[1] it accords with the relative absence from the major United Kingdom macroeconometric models of convincingly detailed and powerful monetary influences.

There is ample room for speculation on why this state of affairs prevails and it is worth dwelling for a moment on some of the conditions required for the effects of monetary policy, whether at an aggregated or disaggregated level, to be isolated and measured. In the first instance it is obviously necessary for monetary policy (or more modestly monetary variables), somehow measured, to have varied sufficiently to exert a measurable influence on real factors – a condition which is met by only a few monetary variables (hire purchase terms, for example) in our period; indeed, a popular broad-brush view of British monetary policy in the 1960s is that it was essentially passive. It is also necessary to establish that any variation in monetary policy was independent of other factors; but here there is the awkward fact of a very intimate relationship between fiscal and monetary policy in British conditions –

---

[1] See, for example, the Bank of England's paper 'The operation of monetary policy since Radcliffe' in D. R. Croome and H. G. Johnson (eds.), *Money in Britain 1959–1969*, London, Oxford University Press, 1970. However, there are some monetarists who have attached unequivocal importance to the price and real output consequences of variations in the money supply; two recent examples are D. E. W. Laidler's 'Brief note on fiscal policy, inflation and the balance of payments' presented to the House of Commons Expenditure Committee (see House of Commons, *Ninth Report from the Expenditure Committee, Session 1974*) and J. M. Parkin's ' Where is Britain's inflation going?', *Lloyds Bank Review*, no. 117, July 1975.

a relationship which is liable to frustrate attempts to demonstrate the effects of monetary policy alone even by the most convinced *aficionados* of its potency.[1] Then, as a third requirement, it has to be possible to quantify monetary policy, but in those views of its transmission mechanism that stress the significance of volatile expectations – 'threshold effects' and the imperfection of capital markets – quantification is by no means straightforward. Finally, the task is made more difficult by evidence that the monetary reforms of 1971 introduced under the title 'Competition and credit control'[2] constituted a structural break with the 1960s; thus, later observations, relating to a period in which several important monetary variables conveniently (at first sight) varied much more than they had in previous years, fail to confirm the significance of relationships established for the earlier period.

These considerations suggest that it will be best to consider separately the problems raised by the conceptual isolation and measurement of monetary policy, the nature of the transmission mechanism and the events following the publication of 'Competition and credit control'.

INSTRUMENTS, INDICATORS AND OBJECTIVES

The theory of macroeconomic policy provides a framework in which instrumental variables[3] – those over which the authorities have direct control – are sharply distinguished from goal variables – those whose magnitudes 'really matter' to policy-makers. Between these two sets stand 'intermediate' variables, whose values are capable of being closely determined by the authorities through their instrument setting and which can be thought of, in turn, as either influencing, or being an early indicator of, the goal variables of the system.[4] According to this approach monetary policy could be defined as changes in those instruments which have, on some principle, been classified as monetary instruments; the effects of monetary policy can then be identified, in two stages, with the effects of monetary actions on the intermediate variables and the effects of changes in these upon the goal variables of the system. Alternatively the sequence can be viewed in reverse, and attention focused upon the response of monetary instruments to

---

[1] Walters, for example, whilst clearly stating his belief in the 'power' of money, rightly draws attention to this problem in *Money in Boom and Slump*.

[2] *Bank of England Quarterly Bulletin*, vol. 11, June 1971.

[3] This term, used here in a policy context, appears also in the literature on econometric estimation, where it has a different meaning.

[4] This account is oversimplified to some degree: the authorities may have grounds for thinking that intermediate variables 'really matter' too, apart from their significance for the goal variables of the system; an example would be the rate of interest on government debt. Most studies of the monetary authorities' reaction functions also seem to assume that the authorities attach 'disutility' to *changing* their instrument variables.

deviations in the goal variables from their preferred values; this is the object of the authors of various investigations into the 'reaction functions' of the authorities (see pages 279–80 below).

This scheme invites us to look at monetary policy actions and effects in a relatively disaggregated fashion, at least to the extent of the multiple goals and instruments which can be identified. As such, it stands in some contrast to the emphasis of a large bulk of literature, both theoretical and empirical, where the effect of monetary policy is identified with the impact of changes in the money supply or the monetary base. There are some considerations (commented upon further below) which can help to resolve the apparent contrast between the two approaches, but our view of the transmission mechanism of monetary policy and of the monetary authorities' goals implies that it cannot be completely removed. Accordingly, some analysis of the effects of changes in individual instrumental variables is in order.

Regulatory instruments

Monetary instruments are classified in the preceding chapter into instruments of a regulatory character and those involving the authorities in direct market transactions. Among the former are bank lending 'requests', Special Deposits and variations in the terms of hire purchase borrowing. Each of these has been the subject of academic enquiry and the use of these instruments, more especially of the last two, was perhaps the most obvious outward sign of monetary action in the period up to 1971 with which we are concerned at this point.

The occasions on which *bank lending requests* were used and their general character have already been described in the preceding chapter; a summary is given here in table 6.1. It is perhaps surprising in view of the importance of this instrument in the 1960s that relatively little attention should have been paid to quantifying its effects. Published investigations appear to be restricted to three papers, of which only that by Norton is of much help.[1] His procedure was to classify the requests into two groups, 'severe' (calling for zero or negative growth) and 'mild' (allowing for restricted but positive growth), and then to use this scoring as a dummy variable in a multiple regression analysis to explain the level of bank advances.

---

[1] F. P. R. Brechling and G. Clayton, 'Commercial banks' portfolio behaviour', *Economic Journal*, vol. 75, June 1965, pp. 290–316; W. E. Norton, 'Debt management and monetary policy in the United Kingdom', *Economic Journal*, vol. 79, September 1969, pp. 475–94; W. R. White, 'Some econometric models of deposit bank portfolio behaviour in the United Kingdom, 1963–1970' in Renton (ed.), *Modelling the Economy*. Brechling and Clayton are mainly concerned with the 1950s, whilst White (who was at the Bank of England at the time) gives an econometric expression to requests and the series affected by them which cannot be replicated from published sources; it is therefore difficult to derive from them any illustrative order of magnitude for the effect.

Table 6.1. *Ceilings on lending to the private sector,[a] 1961–71*

	London and Scottish clearing banks	Other banks	Larger finance houses
July 1961	Unquantified request for restraint[b]		
Oct. 1962	Restraint removed		
May 1965[c]	105% of mid-March 1965	105% of March 1965	
April 1967	Ceiling removed	Unchanged	
Nov. 1967	100% of mid-Nov. 1967		100% of end-Oct. 1967
May 1968	104% of mid-Nov. 1967		Unchanged
Nov. 1968	98% of mid-Nov. 1967[d]	102% of mid-Nov. 1967	98% of end-Oct. 1967
April 1970	105% of mid-March 1970[e]	107% of mid-March 1970	105% of end-March 1970
March–June 1971	107½% of mid-March 1970[e]	109½% of mid-March 1970	107½% of end-March 1970

SOURCE: 'Monetary surveys' in *Midland Bank Review* (May issues).

[a] Requests covered commercial bills as well as advances from May 1965 onwards, and leasing facilities from November 1967 onwards.

[b] Interpreted by London and Scottish clearing banks as 100 per cent of mid-June 1961.

[c] Followed a request to all institutions in December 1964 to slow down the rate of growth of lending. Institutions were told in February 1966 that the ceiling for the ensuing year would remain at 105 per cent of the March 1965 figure.

[d] This level was to be attained by March 1969; in October 1969 it was unofficially relaxed to 104 per cent of the official ceiling.

[e] Ceilings applied to London and Scottish clearing banks in aggregate, not to individual institutions.

A similar procedure was followed in estimating the equations reported in table 6.2; the incidence of requests, scored in the same manner, is shown against a time-series graph of London clearing bank net advances in chart 6.1. The results in table 6.2 are an excerpt from a long series of trials, using alternative formulations of the dependent variable and a wide array of independent variables. Requests were regularly highly significant with the appropriate sign, and virtually all the equations indicated a very slow rate of adjustment, often not significantly different from zero. Two basic models were employed: in the first, advances were treated (following Norton) as demand-determined, subject to requests acting as constraints upon the adjustment process;[1] in the second, a reduced form of supply and demand was estimated, with structural equations based on the assumption that market-clearing occurred in

[1] That is, the long-run demand for advances, A^*, was thought of as subject to the partial adjustment process, $A - A_{-1} = \alpha(A^* - A_{-1}) + \beta D$, where the subscript indicates a one-period lag, α the coefficient of adjustment and D the request dummy, acting as a constraint upon the adjustment process.

Table 6.2. *The effect of lending requests on bank advances,^{a} 1956 III–1971 III*

	Equation numbers				
	1	2	3^b	4	5
Constant term	128·25 (2·05)	218·18 (2·80)	−66·59 (3·25)	−1077·24 (1·91)	−739·30 (1·31)
Regression coefficients for:					
Permanent income^e	0·17 (3·76)	0·18 (3·31)	n.a.	0·15 (3·78)	n.a.
Disposable income^d	−0·17 (3·6c)	−0·17 (3·17)	−0·04^e (3·98)	−0·16 (4·15)	−0·07 (2·89)
Bank Rate^f	−4·81 (0·39)	−42·04 (3·73)	n.a.	n.a.	−2·17 (0·19)
Short bond rate	n.a.	n.a.	−1·81 (2·39)	n.a.	n.a.
Special Deposits	n.a.	n.a.	1·36 (2·73)	n.a.	n.a.
Banks' free resources^g	n.a.	n.a.	n.a.	0·07 (2·35)	0·01 (0·84)
Total private investment	n.a.	0·07 (0·87)	n.a.	n.a.	n.a.
Stockbuilding^h	0·01 (0·80)	n.a.	n.a.	n.a.	n.a.
Capacity utilisation^i	n.a.	n.a.	124·45 (5·94)	1193·18 (2·01)	1305·41 (1·89)
Lagged dependent variable	0·98 (41·29)	0·97 (32·17)	n.a.	0·93 (35·24)	0·82 (15·59)
Time trend	n.a.	n.a.	0·83 (7·08)	n.a.	10·84 (3·05)
Lending request dummies:^{j}					
Mild	−74 80 (2·89)	−0·29^k (1·93)	−2·37 (2·11)	−83·59 (4·06)	−65·96 (2·74)
Severe	−139·20 (5·29)		−3·79 (3·50)	−157·58 (8·98)	−137·17 (5·64)
$\bar{R}^2$	0·999	0·999	0·900	0·998	0·998
DW	2·04	1·55	1·11	2·14	2·11

SOURCE: M. J. Artis and P. Meadows, 'Lending requests' and 'Lending requests: addendum' (unpublished NIESR working papers), 1974.

^{a} Net advances by the London clearing banks, excluding those to nationalised industries. Seasonal dummies not listed. t-statistics shown in brackets.

^{b} Dependent variable scaled by deposits.

^{c} As defined in Norton, 'Debt management and monetary policy in the United Kingdom': $(1-k) \Sigma_{i=0}^{10} k^i Y_{t-i}/(1-k^{11})$, where Y is GDP at factor cost and $k = 0.95$.

^{d} Also as defined by Norton: $Y-T$, where T is total direct tax payments.

^{e} Coefficient multiplied by 10. ^{f} Quarterly average.

^{g} Deposits minus required liquid assets and Special Deposits.

^{h} Value of physical increase in stocks. ^{i} Deviation from trend.

^{j} Taken as zero: 1958 III–1961 II, 1962 IV–1964 IV, 1971 III; mild: 1962 III, 1965 I–1966 I, 1967 II–1968 II, 1970 II–1971 II; severe: 1956 III–1958 II, 1961 III–1962 II, 1966 II–1967 I, 1968 III–1970 I. ^{k} A 0, 1, 2 dummy scaled by the consumer price index.

non-observable 'quality' variables.[1] The dependent variable of the estimated equation is defined for equations (1), (2), (4) and (5) as London clearing bank net advances and for equation (3) as advances scaled by deposits; in equation (2) the dummy variable was also scaled by the consumer price index.

Chart 6.1. *Bank advances and their ratio to personal disposable income,*
1957–72

SOURCES: Bank of England, *Statistical Abstract*, no. 1, table 9(1); CSO, *Financial Statistics* and *National Income and Expenditure* (annual).

Notes: (i) London clearing bank advances (excluding those to nationalised industries), seasonally adjusted.

(ii) Personal bank advances and personal disposable income (at current prices) not seasonally adjusted.

These equations reflect the generality of results obtained in the investigation of bank advances. Interest rates were of variable significance in determining bank advances, and Special Deposits hardly ever significant (although they do influence the value of the variable 'banks' free resources', which was occasionally significant – as in equation (4)).[2] But bank lending requests proved significant on almost any specification of the equations, the 'mild' request having an impact effect of the order

---

[1] That is, assuming that $A_s = a + bQ + cS$ and $A_d = a' - b'Q - c'Z$, where Q is the unobservable market-clearing factor and S and Z are exogenous influences on supply and demand, the weighted sum of A_s and A_d is formed as $w_1 A_s + w_2 A_d = A$, with $w_1 = b'(b'+b)$ and $w_2 = b(b'+b)$, so as to yield an estimating equation, $A = w_1 a + w_2 a' + w_1 cS - w'_2 cZ$. A similar procedure was employed by M. H. Miller in 'An empirical analysis of monetary policy in the UK, 1954–1965' (unpublished Ph.D. thesis, Yale), 1971.

[2] In equation (3) Special Deposits, though significant, have the 'wrong' sign.

of £70 million and the 'severe' dummy an effect approximately twice as large. The results suggest that the cumulative effect of requests on the *level* of bank advances was considerable, building up slowly over a long period. For example, they imply that the requests imposed at the beginning of 1965 and maintained until 1971 were responsible by the end of this period for reducing the demand for bank advances by some £1500 million. It seems, indeed, reasonably clear that the requests affected the level of bank advances significantly and that their prolonged use resulted in a substantial frustration of the demand for bank credit.[1] This was probably especially true of advances to the personal sector, as was the evident intent of the qualitative advice accompanying the requests and as is strongly suggested by chart 6.1. It is, of course, a matter for separate consideration how far the effect of requests on advances was reflected in a parallel modification of spending behaviour.

It is difficult to find any reason (or evidence) for believing that *Special Deposits* played a significant part in monetary policy in the 1960s. The authorities appear to have regarded them, alternately, as possible substitutes for, or as complements of, bank lending requests. But in the latter role they were essentially redundant and in the former largely ineffective. The suggestion that they were largely ineffective is reinforced by the relatively small scale on which they were employed: as table 6.3 shows, up to September 1971 cumulative calls never exceeded $3\frac{1}{2}$ per cent for the London clearing banks and $1\frac{3}{4}$ per cent for the Scottish banks. After 'Competition and credit control', however, calls for Special Deposits cumulated to 6 per cent of eligible liabilities.

That Special Deposits were largely redundant as a complement to bank lending requests follows from the apparently high degree of compliance with those requests by the institutions concerned. Only once, in 1969, did the Bank of England publicly display concern at non-compliance (and temporarily penalised the banks for it by restricting the interest paid on Special Deposits), although it is true that the series to which requests were applicable are not available in detail in the

---

[1] This is not to claim that the determination of bank advances and the role of requests is well understood, however. For example, although the equations in table 6.2 point to the existence of a large pent up demand for advances by 1971, their technical characteristics actually suggest that the response of advances to the removal of requests (as to their imposition) should have been very gradual; as is evident from the value of the coefficients obtained on the lagged dependent variable, the results could have been generated from an instantaneous flow model rather than the partial stock adjustment model outlined in footnote 1, page 261 – that is, the value of α could have been taken as zero. Yet the evidence is that the response of advances to the removal of the requests was in fact very rapid, an observation which can be squared with the results reported only by appealing to the argument that conditions changed so fundamentally in 1971 that observations before and after 'Competition and credit control' must be regarded as belonging to structurally distinct regimes (see pages 298–9 below).

Table 6.3. *Special Deposits required from the clearing banks, 1960–73*

Percentages

	Called		Released		Cumulative total	
	London	Scottish	London	Scottish	London	Scottish
April 1960	1	½	—	—	1	½
June 1960	1	½	—	—	2	1
July 1961	1	½	—	—	3	1½
May 1962	—	—	1	½	2	1
Sept. 1962	—	—	1	½	1	½
Nov. 1962	—	—	1	½	—	—
April 1965	1	½	—	—	1	½
July 1966	1	½	—	—	2	1
April 1970	½	¼	—	—	2½	1¼
Oct. 1970	1	½	—	—	3½	1¾
Sept. 1971	—	—	3½	1¾	—	—
Nov. 1972	1		—		1	
Dec. 1972	2		—		3	
July 1973	1		—		4	
Nov. 1973	2		—		6	

SOURCES: *Bank of England Quarterly Bulletin* (various issues); CSO, *Financial Statistics*.

published statistics, so that it is not possible to be sure how far non-compliance was a significant (if unpublicised) problem in other periods. However, the data that are available do not suggest there could have been major difficulties of this kind.

The ineffectiveness of Special Deposits as a substitute follows from different considerations, of which two are important. First, there is reason to believe that throughout the period the banks were adjusting their portfolios to increase the ratio of advances to deposits far above the level prevailing in 1960; thus, the prewar ratio was in the region of 60 per cent, by which criterion the steady upward trend shown in chart 6.2, depressed as it was by the incidence of requests, strongly suggests that, when Special Deposits were imposed on bank portfolios, the assets for which they were substituted were bonds and not advances. Seen in this light, the analysis appropriate to a situation in which a call for Special Deposits fell upon banks initially in a position of equilibrium can be dispensed with.[1] Secondly, the policy followed by the authorities in the bond market, was as described above (chapter 5) one of 'leaning against the wind' – implying a willingness to absorb the greater part, if

[1] In this situation, there are two counter-posed factors to consider: to the extent that Special Deposits reduce liquidity, banks may wish to hold more bonds to compensate; but, to the extent that profitability per unit of assets is reduced, there is an 'income effect' operating to increase advances. A useful review of these and associated issues appears in A. D. Bain, *The Control of the Money Supply*, London, Penguin, 1970.

not all, of the bond sales induced by a call for Special Deposits. Taken together, these two factors suggest that calls for Special Deposits were largely absorbed by a reduction in bond holdings in bank portfolios, with little or no repercussion upon the total volume of deposits or advances. Researchers into the effects of Special Deposits have usually concluded in this vein,[1] although most have placed greater emphasis

Chart 6.2. *Ratios of advances to deposits and of Special Deposits to gross deposits, 1960–71*

SOURCES: Bank of England, *Statistical Abstract*, no. 1; *Bank of England Quarterly Bulletin*.
Notes: (i) Ratio advances/deposits, quarterly averages, not seasonally adjusted.
          (ii) Ratio Special Deposits/gross deposits, end-quarter figures.

upon the effects (or lack of them) on deposits – an emphasis that was misplaced, since the authorities firmly singled out advances as the goal of Special Deposits. One investigation, however, revealed some effect of Special Deposits upon advances,[2] although no such impact was

[1] For example, N. J. Gibson, 'Special deposits as an instrument of monetary policy', *Manchester School of Economic and Social Studies*, vol. 32, September 1964, and 'Monetary, credit and fiscal policies' in A. R. Prest (ed.) *The UK Economy: a manual of applied economics* (2nd edn), London, Weidenfeld & Nicolson, 1968; R. L. Crouch, 'Special Deposits and the British monetary mechanism', *Economic Studies*, vol. 5, no. 1, 1970. J. M. Parkin, M. R. Gray and R. J. Barrett, 'The portfolio behaviour of commercial banks' in Hilton and Heathfield (eds.) *The Econometric Study of the United Kingdom*, found it appropriate to assume that both deposits and advances were exogenously determined; they concluded that a call for Special Deposits would induce a more than equivalent shift out of bonds with an accompanying increase in holdings of Treasury bills and call money.

[2] R. T. Coghlan, 'Special Deposits and bank advances', *The Bankers Magazine*, vol. 216, August 1973.

discernible in any persistent manner in the investigations described earlier in this chapter.

Hardly less than bank lending requests, changes in the terms of *hire purchase credit* typified monetary action in the 1960s. The terms controlled were the minimum down-payment and maximum repayment period applicable to credit for particular goods; table 6.4 summarises the changes imposed.

Table 6.4. *Hire purchase controls, 1960–71*

	Minimum deposit				Maximum repayment period			
	Cars	Motor cycles	Radio, TV, etc.	Furniture[a]	Cars	Motor cycles	Radio, TV, etc.	Furniture[a]
	(percentages)				(months)			
April 1960	20	20	20	10	24	24	24	24
Jan. 1961	20	20	20	10	36	36	36	36
June 1962	20	20	10	10	36	36	36	36
June 1965	25	25	15	10	36	36	36	36
July 1965	25	25	15	10	30	30	30	36
Feb. 1966	25	25	25	15	27	27	24	30
July 1966	40	40	33⅓	20	24	24	24	24
April 1967	40	25	33⅓	20	24	27	24	24
June 1967	30	25	33⅓	20	30	27	24	24
Aug. 1967	25	25	25	15	36	36	30	30
Nov. 1967	33⅓	25	25	15	27	36	30	30
Nov. 1968	40	33⅓	33⅓	20	24	24	24	24
July 1971	—	—	—	—	—	—	—	—

SOURCE: *Board of Trade Journal/Trade and Industry.*

[a] Excluding cookers, on which the minimum deposit was 10 per cent and the maximum repayment period 48 months throughout.

Investigations of the effect of these controls have usually proceeded in two stages – by first identifying the change in outstanding debt due to specified changes in the controls and then the associated change in consumers' expenditure.[1] The change in outstanding debt can be identified with the difference between new credits and repayments. In Garganas's recent study, the latter are considered to arise as a distri-

[1] These investigations leave no doubt that outstanding debt responded significantly to the controls (see R. J. Ball and P. D. Drake, 'The impact of credit control on consumer durable spending in the United Kingdom, 1957–1961', *Review of Economic Studies*, vol. 30, October 1963, pp. 181–94). This was confirmed more recently by Garganas, using an approach based on the earlier study, but modified to take account of additional factors (see N. Garganas, 'An analysis of consumer credit and its effects on purchases of consumer durables' in Renton (ed.) *Modelling the Economy*). Additional confirmation is provided by A. M. El-Mokadem in *Econometric Models of Personal Saving. The United Kingdom, 1948–1966*, London, Butterworths, 1973.

buted lag of the former, in which the profile of the lag distribution depends on the repayment requirements in force and the deviation of disposable income from its trend. New credits are explained in a stock adjustment framework, with significant determinants including disposable income, an index of hire purchase terms, an interest-rate variable and unfilled vacancies (the latter being interpreted as an attitudinal index). Since the two dimensions of hire purchase control are multi-

Chart 6.3. *Ratio of hire purchase debt to disposable income with and without controls, 1960–73*

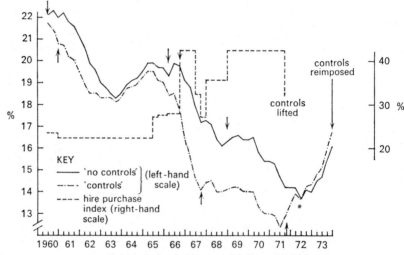

SOURCES: *Board of Trade Journal/Trade and Industry*; NIESR estimates.

Notes: (i) Hire purchase index calculated as $d + (100 - d)/m$, where d is percentage minimum deposit and m maximum repayment period in months. End-quarter figures for cars only are used.
(ii) Arrows indicate major interventions.

collinear, either one of them may be dropped, or they may be combined into a composite variable; the latter is the course followed by Garganas and the value of this composite index for one major group of durable goods (cars) is superimposed on chart 6.3.[1] It is fairly clear that a restriction on hire purchase terms has a largely short-term effect; the initial reduction in new credits is subsequently offset by the lower rate of repayments on outstanding debt, which is smaller than it otherwise would be.

Garganas's system can be used to simulate the effect of the controls on outstanding debt. First, outstanding debt is estimated in the presence

[1] The composite variable is defined as $dp_a + (100 - d)p_a/m$, where d is the minimum average deposit, m the maximum average repayment period and p_a the relative price of consumer durables. For purposes of chart 6.3 variations in the term p_a were suppressed.

of the controls; this is shown, as a proportion of disposable income, by the 'controls' line in chart 6.3; next the level of debt is recomputed on the assumption that the controls remained at their (minimal) 1959 level – this is shown in chart 6.3 as the 'no controls' line, again expressed as a ratio of disposable income. Within the limits of what can be expected from such a simulation, the results indicate that the controls may have frustrated hire purchase credit to a maximum of some $2\frac{1}{2}$ per cent of disposable income (the level of disposable income being regarded as exogenous). The controls were suspended in 1971 and not renewed until 1973; thus, in the intervening period, as might be expected, the two simulation runs come close together, the 'controls' run lying slightly above the 'no controls' because of the lagged effects of lower inherited debt levels (implying, for comparable demands for new credit, reduced repayments and a faster rate of rise in outstandings). The major interventions are shown by arrows in the chart, and it is worth noting that, although the 'controls' simulation shows quite a marked response to the severe restrictions of 1965 and 1966, there would still have been a fairly steady decline in the debt–income ratio in a 'no controls' situation. Indeed, the extent of this decline might lead one to suspect the 'no controls' simulation was biased downwards were it not for the fact that the value of the ratio in the 1973 period of 'freedom' showed no signs of approaching the 1959 levels, despite a probable incentive to anticipate the reimposition of controls. It seems likely that by this time bank credit had become an increasingly effective substitute for hire purchase debt; as we have seen, the debt–income ratio for personal sector bank advances displayed a very marked rise in this period (chart 6.1). As in the case of bank advances, econometric investigation of a period dominated by controls can always be suspected of failing to deliver an accurate verdict, but there appears little reason to doubt that variations in hire purchase terms had a significant short-run impact on levels of debt; but once again, the question of how this impact was transmitted to the demand for consumer durables remains to be investigated (see page 295).

Market instruments

Bank lending requests, calls for Special Deposits and variations in hire purchase terms have all been considered as instruments falling in the general category of monetary regulations. The authorities also had at their disposal the instruments of 'classical' monetary policy – the ability to buy and sell government debt – through which they are traditionally thought of as being able to influence the supply of money and the maturity composition and sectoral holdings of the national debt, or to control decisively the general level and structure of interest rates. It is axiomatic that they are unable to follow independent policies in these respects – to determine *both*, say, a certain growth rate for the money supply *and* any level of interest rates they choose.

As indicated in chapter 5, in the 1960s the monetary authorities pursued distinct policies in the short and longer ends of the market in government debt. In the former they appear to have been overwhelmingly concerned with steering interest rates so as to stabilise the spot exchange rate with the assistance of other devices such as intervention in the forward market. At the long end they followed a policy designed, as they saw it, to maximise sales of debt in the long run and so achieve their objective of funding. However, their view of the bond market led them to pursue a policy of smoothing out the fluctuations around the trend of bond prices ('leaning against the wind') which in effect removed their ability to control the money supply in the short run except through bank lending requests. It was in modifying this policy in the bond market (or rather, in accelerating the previous gradual shift in policy) that 'Competition and credit control' was particularly significant, for the authorities continued, as before, to display a desire to control interest rates at the short end of the market quite firmly, although in a context which had changed markedly.

The significance of movements in Bank Rate (and operations to make it effective) is a well-worn theme in British monetary history. Throughout the period covered by this book, changes in Bank Rate (after October 1972, minimum lending rate) were almost invariably rationalised by reference to the external situation,[1] the desire to exploit the confidence effects of adjustments meaning that increases typically occurred in steps of one or two percentage points (sometimes accompanied by a 'package deal' of other measures) and decreases were usually by half a point (table 6.5). Estimates of reaction functions (pages 279–80 below) confirm that Bank Rate is sensitive to external considerations and suggest that it will eventually rise by something approaching half a point in response to a loss of £100 million in the published reserves.[2]

[1] On the basis of the various statements made in the *Bank of England Quarterly Bulletin* and other official sources, the only possible exceptions seem to be the increases from 4 to 5 per cent on 27 February 1964 and from 7 to 8 per cent on 27 February 1969, when domestic objectives were given pride of place. Decreases in Bank Rate were regarded as almost always desirable domestically whenever external considerations permitted.

[2] See D. Fisher, 'The instruments of monetary policy and the generalised trade-off function for Britain, 1955–1969', *Manchester School of Economic and Social Studies*, vol. 38, September 1970; C. A. Pissarides, 'A model of British macroeconomic policy, 1955–1969', *Manchester School of Economic and Social Studies*, vol. 40, September 1972. R. T. Coghlan, 'Bank competition and bank size', *Manchester School of Economic and Social Studies*, vol. 43, June 1975, relates Bank Rate to changes in net reserves, defined as published reserves minus official short-term and medium-term borrowing, and finds that it would require a loss of something like £500 million in reserves so defined to provoke a half point adjustment in Bank Rate. The 'window-dressing' of published reserves was quite substantial in this period (see table 6.7 on page 280 below).

Table 6.5. *Changes in Bank Rate,[a] 1960–72*

No. of changes

	Total	In 'package deals'
Increased by:		
½%	2	—
1%	6	3
1½%	1	1
2%	2	1
Decreased by:		
½%	15	—
1%	3	—
1½%	—	—
2%	—	—
All changes	29	5

SOURCE: *Bank of England Quarterly Bulletin* (various issues).

[a] Minimum lending rate from October 1972.

As well as improving confidence, increases in Bank Rate were intended to provide or restore an incentive to capital inflows. However, studies of the general effect of interest-rate changes on capital flows provide only indirect evidence on this aspect, because these studies use local authority rates as the representative short rate in the United Kingdom. Chart 6.4, however, shows a broad sympathy of movement between Bank Rate and local authority rates, although it is difficult to be specific about the direction of causation. But, up to the time of 'Competition and credit control', a change in Bank Rate did have immediate effects upon a number of important administered rates (especially those of the London clearing banks) and these, together with reinforcing operations in the money markets, could be expected to lead through arbitrage to sympathetic movements in yields on local authority paper. Even so, this control was indirect and palpably less precise than that of the Treasury bill market, which became in this period a largely captive market of overseas monetary authorities and domestic institutions required to hold such paper.

Subject to these caveats, the estimates provided by Hodjera and, more recently, Hutton can be thought of as indicating an order of magnitude for the short-term capital inflow consequent upon a change in the relevant interest differential.[1] A key result of

[1] See Z. Hodjera, 'Short-term capital movements of the United Kingdom, 1963–1967', *Journal of Political Economy*, vol. 79, July–Aug. 1971, pp. 739–75; J. P. Hutton, 'A model of short-term capital movements, the foreign exchange market and official intervention in the

Chart 6.4. *Bank Rate and the local authority three-month rate,*[a] *1963–73*

SOURCES: Bank of England, *Statistical Abstract*, no. 1; *Bank of England Quarterly Bulletin*.
[a] Taken at the last Friday in each month.

Hodjera's study is provided in the equation (estimated quarterly for 1963–7):

$$SC_t = 109 \cdot 6\Delta UD_{t-1} - 0 \cdot 80\Delta BT_t + 1 \cdot 6\Delta \overline{BT}_{t-4/3} - 140 \cdot 2D$$

where SC is short-term capital inflow defined to include the balancing item, UD the uncovered differential between the 90-day local authority rate and the Eurodollar rate, BT the visible balance

UK 1963–1971' (mimeo.), 1974. A revised version of this paper giving estimates for 1963–70 was subsequently published in *Review of Economic Studies*, vol. 44, February 1977. A further study (OECD, *Capital Movements in the OECD Area: an econometric analysis* by W. H. Branson and R. D. Hill, Paris, 1971) of the combined capital account in the United Kingdom failed to produce plausible interest-rate effects and has been ignored in what follows. The determinants of direct investment have been studied in B. D. Boatwright and G. A. Renton, 'An analysis of United Kingdom inflows and outflows of direct foreign investment', *Review of Economics and Statistics*, vol. 57, November 1975.

of trade, $\overline{BT}_{t-4/3}$ the lagged two-quarter moving average of the balance $= \frac{1}{3}(2BT_{t-1} + BT_{t-2})$, and D a dummy variable for speculation based on the relationship of the forward rate to the lower limit of the permitted swing in the value of the spot rate. The lagged visible balance is interpreted as a speculative variable, with a (therefore) appropriate positive sign, the negative sign on the current value of the visible balance being taken to indicate trade financing. Further analysis by Hodjera showed that, when capital inflows are related to the covered differential, a 1 per cent rise in the latter encourages an inflow of some £475 million (with a one-quarter lag); this is, however, clearly not an alternative estimate of the effect of a rise in the United Kingdom rate of interest, since the cost of cover can be expected to increase as a result of any induced inflow. This mechanism is made explicit in Hutton's treatment, where again a key result is that a rise of 1 per cent in the uncovered differential will lead to an inflow of just over £90 million – the same order of magnitude as the £110 million suggested by Hodjera.[1] The confidence effect of a Bank Rate increase is omitted from these estimates, and it is impossible to impute anything to such an effect *per se*, particularly when reactions can be perverse.[2]

Whilst the close interest of the authorities in controlling short rates primarily for external reasons remained an unvarying theme, policy in the longer end of the market underwent significant changes. The emphasis on damping fluctuations in the price of bonds (whilst not resisting their 'trend') gave way after the mid-1960s to a series of modifications culminating in 'Competition and credit control' (see pages 239–45 above). This change in priorities is reflected in chart 6.5, which shows that an index of the variability of bond prices effectively doubled in value between the mid-1960s and the early 1970s.

---

[1] Hutton models the determination of short-term capital flows (1963–71) by considering separately the behaviour of arbitrageurs (who obtain forward cover) and of spot speculators (who do not). An amalgamated equation provides:

$$SC_t = 5\cdot515\Delta UD_t - 2\cdot673\Delta C_t + 1\cdot867G + 1\cdot075BT_{t-1}$$

where, of the new variables, C_t is the cost of forward cover and G a dummy variable covering specific speculative crises. A second equation determines the forward rate as:

$$F_t = 0\cdot682(S-UD) + 0\cdot313(S-100) + 0\cdot055BT_{t-1} + 0\cdot120BT_{t-2} - 0\cdot846D_1 + 0\cdot273D_2$$

where F is the forward rate, S the spot rate, and D_1 and D_2 are speculative dummies. When the effect on the forward rate of an increase in UD is allowed for in the second equation and the resultant effect on the cost of cover accounted for in the first, the net result for an increase in the uncovered differential of 1 per cent is an inflow of capital in the same quarter of $\frac{1}{4}(5\cdot515 - 2\cdot673 \times 0\cdot682) = £92\cdot3$ million. (In the revised 1977 version Hutton obtains a slightly higher estimate of £126·8 million.)

[2] Perhaps the most notorious example of such a perverse effect occurred after the rise in Bank Rate from 5 to 7 per cent on 23 November 1964, which took place, unusually on a Monday. Sales of sterling on the succeeding days were reported to be even higher than those that had taken place before the increase.

Chart 6.5. *Bond prices and sales of government debt*

SOURCE: CSO, *Financial Statistics*.

Note: Bond price variability measured by the standard error of a 36-month moving average of logarithmic first differences in the Consol rate, end-quarter values.

Both the policy of 'leaning against the wind' and the withdrawal from it were based upon the authorities' (changing) beliefs about the stability of the bond market. It is difficult to confirm or refute these beliefs. The inference that open-market operations feeding speculative demand for gilt-edged stocks would lead to a positive correlation between sales of debt and increases in bond prices seemed to be borne out for earlier periods by graphical evidence produced in the *Radcliffe Report* and confirmed by a regression result quoted by Goodhart.[1] This correlation is less obvious for the period with which we are concerned (see chart 6.5) and an attempt to replicate Goodhart's equation with data for this period failed. Most probably this should be attributed to the fact that the available data are quarterly, so that the relevant day-to-day movements may be obscured; similarly, the movement of Consol prices may be a poor indicator of changes in the complex of gilt-edged prices. Norton has suggested that the speculative behaviour observed by the authorities was the mirror-image of their own counter-speculative operations, which, being known to the market, caused a fall in bond prices to be taken as the herald of a continuing decline as the authorities sought to ease the rate of fall, and consequently as the signal for immediate speculative sales.[2] Although this suggestion was not in fact rigorously confirmed by Norton's results, it seems to have been seriously entertained by the authorities as good cause for modifying their strategy.[3]

By attempting to steady the price of government securities, the authorities removed the possibility of using their operations to effect quantity adjustments designed, say, to influence the growth rate of the money supply. The cash ratio became otiose as a fulcrum of open-market operations, since the authorities had to be prepared to defend the level of short rates at any time. This point was clearly taken by the Radcliffe Committee, which was, however, associated with the view that the liquid asset ratio could be substituted for the cash ratio as such a fulcrum: '...the effective base of bank credit has become the liquid assets (based on the availability of Treasury Bills) instead of the supply of cash'.[4] This would have been true if the authorities could have controlled the supply of assets which might be substituted for Treasury bills to satisfy the liquid asset ratio, and if they had been prepared to accept the implications for the prices of longer bonds of any move designed to squeeze the banks' reserve of liquid assets,[5] but in the event neither of these conditions was met. A number of studies have shown

[1] Treasury, *Radcliffe Report*, p. 204; C. A. E. Goodhart, 'Monetary policy in the United Kingdom' in K. Holbik (ed.), *Monetary Policy in Twelve Industrial Countries*, Boston (Mass.), Federal Reserve Bank of Boston, 1973, where the regression is of bond sales on the change in Consol yield, the latter having a significant negative sign.

[2] Norton, 'Debt management and monetary policy in the United Kingdom'.

[3] At least, this is a possible interpretation of the Chief Cashier's remarks published in 'Competition and credit control'. Norton's results suggest that the public's demand for government bonds contains a speculative element; they also indicate that the authorities responded to increased demand for stock by gradually letting the price rise. The idea that the former behaviour depends on the latter is, however, an embellishment of the results not necessary to their interpretation.   [4] Treasury, *Radcliffe Report*, para. 376.

[5] The Radcliffe Committee accepted the latter point (ibid. para. 378), although the significance of controlling the Treasury bill issue seems to have been overstressed at the expense of ignoring the problem posed by the existence of substitutable liquid assets.

that the decline in the supply of Treasury bills relative to the banks' needs could be, and was, countered by substituting alternative liquid assets eligible for inclusion – commercial bills, call money placed outside the discount market, and so on – and also by increasing the proportion of discount market call money secured on assets other than Treasury bills.[1] In any case, even had the assets eligible as liquid reserves been such that their supply was clearly in the hands of the authorities, a policy of varying this stock with a view to influencing the supply of money would not have been consistent with the defence of bond prices in the short run at something close to their existing levels. Pressure on the banks' technical liquidity, granted their excess holding of government bonds, would have evoked sales of bonds, decreases in bond prices and intervention by the authorities to temper the fall by purchasing bonds, thus undoing the effect of the liquidity squeeze. This explains why Special Deposits could not be expected to function as a variable reserve requirement, and perhaps also why the authorities did not bother (before 'Competition and credit control', that is) to redefine eligible liquid assets so as to preclude the substitution of alternative assets for Treasury bills. The stock of money in this period was not the immediate object of the monetary authorities' operations; when and to the extent that it became so, it is not surprising to find that policies in the bond market changed.[2]

Thus, a textbook caricature of the 1960s system would be that the authorities assured a horizontal 'LM' schedule (at a shifting interest rate 'peg')[3] – a policy which can be rationalised as consistent with the belief that the demand for money was unstable.[4] It is tempting, at this level of abstraction, to bring together the rising tide of research findings

[1] See, for example, R. L. Crouch, 'A re-examination of open-market equations', *Oxford Economic Papers*, vol. 15 (new series), July 1963, and 'The inadequacy of "new orthodox" methods of monetary control', *Economic Journal*, vol. 74, December 1964; also, D. J. Coppock and N. J. Gibson, 'The volume of deposits and the cash and liquid assets ratios', *Manchester School of Economic and Social Studies*, vol. 31, September 1963; W. T. Newlyn, 'The supply of money and its control', *Economic Journal*, vol. 74, June 1964. At the beginning of the 1960s Treasury bills were the largest single component of bank liquid assets – as compared with notes, coins and Bank of England balances, money at call, commercial bills and 'other' bills – but by 1970 they were the smallest of these components.

[2] See chapter 5 above, pages 246–8.

[3] Following the analysis originally due to J. R. Hicks ('Mr. Keynes and the "classics": a suggested interpretation', *Econometrica*, vol. 5, April 1937) and subsequently embodied in most macroeconomic texts, the LM schedule is taken as tracing out combinations of the interest rate and income at which money demand and supply are equal. A horizontal LM schedule is immediately implied by an infinitely interest-elastic *demand* for money, or (as here) by an infinitely elastic *supply* schedule. Cf. B. Griffiths, 'Resource efficiency, monetary policy and the reform of the UK banking system', *Journal of Money, Credit and Banking*, vol. 5, February 1973 (pt 1).

[4] Cf. W. Poole, 'Optimal choice of monetary policy instruments in a simple stochastic macro model', *Quarterly Journal of Economics*, vol. 84, May 1970.

that the demand for money was stable, and the theoretical proposition that in the face of such a stable demand policies should 'aim at' the money supply rather than at interest rates – that is, that the horizontal 'LM' schedule should be abandoned. Such a conjunction provides an appealing analytical rationale for 'Competition and credit control' – and one with an awkward twist in its tail in the light of the re-emergent doubts about the stability of the demand for money in the last few years. But, whilst these caricatures serve to highlight the role of changing beliefs about the demand for money and the consequent irony of experience since 'Competition and credit control', it should be emphasised that the positions described are no more than caricatures. In particular, before 1971 the authorities did not, even in their most rigid phase, aim to peg bond prices and interest rates, only to reduce their fluctuations; nor, since 1971, did they abandon their predilection for selling on a rising market and, more certainly still, did not come to regard fluctuations in bond prices with complete indifference.[1]

Fiscal and monetary policy

Inhibitions about using interest rates as an aid to funding the national debt implied also that additions to the debt arising from a positive public sector borrowing requirement were in general closely associated with an expansion of the money supply; because the non-bank public's demand for such debt rose only to the extent dictated by long-term factors – essentially increasing wealth (including some wealth effects associated with the deficit itself) – the residual supply, to the extent it was not sold overseas, had to find its way into the portfolios of the banks. Thus, to this extent, fiscal policy, as measured by the public sector deficit, and monetary policy, as measured by the change in the stock of money, tended to be highly correlated. At the same time, a monetary policy of this character tended to imply a (short-run) 'high multiplier' fiscal policy, and helped to validate calculations of the effect of tax changes which ostensibly take no account of the means of financing the deficit.[2] Also at the same time, this strong connection between monetary and fiscal policy inevitably frustrated the attempt to measure separately the contributions of fiscal and monetary policy to changes in the level of income.

However, whilst these propositions seem to hold true in a rough and ready way of the 1960s, they do not hold true of experience in more recent years. Table 6.6 shows that the public sector borrowing require-

[1] For an account of the authorities' move in the direction of controlling the 'monetary aggregates' and their actions in the bond market, see pages 245-6.
[2] Such calculations have frequently appeared in, for example, the *National Institute Economic Review*. In the language of the 'IS–LM' macro-model, the horizontal 'LM' curve validates the assumption of an unconstrained multiplier process.

Table 6.6. *The fiscal deficit and monetary expansion, 1963–74*

£ million

	Public sector financial deficit[a]	Public sector borrowing requirement	External financing	Domestic borrowing requirement[b]	Increase in money supply (M₃)
1963	833	832	40	729	766
64	1004	989	571	418	653
65	851	1205	22	1183	938
66	854	961	413	548	479
67	1472	1863	503	1360	1345
68	1033	1279	1111	168	1152
69	−429	−466	−593	127	503
1970	−740	−17	−1353	1336	1586
71	421	1373	−2670	4043	2366
72	1612	2047	1564	483	5299
73	2585	4168	−121	4289	7232
74	4857	6336	1462	4874	4221

SOURCES: CSO, *National Income and Expenditure* and *Financial Statistics*.

[a] Net acquisition of financial assets with the sign reversed.

[b] Public sector borrowing requirement minus external financing.

ment (which represents the financing problem) has become less closely identified with the public sector deficit, and the domestic borrowing requirement (after allowing for external financing) less closely identified with the total public sector borrowing requirement;[1] finally, the domestic borrowing requirement has become less closely identified with changes in the money supply. In consequence, 'Kaldor's rule' of the association of changes in the money supply and the public sector borrowing requirement has ceased to hold.[2]

Even under conditions in which the monetary authorities have gained substantial freedom to use interest rates actively, fiscal and monetary policy are, of course, quite likely to be closely connected in practice. The principle which might separate one from the other – fiscal policy being identified with alterations in public sector indebtedness, monetary policy with the management of the distribution (by sector and by maturity)[3] of the *stock* of debt (including its increment) –

[1] The difference between the public sector deficit and the borrowing requirement is approximately the net amount of transactions in existing assets in which the public sector is involved.

[2] N. Kaldor, 'The new monetarism', *Lloyds Bank Review*, no. 97, July 1970, maintained, on the basis of simple correlation analysis, that the money supply increased almost pound for pound with the public sector borrowing requirement.

[3] Account needs to be taken here of government debt which may change its effective maturity in the hands of the public (for example, when acquired by banks). Also 'management' needs to be defined to include control of the secondary effects of debt management, for example when controls over bank advances frustrate the expansion to which the banks' acquisition of government debt would otherwise give rise.

does not in itself permit the presumption that the two will be independent in practice. It is fairly clear, for example, that very expansive
fiscal policies (as in 1972/3) tend to lead to correspondingly expansive
monetary policies, whilst policies for containing the growth of the
money supply are usually associated with a tighter rein on the borrowing
requirement.

Reaction functions

We have reviewed above evidence on how far certain monetary
instruments are effective in influencing intermediate variables. The
theoretical framework of the instruments–objectives view of economic
policy readily allows the complementary study of the authorities'
reaction functions. Such studies seek to reveal how far changes in instruments are prompted by deviations from their preferred values of the
variables measuring the authorities' ultimate 'goals'.

Table 6.7 draws upon three published studies; it indicates for the
three instruments mentioned, and for Bank Rate, a reasonably systematic relationship with the 'goal' variables distinguished. Increases in
the price level and decreases in foreign exchange reserves and unemployment are associated with deflationary changes (increases) in the
instrument variables, the greatest doubt about the significance of the
relationships concerning that between Special Deposits and reserves,
whilst the response of lending requests to changes in the price level
appears insignificant when other objectives are considered.

It is tempting to try to wring more out of these estimates and in some
of the studies cited an attempt is made to do so, but at this stage of
sophistication it is far from clear that much can be gained from such
attempts. The estimates allow at best for only a limited range of substitution between policy instruments;[1] they are also poor material from which
to draw conclusions about the destabilising effect of policy[2] and do not
allow us to deduce the trade-off between policy goals implied by the
authorities' actions, unless we have convincing estimates of their 'model'
of the effect of instruments on goals. The interpretation of the presence of
the lagged dependent variable on the right hand side of the equation is
open to question, as are also the underlying assumption that the authorities minimise a quadratic disutility function[3] and the disregard of their
use of forecasting apparently implied by the presence of current values

[1] See A. R. Nobay, 'A model of the United Kingdom monetary authorities' behaviour
1959–1969' in H. G. Johnson and A. R. Nobay (eds.), *Issues in Monetary Economics*, London,
Oxford University Press, 1974, for effective criticism on this point.

[2] For a detailed argument to this effect see Worswick, 'Fiscal policy and stabilization in
Britain'.

[3] For an alternative model see P. Mosley, 'Towards a "satisficing" theory of economic
policy', *Economic Journal*, vol. 86, March 1976, pp. 59–72.

Table 6.7. *Reaction function estimates*^{a} *by Fisher, Pissarides and Coghlan*

	Reserves^b	Unemployment rate	Price level^c	Lagged dependent variable	R^2
			Regression coefficients for:		
Fisher (1955–68)					
Bank Rate	−0·68	−0·76	0·10	0·45	0·734
	(2·72)	(2·85)	(2·00)		
Special Deposits	13·49	−28·59	0·99	0·91	0·954
	(1·13)	(2·96)	(2·30)		
Hire purchase deposit^d	−4·17	−5·05	0·19	0·70	0·803
	(1·31)	(2·02)	(1·97)		
Pissarides (1955–68)					
Bank Rate	−0·20^e	−0·63	0·78	0·57	0·752
	(2·30)	(3·12)	(3·70)		
Tax rate^f	−0·05^e	−0·44	2·62	0·56	0·808
	(1·22)	(3·47)	(3·98)		
Hire purchase deposit^d	−0·02	−6·32	26·04	0·66	0·689
	(1·84)	(2·56)	(2·57)		
Coghlan (1962–70)					
Bank Rate	−0·07^e	−0·77	0·04	0·15	0·863
	(4·40)	(2·91)	(2·80)		
Special Deposits	—	−0·24	0·04	0·62	0·914
		(1·50)	(4·99)		
Bank lending requests^g	−0·03^e	−0·47	0·01	0·59	0·841
	(3·47)	(2·98)	(1·03)		

SOURCES: Fisher, 'The instruments of monetary policy'; Pissarides, 'A model of British macroeconomic policy'; Coghlan, 'Bank competition and bank size'.

^{a} *t*-statistics shown in brackets, but suppressed for the lagged dependent variable, where not given by Fisher. Constant terms also suppressed as not given by Fisher.

^{b} Official gold and foreign exchange reserves (Fisher and Pissarides); net reserves, i.e. minus official short-term and medium-term borrowing (Coghlan).

^{c} Consumer price index (Pissarides); retail price index (Coghlan); unspecified (Fisher).

^{d} Minimum percentage down-payment on cars. ^{e} Coefficients multiplied by 10^2.

^{f} Discretionary change in tax yield as a percentage of GDP.

^{g} Dummy variable scored 0 = no request, 1 = mild request, 2 = severe request.

only of the goal variables.[1] Whilst these studies open a promising avenue for further research, their present value in illuminating the use of monetary policy seems accordingly rather limited.

Indicators

Within the spirit of the instruments–objectives model, an intermediate variable can be justified as a measure of economic policy. Popular measures of this kind in the fiscal field include the initial fiscal stimulus

[1] However, this *might* be regarded as 'allowed for' (in a naive fashion) by the presence of the lagged dependent variable.

and the full-employment budget deficit. It can be argued that, although such indicators are inferior in principle to comprehensive simulation results, they command attention where such results are not available and it is desired to have a measure of policy, necessarily approximate. The suggestion that an intermediate variable be chosen for this role stems from the problem that the 'actions' of the authorities – in the case of the monetary authorities, sales and purchases of bonds, calls for and releases of Special Deposits, imposition and cancellation of lending requests, and the like – lack in themselves a common scale upon which they can be aggregated. An intermediate variable is expected to provide just such a common scaling; it should also register and reflect the actions of the monetary authorities without being overwhelmingly determined by forces exogenous to those actions. A further requirement is, however, that changes in the variable concerned should, *ceteris paribus*, have an influence over the goal variables of the system, and this requires some presumption that it has a stable relationship with its determinand. In short, the selection of a policy indicator requires some presumption about the transmission mechanism of monetary policy.

How do these considerations work out in the choice of a policy indicator of monetary action?[1] Is there an obvious analogue with the measures used in the analysis of fiscal policy?

Perhaps the least of the difficulties involved in selecting an indicator is the multiplicity of the monetary authorities' goals. The same consideration applies, after all, to fiscal policy indicators and it can be finessed in the same way by explicitly selecting aggregate demand as the policy goal of interest, setting other goals aside. Using this simplification, it becomes clear that a source of contention will be different views of the transmission mechanism. We present our own view of that mechanism in the following section; at this stage the main point to be noted is that we give some emphasis to rationing and expectational effects in the operation of monetary policy, and to that extent suggest that there are discontinuities and threshold effects. This is in contrast with, or at least an important modification of, the customary 'textbook' view, as exemplified in the use of the 'IS–LM' framework of analysis. However, it is worth enquiring what are the requirements of such a framework in the choice of an indicator.

In a stochastic version of such a framework,[2] variations in the money supply are a good indicator of policy and superior to interest rates to the extent that the demand for money is stable, whilst to the extent

---

[1] For further discussion of these issues the reader may consult, *inter alia*, M. J. Artis, 'Monetary policy in the 1970s in the light of recent developments' in Johnson and Nobay (eds.), *Issues in Monetary Economics*; D. Fisher, 'Targets and indicators of British monetary policy', *The Bankers' Magazine*, vol. 216, August 1973, pp. 97–116.

[2] Poole, 'Optimal choice of monetary policy instruments'.

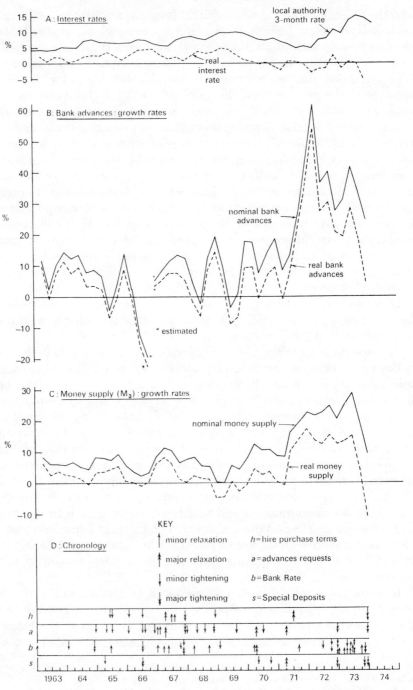

Chart 6.6. *Indicators of monetary policy, 1963–73*

A : Interest rates

local authority
3-month rate

real
interest
rate

B : Bank advances : growth rates

nominal bank
advances

real bank
advances

* estimated

C : Money supply (M₃) : growth rates

nominal money supply —

real money
supply

KEY

↑ minor relaxation   *h*=hire purchase terms

⬆ major relaxation   *a*=advances requests

↓ minor tightening   *b*=Bank Rate

⬇ major tightening   *s*=Special Deposits

D : Chronology

h

a

b

s

1963   64   65   66   67   68   69   70   71   72   73   74

SOURCES: Bank of England, *Statistical Abstract*, no. 1; CSO *Economic Trends* (monthly) and *Financial Statistics*.

that the demand for money is unstable the reverse conclusion holds. This seems plausible; it is, however, arguable by appeal to modern monetarist analysis that, since in an open economy it is domestic credit rather than the supply of money over which the monetary authorities ultimately have control, the former should be the indicator. This proposition is, however, only applicable to the long run; besides assuming a stable demand for money, it also assumes a degree of capital market integration and stability of the real economy that makes it uncertain at best in the short run.

It may, therefore, seem reasonable to say that, to the extent to which the demand for money is stable, the growth rate of the money supply is a reasonable proxy indicator of monetary policy. But this assumes that any actions which do not affect the money supply can be neglected and so cuts across the line of argument that stresses the significance of credit flows (particularly bank advances) in an imperfect capital market. The same point applies, *mutatis mutandis*, to interest rates and in both cases inflation is an additional complication. Both the monetary growth rate and interest rates should allow for inflation (strictly, expected inflation) when used as indicators and there is no simple way of doing this. It is sometimes suggested that inflation improves the claims of the former as opposed to the latter, but this is not as obvious as it sounds. Certainly the same nominal rate of interest differs in significance with different levels of on-going ('expected') inflation, but the same is true of the monetary growth rate. The consequences for *real* demand of a monetary growth of 20 per cent differ according to whether inflation is occurring at zero or at 20 (or any other) per cent.[1]

Enough has perhaps been said to show that there is no very clear presumption in favour of any particular indicator; an eclectic viewpoint therefore seems most appropriate. This conclusion is reflected in the set of graphs shown in chart 6.6, the third panel of which shows the rates of growth of M_3 and the 'real' money supply, the second panel growth in bank advances and the top panel the level of interest rates. At the bottom, the chronology of monetary policy 'actions', given a partial subjective scoring, is also shown. The adjustments made to each series are indicated in the footnotes. Finally, an indicator of financial

---

Chart 6.6 (*cont.*)

Notes: (i) 'Real' rate of interest calculated as $100 (R_t - \dot{P}_t)/(100 + \dot{P}_t)$ where R_t is local authority three-month rate and $\dot{P}_t$ is the first central difference of the rate of change in prices measured by the deflator of total final expenditure.

    (ii) Bank advances to 1966 IV, quarterly totals; no distinction between residents and non-residents, or between currencies available. From 1967 I, quarterly advances to United Kingdom residents.

[1] A different presumption in favour of the money supply arises, of course, from the assumption that the real economy is stable over not too long a run, so that monetary policy, and consequently a monetary indicator, is focused on the control of the price level or its rate of increase. From this viewpoint is seems clear that the monetary growth rate is preferable to nominal interest rates.

stringency was taken from the regular CBI survey, in which firms are asked to indicate the most important factor or factors limiting their output on a check list of seven possibilities (including a residual category). The proportion of respondent firms indicating 'credit or finance' as a constraint is plotted in chart 6.7 against the real money supply to see whether the two series show any sympathy, and there is, it would seem, a loose degree of sympathy, at any rate in the case of the larger movements.[1]

Whilst the quarter-to-quarter concurrence of the various possible measures is not very close, there is some uniformity in the story they tell about the major movements: in particular, it seems that monetary policy was relatively stringent in 1966, and again in 1969 and 1974/5, and

Chart 6.7. *The growth rate of the 'real' money supply and the CBI credit stringency factor, 1963–74*

SOURCES: *Bank of England Quarterly Bulletin* (various issues); CSO, *Economic Trends*; CBI, *Industrial Trends Survey* (4-monthly).

Note: CBI Survey 3-monthly from 1972.

particularly 'easy' in 1967, the latter part of 1971, and in 1972 and 1973. Much the same could be inferred from a chronology of monetary policy actions. It does not seem possible to advance much upon this position; the fiscal policy indicators do not have any very precise analogue in monetary policy and, although the strength of this dichotomy may be partly misleading (in as much as it attributes more cer-

[1] This must be seen, however, in the context of the source of data. Since firms responding to the questionnaire are asked to tick the *most important factor or factors* limiting output, cyclical behaviour in the computed 'ratio of importance' of 'credit or finance' could be induced by the pressure of a cycle in other factors, even where there has been no cycle in monetary conditions.

tainty to the effect of fiscal actions than is probably warranted), it reflects in large part our relatively sketchy understanding of the effects of monetary actions, or, to put it in a more flattering way, the complexity of the transmission mechanism of monetary policy. Two points are, perhaps, most crucial: first, the question of the stability of the demand for money and, second, the significance of capital market imperfections. The interaction of these and other considerations is considered more extensively below.

THE TRANSMISSION MECHANISM

The transmission mechanism of monetary policy consists in the linkages between changes in the instruments of monetary policy (or, going forward one stage, the intermediate variables affected by these instruments) and the goal variables of the system. An account of this mechanism is thus a description of the process whereby changes in monetary variables affect the economy. Clearly an understanding of this process is important in appreciating the potential for monetary policy of the design of policy in terms of the instruments used and the size of adjustments made; also, as suggested above, in the selection of a monetary indicator or proximate target of policy. Accordingly, differences of opinion about the transmission mechanism and changes in the balance of these opinions over time can be seen as underlying dissension over the effectiveness of policy and contributing towards change in policy design – of which 'Competition and credit control' is an example in our period. In principle, then, some of the differences of opinion about monetary policy should be resolved as firm knowledge of the transmission mechanism is obtained by empirical study. To that extent, the disparity of prevailing views attests to the still very incomplete knowledge of the mechanism that we possess, with considerable room left for speculative views and hunches, in some apparent contrast to fiscal policy, where the effects are thought to be known with a much higher degree of certainty.

In default of detailed accounts of the mechanism, some attention has been paid in recent years to the study of so-called 'reduced form' relationships, in which, with details suppressed, attention is focused upon the strength and nature of the relationship between an indicator variable, usually the money supply, and a goal variable, typically GDP or the price level. Studies of this kind have commonly, if not exclusively, been associated with examining propositions due to the monetarist school and have very often taken the form of replicating with British data hypotheses first tested on American data. Certain caveats are necessary in interpreting this kind of evidence. First, since such studies explicitly bypass the exploration of the transmission mechanism, they are open to the charge that all they provide in place of such an exploration is a 'black box'. This would be less troublesome if the reduced form under study could be shown to be a valid reduced form, rather than a casual single equation; unless this is the case there remains an unresolved technical difficulty in interpreting the coefficients obtained, and an ambiguity about what structural system the reduced form results are supposed to be consistent with. Secondly, many of the studies rely implicitly upon time-lags to free the results from the attribution of 'reverse causality', but precedence in time is a treacherous indicator of causality, however attractive superficially.[1]

It so happens, however, that as far as British studies are concerned these cautions are somewhat otiose. Single equation estimates of the 'money multiplier' for the United Kingdom seem to destroy the theory that 'money is all that matters', if indeed the sign and size of the coefficient obtained carry any unambiguous implication.[2] A test on British data by Artis and Nobay was notable chiefly for the lack of statistical significance achieved,[3] not dissimilar results being obtained subsequently by Goodhart and Crockett.[4] Evidence based more explicitly on timing is similarly weak in suggesting any significant relationship between the money supply and either income or prices.[5] Finally, the assertion that the timing profile of the effects of a change in the money stock involves first and soon a change in real output and then (after a lag of 18–20 months) an effect upon the price level, which has become a standard prediction of the monetarist school,[6] has at best a somewhat ambiguous validity. Chart 6.8 shows a scatter diagram of inflation rates and money supply growth rates, with the latter lagged

---

[1] The classic demonstration of the pitfalls involved in using timing as evidence of causality is given in J. Tobin, 'Money and income: post hoc ergo propter hoc?', *Quarterly Journal of Economics*, vol. 84, May 1970, pp. 301–17.

[2] The money multiplier in question here may be identified with the value of the coefficient b in an equation of the general form:

$$\Delta Y_t = a + b\Sigma_{i=0}^{n}(w_i \Delta M_{t-i}) + c\Sigma_{i=0}^{n}(x_i \Delta Z_{t-i})$$

where $\Sigma w_i = \Sigma x_i = 1$, Δ indicates a first difference and Y, M and Z stand for GDP (nominal), money, and other factors (e.g. fiscal policy), respectively. Quite often Z is omitted from equations of this type.

[3] M. J. Artis and A. R. Nobay, 'Two aspects of the monetary debate', *National Institute Economic Review*, no. 49, August 1969, which was modelled on an American study, L. C. Anderson and J. L. Jordan, 'Monetary and fiscal actions: a test of their relative importance in economic stabilization', *Federal Reserve Bank of St. Louis Review*, vol. 50, November 1968.

[4] C. A. E. Goodhart and A. D. Crockett. 'The importance of money', *Bank of England Quarterly Bulletin*, vol. 10, June 1970, where it was found, however, that money multiplier relationships could be strengthened by substituting industrial production (scaled by the wholesale price index) for GDP.

[5] See A. D. Crockett, 'Timing relationships between movements of monetary and national income variables', *Bank of England Quarterly Bulletin*, vol. 10, December 1970.

[6] For example, the contributions by Laidler and by Parkin (see footnote to page 258).

Chart 6.8. *Inflation and monetary growth, 1963–75*

SOURCE: CSO, *Financial Statistics* and *Economic Trends*.

Note :   End-year rates centred on fourth quarter, as $100(Q_2 - Q_{2_{-1}})/Q_{4_{-1}}$, where Q denotes the quarterly value and the subscript a lag of one year. The retail price index is plotted two years ahead of M_3, for example, RPI for 1974 with M_3 for 1972.

two years on the former. As is evident, confirmation of this two-year lag by a line of best fit would turn upon treating the more recent and the earlier observations as derived from the same sample; taken by themselves the earlier observations do not support such an association.[1] It therefore remains an open question, on statistical grounds alone, whether such a relationship has a solid foundation. The assertion that a lag of this length can be supported by reference to structural estimates of the demand for money and the relationship between inflation, excess demand and expectations has recently been examined by Miller.[2]

The British evidence does not, therefore, seem to confirm 'reduced form' relationships between 'money' and demand or prices; although

[1] Elsewhere, of course, the *variability* of the lag has been emphasised. For a sympathetic and subtle account see J. S. Flemming, *Inflation*, London, Oxford University Press, 1976.

[2] M. H. Miller, 'Money, output and inflation: a critique of some recent monetarist developments in the UK', *Manchester School of Economic and Social Studies* (forthcoming).

we have already noted that evidence of this kind, even if confirmed, would be far from conclusive, it appears that British evidence is out of line with that derived from American data. This suggests at least two possibilities: that British evidence should be treated as an instance of the non-universality of the monetarist association and to that extent a counter-example to the doctrine, or that there are features of the British economy which make these tests inapplicable and their results correspondingly irrelevant. An argument of the latter kind is that, for most of the period with which we are concerned, the money supply in the United Kingdom has been demand-determined because the monetary authorities have been overwhelmingly interested in defending the level of interest rates at any point of time. A suggestion to similar effect derives from the more recent amendment of monetarist theory to apply to 'small' open economies, according to which, at least in the long run, the stock of money is endogenous to the economy. The latter argument, except to the extent it is mirrored in the first, is the less easy to accept, insofar as the monetary authorities may be assumed to be able to sterilise money flows and inhibit adjustment through the use of exchange controls. However, if the stock of money is demand-determined, then the reduced form regressions are 'incorrect', in as much as the regressor – the stock of money (or a transformation of it) – is not exogenous, so that the results of such estimation will be biased; whilst this clearly does not imply that money has no effect, it does mean that the magnitude of the effect cannot be properly estimated in this way. A test which might help to clarify matters in this respect was carried out by Williams, Goodhart and Gowland,[1] in an attempt to determine whether it could be inferred either that the money supply was demand-determined or that it was exogenous to income. Their results were, however, less than clear-cut and cannot be said to provide very strong support for either view – again in some contrast to the American evidence, which rather strongly favours the view that money is exogenous to income.[2]

However, to the extent that it is accepted that the money supply was demand-determined during the 1960s, it would seem that there should be little ambiguity in the results of single equation estimation of the demand for money – that is, technically there is no identification

[1] D. Williams, C. A. E. Goodhart and D. H. Gowland, 'Money, income and causality: the UK experience', *American Economic Review*, vol. 66, June 1976, pp. 417–23. They applied to British data the Sims–Granger test for 'causality' (see C. A. Sims, 'Money, income and causality', *American Economic Review*, vol. 62, September 1972, pp. 540–52).

[2] Williams, Goodhart and Gowland, 'Money, income and causality', found some evidence of 'causality' running from nominal incomes to money, but *also* some evidence of 'causality' running from money to prices. The Sims–Granger test leans heavily on *post hoc ergo propter hoc* principles and does not exclude simultaneous causality in either direction, as the authors point out (ibid. p. 423).

problem and so no real doubt that such estimates are indeed estimates of the demand for money function and not of the supply function or of some indeterminate mix of the two. Such estimates were made by a number of investigators,[1] and were generally felt to confirm that a stable function for demand for money did exist, that it was characterised by a significant but low interest elasticity and an income elasticity in the region of unity, and that differences between the various measures of money supply caused no technically insuperable problems.

Findings like these, to the extent they can be regarded as robust (and this is commented upon further below in the light of experience since 'Competition and credit control'), have been widely regarded as highly significant for the interpretation and formulation of monetary policy. It is true, of course, that they cut across the line of thinking about monetary policy which stresses the instability and high interest elasticity of the demand for money, views characteristically attributed to the *Radcliffe Report*; by the same token, they reinforce the case for regarding the money stock or its growth rate as a suitable indicator of (and target for) monetary policy. Finally, by suggesting the viability of a policy of controlling the money stock through interest-rate adjustments, these findings very probably accelerated the 1971 reforms and reinforced the case for moving away from the previous controls with their heavy emphasis upon bank lending ceilings.[2]

But whilst the existence of a relatively stable demand for money is of significance in these ways, it does not in itself illuminate the transmission mechanism, nor guarantee the potency of monetary policy.[3] It leaves open the questions how, and by how much, demand is influenced by monetary factors. It is these questions which continue to vex investigators and to which the answers remain somewhat untidy and unsatisfactory.

The modern theory of portfolio analysis suggests that intervention by the monetary authorities causes a rearrangement of portfolios across a wide spectrum of assets. Because the point of intervention of classical monetary policy is the government bond market, the effect will be felt in that market first. But, as Friedman has reiterated on a number of

[1] For example, D. E. W. Laidler and J. M. Parkin, 'The demand for money in the United Kingdom, 1956–1967: preliminary estimates', *Manchester School of Economic and Social Studies*, vol. 38, September 1970, pp. 187–208.

[2] Cf. C. A. E. Goodhart, 'Problems of monetary management: the UK experience' in A. S. Courakis (ed.), *Inflation, Depression and Economic Policy in the West: lessons from the 1970s*, Oxford, Mansell & Alexandrine Press, 1979

[3] Within the framework of textbook IS–LM analysis, it can be shown that the size and stability of the money multiplier depends both upon the characteristics and fit of the money demand and supply functions, and upon the nature of the real expenditure functions (see D. E. W. Laidler, 'The influence of money on economic activity – a survey of some current problems' in G. Clayton, J. C. Gilbert and R. Sedgwick (eds.), *Monetary Theory and Monetary Policy in the 1970s*, London, Oxford University Press, 1971).

occasions, this is only a 'first round' effect,[1] which upsets the overall portfolio equilibrium and leads to further adjustments involving a wider range of assets, including real assets and paper claims to them. Eventually these adjustments may be expected to spill over from the 'capital account' to the 'current account' at the point where the rise in price of existing assets makes it profitable to buy new ones; thus, new investment will be stimulated.[2]

At the customary level of abstraction it is supposed that these adjustments take place in a perfect capital market. It seems clear, however, that in practice much of the flavour of how monetary policy works, and particularly how it worked in Britain in the 1960s, is lost if this assumption is accepted unquestioningly. The inescapable contingency of bankruptcy and the mediation of capital markets by financial institutions with lending rules and administered interest rates make alterations in the availability of internal funds and in the degree of credit rationing significant sources of stimulus or constraint, in addition to the impetus supplied by calculations of the rate of return and the cost of capital, such as dominate the conventional account of the transmission mechanism of monetary policy. In particular, there appear to be significant differences in ease of access to funds for the personal and for the corporate sectors, which are important in the *modus operandi* of monetary policy and indeed were deliberately exploited by such policy in Britain. One of the consequent dilemmas of the monetary authorities was the conflict between the short-run exploitation of capital market imperfections and the desire to improve the efficiency of those markets.

Finally, because the calculation of expected returns involves anticipating the actions of others and prognosticating the effects of current and future monetary (and other) policies, a monetary intervention can affect current demand by influencing expectations of the future. The monetary authorities cannot avoid this effect and may indeed choose to use it deliberately, as seems often to have been the case when monetary intervention has been announced in 'package deals'.

Traditional theory suggests that one should look to fixed investment

---

[1] For example, M. Friedman, 'A theoretical framework for monetary analysis', *Journal of Political Economy*, vol. 78, March–April 1970, pp. 193–238.

[2] This way of putting it is 'Keynesian' in the distinction which is drawn between adjustments to 'capital account' and to 'current account' – a dividing line which is blurred or eschewed in much monetarist analysis. Nevertheless, the accounts of the transmission process detailed by, for example, M. Friedman in several places (see his joint work with A. J. Schwartz, 'Money and business cycles', *Review of Economics and Statistics*, vol. 45, February 1963, and his paper with D. Meiselman, 'The relative stability of monetary velocity and the investment multiplier in the United States 1897–1958' in Commission on Money and Credit, *Stabilization Policies*, Englewood Cliffs (NJ), Prentice-Hall, 1963), appear to differ not in principle, but rather in the range of possible substitutions, and (implicitly) the scale and perhaps the speed of the process.

as the lever to which monetary policy is applied. But for the period and for type of interventions with which we are concerned this seems unhelpful. It is not so much that there is little firm evidence of variations in interest rates having significant effects on such investment, although this still continues to be true,[1] but rather that monetary interventions were not aimed directly at this target. Variations in real long-term interest rates were not large and, insofar as the exploitation of market imperfections was concerned, policy was usually intended to squeeze the personal sector, whilst cosseting manufacturing investment, in which the more significant policy interventions were fiscal ones (see pages 144–9).

Chart 6.9. *Building societies' differentials and the flow of funds, 1960–73*

SOURCE: CSO, *Financial Statistics* (and supplement), February 1973, table B.

Notes: (i) Debt outstanding equals building society liabilities, deflated by an index of house prices.
 (ii) Interest-rate differential calculated as minimum lending rate (or Bank Rate) minus the building society rate.

The case of dwelling investment was rather different. The conventional wisdom has it that variations in monetary conditions affect the rate of such investment in a number of ways; indeed that these effects have been sufficiently powerful and their associated political repercussions sufficiently important to provide a constraint on monetary action in the form of a politically determined 'ceiling' on interest rates.[2] The routes by which monetary conditions affect the housing market

---

[1] But cf., for example, the study by A. G. Hines and G. Catephores, 'Investment in UK manufacturing industry, 1956–67' in Hilton and Heathfield (eds.), *The Econometric Study of the United Kingdom*. There has as yet been no convincing examination of the attractive hypothesis that the rate of adjustment of the capital stock is significantly influenced by the availability of funds, so that monetary policy can play an indirect role in determining the current rate of investment in this way (see S. Nickell, 'Tax structure and financial policy' in M. J. Artis and A. R. Nobay (eds.), *Studies in Modern Economic Analysis*, Oxford, Blackwell, 1977).

[2] Goodhart, 'Monetary policy in the United Kingdom'.

comprise the influence of mortgage rates on the demand for mortgages and of bank lending rates on the building trades; also, there is the impact of mortage rationing and the general portfolio adjustment through which an excess supply of money may spill over into an increased demand for housing. However, despite public concern, surprisingly little quantification of these effects has been attempted and it is difficult to be precise about their relative importance. Nevertheless, it is well known that, due to the stickiness of their administered interest rates, the building societies' inflow of funds is very volatile; when market rates rise the inflow tends to decline until the share and deposit rates are brought in line (chart 6.9, which uses the minimum lending rate as an index of market rates, illustrates this point). At the same time, mortgage rates appear to be determined primarily as a mark-up on share and deposit rates, so that in periods when the inflow of funds is restricted the societies adopt non-price rationing to restrain the demand for mortgage finance.[1] A study by Artis, Kiernan and Whitley set out to explore the links between the mortgage market and dwelling investment; in a subsequent (unpublished) extension of this work it was found that both mortgage rationing and the mortgage rate were significant influences (the latter with an implied elasticity of -0.35), and that a speculative term in the increase in (real) house prices was also significant.[2] The implication is that an easing of rationing and a decline in mortgage rates are capable of stimulating the volume of dwelling investment considerably, both directly and also because the induced tendency for (real) house prices to rise will tend

[1] C. St J. OHerlihy and J. E. Spencer, 'Building societies' behaviour, 1955–70', *National Institute Economic Review*, no. 61, August 1972, pp. 40–52, showed that deposits and withdrawals were highly sensitive to variations in Bank Rate and the share rate. The following results indicate the long-run effect on deposits and withdrawals of a 1 per cent increase in each of these rates:

Percentages

	Effect on	
	Gross deposits	Withdrawals
1 per cent rise in:		
Bank Rate	-12	$+5$
Share rate	$+50$	-8

[2] See M. J. Artis, E. Kiernan and J. D. Whitley, 'The effects of building society behaviour on housing investment' in A. R. Nobay and J. M. Parkin (eds.), *Contemporary Issues in Economics*, Manchester University Press, 1975. In the original study rationing of mortgage funds was not found to be significant. This seems to have been due to mis-specification of the rationing variable and failure to allow for a lag between changes in mortgage rationing and the impact on investment. In the later study 'rationing' was identified with a variable involving the ratio of the current quarter's inflow of funds into building societies to the average of the previous twelve quarters' inflow, the effect of changes in this variable being registered upon investment with a lag of four quarters.

to be extrapolated, thus stimulating a speculative demand. As the process is subject to considerable lags, this goes some way to making sense of the sequel to the authorities' deliberate policy of stimulating the housing market in 1971/2; this resulted in a significant increase in dwelling investment in 1973 and a strong rise in house prices (which the authorities clearly regretted).[1]

Except for the positive stimulus in late 1971 and 1972, however, dwelling investment does not seem to have been the main object of the monetary authorities' attention, although it was a frequent casualty of their policies and a constraint upon them. Indeed, the history of the period is littered with attempts to insulate the mortgage market, usually the mortgage rate, from the effects of monetary action.[2] In contrast, consumers' expenditure (particularly on durable goods) was the frequent object of monetary interventions in the form of hire purchase controls and bank lending ceilings. There is evidence that these interventions were successful in their limited aim. Moreover, simply by reason of its relative scale, consumption rather than investment may well be the component of expenditure through which monetary policy has its greatest impact on aggregate demand.[3] General considerations suggest three main ways in which monetary factors might bear upon consumers' demand. First, in several popular forms of the consumption function wealth has an important role and short-run fluctuations in the value of measured wealth are usually dominated by changes in stock and bond prices; secondly, changes in the rate of interest may exercise a general influence apart from their wealth effects upon the decision to save or consume; finally, credit rationing by financial institutions and its formal reinforcement by official controls also affect consumer spending.

There is little firm evidence that changes in the rate of interest, apart from their revaluation effects, influence overall savings levels and there

---

[1] Whereas the 'Commentary' in the *Bank of England Quarterly Bulletin*, vol. 11, December 1971, noted with apparent satisfaction that 'monetary relaxations have helped to stimulate a pronounced increase in personal spending on cars and other durable goods and on housing' (p. 453), in the issue for December 1972 the Governor is quoted as having said 'the state of the property and housing market had become unruly with prices moving wildly ahead, unnecessarily far to provide an incentive for new building' (p. 517).

[2] These measures have included temporary government loans to the building societies and control of competitive bank deposit interest rates (both in 1973); earlier, building societies were asked to defer mortgage rate increases, were referred to the NBPI and were encouraged to merge with a view to reducing the mark-up of mortgage rates over share rates.

[3] Modigliani has indeed reported simulations for the United States which show that monetary policy (interest-rate) effects which work through consumption are larger and faster than those which work through investment, a result due to the greater relative scale of consumption offsetting its smaller elasticity (see F. Modigliani, 'The channels of monetary policy in the Federal Reserve–MIT–University of Pennsylvania econometric model of the US' in Renton (ed.) *Modelling the Economy*).

is a well-known ambiguity about the direction of the effect to be expected.[1] On the other hand, two studies of the United Kingdom consumption function have obtained results consistent with capital gains and losses having an impact on consumption,[2] but the scale does not appear to be large. To quote Deaton: '...in normal circumstances ignoring wealth effects causes little error; [although] in times when stock market values change very rapidly...there is a significant impact.'[3] A similar analysis motivated a suggestion in the *National Institute Economic Review* for November 1968 that the stock market boom of that period might have boosted consumption.[4] Nevertheless, it must be noted that empirical studies of these models have usually measured wealth, implicitly or explicitly, by the integration of current savings, thus leaving revaluation effects out of account;[5] also, most observers have reservations about the influence of revaluation effects, partly because capital gains and losses are likely to be associated in the short run with speculative effects and partly because the ownership of stocks and bonds is highly skewed.[6]

As for credit rationing, it was argued above that the officially approved changes in bank and hire purchase lending terms seem to have affected the outstanding totals of bank and hire purchase debt. For such instruments to influence consumption it is also necessary that consumers should not have ready access to alternative forms of finance, or be able easily to liquidate assets to make good the frustration of their borrowing potential. The widely voiced criticism of the inequity and narrow effectiveness of hire purchase controls (falling with particular severity upon certain industries producing durables) is in itself testimony to the fact that the controls worked in this sense, but the extent to which bank lending ceilings were similarly effective is less

---

[1] Recent work offers some suggestive evidence in favour of a positive effect, but so far it stands alone in this regard and cannot be considered conclusive (see El-Mokadem, *Econometric Models of Personal Saving*).

[2] See K. Hilton and D. H. Crossfield, 'Short-run consumption functions for the UK, 1955–66' in Hilton and Heathfield (eds.) *The Econometric Study of the United Kingdom*; also A. S. Deaton, 'Wealth effects on consumption in a modified life-cycle model', *Review of Economic Studies*, vol. 39, October 1972.

[3] Ibid. p. 451.

[4] *National Institute Economic Review*, no. 46, November 1968, pp. 9–11. Hilton and Crossfield concurred with this suggestion ('Short-run consumption functions for the UK', p. 80).

[5] A prominent example is the study by R. Stone, 'Private saving in Britain past, present and future', *Manchester School of Economic and Social Studies*, vol. 32, May 1964, and most of the studies reviewed in F. Modigliani, 'The life cycle hypothesis of saving twenty years later' in Nobay and Parkin (eds.), *Contemporary Issues in Economics*, share this feature.

[6] See J. J. Arena, 'Postwar stock market changes and consumer spending', *Review of Economics and Statistics*, vol. 47, November 1965, pp. 379–91; Modigliani, 'The life cycle hypothesis of saving twenty years later', however, reported on unpublished work by Ando which showed that there was no significant difference between the response of consumption to capital revaluations and to other changes in wealth.

well documented.[1] However, for the bulk of the period covered by our study, forecasting practice at both the Treasury and the National Institute incorporated a consumption function in which the change in debt outstanding (bank advances and hire purchase debt combined) appeared as an important determining variable.[2] This form of consumption function was investigated in some detail by Surrey;[3] similar estimates are shown in table 6.8. From there it will be seen that the equation containing the amalgamated (unweighted) debt term fits marginally better overall than that containing the two forms of debt separately, and that the long-run coefficient for the change in debt is approximately unity. The justification for estimating such an equation is that the 'change in debt' is primarily due to variations in monetary controls; the results can therefore be taken as implying that these controls were effective in stimulating or restraining consumer spending. This suggestion can be further elaborated for hire purchase terms alone by extending the simulation exercise described earlier, where the object was to determine the effect of variations in hire purchase controls on the level of outstanding hire purchase debt. On the assumption that the system is recursive, these simulation results can be extended to measure an impact upon consumption.[4] When this was done, it was found that the *cumulative* restraint of consumers' expenditure attributable to all variations in the controls over the period from 1959 reached a peak of some $3\frac{1}{2}$–4 per cent in 1969/70, broadly similar results being obtained whether an aggregated or disaggregated consumption function was employed; in either case, the impact of any isolated change in the controls was found to be short-lived, with a strong tendency to reverse itself after about a year.

The effectiveness and *modus operandi* of monetary policy depends on the instruments employed and the transmission mechanism by which changes in monetary factors affect demand and output. The Bank of England in 1969 described its policy as having been 'Radcliffean'. In some important respects this could be said to be misleading for, as demonstrated elsewhere, policy in practice ran clean against some of

[1] It might be presumed that bank customers would have easier access to alternative forms of finance and greater ability to liquidate existing assets in face of a frustrated demand for credit. This would at any rate be consistent with Norton's finding in 'Debt management and monetary policy in the United Kingdom' that dummies representing controls on bank advances were significant in determining the public's demand for national savings, and perhaps also with the puzzling experience of conditions since 'Competition and credit control' (see pages 298–9).
[2] See, for example, the paper by A. D. Roy, 'Short-term forecasting for central economic management of the UK economy', and that by M. J. Artis, 'Short-term economic forecasting at NIESR', in Hilton and Heathfield (eds.), *The Econometric Study of the United Kingdom*.
[3] Surrey, 'Personal income and consumers' expenditure'.
[4] Garganas, 'An analysis of consumer credit'.

Table 6.8. *The effect of income and credit rationing on consumption,*[a]
1958 II–1969 IV

Eqn no.	Constant term	Regression coefficients[b] for:					
		Personal disposable income	Change in bank advances[c]	Change in hire purchase debt	Lagged dependent variable	$\bar{R}^2$	DW
(1)	319·30 (2·46)	0·42 (5·66)	0·22 (0·48)	0·70 (2·31)	0·50 (5·53)	0·989	2·19
(2)	298·80 (2·38)	0·42 (5·65)	0·52[d] (3·25)		0·51 (5·70)	0·990	2·26

SOURCE: NIESR estimates.

[a] All data quarterly, seasonally adjusted, at 1970 prices. Dependent variable is consumers' expenditure.
[b] Short-run; long-run coefficients are as follows:

	Eqn (1)	Eqn (2)
Personal disposable income	0·84	0·85
Change in bank advances	0·43⎱	1·04
Change in hire purchase debt	1·38⎰	

[c] To persons.
[d] For combined variable of change in bank advances plus hire purchase debt.

the leading Radcliffe prescriptions,[1] but insofar as it was based on influencing credit flows policy could claim to be 'Radcliffean' at root. The *Radcliffe Report* had argued on a geological analogy that the capital market contained certain major faults,[2] of which one, very roughly, divided the corporate and personal sectors, and policy consisted, to a large extent, in exploiting this fault by the devices of hire purchase controls and bank lending ceilings. This was deliberate, and to some degree effective, but monetary policy also clearly affected the housing market, where most of the fluctuations do not seem to have been intended. Otherwise, the main purpose of monetary policy was to influence the balance of payments by a combination of confidence effects and incentives to flows of funds, whilst seeking to protect manufacturing investment from the worst rigours of the direct effects of policy (it could not, of course, be insulated from indirect effects stemming from the induced fluctuations in consumer demand). The most appropriate model of the transmission mechanism of these years seems, therefore, to be 'Radcliffean' in the loose sense that it used credit flows to exploit the limits which exist in some major sectors of the

[1] See pages 230 and 235–6 above. [2] Treasury, *Radcliffe Report*, para. 319.

economy on the extent to which one form of finance can be substituted for another.

A dilemma underlying such a model is readily apparent; in exploiting imperfections in the capital market the short-run goals conflict with the long-run target of an improved and less imperfect market; it can also be argued that such a policy is inevitably inequitable in requiring disproportionate sacrifice from certain sectors of industry and the community for its success. It may, however, have appeared to policymakers in a slightly different guise. Over the course of time it is fairly certain that a policy based on rationing will breed 'black markets' or their legal equivalent, and as a result it must become less and less certain what the effects of policy actually are (we have already noted the difficulties of interpreting evidence from a period dominated by controls, which is another aspect of the same problem). In these circumstances it might have seemed that the effects of the policy, as well as increasingly uncertain, became increasingly small. Such a judgement might not be wholly justified, but it is a natural one and would be an argument against continuing active discrimination and in favour of a more anonymous and generalised policy. It is not implausible that this was an element in the radical change associated with the introduction of 'Competition and credit control'.[1]

'COMPETITION AND CREDIT CONTROL'

The purpose of this section is not to provide a detailed account of the period which begins with the inauguration of 'Competition and credit control' (such an account appears in chapter 5 above), but rather to draw attention to the interruption in this period – real or apparent – of two of the more significant 'regularities' which characterised the 1960s. The first of these is the role of credit factors in the consumption function and the second the demand for money. The stability of these relationships is relevant to the analysis and interpretation of monetary policy in the 1960s, as is already evident from the preceding account, and in this light evidence of their possible interruption takes on a special significance.

Table 6.9 shows for various estimation periods the coefficients for personal disposable income, lagged consumption and the change in consumer debt (bank advances and hire purchase debt combined) used as variables explaining the level of consumption. Such a relationship, as we have already seen, characterised forecasting practice in the 1960s, and equation (1) (the same as equation (2) in table 6.8 above) may be taken as broadly representative, being estimated on data for

[1] Goodhart, 'Problems of monetary management'

Table 6.9. *The effect of income and credit rationing on consumption[a] in different periods*

Eqn no.	Period of estimation	Personal disposable income	Change in consumer debt[c]	Lagged dependent variable
(1)	1958 II–1969 IV	0·42	0·52	0·51
(2)	1958 II–1973 III	0·41	0·37	0·49
(3)	1970 IV–1973 III	0·34	0·88	0·40

Regression coefficients[b] for:

SOURCE: NIESR estimates.

[a] All data quarterly, seasonally adjusted, at 1970 prices. Dependent variable is consumers' expenditure.

[b] Short-run; long-run coefficients are as follows:

	Eqn (1)	Eqn (2)	Eqn (3)
Personal disposable income	0·85	0·80	0·57
Change in consumer debt	1·04	0·73	1·48

[c] Bank advances to persons plus hire purchase debt.

the period 1958 II–1969 IV. The other two equations in the table show the changes in coefficient values observed when the data period is extended to include, or is confined to, the 1970s and indicate that such data cannot be assimilated in the relationship measured in equation (1). This was confirmed by a simulation of equation (1) using actual values of lagged consumption, which produced very substantial over-predictions of consumption.

Although not obvious from the table, it is clear from graphical inspection and from the apparent stability of relationships involving hire purchase debt alone, that this difficulty is associated with the very rapid rise in bank advances after 1971 (cf. chart 6.1). This poses an awkward problem. The principal justification for estimating equations like those in tables 6.8 and 6.9 is that the values of the 'change of debt' terms were constrained by monetary controls; otherwise they would be choice variables determined simultaneously with consumption and of dubious value as independent regressors. If the controls were successful in suppressing consumption, as such equations suggest, their removal should stimulate it. It is true that, at some point, when consumers have re-established an equilibrium in the absence of controls, the justification for fitting such equations would not be so obvious, but in the intervening period it would not seem unreasonable to suppose that the release of controls would lead to an increase in consumption which could be predicted by such an equation, whereas in fact consumption is substantially over-predicted. Indeed, it is not easy to see where the effect of the increase in bank advances was felt. There is no sign that it significantly affected Stock Exchange prices (which did not rise strongly after the first half of 1971); it may perhaps have helped to boost the rise in house prices, but the series in question purports to exclude loans for house purchase; neither does it seem that an explanation involving broader expenditure categories is of any help.[1] The most likely explanation seems to be that following the release of controls a large part of the expansion in bank advances accommodated a reshuffling of asset (and debt) portfolios, which involved the substitution of bank credit for less preferred forms of debt. This would indeed have been consistent with one of the purposes of 'Competition and credit control', but by the same token it suggests that rather more of the 'effect' of bank lending controls than first appeared may have been offset by drawing down financial assets and repaying other forms of credit, perhaps including trade credit for which data are very inadequate.[2] It must, of course, be admitted that the case for including bank advances together with hire purchase debt was never very firmly established in the first instance and the success of the composite term may merely have reflected a statistical correlation with little of the economic justification suggested. On the other side of the balance sheet, it is still too early to be sure how far this apparent breakdown in the relationship reflects a transitional shock associated with the new conditions. Whatever the case, it would seem that the experience of the recent period implies the need for some caution when interpreting the use of bank lending ceilings in the 1960s.

However, perhaps a more problematic (but not unrelated) issue concerns the demand for money. As already mentioned, one of the achievements of empirical monetary economics in the 1960s had been to demonstrate the existence of a stable function for the short-run demand for money, sensitive, but not greatly so, to variations in the rate of interest, very simply specified, and applicable with minor and plausible modifications to any of the definitions of the money stock available.[3] Fitting in as it did with comparable evidence for other

[1] Indeed, it is noticeable that in the econometric explanation of private expenditure afforded by Cripps, Godley and Fetherston (in the 'New Cambridge' tradition), bank advances for the period in question were replaced by a transformation of hire purchase debt (see House of Commons, *Ninth Report from the Expenditure Committee, Session 1974,* Minutes of Evidence, pp.1–12).

[2] There was a debate about the role of trade credit in the *Economic Journal*, commencing with the investigation published there by F. P. R. Brechling and R. G. Lipsey, 'Trade credit and monetary policy', *Economic Journal*, vol. 73, December 1963, pp. 618–41. It seems fair to say that no conclusive evidence has been produced as to whether movements in trade credit amplify, offset, or are simply neutral with respect to variations in monetary conditions.

[3] The stability of the demand for money is of course crucial to monetarist models of the economy – an intellectual fashion of growing importance in the period – but it is also quite

countries, and running clean contrary to the views of the *Radcliffe Report*, this relationship allows one to suggest that, whilst monetary policy was primarily accommodating in that period, it might possess the potential for more active use; it also allows one – as indicated earlier – to conceive of a monetary policy which did not rely upon bank lending ceilings and direct controls in the manner of the 1960s. The significance of an interruption to the previously observed relationship between money, income and interest rates is then obvious, for, if genuine, it undermines all these conclusions.

It should not have been surprising that the simply-specified demand for money should begin to appear an inadequate explanation of the behaviour of the money stock in the 1970s, for the 'own rate' on money was omitted from the calculations, whilst 'Competition and credit control' allowed the banks to compete for funds.[1] Artis and Lewis argued that allowance should also be made for the increased variability of bond prices in the 1970s, since, *ceteris paribus*, this would diminish the attractiveness of bonds and increase that of money.[2] However, even when these variables were included, the demand for money exhibited considerable instability when the 1970s were added to the estimation period: table 6.10 illustrates this for the broad definition of the money stock (M_3), where, admittedly, the problem was the most pronounced.[3] When demand functions estimated from data for the 1960s were used to predict the level of the money stock in the 1970s, given the actual levels of income and interest rates prevailing, a substantial degree of under-prediction was discovered.[4] Three hypotheses might explain this

---

acceptable to other schools of thought, including the Keynesian; indeed there is an argument that many typical monetarist propositions turn on the assumption of an interest-*in*elastic demand for money (see, for example, J. Tobin, 'Friedman's theoretical framework', *Journal of Political Economy*, vol. 80, Sept.–Oct. 1972) – a characteristic definitely rejected by the United Kingdom evidence. (An early finding by Laidler and Parkin of interest inelasticity seems to have been due to an inappropriate choice of the interest-rate variable. See Laidler and Parkin, 'The demand for money in the United Kingdom, 1956–67'.)

[1] This omission might seem a curious one, but it can be related to the absence of an obvious data series for the 'own rate' and perhaps to its presumed relative lack of variation. In any event, the functions for the demand for money estimated without it were widely judged to be satisfactory.

[2] M. J. Artis and M. K. Lewis, 'The demand for money in the United Kingdom 1963–1973', *Manchester School of Economic and Social Studies*, vol. 44, June 1976, pp. 147–81.

[3] The results of equation (1) can be used to estimate long-run elasticities (for income $+1 \cdot 08$ and for interest rates $-0 \cdot 25$) obtained by dividing the short-run coefficients by the complement of the coefficient on the lagged dependent variable. Such a procedure is implausible for equation (2) because of the value (in excess of unity) obtained there on the lagged dependent variable.

[4] See M. J. Artis and M. K. Lewis, 'The demand for money, stable or unstable?', *The Banker*, vol. 124, March 1974, pp. 239–47; also G. Hacche, 'The demand for money in the United Kingdom: experience since 1971', *Bank of England Quarterly Bulletin*, vol. 14, September 1974.

phenomenon: first, that the demand for money is indeed unstable; secondly, that it was subject to a shock associated with the introduction of 'Competition and credit control'; thirdly, that the under-prediction reflected a disequilibrium position of excess supply which the market had failed to clear within the periods of observation.

Table 6.10. *Estimates of the demand for money function* M_3^a

		Regression coefficients for:					
Eqn no.	Period of estimation	Constant term	GNP at market prices	Interest rates[b]	Index of bond price variability[c]	Lagged dependent variable	R^2	DW
(1)	1963 II–1970 IV	0·13 (0·95)	0·24 (2·17)	−0·06 (1·91)	0·03 (1·80)	0·78 (7·05)	0·998	1·96
(2)	1963 II–1973 I	−0·21 (1·38)	0·05 (0·41)	−0·07 (1·80)	0·06 (3·36)	1·01 (9·34)	0·998	1·94

SOURCE: Artis and Lewis, 'The demand for money in the United Kingdom', table 2.

[a] Data quarterly, GNP and M_3 seasonally adjusted in nominal terms; dependent variable is M_3 logarithmic.

[b] The differential between the Consol rate and the 'own rate' on money.

[c] Based on the standard deviation of a moving average of logarithmic first differences in Consol prices (see source).

Investigations by the Bank of England using disaggregated functions favour an interpretation along the lines of the first or second of these explanations.[1] They suggest that the behaviour of the corporate sector was particularly important and was strongly influenced by an unusual combination of lending and borrowing rates which made it worthwhile for companies both to lend and to borrow from banks simultaneously; also, that competition for bank deposits was much sharper after 'Competition and credit control'. Nevertheless, these factors, insofar as they could be measured, did not appear to provide a full explanation, so it was concluded that 'it is unwise to be confident in the survival of stable demand-for-money relationships when there are changes in regulations affecting banks'.[2] On the face of it, this statement seems to impugn the independence of demand and supply which is normally assumed, but it would be naive to reject the conclusion solely for this reason. It must, after all, be acknowledged that there are many measurement problems where, although the 'true' demand function is independent of supply conditions, the quantification of the relevant relationships is unable to capture the true function. These measurement problems embrace, in particular, lack of data on the 'own rate' and

[1] Ibid.   [2] Ibid. p. 297.

the poor quality of the disaggregated data on sectoral money holdings. Secondly, even assuming no difficulties of measurement, the extent of the change in the supply regime was arguably such as to imply that at least the associated lag structure – if not strictly the form of the demand function – might be altered.[1]

Artis and Lewis attempted to pursue this line of argument. They adopted as an initial hypothesis the position that the demand for money had remained stable,[2] but that variations in supply conditions were responsible (in the absence of a full market-clearing in the short run) for the appearance in later years of a marked disequilibrium and excess supply, which gave the (misleading) appearance of a 'breakdown' in the demand for money. This they associated particularly with the release of bank lending controls in 1971 and the size of the budget deficit in 1972 and 1973. The data available were insufficient to avoid some compromise with the theoretical standpoint they had adopted initially and the final results were somewhat inconclusive.[3]

At the time of writing, therefore, the question still remains unsettled. Confidence in the stability of the demand for money has been impaired but not destroyed, which implies that confidence in the further implications of a stable demand for money has also been impaired, if not destroyed.

CONCLUSIONS

At the beginning of this chapter we remarked that it was not feasible to represent the effects of monetary policy by a set of figures and that in only a few instances can we have much confidence in relationships bearing upon these effects. They seem clear enough in the case of hire purchase controls, the housing market and capital flows; otherwise, it cannot be claimed that much is known. Bank lending controls were unquestionably effective in controlling advances and, probably there-

[1] Brechling offered a perceptive comment on this problem in his contribution to the proceedings of a conference held in 1968. He argued in part that: 'It seems especially plausible to suppose that the demand for money adjusts to its equilibrium position quite rapidly when the supply of money is infinitely elastic and that interest rates, prices and permanent income react sluggishly to exogenous changes in the money stock, thus causing considerable disequilibrium in money holdings. In such a case, the existence of a stable demand function in the sample period may not tell us much about this function in the period of active money supply policy.' (See F. P. R. Brechling's discussion paper on the paper by Laidler in Clayton, Gilbert and Sedgwick (eds.), *Monetary Theory and Monetary Policy in the 1970s*, p. 138.)

[2] Artis and Lewis, 'The demand for money, stable or unstable?'. However, they allowed for the influence of the 'own rate' on money and variability in bond prices – variables suppressed in earlier estimates of the demand function.

[3] Some support was revealed for the proposition that the 'narrow' money supply series M_1 had not been so severely disturbed as M_3, which was compatible up to a point with the findings of Hacche, 'The demand for money in the United Kingdom', and explicable on the argument that M_1 remained primarily demand-determined even in periods when M_3 was in excess supply.

fore, the money supply; that they had much direct effect on spending is more questionable. Variations in the money supply were not particularly marked until the 1970s and the model of a largely accommodating monetary policy seems the most appropriate, for, whilst interest rates were not pegged, the authorities pursued a policy of 'leaning against the wind' in an endeavour to increase the stability of bond prices and the attractiveness of bonds as an asset to hold. This policy in the bond market had to be accompanied by a comparative and complementary stability of rates at the short end of the market, subject, however, to the need to offset incipient balance of payments crises by interest-rate adjustments designed to attract capital inflow, or to stem the outflow. The premise that policy could have had larger positive effects depends on a view of the demand for money which has come under a cloud recently, also upon evidence of the sensitivity of expenditure to interest-rate changes which most investigators have found it difficult to obtain. Clearly the period in which monetary policy was most open to criticism was that of the strong expansion in 1971–3, although this has to be considered in conjunction with fiscal policy in that period, which is discussed elsewhere in this book (chapter 4) as an important episode in its own right. Apart from this, it seems unlikely that monetary policy did very much for good or bad in this period; it did not do very much at all, and was not supposed to.

CHAPTER 7

POLICIES AIMED AT IMPROVING THE BALANCE OF PAYMENTS

by *J. H. B. Tew*[1]

INTRODUCTION

In every year from 1961 to 1968, except for a temporary respite in 1962 and 1963, balance of payments difficulties were serious enough to threaten the exhaustion of the reserves of gold and foreign currencies held by the Exchange Equalisation Account. The government was at intervals faced with crisis situations, which were resolved partly by improvised measures designed to make the external balance less unfavourable, partly by hastily negotiated rescue operations to supplement the reserves. The task was not made easier by the fact that confidence in sterling was at best precarious, each crisis being characterised by large outward short-term capital movements, motivated by the fear that the United Kingdom would be forced to devalue – a fear that was eventually justified in November 1967, when the pound was devalued from $2.80 to $2.40.

In the course of 1969, and at any rate in part as a delayed reaction to the devaluation, there began an improvement in the United Kingdom's external position so dramatic as to exorcise, albeit only temporarily, the anxiety about the balance of payments. From 1972, however, there was a growing suspicion that the old spectre had not after all been finally laid, as the balance started to deteriorate again. In June 1972 sterling was allowed to float and exchange control was extended to transactions with the sterling area, but by 1973 there was once again a large deficit on the current balance.

Intermingled with emergency measures intended to tide over the periodic crises were longer-term reforms intended permanently to reduce the net flow overseas of government payments and private investment. It was hoped prior to November 1967 that these reforms, together with others described elsewhere in this book aimed at countering inflation and improving the efficiency of British industry, would so strengthen our balance of payments in the longer term that, without

[1] The sections on the import surcharge and the temporary import deposit scheme (pages 344–9) are by M. J. Artis; appendix 1 is by A. D. Morgan.

recourse to devaluation, emergency measures could be dispensed with eventually. Some of the measures adopted at times of crisis come under the headings of demand management, priorities in bank lending, or interest-rate policy and, as such, have already been treated in chapters 5 and 6; others, such as more drastic exchange control or the imposition of the import surcharge, will be considered in the present chapter.

EVIDENCE OF BALANCE OF PAYMENTS DIFFICULTIES

At the start we need to be clear about what is meant by 'balance of payments difficulties'. Broadly there are four kinds of evidence that such difficulties may exist.

Table 7.1. *United Kingdom current and basic balance of payments, 1958–73: private and government transactions distinguished*

£ million

	Current balance			Basic balance		
	Government a/c[a]	Private a/c	Total	Government a/c[a]	Private a/c	Total
1958	−360	+704	+344	..	..	+148
59	−355	+510	+155	..	..	−100
1960	−430	+185	−245	..	..	−437
61	−496	+518	+22	−490	+574	+84
62	−506	+634	+128	−589	+611	+22
63	−514	+645	+131	−578	+554	−24
64	−550	+195	−355	−651	−61	−712
65	−578	+552	−26	−675	+422	−253
66	−626	+727	+101	−672	+688	+16
67	−630	+332	−298	−635	+236	−399
68	−696	+424	−272	−663	+264	−399
69	−791	+1251	+460	−946	+1245	+299
1970	−743	+1476	+733	−957	+1525	+568
71	−720	+1804	+1084	−886	+2020	+1134
72	−707	+861	+154	−849	+230	−619
73	−1005	+269	−736	−1089	+9	−1080

SOURCES: CSO, *United Kingdom Balance of Payments 1972*, table 3, and *1965–75*, tables 2, 3 and 13; CSO, *Economic Trends*, no. 200, June 1970, p. xxxi.

[a] Includes public sector interest, profits and dividends.

In the first place there are statistical series of the external balance defined in various ways. On a monthly basis there has always been the balance of visible trade, preliminary figures for which have been available with little delay. On a quarterly basis there have been a number of other statistical series, of which the current balance (of visible and invisible trade) and the basic balance (the current balance together with the balance of long-term capital transactions) were the most widely used in the 1960s (see table 7.1); a difficulty with these quarterly series is that they become available only after a time-lag and are subject to considerable retrospective revision. Originally officials preferred the current balance, but in 1957 preference shifted to the basic balance. In 1970 it was back to the current balance, when the Treasury concluded that the basic balance had become less useful,

Chart 7.1. *Short-term sterling liabilities (net of claims), 1959–69*

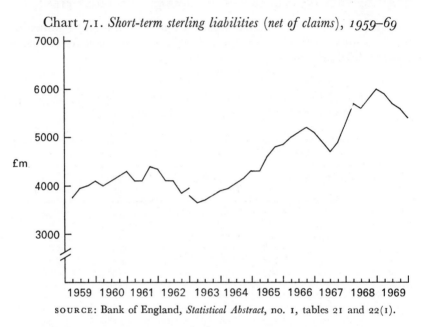

SOURCE: Bank of England, *Statistical Abstract*, no. 1, tables 21 and 22(1).

mainly because of the increasing difficulty of distinguishing long-term from short-term capital investment.[1] From then on the balances judged to be most significant were the current balance, as showing success or failure in paying our way, and the total currency flow, for the facts about our ability (or inability) to build up reserves and repay official borrowing.

A second type of evidence is changes in the stock of British external assets and liabilities. In the 1960s total assets always comfortably exceeded total liabilities, so that the only cause for concern was the balance of short-term assets and liabilities, which was much less satisfactory. The so-called 'sterling balances' held overseas were widely accepted as a measure of short-term sterling liabilities; these were usually taken net of certain short-term sterling claims, as shown in

[1] Treasury, *Economic Progress Report*, no. 7, September 1970.

chart 7.1. The short-term assets were official reserves in various forms: holdings of gold, foreign currencies, IMF Special Drawing Rights (as from 1970) and the reserve position in the IMF general account, and these are shown in the first column of table 7.2. To be offset against these resources were official liabilities contracted specifically to replenish reserves, so that the latter can best be judged when taken net of such liabilities, which are also shown in table 7.2. These statistics were known to officials accurately and without delay, and may well on that account have weighed heavily with them in deciding on urgent official action. Unfortunately no published information is available about official *forward* commitments, which at times were very large and which would be as important as outstanding official borrowing.

A third type of evidence consists of the spot and forward exchange rates. Since the spot pound–dollar rate was pegged throughout the 1960s, initially at $2.80 and later at $2.40, pressures against the pound revealed themselves as a fall in official reserves, or as a rise in official indebtedness, rather than in the spot exchange rate. The latter was therefore an important indicator of our external position only from the time that the pound was floated in June 1972. The forward pound–dollar rate is also a possible indicator, but its value as such was much reduced when (mainly in the years 1964–7) it too was being officially supported. At such times pressures against the pound in the forward market would be revealed better by the outstanding official position in forward dollars, which, though never published, would be known to officials. At other times, thanks to arbitrage, the discount or premium on forward sterling would normally tend to reflect the differential between sterling and dollar market interest rates; hence those occasions when the discount appreciably exceeded the interest-rate differential can fairly confidently be regarded as occasions of considerable pressure against sterling in the forward market. As may be seen from chart 7.2 there were a number of such occasions, in particular in 1968 and 1969.

The fourth kind is qualitative evidence about confidence in sterling coming into the official machine through the Bank of England, which enjoys privileged access to such information by virtue of its close relations with other City institutions and overseas central banks. We know from Harold Wilson's memoirs that such information was of vital importance in government decision-making, particularly on the timing of official action.[1]

The years in the 1960s in which the British authorities judged the United Kingdom to be in balance of payments difficulties were those in which outstanding official short-term and medium-term borrowing

---

[1] Wilson, *The Labour Government 1964–1970*.

Table 7.2. *United Kingdom reserves and outstanding official short-term and medium-term borrowing from abroad, 1959–73*

$ million

		Reserves[a] and related items[b]	Official financing and liabilities[c]			
			Net drawings from IMF[d]	Borrowing from other monetary authorities[e]	Public sector borrowing[f]	Total
1959	Dec.	2736	325	—	—	325
1960	June	2892	232	—	—	232
	Dec.	3231	—	—	—	—
1961	June	2772	—	904	—	904
	Dec.	3318	1040	—	—	1040
1962	June	3433	535	—	—	535
	Dec.	2806	—	—	—	—
1963	June	2713	—	—	—	—
	Dec.	2657	—	—	—	—
1964	June	2704	—	15	—	15
	Dec.	2316	1000	605	—	1605
1965	June	2792	2383	629	—	3012
	Dec.	3004	2370	913	—	3283
1966	June	3276	2430	683	—	3113
	Dec.	3100	2410	1738	—	4148
1967	June	2834	1862	628	—	2490
	Dec.	2695	1508	3453	—	4961
1968	June	2683	2908	4538	—	7446
	Dec.	2422	2723	5348	—	8071
1969	June	2443	2700	4543	50	7293
	Dec.	2528	2650	3744	120	6514
1970	June	2791	2381	1125	120	3626
	Dec.	2827	2328	958	120	3406
1971	June	5319	1620	—	316	1936
	Dec.	8832	1081	—	366	1447
1972	June	8115	—	2608	366	2974
	Dec.	5646	—	—	366	366
1973	June	7012	—	—	1337	1337
	Dec.	6476	—	—	2982	2982

SOURCES: Bank of England, *Statistical Abstract*, no. 1, table 27; *Bank of England Quarterly Bulletin*, vol. 16, March 1976, table 23 and pp. 79–80.

[a] Sterling reserves converted at $2.80 to the pound up to mid-1967 and then at $2.40 until 1969; thereafter reserves are valued as in *Bank of England Quarterly Bulletin*, vol. 16, March 1976, table 23.

[b] Foreign currency taken out of reserves by official swaps with overseas monetary authorities included as follows: June 1971 $1700 million, December 1971 $2251 million, June 1972 $1150 million.

[c] Non-dollar borrowing valued as in *Bank of England Quarterly Bulletin*, vol. 16, March 1976, pp. 79–80.

[d] Drawings net of repayments by the United Kingdom and of drawings of sterling by other countries; interest and charges in sterling excluded.

[e] Foreign exchange obtained by the Bank of England as deposits or by swaps.

[f] Foreign currency borrowing (net of repayments) by the British government and by other public sector institutions under the 1969 and subsequent exchange cover schemes.

increased, namely 1961 and 1964–8 inclusive (see table 7.2). The only year in which other evidence appears to conflict with this table is 1960, when the current balance and the basic balance both suggest a 'difficult' year (table 7.1). However short-term capital inflows in that year (reversed in 1961) delayed the strain on our reserves until 1961, and it was only then that decisive official action, appropriate to balance of

Chart 7.2. *Covered interest-rate differential between local authority temporary loans and Eurodollar deposits in London, 1966–73*

SOURCES: Bank of England, *Statistical Abstract*, no. 1, table 28, and no. 2, table 28.

Note: The differential represents the excess of the sterling rate over the dollar rate, minus the forward premium (per cent per annum) on the dollar.

payments difficulties, was taken. (The only action taken in 1960 was to raise Bank Rate and impose controls on hire purchase.) In the 1970s there was a temporary anxiety about the middle of 1972, associated with the floating of sterling in June, and this accounts for the $2.6 billion of official borrowing shown in table 7.2. Then balance of payments troubles resumed in earnest in 1973 and led to strong official encouragement to public sector institutions to borrow in foreign currencies to improve our reserves.

EXCHANGE-RATE POLICY

An issue which claims our attention at the outset of any discussion of policies to improve the balance of payments is why the authorities were so reluctant to devalue the pound. The spot value of sterling had been pegged within the limits $2.78–$2.82, giving a small margin on either side of the $2.80 parity, ever since the devaluation of 1949. The government's attitude to this rate had, however, been subject to vicissitudes during the 1950s. The Conservative administration which came to power in November 1951 had initially toyed with a scheme 'Operation Robot' for introducing non-resident convertibility with a floating rate for the pound, or at any rate widening the swing on either side of $2.80, and discussions were held within the OEEC about the technical implications of such a move.[1] But as the news of the discussions leaked out there followed a run on sterling, which was only stopped by the Chancellor of the Exchequer's firm denial, in his speech at the annual IMF meeting in September 1955, that any change in the pegging arrangements for sterling was contemplated.[2]

Thereafter the government's commitment to $2.80 hardened. Peter Thorneycroft, in his budget statement of 1957, spoke of the austere policies he had adopted to improve our balance of payments at the existing dollar value of sterling and in the following year his successor, Heathcoat Amory, said that the strength of sterling remained the primary objective of economic policy. Harold Macmillan was no less determined to avoid devaluation, though his grounds were political rather than economic. He stated that devaluation mattered politically because sterling had become a symbol, but he seemed doubtful whether, otherwise, maintaining the parity 'matters as much as we all think'.[3]

Outside comment did not give such unqualified approval to the $2.80 peg. For example, in 1955 James Meade was writing in favour of a floating rate,[4] while the deterioration of the balance of payments in the first half of the 1960s provoked considerable public controversy on the merits of abandoning $2.80 in favour of either a lower peg or a floating rate. However outside opinion, and particularly academic opinion, was deeply divided.[5] At that time none of the protagonists seemed to think it necessary, or indeed possible, to quantify with any

---

[1] The Earl of Birkenhead, *The Prof in Two Worlds*, London, Collins, 1961, pp. 284–92.

[2] A. Shonfield, *British Economic Policy since the War*, Harmondsworth, Penguin, 1958, p. 201.

[3] Macmillan, *Pointing the Way, 1959–1961*, p. 376.

[4] J. E. Meade, 'The case for variable exchange rates', *Three Banks Review*, no. 27, September 1955.

[5] T. W. Hutchison, *Economics and Economic Policy in Britain 1946–1966*, London, Allen & Unwin, 1968, pp. 219–33.

accuracy the fall in the exchange rate appropriate to improving our external balance by the required amount, or even to specify what the required amount was. Yet without quantification the debate was almost bound to be inconclusive, since the possible adverse side effects of a departure from the $2.80 peg (retaliation by other countries; speculation against the pound; deterioration in our terms of trade; a rise in the cost of living, leading possibly to a wage–price spiral; breaking faith with overseas holders of sterling; damage to the City's prestige) all depended very much on the percentage by which the pound's external value would have to fall. (As was pointed out in a more sophisticated public controversy which took place in 1967, the disadvantages of a large devaluation were disproportionally greater than those of a moderate one.[1])

In any case, the inconclusive public controversy in the first half of the 1960s seems to have had no impact on the policy of the Conservative government. The various measures adopted in 1961 enabled us to weather the storm without altering the exchange rate and, when our external balance began to deteriorate again in the course of 1963, Reginald Maudling rejected the proposition that a vigorous economy and a strong position for sterling were incompatible, and planned to deal with what he diagnosed as only a temporary external deficit by drawing down reserves and by recourse to external credit.[2]

Despite Maudling's optimism, the Labour Chancellor James Callaghan, who succeeded him in October 1964, was faced with a formidable balance of payments problem: the basic balance for the year was £717 million in deficit and was believed at the time to be even worse. The incoming Labour government was therefore faced immediately with the major issue of whether to maintain the $2.80 peg or to abandon it. Some of the academics who moved into Whitehall in 1964 had participated on both sides of the public controversy several years earlier and this suggests that there must have been a debate of some kind.[3] Indeed Samuel Brittan says the issue was discussed very thoroughly.[4] But if we are to believe Brandon's account of what happened behind the scenes,[5] whatever debate there may have been was cut short by a decision to hold fast to the $2.80 peg, taken by Harold Wilson and a small group of colleagues at a meeting on 17

---

[1] M. FG. Scott, 'Should the pound be devalued?', *The Bankers' Magazine*, vol. 203, April 1967, p. 227.

[2] Budget statement, 1963.

[3] For example, T. Balogh was in favour of holding to the $2.80 peg, R. R. Neild and N. Kaldor were in favour of abandoning it (Hutchison, *Economics and Economic Policy*, pp. 219–22).

[4] Brittan, *Steering the Economy* (rev. edn), p. 393.

[5] H. Brandon, *In the Red: the struggle for sterling 64/66*, London, Deutsch, 1966, p. 43.

October 1964 immediately after taking office. Callaghan, according to Brandon, had already for some time been committed to $2.80, and he and Wilson remained steadfast to their commitment right up to 1967, when there was no feasible alternative to abandoning it. Indeed, once the decision had been taken, Brittan tells us that all reference to the subject was forbidden and it became known as 'the great unmention-able'.[1]

Wilson's own account of the decision gives more prominence to the political implications of devaluation than the economic ones.[2] He says that he and his colleagues were obviously tempted by the idea, since the responsibility could have been put on the previous government. His first argument against devaluation is that international opinion, remembering that the decision to devalue in 1949 had been made by a Labour government, would conclude that Labour would always take the easy way out by devaluing. Secondly, he argues that – whereas by 1967 there was general international acceptance of devaluation – this would not have been the case in 1964. On the economic side, he argues that devaluation would have required a 'severe and rapid' shift of resources from the home to the overseas sector. In addition, he was strongly influenced by the view that the physical and structural improvement of the British economy, to which he was deeply com-mitted, would make Britain so much more competitive with other countries that our balance of payments would in due course improve adequately without devaluation.[3] Of course, the physical and structural reform of the British economy would take time, but meanwhile the deficit could be reduced by various expedients and whatever balance remained could probably be financed with official help from other major powers, especially the United States. The United States was indeed anxious to help with any policies which offered a credible alternative to a British devaluation, which was seen as menace to confidence in the dollar and hence to the whole international monetary system.

The view that the devaluation of sterling would have such catas-trophic consequences is clearly one which was put to Wilson in 1964 by the Governor of the Bank of England, who advocated draconian alternatives, including all-round cuts in public expenditure, to relin-quishing the $2.80 peg.[4] Another consideration which may have weighed in 1964 was that devaluation or a free float could jeopardise

---

[1] Brittan, *Steering the Economy* (rev. edn), p. 292.

[2] Wilson, *The Labour Government 1964–1970*, p. 6.

[3] Balogh had argued in a similar vein in his written evidence to the Radcliffe Committee (Treasury, *Committee on the Working of the Monetary System. Principal Memoranda of Evidence*, vol. 3, London, HMSO, 1960, p. 40).

[4] Wilson, *The Labour Government 1964–1970*, p. 37.

the success of a prices and incomes policy, which was itself an alternative way of making British goods more competitive. This point of view was being advanced at that time by the National Institute.[1]

Alongside the various arguments against devaluation, there developed in the 1960s a quite different approach, pioneered by Paish,[2] which cannot be so readily reconciled with the views of the Labour leaders at the time of the crucial decision of October 1964. The central idea was that the problems which beset the British economy, including the balance of payments problem, were mainly attributable to excess demand. For, unlike other critics of 'stop–go' policies of demand management, who favoured stabilising demand at the level achieved in the 'boom' phase of the cycle, Paish wished to stabilise it at the level of the 'recession' phase, corresponding to an unemployment rate of 2 per cent or slightly more. Such a margin of excess capacity would serve to maximise the rate of real growth in the long term and at the same time contain the annual rise in wages and prices within acceptable bounds; a highly desirable side effect of the policy would be the avoidance of the balance of payments troubles associated with the high-demand phase of previous cycles.

To those economists, inside as well as outside the government, whose views on the British economy came to be broadly in line with Paish's, the $2.80 peg, at any rate up to mid-1966, was never an undesirable constraint on demand management, since from the end of the war up to that time demand had almost never been inadequate – and had intermittently been excessive. In the high-demand phase the constraint had been beneficial, in that it served to reinforce the government's resolve to deflate demand to a level which this school of thought regarded as more appropriate to the domestic objectives of demand management.

'The great unmentionable' remained unmentionable in government circles until 1966, when George Brown insisted on raising the devaluation issue with his colleagues.[3] But only a minority, though a substantial one, was in favour, so instead of devaluation there was in July a further package of deflationary measures.

Mid-1966 was thus an important milestone on the road to eventual devaluation, in that from then onwards the Cabinet was alive to the issue, and indeed as seriously divided on it as outside opinion.[4] More-

[1] *National Institute Economic Review*, no. 33, August 1965, p. 18.
[2] See F. W. Paish, *Studies in an Inflationary Economy: the United Kingdom 1948–1961*, London, Macmillan, 1962, in particular his chapter on 'Output, inflation and growth'.
[3] Brown, *In My Way*, p. 114.
[4] D. J. Robertson in his introduction to a symposium on the British balance of payments in the *Scottish Journal of Political Economy*, vol. 13, February 1966, said that few of the contributors believed that devaluation alone would help the British balance of payments in any

over, arguments in favour of holding to the $2.80 peg were advanced
with noticeably less conviction. In particular, those who (on Paish's
line of argument) had previously regarded it as more or less compatible
with the domestic aims of demand management began to lose faith in
this harmony of objectives. It still had its defenders, but they were
mainly people burdened with especially heavy responsibilities in the
field of international monetary affairs – Wilson and Callaghan in the
Cabinet,[1] officials on the international side of the Treasury and the
Bank of England, City bankers concerned with international business –
plus a number of outside commentators. Many of the statesmen and
officials concerned had so solemnly pledged themselves to maintain
the $2.80 peg that they would have found it embarrassing to escape
from their commitment, but there is no reason to doubt the sincerity
of their professed dread of the consequences. The last major change in
exchange rates that they remembered – the revaluation of the German
and Dutch currencies in 1961 – had provoked speculative movements
of short-term funds on a scale which they hoped never to experience
again.[2] They feared defections from the sterling area; they feared for
the continued prosperity of the City if sterling should go out of favour
as a commercial currency throughout the world; they were impressed
(unduly so, as we now know from subsequent experience) by the incon-
veniences which varying exchange rates occasion for firms engaged in
international trade. Moreover, those who were critical of the government's administrative competence also noted that our balance of
payments was in deficit almost entirely because of the large deficit
on official transactions (table 7.1) and believed that if only the government were less spendthrift the problem would disappear without any
need to tamper with the $2.80 peg.[3]

The decision taken in mid-1966 to hold to the $2.80 peg remained
the basis of official policy until late in 1967, when it had to be abandoned. The decision to devalue to $2.40 was taken in the crisis atmos-
phere of November 1967 and is described by Wilson in his memoirs.
He characterises the IMF's conditions for supporting sterling as

permanent way, though some might feel that a price advantage would be immediately
beneficial. However, the pro-devaluationists were at this time cautious about presenting their
case in public lest they should rock the boat. One of the rare published arguments in favour
of devaluation was presented by M. FG. Scott ('Should the pound be devalued?') in *The
Bankers' Magazine* of April 1967, p. 225, together with a criticism by R. J. Ball ('The case
against devaluation of the pound').

[1] Wilson suggests (*The Labour Government 1964–1970*, p. 452) that Brown's move to the
Foreign Office caused him to become very mindful of the international consequences of
devaluation, which he came to view less favourably than he had in July 1966.

[2] Macmillan, *Pointing the Way, 1959–1961*, pp. 371–2.

[3] Richard Fry explains this view, which however he did not himself share, in 'Government
spending overseas: how it has risen', *The Banker*, vol. 118, June 1968, p. 493.

unacceptable: they included stricter credit control, a tighter prices and incomes policy, and a pledge that sterling would not be floated.[1]

The die-hard defenders of the $2.80 peg, including Wilson and Callaghan, came to be criticised in post-mortems on devaluation conducted in 1970 and subsequently. But in the period up to the second half of 1969 few commentators dared to interpret what was then still recent history in this way. For initially it was the unwanted consequences of devaluation which were most in evidence, while the desired consequences – export-led growth and a marked improvement in the balance of payments – were delayed longer than anyone, including the Treasury and the National Institute, had expected. The National Institute had by May 1968 revised downwards from £500 million to between £300 and £400 million the surplus on current account for 1969 forecast immediately after devaluation.[2]

In the course of 1969 the belated improvement in the balance of payments became apparent and in 1970 there followed a massive swing into unprecedented surplus, which most people were well content to attribute to the 1967 devaluation without much allowance for other factors operating in the same direction, notably further deflationary measures in 1968 and 1969 and an upsurge of world demand for exported manufactures. More careful assessment of the probable effects of the 1967 devaluation, as they would have been had other things remained equal, suggests a more qualified enthusiasm for its efficacy. This is apparent from appendix 1, which sets out various estimates, made at the time and subsequently, of the consequences of devaluation.

The new $2.40 parity seems not to have come up for reconsideration before President Nixon's speech of 15 August 1971, which suspended the gold convertibility of the dollar and ushered in a regime of floating rates until the Smithsonian conference in December 1971, at which sterling and many other currencies were re-pegged with different dollar parities. The lesson drawn by the major powers from this episode was, however, that parities would probably need to be more adjustable in the 1970s than in the 1960s; with the possible exception of Canada none of them (and certainly not Britain) then favoured floating rates. Indeed, as late as his 1972 budget speech (only about three months before he unpegged sterling) Anthony Barber's pronouncements on exchange rates contain no explicit reference to the case for floating.

The float of June 1972 was always described as temporary, but the government was in no hurry to re-peg. Our national interest was

[1] Wilson, *The Labour Government 1964–1970*, p. 453. Right up to the last minute Wilson seems to have favoured floating the pound to devaluing to a lower peg, so the freedom to float was presumably important to him (ibid. pp. 38 and 448).

[2] *National Institute Economic Review*, no. 44, May 1968, p. 11. The Institute's analysis includes the first published reference to the now famous J-curve (see appendix 1, page 356).

probably thought to be best served by encouraging other countries to peg while ourselves retaining the freedom to float. All the same, our readiness to float, even on this basis, reflects an appreciable shift of government opinion in the first half of 1972. Outside commentators who favoured floating rates had certainly been pressing their case in the preceding year.[1] Moreover, recent experience had shown that floating was practicable and could be efficacious, at any rate as a means of discouraging excessive short-term capital movements. The Canadian dollar had been floating since 1 June 1970; the mark had floated between 29 September 1969 and the following 24 October, while both the mark and the florin floated from May 1971 until the Smith-sonian settlement of December 1971; almost all currencies had floated between 15 August and 21 December 1971. Thus Barber's action in June 1972 was not without precedent.

His resolve to continue the float was soon backed by other countries' actions. The Swiss franc was floated as from January 1973; the crisis of February 1973 left the lira and the yen floating; that of March 1973 left all the major currencies floating, though eight countries of conti-nental Europe operated a joint float. The United Kingdom was invited to join the joint float, but the Chancellor laid down conditions which were so far-reaching that his EEC partners were unable to accept them and the pound continued to float individually. The conditions were that:

(1) The initial exchange rates must be acceptable to each member state and each member state must have the 'unimpaired right', after consultation with the Council of Ministers, to alter the value of its currency in relation to currencies of other members.

(2) There must be financial support of the most far-reaching kind – all EEC countries being prepared to grant unlimited support without conditions and without obligation to repay.[2]

At the beginning of the floating regime the pound was allowed to find its own level, but in 1973 the Bank of England intervened in the market. In mid-May intensifying speculative pressures against the dollar propelled the pound to $2.58 and the Bank of England entered the market to moderate the pace of advance. Thereafter, however, the Bank's intervention was in support of the pound, the first occasion being in July.[3]

[1] For example Brittan in the *Financial Times*, 31 March 1971.

[2] The Chancellor said that the system could only be made proof against speculative capital flows if there was clear knowledge that support was unlimited (*Financial Times*, 5 March 1973).

[3] *Bank of England Quarterly Bulletin*, vol. 13, September 1973, pp. 275–6.

'BRITAIN ALONE' POLICIES

M. FG. Scott, writing at the end of the 1950s, identified a strand of economic thought, as exemplified in the then recent writings of Alan Day and Andrew Shonfield, as favouring what he called a 'Britain alone' solution to our external problems.[1] This solution envisaged that the United Kingdom should shed her international commitments in various ways; it had two facets – remedies for the weakness of the balance of payments and remedies for the illiquidity of the country's balance sheet of external assets and liabilities. The former, according to Shonfield writing in 1959, required both a drastic cut-back in long-term investment overseas and a thorough-going reappraisal of government expenditure abroad, although (on Shonfield's priorities) expenditure on aid to the developing countries was to be reviewed more sympathetically than expenditure for military and political objectives.[2]

The case for discouraging investment was partly fiscal: the investor in his private interest preferred an overseas investment to one in the United Kingdom whenever the yield after tax on the former exceeded the yield after tax on the latter, whereas in the national interest the comparison ought to be made net only of overseas taxation paid on overseas investments, since the tax revenue collected by the British government was enjoyed by the British economy no less than the interest or dividends received by United Kingdom residents. In addition, however, Day questioned the wisdom, from a national point of view, of permitting British companies to maintain their foothold in overseas markets by setting up local production facilities whenever this became more profitable than exporting from the United Kingdom.[3]

The remedy for excessive investment abroad was mainly to be sought in a stricter exchange control on outward capital transactions, and especially in putting an end to the exemption of sterling area transactions from the provisions of United Kingdom control.[4] There were admittedly other devices available for discouraging investment in the sterling area, but these had hitherto been only very mildly restrictive.

The second facet of the 'Britain alone' solution was, according to Day, 'that of reducing the risks arising from our illiquid capital position'.[5] The relation between Britain's short-term assets and liabilities made her (in a banking sense) illiquid and, since a substantial and allegedly volatile part of her short-term liabilities was the liquid

[1] M. FG. Scott, 'What should be done about the Sterling Area?', *Bulletin of the Oxford University Institute of Statistics*, vol. 21, November 1959, p. 228.
[2] Shonfield, *British Economic Policy since the War*, p. 265.
[3] Radcliffe Committee, *Principal Memoranda of Evidence*, vol. 3, p. 74.
[4] Shonfield, *British Economic Policy since the War*, pp. 252 and 273.
[5] Radcliffe Committee, *Principal Memoranda of Evidence*, vol. 3, para. 34 on p. 74.

sterling debts, such as Treasury bills, held overseas, both Day and Shonfield were concerned to find remedies for the 'problem of the sterling balances'.

Various kinds of relatively minor alleviations were proposed, several of which were later adopted by the British authorities. Thus both Day and Shonfield recommended an exchange-rate guarantee on sterling balances, and this was given on the bulk of such balances under the Basle Group Arrangement of 1968 (see page 352 below). Another suggestion was to sell British-owned long-term investments, as Callaghan subsequently did in 1966 and 1967 in the case of the official portfolio of dollar securities. Yet another was to tighten up the exchange control on short-term credits extended by London banks to overseas customers, as was actually done by a series of modifications to the exchange control regulations in September 1957 and on various subsequent occasions.

Apart from such minor alterations Day recommended a much more fundamental change which is strongly reminiscent of the stillborn Barber Plan put forward at the IMF Annual Meeting in 1971.[1] He wrote:

The direction to explore, therefore, is that of finding some international organ to act as financial intermediary and, in effect, to take over London's work as an international central banker...If we could judiciously hand over to an international organisation sterling's functions as a reserve currency, it should be possible to retain most of our commercial banking business, making London into a sort of super-Amsterdam.[2]

This point of view gained more and more adherents, especially as in the course of the 1960s the City had demonstrated its ability to do business in non-sterling currencies, particularly dollars.[3] The overseas sterling area had been diversifying its reserves and was liable to switch out of sterling at times of balance of payments difficulties; from 1968 dollar-value guarantees had to be given to holders of sterling in the overseas sterling area. Moreover, overseas holdings of sterling represented a constraint on our interest-rate policy. Finally, our future EEC partners were unhappy about the role of sterling as a reserve currency and we had to give assurances, as a condition for joining, that we were prepared to contemplate the possibility that this role should be ended.

[1] Barber suggested that IMF Special Drawing Rights should become the *numéraire* in terms of which parities should be denominated, should eventually replace national currencies held as reserve assets (apart from working balances of intervention currencies) and should be issued in future in amounts adequate to meet the total need for additional reserve assets.

[2] Radcliffe Committee, *Principal Memoranda of Evidence*, vol. 3, pp. 75 and 76.

[3] Speech on 8 December 1971 by the Governor of the Bank of England (*Bank of England Quarterly Bulletin*, vol. 12, March 1972, pp. 84–5).

The more important of the 'Britain alone' policies actually adopted – the measures to reduce government expenditure overseas, changes in taxation of overseas profits and the tightening up of exchange controls – are considered in the next three sections.

GOVERNMENT EXPENDITURE OVERSEAS

In the 1960s both political Parties professed to be aware of the need to economise on government expenditure overseas in the interests of a healthier balance of payments. Harold Macmillan's memoirs relating to mid-1961 record the need to cut down defence expenditure and overseas aid in the light of the serious fall in invisible earnings.[1] Selwyn Lloyd, in his budget statement of 1962, said that the country still had a considerable way to go to achieve a satisfactory balance of payments surplus having regard to heavy and continuing obligations for defence, aid and investment overseas. The first Chancellor in the 1964 Labour government, James Callaghan, held substantially similar views; in particular, in his budget statement on 3 May 1966 he referred to the fact that the scale of government investment overseas, which over the last decade had been allowed to grow out of proportion to resources, imposed a heavy burden on the balance of payments. But the resolve to effect economies in such expenditure is not so apparent (at any rate as measured in current values) in the *ex post* statistics as set out above in table 7.1.

The first item of overseas expenditure to consider is aid to developing countries, which would have been exempt from Shonfield's proposed economy campaign but which the British government made determined efforts to contain within a ceiling.[2] Aid did rise slowly in the first half of the 1960s, but it remained static in the second half (chart 7.3).

The limitation of the aid programme was a policy which both political Parties adopted only with reluctance. In the case of the Labour Party, Harold Wilson had constantly argued in favour of the need for large capital flows to the developing countries as part of an international plan;[3] while in the 1964 election manifesto there was a promise to 'increase the share of national income devoted to essential aid programmes, not only by loans and grants but by mobilizing unused industrial capacity to meet overseas needs'. In the case of the Conser-

---

[1] Macmillan, *Pointing the Way, 1959–1961*, p. 374.

[2] In the fiscal year 1965/6 official aid was subject to a ceiling of £205 million (*House of Commons, Seventh Report from the Estimates Committee, Session 1967–68. Overseas Aid*, London, HMSO, 1968, p. vii, para. 11); in 1966/7 it was £225 million and in 1967/8 £205 million (Bank of England, *Report for the year ended 28 February 1967*, p. 5). The ceiling remained at £205 million up to and including 1970/1; in 1971/2 it was raised to £251 million.

[3] D. Seers and P. Streeten, 'Overseas development policies' in Beckerman (ed.), *The Labour Government's Economic Record, 1964–1970*, pp. 118–19.

vative Party, Edward Heath, then Secretary of State for Industry, reaffirmed at the United Nations' Conference on Trade and Development (UNCTAD) in Geneva on 16 June 1964 the United Kingdom's support for the multilateral aid programme of the United Nations and gave a list of additional British multilateral aid to be given.[1]

Chart 7.3. *United Kingdom expenditure on overseas aid, 1961–73*

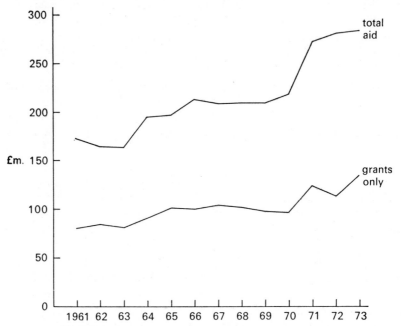

SOURCES: CSO, *United Kingdom Balance of Payments 1972*, table 42 and *1964–74*, table 36; column 4 of table 7.3.

But aid was recognised as a burden on our balance of payments. Heathcoat Amory's budget statement in April 1960 quoted from a speech by the Prime Minister in March arguing that overseas aid required the limiting of the growth of consumption at home and an increase in exports so as to provide a margin of foreign exchange.[2] The National Plan of 1965 argued that it would be necessary to scrutinise the aid programme with particular care so long as the balance of payments was under strain,[3] and the Labour government remained cautious in

[1] *Board of Trade Journal*, 19 June 1964, p. 1326.
[2] Speech delivered on 15 March 1960 to the Commonwealth and Empire Industries Association.
[3] Department of Economic Affairs, *The National Plan*, p. 71.

its attitude to aid throughout its period of office – some Labour supporters indeed thought that the Party had betrayed its ideals.[1]

Apart from aid to the developing countries, the main items of government expenditure overseas (table 7.3) are 'administrative and diplomatic' and 'military', the latter being much the more important. Callaghan, in his budget statement of April 1965, drew attention to the serious consequences of the growth of overseas military expenditure, which since 1959 had 'gone up year by year and from about £175 million to over £300 million'. *The National Plan*, published in the same year, quoted the Prime Minister as saying that the government 'are determined to achieve a saving of £50 to £100 million in overseas military expenditure' and noted the government's intention 'to restrict the Defence Budget at constant prices to the level of the 1964/5 Estimates, and to bring about an absolute reduction in that part which is incurred overseas'.[2]

From 1965 the balance of payments implications of defence were a constant theme in the annual *Statements on the Defence Estimates*. That of February 1965 drew attention to the heavy burden on our

Table 7.3. *Balance of payments on government services and transfers, 1960–73*

£ million

	Credits		Debits		
	Military	Other	Military	Aid grants[a]	Other
1960	41	4	213	..	..
61	41	5	239	80	59
62	33	6	257	84	58
63	35	5	272	81	69
64	38	7	306	91	80
65	25	21	293	101	99
66	25	17	307	100	105
67	25	11	292	104	103
68	28	16	294	102	114
69	27	21	298	98	119
1970	29	22	314	97	125
71	28	31	334	125	127
72	41	31	369	114	153
73	40	103	444	139	358

SOURCES: CSO, *United Kingdom Balance of Payments 1971*, table 12, *1972*, table 42, and *1964–74*, tables 8 and 36.

[a] The items in CSO, *United Kingdom Balance of Payments 1964–74*, table 36, with a cross-reference to table 8.

[1] Seers and Streeten, 'Overseas development policies', p. 150.
[2] Department of Economic Affairs, *The National Plan*, p. 71.

balance of payments of our forces in Germany.[1] In February 1966 it was argued that the maintenance of military tasks and capabilities outside Europe would impose an unacceptable strain on the economy and on our reserves of foreign exchange; consequently it had been decided that Britain would not undertake major operations of war except in cooperation with allies, nor would she provide another country with military assistance unless it was prepared to provide us with the facilities we needed to make such assistance effective in time; finally, there was to be no attempt to maintain defence facilities in an independent country against its wishes.[2]

Various policy measures were adopted in the course of the 1960s to mitigate the burden of military expenditure. In the first place, sterling expenditure in the United Kingdom was seen to have implications for our balance of payments and procurement policies were modified accordingly. Thus, in 1965, when the TSR-2 was cancelled, Callaghan (in his budget statement) emphasised that this would release resources to assist the balance of payments. However, more concern was apparent in the case of expenditure in foreign currencies. The policy was spelt out in February 1966: the British contribution in Europe was to be kept at roughly the same level, but only if some means were found of meeting the foreign exchange costs; substantial savings were to be made in the Mediterranean and the Middle East; in the Far East there was to be some limitation to the scale and nature of our military effort.[3] Little could be done to reduce expenditure in Europe (which in practice meant mainly in Germany) and in the event little was done, as table 7.4 shows. Instead the main effort was directed to finding some means of meeting the foreign exchange costs, in practice through the so-called 'offset agreements'. Table 7.4 also shows that the reductions in forces in the Mediterranean (Gibraltar, Malta and Cyprus) did not succeed in reducing costs measured in current values; the really important run-down in overseas military expenditure occurred east of Suez. This run-down eventually proceeded further than envisaged in February 1966, or even February 1967, when, though it was noted that on the independence of South Arabia in 1968 'we shall withdraw all our forces', nonetheless our continuing intention to maintain a military presence east of Suez was emphasised.[4] By July 1967, however, we had 'declared our intention to withdraw from South Arabia and

---

[1] Ministry of Defence, *Statement on the Defence Estimates 1965*, Cmnd 2592, London, HMSO, 1965, p. 8.

[2] Ministry of Defence, *Statement on the Defence Estimates 1966*, Part 1: *Defence Review*, Cmnd 2901, London, HMSO, 1966, p. 7.

[3] Ibid. p. 14.

[4] Ministry of Defence, *Statement on the Defence Estimates 1967*, Cmnd 3203, London, HMSO, 1967, p. 7.

the Aden base in January 1968'. In the Far East, we had 'decided to reach a reduction of about half the forces deployed in Singapore and Malaysia during 1970–71'.[1]

Table 7.4. *Overseas expenditure on military services, 1960–73*

£ million

	Western Europe	Gibraltar, Malta and Cyprus	Persian Gulf, S. Yemen	Far East	Other	Total
1960	63	39	12	53	36	203
61	73	40	18	57	36	224
62	84	41	19	59	40	243
63	94	40	22	62	32	250
64	101	37	23	71	38	270
65	101	35	25	82	27	270
66	108	34	27	86	28	283
67	107	34	25	78	20	264
68	119	35	14	80	27	275
69	130	40	10	69	33	282
1970	150	41	9	65	36	301
71	169	46	7	55	45	322
72	211	60	—	41	43	355
73	279	70	—	33	47	429

SOURCE: CSO, *United Kingdom Balance of Payments 1971*, table 14, and *1964–74*, table 9.

In February 1968, nine major decisions which the government had taken were listed:

(1) Britain's defence effort would be concentrated mainly in Europe and the North Atlantic area.

(2) The withdrawal of forces from Malaysia, Singapore and the Persian Gulf would be completed by the end of 1971.

(3) Service manpower would be reduced eventually by more than the 75,000 forecast in July 1967, and more quickly.

(4) The carrier force would be phased out and naval construction reduced.

(5) The Brigade of Gurkhas would be run down to 6000 by 1971.

(6) The order for 50 F111 aircraft was cancelled and the Royal Air Force transport force would be cut.

(7) Support facilities, including headquarters and the Ministry of Defence, would be cut.

(8) No special capability for use outside Europe would be maintained.

(9) A general capability, based in Europe including the United

[1] Ministry of Defence, *Supplementary Statement on Defence Policy 1967*, Cmnd 3357, London, HMSO, 1967, p. 5.

Kingdom, would be retained for use overseas as circumstances demanded, and for supporting United Nations operations as necessary.[1]

In a Report dated 1969 it is stated that, in spite of the 1967 devaluation, the sterling cost of our 'local defence expenditure in areas other than Germany will be cut by one-third by 1970/1, and by a further third in 1972/3 compared with the 1967 rate of expenditure'.[2] In addition to such economies achieved in respect of British forces and installations located overseas, reductions in foreign exchange expenditures were achieved by cuts in expenditure on armaments, especially United States military aircraft and missiles.[3]

The defence burden could also be reduced if some means were found of offsetting the foreign exchange costs either by a cash contribution or by 'offset purchases' of British equipment. Cash contributions were obtained to counterbalance expenditure in Germany in the years from 1955/6 to 1960/1;[4] thereafter the Germans helped by means of offset purchases. From 1961 to 1963 roughly half our foreign currency stationing costs were offset by German defence and other contracts. Thereafter the proportion increased, and in 1967/8 there were United States as well as German offset purchases. By 1968/9 about 90 per cent of our costs were offset, the sale of defence equipment playing a substantial part in this achievement.[5]

TAXATION OF OVERSEAS INVESTMENT INCOME

According to the National Plan, the tax system had tended to give too favourable a treatment to overseas compared with domestic investment.[6] This was emphasised by James Callaghan in his budget statement in 1965 in defence of some of the provisions of the new corporation tax which he was introducing. He said that the return we received from our long-term investments overseas was on average considerably less than the return on home investments, because income earned abroad bore tax in the country of origin, so that the benefit to the United Kingdom was measured by what remained after the payment of foreign taxes, whereas in the case of home investment the benefit to the national economy was measured by the return before tax.

---

[1] Ministry of Defence, *Statement on the Defence Estimates 1968*, Cmnd 3540, London, HMSO, 1968, pp. 2 and 3.

[2] Department of Economic Affairs, *The Task Ahead*, p. 49.

[3] Payments to United States manufacturers for military aircraft and missiles were only £2 million in 1964; they rose to £98 million in 1967 and £109 million in 1968, then declined to £61 million in 1969 and to only £20 million in total in the three years 1970–2 (CSO, *United Kingdom Balance of Payments 1963–73*, London, HMSO, 1974, p. 65).

[4] CSO, *United Kingdom Balance of Payments, 1972*, London, HMSO, 1972, p. 67.

[5] Ministry of Defence, *Statement on the Defence Estimates 1969*, Cmnd 3927, London, HMSO, 1969, p. 49.   [6] Department of Economic Affairs, *The National Plan*, p. 71.

His remedy for this state of affairs comprised three main changes. The first concerned portfolio investment overseas, where he proposed to phase out relief given to a British shareholder for 'underlying' tax – that is, tax levied by overseas governments on the *earnings* (not just the remitted dividends) of his foreign shareholdings.[1] The second change was relevant to direct overseas investment by British companies, and concerned the treatment of dividends paid by British companies out of overseas income; credit for overseas tax paid by the British company would be given only against the corporation tax for which the company was liable, not against the income tax due from a shareholder on his dividends. Thirdly, it was proposed to abolish the special tax treatment of overseas trade corporations, which had been introduced by the Conservative government in 1957.[2]

The Chancellor thought that his new corporation tax would, after the expiration of various transitional arrangements, improve the balance of payments, but by an amount which was 'not easy to quantify'. But he did attempt to quantify the benefit to the revenue, estimating that tax from companies with overseas income would ultimately be increased by about £100 million a year. In the next section we consider estimates of the combined effect on United Kingdom outward investment of the tax changes of 1965 and of various changes made in the 1960s in exchange controls on capital transactions.

EXCHANGE CONTROLS ON CAPITAL TRANSACTIONS

Until about 1969 changes in exchange controls were mostly designed to increase obstacles to capital outflows while avoiding discouragement to capital inflows. Then, with the desired improvement of the balance of payments in 1969, there was some relaxation of controls. In 1971 official policy also became less favourable to capital inflows; indeed, with the flight from the dollar precipitated by President Nixon's speech of 15 August,[3] there was a temporary imposition of completely new regulations to limit certain kinds of short-term capital inflows;[4] these were however repealed by the end of the year. The improvement in

---

[1] Relief on underlying tax continued where the shareholder was a British company owning 25 per cent or more of the shares in an overseas company.

[2] Overseas trade corporations are companies controlled and managed from this country, but having all their actual trading operations abroad. Since 1957 their trading profits earned abroad (though not, of course, dividends paid to British residents) had been free of United Kingdom tax.   [3] See page 315 above.

[4] From 27 August banks were not permitted to pay interest on any additional sterling deposits from non-sterling countries; also a prohibition was placed on sales to residents of those countries of sterling certificates of deposit or short-dated public sector securities, and on the accepting by local authorities of further deposits from non-sterling countries (*Midland Bank Review*, May 1972, pp. 22–3).

Britain's balance of payments proved, however, to be short-lived; in 1972 sterling was floated and exchange controls extended to the sterling area; in 1973 a number of new measures were adopted to increase capital inflows.

Oil and miscellaneous investment

United Kingdom official statistics, as shown in tables 7.5 and 7.10, distinguish three categories of overseas investment – 'direct', 'portfolio' and 'oil and miscellaneous'. Of these the last is mainly oil.[1] 'Miscellaneous' includes property investment, certain investments by the British insurance industry, London market borrowings by countries outside the sterling area and other minor items.

Sir Alec Cairncross has observed that oil investment continued throughout the 1960s at a remarkably stable rate, with no indication that exchange control was exercising much effect, despite changes in the regulations. There was also no marked divergence between the course of sterling and non-sterling investment.[2]

Portfolio investment outside the sterling area

Throughout the postwar period there have been restrictions on United Kingdom residents acquiring foreign exchange for the purchase of securities denominated in foreign currencies. Prior to 1957 they were permitted to buy such securities from residents of the overseas sterling area, but with the closing of the so-called 'Kuwait gap' in July 1957 sterling might not be used to make net purchases of foreign currency securities from residents outside the United Kingdom. United Kingdom residents have, however, enjoyed considerable freedom to switch from one foreign currency security to another. Moreover, United Kingdom investment trusts and some similar institutional investors have, since the latter part of the 1960s, been fairly readily permitted to buy such securities out of the proceeds of foreign currency borrowing.[3] United Kingdom investors, whether institutional or private, have also been permitted to trade freely among themselves in foreign currency

---

[1] According to CSO, *United Kingdom Balance of Payments 1964–74*, London, HMSO, 1975, table 20, United Kingdom overseas investment in 'oil and miscellaneous' totalled £1145 million in the ten years 1963–72 inclusive. In the same ten years other changes affecting the value of the United Kingdom's overseas 'oil and miscellaneous' assets amounted to an upward revaluation of £90 million (ibid. table 35). Hence the United Kingdom's overseas 'oil and miscellaneous' assets increased in the ten years by £1235 million. But 'oil' assets alone increased from £1100 million at the end of 1962 to £2250 million at the end of 1972 (ibid. table 35). Thus 'miscellaneous' increased by only £85 million.

[2] Sir Alec Cairncross, *Control of Long-term International Capital Movements, Washington* (D.C.) Brookings Institution, 1973, p. 67.

[3] As have also private investors from December 1970, when this permission was extended to 'professional managers of securities' on behalf of resident individual clients.

Table 7.5. *United Kingdom private investment outside the sterling area,[a] 1960–73*

£ million

	Direct investment[b] financed by:			Portfolio investment	Oil and miscellaneous investment	Total
	Unremitted profits[c]	Other means	Total			
1960	34	56	90	−24	55	121
61	38	64	102	−39	64	127
62	39	48	87	−34	39	92
63	47	54	101	13	43	157
64	49	53	102	28	82	212
65	66	56	122	−44	91	169
66	94	63	157	−44	49	162
67	95	44	139	18	73	230
68	157	76	233	79	61	373
69	171	65	236	13	44	293
1970	164	152	316	70	115	501
71	181	307	488	80	115	683
72	259	247	506	705	61	1272
73	437	726	1163	215	695	2073

SOURCES: CSO, *United Kingdom Balance of Payments 1971*, tables 26 and 29, and later figures from the CSO (by convention these sources give the figures with reversed signs from those above).

[a] Up to June 1972 the sterling area comprised the Commonwealth (except Canada), South Africa, the Irish Republic and a number of smaller contries. Membership is taken to be unchanged thereafter.

[b] Other than oil and miscellaneous. The item 'direct borrowing from financial subsidiaries abroad (net)' in table 7.6 is here treated as disinvestment.

[c] Profits of subsidiaries and associated companies.

securities, many of which (predominantly ones denominated in United States dollars) have been regularly quoted on the London Stock Exchange. The shortage of such securities relative to the demand for them has usually raised their sterling price in London to a premium over their dollar price in New York divided by the official sterling–dollar exchange rate. This premium, the so-called investment currency premium, rose to 40 per cent or even higher on occasions (chart 7.4).

Originally there were separate switching arrangements for securities denominated in dollars and those denominated in other foreign currencies, but the two categories were amalgamated in 1962 to form 'investment currency' and residents could then switch freely from one foreign currency security to another, provided that it was quoted.[1]

Further changes in the 1960s to the controls on outward portfolio investment were largely in the direction of greater restriction. As from

[1] *Bank of England Quarterly Bulletin*, vol. 7, September 1967, p. 256.

the budget of April 1965, 25 per cent of the proceeds of all sales of foreign currency securities, including sales abroad for the purpose of switching investments, had to be sold on the official exchange market, leaving only 75 per cent available for sale as investment currency (at a premium) or for reinvestment. At the same time United Kingdom residents were no longer allowed to use investment currency to buy property outside the sterling area for private use, as had been permissible since April 1964; instead they had to purchase foreign currency

Chart 7.4. *The investment currency premium, 1961–72*

SOURCES: Bank of England, *Statistical Abstract*, no. 1, table 28, and no. 2, table 28.

in a separate 'property currency' market.[1] Then in May 1966 a 'voluntary programme' restricted institutional portfolio investment in the non-sterling area as well as in the four developed countries of the overseas sterling area: institutional investors were asked to ensure that any such investment did no more than balance their disinvestment and foreign currency borrowing. The intention of this restriction was presumably to depress the investment currency premium, and hence to encourage the 'bleeding' of the investment currency pool for financing *direct* investment; as from May 1962 British companies had been permitted to draw on the pool for this purpose.

    In 1969 and 1970 there were minor easements in controls: in the

[1] Ibid. pp. 258–9.

1969 budget institutional portfolio investment outside the sterling area was exempted from the voluntary programme, and in August 1970 the property currency pool was once again merged with the investment currency pool.

What effect can be attributed to official actions in the 1960s aimed at discouraging portfolio investment outside the sterling area? The changes in tax arrangements and in exchange controls made by James Callaghan in April 1965 and in May 1966 were not followed by any sustained decrease in such investment, as may be seen from the fourth column of table 7.5. There was admittedly an excess of disinvestment over investment in 1965 and 1966, but this had also occurred in the three years 1960–2, and after 1966 the balance was always in the opposite direction.

Table 7.6. *Methods of financing direct investment^a outside the sterling area, 1967–72*

£ million

	1967	1968	1969	1970	1971	1972
Eurocurrency borrowing by parent companies from UK banks	35	64	48	138	133	87
Direct borrowing abroad by parent companies	39	46	46	68	97	162
Direct borrowing from financial subsidiaries abroad (net)^b	..	23	32	17	61	57
Use of investment currency pool (net)	5	−28	−15	−5	−12	−29
Total	..	105	111	218	279	277

SOURCES: CSO, *United Kingdom Balance of Payments 1971*, table 49, *1972*, table 47, and *1963–73*, table 47.

^{a} Excluding 'oil and miscellaneous'.
^{b} Treated as outward disinvestment in table 7.5.

This net disinvestment in the five years cannot be explained in detail, since the necessary statistics are lacking in the first half of the 1960s, but part of the explanation is that as from May 1962 the investment currency pool could be drawn upon to finance direct investment. However, drawings on the pool for this purpose were not serious as from 1967, when the relevant statistical series starts (table 7.6) – indeed from 1968 direct investment and disinvestment have on balance made a net contribution to the pool. More serious was the bleeding of the investment currency pool by the 25 per cent surrender scheme (table 7.7). Hence the question arises why it was possible for portfolio investment not merely to equal but to exceed portfolio disinvestment, as

Table 7.7. *Yield to United Kingdom official reserves of the 25 per cent surrender scheme, 1965–72*

£ million

	From net sales through investment currency market of:		Other	Total yield
	Portfolio investments	Direct investments		
1965[a]	56	−21	18	53
66	69	3	−2	70
67	58	−2	32	88
68	59	38	7	104
69	126	21	−38	109
1970	52	9	26	87
71	130		−2	128
72	162		−24	138

SOURCE: CSO, *United Kingdom Balance of Payments 1973*, table 25, and *1965–75*, table 20.

[a] Excluding the first quarter.

happened regularly from 1967 onwards. The main answer must be foreign borrowing by institutional investors,[1] and this is broadly confirmed by official statistics of foreign currency borrowing for portfolio investment (see table 7.8).

Table 7.8. *Foreign currency borrowing to finance portfolio investment, 1967–73*

£ million

	Borrowing	Repayments
1967	38·0	—
68	85·0	—
69	96·1	22·2
1970	52·9	3·5
71	111·9	7·5
72	696·7	37·6
73	373·5	221·7[a]

SOURCE: Bank of England.

[a] Excludes £35·6 million repayments with investment currency.

[1] Foreign securities bought with foreign currency borrowing can be switched at will or sold to repay the loan. In either case the transactions do not involve the purchase or sale of sterling; hence the investment currency premium does not apply, nor does the 25 per cent surrender scheme.

Direct (non-oil) investment outside the sterling area

There was a gradual easing of the restrictions on overseas direct investment in the 1950s and by 1956 practically no outward investment which could show a reasonable economic advantage was refused. However, in July 1961 restrictions were tightened on direct investment (other than 'oil and miscellaneous') in countries outside the sterling area and from then on investment qualified for official exchange only if it would yield commensurate benefits to the balance of payments within two or three years.[1] Companies which could not comply with this criterion were, however, permitted to borrow foreign currency to finance their overseas investment. Prior to July 1961 there had been no provision for such borrowing, but thereafter 'long-term' borrowing was permitted for 'non-criterion' projects. By 'long-term' the authorities generally had in mind a period in excess of five years, although in the case of very long-term loans – ten to fifteen years – repayments might start before five years. In any case, however, borrowing could not be repaid except to the extent that benefits from the investment had been received by the United Kingdom in the forms of exports to countries outside the sterling area, of interest, dividends and profits, or of royalties, licence fees, management fees and other payments for technical 'know-how'.

To alleviate the difficulties of companies unable to borrow in foreign currency, it was conceded in May 1962 that direct investment which did not satisfy the July 1961 criterion for finance at the official exchange rate might be financed through the investment currency market at the cost of paying the current premium (then around 3 per cent). This minor easement was, however, followed by changes in the opposite direction in 1965 and 1966. In the first place the 25 per cent surrender scheme introduced in April 1965 was applied to all transactions which could give rise to investment currency, including sales of direct investments outside the sterling area. At the same time the July 1961 criterion for access to foreign exchange at the official rate was tightened up: the extra conditions imposed were that the project must bring a substantial continuing return to the balance of payments and that there should be good prospects that the overall return to the balance of payments would, in the short term, equal or exceed the capital outflow. Where official exchange was denied, investment continued to be financed with investment currency or by long-term borrowing abroad.

Soon after, in July 1965, it was laid down that even projects satisfying the April 1965 criteria could no longer be financed by foreign currency acquired at the official rate, and in May 1966 the same criteria were

[1] *Bank of England Quarterly Bulletin*, vol. 7, September 1967, p. 258.

applied for access to investment currency; henceforth all non-criterion projects had to be financed from foreign currency borrowing.[1] In January 1968 there was a slight easement: the ban imposed in July 1965 was lifted in the case of direct investment outside the sterling area for so-called 'super-criterion' projects; foreign exchange was henceforth obtainable at the official rate for projects directly concerned with promoting British exports up to a limit of £50,000 or half the investment (whichever was the greater) provided that there was a net benefit to the balance of payments within eighteen months and continuing thereafter. This meant that from January 1968 there were three kinds of direct investment project:

(a) 'super-criterion' projects, which could wholly or in part be financed with foreign exchange bought at the official rate;

(b) 'criterion' projects, satisfying the criteria laid down in April 1965, which could be financed only with foreign exchange borrowed 'long-term' abroad, or purchased (more expensively than at the official rate) in the investment currency market;

(c) 'non-criterion' projects, which (if authorised at all) could only be financed by 'long-term' foreign currency borrowing.

In 1971, when the balance of payments had temporarily ceased to be a problem, there were several further easements. From March, categories (b) and (c) were amalgamated, so that *all* projects which did not meet the super-criterion (as well as those that did), could be financed via the investment currency market (as an alternative to borrowing abroad) and from May the upper limit for the finance of 'super-criterion' projects by foreign exchange purchased at the official rate was raised from £50,000 to £250,000. Moreover, in the 1971 budget the previous requirement that foreign currency borrowing had to be 'long-term' was relaxed by permitting 'self-liquidating' borrowing; that is, borrowing might be repaid as soon as it could be shown that equivalent benefits had been received in the United Kingdom from the investment. Then in the 1972 budget statement a further easement was announced in respect of British companies making direct investment in EEC countries, Denmark or Norway.[2]

With the benefit of hindsight and *ex post* statistics, it now seems that neither the tightening of exchange controls on direct outward investment in countries outside the sterling area from July 1961 nor the fiscal discouragement in the 1965 budget had the effect of reversing the rising trend in such investment in the 1960s, or of tilting downwards the more or less level trend in the amount financed otherwise than out of unremitted profits (this is clear from table 7.5); nor to any great

[1] Ibid.
[2] This easement was withdrawn in March 1974.

extent did they result in direct investment being financed through the investment currency pool (at least from 1967, see table 7.6). But (not unexpectedly) the tightening of controls was associated with substantial non-sterling borrowing to finance direct investment outside the sterling area (as also shown in table 7.6).

Would the upward trend of direct investment (excluding oil) outside the sterling area have been much steeper in the absence of restrictions and of fiscal deterrents? Sir Alec Cairncross thinks probably not.[1] As we see from table 7.5, the rising trend in the 1960s was roughly matched by a similar increase in unremitted profits, which could in practice be fairly readily applied to financing further investment. The official restriction which applied to such financing was the 'normal' requirement that at least two thirds of after-tax profits should be repatriated, but official statistics show a ratio of much less than two thirds, indeed as little as 46 per cent in the five years 1963–7 and 39 per cent in the following five years.[2]

This is largely because exchange control applies only to companies where voting control lies within the UK, whereas the balance of payments statistics include also figures for earnings of overseas companies where the UK interest is a minority; and because remittances of royalties, management fees and certain other earnings count towards the two thirds requirement, while stock appreciation is generally disregarded in calculating earnings.[3]

Would the amount of direct investment *not* financed out of unremitted profits have shown a rising (instead of a roughly level) trend in the 1960s if tax arrangements and exchange controls had been left unchanged? In Sir Alec's view the figures suggest that the criterion introduced in July 1961 for access to official exchange cannot have been applied very restrictively. This is supported by the fact that the permission given in May 1962 to use the investment currency market led neither to an upsurge of direct investment nor to an increase in the investment currency premium to much more than 10 per cent. As from April 1965 access to both the official and the investment currency markets was progressively tightened and the premium rose much higher, but by then the practice of borrowing overseas to finance direct investment developed very rapidly and restricted access to the currency markets was no insuperable obstacle.[4]

[1] Cairncross, *Control of Long-term International Capital Movements.*
[2] CSO, *United Kingdom Balance of Payments 1963–73*, table 20. The figures relate to British companies' subsidiary and associated companies in the non-sterling area.
[3] Treasury, *Economic Progress Report*, no. 78, September 1976, p. 1.
[4] Cairncross, *Control of Long-term International Capital Movements*, pp. 63–5.

Overseas borrowing to finance overseas investment

The considerable scale of non-sterling borrowing for outward investment, including 'oil and miscellaneous' as well as 'portfolio' and
'direct' (table 7.9), resulted in a state of affairs in which the grand total
of British private investment outside the sterling area was financed in
the second half of the 1960s without leading to any drain on official
reserves. This is clear from the second column of the same table.
Moreover, the weight of evidence appears to support the view that
British investors who had access to facilities for foreign currency
borrowing were not greatly restrained in their overseas investment
outside the sterling area by exchange controls. On this view, the only
important category of overseas investment that was discouraged (to
the extent of becoming substantially negative) was portfolio investment
by private individuals, who were only permitted to borrow abroad for
this purpose as from December 1970.[1]

Table 7.9. *Financing of net private overseas investment outside
the scheduled territories,[a] 1965–73*

£ million

	Borrowing in foreign currency	Effect on total currency inflow
1965	78	21
66	47	21
67	133	55
68	231	4
69	163	44
1970	265	20
71	388	−53
72	980	201
73	869	26

SOURCE: CSO, *United Kingdom Balance of Payments 1965–75*, table 20.

[a] Up to 23 June 1972 the scheduled territories were the sterling area; thereafter they were
the British Isles (see page 337 below).

This outcome seems to have been broadly in line with the objectives
of government policy. It was reliably reported that the aim of
Callaghan's changes in tax and exchange control arrangements in 1965
was an improvement of £150 million a year in the net balance of the
private capital account.[2] At the time it was accepted, and even

[1] See footnote 3 on page 326 above.
[2] H. F. R. Catherwood, *Britain with the Brakes Off*, London, Hodder & Stoughton, 1966,
p. 124.

expected, that this could be achieved only by a reduction in the overall level or the rate of growth of such investment. But after the middle of the 1960s, and increasingly from about 1968 onwards, it was apparent to the authorities that British companies were readily able to find international sources of finance; this was, of course, linked with the development of the Euromarkets. The most immediate effect was to make foreign currency borrowing the major basis of financing direct investment and to make it possible to authorise foreign currency borrowing for institutional portfolio investment. Certainly in the last two or three years of the decade the objective of the authorities was no longer to limit overseas investment, but only to ensure that its financing did not impose a strain on the balance of payments; overseas investment which met this requirement was not discouraged.

Investment in the overseas sterling area

Up to May 1966 the British exchange control imposed no impediments to capital movements within the sterling area, except (as from July 1957) in the case of foreign currency securities. However, this did not imply that companies from the overseas sterling area could freely make capital issues on the London market, since there was all the time a control on all overseas capital issues and this has always been highly restrictive. On the other hand, up to May 1966 there was no restriction on United Kingdom portfolio investment in securities issued in the overseas sterling area, nor on bank credit or trade credit to the overseas sterling area, nor on direct investment by British companies in branches, subsidiaries, or associated companies in the overseas sterling area.

Measures taken in May 1966 modified these rules in respect of Australia, New Zealand, South Africa and the Irish Republic. British companies which had plans for direct investment in these sterling area countries which did not satisfy the criteria applied outside the sterling area were asked if the plans could be postponed for the time being; or if that was not practicable, whether finance could be raised from local sources. In addition, institutional investors were asked to refrain from any significant increase in their portfolios of securities in the four countries as well as in all countries outside the sterling area.[1] This 'voluntary programme' was in principle only temporary, but it was renewed from time to time until its termination was announced in the 1972 budget statement.

What was the effect on the United Kingdom balance of payments of the voluntary programme? The Chancellor's statement answered this question in a roundabout way, which the National Institute took to imply that he was hoping for an improvement of perhaps £35 million

[1] *Bank of England Quarterly Bulletin*, vol. 7, September 1967, pp. 259 and 260.

a year.[1] Whether such a saving was in fact achieved cannot be established with any confidence. The relevant official statistics (see table 7.10) do not reveal any sustained discouragement of portfolio investment, either by the budget of April 1965 or by the voluntary programme of May 1966. The statistics do show, in the case of direct investment net of unremitted profits, a run of relatively low annual amounts in 1966–8, but this may have been fortuitous; the 1969 and 1970 figures are higher, despite the fact that tax arrangements continued unchanged and that the voluntary programme remained in operation until April 1972. Thus the *ex post* evidence is inconclusive.

Table 7.10. *United Kingdom private investment in the overseas sterling area,[a] 1960–73*

£ million

	Direct investment[b] financed by:			Portfolio investment	Oil and miscellaneous investment	Total
	Unremitted profits[c]	Other means	Total			
1960	51	109	160	−13	54	201
61	36	88	124	11	51	186
62	56	66	122	−5	33	150
63	71	64	135	−8	36	163
64	98	63	161	−25	51	187
65	101	85	186	−50	63	199
66	89	30	119	−39	61	141
67	95	47	142	41	43	226
68	120	57	177	157	20	354
69	150	163	313	21	52	386
1970	157	73	230	20	35	285
71	148	39	187	−60	25	152
72	208	23	231	−120	—	111
73	410	51	461	−510	−165	−214

SOURCES: CSO, *United Kingdom Balance of Payments 1971*, tables 26 and 29, and later figures from the CSO (by convention these sources give the figures with reversed signs from those above).

[a] Membership of the sterling area taken as unchanged from June 1972.
[b] Other than oil and miscellaneous.
[c] Profits of subsidiaries and associated companies.

In June 1972, when sterling was allowed to float, exchange control was extended to transactions with the sterling area almost as strictly as to countries outside the area.[2] According to Anthony Barber the

[1] *National Institute Economic Review*, no. 36, May 1966, pp. 7–8.
[2] Concessions for investment in the overseas sterling area which remained operative until March 1974 were exemption from the 25 per cent surrender rule for portfolio investment (so that 100 per cent of the overseas currency proceeds of disposals of overseas sterling area securities could be sold at a premium in the investment currency market) and permission

two decisions were related, because a speculative outflow to these countries might follow the float; he announced that pending consultation with the governments concerned he had taken immediate temporary measures to apply exchange control to transactions with the sterling area.[1] However, one is left in some doubt as to whether the two decisions can have been so closely linked; the Chancellor offered no evidence that floating would be likely to provoke a speculative capital outflow to the overseas sterling area, nor have the restrictions he imposed been only temporary.

As a result of the new restrictions, the scheduled territories (the area in which exchange control permitted free capital movements) were reduced from the whole of the sterling area to the British Isles (plus Gibraltar from January 1973). Thus, at last, the step was taken which had been advocated by Day and Shonfield in the 1950s. Since that time the course of events had made the case for it more persuasive, quite apart from the temporary reason adduced by Barber. The whole idea of privileges to the sterling area (other than the Irish Republic) was difficult to reconcile with membership of the EEC; this had been realised as early as 1961. Freedom to invest in the overseas sterling area was also seen as inconsistent with our determination, dating from 1961, to be more discriminating in our official attitude to overseas investment. There had been a heavy capital outflow to Australia and South Africa in 1968 and 1969, which suggested that the 1966 voluntary programme was not very restrictive. This may explain why the programme was abandoned in the budget statement of 1972, only to be replaced by tighter control at the next convenient opportunity.

We have not yet assessed the effect of extending exchange controls to the overseas sterling area and thereby bringing investment in these countries within the scope of the investment currency pool. However, it is probably one of the reasons for the massive portfolio disinvestment in the overseas sterling area in 1973 (table 7.10). The proceeds of such disinvestment could be sold at a premium in the investment currency market (the 25 per cent surrender rule not being applied to the sterling area until March 1974) to finance investment in the non-sterling area, which in 1972 and again in 1973 reached record heights (table 7.5).

Measures to increase the capital inflow

In January 1968 the government adopted a policy of financing our balance of payments deficit by encouraging the nationalised industries and local authorities to borrow in non-sterling currencies. This policy

for all direct investment in the overseas sterling area approved by the British authorities to be financed by buying overseas currency at the official rate.

[1] Treasury, *Economic Progress Report*, no. 30, August 1972.

was implemented by introducing forward exchange cover, given by the Treasury, for dollar borrowing by public sector bodies. However, in July 1971, with the improvement in the balance of payments, the cover was restricted to maturities of ten years or more, and at the time of the 1972 budget it was withdrawn altogether.

In March 1973 foreign exchange cover facilities were reintroduced in respect of dollar borrowing by public sector institutions and in October they were extended to other currencies. Much the biggest public sector borrower in 1973 was the Electricity Council, which raised a dollar loan of $1000 million; the total of all public sector non-sterling borrowing in 1973 net of repayments was $2600 million.[1]

Private sector foreign currency borrowing to finance domestic investment was, like public sector borrowing, affected by the improvement in the balance of payments in 1971 and by its subsequent deterioration. In January 1971 a ban was imposed on such borrowing for domestic use by United Kingdom firms with a maturity of less than five years, but in October 1973 the minimum maturity was reduced from five to two years.[2]

EXPORT PROMOTION AND IMPORT-SAVING

Throughout the 1950s a great deal of help, advice and information on selling abroad was available to firms from government sources through the Export Services Branch and the regional offices of the Board of Trade, and through the commercial officers of the Diplomatic Service; credit insurance for exports was available through the Export Credit Guarantee Department (ECGD). In 1964 the Labour government introduced a number of additional measures to promote exports, some of them aimed particularly at smaller firms. The export rebate scheme was introduced,[3] credit insurance facilities were greatly improved and a list of some 400 established exporters willing to help firms making complementary products to export was published – the so-called 'pick-a-back' scheme. Government finance was made available through the British National Export Council to encourage selling missions abroad and buying missions to Britain, and to support collective market research. A study was made of the feasibility of setting up 'a new form of export selling organisation which will give special attention to the needs of those smaller companies which at present export either very little or not at all'.[4] The evolution of the Export Credit Guarantee Department's facilities for medium-term export

---

[1] *Bank of England Quarterly Bulletin*, vol. 16, March 1976, p. 80.
[2] *Financial Times*, 19 October 1973.
[3] See below page 344.
[4] Department of Economic Affairs, *The National Plan*, p. 73.

credit and of the various other arrangements made between the Bank of England and the commercial banks to improve the credit facilities available to British exporters (and subsequently to British shipbuilders) is set out below in appendix II. The increase in medium-term and long-term credit extended under ECGD guarantees is shown in table 7.11.

Table 7.11. *Increase in medium-term and long-term export credit extended under ECGD guarantees, 1965–73*

£ million

	Buyer credit schemes	Bank guarantees	
		Specific	Comprehensive
1965	42	− 1	—
66	37	28	—
67	77	34	41
68	116	37	53
69	125	77	40
1970	150	119	62
71	229	124	25
72	259	53	10
73	259	− 5	45

SOURCE: CSO, *United Kingdom Balance of Payments 1965–75*, table 22 (by convention this source gives the figures with reversed signs from those above).

Among these new arrangements for export promotion, there was at least one failure: the Overseas Marketing Corporation Limited (which was the 'new form of export selling organisation') did not achieve the expected results and was wound up at the end of 1970 at a loss to the taxpayer of £½ million.[1]

Turning now to import-saving, the National Plan of 1965 refers to 'measures to reduce the growth of manufactured imports';[2] on this issue the Economic Development Committees had already set in hand action to save imports in their fields.[3] Specific mention was made of the work of the Economic Development Committees for machine tools, chemicals and mechanical engineering, and to a Report by the NEDC.[4]

The progress made in import-saving over the subsequent four years or so by the three named industries may be judged from Reports by

[1] Report of the Comptroller and Auditor General in Treasury, *Appropriation Accounts 1972–73* (Classes I–V, Civil), London, HMSO, 1974, pp. xvi and xvii.
[2] Department of Economic Affairs, *The National Plan*, p. 73.
[3] Ibid. p. 46.
[4] NEDC, *Imported Manufactures: an inquiry into competitiveness*, London, HMSO, 1965.

their Economic Development Committees.[1] The impression left is that there were only modest achievements to record and that such as there were owe little to government policy. The share of imports in the home market showed little sign of falling: in machine tools, it was 26 per cent in 1960–5, but seemed 'likely to account for 30 per cent of total home consumption in 1972'; in chemicals, imports were 'expected to continue to grow at $11\frac{1}{2}$ per cent a year', or considerably faster than the rate suggested by the Department of Economic Affairs in 1969 in *The Task Ahead*; in mechanical engineering, imports in 1971 and 1972 were expected to increase at less than the past trend rate, but this had been about 10 per cent a year at constant prices. The only decisive intervention by the government in manufacturing industry in the interests of import-saving was not in any of the three industries specifically mentioned, but in respect of three new smelters in the aluminium industry.

OFFICIAL TRANSACTIONS IN THE FORWARD MARKET

The traditional instrument for discouraging a capital outflow from London and encouraging an inflow was to increase Bank Rate, which raised the level of short-term interest rates prevailing in London relative to those in other countries. But, as the Radcliffe Committee reported in 1959: 'The general tenor of the evidence submitted to us was that in post-war conditions no large-scale transference of funds was to be expected in response to changes in short-term interest rates unsupported by other measures. Two important influences limiting this response have been fear of official interference with the movement of funds and fear of depreciation of sterling.' In consequence, 'such movement of funds as there has been has almost always, at least until lately, been covered in the forward exchange market; that is to say, the foreign holder of sterling has generally taken the precaution of selling it forward at a discount so as to avoid any larger loss through a possible devaluation of the pound.'[2]

If, however, all short-term investment in London is so covered, in the absence of official support in the forward market there will be a rapid fall in the forward value of sterling to the point where covered investment in London is no more profitable than elsewhere. The monetary authorities can, however, maintain the attractiveness of London by supporting the forward pound, and this is what two witnesses to the

[1] NEDO, *Industrial Report by the Chemicals EDC on the Economic Assessment to 1972*, *Industrial Report by the Machine Tools EDC on the Economic Assessment to 1972* and *Industrial Report by the Mechanical Engineering EDC on the Economic Assessment to 1972*, London, 1970.

[2] Treasury, *Radcliffe Report*, para. 697.

Radcliffe Committee recommended should regularly be done.[1] Jasay's evidence recommended official support for the forward rate as a means of making sterling assets adequately attractive *in yield* to investors who have the option of investing in other currencies; his point is that many such investors are (as the Radcliffe Committee believed) interested in comparing covered yields, so that a forward discount on sterling reduces its attraction no less than an unfavourable interest-rate differential. Spraos, on the other hand, had in mind the need to protect the official reserves from a 'speculative attack' on sterling, conducted by transactors seeking to make a capital gain or avoid a capital loss. The Radcliffe Committee's findings gave support (though not very strong support) to the case for forward intervention, but only as a means of retaining a steady clientele of investors in sterling, not as a means of meeting a speculative attack.

The Committee did not spell out its reasons for rejecting the argument put to it by Spraos. It is, however, reasonable to suppose that their view was akin to that of Oppenheimer, who maintained that, in the face of speculation against the pound, the authorities had the choice between holding spot sterling near to its $2.80 parity either by buying it spot or by buying it forward, and that there was not much to choose as between the two.[2] The case put to the Committee by Jasay was more persuasive since, insofar as investors require forward cover, the yield they get on their sterling investments incorporates the difference between the spot and forward rate; thus, if the latter is not officially supported, a flow of covered investment into sterling will quickly widen the difference to the point at which the covered yield on sterling assets becomes unattractive.

The Treasury's oral evidence to the Radcliffe Committee argued 'that there is bound to be at times some participation by the Exchange Equalisation Account in the forward market. But that is quite a different thing from having a definite policy of supporting the rate, which would cast great doubt, which does not exist at present, over the value of the published figures'.[3] And this seems to represent official policy up to the time of the prolonged sterling crisis which began in November

---

[1] A. E. Jasay, 'Alternative ways of defending the exchange rate' in Radcliffe Committee, *Principal Memoranda of Evidence*, vol. 3, p. 132; J. Spraos, 'Speculation, arbitrage and sterling', *Economic Journal*, vol. 69, March 1959.

[2] Spraos would not accept that there is 'not much to choose', since if the authorities support the spot rate the amount of support needed is revealed in the published figures for official reserves, whereas the amount of forward support is never published. It can therefore be argued that bear speculation against sterling is encouraged more by the knowledge that official support has been needed to hold the spot rate than by the suspicion that official support has been needed to hold the forward rate.

Oppenheimer's views are quoted on page 342, below.

[3] Radcliffe Committee, *Minutes of Evidence*, reply to question 9704.

1964. Thereafter, however, until the devaluation of sterling in November 1967, the Exchange Equalisation Account intervened to prevent the forward rate falling to a serious discount,[1] and the intervention is believed to have been on some occasions on a massive scale.[2]

Thus, there was in November 1964 an important change in official tactics in the forward market. Oppenheimer, writing in February 1966, was clearly rather unhappy about the change of policy, but conceded that 'the authorities did keep some short-term money in London by dint of accumulating vast forward commitments. But they might easily have borrowed more from the central banks instead. In effect, they used part of the central-bank credit arrangements to back their forward commitments. It is these arrangements that were in every way the decisive factor. Forward intervention did not make a great deal of difference'.[3] However, he obviously thought that the authorities had been lucky in 1964/5 and might not be equally so in the future; in the event his misgivings were vindicated in the crisis of 1967, when the support operation failed and the authorities were forced to devalue. On that occasion a policy initially adopted to retain a loyal clientele of foreign investors ended up, in the weeks preceding devaluation, by affording unlimited facilities for bear speculation at the expense of the Exchange Equalisation Account. Moreover, it is difficult to see how this outcome could have been avoided, given that the policy of support had been adopted and become known to market operators. Any subsequent withdrawal of support would have been interpreted as a sure sign that the authorities were no longer committed to avoiding devaluation, and the resulting flight from the pound would have forced the immediate abandonment of the $2.80 peg. After devaluation the Account apparently reverted to its earlier policy of severely limiting its intervention in the forward market.[4]

---

[1] *Bank of England Quarterly Bulletin*, vol. 10, March 1970, p. 39.

[2] The CSO's *United Kingdom Balance of Payments 1972*, p. 7, quotes figures for 'EEA loss on forward commitments' amounting to £105 million in 1967 and £251 million in 1968, or £356 million in total. We are also informed (p. 78) that 'this item records the loss arising from the fact that the forward commitments of the Exchange Equalisation Account with the market entered into before devaluation in 1967 have been recorded as being settled on maturity at the new parity'. Since the parity fell by $\frac{1}{7}$, the implication is that at the time of devaluation the Account had outstanding forward commitments to the tune of $5981 million (the devaluation loss of $\frac{1}{7} = $854 million being £356 million at $2.40).

[3] P. M. Oppenheimer, 'Forward exchange intervention: the official view', *Westminster Bank Review*, February 1966, p. 13.

[4] *Bank of England Quarterly Bulletin*, vol. 10, March 1970, p. 39.

PALLIATIVES AFFECTING THE CURRENT BALANCE

Four of the devices used in the 1960s to improve the external balance raised the issue of whether they were compatible with our obligations under the IMF Charter and GATT. They were the travel allowance, the export rebate, the import surcharge and the import deposit scheme.

The travel allowance

Postwar restrictions on expenditure on personal travel abroad had been removed by the end of the 1950s, but they were reimposed in the second half of the 1960s. In July 1966 a basic travel allowance of only £50 a year was introduced for travel in countries outside the sterling area, to operate as from 1 November. A waiver from the IMF was obtained for this restriction, which remained in force until January 1970, when the allowance was raised from £50 a year to the virtually unrestrictive ceiling of £300 a trip. The National Institute, in noting the lifting of the restriction, estimated the effect on the balance of payments in 1970 as something like £40 million, a rather higher figure than that of

Chart 7.5. *The share of overseas travel in consumers' expenditure, 1952–75*

SOURCES: CSO, *United Kingdom Balance of Payments 1965–75*, table 2, and *National Income and Expenditure 1965–75*, table 1.1.

£25 million suggested by official spokesmen.[1] In retrospect, chart 7.5 strongly suggests that the trend of the share of travel in consumers'

---

[1] *National Institute Economic Review*, no. 51, February 1970, p. 30.

expenditure was deflected by the travel allowance; had the curve followed an horizontal path, corresponding to the actual value of travel debits in 1970 as a percentage of consumption, the total difference in travel debits over the three years 1967–9 would have been some £125 million. This must not, of course, be regarded as an estimate, even an approximate one, of the improvement in the balance of payments achieved by the imposition of the travel allowance, since the measure may well have affected expenditure on things other than overseas travel, and thereby have, directly or indirectly, affected other kinds of external transactions.

The export rebate

The export rebate, introduced in October 1964 and repealed at the end of March 1968, provided for the refund of certain indirect taxes on exports to a value of about 2 per cent of total exports or somewhat more than £80 million a year. It was expected that about £10 million would go to the motor industry, £5½ million to the electrical machinery industry and £1 million to the whisky industry.[1] Its ostensible purpose was to recompense exporters for otherwise unrebated indirect taxes, in particular the hydro-carbon duties, paid on goods 'incorporated' in the products exported. Since we maintained that it was a rebate and not an export subsidy, we were able to claim that it did not contravene our obligations under GATT; all the same it was very unpopular with other parties to GATT and hence was repealed when, thanks to devaluation, it was no longer considered a necessary palliative for our external deficit.

The import surcharge

A temporary surcharge of 15 per cent on the value of imports of most manufactured and semi-manufactured goods was introduced in October 1964. Following strong representations from other countries, especially members of EFTA, it was reduced to 10 per cent in April 1965; in May 1966 the termination of the scheme was announced, and the surcharge duly ended on the last day of November 1966.

The surcharge was undoubtedly in breach of our obligations under GATT, which provides that a country in balance of payments difficulties may temporarily impose quantitative restrictions on imports, but not what was in effect a temporary tariff. Nevertheless the United Kingdom's action was not without precedent, in that Canada had imposed a similar surcharge from June 1962 to April 1963. The action was all the same strongly criticised by other contracting parties.

The imposition of a temporary import surcharge might be expected

---

[1] Department of Economic Affairs, *The National Plan*, pp. 72–3.

to exert at least three distinct effects upon the value of the import bill. First, its temporary nature might have induced some overseas suppliers to shade their prices, thus absorbing part of the surcharge and correspondingly improving the United Kingdom's terms of trade. Secondly, one would expect it to lead to some reduction in the volume of imports. Thirdly, the explicitly temporary nature of the scheme might have exerted some temporary, reversible effects on consumption and purchase of imports for stock, any reduction being made good after the removal of the surcharge. There is, in addition, a tax effect on real disposable incomes to the extent that the surcharge is passed on in higher prices; but this effect has been neglected here, on the grounds that it is shared by other instruments of fiscal policy and is not peculiar to the surcharge *per se.*

Post-mortems have concentrated almost exclusively upon the substitution effects of the scheme; however, the terms of trade effect was not entirely negligible. Cooper notes, for example, that the government of the Irish Republic refunded half the surcharge to its exporters[1] and, from the reaction of the import unit value index for manufactures to the removal of the surcharge, it would seem that suppliers may have absorbed something like 2–3 per cent of the surcharge rate. On this basis, the United Kingdom would have gained something like £40–£50 million per annum from the surcharge by way of an improvement in her terms of trade.

Table 7.12 compares various estimates of the surcharge effect and indicates which method was used to arrive at the result. First there is the 'residuals method', where the technique is to estimate an equation in the demand for imports prior to the surcharge period, and then to forecast with it over the surcharge period using the equation residuals as an estimate of the surcharge effect. In order to deduce an elasticity of demand from the residuals some allowance must be made for the reversible stock effects and for absorption by suppliers of part of the surcharge. The second method is the 'dummy variable' approach, in which the surcharge effect may be identified with the coefficient of a dummy variable in an import demand equation; further modifications are again required to arrive at an estimate of the operative elasticity of demand. The third method employs direct estimates of the elasticity of demand, together with a calculation of the effect of the surcharge on prices, to derive a surcharge effect which, *a priori*, excludes the reversible stock fluctuations. All the methods have disadvantages, but the last is possibly the most satisfactory.

The figures in table 7.12 are on a variety of different price bases, but there is not much difference between them and 'current' prices for

[1] R. N. Cooper, 'The balance of payments' in Caves *et al.*, *Britain's Economic Prospects*.

Table 7.12. *Estimates of the effect of the 1964 import surcharge*

	Price base		Method used	
		Residuals	Dummy variable	Price elasticity
			(£ million)	
Johnston and Henderson ⎫		⎧100–150	n.a.	n.a.
Black, Kidgell and Ray ⎬ 1958		⎨ 200	350	n.a.
Burns ⎭		⎩300–364	230–300	n.a.
Barker[a]	1960	134	n.a.	462
Treasury[b]	1961	200	330	n.a.
NIESR ⎫ 1963		⎧ n.a.	390	n.a.
Fane and Whitley[c] ⎭		⎩ n.a.	n.a.	200

SOURCES: Johnston and Henderson, 'Assessing the effects of the import surcharge'; I. G. Black, J. E. Kidgell and G. F. Ray, 'Forecasting imports: a re-examination', *National Institute Economic Review*, no. 42, November 1967; T. Burns, 'An econometric analysis of UK imports 1959–68' (London Graduate Business School discussion paper), 1969; T. S. Barker, 'Aggregation error and estimates of the UK import demand function' in Hilton and Heathfield (eds.), *The Econometric Study of the United Kingdom*; NIESR, 'The effects of the devaluation of 1967 on the current balance of payments'; Treasury, *The Determination of UK Imports* by Rees and Layard; Fane and Whitley, 'Imports of goods and services'.

[a] Assumed elasticities $-1 \cdot 1$ for manufactures, $-1 \cdot 43$ for semi-manufactures.
[b] Assumed elasticities:

	Finished capital goods	Semi-manufactures	Consumer goods
Initial	$-0 \cdot 9$	$-0 \cdot 9$	$-0 \cdot 8$
Under surcharge	$-1 \cdot 3$	$-1 \cdot 2$	$-1 \cdot 8$

[c] Assumed elasticity $-0 \cdot 68$ for all goods.

the period of the surcharge; thus, the multipliers to be attached to the figures to bring them to a current price basis (average for 1965/6) appear to vary only within the range of approximately $1 \cdot 05$ to $1 \cdot 10$, so they can reasonably be compared with each other as they stand.

The estimates by Johnston and Henderson are among the lowest.[1] Cooper, who included in his presentation of the Johnston–Henderson results some credit for what appears to be a reversible stock run-down effect at the end of 1966 and thus inflated the result, suggested that the implied elasticities (0·8 for 1965, 0·5 for 1966) were unexpectedly low,[2] and the original authors themselves concluded their investigation by speculating on why the substitution effect was so weak. Most of the remaining estimates give grounds for thinking that the elasticities may

[1] J. Johnston and M. Henderson, 'Assessing the effects of the import surcharge', *Manchester School of Economic and Social Studies*, vol. 35, May 1967.
[2] Cooper, 'The balance of payments'.

have been rather higher than implied by the original Johnston–Henderson investigation, although there is a suspicion in almost all cases that the calculated effects include reversible stock effects. The most recent estimates by Fane and Whitley go further than the others in attempting to confine the calculation to the elasticity effect;[1] the elasticity used in the computation is, however, probably biased downwards, since it relates to total imports of goods and the presumption is that the elasticities of demand for manufactures and semi-manufactures are higher than average; on the other hand, these authors assumed no absorption of the surcharge by overseas suppliers.

The evidence provided by the surcharge episode on the elasticity of demand was thus less than clear-cut for a variety of reasons. The government had in mind an effect of £300 million a year when this scheme was first introduced;[2] this figure should be taken, after adjustment for the subsequent change in the tariff rate and the length of its operation, as something over £440 million.[3] In the light of the estimates in the table, the government figure seems to have been on the optimistic side. The imposition of the surcharge did involve temporary stock run-downs, so that there was quite a powerful immediate effect and some catching up after the end of the scheme. The difficulty of capturing these reactions is one of the reasons why estimates of the effect differ. It does seem that there was a mild terms of trade effect in Britain's favour as a result of the scheme. Taking the Fane–Whitley estimate as a base, but allowing for price absorption of 2–3 percentage points, the combined terms of trade and elasticity effects of the scheme might be said to amount to something like £250 million at current prices over two years; this is an underestimate to the extent of the bias in the overall elasticity calculation.

The temporary import deposit scheme

In November 1968, when a number of additional deflationary measures were taken, details of a new scheme for controlling imports were announced. Importers of certain classes of goods, broadly those which had been covered by the import surcharge, were required to deposit with the government for six months an amount equal to half the value of such goods purchased for import.[4] The scheme was modified in

[1] G. Fane and J. Whitley, 'Imports of goods and services' (unpublished, NIESR), 1973.

[2] House of Commons, *Hansard*, 11 November 1964, cols. 1027–8.

[3] Obtained by scaling the government's initial £300 million estimate by 11·2/15·0 (the ratio of the average rate of surcharge to the initial rate) and doubling to allow for the fact that the scheme ran for just over two years.

[4] Details of the mechanics of the scheme are given in the notice of credit restriction published in the *Bank of England Quarterly Bulletin*, vol. 8, December 1968, pp. 358–9. Technically, the deposits were regarded as Customs duties. The value of imports covered by the scheme at the time of its introduction is put by the Bank at about £2800 million a year.

December 1969 to require a deposit of only 40 per cent of the value of the imported goods; there were further reductions to 30 per cent in May and 20 per cent in September 1970; the scheme ended in December 1970. Perhaps surprisingly, it did not run into difficulties with either the IMF or GATT; somewhat analogous schemes had been used in other countries, though close parallels were denied by the Chancellor.

The scheme may be regarded as having two components. It can be seen as, on the one hand, analogous to a surcharge, on the other, as a monetary measure designed to reduce the rate of importing by creating a shortage of finance unless the overseas sellers could supply it.

The surcharge effects could never have been thought to be particularly severe, for with a deposit rate of 50 per cent the equivalent surcharge rate could not have been more than about 2–3 per cent.[1] To the extent that the equivalent cost of the surcharge was borne by foreign suppliers the United Kingdom would gain a terms of trade advantage; otherwise import demand would be reduced to an extent dependent on the relevant elasticities.

The availability effects of the scheme arose in theory when importers were unable to find the deposit on any tolerable terms. Banks were asked specifically to avoid lending to customers for the purpose of paying the deposit, particularly on imports for stock.[2] However, overseas suppliers might make good the shortage of funds by loaning the deposit to the customer, or by delaying claims for payment. During the first few weeks of the scheme permission to borrow abroad was in fact granted quite freely, but on 18 December the scheme was reinforced, when it was announced that United Kingdom importers would no longer be allowed to borrow foreign currency, or sterling owned by overseas residents outside the sterling area, in order to pay deposits.[3] However, nothing could be done to prevent overseas suppliers from accommodating British importers by delaying settlement.

Official sources were reticent in providing any estimate of the anticipated effects of the scheme. The Bank of England did suggest that they looked for a quick stock run-down in the first six months, as well as for some continuing cost effect.[4] The National Institute suggested an effect on imports in 1969 of some £80 million (at 1958 prices), of which it was anticipated that £20 million would be reversed in the first quarter of 1970. Of the net effect of £60 million, one third was attributed to

[1] The equivalent surcharge rate, s, may be expressed in terms of the duration of the forced loan, l (measured in years), the annual rate of interest for the period of the loan, r, and the deposit rate, d, as $s = d.l.r$; that is, with d and l both 50 per cent, as one quarter of the rate of interest.

[2] *Bank of England Quarterly Bulletin*, vol. 8, December 1968, pp. 358–9.

[3] *Bank of England Quarterly Bulletin*, vol. 9, March 1969, p. 6.

[4] *Bank of England Quarterly Bulletin*, vol. 8, December 1968, p. 343.

the surcharge-like effects of the scheme and two thirds to availability effects.[1]

Very little detailed work providing estimates of the scheme's effects is available. Rees and Layard reported no discernible effect of the scheme on the residuals of their import demand equations, arguing that the effect was so small as to be negligible.[2] The National Institute subsequently reported its inability to detect any post-devaluation effect on imports, so that the question of distinguishing the effects of the scheme from those of devaluation did not arise.[3] Fane and Whitley, however, estimated a total effect over the whole period of the surcharge of £50 million (1963 prices), an estimate arrived at by considering the surcharge-like effects alone; as in the case of their estimate of the import surcharge, the figure was arrived at by applying an elasticity of −0·68 (in this case to the equivalent surcharge rate), and may be biased downwards because the elasticity in question is an aggregate for all goods.

It is probably justified to neglect availability effects, especially in the light of the Treasury's estimates that a significant proportion of import deposits was financed by overseas suppliers. Although the data are admittedly rather inadequate, the Treasury estimate was that about half of the deposits (some £130 million) paid in the first quarter of 1969 were supplied from overseas.[4] Subsequently the balance of payments statistics have recorded a total of £60 million as 'import deposits paid directly from overseas' in 1968 and 1969, which were repaid in 1970 and 1971, and other 'credit received in connection with import deposits' is located in figures for 'import credits received by United Kingdom businesses (other)'; these show a sharp jump upwards in 1968 and 1969 (the figures are: 1967 £9 million, 1968 £50 million, 1969 £70 million, 1970 £12 million, 1971 £12 million, 1972 £17 million).[5] On this basis, then, it might not be too far off the mark to suggest that, of the total outstanding deposits received by the end of 1969 of £544 million (the quarterly peak in outstandings came in mid-1969 at £565 million), more than a quarter was supplied from overseas.

By the same token it would therefore appear that the deposit scheme had much bigger (but reversible) effects on the capital account than it had on the current account. To put it no higher, there is no indication that this was what was initially anticipated or intended.

---

[1] *National Institute Economic Review*, no. 47, February 1969, p. 35.

[2] Treasury, *The Determinants of UK Imports* by R. D. Rees and P. R. D. Layard, London, HMSO, 1972.

[3] NIESR, 'The effects of the devaluation of 1967 on the current balance of payments', *Economic Journal*, vol. 82, March 1972 (supplement).

[4] CSO, *Economic Trends*, no. 188, June 1969, pp. xiv–xv.

[5] CSO, *Economic Trends*, no. 209, March 1971 and no. 242, December 1973.

FINANCING THE DEFICIT

Despite all the efforts made to improve the balance of payments in the 1960s, both by operating on the general level of demand and by the various policies described in this chapter, large deficits had nevertheless to be financed either by drawing on the reserves held by the Exchange Equalisation Account or by other kinds of official financing.

As table 7.2 shows, the deficits in the 1960s were not to any great extent financed by drawing down our reserves, presumably because the authorities thought it harmful to confidence in sterling. Our transactions with the IMF were mainly the result of drawings in 1961, 1964, 1965 and 1968. These drawings were substantial, but involved no new principle; we had made a large drawing in the 1950s to deal with the financial aftermath of the Suez affair, so that by and large it was a matter of following established procedure.

Support from other central banks (table 7.2) did, however, involve recourse to new procedures. The first step was taken in 1961 with the prototype of what came to be known as 'Basle Arrangements'. Following the German and Dutch revaluations by 5 per cent in the first week of March, there was a wave of speculation, which was discussed on 13 March at the normal monthly meeting of central bank governors at the Bank for International Settlements in Basle. The governors reacted to the danger by agreeing on mutual short-term banking accommodation to finance the speculative movement of funds – such accommodation to be repaid either by the reflux of the speculative funds or, if the reflux did not occur reasonably quickly, by recourse to the IMF. Britain duly obtained accommodation under this prototype Basle Arrangement, partly in the form of an exchange of currencies, partly in foreign currency deposits; the largest amount outstanding was £325 million.[1] The repayment of this sum, which had nearly been completed by the end of September 1961, required (as had been foreseen) recourse to the IMF, from which we made a drawing in August. In subsequent balance of payments crises the same scenario was followed, but in addition we were able to get assistance from the United States central banking system under the reciprocal swap network negotiated by the Federal Reserve Bank of New York.

Assistance afforded by one central bank to another conventionally requires repayment within one year[2] and the United Kingdom made every effort to respect this convention, if needs be by following the

---

[1] *Bank of England Quarterly Bulletin*, vol. 1, September 1961, pp. 9 and 10.

[2] R. A. Young, *Instruments of Monetary Policy in the United States*, Washington (DC), International Monetary Fund, 1973, p. 91. This convention did not apply to the 'Basle Group Arrangements' (see page 351 below).

1961 precedent of refinancing any outstanding amount by drawing on the IMF. But continuous balance of payments difficulties from 1964 onwards forced the British authorities on occasions to have recourse to central bank assistance at times when the IMF drawing limit had already been reached. This issue first arose in May 1965, when a drawing of $1400 million following one of $1000 million the preceding December took Britain to the limit of her drawing rights. The May 1965 drawing enabled outstanding debts to be repaid to other central banks and added $343 million to the reserves, but in June borrowing began again from the Federal Reserve Bank of New York. Then in November 1967 a $250 million credit was negotiated (mainly from other central banks) through the good offices of the Bank for International Settlements, so as to permit repayment of the final instalment of the December 1964 drawing. The permitted IMF limit was again reached in June 1968 with another drawing to repay short-term debts, in particular to the Federal Reserve Bank of New York, 'but in the latter part of the year it became necessary to draw again on the Federal Reserve Bank facility, and by the end of December $1150 million (£480 million) was outstanding'.[1]

In addition to the periodic recourse to 'normal' Basle Arrangements, the United Kingdom benefited from the so-called 'Basle Group Arrangements'; the first was negotiated in June 1966 (renewed in March 1967 and March 1968) and the second in September 1968 (likewise renewed at intervals until September 1973). The Basle Group Arrangements were unusual in being specifically intended to counter the threat to United Kingdom reserves arising from the possible conversion of sterling balances held overseas. Under the 1966 Arrangement the central banks of Austria, Belgium, Canada, Italy, Japan, the Netherlands, Sweden, Switzerland and West Germany, and the Bank for International Settlements collaborated in affording the United Kingdom swap facilities to offset most of any reduction in the United Kingdom reserves caused by fluctuations in overseas countries' sterling balances, whether held by monetary authorities or privately. Such fluctuations were to be measured by reference to a base date early in 1966.[2]

Continued nervousness about the pound after devaluation and about the stability of the international monetary system caused sterling area countries to speed up the process of diversifying their reserves and this led to the second Basle Group Arrangement in 1968. This differed from its predecessor in relating only to sterling balances held within the sterling area. The Basle Group of central banks and the Bank for

[1] Bank of England, *Report for the year ended 28 February 1969*, p. 12.
[2] *Bank of England Quarterly Bulletin*, vol. 6, September 1966, p. 209.

International Settlements provided a medium-term facility of $2000 million, on which the United Kingdom could draw during a three-year period in order to offset fluctuations below an agreed base level in the sterling balances of sterling area holders, both official and private. Then a series of agreements, mostly for three years with provision for an extension to five, was negotiated between the United Kingdom and individual overseas sterling area countries, whereby each undertook to hold a specified proportion of its reserves in sterling and in return obtained a dollar-value guarantee on its official holdings of sterling in excess of 10 per cent of its total official external reserves. At the same time it was announced that the earlier facility, negotiated in June 1966 and subsequently renewed, which related to fluctuations in all overseas countries' sterling balances, would be progressively liquidated and cease by 1971.[1]

At the conclusion of the negotiations in 1968 the United Kingdom was entitled to draw some $600 million to finance earlier reductions in the sterling balances. In 1969 and 1970, when sterling holdings increased, the United Kingdom's net entitlement was correspondingly reduced.[2] By mid-1969 almost all the amount outstanding under the 1968 facility had been repaid.[3] The facility remained in force until September 1973, when it was replaced by a six-month unilateral guarantee by the United Kingdom on most of the sterling reserves held by the sterling area countries, on terms which afforded compensation to the holders if the pound should, on average over the next six months, fall below $2·4213. The exchange rate guarantee was not in this case underwritten by the Basle Group.

The floating pound was costly for the United Kingdom in respect of both the exchange rate guarantee associated with the Basle Group Arrangement of 1968 and the unilateral guarantee which superseded it in September 1973. The former called for payments totalling £59 million; the latter had cost £80 million before it was in turn superseded in March 1974 by yet another scheme.[4]

The improvement in Britain's balance of payments which eventually followed devaluation permitted the repayment of all borrowing from central banks before the end of the first quarter of 1971 and of all drawings from the IMF by the middle of 1972. Further temporary help from other central banks was needed around the time of the floating of sterling in June 1972, but thenceforth borrowing was not needed again to bolster the official reserves until 1973, when the novel device

[1] Bank of England, *Report for the year ended 28 February 1969*, pp. 13 and 14.
[2] Ibid. p. 14.
[3] *Bank of England Quarterly Bulletin*, vol. 9, September 1969, p. 280.
[4] *The Banker*, vol. 124, April 1974, p. 313.

was adopted of encouraging public sector institutions, such as the Central Electricity Generating Board, to borrow in the Eurocurrency market and to sell the currencies thus acquired to the Exchange Equalisation Account for sterling (table 7.2), forward cover being provided by the Treasury.

CONCLUSION

There had been a succession of balance of payments crises in the 1940s and 1950s – notably in 1947, 1949, 1951, 1955, 1956 and 1957 – and this phenomenon continued, though with less regularity, in the 1960s and 1970s. The main remedies applied had much in common throughout these decades: deflationary demand management to improve the current balance and short-term interest-rate management to help the capital balance. These well-tried devices were supplemented by miscellaneous temporary expedients in the crises of the 1960s – for example, the travel allowance, the export rebate, the import surcharge and import deposits – but these were only minor palliatives.

In addition to measures applied specifically to deal with crises, there were others which were aimed at a permanent improvement, even though in many cases their adoption was immediately triggered by one or other of the crises. Included under this heading are exchange control on capital outflows, which was in operation throughout the postwar period; the dam was made more watertight in the 1960s, but its restrictive effect on outward investment was substantially offset by the growth of facilities for financing it by foreign currency borrowing. Then there was devaluation; this had been resorted to in 1949, but was then eschewed for eighteen years. It was resorted to again, with extreme reluctance, in November 1967 and as from June 1972 the exchange rate was allowed to float. The unwanted side effects of exchange-rate depreciation, though unpalatable, turned out to be less serious than had been feared earlier in the 1960s, but the beneficial effect on the current balance proved to be rather disappointing. Additional, and more novel, measures adopted in the 1960s were the tax changes made in 1965 to discourage overseas investment and the determined efforts made throughout the decade to reduce government expenditure overseas; these measures admittedly did not produce any improvement in the relevant items in the British balance of payments, but may well have served to prevent a deterioration.

APPENDIX I
EFFECTS OF THE 1967 DEVALUATION

Five detailed estimates of the balance of payments effects of the 1967 devaluation of sterling have been published; they are summarised in table 7.13, which also shows the actual changes recorded in various items between 1967 and 1969 or 1970. These latter figures reflect, of course, *all* influences on the United Kingdom current account, not merely the devaluation; they are included for comparison with estimates of the 'devaluation effect', so that the importance of the latter's contribution to the improvement in the United Kingdom balance of payments over this period can be gauged.

The first estimate listed – that made by the NIESR *ex ante* at the time of devaluation[1] – is of historical interest as reflecting a degree of optimism about the balance of payments effects which was soon to be dispelled by events. The NIESR used elasticities for merchandise trade that would have been widely accepted as plausible at the time, and made rough estimates of the effect on invisibles. Various statements by the Chancellor to Parliament and in the Letter of Intent to the IMF, which mentioned a preliminary swing of £500 million in the current account in 1968 and later a surplus of between £300 million and £500 million (implying a swing of between £800 and £1000 million), suggest that official forecasts of the likely effect of devaluation were of the same order of magnitude.

The first *ex post* estimate was made by Worswick in 1970, when the payments figures for 1969 were already available.[2] Estimates of export gains were made by calculating the growth of exports assuming that the pre-devaluation relationship between world and United Kingdom exports continued into 1969, and taking the difference between these calculations and observed exports as the 'devaluation effect'. The results implied a lower export elasticity than that used by the NIESR *ex ante*. Furthermore, it was necessary to assume that devaluation had had no effect on the volume of imports, because an estimate of 1969 imports using an unchanged exchange rate gave a lower figure than the actual level. The NIESR *ex post* estimates for 1970 were a refinement of this approach.[3] A similar assumption was made about imports of goods, but the export figures were estimated from a more detailed examination of United Kingdom shares in world exports of manufactures, while major flows of invisibles were separately

---

[1] *National Institute Economic Review*, no. 42, November 1967, pp. 4 *et seq.*
[2] G. D. N. Worswick, 'Trade and payments' in Cairncross (ed.), *Britain's Economic Prospects Reconsidered*.
[3] NIESR, 'The effects of the devaluation of 1967 on the current balance of payments'.

Table 7.13. *Estimates of the effects of devaluation and actual changes in the balance of payments*

	Estimates of devaluation effects					Actual change in value from 1967 to:	
	For 1969		For 1970				
	NIESR[a]	Worswick	NIESR[b]	LBS[c]	Artus	1969	1970
	(£ million)						
Goods							
Exports	986	1240	1255	1116	1243	1939	2769
Imports	314	880[d]	1125	899	517	1525	2221
Balance	672	360	130	217	726	414	548
Services							
Credits	250	250[e]	390	435 ⎱ 240 ⎰		666	1241
Debits	225	180[de]	140	273		445	943
Other (net)	128	80[f]	45	89	70	126	162
Invisible balance	153	150	295	251	310	347	460
Current account	825	510	425	468	1036	761	1008
Elasticities[g]							
Exports	−2·0	−1·5	−1·4	−1·2	−1·3	.	.
Imports	−0·7	—	—	—	−0·4	.	.
	(percentages)						
Price changes[g]							
Exports (£)	9·0	7·6	8·5	7·0	6·1	.	.
($)	−7·0	−7·8	−7·0	−8·3	−9·1	.	.
Imports (£)	13·5	12·3	16·7	10·0	12·9	.	.

SOURCES: *National Institute Economic Review*, no. 42, November 1967; Worswick, 'Trade and payments'; NIESR, 'The effects of the devaluation of 1967 on the current balance of payments'; Ball, Burns and Miller, 'Preliminary simulations with the London Business School macro-economic model'; Artus, 'The 1967 devaluation of the pound sterling'; CSO, *United Kingdom Balance of Payments 1973*.

[a] *Ex ante* forecasts.   [b] *Ex post* estimates.
[c] Includes additional imports induced by rise in GNP. If GNP was held constant, as in other estimates, estimates for goods imports would be £697 million and for service debits £235 million, giving surpluses of £419 million for visibles, £289 million for invisibles and £708 million on current account.
[d] Goods and services originally calculated together; split estimated here.
[e] Excludes government services.   [f] Investment income only.   [g] Goods only.

estimated in relation to trade, income or some other appropriate indicator.

The estimate for 1970 by the London Business School[1] cannot be compared with others in the table, since, unlike them, it does not assume that policies designed to maintain the level of activity unchanged

[1] R. J. Ball, T. Burns and G. Miller, 'Preliminary simulations with the London Business School macro-economic model' in Renton (ed.), *Modelling the Economy*.

were implemented after devaluation. If imports are adjusted to allow for this, a much larger devaluation effect results than that estimated by the NIESR. This is not due to a fall in the volume of imports – the equations for (disaggregated) imports contain no price terms – but to a much smaller rise in import prices. The NIESR assumed that the changed sterling rate was fully reflected in import prices; the London Business School made import prices a function of the volume of world trade and the level of world prices as well as of the exchange rate.

Artus's more recent estimates for 1970[1] are distinguished by the use of disaggregated import equations with significant price elasticities for manufactures (− 3·4 for semi-manufactures and − 1·0 for finished goods) implying an average elasticity of − 0·4. Here, the fall in the volume of imports implies a smaller rise in their value than in the other estimates and, in turn, yields a 'devaluation effect' more than twice as large as that of the NIESR.

All three 1970 estimates were not only close in the export elasticities and price changes estimated or implied (and hence in the changes in the value of goods exported), but also fairly close in their estimates of the effect on invisibles. They all found evidence to support the existence of the J-curve,[2] though the timing differed from estimate to estimate. The essential difference between the three lies in the calculation of the effect of devaluation on imports, and here Artus's view is now probably most widely accepted. The London Business School can still find no significant price elasticity for imports,[3] but the NIESR, when estimating import equations from data spanning the post-devaluation period as Artus did, has found elasticities of a similar order of magnitude. Thus a significant part, but by no means all, of the change in the United Kingdom current account between 1967 and the early 1970s should, on this evidence, be attributed to devaluation, even though the estimates themselves may be open to criticism for failing to take other influences fully into account or ignoring other consequences of devaluation. But it should also be mentioned that there is still a school of thought that would dismiss all arguments about elasticities and propensities, and would explain the turn-round in the balance of payments by reference to the dramatic change in the government's finances between 1967 and 1970.

[1] J. R. Artus, 'The 1967 devaluation of the pound sterling', *IMF Staff Papers*, vol. 22, November 1975.
[2] The J-curve describes the initial deterioration in the balance of payments after a devaluation as import prices rise more quickly than export prices, followed by an improvement as the volume of exports rises and the volume of imports falls in response to price changes.
[3] R. J. Ball, T. Burns and J. S. E. Laury, 'The role of exchange rate changes in balance of payments adjustment', *Economic Journal*, vol. 87, March 1977.

APPENDIX II

MEDIUM-TERM EXPORT CREDIT[1]

October 1960. The ECGD was authorised to 'insure credit on longer terms than the normal maximum where this is necessary to allow a United Kingdom exporter to match terms offered by a foreign competitor with the backing of an export credit guarantee institution or equivalent official support'. 'Part-period cover' (for the first five years only) was introduced for other cases where it was reasonably sure that longer terms were being offered by foreign suppliers and that the order would be lost unless the United Kingdom exporter could compete on terms.

February 1961. The Bank of England announced it would refinance export credits provided by the banks when they reached eighteen months to maturity, provided the loans were originally for between three and five years and were backed by ECGD guarantees. Such credits could be counted as 'liquid assets' in calculating the London clearing banks' liquid asset ratios.

April 1961. Arrangements for direct guarantees to banks were extended to include 'financial guarantees' on loans for more than five years to creditworthy overseas purchasers. This was intended to facilitate the sale by United Kingdom suppliers of large capital projects costing not less than £2 million.

January 1962. The London and Scottish clearing banks agreed to finance export contracts of £100,000 or more of heavy capital equipment for terms of three to five years at a rate of interest fixed at $5\frac{1}{2}$ per cent per annum at least until 1967. Member companies of the British Insurance Association agreed to make £100 million available for loans exceeding five years at an interest rate of $6\frac{1}{2}$ per cent per annum.

January 1965. The banks took over from the insurance companies loans exceeding five years and henceforth would apply their own interest rate of $5\frac{1}{2}$ per cent. The minimum size of contract was reduced from £100,000 to £50,000 and the limitation to capital goods was removed.

Refinancing facilities by the Bank of England were extended to cover whichever was greater of credits maturing within eighteen months or 30 per cent of the total; such credits counted as liquid assets. A supplementary refinancing facility was provided for new loans of over five years to maturity to cover the longer-term

[1] SOURCES: *Bank of England Quarterly Bulletin*, vol. 1, March 1961, vol. 2, March 1962, vol. 5, March 1965, vol. 7, June 1967, vol. 9, September and December 1969; *Midland Bank Review*, August 1962 and August 1972.

lending taken over from the insurance companies, but such credits did not count as liquid assets,[1] so that the purpose was not so much to obviate liquidity constraints as to meet the growing concern of the banks that the expansion of longer-term lending was pre-empting too large a proportion of their resources.

April 1965. The minimum period for medium-term fixed-rate export credit was lowered from three to two years and ECGD cover was increased from 90 to 100 per cent of the finance provided. The minimum size of contract was further reduced to £25,000.

March 1966. The minimum size of contract was abolished.

May 1967. The London and Scottish clearing banks extended medium-term fixed-rate financing to shipbuilding contracts in United Kingdom yards backed by Ministry of Technology guarantees. Refinancing facilities by the Bank of England were extended to shipbuilding credits repayable over a period of more than eight years from delivery, 30 per cent of such loans being eligible as liquid assets.

May 1969. Refinancing facilities were re-negotiated with the banks, so that:

(i) existing arrangements were to be continued for credits which could be counted by the London clearing banks as liquid assets (that is, 30 per cent of all eligible loans or, for export credits, the total repayable within eighteen months if greater);

(ii) other facilities were replaced by a Bank of England commitment to the London and Scottish clearing banks to refinance any eligible lending which might not be treated as liquid in excess of 5 per cent of the bank's total gross deposits.

October 1970. The fixed rate of interest on medium-term bank financing of exports and shipbuilding was increased from $5\frac{1}{2}$ to 7 per cent.

November 1971. The fixed rate of interest on financing of exports other than ships was reduced to $6\frac{1}{2}$ per cent; on exports of ships and shipbuilding it remained at 7 per cent.

March 1972. The fixed rate of interest on financing of exports other than ships was reduced to 6 per cent; henceforth these interest rates were to be determined by the government, which would recompense the banks for the difference between such rates and market rates.

Since medium-term credits were not eligible to be counted towards the new $12\frac{1}{2}$ per cent reserve asset ratio (which superseded the 28 per cent liquid asset ratio in 1971), any excess of

[1] Except insofar as the 18 months or 30 per cent arrangement applied to the whole of a bank's export credits under the scheme.

such credits over 18 per cent of a bank's current account deposits were to be refinanced by the ECGD (if for exports) or by the Department of Trade (if for shipbuilding for United Kingdom purchasers).

January 1974. The fixed rate of interest on financing of exports was increased to 7 per cent for loans lasting two to five years and to a range of 6–8½ per cent for longer loans.

CHAPTER 8

INCOMES POLICY

by *F. T. Blackaby*

1960 TO 1964

The period began at the end of an *annus mirabilis* for price stability: on 15 December 1959 the index of retail prices was exactly the same as on 16 December 1958. This remarkable, if short, period of price stability had been helped a little by the fall in import prices during 1958. However, the main reason was a rather extraordinary hiatus in wage claims during 1959, when the index of hourly wage rates rose by a mere 1·2 per cent. 1959 showed a 'Phillips-type' pattern; unemployment, which was at a peak at the beginning of the year, had fallen only gradually and in consequence a number of important trade unions had postponed their wage claims until times got better.

It was partly this brief price stability which made the developments of 1960 and 1961 appear disturbing. Wage rates began to rise again during 1960 and were just over 5 per cent higher by the end of the year. The effect on retail prices was, however, still very small – they went up by a mere 2 per cent through the year. By the first half of 1961 the inflationary process appeared to be speeding up to figures which, although they now look insignificant, seemed disturbing then: in the first half of 1961 hourly wage rates and retail prices were rising at annual rates of 7 per cent and 4 per cent respectively. This was part of the background to the wages pause introduced in July.

It was also part of the background at the time that a number of Reports were published stressing the cost element in inflation. The Council on Prices, Productivity and Incomes, in its Report published in July 1959, emphasised costs rather than demand as a cause of inflation; it also reviewed a number of proposals, such as those for a 'guiding light' and a statutory advisory body, which later became incorporated into the government's incomes policy.[1] In 1961 the OEEC published a Report which concluded that certainly in Britain 'excessive wage

[1] Council on Prices, Productivity and Incomes, *3rd Report*, London, HMSO, 1959; see also *4th Report*, London, HMSO, 1961. Sir Dennis Robertson had been the economist member of the Council when its first two Reports were produced in 1958, laying heavy stress on demand rather than costs. Sir Dennis resigned in 1958 and his place was filled by Professor Phelps Brown; in the third and fourth Reports there was a distinct change of emphasis.

increases constituted both an important and independent inflationary force '.[1] We have evidence about the advice which must have been given to the government in an article by Sir Robert Hall, written shortly after he had retired as Economic Adviser to the government. He comments: 'With the passage of time the number of adherents of extreme positions has diminished and a large body of opinion now thinks that some form of wage policy other than leaving wages to free collective bargaining is necessary, if full employment and stable prices are to be combined. In this connection, the OEEC Report on the problem of rising prices is extremely significant since it is very nearly an agreed document, by highly respected economists from a number of western countries who can certainly not be regarded as all belonging to any particular school of thought.'[2] It is noticeable that in his 1961 budget speech the Chancellor referred specifically to the dangers of accelerating cost-inflation.

It was not surprising, therefore, that when crisis measures had to be taken in July 1961 they included a 'pay pause'. Indeed, it is clear that in the Prime Minister's view it was the pay pause that really mattered; he had little sympathy with the other deflationary measures. In his view the country's difficulties 'were not due to an attempt to run the economy at too great a rate or to the strains upon government expenditure, whether at home or overseas'; they were primarily due to an explosion of wages. It was the wages battle which was all important: 'what is the use of our scraping and scrounging to get £50–£150 million of "economies", if the extra wage and salary bill of £1,000 million or more is presented again?'[3]

The pay pause was announced on 25 July 1961. It required no legislation; the government proposed to use its existing powers and its position as an employer to hold back wage increases in the public sector as best it might, hoping that the private sector would follow. Existing commitments would be honoured; otherwise, the general principle was that Civil Service pay increases would be delayed for seven months. The process of arbitration would continue, but the government would reserve its right to decide when and in what steps to implement the decisions. The government could put considerable pressure on nationalised industries to conform; there was, however, no complete prohibition of wage increases and each case was considered separately. The pay pause was, therefore, very far from being a statutory pay freeze.

The administration of the pay pause can best be described as a

[1] OEEC, *The Problem of Rising Prices* by W. Fellner *et al.*, Paris, 1961.
[2] 'Britain's economic problem', *Economist*, 16 September 1961, p. 1042.
[3] Macmillan, *At the End of the Day*, p. 36.

prolonged and rather ragged battle, with ground being gained in some sectors and lost in others. In some cases arbitration awards were postponed until the end of the pause. The Civil Service unions were particularly disturbed at the interference with arbitration and only mollified with the promise that there would be a return to unfettered arbitration once the pause was over. Some awards by Wages Councils were referred back for reconsideration, but when this was refused the government let the awards through. Part of a Post Office award was allowed through and part held back until the end of the pause. There was a major breach, however, in November, when the Electricity Board, which had informally agreed to offer a maximum increase of 1d. an hour from 1 April, declared after prolonged negotiations that they saw no alternative to offering 2d. an hour from 28 January; they informed the Minister of Power, who protested over the telephone but did nothing. The Prime Minister reprimanded both the Minister and the Board, but privately admitted that 'we have retreated...from the one point in the line which it is in fact impossible to hold, for we have no technically effective method by which electric power could be produced on any reasonable scale in the event of a strike'.[1]

During the pause, the government – and the Prime Minister in particular – were wrestling with the problem of establishing a permanent incomes policy. The Prime Minister was in a constant state of exasperation that the Chancellor and the Treasury were doing nothing about it and it was on this issue that he eventually concluded that Selwyn Lloyd would have to go (page 21). Certainly it was some time before the longer-term incomes policy took shape; not until a year after the beginning of the pay pause was the National Incomes Commission announced.

The incomes policy which emerged had three main constituents: a 'norm', a set of criteria or principles by which wage claims should be judged, and an independent body to pass judgements on particular cases. This framework stayed much the same until 1970. The name and constitution of the independent body was, of course, changed, and its scope was widened to include prices; there were also some changes (though not many) in the principles or criteria. The policy was, however, firmly based on the view that costs were mainly responsible for inflation; if wage increases could be controlled, this would also effectively control prices and profits.

The idea of a 'norm' had been around for a long time. In 1956 a White Paper had advanced the proposition that if incomes rose faster than output prices were bound to rise,[2] and a general 'norm' had been

---

[1] Ibid. p. 47.

[2] Treasury, *Economic Implications of Full Employment*, Cmd 9725, London, HMSO, 1956.

extensively discussed in the Reports of the Council on Prices, Productivity and Incomes.[1] There was therefore no particular difficulty in saying what the norm should be; in January 1962 the Chancellor of the Exchequer sent a letter to the TUC asking for their cooperation in keeping earnings increases within the limit set by the Treasury estimate of the probable rise in productivity. This was calculated at $2\frac{1}{2}$ per cent and it became known as the 'guiding light'.

The criteria which were supposed to govern decisions about income increases were set out in a White Paper in February of that year.[2] This White Paper, like those which followed it, considered that increases in the cost of living ought not to be given 'the same weight as hitherto', thus sharply distinguishing the incomes policy then pursued by the Conservative government from its later forms. Increased productivity was only to be a justification for increases if it had been achieved by more exacting work, more onerous conditions, or the renunciation of restrictive practices; an increase might also be justifiable when 'a build up of manpower in one industry relatively to another is plainly necessary'. These were much the same principles as those of the subsequent Labour period of incomes policy, except that low pay was not mentioned as a criterion. The White Paper quoted the Chancellor's declaration in December 1961 that 'as a part of the incomes policy, appropriate corrective action would have to be taken if aggregate profits showed signs of increasing excessively as compared with wages and salaries', but it is fairly clear that this contingency was thought unlikely.

The final component of this incomes policy – the National Incomes Commission – was eventually announced in July; the Prime Minister had clearly been a little uncertain about the support he would get from his Cabinet and the Conservative Party in the House of Commons; there were a number of Conservatives who had little sympathy with this kind of intervention. He records that he addressed the Cabinet at some length on the need for 'an impartial source of wage assessment operating over the whole field, in place of a series of *ad hoc* arbitrations when one group after another felt itself to be left behind'.[3] The idea of giving the Commission powers of compulsion was considered and rejected, partly because it would only be able to consider a relatively small number of settlements rather arbitrarily selected and partly because a great deal of industrial action was unofficial. The Prime Minister hoped that the Commission's rulings would become effective through the pressure of public opinion after full disclosure of the facts. It was

[1] Council on Prices, Productivity and Incomes, *1st–4th Reports*, London, HMSO 1958–61.
[2] Treasury, *Incomes Policy: the next step*.
[3] Macmillan, *At the End of the Day*, p. 70.

envisaged as a permanent body: 'an incomes policy is, therefore, necessary as a permanent feature of our economic life'.[1]

The National Incomes Commission

The new Conservative incomes policy, having been born with such travail, hardly lived up to expectations. The National Incomes Commission had a short and rather undistinguished life; it certainly did not succeed in focusing the wrath of public opinion on excessive wage awards.

There were a number of reasons for this failure to make much impact. First of all, by October 1962 when the Commission was eventually established, unemployment was rising sharply and retail prices – even by the standards of the time – only very slowly: the retail price rise through 1962 was only 2½ per cent and through 1963 only 2 per cent. Unemployment, on the other hand, passed half a million (seasonally adjusted) in the winter of 1962/3. Not surprisingly, the threat of inflation ceased to be the main preoccupation of the government, or of public opinion in general.

The Commission had very limited terms of reference: to review certain pay matters where the cost was wholly or partly met from the Exchequer if the government asked it to do so, and to examine retrospectively any particular pay settlement which the government referred to it. In its two years it received only one reference under the first head and three under the second, producing five Reports in all on the four references.[2] It condemned as being against the national interest an agreement for Scottish builders, national agreements in the engineering and shipbuilding industries, and an agreement in electrical contracting. It acquitted an agreement for Scottish plumbers and, in its one 'non-retrospective' reference, it recommended salary increases substantially above the norm for university academic staff. However, its 'retrospective' Reports were published well after the wage agreements had been concluded; for example, its interim Report on the engineering and shipbuilding industries came five to six months after the agreement had taken effect and the final Report fifteen months later, after a new national agreement (with some important innovations) had been reached. This was one reason for the lack of impact on public opinion.

---

[1] Ibid. p. 105.

[2] National Incomes Commission, *Report no. 1: Scottish Plumbers' and Scottish Builders' Agreements of 1962*, Cmnd 1994; *Report no. 2: Agreements of Feb.–March 1963 in Electrical Contracting in Heating, Ventilating and Domestic Engineering and in Exhibition Contracting*, Cmnd 2098; *Report no. 3: Remuneration of Academic Staff in Universities and Colleges of Advanced Technology*, Cmnd 2317; *Report no. 4 (interim and final): Agreements of Nov.–Dec. 1963 in the Engineering and Shipbuilding Industries*, Cmnd 2583, London, HMSO, 1963–5.

The Commission's procedure was legal in form – presumably because this was the procedure with which the chairman, Sir Geoffrey Lawrence, QC, was familiar; it invited submissions and evidence, and held hearings. It was thus considerably handicapped when the trade unions refused to cooperate.[1]

The Commission did, however, increase the 'norm'; the government had promulgated 2–2½ per cent, but the Commission raised this to 3–3½ per cent, partly on the grounds that the target growth rate which had been accepted by the NEDC implied a 3·2 per cent growth rate in productivity per head; the more important reason was simply that 2–2½ per cent seemed unattainable and the Commission thought it more sensible to take a figure which had 'some real chance of general acceptance'.

The last months of the Conservative government

In the first half of 1964 unemployment was falling fast; retail prices were beginning to rise significantly, after moving very little during the previous year. The Chancellor tried through the NEDC to get some agreed statement of intent from both sides of industry on price and wage restraint, but he was unsuccessful. The trade unions were in no mood to cooperate with a Conservative government, which had set up the National Incomes Commission without first securing their cooperation and, further, was clearly in its last year of office and preparing for an election. A number of prominent trade unionists went on record as saying that, although they were unalterably opposed to Conservative wage restraint, they saw possibilities of cooperating with a Labour government on the 'planned growth of incomes'.

It also became clear during 1964 that the government was unable to keep wage increases in the public sector below 3–3½ per cent. In June a Court of Inquiry recommended increases for electricity supply manual workers ranging from 5 to 12½ per cent; this was soon followed by awards to London busmen and Post Office workers also well in excess of the norm. Thus, by the end of their period in office the Conservative government's incomes policy was in some disarray. Their manifesto suggests that if they had won the election there would have been further moves of some kind: '...an effective and fair incomes policy is crucial to the achievement of sustained growth without inflation. We shall take a further initiative to secure wider acceptance and effective implementation of such a policy.' It is noticeable that the manifesto does not mention the National Incomes Commission, although it does mention elsewhere the Conservative's other institutional creation, the NEDC.

[1] Some academic staff gave evidence in the hearings on their salaries.

THE LABOUR GOVERNMENT'S INCOMES POLICY

Labour came to power with different ideas about an incomes policy; it abolished the National Incomes Commission and set up its own institution. (This was to become a pattern of behaviour in this field: in turn, the Conservative government abolished the NBPI in 1970 and the Labour government abolished the Pay Board in 1974.) The idea of some kind of incomes policy had been discussed within the Labour Party, and indeed within the TUC, for some two years previously. The 1963 annual Congress had adopted a Report on economic development and planning which the General Secretary, George Woodcock, defended in a speech in which he used the famous phrase: 'We left Trafalgar Square a long time ago.' This TUC Report cautiously endorsed the view expressed by the NEDC that 'there would be a need for policies to ensure that money incomes, wages, salaries, profits as a whole rise substantially less rapidly than in the past'.[1] However, the same Congress also passed a motion declaring 'its complete opposition to any form of wages restraint', despite the General Secretary indicating that it would contradict the General Council s own Report.[2] The 1964 Congress moved a little further in allowing for an incomes policy: a composite motion included a sentence saying that the Congress 'reiterates its opposition to the attempted imposition of an incomes policy which has as its aim the restraint of wage and salary increases', but it also contained a section describing the characteristics of an acceptable incomes policy – for example, 'it must be based on social justice, taking into account all forms of incomes including rent, interest and profit...Congress further believes that an acceptable incomes policy must redress the injustices in the existing wages structure, and that Congress would have to establish its own system of priorities to achieve these aims.'[3]

With this degree of trade union support the Labour Party felt able to include a section on incomes policy in its election manifesto of 1964: 'To curb inflation we must have a planned growth of incomes so that they are broadly related to the annual growth of production. To achieve this a Labour Government will enter into urgent consultations with the Unions and employers' organisations concerned...Labour's incomes policy will not be unfairly directed at lower paid workers and public employees; instead, it will apply in an expanding economy to *all* incomes: to profits, dividends and rents as well as to wages and salaries.'

[1] NEDC, *Conditions Favourable to Faster Growth*.
[2] TUC, *Report of the 95th Annual Trades Union Congress at Brighton, 1963*, p. 409.
[3] TUC, *Report of the 96th Annual Trades Union Congress at Blackpool, 1964*, p. 561.

General characteristics

The Labour government's incomes policy went through a number of phases; between 1965 and 1970 there were no fewer than six distinct policy statements and a number of Prices and Incomes Acts. However, the successive phases had certain characteristics in common.

The policy was conceived as permanent, with permanent institutions, and not as a temporary interruption; it did not begin, therefore, with a wages freeze. So far as incomes were concerned, the general concept was a norm, with the NBPI adjudicating on difficult cases. As the Labour manifesto suggested, the new institution differed from its predecessors in that it was to consider prices as well as incomes. It differed in other ways too: the procedure was no longer an imitation of a Court of law; the Board conducted vigorous research work of its own and considered that it had a duty not simply to comment on prices and incomes, but to make general recommendations about the running of the industries and firms concerned.

It is also important in any assessment to realise that the Labour government's incomes policy was not a comprehensive statutory policy in the same sense as that introduced by the Conservatives in 1972. During Labour's term of office, except for the short period of the freeze, the powers of enforcement were very limited indeed: the government could refer a relatively small number of wage claims to the NBPI and could only delay those awards for varying lengths of time.

The first phase

In the Labour government the general responsibility for prices and incomes policy was given to the new Department of Economic Affairs. Within two months the Secretary of State, George Brown, had persuaded representatives of the TUC and the various employers' associations to sign a joint statement of intent on productivity, prices and incomes. Not much space in this document is in fact given to incomes policy; most of it is about raising productivity and increasing exports – indeed about the general objectives of the National Plan. On incomes policy, the parties agreed to cooperate in establishing new machinery to 'keep under review the general movement of prices and money incomes of all kinds' and to examine particular cases. The document shows how incomes policy was envisaged then – very much as one element in the expansionary policies of the National Plan.

The executive measures followed shortly. The NBPI was set up early in 1965 and in March the TUC General Council agreed to a 3–3½ per cent norm – the same figure as that of the National Incomes Commission. In the beginning there were no supporting statutory powers;

the NBPI – like the National Incomes Commission before it – was intended to educate public opinion. In April, a White Paper laid down the criteria for prices and for incomes:[1] for prices these were new; for wage and salary increases above the norm they were much the same as under the Conservatives, except for the addition of low pay as a new criterion.

The first wholly voluntary phase of incomes policy disappointed the policy-makers, though the trial was a very short one; the rise in the wage-rate index accelerated in the first half of 1965. The first moves to tighten the policy were made towards the end of August. There had been a sterling crisis (page 35) and, according to Harold Wilson, the Secretary to the United States Treasury indicated that it might be difficult to get further central bank aid if Britain had no better safeguard against inflation than a wholly voluntary system.[2] It was also observed that the NBPI had the same weakness as the National Incomes Commission – only income settlements already made and price increases already effective were being referred to it. The first move, therefore, was to produce an 'early warning' system.

The early warning system

The main problem, as with any statutory intervention in this field, was to get some kind of agreement from trade union leaders, who were fundamentally opposed to any kind of legislative interference with free collective bargaining. George Brown, summoned home from holiday, had a marathon session with the TUC General Council and the result was a compromise. The General Council reluctantly agreed to a voluntary system of notification – and indeed of vetting – of wage claims; the government would nonetheless go ahead with a Bill to give it statutory powers. However, the Bill needed an Order in Council to activate those powers, which the government agreed would not be done unless the voluntary system did not work.

The Trades Union annual Congress, which was in progress at the time, was also persuaded to back the new policy, though the majority in favour was much smaller than it had been in the spring, with 5·2 million for and 3·3 million against. The Transport and General Workers' Union was among those which voted against the new policy. A case for it was presented in a powerful speech by the General Secretary, George Woodcock. He accepted that the government had reason to be disappointed with the voluntary policy so far: prices and incomes had gone up rather more than in the period when there was no policy,

---

[1] Department of Economic Affairs, *Prices and Incomes Policy*, Cmnd 2639, London, HMSO, 1965.

[2] Wilson, *The Labour Government 1964–1970*, pp. 131–2.

and the interval between one claim and another was getting shorter. He argued that the only way to avoid legislation was 'to produce something that looks awfully good in the light of the Government's difficulties, an awfully good substitute'; consequently, any voluntary policy must aim to achieve the same objectives and results as legislation.[1]

Under the voluntary system, unions affiliated to the TUC were expected to notify the General Council of all impending claims. These claims were then examined by a special vetting committee set up for the purpose, consisting of one member of the General Council from each of the nineteen trade groups. This committee had a month in which to make no comment, to make written observations, or to invite representatives of the union or unions concerned to meet and discuss the claim. In most cases, therefore, the period of delay was no longer than five weeks: unions were expected to refrain from proceeding until they had heard from the General Council. There was nothing, however, to make them pay attention to any observations which the committee might make. This vetting committee operated from October 1965 to January 1970, with a short break from July to November 1966 during the period of the wages freeze. In many ways, it was this committee, much more than the NBPI, which was the Labour government's instrument of incomes policy. The NBPI dealt with only a selected number of wage claims and, on the whole, the big claims were not referred to it: the TUC vetting committee, on the other hand, considered all the major claims.

The TUC undertook to keep the government informed of developments: presumably it let the Ministry of Labour know the size of claims coming before the vetting committee and whether or not the committee had commented on them. The Ministry of Labour also received information about claims and offers from the employers, and unions and staff associations not affiliated to the TUC were expected to notify the Ministry directly. Thus there was an overlapping procedure of notification.

On the prices side the government did not feel the same need to get the CBI's agreement to an early warning system. Manufacturers of some 75 items were asked to inform the appropriate government department not less than four weeks in advance of any price increases proposed for those items. This notification had to be accompanied by a brief justification for the increase in the light of the criteria set out in the White Paper earlier in the year.[2]

These various arrangements for prices and incomes were described

[1] TUC, *Report of the 97th Annual Trade Union Congress at Brighton, 1965*, p. 470.
[2] Department of Economic Affairs *Prices and Incomes Policy*, Cmnd 2639.

in a White Paper towards the end of November 1965,[1] and were introduced on a non-statutory basis pending legislation. The legislation was in fact introduced: it was, as promised, an enabling Act, creating powers to be held in reserve until needed. However, it lapsed with the dissolution of Parliament in March 1966.

These new institutions – the early warning system and the TUC's vetting committee – do not seem to have made much difference to the rate at which earnings and wage rates were rising in the first half of 1966. The TUC had indicated clearly enough that, in any vetting which they did, their treatment of the norm would be 'flexible'. The NBPI was also discovering some of the difficulties of its role. Most awards which were not referred to the Board were higher than would have been warranted by a strict interpretation of the criteria in the White Paper. If the NBPI held back the few awards which were referred to it, it would find its judgements almost universally disregarded; this was one reason for it stressing the need to finance increases above the norm by productivity arrangements of some kind. (In addition, the chairman, Aubrey Jones, considered that one of the functions of the NBPI was to act as a kind of national management consultancy.) Further, the Board found that it had to compete with other arbiters using more lenient criteria. Early in 1966, when the government approved a substantial award to Scottish teachers on the basis of comparability, the Board reminded the government that, according to the White Paper, comparability was to be given less weight than hitherto. Also, when the Wages Council for the road haulage industry made a 7 per cent pay award, the Board pointed out that it had made 'concessions, not in exchange for improvements in productivity, but for a promise to talk about productivity'; nonetheless, the Minister of Labour endorsed the settlement. At about the same time Lord Kindersley recommended substantial increases for doctors and dentists, accepting the principle of comparability with little question.

The freeze

The government finally decided to stand firm – or more precisely, to encourage employers to stand firm – when the National Union of Seamen called a strike on 26 May 1966 in pursuit of a 17 per cent wage claim. The strike was very damaging; the government set up a Court of Inquiry on 26 May, which offered the seamen the equivalent of $9\frac{1}{2}$ per cent over two years, as opposed to the employers' final offer of $12\frac{1}{4}$ per cent over 3 years. These terms were eventually accepted, but not

[1] Department of Economic Affairs, *Prices and Incomes Policy: an 'Early Warning System'*, Cmnd 2808, London, HMSO, 1965.

until 1 July. The strike was one of the factors in the sterling crisis in July; it was by now fairly clear – given the apparent failure of voluntary policies – that the measures taken to deal with the crisis would include more forceful wage and price restraints. Together with the deflationary measures introduced on 20 July (page 38), the government enacted a six-month freeze on wages, salaries, dividends and prices, to be followed by six months of 'severe restraint'. This marked a major change in Labour's incomes policy, which had originally been conceived as a long-term strategy, the national interest being gradually introduced as one criterion of wage bargaining in an economy where output and the standard of living were rising fast. As a short-term crisis measure and part of a package intended to check the rise in output and consumers' expenditure, however, an incomes policy inevitably became identified with restrictions on the rise in the real standard of living.

The government obtained statutory powers for enforcing the freeze by adding an extra section to the Prices and Incomes Bill which was going through Parliament at the time. This Bill was a slightly revised version of the one which had lapsed with the general election in March, providing for compulsory advance notification of price or wage increases. Notification had to be given one month before the increases were implemented and, if during that month the Minister decided to refer the case to the NBPI, the increase could not be implemented until after the Board had published its Report or three months had passed from the date of the reference, whichever was the earlier.[1] The section which was now added gave the government powers to direct that specified prices, charges, or rates of remuneration should not be increased from a certain date; also to enforce recommendations of the NBPI – although this power was never used. As with the rest of the Bill, the powers in this new section could only be brought into operation by an Order in Council and would lapse automatically after twelve months.

The government then encountered – as on other occasions – the problems of interpretation which are associated with a standstill of this kind. They decided to allow 'genuine promotion' and increments due on incremental scales. They dealt with existing commitments, which covered about a quarter of the workforce in one way or another, by saying that they should be honoured after a delay of six months. For the rest, no new agreement could take effect before 1 January 1967.

On 27 July the TUC General Council gave its reluctant support to the freeze. In meetings with Ministers, the Council had outlined all

---

[1] The introduction of this Bill in early June led to the resignation of Frank Cousins from the government.

the various objections: it would involve the dishonouring of agreements already made; it would hit hardest at the lowest paid, many of whom had received no increases for eighteen months; through its application to productivity agreements, it would impose a standstill on 'growth and modernisation'. The Council also seemed doubtful about its effectiveness and disclaimed any responsibility for making sure that it worked; there was much the same reluctant endorsement at the Trades Union annual Congress, where the freeze was accepted by a majority of 4·9 to 3·8 million.

There were in fact very few attempts on the union side to break the freeze. At the end of September the Association of Supervisory Staffs, Executives and Technicians forced the government to activate its statutory powers by bringing a case for the payment of wage increases agreed before the freeze. In fact, however, only seven stand-still orders were made up to the end of January 1967 and they only concerned some 36,000 workers out of a working population of 23 million.

In November the government set out the criteria which were to apply during the period of 'severe restraint' from the end of January 1967 to 12 August of that year.[1] There was to be a nil norm; exceptions might be allowed for productivity agreements strictly interpreted and for some increases to the lowest paid workers. Only in the most exceptional circumstances were the other criteria which had been set out initially – the distribution of manpower and comparability – to be accepted as justification for wage or salary increases. The NBPI was asked to produce a special interim Report suggesting guidelines for judging productivity agreements. This set stringent standards: in particular, payment should not be made before the productivity increases took place and there should be clear benefits to the consumer through a contribution to stable prices.[2] The TUC was strongly hostile to this Report.[3]

The NBPI was also given some 'low pay' references. It had relatively little difficulty in accepting that agricultural workers should receive an increase during the period of severe restraint on this ground. It had more difficulty with the retail drapery, outfitting and footwear trades, where it was anxious that increases should be confined to the lowest paid and tapered as earnings rose. The relevant Wages Council rejected this recommendation, but the Minister drew the employers' attention to the NBPI's view and apparently a number of large employers did in fact pay the increases only to workers on near minimum rates. The

[1] Department of Economic Affairs, *Prices and Incomes Standstill: period of severe restraint,* Cmnd 3150, London, HMSO, 1966.

[2] NBPI, *Report no. 36: Productivity Agreements,* Cmnd 3311, London, HMSO, 1967.

[3] TUC, *Report of the 100th Annual Trade Union Congress at Blackpool, 1968,* p. 543.

NBPI also had considerable difficulties with a low pay reference which concerned rather over a million manual workers in local authorities, the National Health Service, and gas and water supply. The conclusion was that the main problem was inefficient use of labour and consequently low productivity; the claim was in fact agreed, but it was argued that there should also be immediate steps to give productivity incentives.

The periods of freeze and severe restraint had the effect, immediately visible in the figures, of checking the rise in wage rates and earnings. From July to December 1966 the weekly wage-rate index did not move at all; from July 1966 to June 1967 there was a rise of only 2 per cent in both the index of weekly wage rates and the monthly index of average earnings. Of course, a good deal of the effect could have been simply postponement; this point is discussed more fully on pages 390–1 below.

The declining phase

Discussions of what should follow the period of severe restraint had already begun towards the end of 1966. In October of that year the TUC General Council published its views on the form a future incomes policy should take. They considered: 'that the TUC should indicate those areas in which the Government could operate effectively and, equally important, those areas which the Government should leave alone. In the General Council's view incomes policy largely fell into the latter category...An incomes policy would need to be in operation for a considerable time before its benefit started to appear, whereas the Government was seeking quick-acting remedies to meet a crisis situation.'[1] They sketched out the kind of voluntary policy they envisaged: their vetting procedures would continue; in addition, each year they would prepare a report on the economic situation, incorporating the General Council's views on the general increase in wages and salaries that would be appropriate, and submit this to a conference of the executives of affiliated unions.

The first such conference was held in March 1967 and endorsed the proposed return to a voluntary policy by a huge majority. The main quantitative guidance which the General Council gave was in interpreting low pay: 'as a first step the General Council decided that they would regard as compatible with incomes policy claims for increases of up to £1.00 a week in national minimum rates which were less than £14.00 a week...The General Council accepted that they would also have to have regard to the need to reward the acquisition of skills and the acceptance of responsibility, and to the relationship between

---

[1] TUC, *Report of the 99th Annual Trades Union Congress at Brighton, 1967*, p. 322.

supervisors and supervised, but agreed that they should not interpret this as automatically justifying claims based on the maintenance of traditional relativities.'[1] This in effect recognised the great difficulty of raising the income of the low paid without raising the income of the higher paid as well. At the conference the General Secretary stoutly defended the effectiveness of the TUC's voluntary system; he considered that its operation so far had been 'remarkably successful, although apparently no one outside the Trade Union movement thought it was'. Both here and on a later occasion he indicated that the vetting committee could not possibly consider itself tightly bound by the precise criteria of any White Paper: 'above all in this business we need flexibility. We need – I am not ashamed of the phrase at all – room for those shoddy, shabby, dirty compromises which are the essence of practical people trying to do a job. We do not rule out any...considerations...cost of living, comparability, the importance of the need to maintain proper differentials for skill, and so on.'[2]

The government's own statement on prices and incomes policy from mid-1967 was published in March. There was to be no norm: 'there can be no justification at present for returning to the norm of $3-3\frac{1}{2}$ per cent...which in practice tended to be regarded as the minimum increase which everyone expected to receive. Over the twelve months' period beginning 1 July 1967, no-one can be entitled to a minimum increase; any proposed increase...will need to be justified against the criteria set out below'.[3] Basically there was a return to the criteria set out in the initial 1965 White Paper,[4] and these criteria were repeated. A few additional points were made: that twelve months should be regarded as the minimum period between awards; that it might be appropriate for substantial improvements to be achieved by stages; that there should be no attempt to make good increases forgone during the previous year. On enforcement, the government returned in effect to the provisions of the 1966 Act, which enabled them to delay an award while it was referred to the NBPI. However, under a new Bill, it could impose a one-month standstill while examining a claim, order a further delay of up to three months if the proposals were referred to the NBPI and, at the end of three months, if the NBPI so recommended, could impose a further delay of three months, making a total maximum period of delay of seven months. Thus a reference to the NBPI became an essential part of delaying tactics by the government.

---

[1] Ibid. p. 329.   [2] Ibid. p. 539.
[3] Department of Economic Affairs, *Prices and Incomes Policy after June 30, 1967*, Cmnd 3235, London, HMSO, 1967.
[4] Department of Economic Affairs, *Prices and Incomes Policy*, Cmnd 2639.

From mid-1967 to the end of the Labour government's incomes policy there was less and less relationship between the carefully worded criteria set out in the White Paper and actual events. There were many claims of the order 15–17 per cent and many settlements at around 7 per cent – which is roughly the percentage implied by the TUC General Council's recommendation earlier in the year that those earning £14 a week might expect to get an additional £1. There is no evidence of any significant narrowing of relativities. The Trades Union annual Congress passed a batch of motions severely critical of incomes policy and the one motion strongly in favour was lost. A motion urging the government to reassess the functions, purpose and organisation of the NBPI was passed; the trade unions were becoming increasingly dissatisfied with its role.

After devaluation at the end of 1967, the gap between the trade union picture of an incomes policy and government ideas widened even further. By the beginning of 1968 retail prices were rising fast, partly because of devaluation, and, although rises in the cost of living were supposed to be no argument for wage increases, this was certainly not generally accepted by the trade unions. Further, at the beginning of 1968 the TUC's *Economic Review* produced a very optimistic forecast of the possibilities of growth, which it put at 6 per cent for the year ahead; in this light it suggested that a basic 14s. per week increase all round would be in line with incomes policy objectives.[1]

The government reasonably took the view that, if those at the bottom of the income scale got increases of 14s. per week, those higher would get substantially more, and in April they produced a tighter incomes policy, which was to start from 20 March 1968.[2] There was still no norm; all increases in pay would have to be justified by the 1967 criteria, but, in addition, there was a ceiling of 3½ per cent for claims which satisfied the criteria, the only exception being agreements which 'genuinely raise productivity and increase efficiency sufficiently to justify a pay increase above 3½ per cent'. The NBPI's guidelines for judging productivity agreements were repeated. At the same time the government gave notice that, when the relevant sections of the 1967 Act expired on 11 August 1968, they would introduce legislation to enable them to delay price or pay increases for as long as twelve months in the context of a reference to the NBPI; this time these powers would be sought for eighteen months – that is, to the end of 1969.

Since the only justification for an increase above 3½ per cent was

---

[1] TUC, *Economic Review 1968*. See also *National Institute Economic Review*, no. 43, February 1968, pp. 28–9.

[2] Department of Economic Affairs, *Productivity, Prices and Incomes Policy in 1968 and 1969*, Cmnd 3590, London, HMSO, 1968.

now productivity, this became the central point in arguments about the various claims put forward. The stress on productivity was perhaps more marked because in April 1968 responsibility for incomes policy was moved to the Ministry of Labour, which was re-christened the Department of Employment and Productivity. Because Ministers now had to find some productivity justification when they gave way to pressure and allowed increases greater than $3\frac{1}{2}$ per cent, there was a growing laxity over the meaning of productivity agreements, and less and less attention was paid to the stringent guidelines laid down by the NBPI. Thus, in July 1968, although the government at first insisted that there would be no across-the-board increases to railwaymen before a 'copper-bottomed' productivity agreement had been drawn up, after a two weeks go-slow a 3 per cent increase across-the-board was agreed upon vague promises of a productivity agreement; the deal subsequently drawn up in August provided for another 8–9 per cent in return for simplified grade structures and the abolition of job demarcations. In much the same way, in October 1968 the government approved a three-year settlement for the engineering industry which was well above the $3\frac{1}{2}$ per cent ceiling; although it was called a 'productivity deal' it complied with virtually none of the NBPI's guidelines, amounting to little more than the promise of good intentions for the future in such matters as cooperation with job evaluation and shop-floor work-study schemes. It was becoming quite clear that the $3\frac{1}{2}$ per cent ceiling was meaningless. Thus, when the NBPI considered agricultural wages for the second time in 1968, it was faced with the situation that no more than $3\frac{1}{2}$ per cent should be allowed, for there was no possibility of productivity bargains which conformed with the Board's own guidelines. A $3\frac{1}{2}$ per cent increase would, however, have been so unfair compared to the other awards current at the time that the NBPI recommended that the government would be justified in considering 'whether a special exception to the requirements of the White Paper ought to be made in this case',[1] and the government accepted this recommendation.

Not only were the trade unions becoming disenchanted with incomes policy – in September 1968 the motion supporting the TUC voluntary policy scraped home with only the tiny majority of 34,000 – but the government was becoming increasingly disenchanted as well. The view began to take hold that the real problem was the trade unions' inability to control unofficial action by local militants, which was making any incomes policy impracticable. This received some support when the Royal Commission on Trade Unions and Employers'

[1] NBPI, *Report no. 101: Pay of Workers in Agriculture in England and Wales*, Cmnd 3911, London, HMSO, 1969.

Associations eventually published its Report, after three years' work, in June 1968.[1] It stressed how far collective bargaining had become de-centralised: 'Before the war it was generally assumed that industry-wide agreements could provide almost all the joint regulation that was needed, leaving only minor issues to be settled by individual managers. Today the consequences of bargaining within the factory can be more momentous than those of industry-wide agreements.'[2] From mid-1968 the government became more and more concerned with the reform of industrial relations and consequently less concerned with incomes policy. A White Paper was published in mid-January 1969 in which it was envisaged that consultations would proceed up to the end of May, when the drafting of a Bill would begin.[3] Soon afterwards the government decided to accelerate this timetable; one industrial dispute which provoked this was at Ford's, where the management had made an offer well in excess of the $3\frac{1}{2}$ per cent ceiling in exchange for an undertaking not to engage in unofficial strikes. On 11 February the unions voted to accept the terms, but they were almost immediately rejected by shop stewards from 21 out of the 23 Ford plants in Britain. The shop stewards called an unofficial strike, which was subsequently declared official. In mid-March a settlement was reached, which included the full pay increases agreed previously but made no reference to any undertaking on unofficial strikes. The award could not in any sense be called a productivity deal and, in order to save face a little, the Employment Secretary agreed to give it 'provisional approval' only. The government then decided to press ahead with an early Bill on industrial relations; the Prime Minister told the General Council that the public were looking for action against unofficial strikers who 'brought about industrial anarchy'. In the event the government was forced to abandon this Bill in exchange for a 'solemn and binding undertaking' from the TUC.

The government, having diverted its attention from incomes policy to legislation on unofficial strikes, found it had insufficient support to get that legislation through and, as a result of this defeat, was no longer in a position to enforce its incomes policy in any way. Indeed, it had already been announced in the budget that the government would not seek to renew its extended powers over prices and incomes when they expired at the end of the year. By the autumn of 1969 Labour's incomes policy was moribund. In October, Aubrey Jones announced his retirement as the chairman of the NBPI. There was no longer any relationship between the size of awards and the criteria they were supposed to

---

[1] This was generally known as the *Donovan Report*.
[2] Ibid. p. 14, para. 57.
[3] Department of Employment and Productivity, *In Place of Strife*.

observe; in October both the miners and the dustmen won very large pay increases. Nonetheless there was one last White Paper in December 1969,[1] which indicated the longer-term intention of the government to merge the NBPI with the Monopolies Commission; it also returned to the minor delaying powers (four months only) of the 1966 Act and suggested a norm of $2\frac{1}{2}$–$4\frac{1}{2}$ per cent for 1970. By January 1970 most of the settlements being made were well into double figures and at this point the TUC wound up their vetting committee.

INCOMES POLICY, 1972–4

Introduction

After the fall of the Labour government in June 1970, a period without an incomes policy followed. The Conservative government came to power devoted to the principle of non-intervention in wage negotiations. This period is described in chapter 2 (pages 52–62), which also gives an account of the search for an agreement with the trade unions after the miners' strike in January and February 1972, leading up to the freeze on wages and prices in November of that year. That ground is not covered again here; this section is concerned with the detailed provisions and problems of the three stages of the Conservative government's incomes policy, and with a discussion of their effects.

The general economic background is important (page 63). First, this was a period of reasonably rapid – but certainly not phenomenally rapid – economic expansion. Between the fourth quarters of 1971 and 1973 national output was rising at about 3 per cent a year[2] and from the first quarter of 1972 onwards unemployment fell rapidly. Secondly, throughout this period of incomes policy there was a mounting explosion of import prices helped by the falling exchange rate for sterling. In the second half of 1972 import prices (in sterling terms) rose at an annual rate of 16 per cent; in successive half years after that the rates of increase were 28, 42 and 64 per cent respectively.

The Conservative incomes policy began with a standstill on pay, prices, rents and dividends announced by the Prime Minister on 6 November 1972. This was to take effect immediately and to last 90 days – with provision for an extension of up to 60 days. A number of trade unions, anticipating some kind of restriction on free bargaining, had already negotiated settlements, and some important agreements – in particular that for 100,000 manual workers in the electricity supply

---

[1] Department of Employment and Productivity, *Productivity, Prices and Incomes Policy after 1969*, Cmnd 4237, London, HMSO, 1969.

[2] The year-on-year estimates are distorted because output fell in the first quarter of 1972 with the miners' strike. Over the same period, total final expenditure rose about 5 per cent a year and the foreign balance worsened sharply.

industry – just managed to get through; so long as the operative date was on or before 6 November, the increase could be implemented. The settlement with the electricity supply workers certainly removed one threat to the early stages of the policy. The main settlements which were caught and had to be deferred to the end of the freeze were for agricultural workers, for those employed by the clearing banks and for employees in the furniture industry; these three groups together involved some 600,000 workers. Wages Council settlements for another 600,000 were also deferred.

The freeze on wages presented the usual problems – increments, merit awards, Christmas bonuses, payment by results, and so on. However, as is usual with short freezes, there was very little leakage; between November 1972 and March 1973 average earnings rose less than 1 per cent.

The freeze on prices excluded fresh foods. There was some provision for firms to apply for increases if material prices rose sharply, and a number of food manufacturers in particular were allowed to raise prices, for between November 1972 and February 1973 the cost of basic material and fuel inputs into food manufacturing rose some 15 per cent. Between November and March the retail price index rose 2·4 per cent. Food prices – particularly for seasonal food – accounted for most of this; excluding food the rise was 0·7 per cent. However, the divergence between the movements of prices and of earnings over this short period prompted the General Secretary of the TUC to say that the proposition that price rises were a consequence of wage increases had been 'blown sky-high'.

For pay the freeze ended partly at the end of February, when deferred settlements whose operating date had been before the end of November 1972 became payable, but mainly at the end of March, when other deferred settlements were payable. This backlog consisted of settlements reached in 1972 when the going figures were high; it is part of the explanation for the relatively large rise in earnings between March and November 1973. For prices the freeze was extended to the end of April to cover the transition to VAT in place of purchase tax.

Throughout November and December 1972 the government had been preparing the next stage of their incomes policy. There were separate consultations with the CBI and the TUC; the latter re-emphasised its opposition to any form of statutory policy. The policy in fact followed the model set up in the United States in August 1971;[1]

---

[1] The American model of incomes policy is analysed in detail in the *National Institute Economic Review*, no. 62, November 1972, pp. 6–11; the designers of that model had in turn attempted to avoid the pitfalls of earlier British experience.

it was very different from the incomes policy of 1964–9, which illustrates the wide range that the term 'incomes policy' covers.

On the wages side the main distinguishing characteristics were as follows. First, the policy was universal and the newly established Pay Board was responsible for ensuring it was observed; there was no question of a few settlements being referred to the Board at the government's discretion. Secondly, the limitation was on the average amount per head actually paid by the firm; in this way the policy dealt with the problem that percentage increases on wage rates agreed in national negotiations often end up as very different percentage increases in actual earnings paid at individual plants. Thirdly, the policy had no productivity provisions, thus avoiding one of the major loopholes of the later stages of Labour's policy. Fourthly, notification requirements were more onerous for big firms than for small ones, the belief being that if the big settlements were held the smaller settlements would be kept in line.

On the prices side too the American model was followed. A separate body – the Price Commission – was set up and again the requirements were more onerous for big firms than for small ones. Price controls were based on two principles: firms could apply for increases on the basis of 'allowable costs per unit'; also, they had a reference level of net profit margins – the average of the best two years of the last five – and were not to exceed that level. Distributors were not controlled by allowable costs, but by a combination of net profit margins and gross percentage margins. Export sales were not controlled. Allowable costs were specified, but not non-allowable costs. Initially, advertising expenditure, depreciation, and research and development were the main non-allowable costs, but later the last two items were allowed. British practice differed from American in its treatment of productivity. The American Price Commission established productivity trends for a large number of industries and used them to calculate the allowable increase in costs per unit, so that a firm whose productivity record was better than average stood to gain. In Britain firms had to demonstrate that their own costs per unit had risen; that is, they gained no advantage in profits per unit from a productivity record better than average (though they might, of course, gain in total profits through an increase in market share). In addition, there was at first a productivity deduction of 50 per cent; that is, only half the rise in wage costs per unit of output was allowable.[1]

---

[1] The Price Commission justified this double deduction with the rather curious argument that, whereas the cost per unit calculation allowed for past increases in productivity, the 50 per cent disallowance allowed for future increases in productivity. This would only be valid if no firm went back to the Price Commission a second time.

Pay policy under Stage II

Under Stage II the pay limit per head – 'the maximum amount by which the average pay per head of the group may be increased in a 12 month period' – was the sum of 4 per cent of the average per head of the group's pay bill for the preceding twelve months and £1 per week. In calculating the total past wage bill non-contractual overtime was excluded and no individual might be paid an increase of more than £250 a year. In administering this policy, a number of employers – for example, the Post Office – found it very difficult to establish a figure for average pay in the past twelve months; in some cases the Pay Board permitted them to use figures from the Department of Employment's *New Earnings Survey*. Once the total sum had been established it could be distributed as the negotiators decided – favouring the low paid if they wished.

How did Stage II of the pay policy in fact work out? The trade union movement reluctantly acquiesced; there was little overt opposition, the number of days lost in strikes being lower not only than in 1972 (when there was the miners' strike), but also substantially lower than in either 1970 or 1971. There was a fairly clear effect on the rise in earnings; in the absence of some kind of incomes policy, there was every reason to think that the rise in money earnings would have accelerated during 1973. Unemployment was coming down quite briskly throughout the year and, pushed by the rise in import prices, retail prices were going up a good deal faster in 1973 than in 1972; nevertheless, the rise in earnings during 1973, excluding the effect of overtime, was significantly lower than during 1972.

However, although it is reasonably certain that the first two stages of incomes policy brought down the rise in money earnings, the increase still seems big when compared with the incomes policy 'norm'. The Pay Board claimed that the average pay increase resulting from approved Stage II settlements was $7\frac{2}{3}$ per cent, but, on national figures and excluding overtime, the increase in average hourly earnings between October 1972 and October 1973 was $13\frac{1}{2}$ per cent. Unlike the Price Commission, which related its figures to the national published series, the Pay Board made no attempt to analyse the reasons for this difference. Part of the explanation clearly lies in settlements postponed by the freeze, which were generally in line with the very large increases in the 1972 wage round. Then, movements towards equal pay could be made outside the pay limit and, according to the Pay Board, nearly three million benefited from this exception. There were also certain reductions in hours and improvements in holidays which were outside the limit, but these were not in fact very important.

How far was the pay code infringed? The Pay Board conducted a number of spot checks to see in particular whether the code was observed in settlements affecting under a hundred employees, which did not need to be reported. In the whole period of Stage II and Stage III spot checks on firms employing 614,000 in all showed that some 40,000, or about 6½ per cent, had been paid too much; the average excess was £1·54, which was 4–5 per cent of average earnings. If we assume that this represents the average degree of non-compliance – and this is a considerable assumption – it still explains only about 0·3 per cent out of the 13½ per cent rise in money earnings. It seems therefore that the settlements postponed by the freeze, the move to equal pay, payments by results systems, increases in overtime and the permitted continuance of incremental awards must explain most of the discrepancy between the national figure and the Pay Board's estimate of the average size of settlements approved.

Stage III

Stage II had an expected life of only seven months – from April to November 1973 – so that from its beginning the government was concerned with the problems of the third stage. The Pay Board was instructed to prepare two Reports, on anomalies and on relativities, and to have the former ready well before November.[1]

Throughout the summer the government discussed the shape of Stage III with the TUC and the CBI – though how much difference the discussions made eventually is uncertain. The TUC agreed to the talks on the grounds that the government ought to be given its views, but one important union, the Amalgamated Union of Engineering Workers, instructed its General Secretary not to join in and at the Trades Union annual Congress the General Council's policy of agreeing to talk was endorsed by only a small majority. In the discussions, the TUC representatives seem mainly to have reiterated their strong opposition to any statutory interference in wage bargaining; during the year various spokesmen for the TUC issued statements suggesting that, while wage increases were held back, price increases were 'let through in droves'.

The government issued a statement in July announcing that it intended to include a threshold clause in the next stage of incomes policy. This idea had been around for a long time, but it represented

---

[1] This was to deal with the unfair situations which had arisen specifically from the standstill introduced in November 1972; the other was to have a wider coverage: 'Within any system for the determination of pay, groups from time to time feel that they deserve special treatment . . . If a policy for controlling inflation is to be effective and fair, it must have procedures for considering such claims objectively' (Pay Board, *Advisory Report no. 2: Problems of Pay Relativities*, p. vi).

a radical change from previous government policies. In the period 1962–9 the official incomes policy had always stressed that price increases were no longer to be considered a justification for wage increases. On occasions the trade unions had put the idea forward and the government had turned it down; this time, it was a government proposal, which had a lukewarm reception from the trade unions.

The government's other main concern was to introduce greater flexibility into the next stage; apart from a general need, there was a specific problem in regard to the miners. The government had early warning of this; at the National Union of Mineworkers' annual conference in July there was unanimous approval for a claim for increases ranging from 22 to 46 per cent.[1] Thus, the provisions for greater flexibility in Stage III had both a general and a specific objective. They included a 1 per cent margin to deal with changes in pay structures or arrangements making possible better use of manpower; also extra payments were allowed for genuine efficiency schemes, but the savings had to be achieved first and the Pay Board presented with evidence from three months' operation. Further progress towards equal pay for women was also permitted, the Pay Board was instructed to produce recommendations on London allowances and (the provision proposed particularly to help the miners) premium payments above the limit were allowed to those working 'unsocial hours'.

Apparently the Prime Minister did attempt to check with the president of the National Union of Mineworkers that the concessions would be sufficient, and was certainly given the impression that they would be. It may be that the latter misjudged his executive committee; it may be that he got the wrong impression that during the negotiations there would be special concessions for the miners alone, rather than general provisions in a code available to all.

The new code for pay came into operation on 7 November 1973; the basic limit on increases was £2.25 per head per week or 7 per cent, with a limit of £350 a year for any individual; groups had to choose either the lump sum or the percentage; the various flexibility provisions described above were also included. Agreements could include the threshold provision, which provided that when the retail price index had risen 7 per cent above the figure for October 1973 a pay increase of 40p a week could be given, and the same increase for every further 1 per cent rise in the index. (This compensated in full on gross earnings of the average worker.) Presumably at the time the threshold was set – probably early in October 1973 – the Treasury price forecast for the

---

[1] The conference set targets for minimum weekly rates of an increase for surface workers from £25.29 to £35, for underground workers from £27.29 to £40 and for face workers from £39.79 to £45.

year from October stood at around 7 per cent; even allowing for the impossibility of forecasting the rise in oil prices, this was rather optimistic, given the increases which had already occurred in other commodity prices and the fall which had already occurred in the sterling exchange rate.

On prices the main change was that all category II firms (in manufacturing, those with sales between £5 million and £50 million a year) were required to notify price increases to the Price Commission. Increases in depreciation were made allowable costs and various safeguards were included to prevent an indefinite erosion of profit margins.

The whole of Stage III was, of course, overshadowed by the struggle with the National Union of Mineworkers. The Coal Board, making full use of the flexibility provisions in the new code, made an offer which was worth about 13 per cent on average, of which the shift premium for 'unsocial hours' accounted for 4·4 per cent. The miners rejected this offer and began an overtime ban on 12 November. The Electrical Power Engineers' Association had also begun a ban on out-of-hours working on 1 November because they considered it impossible under the new code to resolve a dispute over stand-by payments which had begun in December 1972. The sequence of events which led up to the miners' strike and the fall of the Conservative government is set out in chapter 2.

The procedural problem was that Stage III had no adequate mechanism for dealing with special cases on their merits. The Pay Board had to interpret the code as it stood, using only lawyers' ingenuity to see if special payments could not be squared with it. They were empowered to deal with 'anomalies', as recommended in their Report,[1] but these were defined as cases where a clear and identifiable link had been broken by the standstill. The Report on relativities had not yet appeared; when it did appear in January 1974,[2] it recommended a process for selecting and examining cases which could have been used, but by then it was very late. The government did in fact ask the Pay Board to turn itself into a relativities board and consider the miners' case; it reported after the election was over. There was an escape clause in the counter-inflation legislation which provided that, if the Secretary of State for Employment was satisfied that there were exceptional circumstances, he could overrule the Pay Board and give his consent to an increase, but this particular route would have seemed very much a surrender. Apart, then, from all the problems which arose in running an incomes policy to which the trade union movement was hostile,

[1] Pay Board, *Advisory Report no. 1: Anomalies arising out of the Pay Standstill of Nov. 1972*, London, HMSO, 1973.
[2] Pay Board, *Advisory Report no. 2: Problems of Pay Relativities*.

Stage III did not contain adequate mechanisms for dealing with special cases in time.

While the struggle with the miners was going on, the Pay Board proceeded with the administration of the new code – and indeed continued to do so for some months after the change of government. Up to the end of June 1974 it approved settlements covering some $14\frac{1}{2}$ million employees and calculated that the average pay rise was around 9 per cent excluding threshold components. On the whole, negotiating groups preferred the lump sum to the percentage system of calculating the total. Up to the end of June only about a third of the settlements had taken advantage of the threshold provisions; no doubt many of these included threshold provisions later. Perhaps not surprisingly there is evidence of rather more extensive infringement of the code in its dying stages. When infringements were discovered their average size in the quarter to the end of May 1974 was £2.75, against the figure for the whole incomes policy period of £1.54. The Pay Board ceased to exist on 25 July 1974.

AN ASSESSMENT OF INCOMES POLICY

Introduction

Were incomes policies successful? Does the experience of 1960–74 suggest that future governments should continue with experiments of this kind or abandon them?

There are some preliminary points to be made. First, 'incomes policy' covers a wide range of different types of attempt to intervene in the process of fixing incomes; it is not a single instrument like, say, VAT. The incomes policy of 1964–5, with a voluntary statement of intent and the NBPI, whose effect was to be selective and educative, was very different from the statutory £1 plus 4 per cent policy of April–November 1973. Indeed, it is not at all easy to distinguish satisfactorily between periods when incomes policy was 'on' or 'off'. In 1970 and 1971 the Conservative government tried to make each settlement in the public sector 1 per cent lower than the previous settlement – the 'N–1' policy – is this to be counted an 'on' period or not?

Secondly, before discussing the success of any policy, we must establish what policy-makers were trying to do. Clearly their dominant objective was to bring down the rate of inflation, but there were other secondary objectives as well. Most incomes policies were supposed to favour the low paid, so that one measure of success is whether or not the differential between low wages and the average wage narrowed. There are other consequences to be considered: incomes policies may reduce or increase the number of industrial disputes, improve or worsen industrial relations, or (conceivably) affect productivity. However, the main criterion is undoubtedly success or failure in reducing the rate of inflation.

Thirdly, the success of an attempt to change some institution in society must necessarily be judged in a different way from the efficacy of a more conventional instrument, such as a change in tax rates. It may take a long time for new workable institutions to evolve; there can be a slow learning process and the early attempts may be unsuccessful partly because those involved are reluctant to accept the need for change. It is not enough simply to consider the success or failure of early attempts; there is also the question of whether or not these early moves were along a road with a dead end. If incomes policy proves to be an idea with no future, then the early experiments were a waste of time; if, on the other hand, they were steps towards an eventual and necessary acceptance of some form of intervention in free collective bargaining, then the judgement has to be different.

There are therefore basically two questions. First, whether the whole series of attempts at various kinds of incomes policy was a mistake; if so there is little more to be said. If, however, the idea is not wholly rejected, then there is the second question of the lessons to be learned by comparing the various forms of incomes policy which were attempted.

The general argument

The general argument for an incomes policy presented in this country is that without it a very high rate of unemployment would be needed to bring about an acceptable degree of price stability; further, this rate of unemployment was probably higher at the end of the period than at the beginning. Proponents of incomes policy tend to view inflation in terms of wage bargaining; they picture the rate of inflation as being largely determined by trade union bargains in any particular year. Also, a relatively small number of 'leading' wage bargains, which may not be the same ones each year, set the standard which other unions follow, for one of the main concerns of a trade union negotiator is that the group he represents should not be left behind. In any year the leading wage bargains will obviously be strongly influenced by past price rises and increases in real incomes (before or after tax), but not so strictly that they cannot also be influenced by policy, or by willingness or unwillingness to cooperate with the government of the day. Single events can affect the figures; for example, after the successful miners' strikes in 1972 and 1974 the general increase in average earnings was probably much higher than it would have been had the strikes failed. Longer-term trends might also drive the figures up. The advocates of incomes policy see the structure of free collective bargaining in this country, with a very large number of separate bargains following each other throughout the year, as being particularly conducive to high money wage settlements; they therefore believe there may well be some advantage in modifying this institution.

The arguments against incomes policy are that it is, at best, ineffective (except in the very short term) and, at worst, damaging – in preventing desirable changes in relativities. On this view the rate of increase in money earnings is determined by factors which no incomes policy can alter for any appreciable period – predominantly, of course, the demand for labour; governments are therefore wasting their time.

The arguments about incomes policy are part of the wider debate about the desirable degree of intervention in the economy; an incomes policy implies a considerable extension of that intervention, in that, whether the policy is statutory or voluntary, those who negotiate wage or salary increases are subject to constraint. It is natural that those who are anxious to limit government intervention in the working of a market economy should be dubious about incomes policies. There is also a natural disinclination among economists to accept that the rate of increase in earnings cannot be explained in terms of other economic variables – for economists are essentially in the business of explaining the movement of one economic variable in terms of others.

So far as the past is concerned, therefore, the question is whether or not year-to-year movements in average earnings – or some other indicator of income from employment[1] – can be satisfactorily explained using variables which incomes policy could not be expected to influence. If so, there is a strong case for saying that past incomes policies have been ineffective, at least in their main objective of holding back the rise in money incomes. It would not, of course, follow that all forms of incomes policy would necessarily be ineffective; it would simply be evidence on the past performance of the forms tried so far.

The obvious candidate as an economic determinant of the rate of rise in money earnings is the pressure of demand for labour, and in the late 1950s and early 1960s it was widely argued that changes in unemployment adequately explained fluctuations in the increase in money earnings.[2] F. W. Paish was an influential advocate of the view that in this period it was excess pressure of demand for labour which

[1] Attempts at explanation have sometimes used wage rates and sometimes earnings, either hourly or weekly; more recently an attempt has been made to calculate a series for wage settlements. Another possible series is the average wage or salary per unit of employment.

[2] The arguments were generally based on the article by Professor A. W. Phillips, 'The relation between unemployment and the rate of change of money wage rates in the United Kingdom, 1861–1957', *Economica*, vol. 25 (new series), November 1958. It was from this article that Professor Paish deduced that a rise in unemployment from 1 to 2 per cent would be accompanied by a fall in the rate of increase in wage rates from 9 to 3 per cent a year.

mattered; the demands of trade unions were irrelevant. In a memorandum presented to the Council on Prices Productivity and Incomes in November 1957, he wrote:

The causal factor in the rise in wages and salaries has been, not the demands of Trade Unions, but the ability of employers to grant them without reducing their demand for labour...it is probably true that the very existence of collective bargaining, with its administrative delays, has caused wage rates to rise more slowly than they would have done under similar conditions of excess demand in a free labour market, where there were neither Trade Unions nor employers' associations.[1]

In 1964 Paish put forward the view that if wages increased at an excessive rate when unemployment was below 2 per cent the proper course was to restrain demand, if unemployment was above $2\frac{1}{4}$ per cent a 'wages policy' was unnecessary but harmless, in the narrow area where unemployment lay between 2 and $2\frac{1}{4}$ per cent restriction of demand might be usefully supplemented (though probably not replaced) by a 'wages policy'. At that time he considered the level of unemployment a powerful determinant of the rate of increase in wages and earnings.

However, in the late 1960s and early 1970s unemployment was rising and the increase in money earnings accelerating at the same time. The view that the rise in earnings could be explained by the pressure of demand for labour as measured by unemployment then clearly became untenable. Various amendments were tried. It was argued that with the introduction of earnings-related supplements to unemployment benefit as from October 1966 those who became unemployed were not under the same pressure to find another job immediately and so took longer in their search. Hence, for any given pressure of demand for labour, after October 1966 the figure for unemployment was higher than it had been before. However, subsequent studies showed that not many of the unemployed in fact received earnings-related supplements; a Department of Employment working party concluded that the additional unemployment from this cause in November 1973 'was very probably less than 50,000' males.[2] Another amendment was to add price expectations to the pressure of demand as part of the explanation of the movement of earnings or wage rates,[3] but various difficulties were

---

[1] Paish, *Studies in an Inflationary Economy*, p. 116. Paish is referring here to the experience of the 1950s; he did not suggest that excess demand for labour was the sole explanation of inflation in the late 1960s, but concluded that trade union activity was an important component in that period.

[2] The Report was summarised in 'The changed relationship between unemployment and vacancies', *Department of Employment Gazette*, October 1976.

[3] This followed the work of M. Friedman in the United States (see, for example, 'The role of monetary policy', *American Economic Review*, vol. 58, March 1968). The inclusion of price expectations is possibly more plausible in the United States, where labour contracts are for a set term, than in the United Kingdom, where they are not.

encountered: first, it was the term for expected prices which then provided virtually all the explanation of the movement in wage rates or earnings, and unemployment tended to drop out of the picture altogether;[1] secondly, since price expectations are usually made to depend on the movement of past prices (or constructed from a series which is heavily dependent on past prices), there is the much more straightforward method of using past prices themselves, which does not bring in the complexity of expectations.

By the early 1970s, therefore, it was becoming less plausible to suggest that the movement of wage rates or earnings basically responded to the pressure of demand for labour. An alternative approach put wage bargaining in the centre of the picture and attempted to model the main forces acting on the wage bargaining process. The suggestion was that negotiators were concerned to make good the loss in real income from the increase in prices since the last settlement and then to add a further sum to ensure some real gain. This view was in some ways a rediscovery of a relationship suggested by Dow as long ago as 1956 – that it seemed reasonable to believe 'that full compensation for price increases is something which trade unions aim at and which both sides to wage negotiations accept as a standard of reference'.[2] One question which arises is whether the negotiators also take account of changes in tax or national insurance deductions, so that they are concerned with the post-tax income of their members.[3] However, neither the demand for labour nor the wage bargaining view provides a good account of the year-to-year movements of money wage rates or earnings, particularly in the 1970s. There were clearly other forces at work.

By the early 1970s none of the main bodies engaged in short-term economic forecasting in Britain were using econometric relationships for forecasting wage rates or earnings. It is reasonable to suppose that a sharp increase in prices will tend to put wage settlements up and that there is some level of unemployment which will tend to push them down, but it is not possible to quantify those influences with any precision. It follows that there is no way of saying what would have happened in the absence of incomes policy; it certainly does not appear that the year-to-year movement of wage rates or earnings is precisely

[1] For a general discussion of the problem of various forms of wage equation, see M. J. Artis, 'Is there a wage equation?' in Courakis (ed.), *Inflation, Depression and Economic Policy in the West*. See also the discussion in 'Spare capacity and full employment', *National Institute Economic Review*, no. 79, February 1977, p. 45 *et seq.*

[2] J. C. R. Dow, 'Analysis of the generation of price inflation', *Oxford Economic Papers*, vol. 8 (new series), October 1956.

[3] Equations of this kind are set out in S. G. B. Henry, M. C. Sawyer and P. Smith, 'Models of inflation in the United Kingdom', *National Institute Economic Review*, no. 77, August 1976; also, K. Coutts, R. Tarling and F. Wilkinson, 'Wage bargaining and the inflation process', *Economic Policy Review*, no. 2, March 1976, p. 20.

determined by economic factors which incomes policy could not influence. It also follows that assessments of incomes policy effects have to be rather rough and ready. Chart 8.1 sets out experience in various periods, from which the following conclusions are tentatively suggested.

First, short wage freezes are certainly and undoubtedly effective. The clearest evidence is provided by the period of freeze followed by severe restraint from the middle of 1966 to the middle of 1967. Before and after that period average earnings were rising at roughly 8 per cent a year; during that period they rose only 2 per cent a year. There can

Chart 8.1. *Changes in average weekly earnings, 1959–76*

SOURCES: CSO, *Economic Trends, Annual Supplement 1976*; Department of Employment, *British Labour Statistics: historical abstract, 1886–1968*, London, HMSO, 1971, and *British Labour Statistics Yearbook 1972*, London, HMSO, 1974.

Note: For 1959–64 the figures are for male manual workers aged 21 and over in the United Kingdom; from 1964 they are for wages and salaries combined in all industries in Great Britain. The series ran closely together in the period 1964–70 and can be assumed to be comparable.

be no other sensible explanation of that difference. The period of freeze under the Conservative government was even shorter – effectively from November 1972 to March 1973. There was the same sharp deceleration: in the year to November 1972 average earnings rose just on 17 per cent; in the next four months they rose at an annual rate of only 3 per cent.

Assessing longer periods of incomes policy is more difficult. First, they did not achieve the ambitious objectives which their originators set. The basic intention of the Labour government was to bring the rise in money earnings down to a figure close to the trend in national output per head, so that the target was probably an average increase of something like 4–5 per cent a year. In fact, apart from the period of freeze and severe restraint, the rise was roughly 8 per cent a year. During the Conservative government's short incomes policy the objective was probably to bring the rise in earnings down to something like 8 per cent; in fact the figure was about $12\frac{1}{2}$ per cent. However, this is perhaps too severe a criterion of success. The question might rather be whether or not these policies brought the rise in money earnings down to a figure lower than it would otherwise have been.

In any assessment of an incomes policy, it is important to compare the experience of that period not simply with the years that went before, but with the years after as well, because there may well be forces producing a long-term upward trend in the increase in money wages and earnings. Taking the period from the fourth quarter of 1964 to the second quarter of 1969,[1] which included a year of freeze and severe restraint, the annual rise in average earnings was $6\frac{1}{2}$ per cent. This seems very little improvement on the annual rate which prevailed in the two years before the beginning of the period, of around $7\frac{1}{2}$ per cent. However, the period was one in which some of the pressures making for large increases in money earnings were particularly strong; the effect of devaluation on prices and the successive increases in taxation meant that the real post-tax earnings of the average wage earner rose little. The effectiveness of the policy also looks rather different if one takes into account what happened after it ended: the rate of increase in money earnings moved up sharply to 12 per cent a year between mid-1969 and mid-1972, which suggests that up to mid-1969 the policy was having some effect in making trade unions settle for figures lower than they would otherwise have accepted.

To some extent the same kind of assessment applies to the Conservative government's incomes policy. From the fourth quarter of 1972 to the fourth quarter of 1973 average earnings rose about $12\frac{1}{2}$ per cent,[2] which was about the same as the rate of increase during the previous two years. However, again 1973 was a year when one would normally have expected the rise in earnings to accelerate, partly because import prices were rising very fast and partly because output was rising fast and unemployment falling. And again the end of the policy was followed by a very sharp acceleration – to an annual rate of 24 per cent between the end of 1974 and the middle of 1975.

Perhaps the strongest evidence for the effectiveness of incomes policy lies strictly outside the period covered by this book; it is hard to believe that the sharp deceleration in the increase in money earnings which

---

[1] It seems sensible to pick mid-1969 as the terminal date, because during 1969 the government in effect abandoned the incomes policy approach and turned to an attempt to bring the trade unions within the framework of the law (page 377 above).

[2] In the first quarter of 1974 the figure for average earnings fell, mainly because of the effect of the miners' strike.

followed the reintroduction of an incomes policy after mid-1975 would have been so sharp in its absence. Indeed it is highly uncertain whether it would have happened at all.

In sum, if we suppose that over this period there was a variety of forces tending to produce a rising trend in the increase in money earnings, then the experience of the late 1960s and early 1970s is consonant with the view that the two incomes policies during that period were successful, so long as they were in force, in holding back this process. Given that conclusion, it is reasonable to look at the various forms which incomes policy took and the problems which arose to see what lessons can usefully be drawn about different types of attempt at institutional change.

The structure of incomes policies

The problems of incomes policy throughout were not so much conceiving what it should be ideally, but rather the practical and political difficulties of devising machinery which worked. There was the choice between attempting a temporary or a permanent policy and the need to decide on a norm (here the question of compensation for past price rises comes up). Criteria were required for exceptions from the norm; also – and this was easily the most formidable difficulty – some way of administering the policy had to be found; in particular, the choice had to be made between seeking cooperation, imposing a compulsory system, or adopting some mixture of the two. Finally, a decision was needed on any concomitant action on non-wage incomes and prices. In what follows we consider each of these difficulties.

On the choice between temporary and permanent policies, governments alternated between attempts to bring in long-lasting reforms and emergency action to halt inflation. In 1962 the National Incomes Commission was to be a permanent body whose main function was educational. In 1964 the Labour government's initial conception was again a permanent policy, with an annual decision about the norm and the NBPI to adjudicate on cases referred to it. However, in mid-1966 short-term emergency action was superimposed for a year and the more permanent underlying policy had effectively come to an end by the middle of 1969 as government preoccupation moved elsewhere. The Conservative government's policy in 1972 can be labelled 'medium-term temporary'; it was initially envisaged that it would last for perhaps three years.

In neither 1964 nor 1972 was the 're-entry problem' of transition back to free collective bargaining dealt with successfully. Part of the reason is that both policies ended with changes in government. However, clearly a great difficulty with temporary policies is that they are inherently unstable. They tend to be followed by a rash of large claims, with negotiators trying not only to catch up what they think they have lost, but also to obtain a large award before the introduction of the next policy. One of the most obvious things about the rise in money earnings since the mid-1960s is the way in which it accelerated when incomes policies ended. This is part of the case for more permanent institutional changes.

The successive incomes policy White Papers during the 1960s were largely concerned with the theology of the norm and the criteria for exceptions. The norm, both under the Conservatives up to 1964 and under Labour up to 1969, tended to be set theoretically at a figure which would have brought about virtual price stability had it been observed. The initial 'guiding light', set in 1961, was the trend rate of growth in output per head of $2\frac{1}{2}$ per cent. This was later raised by the National Incomes Commission to $3-3\frac{1}{2}$ per cent, partly on the grounds that incomes policy should be geared to the faster rate of growth which it was supposed to help to bring about, but also partly to make the figure a little more realistic. In the period 1964-9 the norm varied between 3 per cent and zero; it was still set at the figure which would bring about virtual price stability. In 1972 the Conservative government's incomes policy was introduced at a time when prices were rising much faster. The objective was the less ambitious one of bringing the rate of inflation down, so that the norm of Stage II was around 7-8 per cent and the Stage III figure if anything rather higher.

Between 1964 and 1972 there was a change of view about indexation. Up to the end of the 1960s it had been emphasised that past price increases should not be considered a justification for future wage increases – this would simply perpetuate the inflationary process. During the early 1970s various means of indexation were being extensively discussed, and Stage III of the Conservative policy permitted negotiators to include in their agreements a guarantee which effectively compensated the average wage earner if the retail price index rose by more than 7 per cent during the year from October 1973 to October 1974. This particular guarantee was most unfortunately timed, since the retail price index passed the 7 per cent threshold in April 1974; indeed the April figure for retail prices was 9·7 per cent above the threshold base and the first three threshold payments were triggered. Under some agreements threshold payments were triggered eleven times during 1974, which shows the danger of any form of indexation in a country with a large foreign trade. If the terms of trade worsen for any reason – because of sharply rising import prices, from devaluation, or from a deliberate 'managed downward float' – real wages and salaries should fall (or rise more slowly) in consequence, but indexation by inhibiting the transfer of real resources into exports prevents the downward movement of the exchange rate from working.

Criteria for exceptions

The main criteria for exceptional pay increases which were put forward at one time or another during this period were as follows:

(1) Low pay: 'where there was general recognition that existing wage or salary levels are too low to maintain a reasonable standard of living'.[1]

(2) The reallocation of labour: 'where it is essential in the national interest to secure (or prevent) a change in the distribution of manpower, and a pay increase would be both necessary and effective for this purpose'.[2] Linked to this criterion was that of comparability – where there was widespread recognition that the pay of some group had fallen out of line with the pay for similar work elsewhere in the United Kingdom – which was behind the Conservative government's proposal to rectify in its Stage III the anomalies brought about by the timing of the freeze in November 1972.

(3) Productivity: initially the principle was that employees had to make a direct contribution by accepting more exacting work or by a major change in working practices, and that some of the benefit should accrue to the community in the form of lower prices. Later, under the Labour government, the NBPI recommended tighter provisions, in particular that the productivity gains should come before the additional payment; this was written into the productivity clauses in the Conservatives' Stage III policy.

Two additional criteria added later were reorganisation of wage and salary structures which could be justified on grounds of economic efficiency and increased productivity (1968), and the implementing of equal pay legislation (1970).

The success of criterion (1) above must be judged on whether or not it in fact improved the position of the low paid in relation to the average. This question can be asked about earnings alone, or about the spread of employment incomes through the economy as a whole; incomes policy was, of course, simply concerned with gross earnings from employment, so that these are the figures which should be used to measure any effect. The figures for the dispersion of gross weekly earnings in fact show a remarkable stability (table 8.1). For both men and women manual workers there is a very slight widening of dispersion between 1960 and 1970, followed by a very slight narrowing between

---

[1] The criterion is described in this way in successive White Papers, for example, Department of Economic Affairs, *Productivity, Prices and Incomes Policy in 1968 and 1969*.

[2] Ibid.

1970 and 1976. However, the movements were very small. For non-manual men (but not for non-manual women) there was some reduction in the relative position of the higher income groups between 1970 and 1976. In general, the figures suggest strongly that it is very difficult to change the distribution of gross earnings, and particularly difficult to improve the relative position of the low paid. This is in spite of the fact that the Conservatives' incomes policy was deliberately designed to help this group; in their Stage II firms were expressly permitted to distribute the total sum available in such a way as to benefit the low paid.

Table 8.1. *Dispersion of gross weekly earnings,[a] Great Britain, 1960–76*

Percentages of median

	Manual workers		Non-manual workers		All workers	
	Highest decile	Lowest decile	Highest decile	Lowest decile	Highest decile	Lowest decile
Men						
1960	145·2	70·6	..	..	..	..
1965	143·9	69·7	..	..	..	..
1970	147·2	67·3	175·1	61·8	160·6	65·4
1974	144·1	68·6	171·6	62·9	157·0	66·8
1976	144·9	70·2	167·5	62·5	159·5	67·6
Women						
1960	138·3	72·0	..	..	..	..
1965	138·7	66·5	..	..	..	..
1970	144·8	69·0	173·7	64·2	170·4	66·4
1974	143·4	69·1	162·0	66·5	159·1	67·7
1976	140·6	67·8	172·9	65·1	165·9	66·1

SOURCES: Department of Employment, *British Labour Statistics Yearbook 1974*, London, HMSO, 1976, and *New Earnings Survey 1976*, London, HMSO, 1977, part A.

[a] For full-time men aged 21 or over and full-time women aged 18 or over, whose pay was not affected by absence.

Criterion (2), although it was available to the NBPI, was in fact hardly ever used. This is perhaps surprising, in that one of the standard arguments against incomes policy is that it abolishes the natural mechanism by which labour is channelled from industries with a low marginal product to industries with a high one. The NBPI tended to take the view that, if there were insufficient workers with the particular skill required for a particular job, a short-term increase in pay was not the best way of increasing the numbers available; the problem was better dealt with by improved long-term prospects, or by an extension of training. The principle of comparability was also used very sparingly; if it were used extensively, an incomes policy might simply reproduce the workings of the existing system, since there is always some com-

parison which can justify virtually any increase. In the allowance for
anomalies made by the Conservatives it was only where the freeze had
broken a relationship which was very well established indeed that the
case was accepted.

Productivity as a criterion has considerable theoretical attractions,
in that its rate of increase in an economy could then be accelerated by
an incomes policy. However, productivity agreements fell into some
disrepute in the later years of the Labour government; in spite of the
fairly stringent conditions which the NBPI attempted to lay down,[1]
these were very frequently not observed.[2] From 1968 onwards there
was what has been described as 'an uncritical campaign for productivity
bargaining',[3] the surveillance of the NBPI was weakened by insufficient
and inadequate references, and productivity bargains became one of
the main routes by which wage awards evaded control. For this reason
stringent criteria were imposed for productivity agreements in the
Conservatives' Stage III; in subsequent incomes policies up to mid-1977
no provision for them was made at all.

The incomes policies of this period did not provide an adequate
structure for dealing with exceptional cases. The NBPI could only
consider the cases which the government chose to refer to it; the intention was that it should establish a kind of case law, but for case law to
be effective its rulings have to be copied by other adjudicators and there
is no evidence that the TUC vetting committee, for example, took
much notice of the principles which the NBPI laid down. The Conservative government's statutory policy did not provide a satisfactory
alternative; the Pay Board could do no more than interpret the pay
code. A basically judicial system has to have greater coverage than the
NBPI had to be effective; on the other hand, a statutory pay code
which allows no discretion to the institution administering it is not
flexible enough for the later stages of an incomes policy.

The administrative machinery

Part of the attraction of incomes policies is that basically the idea is
simple: that there is little point in high nominal wage and salary
awards, which lead to higher prices; it is more sensible to have lower
money awards all round with smaller price rises. However, the problems which arose from the attempts to find new institutions to bring that
result about proved formidable. This section sets out some of the problems encountered and describes the main attempts to find solutions.

[1] NBPI, *Report no. 36: Productivity Agreements*.
[2] In a survey of 24 cases of productivity bargaining, Clegg found over half to be either
spurious or seriously defective (H. Clegg, *How to Run an Incomes Policy and Why We Made
Such a Mess of the Last One*, London, Heinemann, 1971, p. 38).
[3] Ibid. p. 39.

First, there was the choice between a voluntary and a statutory policy. A voluntary policy has the considerable advantage that it can be run in cooperation with the organised trade union movement, which may find it difficult to deliver an incomes policy – particularly a long-term one – but has considerable power effectively to destroy a policy to which it is opposed. The disadvantages of a voluntary policy are that it runs the risk of being weak – little more than a statement of good intentions – and once one union has 'broken through' it is virtually impossible to prevent others (who have the duty to protect the interests of their members) from following. A voluntary policy has to be very simple, so that it can be monitored without difficulty, and such a policy cannot make sufficient allowance for exceptional treatment for one reason or another. The trade union movement is opposed to 'outside bodies' exercising any kind of judicial function in wage negotiations; it was never reconciled to the NBPI.[1] Thus the voluntary incomes policy of the period 1964–9 proved to be weak. It is true that it appears less unsuccessful in retrospect than it did at the time; nonetheless, the norm was exceeded by a very wide margin indeed. However, voluntary policies with a single simple figure and no provision for exceptions have had considerable success.

There are possibilities for mixing statutory and voluntary elements. The period of freeze and severe restraint from mid-1966 to mid-1967 began as a voluntary policy, with the threat of statutory enactment if the policy was broken; in fact one union forced the government to introduce statutory provisions. Another mix is to make the policy basically voluntary for the unions, but in effect statutory on the paying agent. There is indeed no example in any period of statutory policy of a union or union negotiator being penalised for breaking the rules; insofar as there has been any enforcement it has always been on the paying agent, as, for example, under the Conservative government's statutory policy. (The method of enforcement was also very similar in what was labelled a voluntary policy under the Labour government from mid-1975 onwards.) Thus the dividing line between a statutory and a voluntary policy is not distinct.

In fact, the main difficulty of statutory policies proved to be much the same as the main difficulty of voluntary policies – that of making reasonable provision for exceptional treatment where justified. Statutory periods of wage freeze were effective, but the Conservative government did not develop in time any adequate system for dealing with exceptions. Thus, when confronted by the miners' claim to be an

[1] It does not have the same objection to an arbitral body which simply attempts to reconcile the conflicting views of the two sides; the objection is to a body which uses criteria of its own to judge whether a wage award is warranted or not.

exception – a claim which the trade union movement in general supported – they had no adequate machinery; the Pay Board Report on relativities, which suggested such a mechanism, came too late.[1]

Another problem arose from the great complexity of systems of payment in the British economy. In the period 1964–9 the claims and awards considered by the three bodies concerned with the policy – the TUC vetting committee, the Department of Employment and the NBPI – usually arose from national negotiations about changes in basic rates. It was often very difficult to establish what such awards might mean as an annual percentage increase in actual earnings.[2] Incomes policy in this period never grappled with the problem posed by payment by results schemes, for example, although about eight or nine million workers were employed in undertakings where such schemes were used and were directly or indirectly affected by them. The NBPI commented:

The essence of the problem of applying the incomes policy to PBR systems is that a large part of the increase in earnings under them does not arise from 'claims' or 'settlements' in the accepted sense at all. The setting of piece work prices, standard times for new jobs and so forth are not 'settlements' in the accepted sense of the word, and they are often negotiated by individuals or small groups of workers with foremen, rate-fixers or first-line management ...Thousands of such bargains are struck every day...we came across only one instance where a firm was attempting to apply the [incomes] policy to PBR earnings in any way.[3]

Later incomes policies attempted to take this problem into consideration. The Conservatives' incomes policies set a limit to the total increase in the wage bill which firms or other paying agents were permitted to make. Labour's policies after mid-1975 fixed sums which were explicitly additions to earnings, not to basic rates.

Finally there is the choice – which has already been touched on in the discussion of statutory or voluntary policies – between simplicity and flexibility. The advantages of a simple policy are clear – there is much less scope for evasion and it is much easier to monitor – therefore, in the short term, it is likely to be more effective. However, simple policies are short-term policies only – they lead to strong pressures either to restore relativities which have been altered by the policy, or to change relativities when new circumstances have arisen – and short-term policies tend to be followed by a rush of very large claims and

[1] Pay Board, *Advisory Report no. 2: Problems of Pay Relativities.*

[2] For example, the award to electricity supply workers in February 1971 was claimed by some to represent a rise of some 20 per cent and by others to represent a rise of little over 10 per cent.

[3] NBPI, *Report no. 65: Payment by Results Systems,* Cmnd 3627, London, HMSO, 1968, para. 220 *et seq.*

awards. A long-term policy must have some provision for judging exceptions to the norm. No adequate mechanism for doing this was found
during the period: the NBPI (for various reasons) tended to act more as
an advocate for industrial reform than as an adjudicator on particular
settlements; the Pay Board's Report on relativities suggested a possible
mechanism, but too late for it to be tried.

Control of other incomes and prices

The main objective of incomes policies throughout this period was to
bring down the size of wage and salary awards, in the belief that these
were the driving force in the inflationary process in this country. In
the view of those concerned with these policies, there was little risk
that moderation in wage increases would lead to excessive increases in
profits; price moderation would follow from wage moderation. Evidence about the behaviour of prices in this country strongly suggests
that this is true. Nonetheless, all incomes policies concerned themselves
with prices as well – indeed a number were presented so as to give the
impression that price control was on an equal footing with income
control. This was basically a cosmetic exercise, based on the view that
income control without price control would not be acceptable to wage
and salary earners. In much the same way the policies also laid down
rules – admittedly unenforceable – for self-employment incomes and
frequently included statutory control of dividends. These additional
controls were in the interests of 'fairness', not because the designers of
incomes policies believed that these incomes were important in their
own right in the inflationary process.

It is true that a view existed that sufficiently tough price control
could also serve as an incomes policy – in that if firms were prevented
from raising their prices they would be forced to resist excessive wage
demands. However, this particular policy was never tried during the
period covered in this book, and subsequent experience between April
1974 and June 1975, when there was a weak incomes policy together
with price control, was not encouraging.

The guidelines for the various incomes policies normally prescribed
that incomes from self-employment should follow the general rules
which applied to incomes from employment. However, there was no
way of monitoring whether this in fact happened, and certainly no
way of enforcing the rules on the self-employed during periods of
statutory incomes policy; the one exception was fees charged by
professional groups, which could be referred to the NBPI. However,
the general assumption was that this was a 'passive' sector.

The policy towards dividends was more active. Up to 1968 companies were requested to exercise moderation; during the standstill

and period of severe restraint they were asked not to increase dividends at all and indeed dividends did not rise. In 1968 the government introduced a $3\frac{1}{2}$ per cent limit for dividend increases, which was abolished at the end of 1969. Under the Conservatives' incomes policy there was a statutory 5 per cent limit on dividend increases, administered by the Treasury, which was empowered to consent to companies exceeding the limit under certain circumstances – take-over defence, new companies, newly quoted companies, increases in share capital, recoveries and pre-standstill commitments. It is hard to say what effect the various voluntary and statutory limitations on dividends had, for the usual reason that it is virtually impossible to say what dividends might have been paid in their absence. This was a period when there was fairly general pressure on company profits and their share in national income was falling, so that in any case capital consumption and the financing of stocks (including stock appreciation) and new investment might have been expected to take a larger share of company income. Further, during this period companies were tending to raise new money by issuing fixed-interest stock more than ordinary shares; also, there were successive changes in the system of company taxation, including a period from 1965 to 1972 when distributions were differentially taxed.

The legislation concerning the rents of private housing – the Rent Act 1965 and the Housing Finance Act 1971 – was essentially a separate matter outside the scope of incomes policies. However, the operation of this legislation was modified from time to time in the interests of incomes policy. Thus, under Part III of the Prices and Incomes Act 1968, rent increases during the later half of 1968 and 1969 were spread out. As part of Stage II of the Conservative government's incomes policy, there was a specific modification to the size of the rent rebates and allowances in their Housing Finance Act, so that a low income family living in local authority housing would not have to pay a significant rent increase. Essentially, however, these were marginal modifications to housing legislation which had other objectives. During the first year of the Conservatives' incomes policy, there was also a standstill on business rents, which was extended to May 1974.

The system of price control under the Labour government was, like the system of intervention in incomes, basically a voluntary one. Guidelines were promulgated setting out what were considered to be legitimate justifications for price increases, also indicating the circumstances in which prices should be reduced. Then in November 1965 an early warning system was introduced for prices in parallel with the early warning system for wage increases. For an initial list of about 75 items, firms were required to give four weeks notice of their intention to raise prices; there was a supplementary list of food prices 'under constant watch' by the Ministry of Agriculture, Fisheries and Food. The government could ask a firm to defer a price rise for further enquiry or for reference to the NBPI, but the total period of delay – including any NBPI Report – could not exceed three months. This remained the basic system throughout the period, except during the period of wages and prices freeze, when firms were not expected to raise their prices at all.

The system under the Conservative government was considerably more elaborate: its prices policy, like its pay policy, followed the pattern set by the Americans (see page 379 above). Firms were divided into three categories by size: category I had to give prior notification before raising prices, category II had to submit regular reports, and category III were subject to spot checks. In Stage III of the policy category II firms were also required to notify price rises in advance.

It is doubtful whether the Labour government's early warning system had any substantial general effect; certainly some prices were held back when references were made to the NBPI, but it is quite possible that firms cross-subsidised the prices of the products in the early warning list. The effects of the price code under the Conservative government may have been a little more significant. The Price Commission's own quantification of its effects was probably optimistic, in that it was based on the money consequences of its rejection or amendment of applications for price increases. However, we know from firms whose applications were approved that their actual increases were frequently less than those approved. Further, the Price Commission did not have any apparatus for checking that its rulings were observed.

An inquiry addressed to a small group of firms in May 1976 suggested that the prices of that group were $2\frac{1}{2}$ per cent lower on average than they would have been in the absence of the price code;[1] that was after the code had been in operation for three years. Further, a number of the firms stated that they could have raised their prices within the terms of the code, but that market conditions prevented this. The general conclusion is that the effect of the price code was not substantial.

[1] R. W. Evely, 'The effects of the price code', *National Institute Economic Review*, no. 77, August 1976.

CHAPTER 9

GENERAL APPRAISAL

by *F. T. Blackaby*

THE AMBIT OF POLICY

This shortened version of *British Economic Policy 1960–74* analyses the fiscal and monetary policies adopted during this period. It also includes a discussion of the policies which were tried to improve the balance of payments, since this was a major concern of the government, and it discusses incomes policy, which again at various times became a dominant policy preoccupation. However, the full range of government economic intervention covers a rather wider area; this section briefly surveys these other areas of economic policy.[1]

At much the same time as the first experiments with incomes policy, the government also began to experiment with the idea of national planning. The model used was French; the underlying idea was indicative planning – that the stating of a growth target would induce the investment which would help to bring the target rate of growth about. Under the Conservative government the plan was to be formulated by the NEDC; under the Labour government it became the National Plan, prepared by the new Department of Economic Affairs and published in 1965. In both cases, the target set for the growth rate was 4 per cent. However, the plans were based on over-optimistic balance of payments assumptions – particularly about imports; so far as the National Plan was concerned, it was already clear by 196ϵ that the growth target could not be met. As the figures in the National Plan became increasingly irrelevant, the concept of aggregate national planning fell into disrepute. The NEDC increasingly turned its attention to the discussion of ways of improving efficiency in individual industries.

Governments also intervened in the working of the market economy by their industrial policies – by setting the general rules for competition, by looking for other ways of stimulating industrial efficiency and, finally, by fairly extensive intervention in certain individual industries. The government's competition policy did not change a great deal during this period, apart from the Resale Prices Act of 1964, which made it in general unlawful for manufacturers to fix retail prices, and

---

[1] The omitted chapters of *British Economic Policy 1960–74* are listed in the Preface.

the establishment of the Office of Fair Trading in 1973. Government policy towards mergers was ambivalent; in the late 1950s and early 1960s most Conservative and Labour governments tended if anything to encourage mergers, on the grounds that only large firms could stand up against foreign competition. Indeed the main function of the Labour government's IRC was to create larger units. On the other hand, the Monopolies and Mergers Act of 1965 required that the Board of Trade should review proposed mergers above a certain minimum size – although in fact between 1965 and 1973, of 875 mergers or proposed mergers reviewed, only six were in the end forbidden. The main industries in which the government intervened specifically were the computer industry, the machine tool industry, the aircraft industry, shipbuilding and the textile industry. The government gave substantial financial aid to the newly formed computer firm of International Computers and gave it priority in government purchases. Its assistance to the machine tool industry in this period was on a smaller scale, mainly through pre-production purchasing of certain machines and by assisting firms to buy numerically controlled machine tools. The government was deeply involved in the aircraft industry, not only on the military but also on the civil side, since private firms were in general not in a position to finance the development of new civil aircraft out of their own resources; the initial decision to develop Concorde was made in March 1962. There was a long succession of various 'temporary' financial devices to help the British shipbuilding industry. For textiles, the government during this period was administering the Cotton Industry Act of 1959, which compensated firms for scrapping existing machinery; later there was small-scale assistance to help firms in the wool textile industry to modernise and rationalise; in addition, the textile industry was given some quota protection. A great deal of industrial policy consisted of crisis interventions, requiring swift decisions with little time to consider alternatives; this suggests a case for a better industrial monitoring system to provide early warning.

Governments during this period were trying to hammer out their policies towards nationalised industries. (There was always a certain tension between simply requiring the nationalised industries to conform to certain general commercial rules and intervening in a detailed way in furtherance of some social or economic objective.) A 1961 White Paper was mainly concerned with setting certain financial objectives for these industries; a 1967 White Paper added investment criteria – the use of discounted cash flows and a test rate of discount; it also suggested pricing rules – the elimination of undesirable cross-subsidisation and the relation of prices to long-run marginal costs. (This last recommendation on pricing made little headway.) However, governments have not been able to refrain from *ad hoc* interventions: for example, most packages of public expenditure cuts have included cuts in nationalised industries' investment programmes, and after 1971 *de facto* price control forced a number of nationalised industries into deficit. The idea now seems to have been generally accepted that, if for social reasons the government wishes nationalised industries to undertake certain activities which do not pay, it should be the government which provides the finance. However, it is not wholly satisfactory to require nationalised industries to operate with commercial criteria only; most large private firms now recognise that they have certain social responsibilities and there seems no reason why nationalised industries should not follow this trend as well. Further, the commercial criteria under which nationalised industries operate at present cannot provide full efficiency audits.

Another area of government intervention was that of the institutional structure of collective bargaining. Both Labour and Conservative governments, to some extent as an alternative to incomes policy, tried to impose certain legal constraints on the processes of collective bargaining. The Labour government's attempt in 1969, which was embodied in the White Paper, *In Place of Strife*, was aborted at an early stage. The Conservative government's Industrial Relations Act, in spite of the strenuous opposition of the trade union movement, became law in 1971. The Act required that unions should register if they wished to bring themselves within the legal definition of a 'trade union' and that meant that their rule books had to meet certain minimum standards. (Very few unions did in fact register.) Certain types of industrial action were declared to be 'unfair industrial practices' and it was provided that all collective agreements were presumed to be intended to be legally enforceable unless otherwise stipulated. The Act also included new safeguards against unfair dismissal. However, with the move towards a formal incomes policy, operating if possible with tacit trade union cooperation, the Act became something of an embarrassment; it was repealed when the Labour government returned to power.

On measures to improve manpower policy there was not the same degree of conflict. The main measure was the Industrial Training Act of 1964, under which a number of Industrial Training Boards were set up with powers to make both levies and grants; there was a further change in the organisation of training when the Training Services Agency was established in 1974 as part of the new Manpower Services Commission. The second main measure of importance in manpower policy was the Redundancy Payments Act of 1965.

Finally, the United Kingdom's commercial policy can be tersely summarised. The 1960s saw the biggest change in British commercial policy since free trade was finally abandoned in favour of protection and Imperial Preference in 1932. What started as a largely defensive reaction to the creation of the EEC, evolved into a Europe-oriented policy pursued for its own sake. In purely commercial terms, the aim of policy-makers was to establish preferential trading arrangements with the EEC. Partly in pursuit of this aim, and following the lead given by the United States, the tariff protection given to British industry was drastically reduced. At the same time, in preparation for EEC membership, the system of agricultural protection was reorganised.

AN APPROACH TO AN ASSESSMENT

It is generally accepted that the performance of the British economy during this period was relatively poor as measured by the standard criteria normally used for assessing economic success or failure. This proposition has been widely documented and it is not the purpose of this book to review the evidence at length. The attempts to accelerate the British growth rate failed. The objective in the early 1960s was the modest one of getting the figure up from about 3 to about 4 per cent a year; in the event, the rise in real national product from 1960 to 1973 stayed at 2·9 per cent a year.[1] Britain's share in world trade in manufactured goods[2] fell in every year from 1960 to 1973, with only one exception (1971); at the beginning of the period this share was 16 per cent, by 1973 it was down to $9\frac{1}{2}$ per cent. There does not appear to have been much compensation elsewhere for these failures in economic growth and in foreign trade. Consumer prices rose rather faster, if anything, than the average for other industrial countries and Britain's record on unemployment was no better than average.

This relative failure is an important part of the background to the appraisal of economic policy. By their own criteria, economic policy-makers in Britain have been unsuccessful. The natural conclusion has been that the economy was mismanaged and that the policies which successive governments followed were wrong. Perhaps more than in any country, we have had, as a consequence, a very wide range of alternative diagnoses and prescriptions. It does not, of course, strictly follow that because the policies adopted failed in their objectives they were wrong. It is possible that the defects of the British economy are relatively unamenable to management and that no conceivable policy in this period could have made a substantial difference to performance. While it is not an inevitable conclusion that there were other policies which would have been more successful, it is, however, incontrovertible

---

[1] This is the average of the three estimates of the rate of change of GDP at constant factor cost (CSO, *Economic Trends*, no. 276, October 1976, p. 127).

[2] This is the United Kingdom share in the dollar value of exports of manufactures from the eleven main manufacturing countries.

that the policy-makers were wrong in thinking that the particular methods they chose would be powerful enough to transform the economic situation.

The purpose of this chapter is twofold: to survey and comment on some of the various views which have been put forward about British economic policy in this period, and at the same time to summarise some of the conclusions reached in preceding chapters.

Prefatory questions

There are certain prefatory questions to be answered. One concerns how far the different views about the way the British economy should have been managed arise from the fact that their proponents have different valuations of the main objectives of policy. To the extent that they do, the assessment of those views becomes much more complicated. If it is agreed, for example, that one set of policies leads to high unemployment and a low price rise, while another leads to low unemployment and a high price rise, then the choice between those two policies depends on the valuation put on the objectives, so that there is little more to be said. However, the disagreements about economic policy in Britain have not on the whole taken this form. Most proponents of particular economic strategies have tended to claim that if their prescription were followed British economic performance would be better under most of the various heads, certainly in the medium term. There have been differences of emphasis in the valuation put on objectives, but these have not been central to the different views about policy. To give two examples: Paish, in arguing that the economy should be run with a slightly wider margin of spare capacity, suggested that this would not only reduce the rate of increase in prices and help the balance of payments, but would also accelerate the underlying rate of growth.[1] The argument here was that a relatively small sacrifice in the full-employment objective would give a substantial improvement in the other main objectives. Again, the proponents of export-propelled growth argued that, once the economy had entered the 'virtuous circle', its performance would be better on all fronts.

There is, however, a rather different 'complication of valuations' which makes the comparison of alternative policy recommendations more difficult. There is a certain basic difference which permeates a great deal of policy discussion and applies not so much to the objectives of policy as to the type of instruments used. Among policy-makers and economists there are those who strongly prefer that, if possible, the state should not intervene; also, that any intervention should be as far as possible general rather than selective. At the other end of the

[1] Paish, *Studies in an Inflationary Economy.*

spectrum there are those who are by nature enthusiastic for a greater degree of state intervention. This difference was particularly important in the field of industrial policy, where there were, on the one hand, those who argued that the main requirement for greater industrial success was to reduce state interference in industry and to allow managers and owners to obtain higher post-tax rewards for success, and, on the other hand, those who argued that without state intervention British industry would not invest enough, or in the right pattern. This tension shows up in discussions of short-term policy as well. Those who object to constant government attempts to adjust the level of demand do so at least partly because they want to reduce the overall level of state intervention in the economy; this is one of the advantages claimed for the 'simple rules' (page 422 below).

Apart from this general question – of intervention or non-intervention – the differences in views about economic policy have arisen mainly from disagreements about the likely effects of various actions. This raises the question why it is not possible to take the different policy recommendations, put them into one of the existing models of the British economy and compare the results obtained. There are, after all, a number of models of the British economy which are used both for forecasting and for simulating the effects of alternative policies.

For a number of reasons this would not settle the arguments. First, the different models themselves, although they may during some of the period have had a certain family resemblance, are in no way identical and, since they are in a fairly constant state of flux, the differences change from year to year. To take one example, the forecast for the rise in average money earnings has, at various times and in various models, been made to depend essentially on the demand for labour – either the level of unemployment, or the level of unemployment together with price expectations; alternatively, it has been made to depend on variables which represent the pressures on the wage bargainers – the past movements of prices and post-tax real earnings – again, the figures have been put in exogenously on the grounds that there is no good wage equation at all. These different views of inflation lead to different conclusions about policy. The first may suggest measures which raise unemployment, the second measures which accelerate the rise in post-tax real earnings, and those who take the third view probably allow to a greater extent than the others for the possibility of an effective incomes policy.

Linked in some ways to the different views about inflation, the effects of devaluation have also been modelled in different ways. In one model it is the relative movement of wage costs per unit of manufacturing output which is the important variable; in another it is export prices.

Different conclusions are reached about the reaction of imports to changes in relative prices and about the extent to which a competitive advantage obtained by devaluation is automatically eroded by higher wage increases. These differences naturally lead to a different view on the effectiveness of devaluation as an instrument of policy.

The Cambridge Economic Policy Group held for a time a view about the behaviour of the private sector which had strong implications for fiscal policy: this was that, for the private sector as a whole (the company sector and the personal sector taken together) the net acquisition of financial assets was stable and predictable. Consequently, it was argued that fiscal policy – the public sector's net acquisition of financial assets – should be 'set', not in relation to a short-term forecast, but in such a way that it equalled 1–2 per cent of GNP at full employment (depending on the rate of inflation and the balance of payments objective), so that it would balance the full-employment net acquisition of financial assets by the private sector. This prescription was, of course, peculiar to a model embodying this particular constancy.

The problem of reaching an agreement on policy did not arise simply because existing models of the British economy differed. There were critics of the policies adopted since 1960 who did not accept that any of the existing models properly described the workings of the British economy. This is perhaps particularly true of those who criticised the Treasury model or the National Institute model for 'ignoring monetary factors'.[1] These critics did not generally advance an alternative fully fledged model themselves; they put forward certain individual relationships, such as a lagged one from the movement of the money supply first to output and then to prices. Insofar as they were not prepared to specify a full alternative model fitted to past data, and to use it for regular forecasts of the real future, their position was perhaps not a strong one. Nonetheless they were not prepared to accept the results of policy simulations on any of the models extant during this period.

The second reason that it is impracticable to draw incontrovertible conclusions from feeding policies into current models is that those models can only deal with the consequences of policy instruments which can be assumed to have quantifiable and identifiable short-term effects. They cannot, for example, settle arguments about what policies (if any) might have been successful in accelerating the growth rate. They have no satisfactory way of dealing with the underlying productivity trend in the economy – the most usual assumption is simply to extrapolate the past trend into the future[2] – and obviously they cannot then be

[1] The reply was that monetary factors were treated like any other variable in the construction of the models; they were incorporated when they were found to be significant.

[2] G. D. N. Worswick and F. T. Blackaby (eds.), *The Medium Term*, Heinemann, 1974.

used to evaluate policies which, as their advocates argue, would accelerate economic growth.

The third point, linked to the previous one, is that econometric models cannot in general deal with the consequences of institutional changes designed to have medium-term or long-term effects. Increasingly over this period economic policy has consisted in attempts at institutional change, policy-makers becoming less concerned with the traditional instruments of demand management. There is no model of the economy which can estimate the effects of the IRC or the Industrial Relations Act, or which can forecast the consequences of a new set of incomes policy institutions. Further, there are some policies which, though not institutional changes, have effects which depend heavily on how certain institutions react to them. For example, in the debate about the relative merits of import restrictions and devaluation, one argument is that other countries, rationally or irrationally, are more likely to retaliate against the first of these than against the second. This is a crucial assumption; however, there is no way by which a model can indicate whether or not it is correct.

Fourthly, a model is basically a statement of past relationships; it cannot predict with any certainty when the economy moves into previously uncharted territory. The most obvious example is the rate of inflation. Towards the end of the period prices were rising at a rate which had no recent peacetime precedent and there was no reason to suppose that relationships between the rate of inflation and other variables which held when the rate was 5 per cent a year would necessarily hold when it was 25 per cent.

The main decisions during this period were strategic choices between different types of economic policy. Thus, there was a succession of choices between incomes policy and some alternative; there was the decision in 1972 to attempt to combine a faster rate of growth with a floating exchange rate as a way of avoiding the balance of payments constraints which had halted earlier attempts to raise the growth rate; there were decisions about the forms and the extent of industrial intervention, and about the desirability of attempting to join the EEC; there were attempts at trade union reform. These policies could not be evaluated by running them through some agreed model of the economy, even if such a model existed.

A final prefatory point concerns the difference between diagnosis and prescription. Obviously the analysis of the causes of some phenomenon – such as Britain's slow growth – is a necessary preliminary to any decision about what should be done, but the analysis of causation does not by itself settle the question of policy. Some causes – or predisposing factors – may be virtually unalterable; policy has to concentrate on those which can be altered by government action. For example, it is often argued that British exports are uncompetitive, not because of their relative price, but because of uncertain delivery dates, or poor design, or inadequate salesmanship. Nonetheless, the appropriate government policy to deal with a lack of competitiveness may be a devaluation, since relative price is something which the government can alter, and alter quickly; it may have no instruments to deal with uncertain delivery dates or poor design, and relatively low prices may compensate for other deficiencies. This distinction between the analysis of causes and policy prescription is important in assessing the attempts made to accelerate Britain's growth rate.

One large group of suggested causes for Britain's slow growth is concerned, in one way or another, with the social structure of British manufacturing industry – with, for example, the relatively low level of education of British management, or the failure of the workforce to identify with management's objectives. It is argued later that economic policy should have been more concerned with such matters. Nonetheless it is understandable that policy-makers, even if they agreed that these were the major causes of Britain's slow growth, might still search for policies to affect other minor causes, on the grounds that the major predisposing factors were ones which government policy would find it very difficult to alter.

A brief conspectus

Before turning to a critique of the various economic strategies pursued by successive governments during this period, it is perhaps useful to summarise very briefly what they were.

The beginning of the period (1960) coincided with the end of a short expansion – short and unsatisfactory, in that the rise in output per man tapered off rather quickly and the balance of payments ran into a deficit which led to a run on the pound in the following year. It was a time of growing dissatisfaction with Britain's slow rate of economic growth and with the orthodox techniques of demand management. The government, at the same time as it was taking restrictive measures to stop the run on sterling in 1961, was also beginning the first experiments with planning and incomes policies. Rising unemployment, which passed the then crucial figure of half a million in the winter of 1962/3, set off expansionary policies again; the government indicated it was prepared to accept a temporary loss of gold and foreign exchange reserves in order to keep the expansion going. However, the size of the current deficit which developed in 1964 was unexpectedly large.

The period of the Labour government was one of sharp contrast between the initial intended economic strategy and the actual policy the government was forced to follow. The intention was to follow a long-term strategy based on a national plan, with a permanent voluntary incomes policy and an active industrial policy. Actual policy was dominated by, first, the attempt to hold the exchange rate and, secondly, after November 1967, the attempt to defend the new exchange rate; it consisted largely in a succession of crisis measures whose main aim was to reassure foreign opinion. Only in its last year – from mid-1969 onwards – was the government free of its preoccupation with the balance of payments and, in this last year, dissatisfied with the apparent failure of its incomes policies, it made a tentative move towards some legal restraint on unofficial strikes, but was forced to withdraw by lack of Party support.

The Conservative government, coming to power in June 1970, inherited a strong balance of payments. Initially it was not particularly concerned with demand management; its main object was to reduce the role of government and, with its Industrial Relations Act, to bring the operations of the unions more fully within the framework of the law. The government was not anxious to reduce unemployment until the rapid increase in wage rates and earnings had been moderated; it adopted a partial, covert incomes policy in the public sector. The continuing rise in unemployment and the defeat of the public sector incomes policy by the miners' strike led to a change of strategy in 1972. An expansionary fiscal and monetary policy with a floating exchange rate was adopted, together with an attempt at a voluntary incomes policy, which led to a statutory prices and incomes policy when the government failed to reach agreement with the TUC; this strategy evolved into one more attempt to accelerate the growth rate. In the remainder of its period of office the government was largely preoccupied with the successive stages of its incomes policy; it also moved towards more intervention in industry.

The pattern of criticisms

There is a large number of alternative views about the way in which economic policy should have been conducted – some covering one part of economic policy only and others more general. One group of criticisms is concerned with the short-term demand adjustments made mainly with employment or the balance of payments as objectives. Some of these criticisms are radical, in that they argue that the whole procedure was, in one way or another, misconceived; others simply take issue with the size or timing of the reflationary or deflationary stimuli applied in certain years. Another group of alternative views is more concerned with the policies adopted to accelerate the underlying rate of growth.

DEMAND MANAGEMENT

At the beginning of the 1960s, when *The Management of the British Economy* was written,[1] the idea that the government should 'manage' the economy by intervention based on forecasts was widely accepted. 'Demand management' is, however, something of a portmanteau term and different parts of the procedure have been criticised. Indeed, some criticisms seem to be directed to procedures which were not in fact followed, or to beliefs which were not in fact held. This section first describes and discusses 'demand management' as it was practised during this period; it then considers criticisms and alternative views.

Forecasts and policy actions

The basic idea is that from time to time a forecast is made of the likely trends in the economy for some period ahead; the policy-makers are then able to judge whether or not the performance of the economy, according to the objectives which they have in mind, is likely to be satisfactory or not. If the prospect is considered unsatisfactory, then some of the various instruments available are used to try to improve it. Thus the principles of demand management are the same as the principles of economic policy in general.

The 'normal' process of demand management, which is behind the preparation of a normal rather than an emergency budget, begins with a forecast probably for some eighteen months to two years ahead. This would indicate in particular the expected course of output, employment and unemployment, prices, and the balance of payments on unchanged policies. It would certainly include the tabular material which is normally presented in the regular forecasts published in the *National Institute Economic Review*. The 'budget judgement', of course, involves other considerations too, but, so far as demand management is concerned, it is essentially whether policy intervention can bring about some improvement on balance in the prospect for certain short-term objectives. Obviously there may be a conflict of objectives; a tax change may improve the prospect for output and employment, but worsen the prospect for the balance of payments. Chapter 4 gives examples of the judgements that were made from time to time: for instance, that on unchanged policies output was rising in line with productive potential, so that the budget should make no net change in demand; or, that the pressure of demand showed signs of becoming excessive, so that taxes should be increased; and so on.

It is difficult for any critic to argue with the basic framework of this process – that the government should consider the course which the

[1] Dow, *The Management of the British Economy, 1945–60*.

economy is taking, compare this with certain objectives and intervene to get a better mix of objectives if it can. The critics are, for the most part, not denying that this should be done; they are saying that, in one way or another, the government's picture of the working of the economy has been wrong or incomplete. Essentially they are criticising the models of the British economy which have prevailed in economic policy-making in this country since the war, their criticisms centring mainly on the working of the public sector and the treatment of money. It is therefore useful to describe in general terms how these were treated in the official forecasting process. Obviously the precise methods used evolved substantially during the fourteen years from 1960 to 1974, but the basic structure does not seem to have altered radically.

The forecast of the main categories of expenditure at constant prices has been central to the structure. In this basic forecast the whole public sector does not appear as a single item. The various components are incorporated in ways which seem most appropriate: public authorities' current spending on goods and services appears as a separate item; transfer payments to individuals and taxes on persons are incorporated in the calculations which lead up to a forecast of consumers' expenditure; investment grants are considered in relation to fixed investment in the private sector, so too are tax allowances on investment. On this disaggregated approach the pattern of any changes in government expenditure or in taxation will be important. It will make a difference, for example, whether a given change in the public sector's financial deficit is caused by an increase in an investment programme, a reduction in capital gains tax, or an increase in old age pensions, because these changes, when incorporated into the forecasting process, have different effects on effective demand and on output; consequently any policy adjustment required is also different. Thus the case for this treatment of the components of public sector expenditure is that:

the output-generating (or, in the case of taxes, output-destroying) content differs from item to item. In some 'extreme' cases, for example imports of missiles wholly constructed in the United States, the domestic output content may be zero, and in others, for example the services of school teachers, the output content may be 100 per cent. Similarly, the output generated by public expenditure as a whole may be judged greater than the reduction in competing demands on output implicit in a matching amount of tax revenues raised by the public sector.[1]

There are two main comments on this procedure. First, while it is perfectly possible to produce a measure of the 'push' given by the public sector as a whole, the appropriate measure is not simply the

[1] Artis, 'Fiscal policy for stabilization', p. 294.

public sector financial deficit as it stands, but the 'weighted' budget deficit (page 184), the figures for which are essentially the same as those embodied in the forecast tables. Thus, the production of a weighted budget deficit is not an alternative method of preparing a forecast, but an alternative way of presenting some of the figures. It can also be calculated on a full-employment basis, which helps to establish how far the deficit may simply be due to a recession (pages 183–4).

Secondly, it is possible to deduce from the forecast a set of figures for 'net acquisition of financial assets' by the government sector, the personal sector, the company sector and the overseas sector; towards the end of the period Treasury forecasts produced these figures explicitly. The sum of the balances must, of course, be zero, which is simply a way of saying that each transaction is both a debit and a credit item.[1] In the ordinary process of forecasting consumers' expenditure and private investment, a judgement will already have been made about the plausibility of the savings figures for those sectors; so it is generally unlikely that, when the figures for the balances of each of the four sectors are deduced, they will lead to a revision of the forecasts – certainly a revision has not often been necessary in the National Institute process of forecasting.

'Monetary factors' were incorporated into the forecasting procedure when they were found, on the basis of historical relationships, to have significant effects. These effects were limited (page 291), the main areas of expenditure which were found to have some sensitivity to interest rates being private housing and capital inflows from abroad; changes in hire purchase terms also had effects. Private industrial investment appears to depend heavily on the degree of capacity working and not to respond much to interest-rate changes. Prices were not forecast from the money supply, but from movements in labour costs, import prices and indirect taxes. Wage costs, in turn, which in earlier years were assumed to respond to unemployment, were later forecast on the basis of an *ad hoc* assessment of the situation. Altogether monetary factors were peripheral rather than central to the forecast mainly because examination of past relationships suggested that their influence was not strong.

The model of the economy employed in the forecasts had certain properties with important implications for policy. It had no powerful self-righting properties to bring the economy back without intervention to some natural growth path; it was also one in which changes in government expenditure and taxation had effects on real demand, and did not set in train processes which cancelled out automatically any

---

[1] Except for the residual error – the difference between the income and expenditure estimates of GDP.

effect on output. Certainly an increase in government expenditure might raise the pressure of demand and, under certain circumstances – particularly in the early part of the period, when the level of unemployment was low – this would lead to higher forecasts of wage rates and prices; but it would not lead to a reduction in private expenditure – for example, because the increased government borrowing led to an increase in the rate of interest and so to a reduction in private investment. The effect would depend on the degree of spare capacity in the economy; if the economy was at less than full employment, an increase in public expenditure would normally lead to a rise, not a fall, in private expenditure. Finally, an increase in government expenditure (or a reduction in taxation) would normally, other things being equal, worsen the balance of payments by increasing imports and possibly also affecting exports; but again there was no process by which an increase in government expenditure automatically led to a worsening of the balance of payments of the same order of magnitude.

However, the model was not such as to lead the policy-makers to suppose that, simply by demand management, they could simultaneously achieve all the traditional objectives. They would generally be unable to engineer simultaneously an adequate balance of payments surplus and full employment, so there could very well be circumstances in which the balance of payments was an effective constraint on the use of demand management to achieve full employment. Further, in the later part of the period the rise in earnings was treated as exogenous in the forecasting process – that is, within a fairly wide range of unemployment figures, it was not substantially influenced simply by demand management, so that clearly on this model some other instrument had to be used when prices began to accelerate.

A monetary rule

One main alternative proposed as a short-term management technique is a monetary rule: the government should set a target for the rate of growth of the money supply and allow the rate of interest to clear the market.

The monetarist approach to economic management is centrally concerned with inflation. The argument, it is true, is that once the economy is on a stable path with firm monetary targets, unemployment will settle at the 'natural rate' and output will grow in line with productive capacity. However, the main stress has been on a monetary regime as a corrective for high rates of inflation; hence its greater prominence in recent years.

The basic proposal is that the government should announce targets for the rate of growth of either M_1 or M_3 or both, equal to the trend growth of productive capacity plus an 'acceptable' rate of inflation. Adjustments should not be made on each month's figures, but on a moving average of three or four months. The government should attempt to set the public sector borrowing requirement so that it does not conflict with the monetary growth target; otherwise control should essentially be through the rate of interest.

In some presentations of monetary policy it is stressed that the government should announce its monetary target and emphasise its determination to keep to it. This, it is argued, would discourage trade unions from making claims which are clearly out of line, for if they collectively succeeded in forcing money wages up excessively, this would force up interest rates, which would reduce the growth of output and create unemployment. This unemployment would then be seen to be the responsibility of the trade unions rather than of the government.

This particular prescription for short-term management has not been tried in this country; there is, therefore, no postwar experience which can be used to assess its effectiveness. Experience in other countries is not an adequate substitute, since financial institutions and trade union structures differ a great deal. Such a policy is dependent on the assumption that there is a stable demand function for 'money', on one or other of its definitions, but it is difficult to establish such a function which holds both before and after 1970 (page 300). There is the further possibility that once particular aggregates of liquid assets, such as M_1 or M_3, are subject to tight control, they cease to act as good indicators because other forms of liquid asset are devised or developed which fall outside the controlled definition.

The money supply is, strictly speaking, an indicator and not an instrument of policy, since the term 'instrument' should be kept for changes which the government can itself make directly, such as changes in its purchases or sales of bonds or in the minimum lending rate. The money supply is therefore an intermediate variable, or an indicator of the setting of policy, and as such the information it provides is limited; so long as the demand function for money is stable, it should give an indication of the rate of increase of national expenditure in money terms, but it says nothing about the separate contributions of real output and of prices to any such increase. Thus a figure for the money supply which is observed in practice, although it may be based on a certain rate of real growth and a certain rate of inflation, will not necessarily bring about that particular combination. Even assuming there is a stable demand function for money on some definition or combination of definitions, all that is controlled is a figure of national expenditure in money terms, which can be brought about by a wide range of combinations of output and price changes.

The 'announcement effect' of a monetary target on trade union wage claims and wage awards is, of course, something which has not been tried. Although it might have some plausibility if the trade union movement negotiated as a whole, it is less plausible as a moderating influence on each individual union, which may well consider that its own position is exceptional, and that its above-average wage claim will be offset by below-average wage claims elsewhere. There is also the political question of how far the government could claim that it was the trade unions which were responsible for high unemployment; it might be argued that, if trade union structures or negotiating procedures were such as to lead to high unemployment, then it was the government's responsibility to change them. 'To "leave it to the Trade Unions" to determine the level of unemployment has no more to be said for it than to leave it to Trade Unions to determine the rate of inflation.'[1]

It is not at all certain what kind of variations in the rate of interest would have to be permitted to make a monetary rule effective. One of the objections to the use of monetary policy in this way, as against the use of fiscal policy, is, first, that there is not much evidence on the quantitative effects of interest-rate changes; secondly, those effects are in any case likely to fall heavily in the first instance on particular sectors of expenditure – such as private investment in general and private investment in housing in particular – which the government may not wish to discriminate against. Many of the self-righting characteristics claimed for a regime in which a monetary target is strictly observed arise from the assumption that expenditure is highly sensitive to interest-rate changes. Thus, if a reduction in the public sector borrowing requirement is needed, it is argued that this will not necessarily be deflationary, since at the same time interest rates can be reduced, which will stimulate private investment sufficiently to offset the effects of the reduced public expenditure or higher taxes. However, the sensitivity of expenditure to changes in the rate of interest is difficult to validate; when rates of interest are included in the equations which attempt to explain the movement of investment, stockbuilding, or consumers' expenditure, they are not in general found to have a strong effect.

In the period 1960–74 monetary policy was not in fact called on to do a great deal. The main quantifiable effects were those of changes in direct controls (on hire purchase terms and bank advances), though failure to discern any more general effects is not, of course, proof that they do not exist. It was the personal sector which felt the main brunt of monetary policy – in both directions – and, given the government's decision to shield and subsidise corporate investment, there was some

[1] G. D. N. Worswick, 'The end of demand management?', *Lloyds Bank Review*, no. 123, January 1977.

justification for this. However, it is also true that by 1971 the system of bank lending controls had become very difficult to manage and there was a case for more flexible arrangements. There were large swings in monetary policy (as in fiscal policy), leading – particularly in 1972/3 – to large changes in asset prices, with possible long-lagged effects of which we know little. As with fiscal policy, there is a case for small, more frequent adjustments, as against large infrequent ones.

The public sector financial deficit

Another line of criticism of the process of demand management suggests that policy-makers, rather than coming to an *ad hoc* judgement on the basis of each successive forecast, should follow some fiscal rule. One set of alternative 'rules' concerns the public sector's financial deficit – that is, it brings together out of the forecast both the revenue and the expenditure elements of the public sector, including the current surpluses and capital expenditure of the nationalised industries.

This formulation, which came to be known as the 'New Cambridge' view, is 'that tax rates should be set, not by reference to a short-term forecast, but in such a way that the full-employment yield of taxes falls short of public expenditure by an amount equal to 1 or 2 per cent of GNP'.[1] The rationale for this proposition is that the private sector as a whole increases its expenditure (on both current and capital items) over a period of two years in line with any increase in its disposable income and that its net acquisition of financial assets tends to be predictably 1–2 per cent of GNP. Consequently, given that the net acquisition of financial assets by the private, public and overseas sectors must add to zero, if the net deficit of the public sector exceeds the private sector's net acquisition, there must be a deficit in the balance of payments. Setting tax rates in the way suggested, it is argued, is a necessary (but not sufficient) condition for ensuring that the return to full employment does not lead to a balance of payments deficit. It is not a sufficient condition, because the competitive position of the country may be such that at full employment there is no prospect that exports will be sufficient to finance full-employment imports; that competitive deficiency would have to be dealt with by other instruments.

A further claim made for this approach to demand management is that it avoids constant intervention – 'fine-tuning'. It is argued that it is possible to calculate from the medium-term public expenditure forecasts what full-employment expenditure will be and thus to specify a set of tax rates which will deliver a certain figure of government revenue at full employment. Once these tax rates have been set, it will

---

[1] *Economic Policy Review*, no. 2, March 1976, p. 47. The proposition has a footnote added to it which reads 'depending on the balance of payments target and the rate of inflation'.

not be necessary to change them; given appropriate policies to deal with the balance of payments, this setting of tax rates will bring the economy back to full employment and keep it there.

There are various difficulties with this formulation. First, the relationship between disposable income and expenditure which appears to hold for the private sector as a whole does not appear to hold for the personal sector and the company sector taken separately. It is not easy to see why this should be, or what transactions between the personal and company sectors provide the offsetting effect. Secondly, the relationship between income and expenditure is not wholly straightforward; expenditure depends, not simply on the disposable income of the current and the preceding year, but also on changes in hire purchase debt, bank advances and the book value of stocks.[1]

Secondly, the rule clearly does not hold at times when prices are rising fast; indeed the proponents of the rule recognise that there is a problem here, particularly with stock appreciation. The private sector's net acquisition of financial assets, which was 2·6 per cent of GNP in 1974, rose to 6·2 per cent in 1975 and 5·5 per cent in 1976; clearly any forecast depends very heavily on the assumption which is made about rates of inflation. Further, it is not at all certain that if the rate of inflation returns to a more normal level the private sector's net acquisitions will necessarily return to 1–2 per cent of GNP.

Thirdly, the 'full-employment yield of taxes' is not an unambiguous concept. The return to full employment can take a number of different routes, with different patterns of expenditure and different rates of inflation leading to different revenue outcomes (also different expenditure outcomes). They will vary with different mixes of consumption and investment, and of personal and company income.

If one starts from a position of fairly substantial unemployment, so that it may take some years to return to full employment, it is not easy to see why it should necessarily be right to set tax rates now so that they would be appropriate in two or three years' time when full employment is regained – unless it is considered that there is a very substantial cost in changing tax rates. It is not easy to demonstrate that such a course is better than, for example, reducing taxes now to quicken the early stages of a return to full employment and then increasing them later. The choice between the two policies may depend on the weight given to the unfortunate consequences of unemployment now, as against the possible consequences of too rapid a return to full employment. This is a matter of valuation and there may well be no uniquely 'right' economic answer.

It is not clear that the use of this rule – that tax rates should be set

[1] House of Commons, *Ninth Report from the Expenditure Committee, Session 1974*, p. 3.

so that at full employment the surplus of the public sector is equal to the expected deficit of the private sector – is superior to the following rather less impressive-sounding suggestion: that when the economy is under-employed, policy-makers should look for a succession of fiscal stimuli which, together with measures to safeguard the balance of payments, will produce a reasonably rapid return to full employment, without leaving the economy with a balance of payments deficit when full employment is regained. Sets of measures can be tested using the normal forecasting model to see what the results would in fact be.

Stabilisation

It is probably true that the policy-makers' ideal or Utopian economy, at which they might say they were aiming in the long run, was one of stability in a certain sense; that is, it would be an economy with a steady (rapid) growth rate, a steady level of unemployment, a steady low (or nil) rise in prices,[1] and a balance of payments current surplus which (given stability in the world outside) was roughly constant, or which (in the absence of external stability) fluctuated not too widely around some target figure.[2] However, although this combination of long-term objectives might be summed up as 'stabilisation', this was not in fact a term which was often used by policy-makers themselves – in budget speeches, for example – to describe what they aimed to do.

There are a number of reasons for this. First, the concept of an eventual stable equilibrium of this kind is rather a visionary one and policy-makers' immediate objectives were usually much less ambitious; they were probably doubtful (and probably rightly) whether a stable equilibrium of this kind could be attained with the instruments at their disposal. Secondly, the concept of stabilisation does not include the acceleration of the growth rate, which was one of the objectives of economic policy, including demand management policy. As part of their attempts to accelerate the growth rate, governments on more than one occasion deliberately took action which risked 'destabilising' the balance of payments. Thirdly, on a large number of occasions when governments intervened, the problems of short-term policy did not present themselves as the need for some kind of general stability; rather the situation was that something had to be done, imperatively, about either the balance of payments or unemployment, and action was taken in the full knowledge that an attempt to stabilise one objective was likely to destabilise others.

[1] Perhaps the last serious advocacy of the desirability of a gently falling price level was in Council on Prices, Productivity and Incomes, *1st Report*, para. 109.

[2] When targets for the United Kingdom balance of payments were stated, they were usually for a current surplus in order to improve the ratio of short-term assets to liabilities.

The question whether government intervention did or did not reduce the degree of fluctuation of output around its trend is therefore one to ask about policy – but certainly not the only one, since stabilisation of the trend of output is one of many objectives of demand management. (It would be quite possible, for example, for it to be accompanied by steadily rising unemployment, and there seems no particular reason to assume it has any connection with stable prices.)

The various attempts to answer the question whether or not policy has on balance stabilised or destabilised the trend of output are not conclusive.[1] There are two difficulties: first, it is not at all easy to define precisely what non-intervention would be, either for fiscal or for monetary policy; secondly, given some definition of non-intervention, it is not easy to say with any assurance what would have happened on various occasions if the government had not intervened. The short-term models of the economy in use through most of this period show a certain tendency for the rise in output to flatten out if the models are run on into the medium term; it is not clear how far this is due to the way the models were constructed, or whether it represents what in fact the British economy would do.

For example, from July 1971 the government intervened to stimulate demand – first in a small way and then with a substantial reflationary package in the 1972 budget. If none of these stimuli had been applied, would the economy have recovered on its own, or would it simply have continued with a slow rise in output accompanied by steadily increasing unemployment?

Another approach to the question of stabilisation is to compare the United Kingdom's fluctuation in output around its trend with the experience of other industrial countries; the rather surprising conclusion is that output fluctuations in Britain were usually less marked than elsewhere.[2] Of course, this may not be the consequence of British economic policy; it may be that the British economy is itself in some way less volatile. However, it does suggest that the problem with the British economy was not so much any 'stop–go' pattern imposed by government policy, but rather the slowness of the rise in the underlying trend in output. Possibly the 'stop–go' pattern appeared more marked in the United Kingdom because in other industrial countries output was still rising significantly when it was below trend, whereas in Britain there tended to be virtually no rise at all in the 'stop' phases.

---

[1] See references on page 210, footnote 2.

[2] NEDO, *Cyclical Fluctuations in the United Kingdom Economy*, London, 1975; Whiting, 'An international comparison of the instability of economic growth'.

Fine-tuning

The objections to what has been called 'fine-tuning' are somewhat mixed. Sometimes the term appears to be used as a synonym for demand management, so that the objection is really to any kind of discretionary intervention. Certainly, if it is believed that the economy is self-regulating with some simple rule, then on this view it is a mistake to intervene at all. However, the observance of a simple rule will not necessarily reduce the *number* of government interventions; it will only make them less discretionary. Thus, if the government were to adopt some target figure for the growth of one of the monetary magnitudes, the observance of this rule would probably require frequent interventions in open-market operations, in calls for Special Deposits, or in changes in the minimum lending rate.

Alternatively, the objection may be to the view that it is possible, simply by the adroit manipulation of demand, to steer the economy with a considerable degree of precision on a desired course and, by demand management alone, to bring about a state in which all the major objectives of policy are achieved. Given the experience of the past fifteen years the case against any such view is indeed a strong one, but it is rather difficult to say who held it. Not many of the practitioners of demand management believed that it was an all-purpose technique. From the early 1960s onwards it was doubted whether it could by itself be effective in dealing with inflation, except at a very high cost in unemployment. From the later 1960s onwards there were also not many people who believed that demand management by itself had much to contribute to accelerating the rate of economic growth.

Thirdly, the objection may simply be to the frequency of intervention. This is different from objections to constant reversals of general economic strategy (page 438), such as the alternations between belief and disbelief in an incomes policy, or the changes in industrial policy. The issue here is not whether demand management interventions are needed; it is rather whether it is better for them to be frequent or infrequent. The argument against frequency is that, given the unreliability of economic forecasts, it is better to wait until it is quite clear that action is needed rather than to intervene every time that there are tentative signs of a divergence from the target figures for the objectives. In addition, it is argued that not enough weight is given to the costs imposed on the economy by policy changes – for instance, the constant disturbance to forward plans for production of cars or consumer durables which resulted from the frequent changes in hire purchase controls (pages 226–7).

There is here a difficult problem of balance. It is true that policy interventions have costs (though some create much less disturbance than others) and that forecasts are uncertain. However, although there are some examples during the period of rapid changes in the direction of demand management interventions after short intervals (for example, with public expenditure between 1970 and 1973, pages 117–23), such rapid changes are not all that usual. The National Institute, in its policy appraisals, has tended to take the view it is better to make small frequent adjustments than large infrequent ones. This was on the grounds that there were often fairly long time-lags before policy actions had their effects, and if intervention was left too long there was a danger that it would eventually be excessive. Thus, during the period from July 1970 to the budget of 1972, the National Institute argued consistently for the early application of small stimuli to demand to bring the rise in output in line with productive capacity; it is arguable that this would have produced rather better results than the course actually followed, of giving a very substantial demand stimulus in the budget of 1972.

Other aspects of fiscal policy

On the revenue side of the public sector accounts there was substantial structural reform in the period 1960–74. There was a reduction in the number of rates of both indirect and company taxes, although there was a difference of emphasis here between the two Parties: Labour governments tended to prefer a larger number of rates (and consequently more discrimination) and Conservative governments preferred to reduce the number. The tax base was extended through VAT and capital gains tax. There was also a move towards administrative simplification of income tax, so that the tax threshold is now one of the lowest among industrial countries and the threshold rate of tax by far the highest. On the other hand, the indirect tax system became administratively more complex, first with selective employment tax and then with VAT. Finally, there was a move in the 1970s towards more public consultation about tax reform (through Green Papers).

Particularly in later years, the tax-mix shifted substantially towards direct taxation, as a combined consequence of more rapid inflation, a progressive direct tax system and an indirect tax system relying heavily on specific taxes. This development was hardly a deliberate policy decision; it strengthened demands for *ad valorem* instead of specific indirect taxes and for indexation of tax allowances and thresholds.

On the expenditure side there are the separate questions of the control of public expenditure in the medium term and its use as an instrument of short-term demand management. In the period 1960–74, the public sector, by any measure, expanded a good deal faster than the economy as a whole. In the early and mid-1960s the basic strategy was that public expenditure should rise in volume rather faster than GDP – and the assumption about the future growth of that product was optimistic. In 1969/70 the medium-term strategy shifted to one in which public expenditure, in cost rather than in volume terms, should rise simply in proportion to a less optimistic forecast of the rise in GDP. Finally, there has been a shift to the view that public expenditure, again in cost terms, should rise more slowly than total output. However, these medium-term strategies have tended to be disrupted by short-term interventions. Further, public expenditure planning throughout most of this period was in constant price terms, with an implicit undertaking to finance inflation; it was only after the very sharp rise in relative wages and prices in the public sector between 1972/3 and 1974/5 that cash limits were introduced.

Although most governments agreed in principle with the conclusions of the *Plowden Report*, that short-term changes in public expenditure should be 'a tool of the last resort',[1] nonetheless such interventions were, if anything, probably more frequent at the end of the period than at the beginning. The general picture is one of an unreliable conjunctural instrument, whose timing often proved not to be counter-cyclical in the event. There was, however, no general rule that expenditure cuts were ineffective; sometimes they were under-implemented and sometimes over-implemented. Control over investment by nationalised industries and in housing proved unreliable; it was also difficult to implement cuts in local authority current spending, where control was indirect and incomplete. On the other hand, control over local authority capital programmes (other than housing) proved fairly reliable. In the reflationary counter-cyclical use of public expenditure there was some tendency for a ratchet effect – for counter-cyclical increases to shift the schedule of medium-term expenditure plans upwards as well.

This is one reason for a more extensive use of the concept of the 'full-employment' budget. If each time after a counter-cyclical intervention the long-run full-employment budget was recalculated, this would help to show how far the effects of that intervention were likely to be temporary and how far permanent, which has never been entirely clear in the past, and thus to give some advance warning of any conflict between stored-up resistance to expenditure cuts and equal resistance to tax increases (page 134 and footnote 1, page 190).

---

[1] Treasury, *The Control of Public Expenditure*.

PRICE AND EXCHANGE-RATE POLICIES

PRICE AND EXCHANGE-RATE POLICIES

Price inflation

The amount of academic analysis of inflation during this period was, of course, enormous. So far as policy was concerned, the important issue was between, on the one hand, those who considered that inflation could be controlled by some form of macroeconomic strategy and, on the other, those who thought that free collective bargaining would have to be modified in some way.

The arguments about the nature of inflation – whether it was cost-push or demand-pull, or a mixture of the two, or indeed whether the two were distinguishable – continued in a massive literature. Here only one or two of the more influential examples are noted. Some early work by Dow and Dicks-Mireaux suggested that the movement of past prices was more important in explaining the movement of wage rates than the pressure of demand[1] – a doctrine that was later rediscovered – and that trade union pushfulness was an important independent influence.[2] Those who argued for the importance of the pressure of demand turned their attention away from the goods market towards the labour market; the most influential articles during this period were by Phillips, who presented a study of the relationship over a hundred years between the movement of wage rates and the level of unemployment,[3] and Paish, who concluded that a very modest increase in unemployment, to a figure of around $2\frac{1}{4}$ per cent, would be sufficient to produce price stability.[4] However, others disputed the meaning of this apparent relationship between the level of unemployment and the rate of change in wage rates or earnings; they argued that in the short periods when unemployment was rising trade unions postponed or moderated their demands with every intention of pressing them harder when unemployment began to fall again. It was wrong, therefore, to infer from short periods of relatively high unemployment what would happen to wage rates if the relatively high unemployment persisted for some time.

The state of the debate at the beginning of the period of this book – so far as policy-making was concerned – can be seen in the Reports of the Council on Prices, Productivity and Incomes, a body set up in

---

[1] 'It seemed reasonable to believe that full compensation for price increases is something which trade unions aim at and which both sides accept as a standard of reference' (Dow, 'Analysis of the generation of price inflation').

[2] L. A. Dicks-Mireaux and J. C. R. Dow, 'The determinants of wage inflation: United Kingdom, 1946–56', *Journal of the Royal Statistical Society* (series A), vol. 122, pt 2, 1959.

[3] Phillips, 'The relation between unemployment and the rate of change of money wages in the United Kingdom, 1861–1957'.

[4] Paish, *Studies in an Inflationary Economy*.

1957 with the hope that it would clarify matters. The first two Reports came out categorically upon the side of those who stressed excess demand: 'Viewing the period as a whole, we incline to think that the main cause of the rising trend of prices and incomes has been an abnormally high level of demand for goods and services in general, maintained for an abnormally long stretch of time.'[1] The third and fourth Reports expressed a rather different conclusion: 'How can inflation be stopped? It has sometimes been due to the pull of excess demand, but experience has shown that removing excess demand is not of itself enough. We have been brought to the conclusion that inflation has another cause, an upward push as rates of pay are raised and profit margins are maintained by raising prices. This "cost push" comes into play through a myriad of decisions on wages, salaries and prices.'[2]

Certainly from about 1961 up to the late 1960s anti-inflationary policy was mainly directed at trying to find ways of moderating trade union demands – that is, it concentrated on the cost-push side. However, in 1966 the Labour government tacitly accepted an upward shift in the level of unemployment to around $2\frac{1}{2}$ per cent in the hope that easing the pressure of demand would be of some help. And from the end of the 1960s theorists had to explain why the rate of inflation and the level of unemployment rose together, which was obviously rather more difficult for those who stressed the pressure of demand. Price expectations were added to the explanation, also a term to represent the increased benefit resulting from the earnings-related supplement introduced at the end of 1966. The hypothesis was that, with a higher ratio of unemployment benefit to average earnings, those who became unemployed would take longer to search for a new job, so that the level of unemployment corresponding to any given 'pressure of demand' would be raised. However, the figures for the actual number of unemployed persons receiving earnings-related benefit do not provide much support for this view.[3]

An alternative view – not dissimilar to the one put forward by Dow and Dicks-Mireaux 25 years earlier – was that inflation could be better explained by assuming that trade unions bargained on each occasion to recover what they had lost in real income by the rise in prices since their last settlement and then added something to give themselves a real

---

[1] Council on Prices, Productivity and Incomes, *1st Report*, para. 78.

[2] Council on Prices, Productivity and Incomes, *4th Report*, para. 8.

[3] 'Throughout virtually the whole period from November 1966 to November 1970 the number of men receiving ERS was less than 100,000. Even if it was supposed that receipt of ERS doubled the length of an individual's spell out of work...then the increase in the level of unemployment would be 50,000' (*Department of Employment Gazette*, October 1976). See also *National Institute Economic Review*, no. 79, February 1977, p. 15.

increase; it was further suggested that they looked at the movement of their post-tax rather than their gross earnings.[1] This hypothesis helped to explain the very big increase in money earnings which followed a number of years under the Labour government when real earnings net of taxes and national insurance contributions had hardly risen at all; if it was correct, the level of unemployment was relatively unimportant and the main way to keep down inflation would be to ensure a reasonable rate of increase in post-tax real earnings.

However, neither of these suggestions provide a close explanation of the movement of money earnings – particularly for the period after 1972. It appears that money earnings are not so strictly determined that they cannot be influenced by policy – or by the willingness or unwillingness of the trade union movement to cooperate with the government of the day. In any case, any relationships are presumably partly the product of the particular system of pay bargaining in force, so that there is no reason to think that they would necessarily hold if the system were modified or changed.

Because of the absence of any good wage equation, it is not possible to say what would have happened to money earnings in the absence of any incomes policy; it follows that it is not possible to prove any statement about whether such policies were effective or not. A crude examination of the figures suggests that periods of freeze were effective: for example, between the second quarters of 1966 and of 1967 average weekly earnings rose only 2 per cent. For the longer periods of incomes policy, if one assumes that there were long-term forces tending to push up the rise in money earnings during the whole period, it certainly appears that the rise was held back when an incomes policy was in force, with a rebound when the incomes policy was abandoned.

However, during this period – in spite of a number of attempts to create new incomes policy institutions – no progress was in fact made towards any permanent modification of free collective bargaining. This was partly the consequence of the damaging alternation of policies (page 366), in which new governments reversed the decisions of their predecessors, instead of trying to build on to them. Some things were learnt: it is probably true that, particularly after 1974/5, more trade unionists accepted that there was a connection between wage and price increases, and the experience of 1973/4 showed how dangerous indexation could be when the terms of trade turned against the United Kingdom. Conclusions could also be drawn about how to reconcile an incomes policy with plant bargaining and about the problems posed by productivity agreements. The general assessment, however, must be

---

[1] See Coutts, Tarling and Wilkinson, 'Wage bargaining and the inflation process'; Henry, Sawyer and Smith, 'Models of inflation in the United Kingdom'.

one of failure to develop any satisfactory institutional modifications. There were also, of course, the attempts to use legislation to reduce the incidence of strikes and to set industrial relations more generally within a legal framework. Once again no lasting reforms were achieved.

The exchange rate

In the early 1970s probably most British economists concerned with macroeconomic policy would have agreed that the use of the exchange rate was a desirable addition to the instruments of economic policy; it seemed that a lesson had been drawn from experience. It is true that the apparent effects of devaluation had taken a long time to arrive, but the eventual swing into surplus in 1969 and 1970 was a strong one. Those who had argued that devaluation would have catastrophic effects on Britain's invisible earnings had been proved wrong; in fact it appeared to have had a stronger effect on invisible than on visible credits. Consequently, the main criticisms of exchange-rate policy current in the early 1970s were that the pound should have been devalued earlier and the rate moved down more.

The next decision about the exchange rate was rather different. When in 1972 the Chancellor of the Exchequer indicated that he would not let a fixed exchange rate stand in the way of economic expansion, it was assumed that he had in mind a further devaluation to a fixed rate if necessary. When in fact the pound was floated, it was presented as (and probably intended as) essentially a temporary measure, as a prelude to a new fixed rate. It subsequently proved to be a more radical change in exchange-rate policy.

Further, whereas the arguments at the time of the 1967 devaluation were essentially about whether Britain should or should not devalue, the arguments about the move to floating rates were not specifically in the British context; they were rather concerned with the worldwide breakdown of the system of fixed exchange rates and the desirability or otherwise of floating rates in the world system of trade and payments.

Experience since 1972 has served to shake the consensus of the early 1970s. Certainly there are still strong advocates of exchange-rate changes as the best method available for balance of payments adjustment. However, there are now strong critics as well; a number of economists who strongly favoured devaluation in the 1960s now favour import controls instead, and some take the line that in the long term (though the time-period is not always specified) devaluation does not improve the balance of payments at all.

There are a number of points at issue. First, there is the problem of assessing the size of the price elasticities which indicate the likely balance of payments response to an exchange-rate change; for example, there is a good deal of disagreement about the extent to which British imports of manufactures are sensitive to price changes. Secondly, there are questions about the pricing policies of firms, particularly with a floating rate; it has been suggested that more firms now increase their export prices (expressed in sterling) quickly as the sterling exchange rate falls, and if this is so the effect of a downward floating rate on exports depends on firms' reactions to a possible higher profit margin on exports than on home sales. Thirdly, there is the problem for a devaluing country of holding its competitive advantage; by putting up import prices, devaluation increases the pressure on wages (insofar as they respond to past price movements), which raises the possibility of a cumulative process, in which devaluation helps to bring about a continuation of the relatively rapid price rise which occasioned it in the first place. Thus, in countries where the exchange rate floats down, higher rates of inflation may tend to persist, and so the downward float continues. The critics have suggested that there is a good deal in world experience since 1972 to suggest some cumulative process of this kind.

The experience of floating rates since 1972 – particularly the experience of sterling – does not suggest that the market moves exchange rates smoothly to some point of long-term equilibrium. Those responsible for movements in and out of sterling (including those who can delay or accelerate payments on imports or exports) appear to take short views, often reacting to rather ephemeral items of news; since the amount of funds which can be moved in this way far exceeds the funds which the authorities can use to moderate exchange-rate movements (at least in a downward direction), the course of sterling's exchange rate since June 1972 has been anything but smooth.

ECONOMIC GROWTH

Throughout the period widely conflicting lessons were drawn about the reasons for Britain's slow rate of economic growth – and, again, behind these conflicting views lay different pictures of the medium-term or long-term behaviour of the economic system. A number of commentators have pointed out how difficult it is to validate any conclusions here. At least with short-term policies there is some hope of disentangling and quantifying the consequences of, say, a tax change. It is very hard to see how one could successfully disentangle the consequences of the various policies whose objective was to raise the rate of economic growth. First of all, there are usually quite a number of such policies in existence at any time, with long but varying time-lags assumed before they might become effective, and throughout the period these policies were frequently changed. The basic observation of the last fifteen years is that a large number of policies were attempted – some for a short time, some for longer – and there is no evidence that the growth rate of productive capacity was faster at the end of the period than at the beginning. It is still, of course, open to the proponents of various policies to argue that they were not persisted with for long enough, or that there were other policies being pursued simultaneously which prevented them from being effective, or indeed that without them economic growth would have been even slower still.

International comparisons between fast-growing and slow-growing countries are not particularly helpful. There are relatively few observations and a very large number of possible relevant ways in which an economy (and for that matter a society) like that of Japan differs from an economy (or society) like that of Britain. Further, as Beckerman has pointed out, it is extremely difficult to separate causes and effects, 'since almost anything that might be expected to contribute to growth might equally well be caused by growth'.[1]

The lessons drawn at various times about the causes of Britain's slow economic growth can be put into two groups. First, there are views which lead to the conclusion that there is some central, or general, policy change which could accelerate the growth rate; that is, there are, as it were, some levers which the government can pull which would bring about a change in the underlying rate of growth. Here three such approaches are considered – of Kaldor, of Beckerman and of Bacon and Eltis.[2] Secondly, there is a rather more heterogeneous collection of views – views perhaps of economic historians rather than econometricians – which stress a multitude of assorted institutional factors leading to a multitude of assorted inefficiencies.

Growth and the supply of labour

Kaldor's thesis maintained that the driving force behind rapid economic growth was in the manufacturing sector; further – following Verdoorn – the faster the rise in manufacturing output, the faster the increase in productivity, with the direction of causation from output to productivity. He laid great stress on the need for an elastic supply of labour, pointing out that in France, Germany and Italy the industrial sector could draw on reservoirs of labour either from agriculture or from the poorer countries of Western Europe, whereas in Britain the

[1] W. Beckerman, 'The determinants of economic growth' in P. D. Henderson (ed.), *Economic Growth in Britain*, London, Weidenfeld & Nicolson, 1966, p. 57.

[2] Kaldor, *Causes of the Slow Rate of Economic Growth of the United Kingdom*; W. Beckerman, 'Demand, exports and growth' in W. Beckerman and Associates, *The British Economy in 1975*, Cambridge University Press, 1965; R. W. Bacon and W. A. Eltis, *Britain's Economic Problem: too few producers*, London, Macmillan, 1976.

reduction in the agricultural labour force had already occurred and there were powerful social arguments for checking the immigration from Commonwealth countries. Thus, Kaldor argued, a rise in manufacturing output in Britain was constantly checked by severe labour shortages which emerged during economic expansions, and this caused the United Kingdom's recurring balance of payments crises, with imports rising faster than exports during periods of growth. This view had some influence on policy; one of the arguments behind the selective employment tax was that it would raise the relative price of labour in service occupations and so free workers for manufacturing industry.

A number of difficulties have emerged with this approach to the causes of Britain's slow growth. The relationship which Kaldor observed in 1966 between manufacturing output and productivity appears not to have held since that date; also, it has been suggested that his comparisons were heavily influenced by the figures for a single country (Japan).[1] Secondly, the conclusion that British manufacturing industry was starved of labour during the postwar period conflicts with a number of industry studies, which show that British plants were overmanned in relation to their continental counterparts. Thirdly, it has been argued that both the productivity potential and the export potential are as high in many service industries as in manufacturing; this does not appear from national accounts statistics simply because there is no adequate way of measuring productivity in many service industries. Kaldor himself now takes the view that the United Kingdom's poor performance may be explained more by lack of international competitiveness than by inability to recruit sufficient labour into manufacturing industry.

'Export-propelled growth'

The phrase 'export-propelled growth' is shorthand for a group of views which became prominent in the early 1960s and had some influence on economic policy in the period of planning. The basic proposition was that more rapid economic growth could be brought about if businessmen expected demand for their products to rise quickly; in countries such as the United Kingdom they would only expect this to happen if there was a sufficiently large export content in the expected rise in demand for there to be little risk of a balance of payments 'stop'. A good deal of the discussion was concerned with possible reasons for relatively fast economic growth in some countries and slow growth in others.

[1] R. E. Rowthorn, 'What remains of Kaldor's Law?', *Economic Journal*, vol. 85, March 1975.

Thus, in February 1962, in a chapter on policies for faster growth, the *National Institute Economic Review* commented:

A number of explanations have been put forward for low growth rates – for instance, too much demand, too little demand, an unfavourable structure of output, slothful entrepreneurs, or legacies of the past – such as having come relatively unscathed out of the war. ...none of these factors by itself seems to provide an adequate explanation.

The only important point that can be established is that a necessary, and almost sufficient, condition for rapid growth is for businessmen in general to expect that the demand for their products will continue to grow rapidly... For businessmen to hold confident expectations about the long-run demand for their products, they must also be confident that total demand in the economy as a whole will expand unhampered by balance of payments difficulties or excessive price rises.[1]

The chapter went on to argue that this 'export-propelled' acceleration of the growth rate could come about if Britain achieved and maintained competitiveness for its goods; it also described the concept of the 'virtuous circle', 'by which initial competitiveness brings growth through rapidly rising exports, growth brings a faster rise in productivity, and this faster rise in productivity helps to keep prices stable and so to maintain or indeed increase competitiveness'.[2]

It is, of course, not easy to establish directly that investment responds to businessmen's demand expectations, because there is no quantitative measure of those expectations. Beckerman treats this essentially as a proposition of obvious commonsense.[3] He cites evidence that changes in sales have been shown to have an overridingly important influence on the rate of investment and comments that the past rate of change of sales must be regarded as the variable most likely to be highly corre-lated with expectations. However, although fluctuations in demand expectations may well explain fluctuations in investment in individual countries, it does not necessarily follow that different levels of invest-ment in different countries are explained in the same way. Further, in one country a businessman's demand expectations may cover only the next year or two, while in another he may be looking ten years ahead. For example, a Report on the comparative experience of the British and Japanese motor cycle industries suggested that one of the reasons for the decline of the British industry was that it only looked at short-term sales prospects.[4]

---

[1] *National Institute Economic Review*, no. 19, February 1962, pp. 55–6.
[2] Ibid. p. 56.
[3] Beckerman, 'Demand, exports and growth'.
[4] Department of Industry, *Strategy Alternatives for the British Motorcycle Industry*, London, HMSO, 1975.

Although the proponents of export-propelled growth laid stress on the connection between demand expectations and investment, they did not argue that investment alone could explain the differences in growth rates between countries. Beckerman showed that differences in investment ratios between countries explain only a relatively small part of differences in growth rates: in fast-growing countries a given increase in the stock of capital appears to yield a much higher increase in output, the incremental capital–output ratio being much lower than in slow-growing countries.

The second main element in the strategy of export-propelled growth was an improvement in competitiveness. Many of those who put forward this general view envisaged that it should come about through a devaluation. This was not because they necessarily believed that price competitiveness was all-important in exports, although in the period 1951–61 differences in export performance between countries appear to have been closely related to movements in export prices.[1] (After 1961 the relationship is much less close.) Rather it was because they considered that the government had an instrument in devaluation to alter prices relative to those of other countries, whereas it had no short-term instruments to improve design, delivery dates, or the provision of servicing facilities. However, the proponents of this view tended to refer in general terms to the need to improve competitiveness and then maintain that improvement; they did not put numbers to the requirement.

From 1960 to 1967 there was no improvement in price competitiveness; indeed Britain's relative position worsened.[2] The various attempts at incomes policy during this period did not prove (as some people hoped) an adequate substitute for devaluation. The devaluation at the end of 1967 produced a competitive margin, but by 1970 this had been significantly eroded. It is possible that the advocates of devaluation did not pay enough attention to the problem of preventing such erosion; it was unfortunate that the year of 'freeze and severe restraint' had preceded devaluation, so that it was very difficult to prevent a wage reaction to the rise in import prices. Between 1970 and 1974, partly because of revaluations elsewhere and partly because of the downward float of sterling after mid-1972, there were further improvements in United Kingdom competitiveness measured in this way.

The improvement seems to have accelerated the rate of increase in exports: from 1953/4 to 1966/7 – that is, up to devaluation – the annual

---

[1] Beckerman and Associates, *The British Economy in 1975*, p. 59.

[2] The series used for these propositions is the movement of wage costs per unit of output in manufacturing in Britain compared with the weighted average for other industrial countries, both measured in dollars. This series is used, rather than export prices, since part of the mechanism of export-propelled growth was considered to be the improvement of profit margins on export sales.

average rate of increase in the volume of exports of goods and services was
$3\frac{1}{2}$ per cent; from 1966/7 to 1973/4 it was double that – 7 per cent.
However, this appears to have been largely due to faster growth in
world trade – the rate of fall in the United Kingdom's share in world
exports of manufactures stayed much the same – and it failed to bring
about 'export propulsion'. Part of the reason may have been that this
export rise did not produce adequate balance of payments surpluses;
the rise in exports was insufficient to finance both the turning of the
terms of trade against the United Kingdom (partly the consequence of
the falling value of sterling) and also the acceleration in the rise in
import volume. The comparable figures for the rise in the volume of
imports of goods and services were 4 per cent (1953/4 to 1966/7) and
7 per cent (1966/7 to 1973/4). The balance of payments was only
briefly in significant surplus and the second stage of export-propelled
growth – the effect on investment – did not occur; from 1966/7 to
1973/4 the volume of fixed investment in manufacturing industry rose
less than 2 per cent a year.

The idea that indicative planning might help to accelerate economic
growth was in some ways linked to the idea of export-propelled growth;
it was also put forward forcefully in the early 1960s and intended to
work on businessmen's expectations. The statement of an output target,
with a government commitment to try to reach that target, would, it
was hoped, lead firms to expand their capacity and so bring the higher
growth rate about. The experiment with indicative planning, coinciding
as it did with a period when the government took a long succession of
deflationary measures in defence of the exchange rate, was an obvious
failure. Unfortunately all forms of national medium-term planning were
discredited in consequence, so that there is – for instance – now very
little official material published about the possible evolution of the
economy in the medium term.

Market and non-market sectors

The thesis presented by Bacon and Eltis[1] has a certain similarity to that
put forward by Kaldor in 1966. However, whereas Kaldor was arguing
that the manufacturing sector had been starved of labour, Bacon and
Eltis suggest that the market sector has been squeezed by the non-
market sector – that is, essentially, the public sector.

There are a number of points on this thesis. First, insofar as the rise in
the public sector share is considered to be a trend factor which has been
damaging to economic growth, it is perhaps rather unfair to include the
year 1974, which was the first year of a recession when the share of the
public sector can naturally be expected to be off-trend.

[1] Bacon and Eltis, *Britain's Economic Problem*.

Secondly, the distinction is perhaps not drawn sufficiently emphatically between the different economic effects of the resources which the government uses itself and the resources it transfers within the private sector. If the government itself employs more people in the health or education services, then obviously it is reducing the productive resources available for the market sector. If the government transfers purchasing power from producers to non-producers in the private sector, the effect is simply to transfer the ability to purchase the output of the market sector from one group to another, which has no *direct* effect on the output of that sector (except insofar as different groups may purchase different types of product, pensioners having a different pattern of consumption from people in the labour force, for example). The effect of this transfer, such as it is, is indirect, presumably arising from the unwillingness of the producers happily to accept the transfer to non-producers.

In the postwar period there has been no substantial increase in the share of resources which the public authorities take for their own direct expenditure. Public authorities' current and capital expenditure on goods and services (excluding public corporations) was, at current prices, 24 per cent of GDP at factor cost in the early 1950s and 27 per cent in 1973. A rise of this order over twenty years is hardly powerful enough to be much of an explanation for slow growth, nor is the share particularly high in comparison with most industrial countries.

The marked change in the postwar period has been the increase in transfers within the private sector. These are not exclusively transfers from producers to non-producers; a significant part comes back to the producers themselves, as housing subsidies, food subsidies and subsidies to the prices of nationalised industries, for example. The argument is that producers have been unwilling to accept the burden of these transfers, which have resulted in a rising incidence of taxation on their earnings, and this unwillingness has been one of the driving forces behind wage demands and consequently behind accelerating inflation. This view is another presentation of the 'real wage' theory of inflation, discussed on page 427 above – that wage explosions tend to occur after a period when the real post-tax wage has failed to rise. The essential strength of the argument is, therefore, the strength of the 'real wage' hypothesis and that hypothesis is far from conclusive.

Further, although the slow rise in the real post-tax wage since 1970 may help to explain the acceleration in inflation in the last few years of this period, it can hardly be considered an explanation of the relatively slow rate of growth over the whole postwar period. For this, it is reasonable to look for some factor which distinguishes the British economy from fast-growing economies and it does not appear that the burden of taxation is such a characteristic. Taxes, including social security contributions, are a lower proportion of GNP in the United Kingdom than in many other industrial countries; further, the aggregate tax burden in the United Kingdom fell quite sharply between 1969 and 1973, whereas in most other countries it rose.[1]

'Generalised inefficiency'

Finally, there is a line of thought about Britain's economic growth which starts not so much with models of the economy but with economic history; it moves on to look not primarily at aggregate statistical series but rather at comparative industry case studies, concerning itself with a certain 'generalised inefficiency' in British industry compared with the situation in competing countries.

This particular approach has a long history: comparisons between British industries and their competitors, to the detriment of the British, date back to the turn of the century and beyond, with comments on Britain's excessive reliance on coal and textiles, on her failure to achieve economies of scale in the iron and steel industry and on her relative weakness in electrical, chemical and metallurgical industries.

There are obvious difficulties in drawing general conclusions from analyses of this type. First, it is always the problem industries which tend to get most attention and they are clearly atypical; secondly, it is always possible that one of the less efficient British firms is being compared with one of the more efficient foreign ones. Further, there is a very large number of facets in the detailed comparisons of firms' behaviour in different countries. Comparisons can be made of innovative ability and of design; of research and development expenditure; of capital stock per worker and of the age of installed equipment; of the organisation and manning of the productive processes; of the proportions of management to other staff; of delivery dates; of the effort put into the study of markets, and into salesmanship and after-sales service. The one thing that all these items have in common is that they are basically the responsibility of the management. However, management obviously works under a set of constraints – such as those imposed by government policy towards industry and government tax policy, by the availability of sources of finance for expansion, or by the 'countervailing power' of trade union organisations.

This line of thought leads to inquiries into such matters as management education and training, the rewards and status of industrial managers in comparison with those afforded by universities or the Civil Service, and the factors which contribute to, or detract from, management–worker cooperation in matters of efficiency. Economists have not given a great deal of attention to questions of this kind, tending to con-

[1] CSO, *Economic Trends*, no. 277, November 1976, p. 109.

sider that they fall outside their field. To quote G. C. Allen: '. . . economists tend, very naturally, when dealing with practical problems, to direct their attention to facets that can be illuminated by the methods of inquiry they find congenial. Their instruments are efficient within a range; but they often choose to ignore what lies outside it. . .so it happens that, on occasions, their inquiries do not penetrate beyond the periphery of fundamental problems.'[1] Nor have these matters been in any sense in the forefront of economic policy. There are no obvious instruments at hand to deal with them and any action which the government might take could only begin to have effects over the very long term.

Governments, in their industrial policies, have not given great prominence during the last fifteen years to promoting competition as a way of improving efficiency. Indeed, particularly in the early 1960s, there was a good deal of positive encouragement to mergers; as between encouraging mergers to promote structural change and constraining them to preserve competition, the encouragement clearly outweighed the constraint. Otherwise, direct intervention by governments in industry has largely consisted in rescue operations to preserve employment or to support technology, many of which, initially intended to be temporary (as with shipbuilding), have become permanent. They cannot be said to have made any major contribution to the improvement of economic performance.

Successive governments also found difficulty in adopting coherent policies for industries for which they were more directly responsible – that is, the nationalised industries. The commercial criteria which were elaborated during this period frequently came into conflict with social objectives; they also came into conflict with national economic strategy – notably when the nationalised industries were required to hold their prices down and so run substantial deficits. Since many nationalised industries are monopolies, their pricing policies (and for that matter their general wage and salary decisions) can hardly be left entirely without some supervision. However, the form of supervision during this period was less than ideal; the degree to which the government intervened in detail varied a great deal from time to time and from industry to industry. There is a possible case for some general supervisory body to set a coherent pattern of constraints within which the management of nationalised industries should operate – whether they are commercial criteria, social objectives, or the requirements of national economic policy. It could also conduct efficiency audits.

[1] G. C. Allen, *The British Disease*, London, Institute of Economic Affairs, 1976.

CONCLUSIONS

⁅One main strand of criticism is that there was no continuity of economic policy during this period, mainly because of changes in government, and that this was damaging, particularly to economic growth.⁆This lack of continuity, it is argued, added to the uncertainties of the time; if firms are sufficiently uncertain about the future they will tend not to initiate new ventures and uncertainty about government policy is clearly one element in the total. So the argument has been presented that frequent policy changes – and particularly policy reversals – have a damaging effect on confidence.

There is in addition the cost of policy changes. The public expenditure costs – of creating or altering some institution, for example – are not usually very big. The costs to the economy as a whole are often much greater, since, for example, with a change in company taxation, firms have to devote resources to learning the new rules, and there may well be significant costs of compliance. To take another example, the main costs of running a price control system fall not so much on the central government (in the costs of the Price Commission), but rather on the firms who have to do additional work to meet the requirements of the new laws.

Certainly, in most of the areas of economic policy covered in this book, there were a great many changes, and indeed frequent reversals, in policy. Perhaps anti-inflationary policy is the best example. There was no continuity in the attempt to establish institutions to modify the system of free collective bargaining. The 1964 Labour government abolished the National Incomes Commission and created the NBPI; the 1970 Conservative government abolished the NBPI and two years later created the Price Commission and the Pay Board; the 1974 Labour government abolished the Pay Board. Anti-inflationary policy is not the only example: in fiscal policy, the system of corporate taxation was changed in 1958, changed back again in 1965, and changed once more in 1973; there was also the change from investment allowances to investment grants and back again and, in the field of indirect taxation, there was the introduction and abolition of selective employment tax. In industrial relations there were the attempts to 'bring the trade unions within the framework of the law'; this legislation too was subsequently repealed. In policy towards the nationalised industries there was alternation between encouraging them to act as independent commercial concerns and forcing them to charge low prices in the interests of the government's anti-inflationary policy. In industrial policy the institution of one government – the IRC – was abolished by the next one. One of the few areas where there was a certain consistency was in commercial policy, where it was common ground between successive governments that Britain should if possible join the Common Market; but the reasons were primarily political – the economic gains or losses from EEC membership are uncertain.

There is no way of putting numbers on the effects of these policy changes; nor is it easy to demonstrate in a quantitative way that policy changes were more frequent in Britain than in other major industrial countries. However, the fact that effects cannot be quantified does not mean that they are non-existent; for example, multi-national companies considering in what country to expand must surely give some weight to continuity in economic policy.

Policy-makers in Britain have been faced with the problem of trying to compensate for the fact that Britain has a long history of relative lack of success as an industrial society. In a world where trade barriers have been falling, British industry has not competed successfully in world trade in manufactures: imports have risen very fast and Britain's share in world exports has fallen year by year. In consequence, it has proved increasingly difficult to combine full employment with an adequate balance of payments. Moves aiming at full employment, particularly towards the end of the period, tended to raise the volume of imports to such an extent that exports – with their share in the world market continuing to decline – were unable to finance them.

The second main problem, again emerging particularly towards the end of the period, was the tendency of the particular form of free collective bargaining which exists in Britain to deliver very high figures for the annual increase in money earnings. No doubt there would have been some level of unemployment which would have moderated this tendency, but it is difficult to say what it would have been, except that it would have been very high. Variations in unemployment within a lower range appeared to have little effect on the rate of increase in earnings. Under these circumstances it was not possible simply by demand management to obtain a reasonable combination of the standard objectives of economic policy. This is not to deny that demand management was, in a limited way, effective; that is, that changes in taxation or in government expenditure had effects on the level of employment which were not automatically cancelled by any consequent effects on the price trend (because the rate of inflation was relatively insensitive to unemployment over a wide range). The constraint on the use of demand management was essentially the balance of payments, which hampered moves towards full employment. At the same time, given the insensitivity of the rise in earnings to variations in the pressure of demand for labour, it was not practicable to use demand management to slow down the rise in earnings.

In an attempt to deal with the balance of payments constraint, the government, after initial reluctance, turned to the exchange rate – an instrument whose effectiveness depends, of course, on the reactions of import and export volumes to changes in relative prices.[1] It was not easy, either before or after devaluation, to calculate the size of these price effects; there tended to be a certain alternation of elasticity optimism and elasticity pessimism. The conclusion towards the end of the period was that a shift in relative prices, if maintained, was efficacious in a limited way. The problem with the use of the exchange rate was to retain the competitive advantage – that is, to prevent the rise in import prices triggering off such an acceleration in the rise in earnings that the advantage was rapidly lost. Particularly in the period of floating exchange rates, there appeared to be some danger of a vicious circle, by which a downward float led to an accelerating rate of inflation, so that the exchange rate fell again, and so on.

The problem of dealing with the excessively high increases in money earnings by means other than demand management led to episodic attempts at incomes policy. However, the alternation of policies was such that by the end of the period no permanent modification to the institutional structure had evolved. It is probably true that there had been a certain evolution towards recognising the need for something, but no significant advance to any consensus about what that 'something' should be.

The policy approach to the problems of low productivity, or generalised inefficiency, or low competitiveness – however it might be labelled – was relatively uncertain. This is perhaps not surprising, since it is not at all clear what measures might be effective. Both in the mid-1960s and the early 1970s it was hoped that, given a good prospect of rising demand coupled with an adequate balance of payments, these supply problems would dwindle in importance. How far this might have been true it is hard to say, since the condition of an adequate balance of payments over a reasonably long period of time was never met. In the first period this approach of 'going for growth' was coupled with an experiment in indicative planning, in the hope that this would induce confidence and, by persuading businessmen that faster growth was possible, would encourage them to increase investment and so help to bring it about.

There were not many policy measures *directly* addressed to the problems of low productivity. It is true that throughout the period fiscal encouragement to investment – either in the form of grants or tax allowances – was substantial. The main device tried for improving the general level of management was to encourage mergers (during the

---

[1] Or to changes in the profit margin on exports relative to the profit margin on home sales.

period of the Labour government) and to give a good deal of weight to selecting the best management team for the merged concern. Otherwise, there were a number of studies of the general level of efficiency or competitiveness in various industries. On the industrial relations side an attempt was made (by the Labour government) to impose some legal restraint on unofficial strikes. It failed, and the more extensive attempt to put certain legal limits on unions' industrial action by the Conservative government (the Industrial Relations Act) was also eventually abandoned. There were no government moves during this period to put forward legislation on workers' participation.

In sum, the problem of devising policies appropriate for a country with a relatively inefficient manufacturing sector and an unreformed pay bargaining system remained unsolved.

SELECTED BIBLIOGRAPHY

I. BOOKS, ARTICLES AND PERIODICALS

ALLEN, G. C. *The British Disease*, London, Institute of Economic Affairs, 1976.

ARTIS, M. J. 'Fiscal policy for stabilization' in Beckerman (ed.), 1972, q.v.

ARTIS, M. J. and LEWIS, M. K. 'The demand for money in the United Kingdom 1963–1973', *Manchester School of Economic and Social Studies*, vol. 44, June 1976.

ARTUS, J. R. 'The 1967 devaluation of the pound sterling', *IMF Staff Papers*, vol. 22, November 1975.

BACON, R. W. and ELTIS, W. A. *Britain's Economic Problem: too few producers*, London, Macmillan, 1976.

BALL, R. J. 'The case against devaluation of the pound', *The Bankers' Magazine*, vol. 203, April 1967.

BECKERMAN, W. 'The determinants of economic growth' in P. D. Henderson (ed.), *Economic Growth in Britain*, London, Weidenfeld & Nicolson, 1966.

— (ed.) *The Labour Government's Economic Record 1964–1970*, London, Duckworth, 1972.

BECKERMAN, W. and Associates. *The British Economy in 1975*, Cambridge University Press, 1965.

BEVERIDGE, W. H. *Full Employment in a Free Society*, London, Allen & Unwin, 1944.

BLINDER, A. S. and SOLOW, R. M. 'Analytical foundations of fiscal policy' in *The Economics of Public Finance*, Washington (DC), Brookings Institution, 1974.

BRANDON, H. *In the Red: the struggle for sterling, 64/66*, London, Deutsch, 1966.

BRITTAN, S. *Steering the Economy: the role of the Treasury* (rev. edn), London, Penguin, 1971.

BROWN, G. *In My Way*, London, Gollancz, 1971.

CAIRNCROSS, Sir Alec (ed.) *Britain's Economic Prospects Reconsidered*, London, Allen & Unwin, 1970.

— (ed.) *The Managed Economy*, Oxford, Blackwell, 1970.

— *Control of Long-term International Capital Movements*, Washington (DC), Brookings Institution, 1973.

CATHERWOOD, H. F. R. *Britain with the Brakes Off*, London, Hodder & Stoughton, 1966.

CAVES, R. E. and Associates. *Britain's Economic Prospects*, London, Allen & Unwin, 1968.

CLEGG, H. *How to Run an Incomes Policy and Why We Made Such a Mess of the Last One*, London, Heinemann, 1971.

COPPOCK, D. J. and GIBSON, N. J. 'The volume of deposits and the cash and liquid assets ratios', *Manchester School of Economic and Social Studies*, vol. 31, September 1963.

DIAMOND, Lord. *Public Expenditure in Practice*, London, Allen & Unwin, 1975.

DICKS-MIREAUX, L. A. and DOW, J. C. R. 'The determinants of wage inflation: United Kingdom, 1946–1956', *Journal of the Royal Statistical Society* (series A), vol. 122, pt 2, 1959.

DOW, J. C. R. 'Analysis of the generation of price inflation', *Oxford Economic Papers*, vol. 8 (new series), October 1956.

EVELY, R. W. 'The effects of the price code', *National Institute Economic Review*, no. 77, August 1976.

Federation of British Industries. *The Next Five Years*, London, 1960.

FISHER, D. 'The instruments of monetary policy and the generalised trade-off function for Britain, 1955–1968', *Manchester School of Economic and Social Studies*, vol. 38, September 1970.

FLEMMING, J. S. *Inflation*, London, Oxford University Press, 1976.

GIBSON, N. J. 'Special Deposits as an instrument of monetary policy', *Manchester School of Economic and Social Studies*, vol. 32, September 1964.

GODLEY, W. A. H. and SHEPHERD, J. R. 'Long-term growth and short-term policy', *National Institute Economic Review*, no. 29, August 1964.

GOODHART, C. A. E. 'Monetary policy in the United Kingdom' in K. Holbik (ed.), *Monetary Policy in Twelve Industrial Countries*, Boston (Mass.), Federal Reserve Bank of Boston, 1973.
— 'Problems of monetary management: the UK experience' in A. S. Courakis (ed.), *Inflation, Depression and Economic Policy in the West: lessons from the 1970s*, Oxford, Mansell & Alexandrine Press, 1979.
GOODHART, C. A. E. and CROCKETT, A. D. 'The importance of money', *Bank of England Quarterly Bulletin*, vol. 10, June 1970.
GRIFFITHS, B. 'Resource efficiency, monetary policy and the reform of the UK banking system', *Journal of Money, Credit and Banking*, vol. 5, February 1973 (pt I).
HACCHE, G. 'The demand for money in the United Kingdom: experience since 1971', *Bank of England Quarterly Bulletin*, vol. 14, September 1974.
HALL, Sir Robert. 'Britain's economic problem', *Economist*, 16 and 23 September 1961.
HARROD, Sir Roy. 'Are monetary and fiscal policies enough?', *Economic Journal*, vol. 74, December 1964.
HECLO, H. and WILDAVSKY, A. *The Private Government of Public Money*, London, Macmillan, 1974.
HENRY, S. G. B., SAWYER, M. C. and SMITH, P. 'Models of inflation in the United Kingdom', *National Institute Economic Review*, no. 77, August 1976.
HODJERA, Z. 'Short-term capital movements of the United Kingdom, 1963–1967', *Journal of Political Economy*, vol. 79, July–August 1971.
HOPKIN, W. A. B. and GODLEY, W. A. H. 'An analysis of tax changes', *National Institute Economic Review*, no. 32, May 1965.
HUTCHISON, T. W. *Economics and Economic Policy in Britain, 1946–1966: some aspects of their interrelations*, London, Allen & Unwin, 1968.
HUTTON, J. P. 'A model of short-term capital movements, the foreign exchange market and official intervention in the UK, 1963–1970', *Review of Economic Studies*, vol. 44, February 1977.
Institute for Fiscal Studies. *The Structure and Reform of Direct Taxation* [Meade Report], London, Allen & Unwin, 1978.
JENKINS, P. *The Battle of Downing Street*, London, Charles Knight, 1970.
KALDOR, N. *An Expenditure Tax*, London, Allen & Unwin, 1955.
— *Essays on Economic Policy*, London, Duckworth, 1964.
— *Causes of the Slow Rate of Economic Growth of the United Kingdom*, Cambridge University Press, 1966.
— 'Productivity and growth in manufacturing industry: a reply', *Economica*, vol. 35 (new series), November 1968.
— (ed.) *Conflicts in Policy Objectives*, Oxford, Blackwell, 1971.
KAY, J. A. and KING, M. A. *The British Tax System*, Oxford University Press, 1978.
KING, M. A. *Public Policy and the Corporation*, London, Chapman & Hall, 1977.
KIRSCHEN, E. S. (ed.). *Economic Policies Compared: West and East*, vol. I: *General Theory*, Amsterdam, North-Holland, 1974.
KIRSCHEN, E. S. *et al. Economic Policy in our Time*. vol. I: *General Theory*, Amsterdam, North-Holland, 1964.
LAIDLER, D. E. W. 'The influence of money on economic activity – a survey of some current problems' in G. Clayton, J. C. Gilbert and R. Sedgwick (eds.), *Monetary Theory and Monetary Policy in the 1970s*, London, Oxford University Press, 1971.
LAIDLER, D. E. W. and PARKIN, J. M. 'The demand for money in the United Kingdom 1956–1967: preliminary estimates', *Manchester School of Economic and Social Studies*, vol. 38, September 1970.
LIEBENSTEIN, H. 'Allocative efficiency vs. "X-efficiency"', *American Economic Review*, vol 56, June 1966.
MACMILLAN, H. *The Middle Way*, London, Macmillan, 1939.
— *Riding the Storm, 1956–1959*, London, Macmillan, 1971.
— *Pointing the Way, 1959–1961*, London, Macmillan, 1972.
— *At the End of the Day, 1961–1963*, London, Macmillan, 1973.
Midland Bank Review (quarterly).

MODIGLIANI, F. 'The channels of monetary policy in the Federal Reserve – MIT – University of Pennsylvania econometric model of the US', in G. A. Renton (ed.), *Modelling the Economy*, London, Heinemann, 1975.

MUSGRAVE, R. A. 'On measuring fiscal performance', *Review of Economics and Statistics*, vol. 46, May 1964.

MUSGRAVE, R. A. and MILLER, M. H. 'Built-in flexibility', *American Economic Review*, vol. 38, March 1948.

MUSGRAVE, R. A. and MUSGRAVE, P. B. 'Fiscal policy' in Caves *et al.*, 1968, q.v.

— *Public Finance: in theory and practice*, London, McGraw Hill, 1975.

MUSGRAVE, R. A. and THIN, T. 'Income tax progression, 1929–48', *Journal of Political Economy*, vol. 56, December 1948.

National Institute Economic Review (quarterly).

NIESR. 'The effects of the devaluation of 1967 on the current balance of payments', *Economic Journal*, vol. 82, March 1972 (supplement).

OPPENHEIMER, P. M. 'Forward exchange intervention: the official view', *Westminster Bank Review*, February 1966.

PAIGE, D. C. 'Economic growth: the last hundred years', *National Institute Economic Review*, no. 16, July 1961.

PAISH, F. W. *Studies in an Inflationary Economy: the United Kingdom, 1948–1961*, London, Macmillan, 1966.

PARKIN, J. M., GRAY, M. R. and BARRETT, R. J. 'The portfolio behaviour of commercial banks' in K. Hilton and D. F. Heathfield (eds.), *The Econometric Study of the United Kingdom*, London, Macmillan, 1970.

PECHMAN, J. A. *Federal Tax Policy*, Washington (DC), Brookings Institution, 1977.

PHILLIPS, A. W. 'The relation between unemployment and the rate of change of money wage rates in the United Kingdom, 1861–1957', *Economica*, vol. 25 (new series), November 1958.

PISSARIDES, C. A. 'A model of British macroeconomic policy, 1955–1969', *Manchester School of Economic and Social Studies*, vol. 40, September 1972.

POLAK, J. J. 'Monetary analysis of income formation and payments problems', *IMF Staff Papers*, vol. 6, November 1957.

Political and Economic Planning. *Growth in the British Economy: a study of economic problems and policies in contemporary Britain*, London, Allen & Unwin, 1960.

— 'Economic planning in France', *Planning*, vol. 27, 14 August 1961.

POOLE, W. 'Optimal choice of monetary policy instruments in a simple stochastic macro model', *Quarterly Journal of Economics*, vol. 84, May 1970.

PREST, A. R. *Public Finance: in theory and practice*, London, Weidenfeld & Nicolson, 1st edn 1960 and 5th edn 1975.

PRICE, L. D. D. 'The demand for money in the United Kingdom: a further investigation', *Bank of England Quarterly Bulletin*, vol. 12, March 1972.

REDDAWAY, W. B. *Effects of the Selective Employment Tax: final report*, Cambridge University Press, 1973.

ROWTHORN, R. E. 'What remains of Kaldor's law?', *Economic Journal*, vol. 85, March 1975.

SCOTT, M. FG. 'What should be done about the Sterling Area?', *Bulletin of the Oxford University Institute of Statistics*, vol. 21, November 1959.

SEERS, D. and STREETEN, P. 'Overseas development policies' in Beckerman (ed.), 1972, q.v.

SHANKS, M. 'The comforts of stagnation', *Encounter*, July 1963.

SHONFIELD, A. *British Economic Policy since the War*, Harmondsworth, Penguin, 1958.

— *Modern Capitalism: the changing balance of public and private power*, London, Oxford University Press, 1965.

SPRAOS, J. 'Speculation, arbitrage and sterling', *Economic Journal*, vol. 69, March 1959.

SUMNER, M. T. *The Effect of Taxation on Corporate Saving and Investment*, London, Institute for Fiscal Studies, 1976.

TINBERGEN, J. *Economic Policy: principles and design*, Amsterdam, North-Holland, 1956.

Trades Union Congress. *The Chequers and Downing Street Talks – July to November 1972: report*, London, 1972.

WALTERS, A. A. *Money in Boom and Slump*, London, Institute of Economic Affairs, 1969.

WHITING, A. 'An international comparison of the instability of economic growth', *Three Banks Review*, no. 109, March 1976.

WILLIAMS, D., GOODHART, C. A. E. and GOWLAND, D. H. 'Money, income and causality: the UK experience', *American Economic Review*, vol. 66, June 1976.

WILSON, H. *The Labour Government 1964–1970: a personal record*, London, Weidenfeld & Michael Joseph, 1971.

WORSWICK, G. D. N. 'Fiscal policy and stabilization in Britain' and 'Trade and payments' in Cairncross (ed.), *Britain's Economic Prospects Reconsidered*, q.v.

— 'The end of demand management?', *Lloyds Bank Review*, no. 123, January 1977.

II. OFFICIAL PUBLICATIONS

(a) *United Kingdom*[1]

Bank of England. *Bank of England Quarterly Bulletin.*

— *Report [and Accounts]* (annual).

— *Statistical Abstract*, no. 1, 1970, and no. 2, 1975.

Central Statistical Office. *Financial Statistics* (monthly).

— *National Income and Expenditure* (annual).

— *United Kingdom Balance of Payments* (annual).

Civil Service Department. *The Developing System of Public Expenditure Management and Control* by Sir Samuel Goldman, KCB, HMSO, 1973.

Council on Prices, Productivity and Incomes. *1st Report*, HMSO, 1958.

— *2nd Report*, HMSO, 1958.

— *3rd Report*, HMSO, 1959.

— *4th Report*, HMSO, 1961.

Department of Economic Affairs, *The National Plan*, Cmnd 2764, HMSO, 1965.

— *Prices and Incomes Policy: an 'Early Warning System'*, Cmnd 2808, HMSO, 1965.

— *Prices and Incomes Standstill: period of severe restraint*, Cmnd 3150, HMSO, 1966.

— *Prices and Incomes Policy after June 30, 1967*, Cmnd 3235, HMSO, 1967.

— *Productivity, Prices and Incomes Policy in 1968 and 1969*, Cmnd 3590, HMSO, 1968.

Department of Employment and Productivity. *Productivity, Prices and Incomes Policy after 1969*, Cmnd 4237, HMSO, 1969.

Department of the Environment. *Local Government Finance. Report of the Committee of Enquiry* [Layfield Report], Cmnd 6453, HMSO, 1976.

Department of Industry. *Strategy Alternatives for the British Motorcycle Industry*, HMSO, 1975.

National Board for Prices and Incomes. *Report no. 34: Bank Charges*, Cmnd 3292, HMSO, 1967.

— *Report no. 36: Productivity Agreements*, Cmnd 3311, HMSO, 1967.

— *Report no. 65: Payment by Results Systems*, Cmnd 3627, HMSO, 1968.

— *Report no. 101: Pay of Workers in Agriculture in England and Wales*, Cmnd 3911, HMSO, 1969.

National Economic Development Council. *Conditions Favourable to Faster Growth*, HMSO, 1963.

— *Growth of the United Kingdom Economy to 1966*, HMSO, 1963.

National Economic Development Office. *Cyclical Fluctuations in the United Kingdom Economy*, 1975.

Pay Board. *Advisory Report no. 1: Anomalies arising out of the Pay Standstill of Nov. 1972*, HMSO, 1973.

— *Advisory Report no. 2: Problems of Pay Relativities*, Cmnd 5535, HMSO, 1974.

— *Special Report: Relativity Pay of Mineworkers*, Cmnd 5567, HMSO, 1974.

Prime Minister's Office. *Machinery of Prices and Incomes Policy*, Cmnd 2577, HMSO, 1965.

Department of Trade and Industry. *Consumer Credit. Report of the Committee* [Crowther Report], Cmnd 4596, HMSO, 1971.

Treasury. *Economic Implications of Full Employment*, Cmd 9725, HMSO, 1956.

[1] All published in London.

Treasury. *Committee on the Working of the Monetary System:*
   Report [Radcliffe Report], Cmnd 827, HMSO, 1959.
   Minutes of Evidence July 11, 1957 to April 30, 1959, HMSO, 1960.
   Principal Memoranda of Evidence, vols. 1–3, HMSO, 1960.
— *The Control of Public Expenditure* [Plowden Report], Cmnd 1432, HMSO, 1961.
— *Incomes Policy: the next step*, Cmnd 1626, HMSO, 1962.
— *Public Expenditure White Papers: handbook on methodology*, HMSO, 1972.
— *Price and Pay Code. Consultative Document*, Cmnd 5247, HMSO, 1973.
— *Price and Pay Code for Stage 3. A Consultative Document*, Cmnd 5444, HMSO, 1973.
— *The Counter Inflation Policy: Stage 3*, Cmnd 5446, HMSO, 1973.

(b) *International*

European Communities. Monetary Committee. *Monetary Policy in the Countries of the European Economic Community. Supplement 1974 (The United Kingdom)*, Brussels, 1974.
Organisation for Economic Co-operation and Development. *Fiscal Policy in Seven Countries, 1955–1965*, by B. Hansen, Paris, 1969.

INDEX

(after page numbers, ch = chart, n = text footnote, t = table)

RECENT PUBLICATIONS FOR THE NATIONAL INSTITUTE
OF ECONOMIC AND SOCIAL RESEARCH
BY THE CAMBRIDGE UNIVERSITY PRESS

ECONOMIC AND SOCIAL STUDIES

XXV   *Exports and Economic Growth of Developing Countries*
By A. MAIZELS, assisted by L. F. CAMPBELL-BOROSS and P. B. W. RAYMENT. 1968.
pp. 445. £11.00 net.

XXVI   *Urban Development in Britain: Standards, Costs and Resources, 1964–2004*
By P. A. STONE. Vol. 1: *Population Trends and Housing.* 1970. pp. 436. £12.25 net.

XXVII   *The Framework of Regional Economics in the United Kingdom*
By A. J. BROWN. 1972. pp. 372. £12.50 net.

XXVIII   *The Structure, Size and Costs of Urban Settlements*
By P. A. STONE. 1973. pp. 304. £10.00 net.

XXIX   *The Diffusion of New Industrial Processes: An International Study*
Edited by L. NABSETH and G. F. RAY. 1974. pp. 346. £11.25 net.

XXX   *The Evolution of Giant Firms in Britain*
By S. J. PRAIS. 1976. pp. 340. £10.00 net.

XXXI   *British Economic Policy 1960–74*
Edited by F. T. BLACKABY. 1978. pp. 710. £20.00 net.

OCCASIONAL PAPERS

XXV   *The Analysis and Forecasting of the British Economy*
By M. J. C. SURREY. 1971. pp. 120. £4.25 net.

XXVI   *Mergers and Concentration in British Industry*
By P. E. HART, M. A. UTTON and G. WALSHE. 1973. pp. 190. £6.00 net.

XXVII   *Recent Trends in Monopoly in Great Britain*
By G. WALSHE. 1974. pp. 156. £5.50 net.

XXVIII   *Cyclical Indicators for the Postwar British Economy*
By D. J. O'DEA. 1975. pp. 184. £6.75 net.

XXIX   *Poverty and Progress in Britain, 1953–73*
By G. C. FIEGEHEN, P. S. LANSLEY and A. D. SMITH. 1977. pp. 192. £7.00 net.

XXX   *The Innovation Process in the Energy Industries*
By G. F. RAY and L. UHLMANN. 1979. pp. 132. £6.00 net.

NIESR STUDENTS' EDITION

1   *Growth and Trade* (abridged from *Industrial Growth and World Trade*)
By A. MAIZELS. 1970. pp. 312. £3.95 net.

2   *The Antitrust Laws of the U.S.A.* (2nd edition, unabridged)
By A. D. NEALE. 1970. pp. 544. £5.95 net.

3   *The Management of the British Economy, 1945–60* (unabridged)
By J. C. R. DOW. 1970. pp. 464. £2.95 net.

REGIONAL PAPERS

1   *The Anatomy of Regional Activity Rates* by JOHN BOWERS, and *Regional Social Accounts for the United Kingdom* by V. H. WOODWARD. 1970. pp. 192. £4.50 net.

2   *Regional Unemployment Differences in Great Britain* by P. C. CHESHIRE, and *Interregional Migration Models and their Application to Great Britain* by R. WEEDEN. 1973. pp. 118. £4.50 net.

3   *Unemployment, Vacancies and the Rate of Change of Earnings: A Regional Analysis* by A. E. WEBB, and *Regional Rates of Employment Growth: An Analysis of Variance Treatment* by R. WEEDEN. 1974. pp. 114. £4.50 net.

Published by

HEINEMANN EDUCATIONAL BOOKS

AN INCOMES POLICY FOR BRITAIN

Edited by FRANK BLACKABY. 1972. pp. 260. £4.00 net.

THE MEDIUM TERM: MODELS OF THE BRITISH ECONOMY

Edited by G. D. N. WORSWICK and FRANK BLACKABY. 1974. pp. 256. £4.80 net.

THE UNITED KINGDOM ECONOMY

By the NIESR. 1977. pp. 144. £1.25 net.

DEMAND MANAGEMENT

Edited by MICHAEL POSNER. 1978. pp. 256. £9.50 (hardback), £4.50 (paperback) net.

DE-INDUSTRIALISATION

Edited by FRANK BLACKABY. 1979. pp. 282. £9.50 (hardback), £5.50 (paperback) net.

Available from booksellers

THE NATIONAL INSTITUTE OF ECONOMIC AND SOCIAL RESEARCH

publishes regularly

THE NATIONAL INSTITUTE ECONOMIC REVIEW

A quarterly analysis of the general economic situation in the United Kingdom and the world overseas, with forecasts eighteen months ahead. The first issue each year contains an assessment of medium-term prospects. There are also in most issues special articles on subjects of interest to academic and business economists.

Annual subscriptions, £14.00 (home), and £18.00 (abroad), also single issues for the current year, £4.00 (home) and £5.00 (abroad), are available directly from the NIESR, 2 Dean Trench Street, Smith Square, London, SW1P 3EH.

Subscriptions at the special reduced price of £5.00 p.a. are available to students in the United Kingdom and Irish Republic on application to the Secretary of the Institute.

Back issues for the years 1959–77 and reprints of issues which have gone out of stock, price £4.00 each plus postage, are obtainable from Wm Dawson & Sons Ltd, Cannon House, Park Farm Road, Folkestone, Kent. Microfiche copies for the years 1959–77 are available from EP Microform Ltd, Bradford Road, East Ardsley, Wakefield, WF3 2JN, Yorkshire.

Also available directly from the Institute

THE IVTH FRENCH PLAN

By FRANÇOIS PERROUX, translated by Bruno Leblanc. 1965. pp. 72. 50p net.*y*